Business Essentials

Supporting HNC/HND and Foundation degrees

Marketing Principles

Course Book

In this July 2010 edition:

- Full and comprehensive coverage of the key topics within the subject
- Activities, examples and quizzes
- Practical illustrations and case studies
- Index
- Fully up to date as at July 2010
- Coverage mapped to the Edexcel Guidelines for the HNC/HND in Business

First edition September 2007
Second edition July 2010

Published ISBN 9780 7517 6827 5
(previous edition 9780 7517 4473 6)
e-ISBN 9780 7517 7664 5

British Library Cataloguing-in-Publication Data
A catalogue record for this book is available from the British Library

Published by
BPP Learning Media Ltd
BPP House, Aldine Place
London W12 8AA

www.bpp.com/learningmedia

Printed in the United Kingdom

Your learning materials, published by BPP Learning Media Ltd, are printed on paper sourced from sustainable, managed forests.

We are grateful to Edexcel for permission to reproduce the Guidelines for the BTEC Higher Nationals in Business.

A note about copyright

Dear Customer

What does the little © mean and why does it matter?

Your market-leading BPP books, course materials and e-learning materials do not write and update themselves. People write them: on their own behalf or as employees of an organisation that invests in this activity. Copyright law protects their livelihoods. It does so by creating rights over the use of the content.

Breach of copyright is a form of theft – as well as being a criminal offence in some jurisdictions, it is potentially a serious breach of professional ethics.

With current technology, things might seem a bit hazy but, basically, without the express permission of BPP Learning Media:

- Photocopying our materials is a breach of copyright.
- Scanning, ripcasting or conversion of our digital materials into different file formats, uploading them to facebook or e-mailing them to your friends is a breach of copyright.

You can, of course, sell your books, in the form in which you have bought them – once you have finished with them. (Is this fair to your fellow students? We update for a reason.) But the e-products are sold on a single user licence basis: we do not supply 'unlock' codes to people who have bought them second-hand.

And what about outside the UK? BPP Learning Media strives to make our materials available at prices students can afford by local printing arrangements, pricing policies and partnerships which are clearly listed on our website. A tiny minority ignore this and indulge in criminal activity by illegally photocopying our material or supporting organisations that do. If they act illegally and unethically in one area, can you really trust them?

Contents

Introduction

BPP Learning Media's **Business Essentials** range is the ideal learning solution for all students studying for business-related qualifications and degrees. The range provides concise and comprehensive coverage of the key areas that are essential to the business student.

Qualifications in business are traditionally very demanding. Students therefore need learning resources which go straight to the core of the topics involved, and which build upon students' pre-existing knowledge and experience. The BPP Learning Media Business Essentials range has been designed to meet exactly that need.

Features include:

- In-depth coverage of essential topics within business-related subjects
- Plenty of activities, quizzes and topics for discussion to help retain the interest of students and ensure progress
- Up-to-date practical illustrations and case studies that really bring the material to life
- A glossary of terms and full index

In addition, the contents of the chapters are comprehensively mapped to the **Edexcel Guidelines**, providing full coverage of all topics specified in the HND/HNC qualifications in Business.

Each chapter contains:

- An introduction and a list of specific study objectives
- Summary diagrams and signposts to guide you through the chapter
- A chapter roundup, quick quiz with answers and answers to activities

Other titles in this series:

Generic titles

Economics

Accounts

Business Maths

Mandatory units for the Edexcel HND/HNC in Business qualification

Unit 1	Business Environment
Unit 2	Managing Financial Resources and Decisions
Unit 3	Organisations and Behaviour
Unit 4	Marketing Principles
Unit 5	Business Law
Unit 6	Business Decision Making
Unit 7	Business Strategy
Unit 8	Research Project

Pathways for the Edexcel HND/HNC in Business qualification

Units 9 and 10	Finance: Management Accounting and Financial Reporting
Units 11 and 12	Finance: Auditing and Financial Systems and Taxation
Units 13 and 14	Management: Leading People and Professional Development
Units 15 and 16	Management: Communications and Achieving Results
Units 17 and 18	Marketing and Promotion
Units 19 and 20	Marketing and Sales Strategy
Units 21 and 22	Human Resource Management
Units 23 and 24	Human Resource Development and Employee Relations
Units 25-28	Company and Commercial Law

For more information, or to place an order, please call 0845 0751 100 (for orders within the UK) or +44(0)20 8740 2211 (from overseas), e-mail learningmedia@bpp.com, or visit our website at www.bpp.com/learningmedia.

If you would like to send in your comments on this Course Book, please turn to the review form at the back of this book.

Study Guide

This Course Book includes features designed specifically to make learning effective and efficient.

- Each chapter begins with a summary diagram which maps out the areas covered by the chapter. There are detailed summary diagrams at the start of each main section of the chapter. You can use the diagrams during revision as a basis for your notes.

- After the main summary diagram there is an introduction, which sets the chapter in context. This is followed by learning objectives, which show you what you will learn as you work through the chapter.

- Throughout the Course Book, there are special aids to learning. These are indicated by symbols in the margin:

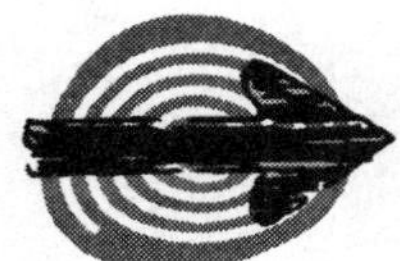

Signposts guide you through the book, showing how each section connects with the next.

Definitions give the meanings of key terms. The *glossary* at the end of the book summarises these.

Activities help you to test how much you have learned. An indication of the time you should take on each is given. Answers are given at the end of each chapter.

Topics for discussion are for use in seminars. They give you a chance to share you views with your fellow students. They allow you to highlight holes in your knowledge and to see how others understand concepts. If you have time, try 'teaching' someone the concepts you have learned in a session. This helps you to remember key points and answering their questions will consolidate your knowledge.

Examples relate what you have learned to the outside world. Try to think up your own examples as you work through the Course Book.

Chapter roundups present the key information from the chapter in a concise format. Useful for revision.

- The wide **margin** on each page is for your notes. You will get the best out of this book if you interact with it. Write down your thoughts and ideas. Record examples, question theories, add references to other pages in the Course Book and rephrase key points in your own words.

- At the end of each chapter, there is a **chapter roundup** and a **quick quiz** with answers. Use these to revise and consolidate your knowledge. The chapter roundup summarises the chapter. The quick quiz tests what you have learned (the answers often refer you back to the chapter so you can look over subjects again).

- At the end of the text, there is a glossary of definitions and an index.

Part A

The Concept and Process of Marketing

Chapter 1 :
MARKETS AND MARKETING

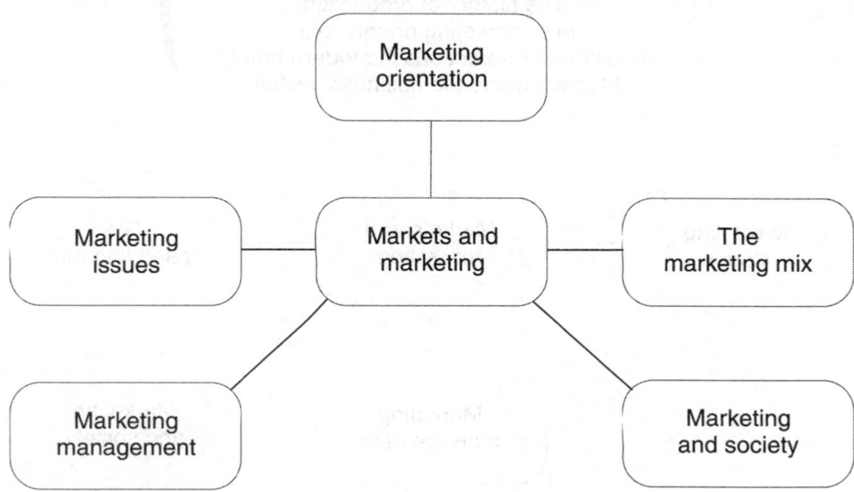

Introduction

In this chapter we describe what a market is and lay the foundations for explaining the marketing process. We also explain the importance of marketing and the **marketing concept**. It is important that you understand marketing as all industries and services have to market their products to their customers. We discuss the development of marketing and describe the role of marketing in different contexts.

Marketing can be thought of as a philosophy for business organisations. It is also a functional area of management located within a departmental structure. The marketing concept means **putting the customer first**. In practice, this consumer orientation should permeate every part of a business if it is to succeed. The theory of marketing is based on the so called **marketing mix** variables of **product, price, place** and **promotion** which will be discussed later in this text.

Often the term 'marketing' is confused with 'advertising'. However, although it is an element of marketing, advertising is only part of a much wider area of business activity.

This chapter aims to give an overview of the marketing concept. It will also investigate the organisation of marketing within the company structure but first we will review the historical development of marketing.

Your objectives

In this chapter you will learn about the following.

(a) The history and development of marketing
(b) What is meant by marketing and the marketing concept
(c) Why organisations need a marketing oriented strategy
(d) The elements that make up the marketing mix
(e) How marketing activities are managed and organised within a marketing department
(f) How the marketing department fits into the organisation as a whole
(g) Marketing and society

1 MARKETING ORIENTATION

1.1 The history of markets and marketing

Markets existed as soon as goods started to be **exchanged**. In the primitive world, each family might have bred its own animals for food and clothes. Soon, however, people found that they were able to produce more food than they needed for themselves. One person might then offer to exchange his spare food for someone else's spare clothes. This is known as **bartering**. As time went on, people became more **specialised**: one person might not produce any food himself, but might get food from other people in exchange for curing their sick animals.

The next stage was to avoid the need to exchange goods, by inventing **money**: a vet who liked mutton could then get cash from one farmer, who only had cows, and spend it with another farmer, who could offer sheep for sale. By this stage, there was a fully fledged **market**.

The growth of markets received a big boost during the Industrial Revolution in the 18th and 19th centuries. **Production** became concentrated in big factories, towns grew bigger and **trade** increased as people became more likely to buy goods than to produce them themselves. Producers and the markets to which they sold became geographically separated. Most industries still had a **production orientation**. This means that they would concentrate on making things efficiently, and assume that someone would buy whatever they made.

FOR DISCUSSION

Think of an organisation you have encountered which you felt did not take its customers' needs sufficiently into account. Did a production orientation show itself? You may think about its product's features, availability, price, adaptability, and so on.

Mass production techniques increased the number and types of goods on the market. Increased productivity also reduced unit costs. With new cheaper products on offer, **demand** was such that until very recently many business problems centred on production and selling rather than marketing, since it was more important to produce enough of a product to satisfy strong demand than to think about **customer needs**.

This was exacerbated in the UK because of its historical pre-eminence in industry and trade. Great Britain dominated world trade up until the First World War when other countries emerged to compete. The United States, Japan and Germany took much of Britain's share in the market for manufactured goods. Present-day UK businesses have to **compete** effectively. Marketing enables them to identify customer needs and to find products that satisfy those needs.

Production is no longer the main problem facing business concerns. Indeed, for most products and services, it is excess supply rather than excess demand which is the problem. In these circumstances, the focus has switched from 'how to produce enough' **(supply factor)** to 'how to increase demand' **(demand factor)**. Marketing techniques have been developed as a result of this switch in orientation.

Initially, **mass marketing techniques** were applied to selling **fast-moving consumer goods** (often referred to as FMCG) such as washing powder, toothpaste and groceries, although these were relatively unsophisticated. Subsequently, marketing methods have been applied to industrial goods and to services. Marketing techniques have grown in importance as competition and consumer choice have increased.

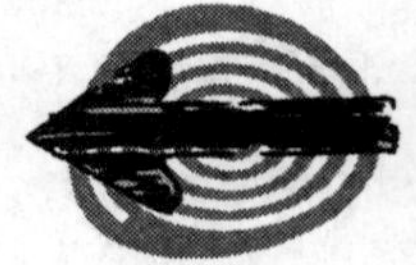

The result of this change in view has been the marketing concept, which is the subject of a later section.

1.2 Marketing defined

Marketing → Identifying / Anticipating / Supplying → Customer needs / Mutually beneficial exchange / Firm's objectives

Figure 1.1: Arriving at a definition of marketing

There are many **definitions of marketing.** Here we will consider four that provide insight into how marketing is used in practice.

Definition

> **Marketing** is the management of exchange relationships.

This emphasises the **role** of marketing in relating to the world outside the organisation. All **relationships** between the organisation and the outside world, especially when they relate to customers, need to be managed. The organisation will be judged by customers, suppliers, competitors and others according to their personal experience. How often have you been put off an organisation by the manner of a telephone operator, or the tone of a receptionist's voice? These contacts are vital in creating a positive image for the organisation with customers and the public.

Another definition is that of the **Chartered Institute of Marketing:**

Definition

Marketing is the management process which identifies, anticipates and supplies customer requirements efficiently and profitably.

This definition emphasises the wide **scope** of marketing, ranging from initial identification of customer needs by means of research, right through to eventual, profitable satisfaction of those needs.

Definition

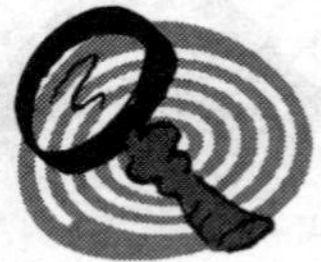

Marketing is concerned with meeting business objectives by providing customer satisfactions.

This definition is important because it stresses the importance of the customer and, more particularly, **customer satisfaction**. When people buy products or services they do not simply want the products, they also want the benefits from using the products or services. Products and services help to solve a customer's problems. It is the **solution** to these problems that customers are buying.

Finally, here is the definition provided by the **American Marketing Association**:

Definition

Marketing is the process of planning and executing the conception, pricing, promotion, and distribution of ideas, goods, and services to create exchanges that satisfy individual and organisational goals.

This definition expands on the previous one and considers what is involved in marketing to satisfy **both the customer and the company.**

These definitions serve to demonstrate useful distinctions between marketing as a **thing that is done** and marketing as an **approach to how something is achieved.**

It is important that you keep these two elements in mind in your approach to the study and practice of marketing. There must be a systematic **method** and there must be a **purpose.**

(a) The main purpose is the **mutual satisfaction** of both supplier and customer.

(b) The method is the process of **shaping and managing the marketing mix** in a way which takes into consideration the needs of the customer and the goals of the organisation at one and the same time.

Activity 1 **(15 minutes)**

When people buy the products listed below, what problems or types of problems are they trying to solve?

(a) Lawn mowers

(b) Life insurance

(c) A particular model of car

1.3 The marketing concept

The marketing concept is the attitude that business decisions should be based on **what the consumer wants**. For example, a company providing public telephones should start by finding out whether people prefer small hoods over the telephones, or complete telephone boxes in which they can stand and shut the door behind them. If people prefer complete boxes, then the company should at least consider providing them, even though small hoods are easier and cheaper to make. Of course the company also has to make a profit, and the extra cost of complete boxes will be important. Would the company have to charge more for telephone calls, and would people mind paying extra? Again, we are asking what the consumer wants, and trying to work out **how to satisfy the consumer while still making a profit**.

FOR DISCUSSION

As part of their product development programme, Cadbury had taken the decision to change one of its ingredients. Information was leaked to the press that the new ingredient contained an animal based product. This news angered vegetarians and led to negative press attention. When they realised the strength of opinion, within days of press coverage, Cadbury quickly apologised to consumers and reverted to their existing recipe.

What could have been the consequences for Cadbury if they had continued with their product modification plans? Would they have been following the marketing concept?

Activity 2 **(15 minutes)**

In small groups, think of one example of a company which has taken into account the marketing concept and one which has not. Give reasons for your choice.

1.4 Customer orientation

The truism that 'without customers, you don't have a business' remains the logic for maintaining a customer orientation. Satisfying customers' needs at a profit should be the central drive of any company.

In contrast to following a market orientation, however, many companies adopt a **sales orientation**. Here, the tendency is to make the product first and then to worry about whether it will sell. Underlying this philosophy is a belief that a good sales force can sell just about anything to anybody.

Levitt distinguishes between sales and marketing orientations in terms of the place of the customer in the marketing process.

Selling focuses on the needs of the seller; marketing on the needs of the buyer. Selling is preoccupied with the seller's need to convert his product into cash; marketing with the idea of satisfying the needs of the customer by means of the product and the whole cluster of things associated with creating, delivering and finally consuming it.

The marketing concept suggests that companies should focus their operations on their customers' needs rather than be driven solely by the organisation's technical competence to produce a particular range of products or services, or by a belief in the sales force.

EXAMPLE

A quotation attributed to Charles Revlon describes the customer orientation of a marketing led organisation.

'In the factory we make cosmetics. In the store we sell hope.'

If new products and services are developed that do not meet customer requirements, the result will be the need for an expensive selling effort to persuade customers that they should purchase something from the company that does not quite fit their purpose.

Taking this to its conclusion: the aim of marketing is to make this kind of selling superfluous.

If the organisation has got its marketing right, it will have produced products and services that meet customers' requirements at a price that customers accept. In theory, at least, little or no sales effort will be needed.

Activity 3 **(10 minutes)**

Quality Goods makes a variety of widgets. Its chairman, in the annual report, boasts of the firm's 'passion for the customer'. 'The customer wants quality goods, and if they don't get them they'll complain. So we don't need to worry, until they do.'

Is this a marketing orientated firm?

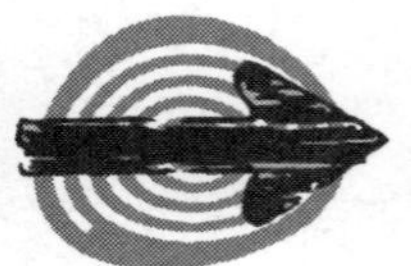

How can businesses take account of the marketing concept? The following section looks at some of the key implications.

1.5 Implications for businesses

If a business accepts the marketing concept, it may have to change the way it works and the structure of its departments. It may need a department of market research, to find out what customers want. It will also need to maintain continuous contact with the market.

A company needs:

(a) An understanding of the market, based on research and not on unsupported hunches

(b) A spirit of innovation: the company must be willing to change as customers' requirements change

(c) Skilled direction and administration of its marketing activities

Consumer research is central to the marketing concept. This is more than counting the potential customers.

Definition

> **Consumer research** has been called the study of the relationship between the personality of the consumer and the personality of the product. It looks at the consumer's motives, which may be unconscious but which still affect his or her choice of products. Techniques such as in-depth interviews and word association tests can be used to find out how consumers are really thinking.

When a company understands consumers, it can design products to appeal to them. For example, a computer game might involve the user fighting enemies on screen: whether those enemies are Martians or dinosaurs could have a big impact on sales, even though the game itself might not be affected by that choice.

> **Activity 4** **(15 minutes)**
>
> The marketing concept is based upon the customer. Why is this so important?

1.6 The history of production and marketing orientations

Definition

> **Production orientation** describes a company which makes what it thinks the customer will buy. It may make good products but will not take the trouble to find out whether there is a market for them.

Until the end of the 18th century, production orientation was the norm. A tradesman or merchant produced something and then found someone to buy it. Remember the statement made by Henry Ford when he pioneered mass car production '*You can have any colour you like as long as it is black*' This comment clearly represents a production orientation. Black was the colour of the cars produced because it was convenient for Ford.

By the middle of the 19th century this was giving way to a consciousness of the role of **sales management**. Companies were beginning to understand and note the power of the consumer. If they did not then other companies would, and these competitors would increase their own business. The depression of the 1920s and 1930s, which made it very difficult for companies to survive, hastened this change.

The next stage was reached with the acceleration of **economic** and **technological development**. By the 1960s, people had significant spare discretionary income which they could spend as they liked. In this new age of **mass consumption,** companies had to persuade people to spend their income on some products rather than others.

Increasingly organisations started to embrace the marketing concept. They realised that in the face of strong competition they had to get closer to their markets and to their customers.

EXAMPLE

A market orientated organisation will have:

(a) A commitment to meeting the needs of customers more successfully than the competition

(b) A structure and processes of operation which are designed to achieve this aim. It is not sufficient that the company employs a marketing manager or has a market research department. All the company's activities must be co-ordinated around the needs of the customer when making decisions about what to produce and, subsequently, how and where the product or service is to be made available.

Underlying all this is the belief that a market orientation is essential to the **long-term profitability** of the company.

In summary the marketing concept has three elements.

- Customer orientation
- Co-ordination of market led activities
- Profit orientation

1.7 The different orientations in modern practice

A company that is production orientated believes that consumers will buy products that are widely available and cheap. Managers of such companies concentrate on achieving high production efficiency and wide distribution. The danger of this approach is obvious with so-called technology worship: high technology products can fail to sell, because consumers' needs are perfectly well satisfied by simpler products.

Between production orientation and marketing orientation lies **sales orientation**. A company with a sales orientation may make products which are not carefully tailored to consumers' needs, but will then use **aggressive advertising and selling methods.**

NOTES

EXAMPLE

The sales orientation is far from dead, as you will know if you have ever been the victim of cold calling by companies selling double-glazing, kitchen replacements and the like. You are called because you happen to have a particular post code or telephone dialling code, not because there is anything wrong with your windows.

The UK energy industry can be described as sales orientated. Since 1999 when the industry was deregulated it has been widely criticised because several companies were found to be using heavy-handed sales techniques in order to persuade consumers to switch suppliers. Forging signatures, falsely claiming telephone agreements and door to door sales people making false claims are a few of the reported tactics used.

In order to protect consumers, in 2001 the Erroneous Transfer Customer Charter was introduced. The charter promises complaints about dubious sales techniques will be dealt with swiftly, and that the customer will be transferred back to their original supplier within a guaranteed 20 days at no cost. To make further improvements, in May 2003 the self regulating Code of Practice for Face to Face Marketing of Energy was launched by the industry. By March 2007, the industry watchdog, EnergyWatch reported that the number of complaints had fallen dramatically to just 780 for the year from April 2006. Despite this fall in complaints about bad sales practice, the industry reputation has remained tarnished.

A market orientated organisation will not only commit itself to meeting the needs of the customer (as in Avis Cars' slogan, 'We try harder'). It will also set up the right **structures** and **processes** to do so. The most significant change over recent years has been the establishment of **customer service departments**, often in highly competitive and low profit margin businesses such as retailing.

The more advanced companies have now entered the relationship marketing era. This is covered in Chapter 3 when we look at 'customer focus' in more detail.

Activity 5 **(20 minutes)**

Think of two organisations that you have direct knowledge of. Are they market oriented or not? What activities show market orientation?

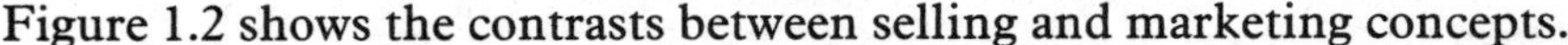

Figure 1.2 shows the contrasts between selling and marketing concepts.

	Starting point	Focus	Means	End
Sales orientation	Factory	Existing products	Selling + promoting	Profit through sales volume
Marketing orientation	Market	Customer needs	Integrated marketing	Profit through customer satisfaction

Figure 1.2: Selling and marketing concepts contrasted

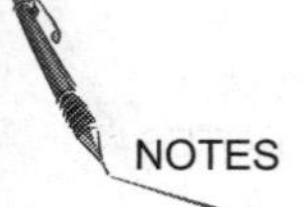

The implications of these contrasts are outlined below.

Marketing orientation

Advantages	Disadvantages/limitations
• Product tailored to the needs of the customer	• Extensive market research needed into customer needs/wants
• Research and development enables the market-led company to keep ahead of the competition	• Expensive and time consuming – time delay for product to market
• Opportunities arise out of a continuous research thrust	• 'Me-too' products that can undercut because there are no costs of research and development
• Knowing your customer enables you to communicate more efficiently, with cost-effective marketing communications	• Irrational consumer behaviour – no amount of research will alter the fickle nature of the average customer
• Produce what you can sell rather than sell what you produce	• Dynamic nature of market place – today's products become tomorrow's throwaways
• Leads to long-term relationships with high customer satisfaction	• Too narrow a focus

Sales orientation

Advantages	Disadvantages/limitations
• Product manufactured relatively inexpensively with minimum time delay to market	• Sell what you produce as opposed to produce what will sell – no product innovation
• Flexibility within production capabilities which ensures swift response to supply-demand imbalance	• Needs extensive sales promotion effort to sell product
• Suits small and medium sized business units that are not particularly well financed – minimises cash flow problems	• No opportunity for long-term profitable growth – concentration on short-term transactional approach
	• Little emphasis on customer satisfaction means limited loyalty and word of mouth marketing

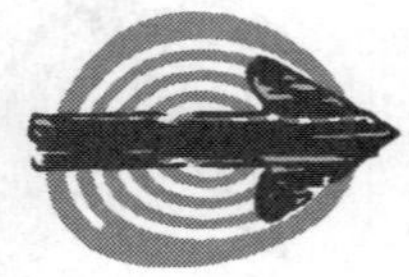

Finally in this section we will consider how marketing fits into the overall business.

1.8 Marketing and the business system

Three aspects of a business are especially important in marketing. These are the distribution system, the information system and the flow of influence.

The distribution system

This is the system for getting goods to customers. It may involve lorries, wholesalers, retailers and mail order. It also includes warehouses and the system for agreeing to supply customers. For example, if a shop buys goods from a factory, it will not want to pay for the goods immediately: there will have to be a system to approve the supply of goods on credit and to collect the money from the shop when it is due.

A distribution system may have the following features.

(a) It may be long or short. If an airline wants to buy a new aircraft, it will probably deal directly with the manufacturer – a short chain. If, at the other extreme, pocket calculators are made in the Far East and sold in Britain there may be a very long chain, involving the maker, an export agent, a shipping company, a wholesaler and retailers.

(b) It may be owned by the producer, for example the branches of a building society, or it may be independent, for example book wholesalers and bookshops which are not owned by publishers.

(c) The customers at the end of the system may be final consumers, or they may produce other goods (for example, the customers of car headlamp bulb makers are mostly car manufacturers).

The information system

A company cannot be market-oriented unless it gets information about its customers, perhaps by conducting interviews or by enclosing a questionnaire with the product. Information also needs to be sent in the other direction: people need to be told what they can buy and why they might like to buy it. This may involve advertising, catalogues and other forms of publicity. The main goal is to get across the special features of a product, which make it a better buy than its rivals. You can see that information travels both ways: from the company to the customer and from the customer to the company.

The flow of influence

Businesses do not operate in isolation: they influence each other, as competitors, and their potential customers are influenced by all sorts of factors. We will examine these influences in detail later in this Course Book.

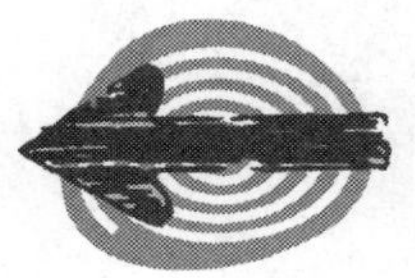

You have seen how marketing developed, and you can differentiate a marketing-oriented business from one which is production-orientated. Refer back to the definitions of marketing in section 1.2.

2 MARKETING ISSUES

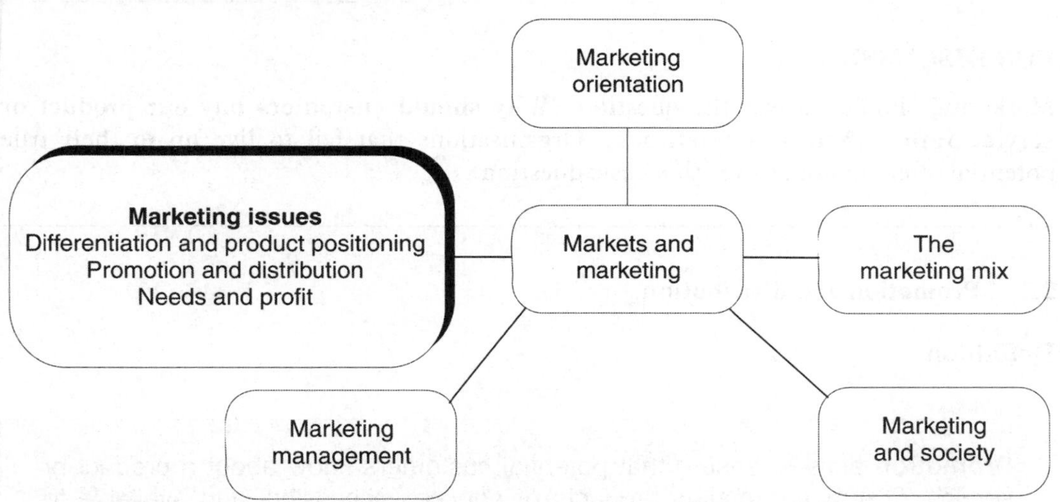

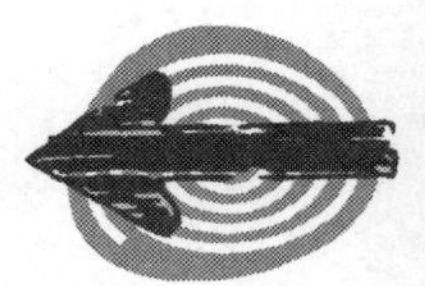

In this section we look at some marketing issues in order to demonstrate the breadth of marketing activity. These are shown in the diagram above and described below by returning to the same recognised definitions of marketing covered earlier in this chapter.

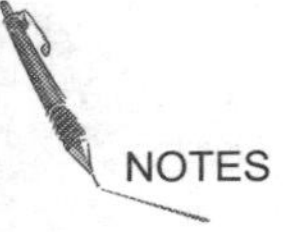

2.1 Differentiation and product positioning

Definition

Product differentiation occurs when specific products or brands each have a specific combination of costs and benefits which a particular set of potential customers seek. This allows the product to be positioned in the market for specific customers.

If you look at many markets you will see that there is very little intrinsic difference between the products supplied. This is particularly noticeable in the area of services. Most of the high street banks offer their customers the same facilities and account structures. Any innovations, such as telephone banking, are easily copied. In order to create improved sales, banks use promotional activity and concentrate on how their products serve to create unique images (such as accounts for young people, or for the very successful). This is called differentiation and also positions the product to appeal to a certain section of the market.

Activity 6 **(15 minutes)**

Try to identify what differentiates one brand of coffee from another. You should be able to think of at least five elements. For example, Carte Noire sells its instant coffee in the UK with USPs of black, gold and white packaging and the fact that it is a French brand.

FOR DISCUSSION

Marketing should answer the question: '**Why should customers buy our product or service rather than a competitor's?**' Organisations that fail to live up to their true potential often do not answer this basic question.

2.2 Promotion and distribution

Definition

Promotion aims to ensure that potential customers know about a product or service. Distribution makes products or services accessible and available to consumers or buyers.

Customers must know about a product before they can buy it. This sounds obvious but many organisations do not give this aspect enough attention. Either they fail to reach their customers, or they give unclear or incomplete messages. Many organisations realise the importance of **communication** and invest heavily in this process. The Body

Shop, for example, sees itself not simply as a retailer but also as an organisation committed to communication.

One of the basic reasons for the evolution of marketing is the distance there now is between the **source of production** and the customer. Organisations now spend a lot of time trying to supply the market in as efficient a way as possible. The **retail network** is often a very effective way of doing this, but producers lose control of how their product is finally presented at the point of sale. Marketing is constantly reviewing methods of distribution and it is common for companies in the same sector to approach the market in different ways.

EXAMPLE

If you compare the sales and distribution methods employed in cosmetics by Avon and Revlon you will be able to see that both methods have their advantages and drawbacks. By going door to door Avon are not reliant upon people going to shops and can offer the service of home delivery. Revlon, by choosing to distribute their products in high street locations, can benefit from the fact that chain stores like Boots have millions of customers weekly.

Activity 7 **(15 minutes)**

Analyse further the strategies used by Avon and Revlon. Can you think of any other pros and cons? What basic decisions would each face in changing their method of distribution?

2.3 Needs and profit

Definition

Marketing is concerned with the matching of an organisation's capabilities with consumers' wants.

This definition recognises the central place that marketing plays in the overall business process. By first examining the wants of the marketplace, and then appraising whether the organisation is capable of satisfying these wants, marketing performs a central role.

EXAMPLE

A good example of this definition in action is when United Biscuits decided to enter the confectionery market by acquiring an established company rather than trying to build a market presence from its existing business. United Biscuits felt that the latter course was

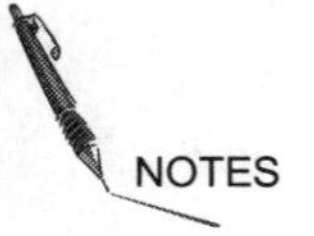

beyond their resources but what they did have was the means to buy the confectionery company Terry's of York.

Activity 8 **(15 minutes)**

It is obviously easier to buy an existing business than to build up a new one from scratch. What is the great advantage of doing this?

Definition

Marketing is the process of determining consumer demand for a product, motivating its sale and distributing it into ultimate consumption at a profit.

Profit is one of the key objectives of most organisations, if not in the short term then certainly in the longer term. There are two key aspects.

(a) Making sure that the **income from sales exceeds costs** so that the product gives a good rate of return.

(b) Conversely, ensuring that costs, including marketing costs, are properly **controlled.**

Definition

Marketing is the management process responsible for identifying, anticipating and satisfying customer requirements efficiently and profitably.

This definition (the CIM one which we saw earlier in this chapter) adds the dimension of anticipating customer requirements and brings in the key function of **forecasting**: what are consumers likely to want in the future? It also acknowledges the existence of not-for-profit organisations such as colleges and libraries whose aim is not profit but efficiency, but for whom marketing techniques and concepts have great importance.

Activity 9 **(15 minutes)**

Consider the marketing activities of an organisation with which you are familiar, perhaps a company you or someone in your family has worked for. Assess whether the organisation does identify, anticipate and satisfy customer requirements efficiently and profitably.

Now that we can define marketing in terms of what it sets out to achieve, we shall look at how it comprises a number of elements which can be combined in the way best served to achieving the given aims.

3 THE MARKETING MIX

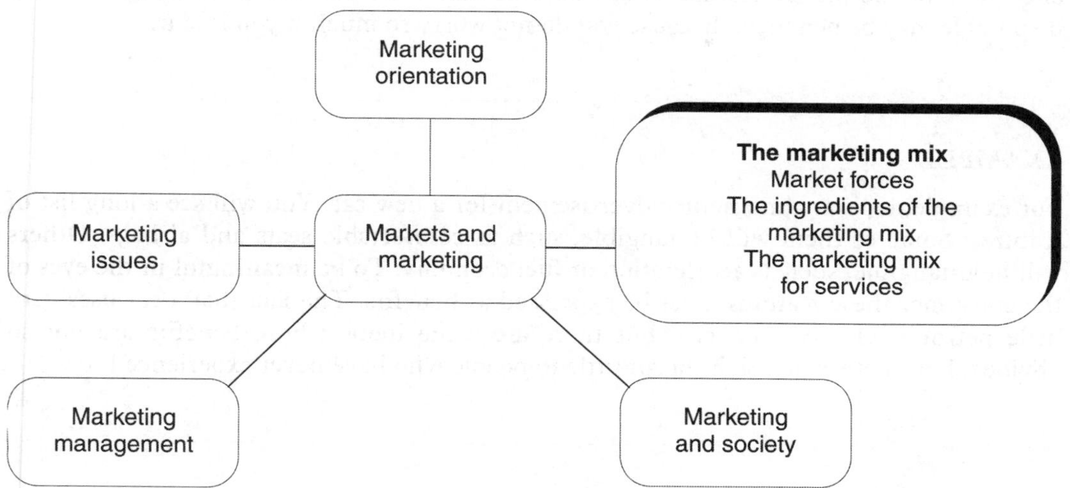

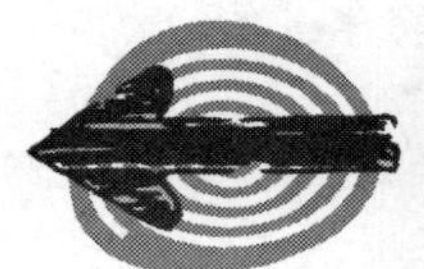

The marketing mix consists of the variables under the firm's control that the marketing manager manipulates in an attempt to achieve tactical marketing objectives.

3.1 The ingredients of the marketing mix

The basic marketing mix has four elements, known as the **four Ps**: product, price, place, and promotion.

This gives rise to a further definition of marketing and its mix.

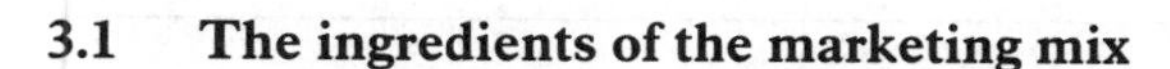

Definition

> **Marketing** is the ability of an organisation to provide the right product, at the right price, via the right outlets (place) and presented in the right way (promotion).

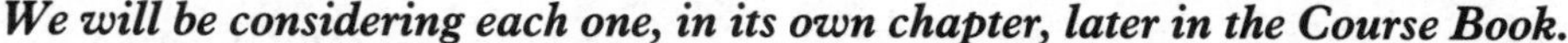

We will be considering each one, in its own chapter, later in the Course Book.

Product

What is a **product**? It is not simply what an organisation produces: it is **what the consumer buys.**

To understand this distinction we need to appreciate the difference between product features and consumer benefits. A product is composed of a bundle of features.

Importantly, consumers buy benefits, not features. To illustrate this point, think about the pen you may be using as you are studying right now. If it is a 'Bic' style pen, it is probably true to say that when you bought it you didn't really want a piece of plastic containing a tube of ink and a metal point at the end. In essence these are the features of a 'Bic' pen. Rather than these features it is probably true to state that what you actually require is an implement that enables you to write. The trail of benefits associated with this is that it means you can write notes in this Course Book, the benefit of doing is that you are more likely to be studying effectively and therefore pass your course!

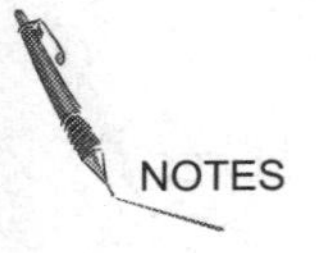

Additional benefits may be that you didn't want to pay a lot for this pen and so the cheapness of the plastic feature would be a benefit. The fact that it is designed to be disposable may be beneficial because you do not worry so much if you lose it.

EXAMPLE

For example, look at a magazine advertisement for a new car. You will see a long list of features. Some of them will be tangible, such as comfortable seats and airbags. Others will be intangible, such as acceleration or fuel economy. To be meaningful in the eyes of the consumer these features must be expressed as benefits. The fact that a car uses very little petrol is clearly a benefit, but there are some items whose benefits are not so obvious. Power steering might mean little to people who have never experienced it

FOR DISCUSSION

Look at an advertisement for breakfast cereals. What is it the customer is buying? What are the various features and what are the benefits? How do the companies ensure that features are expressed as benefits?

When we are thinking about a product, and how to present its benefits to consumers, it is often useful to think in terms of **three product aspects** or levels. The **physical aspect** relates to the components and materials used in the manufacture of the product: for example, a pullover may be 100% pure wool. This is also known as the **actual product**. The second element is the **functional aspect** of the product. This is a statement of how a product performs and the needs it satisfies: for example, a wool pullover should be warm and comfortable. This is also called the **core product.** The last aspect is the wider benefits that the product or service will bestow upon the owner. These may be ancillary benefits such as credit terms or an extended guarantee, or they may be less tangible benefits such as smart appearance. The inclusion of these benefits forms the **augmented product**. The **total product concept** recognises this complexity and influences the processes of promotion and brand management.

Activity 10 **(15 minutes)**

Conduct an analysis of beefburgers in terms of their physical, functional and augmented product aspects.

An important decision for organisations is the **product range**. This consists of two dimensions – **width** and **depth**. A car maker may have products in all parts, known as segments, of the market: luxury cars, family cars, small cheap cars, and so on. This is width. It may then offer a wide variety of options within each segment – a choice of engines, colours, accessories and so on. This is depth.

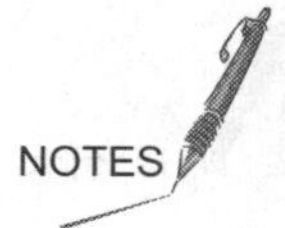

FOR DISCUSSION

What segments of the insurance market might an insurance company offer products in? (To get you started, consider life insurance and household insurance.) To what extent would the company have to market the products in different ways? Can you think of companies which have a presence in all segments, and of companies which stick to just a few segments?

Price

There are many potential influences on price. Here are a few important considerations.

(a) **Costs.** These are split between fixed costs and variable costs. Fixed costs do not change over a given level of production or sales.

For a manufacturer **fixed costs** will include the cost of renting or buying the factory and offices as well as any staff who are paid fixed salaries. **Variable costs** are those that change with the level of production. For example, if a manufacturer sells more he will have to spend more on materials to meet the increased production, more on light, heat and power and more on transportation.

For a retailer fixed costs will include the cost of renting or buying the building and the display stands. Variable costs are costs that change with the level of sales. For example, if a retailer sells more he will have to spend more on packaging and may have to employ extra sales staff. Costs will dictate the minimum price that can be charged in order to make a profit.

(b) The level of **competitors' prices**.

(c) The effect of price on **consumers' perceptions**. Some consumers like to see a product as being good value. Others will expect to pay a high price, because they suspect that a cheap product will be of low **quality**.

(d) **Market conditions.** If there is a strawberry shortage for example due to bad weather, suppliers are able to charge a premium because there will be individuals willing and able to pay a higher price to ensure they can still guarantee they can eat strawberries.

Activity 11 **(15 minutes)**

How do you think competitors' pricing affects the pricing decision for a product of your choice? What problems can you foresee with a method which only takes into account competitors' prices?

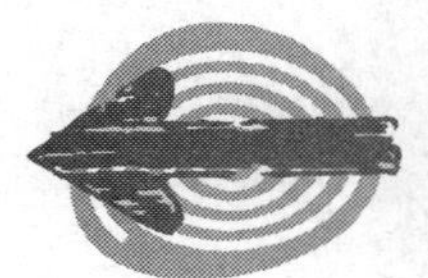

A range of alternative pricing strategies are discussed in Chapter 10.

Place

We have seen that contact is a key element of the marketing process: if you cannot get in touch with your customers, you cannot sell anything. For many products, organisations must rely on third parties to reach the customer. These third parties are collectively known as **middlemen** and the access they provide is called **distribution channels**. There are two major types of middleman.

(a) **Merchants** take title to the goods, that is they become owners of the goods. They then resell them. **Wholesalers** and **retailers** are in this category.

(b) **Agents and brokers** do not own the goods, but merely assist in the transfer of ownership from, say, the manufacturer to the customer. Examples of these are insurance brokers and estate agents: if you sell your house through an estate agent, the agent never actually owns your house. Many services are supplied in this way.

Distribution channels are increasingly sophisticated and in recent times the power of the middlemen in certain markets has grown considerably. Distributors have invested in **information technology**, and have developed it in order to become more efficient, more competitive and ultimately more profitable.

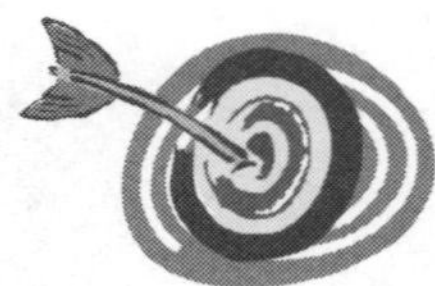

EXAMPLE

In retailing, re-ordering and stock control is made easier with the use of barcode scanners at tills, which record exactly which products have been sold. Innovations such as EFTPOS – Electronic Funds Transfer at the Point of Sale – have greatly improved the process of exchange. This enables a customer's credit or debit card to be electronically read at the till and the total bill is then automatically debited from the customer's account and credited to the retailer's account. Stock records may also be updated.

Disintermediation is a term related to Internet distribution methods. When companies sell directly to customers via their website they cut out the middle men, enabling additional customer convenience by adding an additional method to purchase the product and retaining more control of how their brand is perceived. Unipath adopted this approach by selling their Clearblue branded pregnancy tests from their consumer website. The brand is still distributed via their existing channels of pharmacies and major grocery retailers.

A recent innovation has been the increased use of **franchising** as a means of gaining distribution for a product or service. A franchise operator invests their own money, and receives guidance and support from the company behind the operation. The Body Shop, Dyno-Rod and Kentucky Fried Chicken are good examples of franchises.

Activity 12 **(15 minutes)**

Think of your own example of a franchise and suggest what the benefits may be to the investor.

Promotion

The **promotional mix** has several aspects, including **advertising, personal selling, public relations** and **sales promotion.**

There is a constant attempt to measure the direct results of promotional expenditure.

(a) The number of people seeing a **particular advertisement** is measured by extensive surveys and in the case of television by the use of special meters in a sample of households.

(b) **Direct mail** offers the key benefit of reaching consumers precisely. Order forms are likely to include special codes so that the response from different areas of the country and with different delays after the mailshot can be monitored easily.

(c) **Publicity** activities, such as presentations to journalists, can be monitored by measuring the amount of media exposure gained.

(d) The impact of **personal visits** by sales staff has always been monitored, simply by seeing which staff bring in the business.

(e) Special **sales promotional activities** invariably have inbuilt measurement. Technology has had a big impact, with the use of automatic **information collection** using barcodes on money-off coupons.

Consistency in the marketing mix

An essential feature of the marketing mix is that it must be consistent; that is to say, the various elements must relate sensibly to each other and provide mutual support. A mix is unlikely to be successful if such consistency and support are not present, whether it relates to an individual product, a product range or a brand.

Thus, for example, if a brand is promoted as a cheerful, everyday, value-for-money idea, the price of the products must reflect this promotion. Similarly, if a consumer product is typically purchased on impulse, it must be given the widest possible distribution: chocolate snack bars and ice cream bars are good example here.

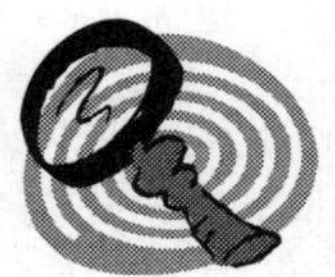

We have now seen what the four elements in the marketing mix are. However, the marketing mix is only one way of looking at marketing. As marketing has evolved, people have found that the four Ps are not always enough: we will now see how the mix has been expanded to apply to services as well.

3.2 The marketing mix for services

Definition

A **service** is any activity or benefit offered by one party to another which is essentially intangible and does not result in the ownership of anything physical. An example is a seat on an aircraft, which the customer uses for the duration of the flight but does not own.

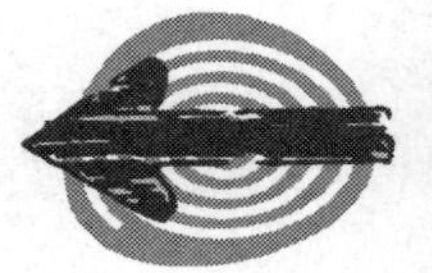

Services marketing is the subject of its own chapter later in the Course Book. What we give here is a brief introduction.

The **services sector** has been one of the fastest growing parts of many economies. Indeed, many of the developed economies of the world can now be called **service economies,** because the services sector contributes the greater part of economic activity. This trend has continued as societies continue to move towards post-industrial economies.

The special **characteristics of services** are:

- Intangibility
- Variability of nature and quality
- Inseparability of production and consumption
- Perishability – following on from the concept of inseparability, services cannot be stored

In addition to the four elements in the marketing mix for tangible products, there are three more ingredients in the mix for services. These are **process, physical evidence** and **people.**

Process

User-friendly systems for selling and buying are essential. Not only should it be easy for organisations to operate efficiently, but customers should not face any unnecessary bureaucracy or delay. Information technology and the widespread use of computers to take the drudgery out of form filling, the ordering of goods and the maintenance of accurate customer records have greatly aided the move to more customer-friendly systems.

EXAMPLE: INSURANCE OVER THE PHONE

Let us look at an example. Do you like filling in forms? You can now buy car insurance over the telephone or online. You give a certain amount of information and with the use of a computer you can get a firm quotation. Driver and vehicle details then have to be confirmed by you. One company may send these details on a computer-generated listing together with a blank form for you to complete. Another company may send a form that had already been completed by the computer. You simply have to check the entries on the form and sign to show that the information is correct. The second company has the advantage, because it has made life easier for you.

A third company Inspop.com Limited launched their online brand Confused.com in May 2005. The site benefits consumers by first not being a broker charging search fees, but its major advantage is that the consumer completes one online form where details are then saved on 94% of the UK motor insurers websites who return a quote to Confused.com within five minutes. The consumer can then see an itemised list of insurers and directly compare policy details and prices. Once the preferred policy is chosen the consumer is then redirected to the insurers website where all forms are already completed and all that is left within the transaction is completion of payment details.

FOR DISCUSSION

'I am the world's worst salesman: therefore I must make it easy for people to buy':

F W Woolworth.

How do shops make the process of buying easy? Can a service provider such as a bank adopt the same approach?

Physical evidence

Services tend to suffer from the **intangible** nature of the offering. Organisations in the service sector are increasingly using devices such as newsletters (often via e-mail) to maintain the customer's desire to have the service.

EXAMPLE

The service provided by a breakdown company like the RAC is a sense of security which only becomes a reality when you have to make use of it. The sense of security tends to fade when you do not make any use of it, and then you start to question the fee. A plastic membership card is issued as a reminder of the service and its provider. The patrolmen drive vehicles with distinctive logos and they wear uniforms as a permanent display of the quality of the service.

People

Variability and inseparability mean that a key element of services marketing is the people who are an integral part of the process. If the staff who deal with customers are poorly motivated or badly trained, this can greatly affect the quality of the service. Many people in organisations come into direct customer contact, not just those whose jobs are staffing counters or in other sales positions, but also others in backroom roles such as accounts and stores may have contact with customers. How they treat customers will greatly impact upon the business. Any problems that arise can be largely overcome by **training** in interpersonal skills, setting **standards of conduct and dress** and creating **customer service teams.** It is important that **internal communication** is effective to ensure that customers are dealt with properly.

EXAMPLE

Saks the UK based hair and beauty company provide conversational training and manuals to help improve the in-salon experience for clients. Cliché hairdresser discussion topics such as '*where are you going on holiday*' that customers were found to dislike are banned.

Consistency again

Clearly, the need for consistency and mutual support already explained in relation to the basic marketing mix also applies to the extended marketing mix for services.

Activity 13 **(15 minutes)**

Travel agents provide the service of booking travel and holidays. In addition to the services they sell how do they address the extra three Ps of the services marketing mix?

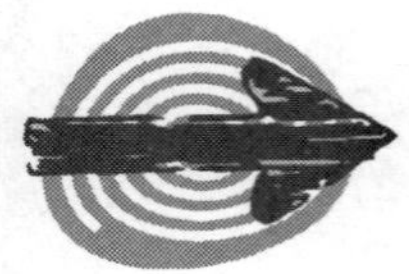

The marketing concept and marketing mix will be applied in differing ways depending on what sort of market an organisation operates in. A consideration of different categories of market follows later in the Course Book.

4 MARKETING MANAGEMENT

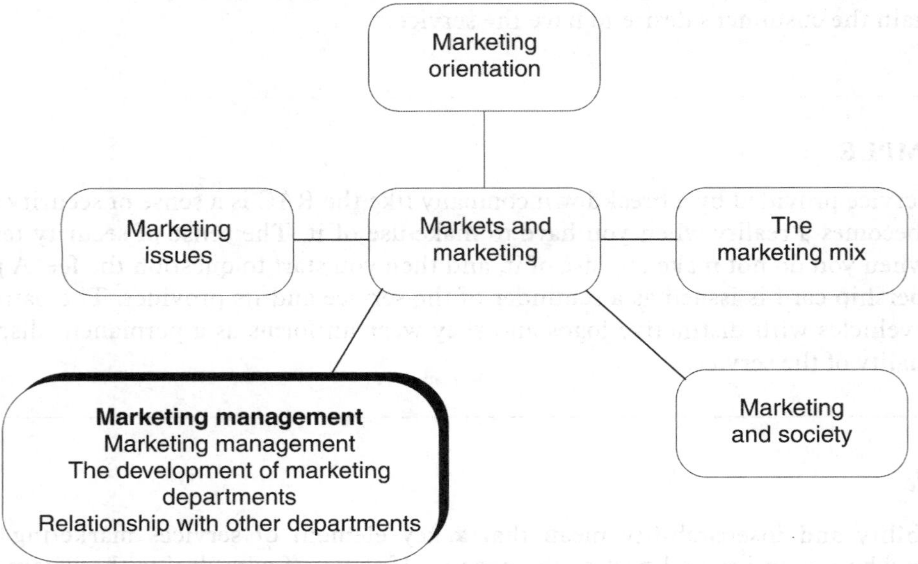

4.1 Marketing management

Definition

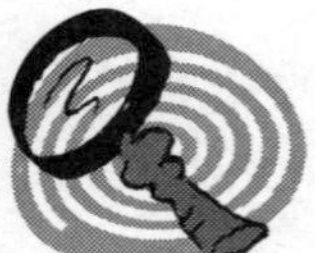

Marketing management is the process of devising, implementing and monitoring the marketing plan.

Marketing management involves **analysis, planning, implementation** and **control.**

Analysis

A marketing orientation begins and ends with the customer. Analysis in marketing management involves identifying **who** are the customers, **why** do they buy the product or service and are they **satisfied** with it? This process includes market research. The process can include **quantitative analysis** (How many customers? What is our market share? How many competitors?) and **qualitative analysis** (Why do people buy? What are their motivations, attitudes, personality?).

In some organisations, market information is integrated into a **marketing information system** which can be used by managers in making marketing decisions. Increasingly, this will be in the form of a **computerised model. Decision support systems** use such information to develop effective marketing decision making.

Planning

Marketing management also uses the information from marketing analysis to develop the organisation's marketing response – the **strategic marketing plan.**

The strategic marketing plan will involve:

- Identification of selected **target markets**
- Forecasting **future demand** in each market
- Setting the levels of each element of the **marketing mix** for each target market

Implementation

It is essential that plans are properly implemented and all resources are available. Individuals who will play a role in the success of the overall strategy should also be aware of their input and are in a position to assist appropriately. It is the implementation stage is one which requires careful management.

Control

Control involves setting **quantifiable targets,** and then checking performance against these targets. If necessary, **remedial action** is taken to ensure that planned and actual performance correspond.

4.2 The development of marketing departments

Although every organisation is different, common patterns appear in the **structure of organisations**. Current departments of marketing are widely thought to have evolved from sales departments. Traditionally all marketplace issues would have been the responsibility of a sales director who would typically report direct to senior management. When the need for a marketing orientated approach became more apparent a marketing director might appear in parallel to the sales director, each having a distinct functional department.

The marketing department plays a key role in **co-ordinating marketing activities.** The **marketing manager** has to take responsibility for planning, resource allocation, monitoring and controlling the marketing effort. In order to ensure that the marketing effort has maximum effectiveness, this co-ordinating role is crucial, involving co-ordination of marketing efforts for different products in different markets as well as ensuring that individual marketing campaigns are themselves co-ordinated and consistent.

4.3 Relationship with other departments

Marketing managers often claim that marketing involves every facet of the organisation's operations. It can be argued that the philosophy of a customer orientation, central to marketing is a central business function which is a prerequisite to success.

However, this is not always the case, even in companies serving consumer markets. The product orientation is still appropriate in many sectors such as pharmaceuticals and

many professional services. However, it is usually combined with exclusive marketing input.

5 MARKETING AND SOCIETY

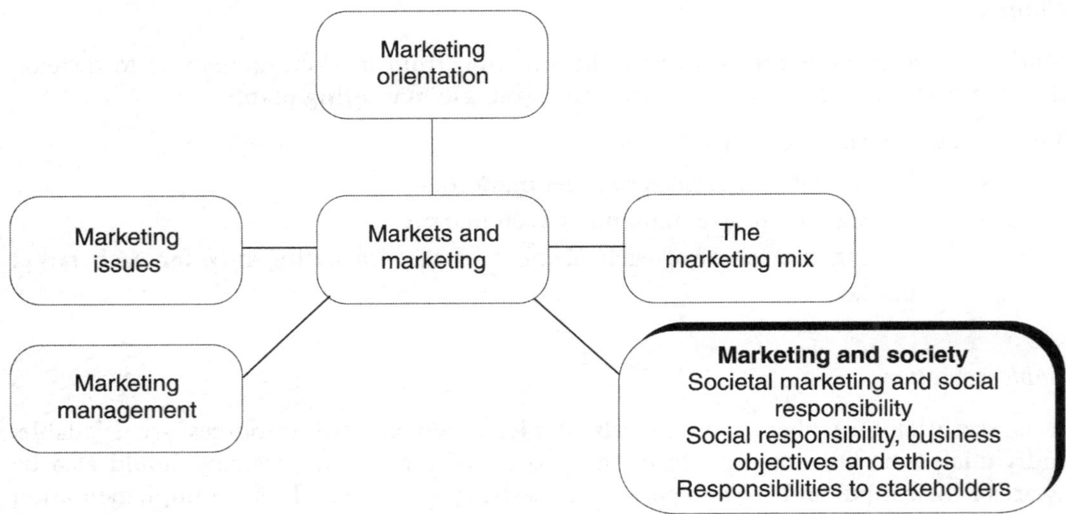

5.1 Societal marketing and social responsibility

Critics of the marketing concept suggest that marketing is so powerful that it can make people want things they don't really need, or worse, create a desire for products and services that are against the long-term interests of customers and of society as a whole. **Cigarettes** are the most obvious example; non-nutritious **convenience food** products are another; another is **instant win scratch cards**, whose 'get rich quick' marketing appeals most to the very poorest members of society, who can barely afford basics like food, never mind gambling.

Such as

A number of writers have suggested that a **societal marketing concept** should replace the marketing concept as a philosophy for the future.

Definitions

The **societal marketing concept** is a management orientation that holds that the key task of the organisation is to determine the needs and wants of target markets and to adapt the organisation to delivering the desired satisfactions more effectively and efficiently than its competitors in a way that preserves or enhances the consumers' and society's well-being.

Social responsibility is accepting responsibilities to the various publics of an organisation which go beyond contractual or legal requirements.

An increasingly popular view is that marketing should aim to maximise customer satisfaction, but within the constraints that all firms have a responsibility to **society** as a **whole** and to the **environment**.

(a) Some products which consume energy (eg motor cars) should perhaps make more efficient use of the energy they consume.

(b) It may be possible to extend the useful life of certain products.

(c) Other products might be made smaller, so that they make use of fewer materials (eg products made using microtechnology).

(d) More ecological alternatives should be actively researched with the product development process.

Activity 14 **(15 minutes)**

Does your own organisation do anything that indicates to you that it takes a responsible attitude towards society and the environment?

5.2 Social responsibility, business objectives and ethics

FOR DISCUSSION

Institutions like **hospitals** and **schools** exist because health care and education are seen to be **desirable social objectives** by government and the public at large, if they can be afforded.

However, **where does this leave businesses?** How far is it reasonable, or even appropriate, for businesses to exercise 'social responsibility' by giving to charities, voluntarily imposing strict environmental objectives on themselves, offering the same conditions of work to all workers, and so on? For example, if someone is made ill by industrial pollution, should the polluter pay the sick person damages or compensation?

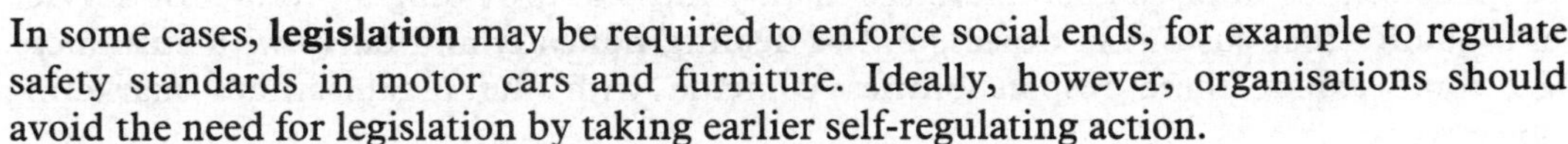

In some cases, **legislation** may be required to enforce social ends, for example to regulate safety standards in motor cars and furniture. Ideally, however, organisations should avoid the need for legislation by taking earlier self-regulating action.

One of the arguments for the 'social responsibility approach' is that in the long term it benefits the organisation. **Enlightened self-interest** leads to socially responsible decisions, so there is no conflict between the objectives of the organisation (eg profit) and its social and ethical obligations.

Social responsibility and cause related marketing initiatives need to be carefully considered so that intentions are not thought to be manipulative.

EXAMPLE

In 2003 Cadbury launched a cause related marketing campaign known as 'Get Active'. The campaign involved several elements all related to the idea of encouraging children to participate more in sports such as: training for 5000 teachers to become sports specialists; research with Loughborough university into activity levels amongst children; the use of celebrity sports ambassadors to promote activity; Cadbury staff involvement through volunteering and adoption of schools to assist with sports; a free activity day event at the National Exhibition Centre and; a consumer on-pack token

scheme to collect and exchange for unbranded sports goods for schools. It was this final element, the most visible aspect which led to controversy. The Food Commission, British Diabetic Association, Consumers Association and National Union of Teachers immediately criticised the campaign for encouraging children to eat more chocolate at a time when child obesity rates are increasing to epidemic levels. The organisations highlighted their concerns with the campaign to the media using example statistics such as the need to consume 2370 chocolate bars to save enough tokens for a cricket set. Very few press reports mentioned that the token collection was only one part of the overall campaign.

Ethics

The terms 'marketing ethics' and 'social responsibility' are often used synonymously – and they may amount to the same thing – but there is a difference.

- Society expects, but does not demand, that organisations will not act in a way which harms the general public or which is thought to be socially irresponsible.
- **Marketing ethics** relate to morality rather than society's interests. Morality is essentially an **individual** judgement about what is right and wrong.

An ethical issue in marketing can be defined as an identifiable problem, situation or opportunity requiring an individual or organisation to choose from among several actions that must be evaluated as **right or wrong**, ethical or unethical.

5.3 Responsibilities to stakeholders

Responsibilities to customers

Responsibilities towards **customers** are mainly those of providing a **product or service** of a **quality** that customers expect, and of **dealing honestly** and **fairly** with customers. To some extent these responsibilities coincide with the organisation's marketing objectives.

Consumerism

The **importance of customer care** has been acknowledged as a result of the growth of consumerism. In the UK a number of consumer rights have been recognised in law.

(a) The right to be **informed of the true facts** of the buyer-seller relationship, eg the true cost of loans (APRs must be published in any advertisement for loans); truth in advertising (watchdog bodies vet any advertisement and consumers complain about advertisements to the Advertising Standards Authority).

(b) The right to be **protected from unfair exploitation** or intrusion. Consumers' trust in organisations must not be abused, eg the sale of mailing lists to third parties can lead to consumers receiving vast quantities of 'junk' mail.

(c) **The right to a particular quality of life**. This right is focused increasingly on environmental protection making suppliers aware of the implications of their actions on the eco-system, and the quality of water, air etc.

Definition

> **Consumerism** is a term used to describe the increased **importance and power of consumers**. It includes the increasingly organised consumer groups, and the recognition by producers that consumer satisfaction is the key to long-term profitability.

Marketers are increasingly responsive to **consumer pressures** to maintain a **responsible** image and reputation. This may deter aggressive marketing tactics, as the need to consider the best interests of customers should be paramount in a marketing strategy. This approach should bring **long-term benefits**, rather than attempting to maximise short-term profits.

Responsibilities towards the community

A business only succeeds because it is part of a wider community. It should be responsible for:

(a) Upholding the social and ethical values of the community

(b) Contributing towards the well-being of the community, eg by sponsoring local events and charities, or providing facilities for the community to use (eg sports fields). Giving to such causes is one way of encouraging a relationship

(c) Responding constructively to complaints from local residents or politicians (eg about problems for local traffic caused by the organisation's delivery vehicles)

Artistic sponsorships, charitable donations and the like are, of course, a useful medium of **public relations** and can reflect well on the business. It can be regarded as a form of promotion, which like advertising, serves to enhance consumer awareness of the business, while not encouraging the sale of a particular brand.

Responsibilities to employees

General principles should take the form of **good pay** and **working conditions**, and **good training** and **development schemes.** They should also extend into:

- Recruitment policy
- Redundancy and retirement policies

Recruitment of new staff should be done as carefully as possible, because if an organisation recruits an individual who turns out to be bad at his job the company has to sack him.

Staff who are about to retire, after years of service with the organisation, should be provided for in their **retirement**.

(a) The organisation might have a **good pension scheme**.

(b) One of the problems for retired people is learning what to do with their leisure time. Some organisations provide **training courses** and discussion groups for employees who are coming up for retirement, to help them to plan their future time constructively.

NOTES

Dealing with **redundancies** is a more difficult problem. In such a situation, the organisation might:

(a) Try to **redeploy** as many staff as possible, without making them redundant

(b) Where necessary, provide **retraining** to give staff the skills to do a new job within the organisation

(c) Take steps to help them to get a job elsewhere

EXAMPLE

Sports shoe manufacturers Nike (www.nike.com) have been fiercely attacked over their alleged mistreatment of workers in third world countries, where most of their shoes are actually made.

Reebok's shoes are also made mainly in third world countries and the company has gone to considerable lengths over the years to stave off criticism.

'More than a decade ago, it set up the Reebok Human Rights Foundation (www.reebok.com/Reebok/US/HumanRights), which gives financial aid to human rights groups such as Human Rights Watch, the Commission for Refugee Women and Children, and The Carter Center.

The company also became the sponsor of the Reebok Human Rights Award, which provides grants of $50,000 to human-rights activists under the age of 30 'who have made significant contributions to the field of human rights strictly through non-violent means. Since the awards were introduced in 1988, more than 60 recipients from over 35 countries have received the award.'

Adapted from *PR Week* (USA edition), 5 August 2002

Responsibilities to suppliers

The responsibilities of an organisation towards its suppliers come down mainly to trading relationships.

(a) The organisation's size could give it considerable power as a buyer. One guideline might be that the organisation should not use its **power unscrupulously** (say to force the supplier to lower his prices under threat of withdrawing business).

(b) Suppliers (especially small businesses) might rely on getting prompt payment in accordance with the terms of trade negotiated with its customers. Another guideline is that an organisation should **not delay payments** to suppliers beyond the agreed credit period.

(c) All **information** obtained from suppliers and potential suppliers should be kept **confidential**.

(d) All **suppliers** should be **treated fairly**, and this means:

(i) Giving potential new suppliers a chance to win some business

(ii) Maintaining long-standing relationships that have been built up over the years with some suppliers. (Long-established suppliers should not

be replaced unless there is a significant commercial advantage for the organisation from such a move.)

Responsibilities to competitors

Some responsibilities should exist towards competitors. Responsibilities regarding competitors are by no means solely directed by social conscience or ethics however: there is also a great deal of **law** surrounding the conduct of fair trading, monopolies, mergers, anti-competitive practices, abuses of a dominant market position and restrictive trade practices.

EXAMPLE

Social responsibility should not be confused with business expedience. For instance Covisint (www.covisint.com) is a co-operative venture set up in 2000 that now includes many of the major competing car manufacturers (Ford, General Motors, Nissan, Peugeot and so on). The purpose is to create a central marketplace for suppliers of car components.

But this has not been done out of social conscience: it is simply in everyone's business interests.

Chapter roundup

- Markets are the places where goods and services are exchanged. Markets evolved as soon as people started making things they did not need, to give to others in exchange for things they did need.
- A business may have a production orientation, concentrating on making things, or a marketing orientation, concentrating on serving customers' needs. A sales orientation is a half-way house between these.
- The definition of marketing provided by the Chartered Institute of Marketing is marketing is 'the management process which identifies, anticipates and supplies customer requirements efficiently and profitably.'
- The marketing concept is the attitude that business decisions should be based on what the consumer wants.
- Marketing can be defined in many ways, but they all focus on getting sales by finding customers, finding out what they want and delivering it.
- The marketing mix is a schematic plan to guide analysis of marketing problems. The four elements in the mix are product, price, promotion, place. Each of these has a chapter to itself later in this book. Three more Ps have also been suggested: people, processes and physical evidence.
- We have seen how the marketing orientation has resulted in increased importance for the marketing department.
- We have also looked at ways of organising the marketing function in an organisation and at the relationship of marketing with other parts of the organisation.
- Marketing has an impact on society. Although social responsibility may conflict with business objectives there is a growing body of opinion that accepts that it is in the organisation's own best interests.

NOTES

Quick quiz

1 What is the marketing concept?

2 Give three different definitions of marketing.

3 How does a marketing orientation affect a business's structure?

4 Give four examples of ways in which a business could contact potential customers.

5 What are the two key aspects of making profits?

6 What are the four Ps?

7 What is the total product concept?

8 What are the two dimensions of product range?

9 How have distribution channels become more sophisticated in recent years?

10 How can the effectiveness of different types of promotional activity be measured?

11 Why is physical evidence important in the marketing of services?

12 What is 'societal marketing'?

Answers to Quick quiz

1 The attitude that all business decisions should be based on what the customer wants

2 See section 1.2.

3 See section 1.7.

4 See section 2.2.

5 Ensuring that revenue exceeds costs and that costs are controlled.

6 Price, product, place and promotion.

7 A product has features which to a consumer are expressed as benefits. These may be grouped into core, actual and augmented product aspects.

8 Width and depth

9 Middlemen have become more important and information technology plays an important role.

10 Surveys, meters, analysis of consumer responses at point of sale, measurement of media exposure for PR, monitoring of sales by sales staff, barcodes and other forms of information technology.

11 It gives a sense of security.

12 See the definition in section 5.1.

Answers to Activities

1 (a) Is fairly straightforward. The gardener is trying to get a task done (mowing the lawn), presumably with the minimum of effort and at economical cost.

(b) Is more complicated. The purchaser of life insurance may be trying to remove a feeling of financial insecurity, or to fulfil a duty of providing for dependants. There may be more immediate problems involved; for example, taking out life insurance is often a pre-condition of getting a mortgage.

(c) Is in some ways the trickiest of all. Although there are some simple facts involved (the need to get from A to B cheaply and conveniently), there are also subtle points of self-image and status in the choice of a particular model of car.

2 You will obviously have thought of companies you know. One example of companies taking account of the marketing concept is the supermarkets, such as Sainsbury. They regularly ask their customers what they want and how they may improve their service, for example by asking what new products should be stocked, or enhancing organic ranges. One company who does not appear to be taking account of the marketing concept, in the sense that an existing customer group could be alienated, is British Airways. They are increasing their focus on higher paying customers, at the expense of economy passengers who are finding the number of seats available being cut.

3 No. A mere absence of complaints is not the same as the identification of customer needs. The firm, if anything, has a product orientation.

4 Because, if a company knows what customers want it can design products and services which they know customers will buy.

5 To decide whether an organisation is market oriented, we should see whether its products are what the customers want. We should also look at how it deals with its customers. Typical activities that demonstrate a market orientation are clearly identified customer service functions, a real understanding of customer needs (as shown by Tesco with their 'every little helps' campaign), trust in the customer (as shown by Marks & Spencer and John Lewis with their almost unconditional goods returns system) and regular customer surveys.

6 Possible elements differentiating a coffee brand: price (easily copied); product quality; brand image; promotional techniques; availability, packaging.

7 Avon depends very heavily on the quality of sales staff who are mostly working without supervision, whereas shop staff are constantly under the surveillance of management. On the other hand, shop staff may be selling a wide variety of competing products, and may not be dedicated to maximising sales of Revlon's own products: even if they are, customers can easily go to a neighbouring shop and look at the products offered by other companies. If either company were to change its method of distribution, it would have to check the distribution method was convenient to customers. Decide what to do with its existing staff, how to get the message about the new distribution method across to customers and whether it should take the opportunity to change its product range.

8 If an existing business is bought, the price will be greater than the value of its factories, machinery and stock. This premium covers the experience, knowledge and expertise present in the business, all of which have a beneficial effect on its profits. This intangible advantage is called 'goodwill'. If the business is not expensive, this may be because its presence in the market is not very good: its brand names may not be well respected among consumers, for example.

9 The solution will depend on the business you chose. However, you should be able to find out whether customers are satisfied with the company or not. If it is a limited company you can obtain a copy of the company report and accounts which will give you answers on profitability.

10 The physical aspect of a beefburger is the meat, the bun and so on. The functional aspect is its property of satisfying you when you are hungry. The symbolic aspect is the culture and values associated with beefburgers: convenience, American culture, worries about BSE and the future of the British beef industry and, in the case of beefburgers eaten in some restaurants (such as the Hard Rock Cafe), status.

11 To some extent the answer depends on the product you have chosen. In a market where your product has many close substitutes the consumer's decision is likely to be very influenced by price, so all products will be similarly priced. Where the product is differentiated and is perceived to offer benefits unobtainable elsewhere, such as availability or quality, a premium price could be obtained. Only considering market price can lead to missed opportunities or even losses. Tesco Stores were making losses at one time by selling too cheaply. They increased their prices, sold slightly less, yet made profits.

12 Two examples of franchises are Kwik-fit and Prontaprint. The benefits to an investor will include assistance in finding suitable premises, immediate well-known brand name and national advertising, help in approaching banks for finance and training in the business.

13 Process: travel agents use computer terminals linked directly to airlines and tour operators so that they can check availability and make bookings quickly. This may be threatened by the Internet, with customers being able to book holidays themselves on-line.

Physical evidence: posters of appealing holiday locations and glossy brochures help customers to imagine what it will be like on holiday.

People: staff are trained to handle customers, and often wear uniforms.

14 Your answer to this will depend upon your chosen organisation's policies and actions.

Chapter 2 : THE MARKETING PROCESS: STRATEGY AND PLANNING

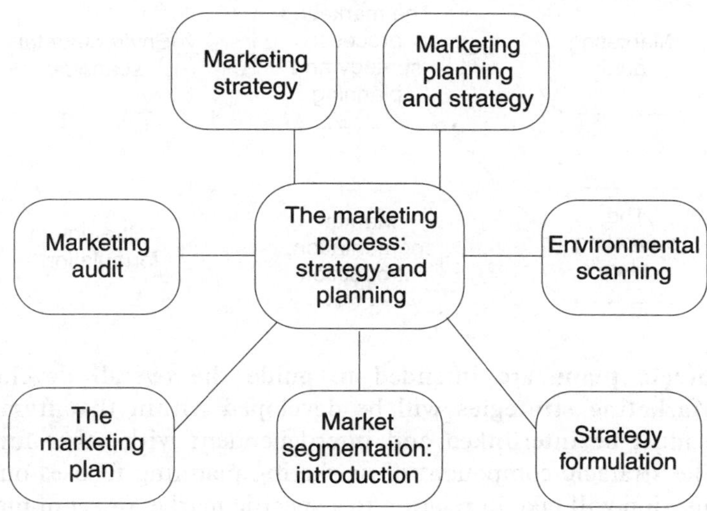

Introduction

Strategy is a big concept as you will no doubt learn in your later studies. For now be content with a simple definition: a strategy is **a course of action to achieve a specific objective**. We shall consider very briefly the link between an **overall corporate strategy** and the **marketing strategy** that is developed within that framework. Then we go on to look at the stages in strategic planning and strategy formulation, in particular SWOT analysis.

In the remaining parts of this chapter we introduce some techniques that are relevant to marketing strategy: **segmentation** is described in outline (there is more detail in Chapter 6) and we consider various aspects of marketing planning, notably **forecasting** and **budgeting**.

Your objectives

In this chapter you will learn about the following.

(a) Why an organisation needs to have a strategy
(b) The stages in strategic planning, including the setting of objectives
(c) The marketing audit
(d) Environmental analysis and where to look for relevant information
(e) SWOT analysis and a variety of competitive strategies and growth strategies
(f) What is meant by segmentation and what a target market is
(g) The stages of marketing planning and in particular discuss methods of sales forecasting and the elements of the marketing budget

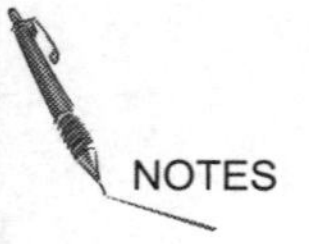
NOTES

1 MARKETING STRATEGY

Corporate strategic plans are intended to guide the overall development of an organisation. **Marketing strategies** will be developed within that framework. To be effective, these must be interlinked and interdependent with other functions of the organisation. The strategic component of marketing planning focuses on the direction which an organisation will take in relation to a specific market or set of markets in order to achieve a specified set of objectives. Marketing planning also requires an **operational component** which details specific tasks and activities to be undertaken in order to implement the desired strategy.

This approach ensures that marketing efforts are **consistent with organisational goals,** internally coherent and tailored to market needs and that the **resources** available within the organisation are systematically allocated.

1.1 Strategies

Strategies develop at several levels. **Corporate strategy** deals with the overall development of an organisation's business activities, while **marketing strategy** focuses on the organisation's activities in relation to its markets. Individual brand or product group strategies are also required in many instances. **Deliberate strategies** are the result of planning. **Emergent strategies** are developed over time as a result of the behaviour and actions of the organisation. Often this behaviour is unconscious but falls into a consistent pattern. It is directly associated with decisions that emerge from individual managers adapting the strategy to meet the needs of the changing external marketing environment. For example imagine a breakfast cereal company planning a deliberate strategy to focus on the adult 'ready to eat' wheat based cereal market category with a number of planned brand extension products. If within society there appeared to be a movement away from wheat based products towards oat based cereal because they were perceived as a healthier option, it would make sense for the marketing manager responsible for ready to eat cereals to adapt the decision to develop wheat based products to oat based ones. The overall strategy to launch new products could still be realised although the focus of the strategy would have emerged from knowledge of changes in consumer preferences.

In practice, most strategies are **part deliberate** and **part emergent.**

Strategic marketing has three key components:

- The **designation** of specific, desired objectives
- Commitment of **resources** to these objectives
- Evaluation of a range of **environmental influences**

Note that the strategy does not just focus on organisational **efficiency**. It is more important that the organisation should be **effective**. Efficiency here relates to **doing a task well**, but effectiveness relates to **doing the right task** – having the right products in the right markets at the most appropriate times.

Strategy also has a dynamic component. To be truly effective the organisation should not only be 'doing the right things now', it needs to be aware of and prepared to anticipate **future changes** to ensure that it will also be 'doing the right things in the future'. Planning and strategy enable managers to think through the possible range of future changes, and hence be better prepared to meet the changes that actually occur.

1.2 Integrated marketing

Marketers cannot control all the information that customers gather and process about products, but nevertheless marketing organisations must develop an effective **integrated marketing communications plan**, and thereby exert some form of control.

Such plans are vitally important in the modern market, because the marketing mix variables on which marketers have traditionally relied to distinguish themselves from their rivals (product design, lower prices, distribution channels etc) have been changed by the march of technology. Competitors can copy what is done quicker than ever before.

EXAMPLE

In July 2004 the retailer Marks and Spencer looked doomed with take-overs expected and revival acquisitions being offered by rival retailer Philip Green. It looked as though Marks and Spencer was a brand stuck in the past.

For many years Marks and Spencer had been regarded as the premium high street food retailer. With increasing numbers of competitors enlarging their premium retailer brand offerings such as Tesco 'Finest' and Sainsbury's 'Taste the Difference' ranges, M&S needed to establish new ways to differentiate their food.

The first execution of a revised food campaign won the top award by the Institute of Practitioners in Advertising and was reported to fuel an advertising-led recovery for the ailing retailer. The campaign featured the voice of actress Dervla Kirwan and the tagline '*This is not just food; this is Marks and Spencer's food*'.

A highly relevant and innovative creative message was used which focussed on the quality, taste and appeal of the individual food items to a point where consumers were reported to drool on viewing the slow motion ads. Some commentators referred to the ad as 'food-porn'. When hot chocolate puddings appeared in one of the commercials, sales increased 288%. The campaign was well integrated with all TV, print, web and radio advertising with the same message in store and within direct mail promotions. Throughout the long running campaign in-store price promotions were also used encourage trial of the food items featured within the adverts running at that time.

The retailer later combined the food promotion with highly successful advertisements featuring the model Twiggy for clothing and an initiative to outline their ethical positioning and to encourage a greater sense of trust in the brand. An end-line of 'Look behind the label' was added to print adverts and was linked to a section of the M&S

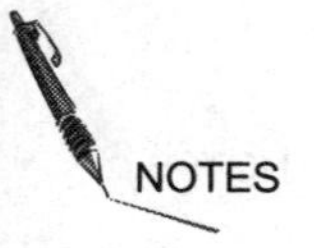

website where consumers could find out information about the sourcing of ingredients, use and selection of suppliers, fair-trade initiatives and other social issues relevant to the retailer.

The success of the overall campaign can partly be attributed to the creative message but also its well integrated nature. In June 2007 Marks and Spencer won the Grand Prix award and was commended in the marketing achievement category at the Marketing Society Awards for Excellence. Furthermore in May 2007 the retailer reported its best profits in a decade.

(*Sources: The Guardian* 18 April 2006; *The Guardian* 6 November 2006; Institute of Practitioners in Advertising; Marks and Spencer; *Marketing* June 2007)

FOR DISCUSSION

It could be said that **marketing communications** is one area where it is still possible to differentiate the product or service – making the customer believe what you want him to believe about the company, product, brand or service.

Major tasks facing those responsible for integrated marketing campaigns

- Who should receive messages
- What the messages should say
- What image of the organisation/brand receivers should retain
- How much is to be invested in the process
- How the messages are to be delivered
- What actions receivers should take
- How the whole process should be controlled
- Determine what was achieved

EXAMPLE

According to Schultz *et al* (*Integrated Marketing Communications – Putting it Together and Making it Work*, 1993):

'What exists in the mental network of the consumer or the prospect is truly where marketing value resides. [It] is what people believe, not what is true. [It] is what people want, not what is available; what people dream about, not what they know that really differentiates one product from another in a parity marketplace. That is why ... communications is rapidly becoming the major marketing force of today and certainly tomorrow.'

So the proper co-ordination of all marketing messages becomes extremely important. What the marketer says about a product must fit with whatever information the customer has already collected.

> **Activity 1** **(10 minutes)**
>
> Do you understand what people mean when they distinguish between efficiency and effectiveness? Give an example to prove to yourself that you do.

2 MARKETING PLANNING AND STRATEGY

2.1 Developing a marketing plan

A marketing plan should follow a logical structure:

(1) Historical and current **analyses** of the organisation and its market

(2) A statement of **objectives**

(3) The development of a **strategy** to approach that market, both in general terms and in terms of developing an appropriate marketing mix

(4) Finally, an outline of the appropriate **methods** for plan implementation

(5) Finally a statement measuring how effective the plan has been should be included so that future plans can be developed according to lessons learnt and/or for corrective action to be taken.

Implementation sometimes may appear at the end of any discussion of marketing plans. Arguably, the process of **monitoring and controlling marketing activities** is the most crucial factor in determining whether a plan is successful or not.

The main function of the plan is to offer management a coherent set of clearly defined guidelines, but at the same time it must remain flexible enough to adapt to **changing conditions** within the organisation or its markets. The **stages in strategic planning** are as follows.

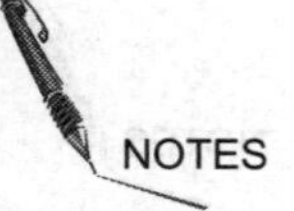

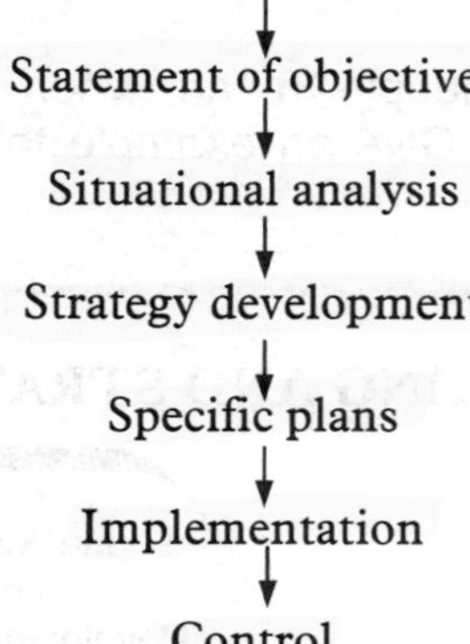

Development of the organisation's mission statement
↓
Statement of objectives
↓
Situational analysis
↓
Strategy development
↓
Specific plans
↓
Implementation
↓
Control

In simple but meaningful terms, a marketing strategy can be thought of as a series of four important questions to be addressed:

1 Where are we now?
2 Where do we what to be?
3 How are we going to get there?
4 How do we know when we have got there?

Philip Kotler, a key marketing guru, refers to the process of creating a marketing plan as being about: analysis; planning; implementation and control.

2.2 Company mission statement

Definition

> The company **mission statement** is simply a statement of what an organisation is aiming to achieve through the conduct of its business. It can even be thought of as a statement of the organisation's reason for existence.

The purpose of the mission statement is to provide the organisation with **focus** and **direction**.

Factors influencing the development of the mission statement include:

- Corporate culture
- Organisational structure
- Product/market scope
- Customer needs
- Technology

This approach forces managers to think about **customer groups** and the particular set of needs/wants which the firm wants to satisfy, and so is particularly relevant to marketing.

A mission statement can offer guidelines to management when considering how the business should develop and in which directions. With the benefits of a clear mission statement, future growth strategies can rely on what are regarded as **distinctive competences.**

Identifying distinctive competences enables the organisation to focus on developing the business in areas where they have experience such as customer groups with similar needs or characteristics or where similar service technologies exist.

EXAMPLE

One reason why Weetabix launched the cereal Oatibix as a breakfast biscuit was because they already were well regarded in this sector with the existing Weetabix product range. Consumers regard Weetabix as the premium biscuit and so the company would be able to transfer this perceived credibility into a new format where they already have considerable production experience and capability. The amount of investment required to launch the new range would be minimal due to the ability to use existing production equipment and so on.

Activity 2 **(15 minutes)**

Here is part of a proposed mission statement. How good do you think it is?

ROYAL MAIL: MISSION

At Royal Mail our mission is to be recognised as the best organisation in the world at distributing text and packages. We shall achieve this by:

- excelling in our collection, processing, distribution and delivery arrangements
- establishing a partnership with our customers to understand, agree and meet their changing requirements
- operating profitably by providing efficient services which our customers consider to be value for money
- creating a work environment that recognises and rewards the commitment of all employees to customer satisfaction
- recognising our responsibilities as part of the social, industrial and commercial life of the country
- being forward-looking and innovative.

2.3 Statement of objectives

Objectives enter into the planning process both at the corporate level and at the market level.

Definition

Corporate objectives define specific goals for the organisation as a whole and may be expressed in terms of profitability, returns on investment, growth of asset base, earnings per share and so on.

These factors will be reflected in the stated objectives for marketing, branch and other functional plans. They will not be identical to those specified at the corporate level and need to be translated into market-specific marketing objectives. These may involve targets for the size of the customer base, growth in the usage of certain facilities, gains in market share for a particular product type and so on, but all must conform to three

criteria: they must be **achievable,** they must be **consistent** and they must be **stated clearly**.

Objectives are therefore hierarchical in nature and can be represented in many instances as shown in the diagram below: *(Please note that the diagram shows how objectives for two specific brands can be traced back to the corporate objectives.)*

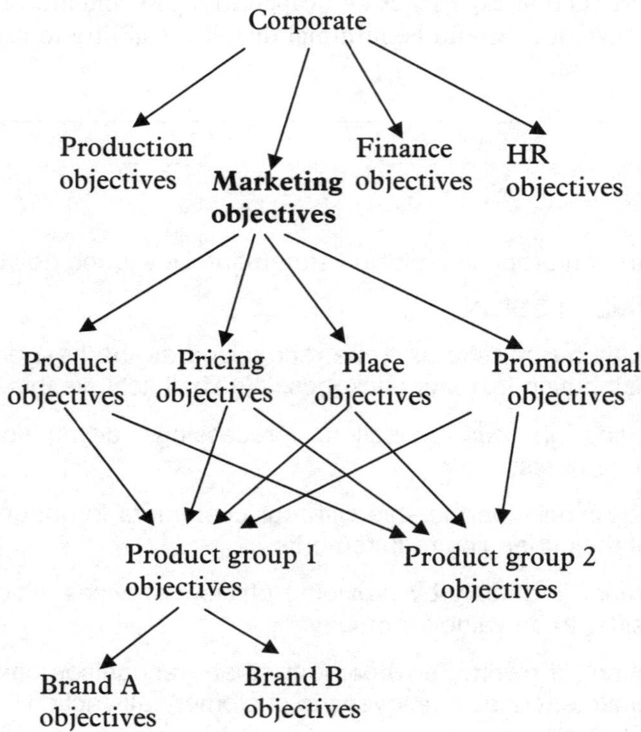

2.4 Situation analysis

Situation analysis requires a thorough study of the **broad trends** within the economy and society, as well as a detailed analysis of markets, consumers and competitors. **Market segmentation** is considered, and also an understanding of the organisation's **internal environment** and its particular **strengths and weaknesses.**

Market research and external databases provide information on the **external environment,** while an **audit** of the organisation's marketing activities provides information on the internal environment.

A **marketing information system** may be used for processing and analysis, while SWOT analysis (see below) may be used to organise and present the results.

2.5 Strategy development

Strategy development links corporate and market level plans. Most large organisations will have important **resource allocation** decisions to make. Financial and human resources must be allocated in a manner consistent with corporate objectives. This process is a key component of corporate strategy and indicates how specific markets or products are expected to develop, enabling the development of market level plans.

Market specific plans relate to particular markets or, in some cases, particular products, but are closely tied to the corporate plan. Situation analysis must supply further

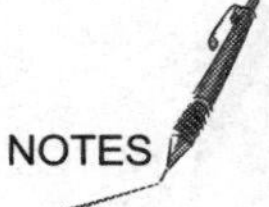

information on patterns of competition, consumer behaviour and market segmentation, as input to the development of marketing objectives and market specific strategies.

Since marketing mix variables are under the control of the marketing department, development is guided by the need to ensure that the product's features, image, perceived value and availability are appropriate to the market involved.

Marketing expenditure rests on resource allocation decisions at corporate level, but nevertheless a suggested **budget** and the way it is to be spent are required.

2.6 Implementation

This requires an **identification** of the specific tasks, allocation of **responsibility** for those tasks and a system for **monitoring** their implementation. It may also include some elements of **contingency planning.** However well thought out the marketing plan may be, markets are dynamic. Planned activities may turn out to be inappropriate or ineffective and need a response.

In developing a marketing strategy, the company is seeking to meet the specific needs of its consumers and to do so more effectively than its competitors. To do this, the company must be able to assess its position, relative to competitors and customers, accurately.

3 MARKETING AUDIT

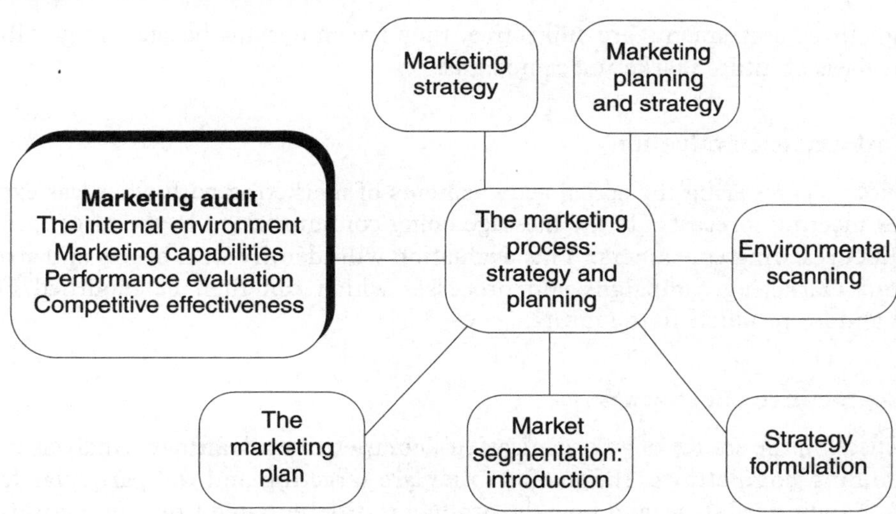

3.1 The internal environment

An understanding of the strengths and weaknesses of the **structure** of the company and of the **personnel** within the company is important. Internal structures may be changing to reflect the increased pressures of a competitive market place.

Marketing audits help an organisation (and the individuals involved in the planning process) to understand the internal environment.

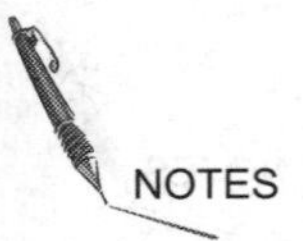

Definition

A **marketing audit** is simply a systematic analysis and evaluation of the organisation's marketing position and performance.

It may cover all activities which are either directly or indirectly connected with the marketing function, or it can simply focus on specific products/markets or specific marketing functions. Further distinctions may be drawn between audits at the corporate level, at the divisional level or at the level of the product/market.

The audit will focus on all the relevant marketing activities, but the following may be singled out as being of particular importance.

3.2 Marketing capabilities

The audit considers in which aspects of marketing the company may be considered to have particular strengths and weaknesses. We may want to know the following.

- How flexible/responsive is the organisation of the marketing department?
- What is the company's image/reputation?
- How strong are particular product lines?
- What is the extent of brand loyalty among customers?

Although these assessments are subjective, they are important because they will often form the basis of future marketing campaigns.

3.3 Performance evaluation

This involves comparing the actual achievements of marketing with what was expected. Are sales meeting forecasts? Is the message being communicated to the target group? Is the product reaching consumers? This evaluation will identify weaknesses and strengths of current marketing campaigns and processes which can then be modified for this product and for products in the future.

3.4 Competitive effectiveness

This focuses on the source of an organisation's **competitive advantage**. Analysis requires understanding **competitors**, the markets they are targeting and the particular features they use to their advantage, and how the product is differentiated from competitors'.

There are a number of tools available for marketing audits. Note that the marketing audit should be **systematic**, should canvass a wide variety of opinions and is frequently based on data gathered by **questionnaire surveys**.

4 ENVIRONMENTAL SCANNING

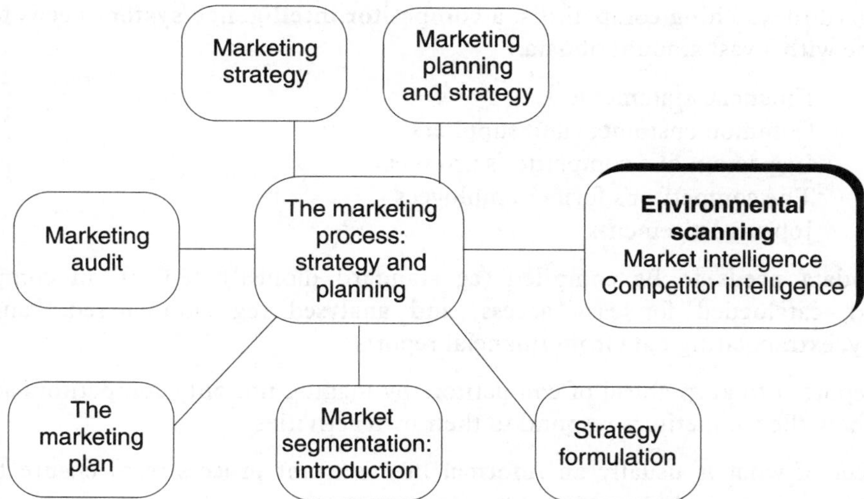

Environmental scanning means keeping one's eyes and ears open to what is going on generally in the market place, especially with respect to competitors, and more widely in the technological, social, economic and political environment.

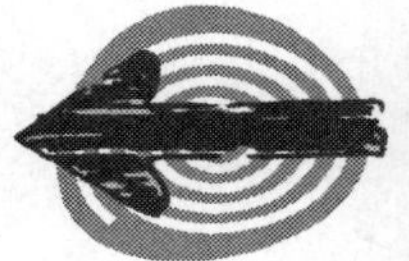

We look at the environment in more detail in Chapter 4.

4.1 Marketing intelligence

The result of environmental scanning is **marketing intelligence**. Its sources include:

- Business and financial newspapers, such as the *Financial Times*
- General business magazines, such as the *Economist* and *Business Week*
- Trade journals, such as *Campaign, The Grocer, Retail Week*
- Academic journals, such as *Harvard Business Review*
- Attending conferences, exhibitions, courses and trade fairs
- Making use of sales force feedback
- Developing and making use of a network of personal contacts
- Monitoring competitors
- Trade associations
- Primary and Secondary Market Research

Activity 3 **(20 minutes)**

Here is a small selection of headlines from newspapers in the UK:

(a) House prices show signs of slow down
(b) Professions in insurance crisis
(c) Protesters halt royal tree felling

In each case what sort of organisations should take note of the articles as part of their environmental scanning for marketing threats and opportunities?

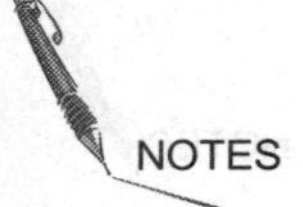

4.2 Competitor intelligence

With regard to watching competitors, a **competitor intelligence system** needs to be set up to cope with a vast amount of data.

- Financial statements
- Common customers and suppliers
- Inspection of a competitor's products
- The competitor's former employees
- Job advertisements

All this data needs to be compiled (eg standard monthly reports on competitors' activities), catalogued for easy access, and analysed (eg summarised, ranked by reliability, extrapolating data from financial reports).

Dell is reported to keep ahead of competitors by logging not only competitors activities but also how the competitors respond to their own activities.

The object of what is usually an informal but constant process is to ensure that the organisation is not caught by surprise by developments.

5 STRATEGY FORMULATION

5.1 SWOT analysis

This technique provides a method for organising information to identify strategic direction. The basic principle is that any statement about an organisation or its environment can be classified as a **Strength, Weakness, Opportunity** or **Threat**. An **opportunity** is simply any feature of the external environment which creates conditions which are advantageous to the firm in relation to a particular objective or set of objectives. By contrast, a **threat** is any environmental development which will present problems and may hinder the achievement of organisational objectives. What constitutes an opportunity to some firms will almost invariably constitute a threat to others.

A **strength** can be thought of as a particular skill or distinctive competence which the organisation possesses and which will aid it in achieving its stated objectives. A **weakness** is simply any aspect of the company which may hinder the achievement of specific objectives.

This information would typically be presented as a **matrix**. Effective SWOT analysis does not simply require a categorisation of information, it also requires some **evaluation**

of the relative importance of the various factors. These features are only relevant if perceived to exist by consumers. Threats and opportunities are conditions presented by the **external environment** and they should be independent of the firm.

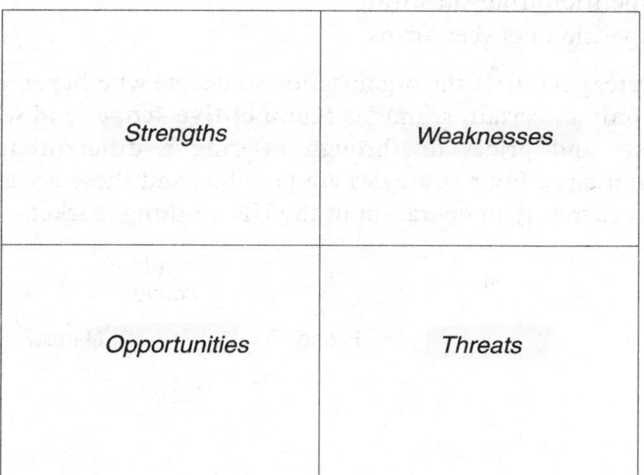

Figure 2.1: SWOT analysis

The two major strategic options from a SWOT analysis are as follows.

(a) **Matching** the strengths of the organisation to the opportunities presented by the market.

(b) **Conversion** of weaknesses into strengths in order to take advantage of some particular opportunity, or converting threats into opportunities which can then be matched by existing strengths.

It is also necessary to consider more specific aspects of strategies, such as how best to compete, or, how to grow within the target markets. A number of analytical techniques can be used, not to offer definitive statements on the final form that a strategy should take, but rather to provide a **framework** for the organisation.

FOR DISCUSSION

Can you carry out a SWOT analysis on yourself? Try it with a group of friends and compare the results.

5.2 Competitive strategies

Management must identify the **way** in which it will compete with other organisations and what it perceives as the basis of its competitive advantage. The American strategist **Michael Porter** (*Competitive Strategy*, 1996) argues that the strategy adopted by a firm is essentially a method for creating and sustaining **a profitable position in a particular market environment.** Profit depends first on the nature of its strategy and second on the inherent profitability of the industry in which it operates. An organisation in a basically profitable industry can perform badly with an unsuitable strategy while an organisation in an unprofitable industry may perform well with a more suitable strategy.

According to Porter, the profitability of an industry depends on five key features. These are known as **Porter's Five Forces,** and we look at them in more detail in Chapter 4.

NOTES

- Bargaining power of suppliers
- Bargaining power of consumers
- Threat of entry of new competitors into the market
- Competition from substitutes
- Competition between firms

A competitive strategy requires the organisation to decide whether to compete across the entire market or only in certain segments (**competitive scope**) and whether to compete through low costs and prices or through offering a differentiated product range (**competitive advantage**). Four strategies are possible, and these are as shown here with example strategies currently in operation in the UK clothing market.

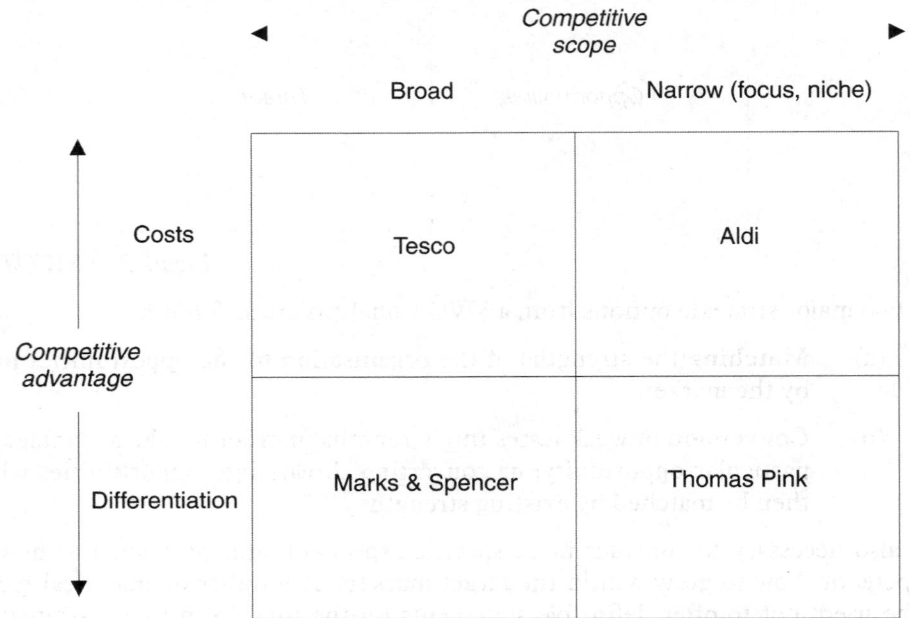

Figure 2.2: Competitive strategies

(a) **Cost leadership** attempts to control the market through being the low cost producer.

(b) **Differentiation** offers leadership or focus products which can be regarded as unique in areas which are highly valued by the consumer, creating customer loyalty which protects the firm from competition.

(c) **Focus/nicheing**, based on either costs or differentiation, aims to serve particularly attractive or suitable segments or niches.

An important feature of this approach is the need to avoid being '**stuck in the middle**' – trying to be all things to all consumers. The firm that doesn't achieve either low costs or good differentiation is likely to lose out to firms concentrating on either one strategy or the other.

5.3 Growth strategies

Ansoff's Product/Market matrix (*Corporate Strategy*, 1987) (see Chapter 7) suggests that the growth strategy decision rests on whether to sell new or existing products in new or existing markets. This produces four possible options.

(a) **Market penetration**

This involves selling **more** of the existing products in existing markets. Possible options are persuading existing users to use more, persuading non-

users to use, or attracting consumers from competitors. This is only a viable strategy where the market is not saturated. Increased promotional activity and ensuring there are maximum opportunities to buy with increased distribution are often tactics used to further penetrate markets. Krispy Crème donuts launched self service kiosks in Tesco extra stores to increase the number of sales opportunities. Previously the brand was only available in their own outlets.

(b) **Market development**

This entails **expanding into new markets** with existing products. These may be new markets geographically, new market segments or new uses for products. Some the most famous marketing success examples involve market development strategies. Johnson and Johnson used this approach to extend the life of their baby lotion product when it was repositioned to appeal to women as a skincare product through the slogan ' Best for baby, best for you'. Lucozade also is now considered a sports brand rather than a drink to provide energy when recovering from illness.

(c) **Product development**

This approach requires the organisation to develop **modified versions** of its existing products which can appeal to existing markets. By tailoring the products more specifically to the needs of some existing consumers and some new consumers, the organisation can strengthen its competitive position. Veet, the hair removal brand, developed an 'in shower' version to appeal to existing consumers who may be more satisfied with the product if they could use it this way but also to appeal to new consumers who may usually shave their legs in the shower due to time pressures.

(d) **Diversification**

Diversification (new products, new markets) is a much more **risky** strategy because the organisation is moving into areas in which it has **little or no experience**. Instances of pure diversification are rare and its use as a strategic option tends to be in cases when there are no other possible routes for growth available. Caterpillar, the plant machinery manufacturer, successfully moved into the footwear and clothing market. The move was possible because the brand represented high quality, durability and dependable. These qualities were also sought by workers using the heavy plant equipment in their work wear and as they trusted the brand the clothing was also successful.

We will now take an initial look at how markets can be subdivided into groups of consumers with specific needs and how this is used in marketing planning.

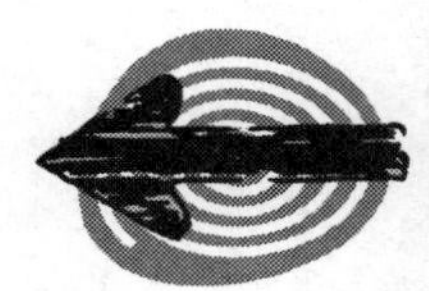

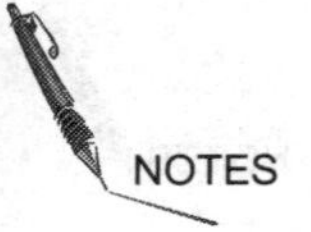

6 MARKET SEGMENTATION: INTRODUCTION

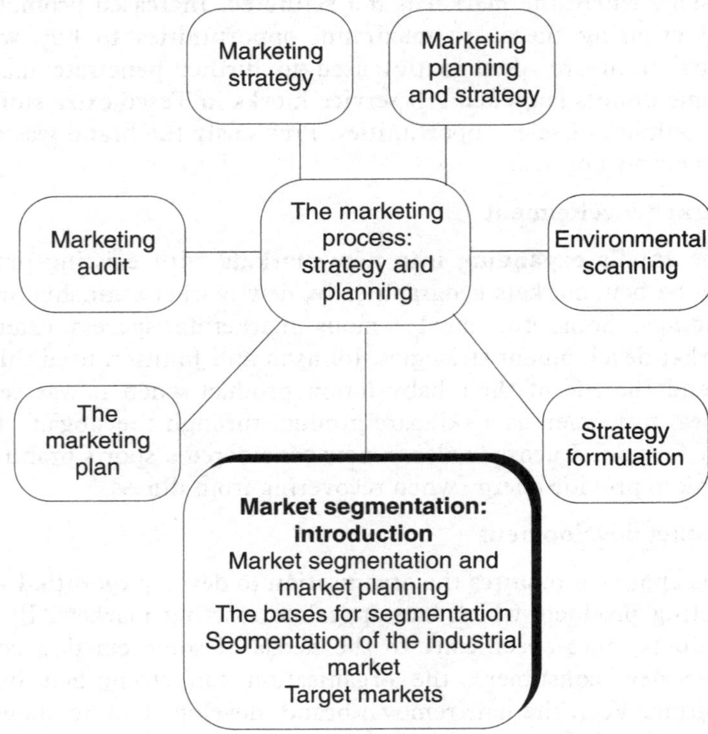

Definition

> **Market segmentation** is the subdividing of a market into distinct subsets of customers, where any subset may conceivably be selected as a target market to be reached with a distinct marketing mix. (Kotler)

The import ant elements in this definition of market segmentation are as follows.

(a) Each segment consists of people (or organisations) with common needs and preferences, who may react to market stimuli in much the same way.

(b) Each segment can become a target market with a unique marketing mix.

Customers differ in various respects – according to age, sex, income, geographical area, buying attitudes, buying habits etc. Each of these differences can be used to segment a market.

6.1 Market segmentation and marketing planning

Market segmentation is based on the recognition of the diverse needs of potential buyers. Different customer attitudes may be grouped into segments. **A different marketing approach is needed for each market segment.**

A total market may occasionally be homogeneous (very similar) but this is rare. A segmentation approach to marketing succeeds when there are identifiable 'clusters' of consumer wants in the market. For example, people differ considerably in their TV viewing habits. Sky would therefore find it impossible to sell their complete range of TV channels to all consumers as one large package. If they adopted this approach they would no doubt loose a large proportion of the market because not everyone would pay large fees to subscribe to hundreds of channels many of which they possibly would never

watch. Instead of taking this approach Sky bundle together channels into packages such as 'kids' 'entertainment', 'music' etc. Customers are able to select they types of channels they are most likely to watch and select a price range they are willing to pay.

Activity 4 **(10 minutes)**

Suggest how the market for umbrellas might be segmented.

6.2 The bases for segmentation

There are many different bases for segmentation. Bases refer to the way individuals can be grouped. One basis will not be appropriate in every market, and sometimes two or more bases might be valid at the same time. One segmentation variable might be superior to another in a hierarchy of variables. We cover this in Part D of the Course Book.

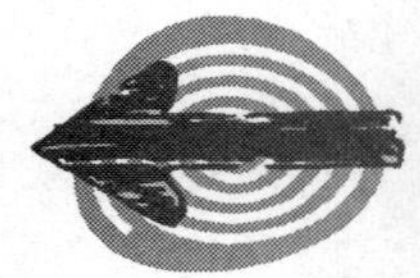

Segmentation in any particular market is to some extent a matter of intuition or interpretation.

6.3 Segmentation of the industrial market

Segmentation can also be applied to an industrial market based on, for instance, the nature of the customer's business.

Components manufacturers specialise in the industries of the firms to which they supply components. In the motor car industry, there are companies that specialise in the manufacture of car components. We look at this topic in more detail in Chapter 6.

6.4 Target markets

Organisations are not usually able to sell with equal efficiency and success to an entire market: that is, to every market segment.

The potential benefits of segmentation and target marketing are as follows.

(a) **Product differentiation**: a feature of a particular product might appeal to one segment of the market in such a way that the product is thought better than its rivals.

(b) The seller will be more **aware** of how product design and development may stimulate further demand in a particular area of the market.

(c) The resources of the business will be used more **effectively**, because the organisation should be more able to make products which the customer wants and will pay for.

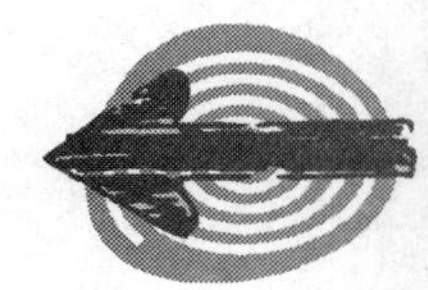

We shall be exploring the topic of segmentation in a good deal more depth in Chapter 6.

7 THE MARKETING PLAN

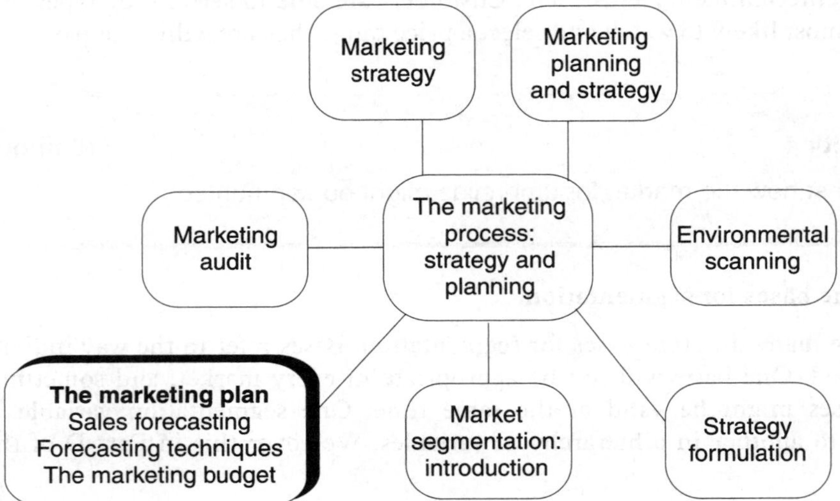

The marketing plan in detail consists of **several inter-related decisions.**

(a) **Sales targets** must be set for each product and each sales division (with sub-targets also set for sales regions, sales areas and individual salespeople).

(b) The **total marketing budget** must be set.

(c) Given an overall marketing budget, **resources must be allocated** between:

- Salaries and other staff costs
- Above the line expenditure (advertising)
- Below the line expenditure (sales promotion items, price reduction allowances etc)

(d) The overall sales target set by top management will incorporate **price decisions**, but within the formulation of the marketing plan there is likely to be some room for manoeuvre. In other words, top management will decide on a rough pricing zone and a specific price within this zone will be fixed later.

(e) Expenditure on marketing will also be allocated to different products or services within the organisation's product or service range. Some products might justify additional marketing expenditure, whereas others, nearing the end of their life cycle, may lose a part of their previous allocation.

None of this can take place without **detailed forecasts** of future outcomes, particularly sales forecasts.

7.1 Sales forecasting

Sales forecasting is a key element in budgeting and in long-term strategic planning, both essential disciplines. Without an accurate idea of a business's future sales it becomes difficult to make any meaningful plans.

Activity 5 **(15 minutes)**

How do you think a manager sets about making a sales forecast? To keep it simple, assume we are talking about a smallish company (say £5m turnover) with computerised accounting systems and a limited range of products.

Companies must be aware of **factors both within and outside their control** so they can plan effectively for the future. Sales figures do not simply depend on how well the sales force is performing or even how well the product fits customer requirements. In the long run performance will depend on many factors including the general economic climate, the level of technology and rate of technological change.

The nature of forecasting also differs considerably according to the nature of the product or industry. Ice cream sales for example are highly seasonal, the demand for milk on the other hand remains fairly stable throughout the year. Sales forecasting can be one of the most complex tasks for the marketer and it often thought of a task requiring skills in both art and science.

There is a vast array of **forecasting techniques** that can be applied to sales forecasting but here we will only deal with a small number. Some forecasting methods are very basic, for instance using last month's sales figures to predict this month's. Others are very complex such as some financial and economic models. The use of computers has aided the development of forecasting techniques.

EXAMPLE

Managers should be aware of the different types of product that exist to serve a particular market before attempting to forecast demand. For example, a coffee producer must decide which forecast suits his objectives: a forecast for the total coffee market, the decaffeinated coffee market or the instant coffee market. The manager must also make a decision about the geographical area the forecast should cover.

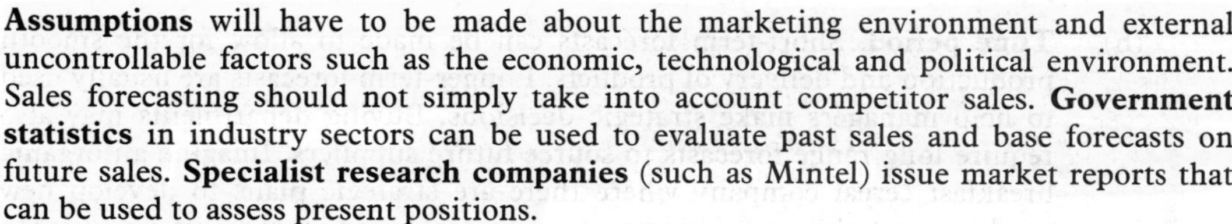

Assumptions will have to be made about the marketing environment and external uncontrollable factors such as the economic, technological and political environment. Sales forecasting should not simply take into account competitor sales. **Government statistics** in industry sectors can be used to evaluate past sales and base forecasts on future sales. **Specialist research companies** (such as Mintel) issue market reports that can be used to assess present positions.

Companies often arrive at sales forecasts in three stages.

- Environmental forecast
- Industry forecast
- Company sales forecast

There are three basic ways forecasts can be made.

(a) By **surveying** the opinions of consumers, sales people or experts within the field. For example, an economist's opinion may be sought to give an assessment of future interest rate levels.

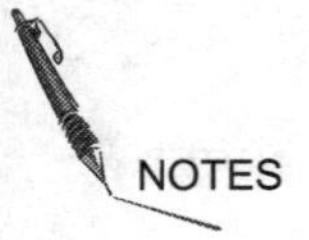

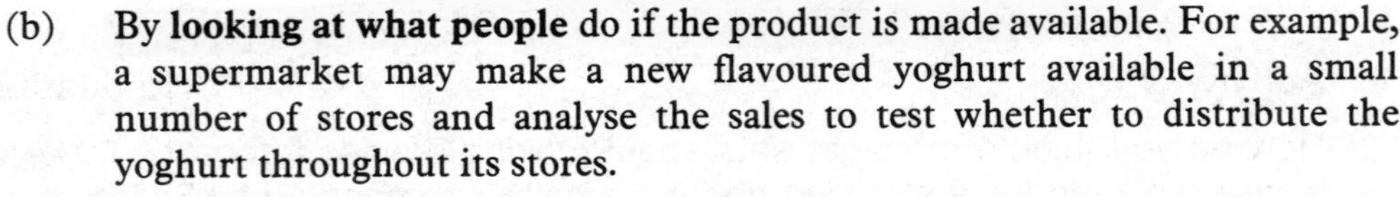

(b) By **looking at what people** do if the product is made available. For example, a supermarket may make a new flavoured yoghurt available in a small number of stores and analyse the sales to test whether to distribute the yoghurt throughout its stores.

(c) By looking at the **past** to evaluate what was purchased and when.

The method which is used to estimate sales will depend upon product characteristics.

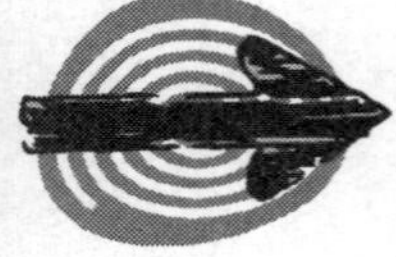

The diagram below shows some examples of why forecasting is needed by a company, illustrating how many different forecast types are required in addition to sales forecasts.

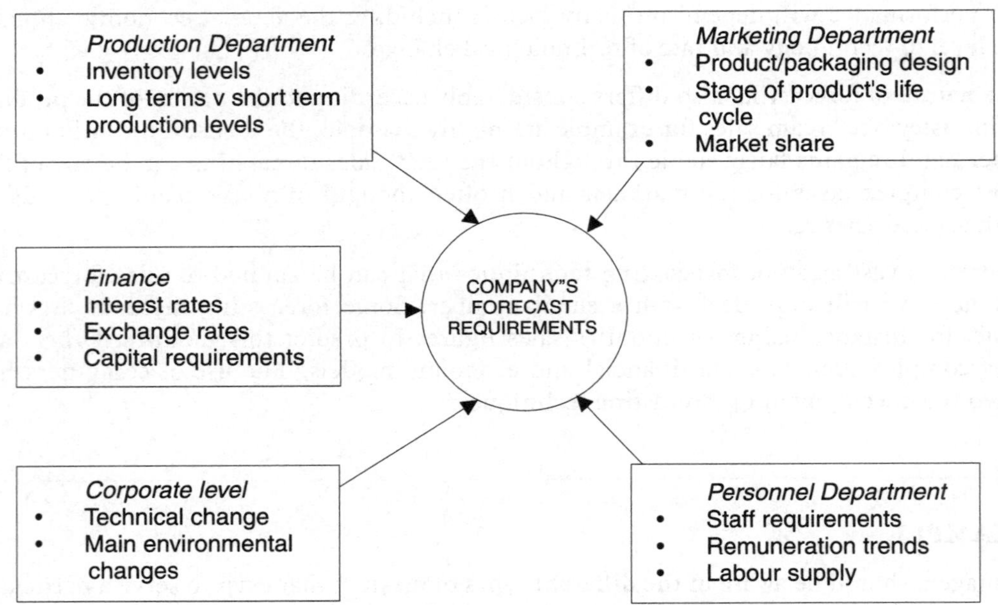

Figure 2.3 The variety of forecasts

Forecasts should take the following into account.

(a) **Accuracy**. Although this seems obvious the level of desired accuracy can differ. The longer the time span involved generally the less accuracy is possible.

(b) **Time period**. Short-term forecasts can be made to allow for the smooth production and delivery of products. Longer-term forecasts are usually used to help managers make strategic decisions. Buying departments may also require long range forecasts to source future suppliers. Imagine an organic breakfast cereal company where there are strategic plans to develop new products over the next five years. Some cereal based ingredients are easier to source than others and so it could mean that the company would have to source additional quantities possibly years in advance. Farmers need to rotate crops and ensure appropriate land usage. An organic farmer also needs specific organic accreditation standards to be reached in order for the land to be used. The cereal company may therefore need to brief their existing suppliers or even source new organic farmers in order to launch the new products when planned.

(c) **Detail**. The level of detail required by a forecast will differ amongst functional departments. Production will want a very detailed assessment of the future demand for the product to enable them to make necessary adjustments to production runs or resource planning.

7.2 Forecasting techniques

There are many different forecasting techniques available at different levels of complexity. Here we shall be evaluating the three broad categories of forecasting methods: **time series, causal** and **qualitative techniques.**

Time series forecasts

Historical (past) data is analysed and **trends or patterns are projected into the future.** This type of analysis is, of course, more useful in stable industries that have been in existence for some time.

Statistical techniques are available that take into account **seasonal variations,** such as occur, for example, in the sales of fireworks. In the long term, fireworks may be used in more displays and entertainments throughout the year rather than the traditional Guy Fawkes night.

Causal models

Causal models use equations to explain the **relationship** between a **dependent variable** (the one being forecast) and a number of **independent variables.** Past data can be used in the model and with the use of computers complex models can be evaluated. Causal models are linked to **probability** so a forecast may be that there is a 95% chance that sales will achieve a certain target. They are useful for longer term forecasting as independent variables can be altered and their impact noted.

As an example of a causal model, demand for electricity may depend upon a number of independent variables such as the price of electricity, the price of alternative energies, electric appliances already in operation (so locked into supply) and past demand for electricity.

The mathematical technique of **regression analysis** is used to analyse causal models.

Qualitative forecasting

Qualitative forecasting techniques do not depend on historical data. They are used mainly in technological forecasting, corporate planning and monitoring changes in consumer tastes and culture. There are two types of qualitative forecasting: **explorative** and **normative.** Explorative techniques start with the current state of affairs and attempt to predict changes. Normative techniques start with a desired state of affairs in the future and work back to consider ways in which to get there. So, for example, qualitative techniques can attempt to forecast new product adoption, technological change and innovations.

Base rate of sales, seasonal and promotional uplifts are often estimated separately in order to make forecasting simpler. It also helps to identify where any elements of inaccuracy may have come from. A drug company selling cold remedies may find that that sales forecast was wildly inaccurate but after investigation it may emerge that their seasonal element to their forecast was inaccurate because for some reason the cold virus hit a month earlier than usual. This information can be used to consider future forecasts. The company would need to use judgement and their knowledge of viruses to decide whether they should adjust their future forecast. It is situations such as this that leads people to think of forecasting as both an art and a science.

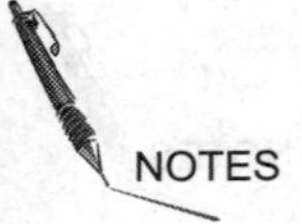

NOTES

7.3 The marketing budget

Top management must set an overall sales strategy and a series of sales objectives. Only then should a more detailed marketing plan be prepared.

There are three types of annual budget planning for a marketing budget.

(a) **Top down planning**: the setting of goals for lower management by higher management.

(b) **Bottom up planning**: employees set their own goals and submit them to higher management for approval.

(c) **'Goals down – plans up' planning**: a mixture of the two styles. Top management sets overall goals and employees formulate plans for achieving those goals. This is well suited to the formulation of sales budgets.

A sales and marketing budget is necessary for the following reasons.

(a) It is an element of the **overall strategic plan** of the business (the master budget) which brings together all the activities of the business

(b) Where sales and other non-production costs are a large part of total costs, it is **financially prudent** to forecast, plan and control them

(c) Since selling rests on **uncertain conditions**, good forecasts and plans become more important. If budgets are to be used for control, the more uncertain the budget estimates are, the more budgetary control is necessary.

Activity 6 **(10 minutes)**

What would you expect to be the largest single item in the marketing budget of a small to medium sized company? What would you expect it to be in a large company?

Chapter roundup

- Use of strategic planning enables organisations to be effective, not just efficient. Information is gathered and used to develop a corporate plan, covering short-, medium- and long-term goals and acting as a framework within which specific functions such as marketing can develop their own plans.
- The marketing audit helps an organisation to understand its internal environment. Factors to consider include: marketing capabilities, performance evaluation and competitive effectiveness.
- An organisation must also keep its eyes and ears open to what is going on in its external environment.
- Techniques used in strategy formulation include SWOT analysis which enables an organisation to choose whether to match its strengths to available opportunities or to convert its weaknesses into strengths or its threats into opportunities.
- Competitive strategies involve deciding whether to compete across the whole market or only in certain segments and whether to compete through low costs/prices or by offering a differentiated product range.
- Possible growth strategies are market penetration or development, product development and diversification.
- Market segmentation should result in increased total sales and profits because products/services will be more likely to appeal to the target segments and pricing policy can be more sophisticated. There are many possible bases for segmentation.
- The marketing plan should include sales targets and a total marketing budget analysed between above the line, below the line and other items.
- Sales forecasts form the basis of much of the activity of an organisation. Methods include using historical data, building causal models and qualitative forecasting.

Quick quiz

1. What is an emergent strategy?
2. List the stages in strategic planning.
3. What is a marketing audit?
4. Why should an organisation carry out an environmental analysis?
5. What do the letters in SWOT analysis stand for?
6. Differentiate between market and product development.
7. What are the three stages by which forecasts are arrived at and what are the three basic ways of making forecasts?
8. Why is a sales and marketing budget necessary?

NOTES

Answers to Quick quiz

1. They are strategies which emerge from activities and behaviour. They are not planned, but rather develop unconsciously.

2. Development of the organisation's mission statement
   Statement of objectives
   Situational analysis
   Strategy developments
   Specific plans
   Implementation

3. A systematic analysis and evaluation of the organisation's marketing position and performance.

4. To ensure that the organisation is not caught out by developments which may affect its markets. It needs to be adaptable to changing circumstances.

5. Strengths, weaknesses, opportunities, threats.

6. Broadly speaking, market development uses existing products in new markets. Product development entails developing existing products to give them more features to appeal in existing markets, to both previous customers and potential new ones.

7. Environmental forecast, industry forecast, company sales forecast.

8. A sales and marketing budget is necessary because it is an element of the overall plan of the business, it enables related costs to be planned and controlled, and encourages proper planning of sales (which can be subject to considerable uncertainty).

Answers to Activities

1 Many people use the words like this: efficiency relates to doing a given task well, making the best use of resources available to do it; effectiveness, however, means working out a way best calculated to achieve a given objective. For example if your objective is to get from London to Bristol quickly, and your resources are a bicycle, then careful route planning and staged rests will get you there as efficiently as possible; but a more effective approach might be to sell the bicycle and buy a rail ticket.

2 If you struggle with this try to put yourself in the position of a branch manager at Royal Mail. Does the statement give you clear guidelines on how you should be developing your branch? How many of the bullet points could apply to *any* organisation?

3 Here are some suggestions. You may have other better ideas.

(a) Property development companies, builders, mortgage providers, estate agents.

(b) Accountants, solicitors, surveyors, insurance companies, clients.

(c) Land developers, environmental groups.

It is a good idea to get into the habit of playing this game whenever you read a newspaper.

4 The market for umbrellas might be segmented according to the sex of the consumer. Women might seem to prefer umbrellas of different size and weight. The men's market might further be subdivided into age (with some age groups buying few umbrellas and others buying many more) or occupation (for example, professional classes, commuters, golfers). Each subdivision of the market (each subsegment) will show increasingly common traits. Golfers, for example, appear to buy large multi-coloured umbrellas.

5 In practice, the starting point is often the historical sales record, product by product. Trend analysis – which in this case may be less sophisticated than it sounds – might give a pointer to how sales are developing. Market information will help – the activities of competitors, the plans of intermediaries such as distributors and so on. Then internal plans must be taken into account: changes in the product mix, changes in the level of advertising, and so on.

In a larger company it all becomes more complicated.

6 There are no hard and fast rules about this. For a small to medium sized company the largest cost is likely to be the salaries of marketing staff. For a large company using expensive media like TV advertising may be the largest item.

NOTES

Chapter 3 : CUSTOMER FOCUS: COSTS AND BENEFITS

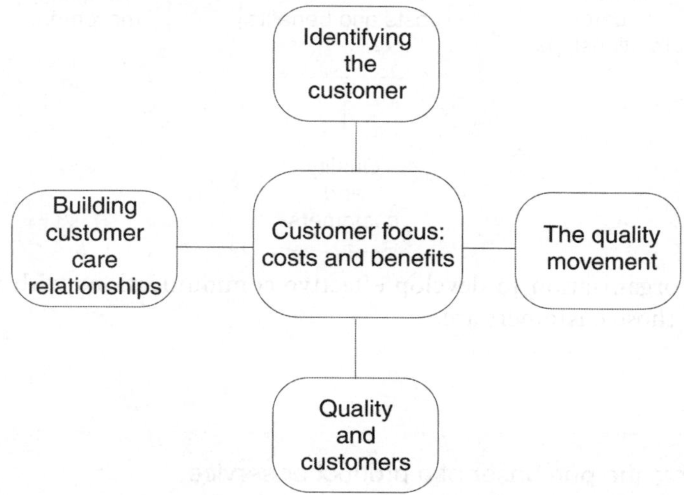

Introduction

Successful organisations focus on the customer. They realise that the organisation as a whole needs to direct its effort at providing the customer with what is required (the **product**) at the right time (**place**), the right **price** and in the right manner (**promotion**). In this way the customer is likely to be satisfied: he will keep the product, pay his bill, buy again, and recommend to others. An organisation that lacks customer focus may find itself unable to compete in the marketplace.

This chapter looks at the benefits of a customer focus.

Customer care emphasises the importance of an organisation's attitude to, and covers every aspect of its relationships with, its customers. It aims to close the gap between customers' expectations and their experience.

Quality has been elevated into a philosophy that guides every activity within a business. This is known as **total quality management** (TQM).

Satisfying the customer – giving 'added value' – is the underlying principle of TQM since quality is judged by the customer, and so the customer is the guarantee of the organisation's continued existence.

Your objectives

In this chapter you will learn about the following.

(a) Identifying the customer
(b) Building a valuable relationship with the customer
(c) Customer care and service
(d) Quality issues, and their implication for customer relationships

1 IDENTIFYING THE CUSTOMER

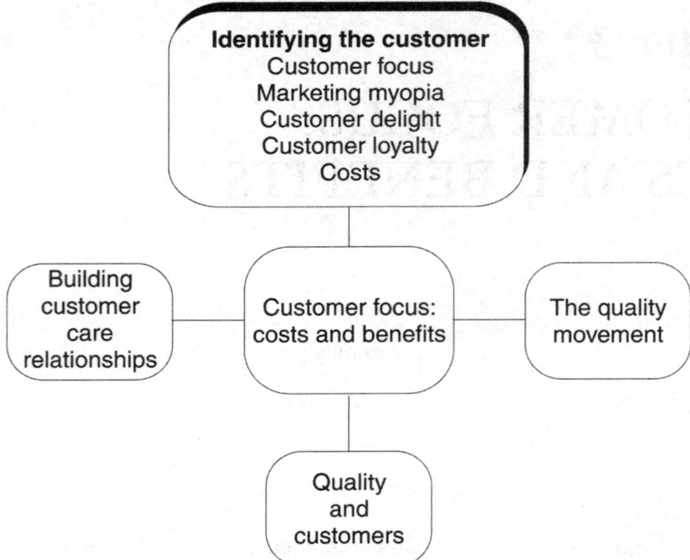

In order for an organisation to develop effective communications with its customers it must know who those customers are.

Definition

A **customer** is the purchaser of a product or service.

A customer is basically an **outsider**. This outsider has a want or need which the organisation can fulfil. Sometimes the customer is not aware of this want or need and so the organisation must communicate with the customer to **raise their awareness**.

Activity 1 **(10 minutes)**

Consider recent examples of products or services which were not necessarily provided to fulfil an existing need or want.

Products which create a need are innovative. Certain products will create more than one need, for example the introduction of dishwashers not only created a need for the dishwashing unit but also dishwashing liquid. The organisation may want to communicate with the customer regarding other issues. These could relate to price cuts, new features to existing products, trade fairs and events.

Marketers also distinguish between customers and consumers. We are very used to using '*customer*' as a 'catch all' term to refer to both. Sometimes the customer is also the consumer but not in every occasion and the needs of each differ considerably.

A customer is the purchaser but they may be an industrial purchaser buying for a company or an individual buying from themselves. Consider, for example, Toys R Us buying a bulk order of Raleigh bicycles to sell in its stores. Toys R Us would be the customer for Raleigh. The person going to Toys R Us to buy the bike would be referred to as the consumer. The consumer is the person who buys and uses the product so in this instance the person who

buys and rides the bike. It could be a small bike for a child and therefore the child would be referred to as the end-user. The needs of each of the parties varies considerably in this example and so it is important to be clear about who is being referred to. Toys R U need a reliable supplier selling good quality products so that their store reputation is preserved. The consumer needs a bike which is suitable as a gift, safe and so on. The end-user needs a bike which will be fun to ride and play on.

1.1 Customer focus

Customer focus represents a major shift in marketing emphasis for many organisations which at one time did not seem to realise that they had customers at all. Indeed, British Telecommunications plc (BT) used to call its customers 'subscribers', and kept them diligently at arm's length; many public-sector service operations were not in any sense '**customer-focused**' simply because they were **monopolies**, supplying services they thought it was appropriate for people to have.

1.2 Marketing myopia

This is a term coined by Harvard professor Ted Levitt in an article in 1960. It refers to the phenomenon whereby sellers confuse wants and needs. Such sellers are so focused on continually improving their product that they ignore customer needs, which exposes them if another product emerges which serves the need either better or more cheaply.

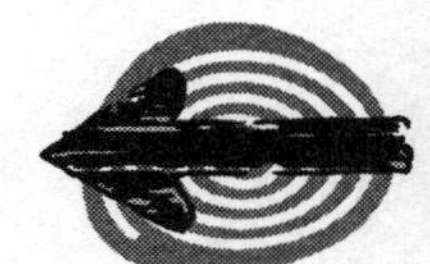

The product concept (or product orientation), discussed in Chapter 1, can lead to this marketing myopia.

A marketer obsessed with his own product may introduce new benefits and improvements that the consumer simply does not want and is not willing to pay for. Technology often drives these enhancements, and the company may be left with a product that has been expensive to develop and is full of amazing features, but which simply does not sell.

1.3 Customer delight

Many organisations have come to realise that customer satisfaction (or, better still, **customer 'delight'**) is the only route to long-term sustainable competitive advantage. Equally, customers themselves have begun to flex their muscles: they are much less inclined to remain silent in the face of indifferent attention. They are much more willing to take their business elsewhere when presented with the opportunity to do so, and attracting and retaining their **loyalty** has become a major issue in boardrooms everywhere.

Despite all this effort, however, **customer service and customer care** still remain problematic for many organisations and even within whole industry sectors.

As well as a lack of explicit **customer service strategies** linked to overall mission and policy, many organisations are still unclear about the role of **customer service** and how to organise it in order to deliver **added-value** and enhanced profitability (which is, after all, the point of the exercise). If an organisation does not know how good it is at delivering customer service, then it will tend to become **complacent**. Problems and obstacles include the following.

(a) The **use** of **vague, generalised** statements like 'quite good', 'getting better', 'world class' (without any comprehension of what being 'world class' might actually entail)

NOTES

(b) The **counting of customer complaints** in the belief that the incidence of complaints is a direct measure of customer satisfaction (without realising that, in most cases, only between **10** and **20 per cent** of customers actually **complain**: the rest simply take their business elsewhere)

(c) Reliance on infrequent survey data about **customer perceptions** and the selective application of the data thus acquired

(d) So-called 'improvements' which only address **front-line 'customer-care' features** like answering the telephone within three rings – when what really matters is how customers are handled once the telephone has been picked up

EXAMPLE

Jack Welch, General Electric's celebrated CEO, once said: 'Companies can't give job security. Only customers can!'

Many organisations make their hard task harder by two failings.

(a) They concentrate on **defending sales margins,** but tend to think about reducing employment levels before they think about redesigning their business processes.

(b) Information about changing customer tastes and opinions is hidden from head office by a culture which emphasises **top-down communication** and **discourages feedback** from below.

FOR DISCUSSION

The front-line staff of the organisation are the key to communication with (and from) customers.

1.4 Customer loyalty

The customer is the basic reason for the **existence** of any business since without customers to sell to, a business cannot operate. Meeting the needs of those customers more effectively than competitors is the key to continued profitable existence for any business. Each customer who deals with an organisation should leave with a feeling of satisfaction. This outcome is important since it can lead to increased sales and/or a willingness to pay higher prices and thus lead to higher profits. If customers are satisfied they may:

- Buy **again** from the same supplier
- Buy **more** of the same item, or more expensive items
- Advise their **friends** to buy from the supplier

When anyone buys they take a risk. Everyone likes to feel that they get **value for money**. There is increased risk of dissatisfaction when buying a new product or buying from a new supplier. It is important that the supplier helps to reduce this risk for new customers so that they are more likely to become regular customers.

Activity 2 **(10 minutes)**

Why is customer loyalty important?

Customer loyalty is promoted, achieved and enhanced in several differing ways.

(a) The **launch of specific initiatives** aimed at **engaging the customer** in schemes which help to **guarantee loyalty**, eg airmiles, the Tesco ClubCard, Sainsbury's Reward Card and various SMART card offers run by retailers and others.

(b) Creating a **customer proposition** offering something which customers may feel they cannot refuse, eg Esso's price-offer advertising campaign.

(c) Engaging the customer in a **dialogue**, thus ensuring that the customer **feels an affinity with the product** or **service** on offer.

1.5 Costs

Customers should be seen as potentially providing a lifetime of purchases so that **the turnover from a single individual over time might be very large indeed**. It is widely accepted that there is a non-linear relationship between customer retention and **profitability** in that a fairly small amount of repeat purchasing generates significant profit. It is far more expensive to convert a non-buyer into an occasional buyer than to turn an occasional buyer into a frequent buyer. The **repeat buyer:**

- Does not have to be persuaded to give the product a try
- Does not need to be tempted by special deals
- Needs less attention from sales staff
- Already has his credit account set up

Customer retention is important because the cost of acquiring new business can be significant. Costs may include some or all of the following.

- Advertising
- Salesmen time
- Credit checks
- Agent commission
- Initial discounts

EXAMPLE

High street banks run student accounts at a loss offering a range of services such as low cost loans, interest free overdrafts, free banking, commission free currency exchange. All these are offered in the hope that once they have graduated and earning a salary, students will remain loyal to the bank. This appears to be a profitable strategy as statistics have shown that customers are more likely to get divorced than change their bank.

Once established, **different costs from customer to customer** can arise out of the following.

NOTES

- Order size
- Sales mix
- Order processing
- Transport costs
- Management time
- Cash flow problems caused by slow payers
- Order complexity
- Stockholding costs
- The customer's negotiating strength

1.6 Competitive advantage and the marketing orientation

Essentially, the marketing orientation is a philosophy of business: it defines the basic nature of the approach the business organisation will take and the methods it will employ as it works towards survival and success. This amounts, in fact, to saying that the fundamental purpose of adopting a marketing orientation is to build and maintain **competitive advantage**.

The only true measure of competitive advantage is long-term profitability. By definition, this depends on the management of both costs and revenues. However, costs and revenues should not be seen as separate and opposed: both are intimately linked with the **creation of customer value**. Creating value for customers both incurs costs and generates revenues; the secret of business success is to manage the overall process profitably. This is how competitive advantage is created.

From the customer's viewpoint, value received depends on a simple algebraic relationship between perceived benefits and perceived sacrifice.

Customer value = perceived benefits – perceived sacrifice

Jobber, 2007

Jobber says that the customer's **perceived benefits** fall into four categories.

(a) **Product benefits** are the most fundamental kind of benefit and are most apparent in physical products; they provide the satisfaction the customer derives from the product itself, such as the taste and nutritional content of a food stuff.

(b) **Service benefits** are provided by the service the customer receives as part of the wider supplier-customer relationship. Here, it is important to remember that very few products can be regarded as purely physical: most involve a greater or lesser degree of service and some are, of course, entirely intangible. Even industrial commodities purchased in bulk for routine delivery involve an element of customer service in the form of order and delivery transaction processing.

(c) **Image benefits** exist when customers perceive that consumption of the product enhances their personal image. This perception can arise on such grounds as celebrity endorsement, the exclusivity or design of the product itself or the reputation of the supplier.

(d) **Relational benefits** arise when customers come to value their relationship with the supplier on such grounds as convenience, reliability, helpfulness and trust.

The customer's **perceived costs** also fall into four categories.

(a) **Monetary, time** and **energy costs** are self-explanatory.

(b) **Psychological costs** arise from the purchaser's perception of the **risk** associated with the buying decision. Purchasers are anxious to select the product that is best for them and wish to avoid the disappointment that will result from a sub-optimal decision. This particular perceived cost is specifically addressed by the provision of detailed product information during the selling process and by such benefits as product standardisation, guarantees and after sales service.

This analysis leads us back to the problem of achieving long-term profitability. There are two obvious but important basic facts.

(a) First, providing benefits to the customer (of whatever type), inevitably imposes costs.

(b) Second, while managers must understand all of their customers' perceived costs, it is obvious that only the monetary cost category generates revenue for the supplier.

In summary, the firm obtains revenue and incurs costs by providing benefits. However, the costs associated with each benefit will not necessarily be proportional to the satisfaction customers derive from it nor, therefore, to the price they are prepared to pay for it. Competitive advantage thus depends on the careful design of targeted products whose benefits generate revenues that exceed the costs they impose.

Great care is needed. Benefits that seem highly desirable and capable of generating substantial revenue should not generally be provided if they are disproportionately expensive. Similarly, marketers should be cautious about benefits that are cheap to provide but are of dubious value to the customer: they are unlikely to enhance either sales growth or product and company image. This balancing of customer benefits, costs and revenues is the essence of business and, in a sense, of the marketing orientation.

1.7 Assessing the impact of a marketing orientation

The marketing orientation is something of a totem in the marketing community. However, there is empirical evidence of its value. Jobber (2007) summarises research into the impact on business performance of adopting a marketing orientation. Positive correlations have been observed with profitability, sales growth, market share, new product success, perception of product quality and overall business performance.

A more complex relationship was observed in a study of 36 commodity businesses (all dealing in forestry products). In this group, a high degree of market orientation was accompanied by high profitability, while a medium degree of market orientation was accompanied by low profitability. However, a low degree of market orientation was accompanied by fairly high profitability. It was hypothesised that in these cases, profit was achieved by a simple low cost strategy.

Jobber D (2007), *Principles and Practice of Marketing,* 5th edition, Maidenhead, McGraw-Hill Education (UK) Ltd

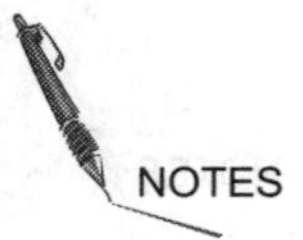

2 BUILDING CUSTOMER CARE RELATIONSHIPS

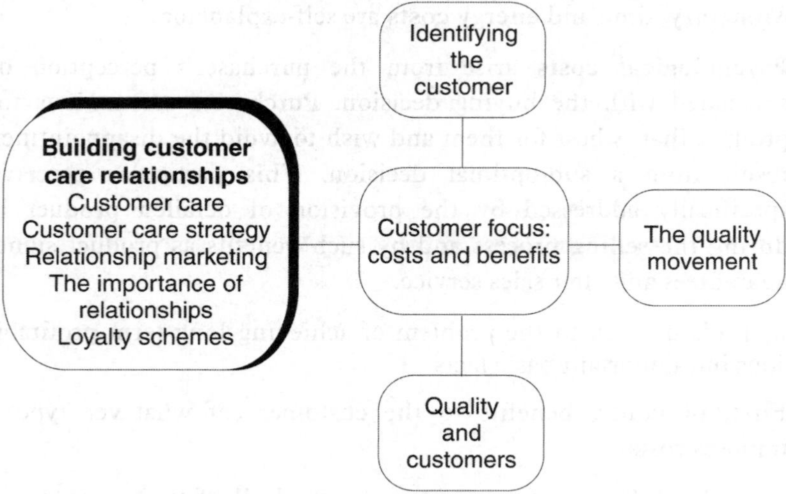

EXAMPLE: CUSTOMER LOYALTY

The problem with profitable customers is retaining them, because they will attract the attention of your competitors. Building customer relationships may be the answer to both types of problem.

Relationship marketing is grounded in the idea of establishing a learning relationship with customers. At the lower end, building a relationship can create cross-selling opportunities that may make the overall relationship profitable. For example, some retail banks have tried selling credit cards to less profitable customers. With valuable customers, customer relationship management may make them more loyal and willing to invest additional funds. In banking, these high-end relationships are often managed through private bankers, whose goals are not only to increase customer satisfaction and retention, but also to cross-sell and bring in investment.

In determining which customers are worth the cost of long-term relationships, it is useful to consider their lifetime value. This depends on:

- Current profitability computed at the customer level
- The propensity of those customers to stay loyal
- Expected revenues and costs of servicing such customers over the lifetime of the relationship

Building relationships makes most sense for customers whose lifetime value to the company is the highest. Thus, building relationships should focus on customers who are currently the most profitable, likely to be the most profitable in the future, or likely to remain with the company for the foreseeable future and have acceptable levels of profitability. The goal of relationship management is to increase customer satisfaction and to minimise any problems. By engaging in 'smarter' relationships, a company can learn customers' preferences and develop trust. Every contact point with the customer can be seen as a chance to record information and learn preferences. Complaints and errors must be recorded, not just fixed and forgotten. Contact with customers in every medium, whether over the Internet, through a call centre, or through personal contact, is recorded and centralised. Many companies are beginning to achieve this goal by using customer relationship management (CRM) software. Data, once collected and centralised, can be used to customise service. In addition, the database can be analysed to detect patterns that can suggest better ways to serve customers in general. A key aspect of this dialogue is to learn and record preferences. There are two ways to determine customers' preferences: transparently and collaboratively.

Discovering preferences transparently means that the marketer learns the customers' needs without actually involving them. For example, the Ritz Carlton Hotel makes a point of observing the choices that guests make and recording them. If a guest requests extra pillows, then extra pillows will be provided every time that person visits. At upmarket retailers, personal shoppers will record customers' preferences in sizes, styles, brands, colours and price ranges and notify them when new merchandise appears or help them choose accessories.

Barbara Kahn, *Financial Times*

2.1 Customer care

In deciding strategic direction and formulating marketing strategy, any company needs to address issues of customer care, because of:

(a) **Legal** constraints

(b) Industry **codes of conduct**

(c) The recognition that keeping existing customers happy is cheaper than acquiring new ones

(d) The **value chain**. Customer care is part of after-sales service and offers an opportunity for differentiation. It is also a valuable source of information.

2.2 Customer care strategy

Stage	Content
Corporate strategy and objectives	Objectives for customer loyalty and customer care A strategy for caring for customers
External environmental analysis	Analyse what makes customers loyal and how well they respond to different policies aimed at encouraging them to do so.
Internal environmental analysis	Analyse suppliers' capabilities in relation to keeping customers
Marketing objectives and strategy	Marketing objectives and strategy should focus on long-term impact on customer loyalty as well as profit, sales and market share
Action plans – marketing operations	Focus on the effect on customers
Results	Track customer movements (ie new customers, repeat business) not just sales and profit.

Figure 3.1: Customer care strategy

2.3 Relationship marketing

Since the mid 1990s the concept of relationship marketing has been gaining steady ground.

Definition

> **Relationship marketing** is the process of creating, building up and managing long-term relationships with customers, distributors and suppliers.

The type of relationship between a buyer and a seller may be of two types.

(a) In a **transaction**, a supplier gives the customer a good or service in exchange for money. The marketer, in offering the good or service, is looking for a response. Transaction-based marketing is based on individual transactions and little else, such as when you buy a bar of chocolate.

(b) In a **relationship approach** a sale is not the end of a process but the start of an organisation's relationship with a customer.

The main justification for relationship marketing comes from the need to **retain customers**. It has been estimated that the cost of attracting a new customer may be five times the cost of keeping a current customer happy.

In terms of the competitive forces, relationship marketing attempts to make it harder, or less desirable, for buyers to switch to another seller. It raises switching costs (emotional, if not financial).

EXAMPLE

'Marketing, used to be a relatively straightforward profession that centered around sales and promotion activities, brand building and the four Ps (product, price, place and promotion).

But now Marketing is about the four Ps plus 1 R and 1 T. The R stands for Relationships and the T stands for Technology.

Creating long-term profitable relationships with your key customers is all the rage today, everyone is talking about it, but few are doing it very well. The fundamental problem with the R in CRM is the way companies define the term relationship.

Many marketers believe they have a relationship with you because they have your name, phone number, email address and profession. What a bunch of rubbish. Relationships cannot be defined by how the company views them; instead they must be defined by how the customer defines them. If you fool yourself into believing you have an enduring relationship with a customer, when you really do not, you will find this out very quickly the next time your competitor offers a similar product or service for 10 per cent less. Relationships are the new battlefield that companies will fight each other on and the traditional metric of market share will take a back seat.

Why? For the simple reason that it typically costs between five and 10 times more to attract a new customer than to keep an existing one.

Extracted from: 'Relationships are the new battlefield for brands in Asia', *Media Asia* 5 April 2002.

Evert Gummesson, a key writer in the field of relationship marketing, went so far as to propose that the 4P's should be changed to 30R's (relationships). Central to his argument was the point that few organisations actually practiced 'total relationship marketing' which recognises that relationships, networks and interaction were at the core of marketing.

2.4 Importance of relationships: the cost of lost customers

If a company loses customers unnecessarily, it sacrifices a potential lifetime of profits. This is known as **lifetime customer value**. It has been suggested that a 5% increase in customer retention can increase total company operating profits by 50%.

Unless an industry is characterised by one-off sales, it is likely that customers will go through a **life cycle** of acquisition, development, maturity and decline. Each of these stages will carry a different level of revenue and profitability.

Existing, loyal customers are profitable because:

- They do not have to be **acquired**
- They buy a **broader range** of products
- They **cost less to service** as they are familiar with the company's ways of doing business
- They become **less sensitive to price** over time
- They can recommend by **word of mouth**

The justification for relationship marketing comes from this need to retain customers. There are five different levels of **customer relationship**.

(a) **Basic**. The salesperson sells the product without any further contact with the customer.

(b) **Reactive**. The customer is encouraged to call the salesperson if there are any problems.

(c) **Accountable**. The salesperson phones the customer to see if there are any problems and to elicit ideas for product improvements.

(d) **Proactive**. The salesperson contacts the customer on a regular basis.

(e) **Partnership**. The salesperson and customer work together, to ensure that all aspects of the deal suit the needs of both parties.

Broadly speaking, the greater the number of customers and the smaller the profit per unit sold, the greater the likelihood that the type of marketing will be **basic**. At the other extreme, where a firm has few customers, but where profits are high, the **partnership** approach is most likely.

EXAMPLE

Some firms convert a basic approach into relationship marketing. Many car dealerships, for example, seek to generate additional profits by servicing the cars they sell, and by keeping in touch with their customers so that they can earn repeat business.

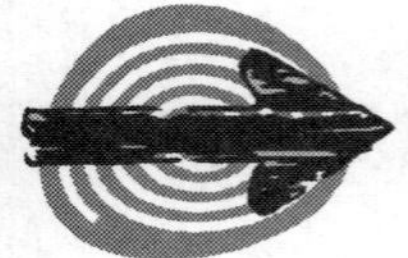

Building up customer relationships requires a change of focus from the 'transaction-based approach' to the relationship approach.

2.5 Relationship marketing

Relationship marketing is defined very simply by Grönroos as the management of a firm's market relationships.

Kotler says 'marketing can **make promises** but only the whole organisation can **deliver satisfaction**'. Adcock expands on this by remarking that relationship marketing can only exist when the marketing function fosters a customer-oriented **service culture** which supports the network of activities that deliver value to the customer.

Relationship marketing is thus as much about **attitudes** and **assumptions** as it is about techniques. The marketing function's task is to inculcate habits of behaviour at all levels and in all departments that will enhance and strengthen the alliance. It must be remembered, however, that the effort involved in long-term relationship building is **more appropriate in some markets than in others**. Where customers are purchasing intermittently and switching costs are low, there is always a chance of business. This tends to be the pattern in commodity markets. Here, it is reasonable to take a **transactions approach** to marketing and treat each sale as unique. A **relationship marketing approach** is more appropriate where switching costs are high and a lost customer is thus probably lost for a long time. Switching costs are raised by such factors as the need for training on systems; the need for a large common installed base and high capital cost and the incorporation of purchased items into the customer's own designs.

Differences between transactional and relationship marketing

Transactional	**Relationship**
Importance of single sale	Importance of customer relationship
Importance of product features	Importance of customer benefits
Short time scale	Longer time scale
Less emphasis on service	High level of customer service
Quality is concern of production	Quality is concern of all
Competitive commitment	High level of customer commitment
Persuasive communication	Regular communication

Figure 3.2: Transaction and relationship marketing contrasted

The process of retaining customers for a lifetime is an important one. Instead of one-way communication aimed solely at gaining a sale it is necessary to develop an effective two-way communication process to turn a **prospect into a lifetime advocate**. This is shown in the following ladder of customer loyalty.

Ladder of customer loyalty

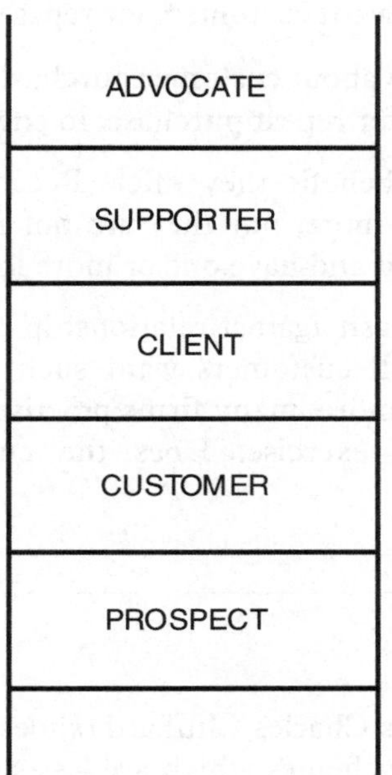

Figure 3.3: Ladder of customer loyalty

The purpose of relationship marketing is to establish, maintain and enhance relationships with customers and other parties so that the objectives of both parties involved are met.

(a) Because **service and industrial companies** have direct, regular and often multiple contacts with their customers (for example, the regular hotel guest who interacts with reception), the importance of 'part-time' marketers is increased. Customer contact with all employees is vital.

(b) **Trust and keeping promises.** To have an ongoing relationship, both parties need to trust each other and keep the promises they make. Marketing moves from one-off exchanges towards co-operative relationships built on financial, social and structural benefits.

(c) **Network of exchange partners.** Customer relationships are important but so too are the relationships which organisations have with other parties such as suppliers, distributors, professional bodies, banks, trade associations etc.

FOR DISCUSSION

What do you think are the differences between:

(a) Loyal customers with whom companies have a long-term relationship, and
(b) Captive markets?

Will customers be able to tell the difference?

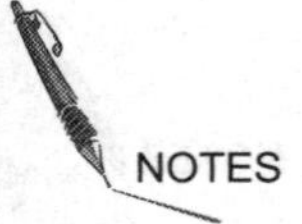

2.6 Loyalty schemes

Loyalty cards are designed to reward customers for repeat purchase. They:

- Collect information about customer purchasing habits
- Reward customers for repeat purchase, to encourage sales volumes.

Loyalty schemes vary in the benefit they offer. Recent UK research indicates that owners of 'loyalty' cards spend more, but they are not necessarily loyal. Furthermore, most customers still shop around and have one or more loyalty cards.

Recently there has been a backlash against relationship marketing, especially as applied to the consumer sector. Not all customers want such a relationship, and resent the potential for intrusion. Furthermore, many firms practise relationship marketing purely as an **information gathering** exercise. Does the customer benefit from such a relationship?

EXAMPLE

A wide range of retailers such as Charles Clinkard (shoes), McDonalds and Waterstones (books) have developed loyalty schemes which are less sophisticated than those used by major grocery retailers. Rather than being used to gather insight into consumer behaviour they simply encourage repeat purchase customers to collect stickers on a card every time they make a purchase to qualify for a free gift of some kind after so many purchases. This tactic stems from concern consumers may have about organisations tracking their behaviour. The scheme works as an incentive for loyalty as consumers may be more likely to visit that retailer particularly once they have collected a few stickers and value the reward.

In June 2007, Sky were reported by *Marketing* magazine to be about to launch a set top box loyalty card to reward individual viewers for watching TV shows rather than the household as a whole. The implementation of such a scheme would enable Sky to understand viewing habits to make better– informed decisions about what customers would want to buy in the future. It would also help with their advertising slot sales as advertisers may possibly be able to identify more accurately the specific target audience watching particular programmes. The report outlining this scheme came at a time when Sky and Virgin Media were in the midst of a fierce competitive battle.

To summarise, these are the distinguishing characteristics of relationship marketing.

- A focus on **customer retention** rather than attraction
- The development of an **on-going relationship** as opposed to a one-off transaction
- A **long time scale** rather than short time scale
- Direct and **regular customer contact** rather than impersonal sales
- **Multiple employee/customer contacts**
- **Quality and customer satisfaction** being the concern of all employees
- Emphasis on **key account relationship management**
- Importance of **trust** and keeping promises
- **Multiple exchanges** with a number of parties

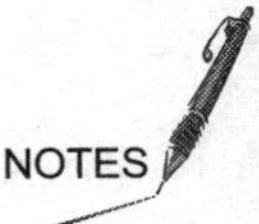

3 THE QUALITY MOVEMENT

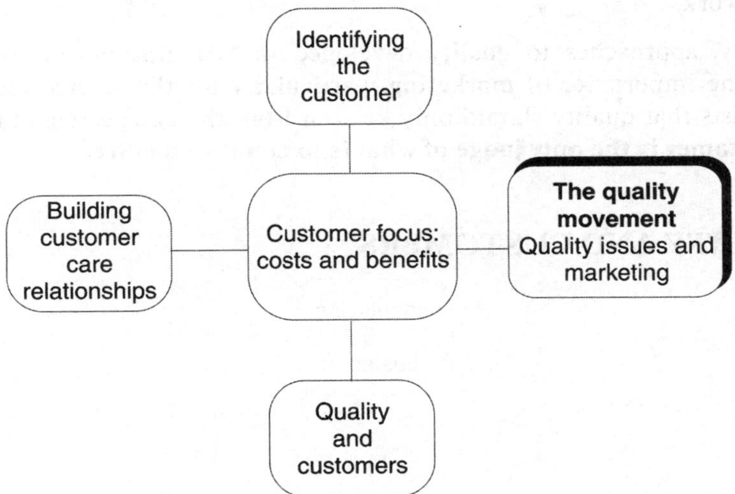

Definition

> **Quality** means 'the degree of excellence of a thing' – how well made it is, or how well performed if it is a service, how well it serves its purpose, and how it measures up against its rivals.

Two approaches to **quality control** are as follows.

(a) Aim for a level of quality which **minimises costs,** like inspection of goods produced or supervision of front line customer service staff on the one hand and the costs of repairing the damage when goods or services fall below standard on the other.

(b) Aim for **zero rejects** and **100% quality**. The desired standard is contained within the product or service specification and every unit produced or service performed ought to achieve this standard; in other words, there ought to be no defects. Zero-defect targets are one aspect of Japanese management philosophy.

Both approaches show a concern for quality and quality control. They both accept the need to incur **quality costs.** With a zero-defect target, there must be costs incurred in preventing defects and testing output. There is, however, a fundamental difference of view in the sense that the first approach accepts some level of defects and the second approach takes the view that all defects are undesirable.

Concern for the quality of the **environment** has matched the increasing concern with the quality of products and services. The two are related in that good quality control reduces waste.

The **quality movement** grew from the general alarm which spread throughout Europe and the US during the 1980s as previously successful manufacturing industries failed, while Japanese cars and electronic goods prospered. Japanese takeovers of failing western companies, and turnarounds based on the application of new managerial practices, underlined the urgency of understanding what this new approach involved, and how it could be applied here in the UK.

In the past, quality has been approached by looking at processes of **manufacturing** and reducing the **variability** and **waste** which such systems can produce, and introducing

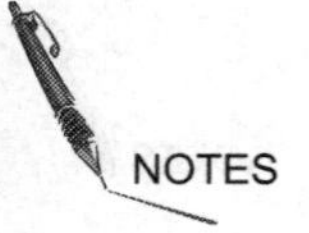

methods of checking to assure quality and reliability. The aim is to remove faults and substandard work.

More recently, approaches to quality developed in Scandinavia and the USA have emphasised the importance of **marketing,** particularly for the service industries. This approach insists that quality should only be seen from the perspective of the customer, since **the customer is the only judge of what is to count as quality.**

4 QUALITY AND CUSTOMERS

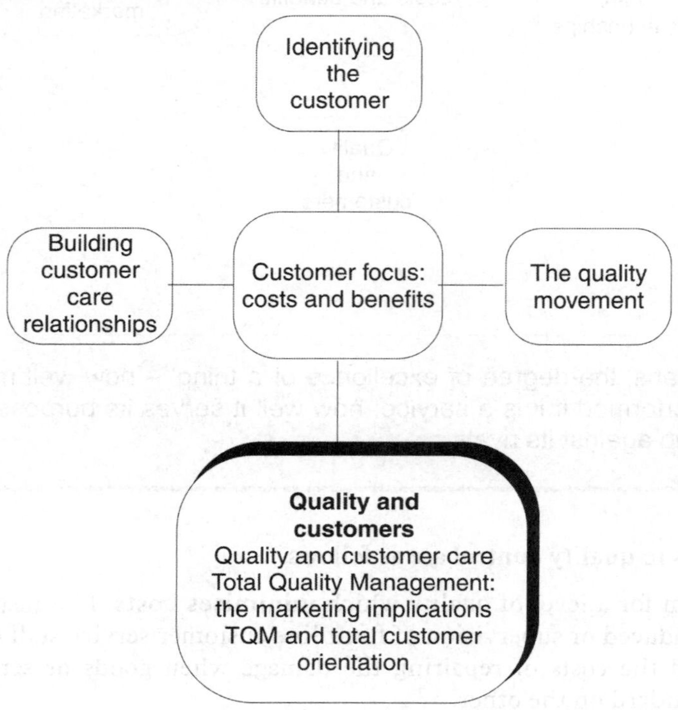

4.1 Quality and customer care

Why should a business embrace quality as a source of **competitive advantage**? The simple answer is that if you don't, someone else will – and, all other things (price, availability or whatever) being equal in the eyes of the consumer, better service or customer care will lead the consumer to choose your competitor's product.

Definition

> **Customer care** emphasises the importance of attitude and covers every aspect of the organisation's relationship with its customers.

It aims to **close the gap** between customers' **expectations** and their **experience.**

Ted Johns, in *Perfect Customer Care,* outlines the following excuses given for bad customer service, and the scenarios whereby the organisation will fall on its face.

Excuse for bad customer service	Likely outcome
Other organisations in the sector don't care about their customers	One will break ranks and compete successfully on the basis of customer care
The organisation competes on other factors, like price	Other factors, like service, have been shown to be more important
The organisation has no competitors	It won't stay a monopoly for ever
Demand for your organisation's output exceeds supply in the market	Success will only last as long as demand keeps up – and it is likely to go elsewhere once another provider arrives on the scene

Figure 3.4: Customer care

Activity 3 **(15 minutes)**

Are factors like service and quality *really* more important to the consumer than price, or is this just a myth put about by clever marketing people?

Think about this in terms of purchases that you make regularly, on the one hand, and very seldom on the other.

4.2 Total Quality Management: the marketing implications

The indications are that from now on, **quality will evolve around marketing-led developments**. As the discussion of the main quality gurus demonstrates, such agreement as exists on the definition of what quality involves refers to customer needs.

Definition

To **deliver quality** is to identify and produce what customers need.

Definition (TQM)

Feigenbaum (1983) identifies **Total Quality Management** (TQM) directly with the customer. TQM is defined as the total composite product and service characteristics of marketing, engineering, manufacture and maintenance, through which the product and service in use will meet the expectations by the customer.

4.3 Total quality and total customer orientation

A customer orientation, seeking to satisfy the customer, is pursued in marketing by recognising that customers buy 'the sizzle, not the steak' – products are bought for the benefits they deliver.

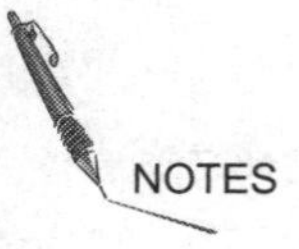

What constitutes a 'quality product or service' must, it seems, be related to what the customer wants. Indeed, quality would have no commercial value unless it delivered **customer benefit**, since the key reason for aiming to produce quality products is to derive extra sales by establishing competitive advantage through tangible and generally perceived superiority in particular product or service features.

Activity 4 **(20 minutes)**

In class, pick three or four different products. Each member of the class should write a list of five features that they would want to find in a high quality version of each product. Then compare your lists.

From a marketing point of view, then, quality is in the eye of the consumer. If quality is meeting the requirements of the consumer, then it should be recognised that throughout and beyond all enterprises, whatever business they are in, is a series of '**quality chains**'.

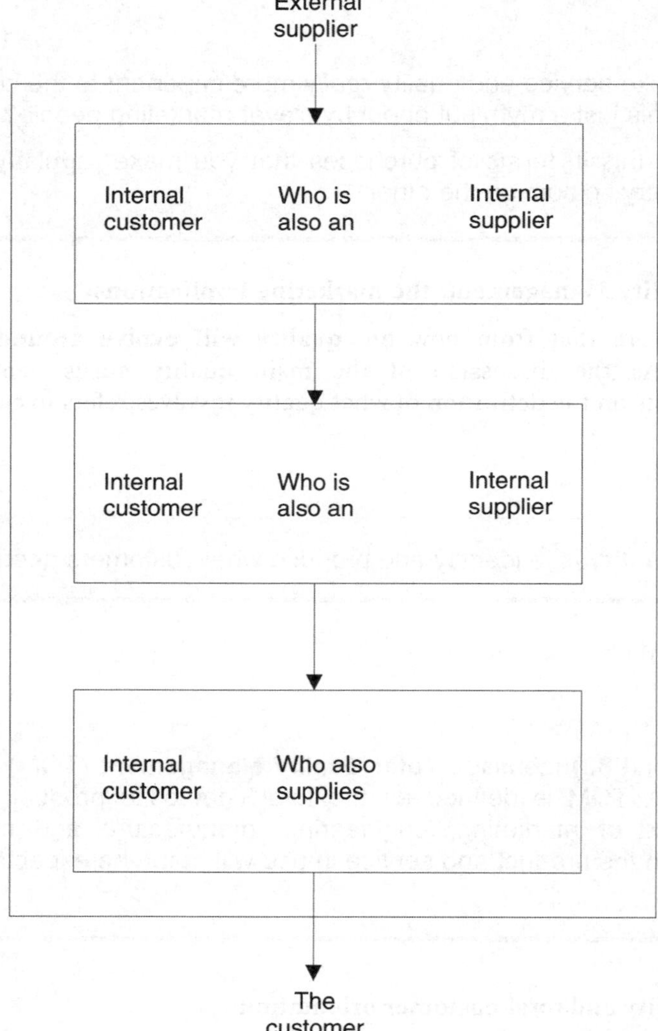

Figure 3.5: The quality chain

Meeting customer requirements is the main focus in a search for quality. While these requirements would typically include aspects such as availability, delivery, reliability, maintainability and cost effectiveness, in fact the first priority is to establish what customer requirements actually are.

If the customer is outside the organisation, then the supplier must seek to set up market research to gather this information and to relate the output of their organisation to the needs of the customer.

Internal customers for services are equally important, but their requirements are seldom investigated. The quality implementation process requires that all the supplier/customer relationships within the 'quality chain' should be treated as marketing exercises, and that each customer should be carefully consulted as to their precise requirements. Each link in the chain should prompt the following questions.

Of customers

- Who are my immediate customers?
- What are their true requirements?
- How can I find out what the requirements are?
- How can I measure my ability to meet the requirements?
- Do I have the necessary capability to meet the requirements?
  (If not, then what must change to improve the capability?)
- Do I continually meet the requirements?
  (If not, then what prevents this from happening, when the capability exists?)
- How do I monitor changes in the requirements?

Of suppliers

- Who are my immediate suppliers?
- What are my true requirements?
- How do I communicate my requirements?
- Do my suppliers have the capability to measure and meet the requirements?
- How do I inform them of changes in the requirements?

It should be noted that this focus on the customer does pose a number of problems.

(a) **Quality is subjective**

  (i) If quality is relative to customer expectations, it cannot be measured in an absolute sense.

  (ii) Different customers will want, need or expect different things from the same product-type.

(b) **Quality is distinctive**

  Product differentiation and highly segmented modern markets mean that the precise requirements of a particular market segment will produce an equally precise and differentiated definition of quality.

(c) **Quality is dynamic**

Expectations, and therefore definitions of quality, are highly dynamic: they change over time as a consequence of experience. A ratchet effect is highly likely, so that expectations will rise relatively easily, but will rarely and very reluctantly fall.

EXAMPLE

When a supplier pulls out all the stops for customers, this can sometimes lead to them making even greater demands. The IKEA furniture and houseware superstore chain, for instance, constantly monitors suppliers' delivery performance. It was greatly impressed that Richardson Sheffield, the cutlery manufacturer, was scoring 100% on its 10-day delivery schedule – so much so that it asked Richardson Sheffield to cut delivery to five days. That enabled Ikea to halve its stocks of cutlery – and thus reduce its inventory costs.

National Westminster Life Assurance has noticed that, where service is concerned, the customer is a bit of a junkie. You make improvements in one area but pretty soon that improvement is taken for granted and the customer ratchets up his expectations a notch or two. Having met customer demand on the time it takes to deliver insurance policies to its customers, NatWest Life is finding that this concern is dropping out of its customer satisfaction surveys, only to be replaced by anxiety over the extent to which the policy documents themselves are written in plain English.

Chapter roundup

- Customer focus concentrates an organisation's efforts on the customer to provide satisfaction or delight.
- Customer care and customer service help provide a competitive advantage.
- Customer retention is important because it can be expensive to attract and retain new customers.
- The total cost of customer care has various elements.
- In recent times emphasis has therefore increased on building and maintaining good long term relationships with customers.
- There is a move away from 'transactions' to relationship marketing. Firms aim to build loyalty.
- Quality is the degree of excellence of a thing - it requires care on the part of the provider, and how well it is achieved can only be measured by the customer.
- Total Quality Management means the management of all the organisation's resources so that a culture of continuous improvement focuses on the customer's needs.
- A key element of TQM is customer care, which involves the following.
  - Constantly collecting information on customer needs
  - Publicising this information in the organisation
  - Using the information to design, produce and deliver the organisation's goods and services so that the customer's needs are fulfilled.
- The heart of quality programmes is the need to define, research and respond to customer need. This is the marketing orientation at work. Quality programmes complement this core element with the formulation of systems which ensure sustained and consistent delivery of the desired processes and products. Further, their insistence on commitment from all parts of the organisation, on monitoring and measurement to check that the systems are working, and the requirement that the very top management should provide leadership on these issues, aims to take this consumer-driven approach to the very heart of management philosophy.
- The result of TQM is to aim to get it right, first time, and to improve service continuously. A very important way of achieving this is to train for quality, and to design quality into every stage of the delivery of the organisation's products and services to its customers.

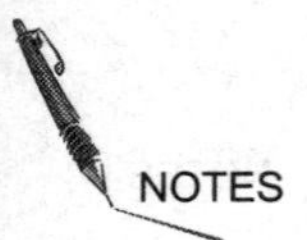
NOTES

Quick quiz

1. Give a definition of a customer.
2. What is better than customer satisfaction?
3. What is marketing myopia?
4. What are satisfied customers likely to do?
5. Give some examples of costs associated with attracting new customers.
6. Define relationship marketing.
7. What are the five different levels of customer relationship?
8. Why might some customers not want a 'relationship' with a company?
9. Give a definition of quality.
10. What is the quality chain reaction?
11. What is total quality management?
12. What does customer care aim to achieve?

Answers to Quick quiz

1. The purchaser of a product or service.
2. Customer 'delight'.
3. A narrow focus on the product, to such an extent that the importance of customer needs is disregarded.
4. Buy again, buy more, recommend to friends.
5. Advertising; salesmen time; credit checks; agent commission; initial discounts.
6. The process of creating, building up and managing long term relationships with customers, distributors and suppliers.
7. Basic; reactive; accountable, pro-active; partnership.
8. They may see it as unwarranted intrusion. If all the company is doing is gathering information (rather than genuine relationship building) then it is difficult to see what the customer is gaining anyway.
9. How well made or how well performed something is.
10. See figure 3.5.
11. The total composite product and service characteristics of marketing, engineering, manufacturing and maintenance through which customer expectations are met.
12. To close the gap between customers' expectations and their experience.

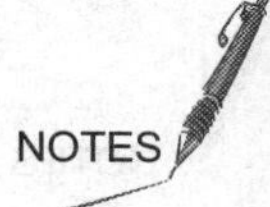

Answers to Activities

1 There are many examples of a product/service effectively creating a need or a want. These include DVD, Internet services, digital TV and even film merchandise, such as South Park, Star Wars or Harry Potter.

2 Here are some suggestions.

(a) It means that regular customers will support the supplier. It will be difficult for competitors to attract customers away from their favoured supplier.

(b) Regular customers provide reliable income and turnover.

(c) It is possible to build a rapport with customers over time. This helps the supplier understand their needs more easily, thus making the marketing process more straightforward.

(d) Customer loyalty is also a source of goodwill. It will enhance the supplier organisation's image and can be a source of very potent advertising in that customers may recommend the supplier to their friends or colleagues.

3 Food is a good example here. Many consumers persist in buying branded beans instead of supermarket brands, due to the perceived quality of the brand. Consider also eating out at a restaurant. Many people would pay premium prices to guarantee good service.

4 The answer to this activity will depend upon the products you have chosen. However, you may find that different people's perceptions of quality vary quite a lot.

NOTES

Answers to activities

1 There are many examples of a product/service effectively creating a brand new want. These include DVD, internet services, digital TV and even merchandise, such as South Park, Star Wars or Harry Potter.

2 Here are some suggestions.

(a) It means that regular customers will support the supplier. It will be difficult for competitors to attract customers away from their favoured supplier.

(b) Regular customers are more predictable in their purchase behaviour.

(c) It is possible to build a rapport with customers over time. This helps the supplier understand their needs more easily, thus making the marketing process more straightforward.

(d) Customer loyalty is also a source of goodwill. It will enhance the supplier's reputation in the market and can be a source of very potent advertising as the customers may recommend the supplier to their friends and colleagues.

3 Food is a good example here. Many consumers will prefer to buy branded foods instead of own-brand products due to the perceived quality of the brand. Consumers may willingly pay a premium. Many people would pay premium prices to guarantee good service.

The answer to this activity will depend upon the products you have chosen. However, you may find that different people's perceptions of quality vary quite a lot.

Part B

Segmentation, Targeting and Positioning

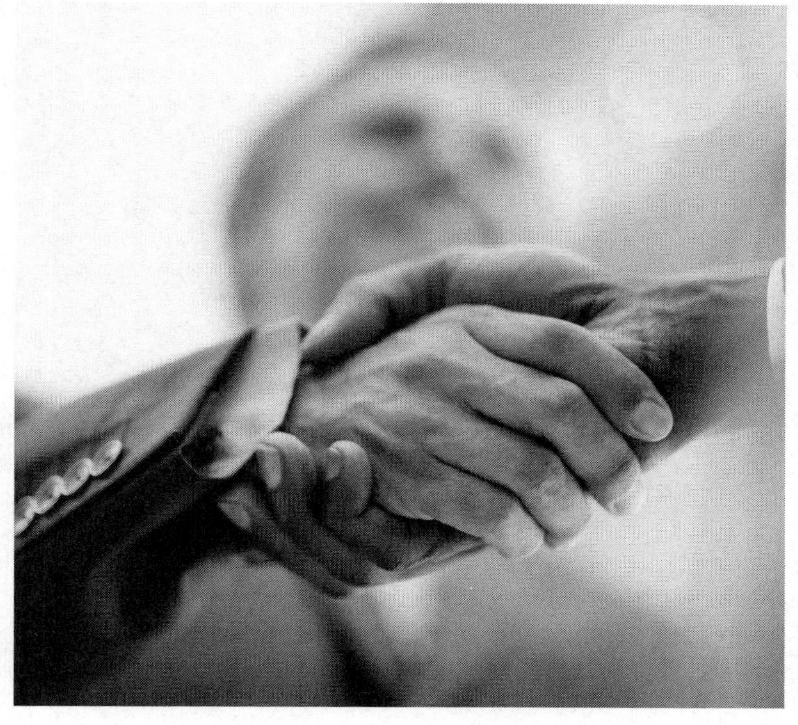

Chapter 4 : THE MARKETING ENVIRONMENT

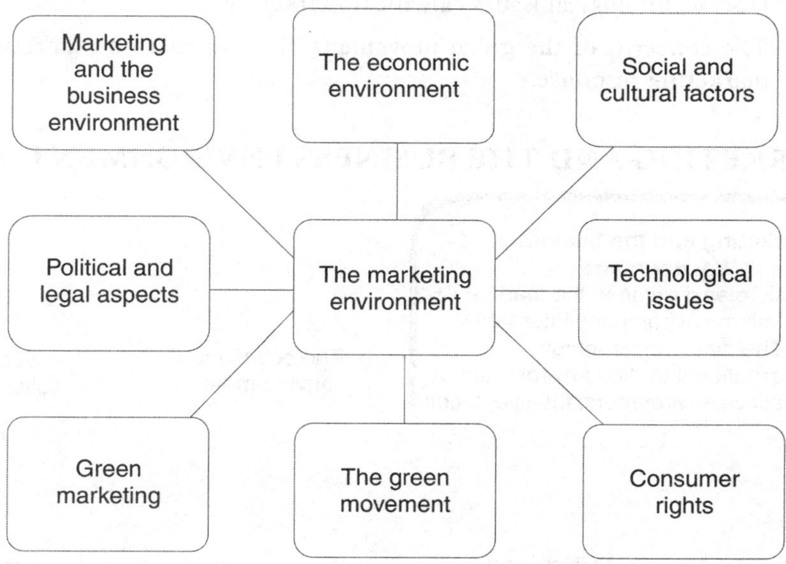

Introduction

An organisation must **understand its environment** if it is to exploit changing market conditions and **target** its market successfully.

The **micro environment** includes all factors which impact directly on a firm and its activities in relation to a particular market in which it operates, and also any internal aspects of the organisation which influence the development of a marketing strategy. The **macro environment** is concerned with broad trends and patterns in society as a whole which may affect all markets, but will be more relevant to some than others. Careful monitoring of the macro environment can enable an organisation to identify opportunities for and threats to its business and will enable it to adopt a proactive rather than a reactive approach in the action it takes.

The environment is large and complex and this is quite a long chapter. We shall look in some detail at the ways in which **economic** factors, at home and abroad, **social** and **cultural** factors within families and larger groups, and **legal** and **political** considerations, can all affect the marketing of goods and services.

Developments in **technology** are happening at an ever-increasing pace. The rapid appearance of completely new products, such as the digital camera, and the obsolescence of those previously thought essential, presents a special challenge to marketers. The Internet is also having a profound effect.

The marketing concept will undoubtedly be increasingly affected by **ecological** issues. In the past there was a tendency to regard business activities as antithetical to 'green-ness', but now it is being recognised that the two are complementary, and that one of the key factors in future business success will be the **sustainability** of business activity. This refers to the idea that resources which are used up must be replaced.

Your objectives

In this chapter you will learn about the following.

(a) Features of the business environment that influence marketing strategy

(b) Consumerism

(c) Political, economic, social, cultural and legal factors, and how they affect customer behaviour and their implications for marketing

(d) How technological issues can affect marketing

(e) The concerns of the green movement, their impact on marketing, and the marketing response.

1 MARKETING AND THE BUSINESS ENVIRONMENT

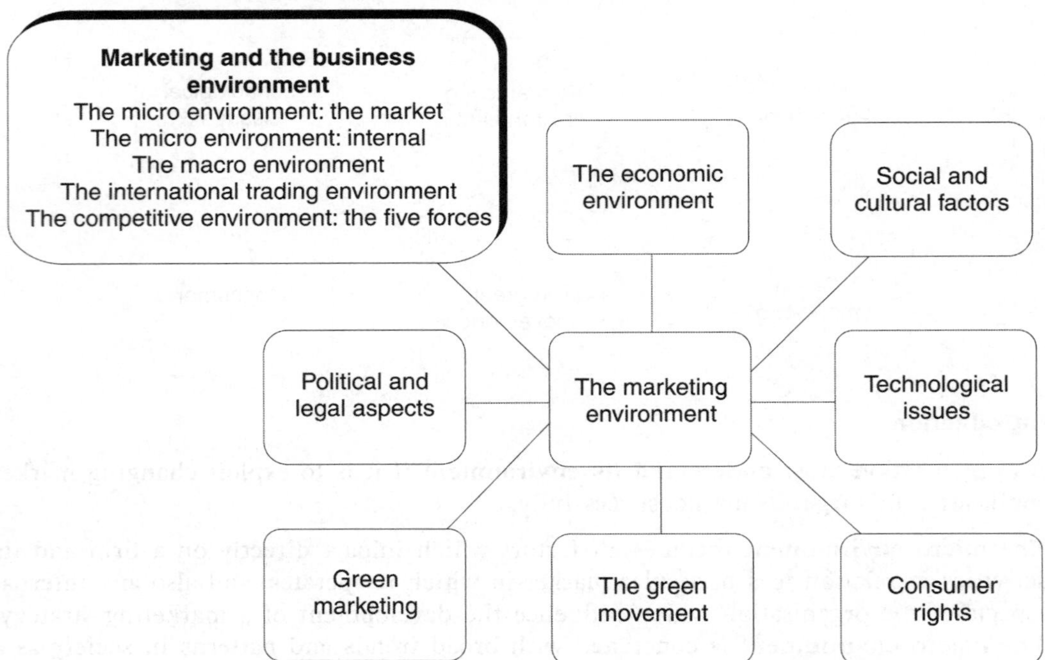

Within the marketing environment an organisation needs to consider both macro and micro factors. Before you read any further into your chapter try to complete the activity below.

Activity 1 **(5 minutes)**

Looking through the list below, try to decide if for your organisation it would fall into the category of the organisation's macro or micro environment. The micro environment refers to your immediate market. The macro environment refers to the factors which extend way beyond your control which are outside of your immediate market.

- Political and legal
- Economic forces
- Suppliers
- Intermediaries
- Social and cultural forces
- Competitors
- Customers
- Technological forces
- Other stakeholders

1.1 The micro environment: the market

The nature of the micro market environment is outlined in the diagram below.

Definition

The **market environment** comprises all aspects of a market that have direct effects on the company's relationship with its customers and their patterns of competition.

Its importance should not be underestimated, not only because it has a major **impact** on the operation of a business, but also because business can, in part, **control and change it**. Suppliers, distributors, consumers, competitors and interest groups have all been identified as key elements of the market environment.

Understanding the **interactions and the behaviour** of these groups enables the firm to use its marketing strategies to encourage loyalty, obtain preference from suppliers/distributors, and influence what competitors do and what consumers think. Equally, through the development of **corporate image,** it can influence the way the business is perceived by various interest groups.

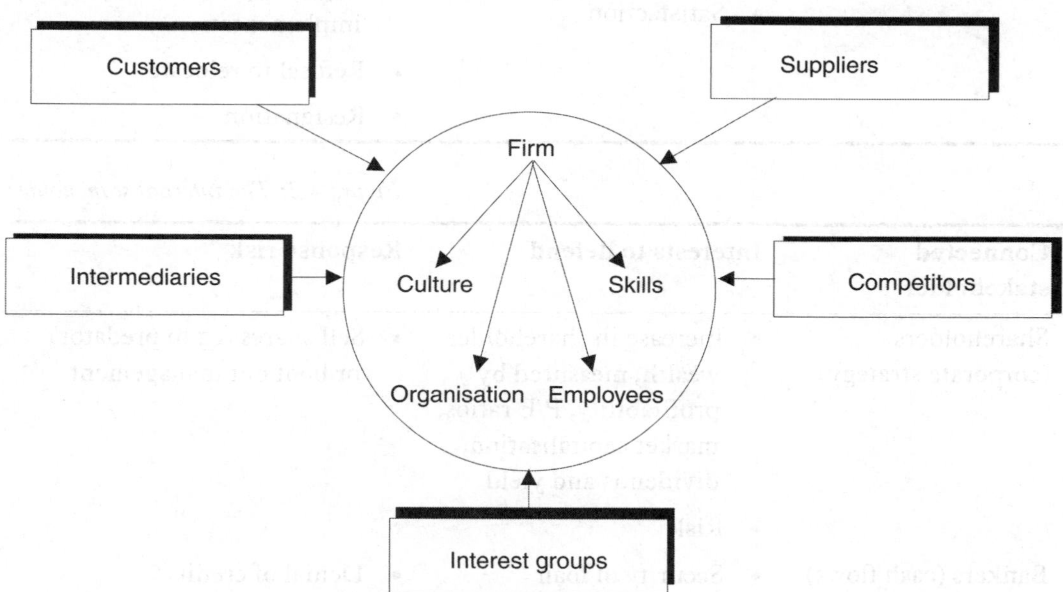

Figure 4.1: The micro environment

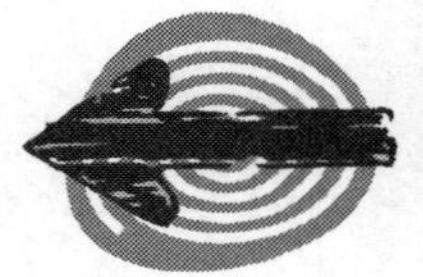

We will now consider the key elements of the market environment in turn, starting with stakeholders.

Definition

Stakeholders are those having an interest in the activities of an organisation, such as customers, employees, the community, shareholders, suppliers and lenders.

NOTES

There are three broad types of **stakeholder** in an organisation, as follows.

- **Internal** stakeholders (employees, management)
- **Connected** stakeholders (shareholders, customers, suppliers, financiers)
- **External** stakeholders (the community, local residents, government, pressure groups)

Because employees and management are so intimately connected with the company, their **objectives** are likely to have a strong influence on how it is run. They are interested in the following issues.

(a) The organisation's continuation and growth. Management and employees have a special interest in the organisation's continued existence.

(b) Managers and employees have **individual interests** and goals which can be harnessed to the goals of the organisation.

Internal stakeholder	Interests to defend	Response risk
Managers and employees	• Jobs/careers • Money • Promotion • Benefits • Satisfaction	• Pursuit of 'systems goals' rather than shareholder interests • Industrial action • Negative power to impede implementation • Refusal to relocate • Resignation

Figure 4.2: The internal stakeholder

Connected stakeholder	Interests to defend	Response risk
Shareholders (corporate strategy)	• Increase in shareholder wealth, measured by profitability, P/E ratios, market capitalisation, dividends and yield • Risk	• Sell shares (eg to predator) or boot out management
Bankers (cash flows)	• Security of loan • Adherence to loan agreements	• Denial of credit • Higher interest charges • Receivership
Suppliers (purchase strategy)	• Profitable sales • Payment for goods • Long-term relationship	• Refusal of credit • Court action • Wind down relationships
Customers (product market strategy)	• Goods as promised • Future benefits	• Buy elsewhere • Sue

Figure 4.3: The connected stakeholder

EXAMPLE

A survey of FTSE 100 companies conducted by the *Financial Times* asked what part leading shareholders play in the running of companies and what top directors think of their investors.

Almost half of those surveyed felt that their main shareholders 'rarely or never' offered any useful comments about their business. 69% of respondents however felt that their major investors understood their business well or very well. 89% did not feel hampered by shareholders in taking the correct long term strategy.

Almost all directors felt their biggest shareholders were in it for the long term. This latter point probably reflects the fact that the top ten fund managers own 36 per cent of the FTSE 100 – few fund managers can afford to move out of a FTSE 100 company altogether and therefore remain long term shareholders whether the investment is liked or not.

There is a perceived trend towards greater involvement and communication. To quote one director: 'Investors are much more sensitive to their responsibilities than in the past because they are looked on as the guardians of the corporate conscience.'

External stakeholder groups – the government, local authorities, pressure groups, the community at large, professional bodies – are likely to have quite diverse objectives. Here are some examples.

External stakeholder	Interests to defend	Response risk
Government	• Jobs, training, tax	• Tax increases • Regulation • Legal action
Interest/pressure groups	• Pollution • Rights • Other	• Publicity • Direct action • Sabotage • Pressure on government

Figure 4.4: The external stakeholder

Distributive network

Although the nature and structure of the **distributive network** is generally treated as a marketing mix variable which can be controlled by an organisation, it is also part of the market environment. There are few instances where a market is so new that there are no existing distribution systems. Normally these systems are in place and they will impose constraints on what an organisation can do, partly because of consumer familiarity with existing systems and partly because of the degree of market power held by the distribution network. For example, in the UK food industry the decisions taken by food manufacturers are heavily influenced by the market power of the large supermarket chains.

Competition

Marketing as an aid to establishing a **competitive position** in the market place has already been stressed; any organisation must develop an awareness and understanding of

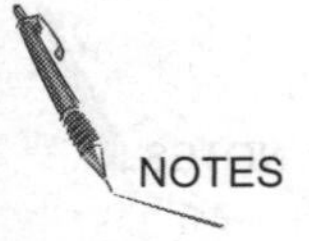

NOTES

its competitors, their strengths and weaknesses and the essence of their strategic approach. We look at Porter's model of the **five competitive forces** later in this section.

1.2 The micro environment: internal

The internal environment is where the firm can exercise greatest control and should possess the greatest knowledge. The **internal capabilities** of the organisation are a key factor in generating marketing success. The analysis of the internal environment rests on an understanding of the nature of the **corporate culture** – the attitudes and beliefs of personnel at all levels. Strategies appropriate for an organisation with a culture orientated towards rapid innovation and risk-taking may be quite different from those available to a company orientated towards high quality and an exclusive image, or those pursued by an organisation which sees itself as a low risk market follower with a reliable product range.

An understanding of the strengths and weaknesses of the structure of the company and of the personnel within the company is equally important. Internal structures may be changing to reflect the increased pressures of a competitive market place.

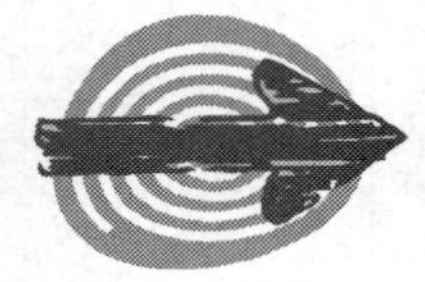

Marketing audits help an organisation (and the individuals involved in the planning process) to understand the internal environment. We looked at these in Chapter 2.

1.3 The macro environment

The macro environment can be described in terms of four key components: political/legal, economic, social/cultural, and technological (PEST factors). The diagram below shows these factors.

The total environment

Figure 4.5: The macro environment

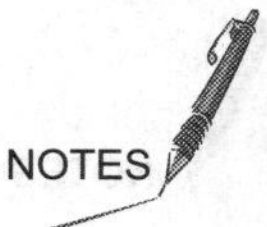

1.4 The organisation in the international trading environment

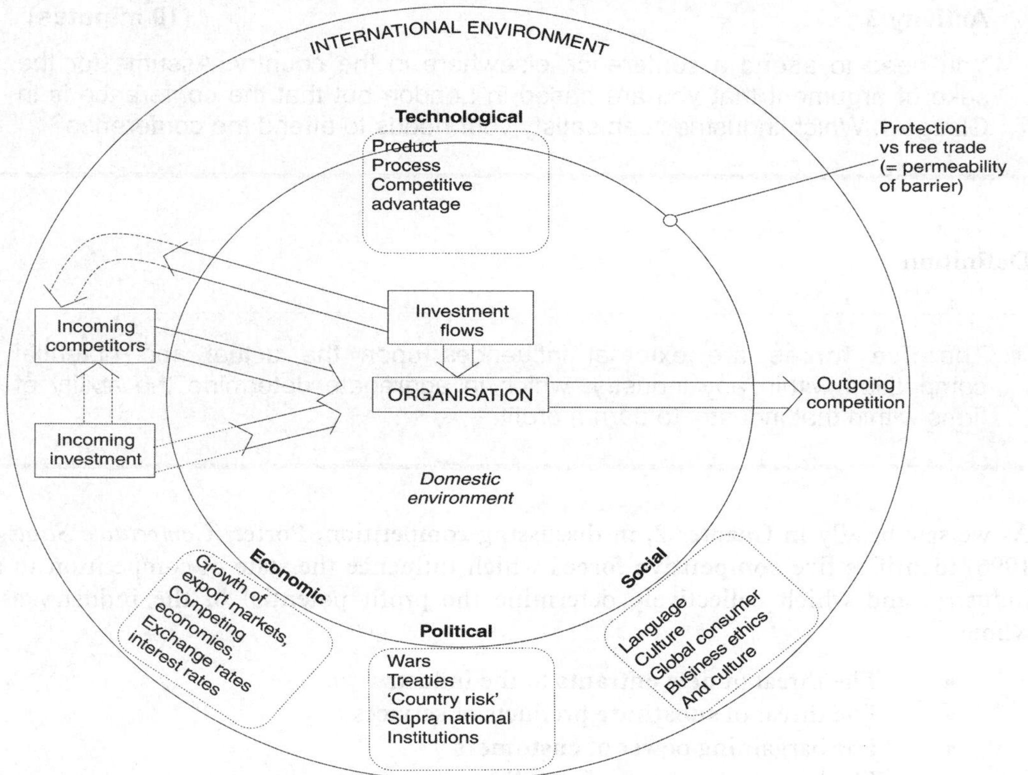

Figure 4.6: International influences on the organisation's domestic conditions

Activity 2 **(15 minutes)**

Tommy's Toys manufactures model cars and trucks, which are normally battery driven. The firm has not gone into exporting very much because of the trouble caused by different product standards and requirements. What would be the effect on Tommy's Toys if the government of its country entered into free trade agreements with neighbouring countries?

1.5 The competitive environment: The five forces

Before we start we should make a basic distinction between the **market** and the **industry**.

Definitions

The **market** comprises the customers or potential customers who have needs which are satisfied by a product or service.

The **industry** comprises those firms which use a particular competence, technology, product or service to satisfy customer needs.

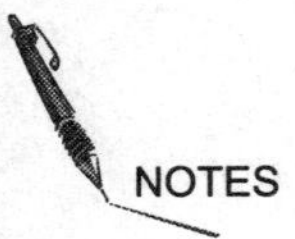

Activity 3 **(10 minutes)**

You need to attend a conference elsewhere in the country. Assume for the sake of argument that you are based in London but that the conference is in Glasgow. Which industries can satisfy your needs to attend the conference?

Definition

The **five forces** are external influences upon the actual and potential competition within any industry, which in aggregate determine the ability of firms within that industry to earn a profit.

As we saw briefly in Chapter 2, in discussing competition, Porter (*Competitive Strategy*, 1996) identifies five **competitive forces** which influence the state of competition in an industry, and which collectively determine the profit potential of the industry as a whole.

- The threat of **new entrants** to the industry
- The threat of **substitute** products or services
- The bargaining power of **customers**
- The bargaining power of **suppliers**
- The **rivalry** amongst current competitors in the industry

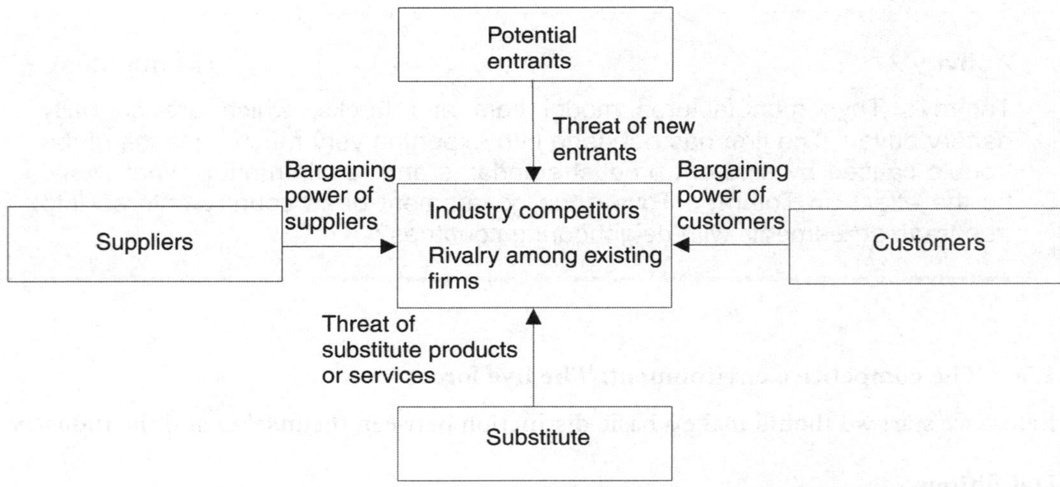

Figure 4.7: The five forces (adapted from Porter)

The threat of new entrants (and barriers to entry to keep them out)

A new entrant into an industry will bring extra capacity and more competition. The strength of this threat is likely to vary from industry to industry, depending on:

- The strength of the **barriers to entry**. Barriers to entry discourage new entrants
- The likely **response of existing competitors** to the new entrant

EXAMPLE

Given that the cola market is shared mostly between the two giants Pepsi and Coca-cola (and a few retailer own brands) few new entrants enter the market due to the anticipated reaction of Pepsi and Coca who are large enough organisations to sustain an expensive period of vastly increased promotional activities. Virgin entered the market and although the product remained on the market it never gained significant market share due to the existing brand strength share between the existing market leaders.

Barriers to entry

(a) **Scale economies**. High fixed costs often imply a high breakeven point, which needs a large volume of sales. If the market as a whole is not growing, the new entrant has to capture a large slice of the market from existing competitors.

(b) **Product differentiation**. Existing firms in an industry may have built up a good brand image and strong customer loyalty over a long period of time.

(c) **Capital requirements**. When capital investment requirements are high, the barrier against new entrants will be strong, particularly when the investment would possibly be high-risk.

(d) **Switching costs**. Switching costs refer to the costs (time, money, convenience) that a customer would have to incur by switching from one supplier's products to another's. Although it might cost a **consumer** nothing to switch from one brand of frozen peas to another, the potential costs for the **retailer or distributor** might be high.

(e) **Access to distribution channels**. Distribution channels carry a manufacturer's products to the end-buyer. New distribution channels are difficult to establish, and existing distribution channels hard to gain access to.

(f) **Cost advantages of existing producers, independent of economies of scale** include:

- Patent rights
- Experience and know-how (the learning curve)
- Government subsidies and regulations
- Favoured access to raw materials

Entry barriers might be **lowered** by:

- Changes in the environment
- Technological changes
- Novel distribution channels for products or services

The threat from substitute products

Definition

A **substitute product** is a good/service produced by another industry which satisfies the same customer needs.

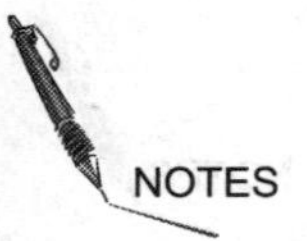

EXAMPLE

Passengers have several ways of getting from London to Paris, and the pricing policies of the various industries transporting them there reflects this.

(a) 'Le Shuttle' carries cars in the Channel Tunnel. Its main competitors come from the ferry companies, offering a substitute service. Therefore, you will find that Le Shuttle sets its prices with reference to ferry company prices, and *vice versa*.

(b) Eurostar is the rail service from London to Paris/Brussels. Its main competitors are not the ferry companies but the airlines. Prices on the London-Paris air routes fell with the commencement of Eurostar services, and some airlines have curtailed the number of flights they offer.

Organisations need to think widely about the source of potential substitute products or run this risk of becoming myopic. Cinemas may think that DVD rental or sales may be their main substitutes however consumers may see the wider entertainment market maybe restaurants, gaming, clubs etc as an alternative to going to the cinema.

The bargaining power of customers

Customers want better quality products and services at a lower price. Satisfying this want might force down the profitability of suppliers in the industry. Just how strong the position of customers is dependent on several factors.

- How much the **customer buys**
- How **critical** the product is to the customer's own business
- **Switching costs (ie the cost of switching supplier)**
- Whether the products are **standard items** (hence easily copied) or specialised
- The **customer's own profitability**
- Customer's **ability to bypass** the supplier or might take over the supplier
- The **skills** of the customer **purchasing staff**, or the price-awareness of consumers
- The importance of **product quality** to the customer

The bargaining power of suppliers

Suppliers can exert pressure for higher prices but this is dependent on several factors.

- Whether there are just **one or two dominant suppliers** to the industry, able to charge monopoly or oligopoly prices
- The threat of **new entrants** or substitute products to the **supplier's industry**
- Whether the suppliers have **other customers** outside the industry, and do not rely on the industry for the majority of their sales
- The **importance of the supplier's product** to the customer's business
- Whether the supplier has a **differentiated product** which buyers need to obtain
- Whether **switching costs** for customers would be high

The rivalry amongst current competitors in the industry

The **intensity of competitive rivalry** within an industry will affect the profitability of the industry as a whole. Competitive actions might take the form of price competition, advertising battles, sales promotion campaigns, introducing new products for the market, improving after sales service or providing guarantees or warranties.

The intensity of competition will depend on the following factors.

(a) **Market growth**. Rivalry is intensified when firms are competing for a greater market share in a total market where growth is slow or stagnant.

(b) **Cost structure**. High fixed costs are a temptation to compete on price, as in the short run any contribution from sales is better than none at all.

(c) **Switching**. Suppliers will compete if buyers switch easily (eg Coke v Pepsi).

(d) **Capacity**. A supplier might need to achieve a substantial increase in output capacity, in order to obtain reductions in unit costs.

(e) **Uncertainty**. When one firm is not sure what another is up to, there is a tendency to respond to the uncertainty by formulating a more competitive strategy.

(f) **Strategic importance**. If success is a prime strategic objective, firms will be likely to act very competitively to meet their targets.

(g) **Exit barriers** may make it difficult for an existing supplier to leave the industry, such as the cost of redundancy payments to employees. One of the issues in BMW's disposal of Rover Cars was the question of who would be liable for workers' redundancy and pension payments.

EXAMPLE

Some companies are in danger of losing lucrative home markets because the Internet has made it easier for customers to access and compare prices.

Geographical price discrimination is becoming harder to sustain in an age where a shopper with a credit card and a computer can sit at home and order from around the world. The Internet has increased competition, and is used by many organisations as a competitive weapon.

2 THE ECONOMIC ENVIRONMENT

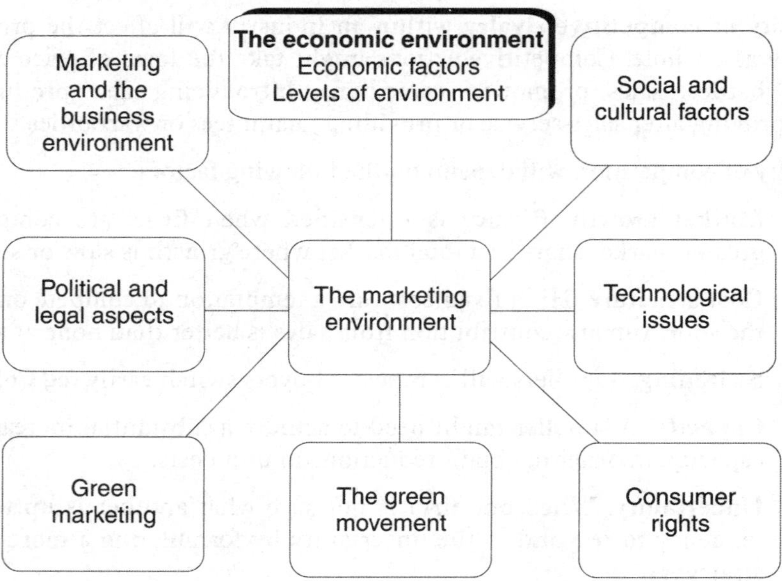

2.1 Economic factors

You will often hear reports of politicians discussing the state of the economy. We all know that this is supposed to be important, but unfortunately vague terms like 'recession' don't give us much useful information. We need much more precise measures of how the economy is doing. These can then be identified as the economic factors which affect businesses and set their economic environment. For example, the rate of inflation is both a measure of how the economy is doing and an important factor for most businesses: if costs are rising, a business must either raise its own prices or save on costs in order to maintain profits. We will therefore identify a number of key measures, and look at why they are important for businesses.

The rate of growth

The rate of growth of the economy is the rate of increase in total economic activity. It can be measured using the **gross national product**, which is (roughly) the total amount of goods and services made in a year. For example, if a country has only one product, cars, and in year 1 it makes 1,000 cars and in year 2 it makes 1,200 cars, the rate of growth is 20%. The rate of growth matters to businesses because the faster the economy grows, the better off people become and the more they will buy. People can also change what they buy. For example, they might buy more cars and fewer train tickets, because they prefer private transport. This could have a knock-on effect: the demand for driving lessons might increase while the demand for sandwiches at stalls in railway stations might fall.

The rate of inflation

This is the rate at which prices are rising. Businesses must take account of how their **costs** might increase, what **wage rises** they might have to pay and the extent to which **competitors** might increase their prices.

Quite apart from general inflation, the prices of certain **raw materials** may go up or down dramatically, having a direct effect on some businesses. For example, the price of crude oil has fluctuated sharply in the past 30 years, affecting not only the price of petrol but also the price of all goods transported by road or sea.

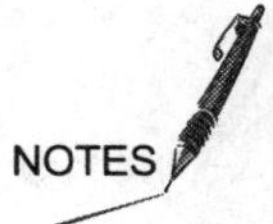

The level of unemployment

The number of unemployed people is particularly important for consumer markets and the retail sector. If people are out of work, they will not spend much in the shops.

Businesses may also be interested in who is unemployed, if they are looking for new workers. Some businesses need workers who already have special **skills**, or who can be trained quickly. If most of the unemployed are unskilled, this may make recruitment difficult.

Interest rates

Most businesses borrow money, either as **overdrafts** or as **long-term loans**. If a business wishes to expand, perhaps buying a new factory and machinery, it may need to take out a large loan. If interest rates are low, this may be easy. If, on the other hand, interest rates are high, it may be too expensive and the expansion plan may have to be abandoned. High interest rates can even drive a business to bankruptcy, if it can no longer afford the interest payments on its existing borrowings.

Taxation levels and policy

Taxation levels and the nature of taxes can greatly affect businesses and their customers.

The opposite of taxes is **subsidies**, when the government grants money to new businesses, businesses in poor areas and so on.

The level of personal saving

If people earn money, they can either spend it or save it. If they spend it, businesses get the benefit straightaway through making sales. If they save a large part of their incomes, businesses may suffer in the short term. However, savings are ultimately invested, and make capital available for industry to expand.

The exchange rate

If the value of the pound increases imports become cheaper. This will help businesses which import, for example a UK dealer in Japanese televisions. However, exporting will become more difficult, since foreign buyers will have to pay more of their own currency for the same goods.

How other countries are doing

If a company exports to, for example, Australia, it is likely to do well if the Australian economy is doing well. This in turn will depend on Australian inflation, unemployment, interest rates and so on.

International barriers to trade

Some countries set up barriers, such as customs duties on imports, so as to make it difficult for foreigners to sell goods into the country. On the other hand, groups of countries can set up free trade areas such as the **European Economic Area**, and remove trade barriers within the area.

EXAMPLE: TRADE BARRIERS

For those who worry about a return of the Great Depression's high tariffs and trade wars, the last several months have been troubling. Figures from the World Bank's Global Antidumping Database released last month show that industry requests for trade barriers globally are up 30% this year to date compared to the same period last year. Yet along with this latest bad news come some trade-policy green shoots that suggest the global economy may still stay on a protrade path.

The recent U.S. government decision against a request to impose new trade barriers on imports from Argentina of aluminum *(sic)* pistons used in diesel engines is one cause for optimism. In January, an Ohio-based piston plant filed a petition with the U.S. Commerce Department alleging that Argentina unfairly subsidizes production of the pistons and that these subsidies were hurting the company. Late last month, the U.S. International Trade Commission ruled that, while the firm may have hit hard times, its injury was not caused by subsidized imports.

Chad P Bown,
The Wall Street Journal, 17 November 2009

Activity 4 **(20 minutes)**

Think about a company which makes personal computers and give one way whereby each of the above economic factors may affect the company.

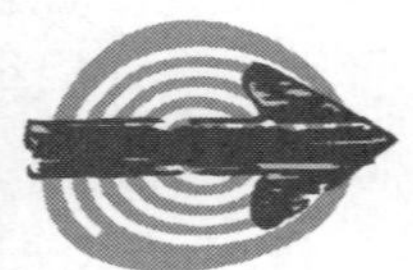

Some of the economic factors we have looked at tell us a lot about a business's local environment, for example the town it is based in. Some tell us more about a business's country. And some are only really important when we look at the whole world. We will now look at examples of economic factors in action at each of these three levels.

2.2 Levels of environment

The local economic environment

A business's local environment is most likely to have a big impact on its prospects if it is a retail business. A shop will only do well if there are customers in the town with money to spend. The most important local factor is likely to be the unemployment rate. A major industrial closure, for example of a coal mine, can destroy shops in the area. On the other hand, the opening of a new factory can bring prosperity to all businesses.

The national economic environment

The national environment affects practically all businesses. Growth, inflation, unemployment, interest rates, taxation rates and the level of personal saving are all relevant. Another factor which affects long term national economic prospects is the make-up of the population. In some countries the retired population is increasing faster than the working population, because people are living longer but having fewer children. This may mean that economic growth will slow down, because too small a proportion of the population is making things to sell.

NOTES

Note that these national economic factors are things which an individual business, even a very big one, can do little or nothing about.

The world economic environment

World economic factors include the balance of payments and exchange rates, the performance of other countries' economies and international barriers to trade or free trade areas. Businesses may be affected by these things directly, if they import or export goods. They may also be affected indirectly, if they buy from an importer or sell to an exporter. For example, a printer may work only for UK publishers and may buy paper only from UK paper makers, but the paper makers will buy their raw material, wood pulp, from Sweden where the trees are grown. If the pound falls in value against the Swedish Krona, the price of wood pulp will go up in pounds and the printer will have to pay more for paper. This in turn may put up the price of books in bookshops, affecting the number of books sold and the shops' profits.

FOR DISCUSSION

Do you feel that the UK economy is doing well or badly at the moment? What are the good signs and what are the bad signs? Are there any big problems looming in the years ahead?

The impact of some changes can be dramatic. Consider, for example, the vast increase in the UK national debt in 2009 and the subsequent fall in value of the pound against many other currencies. This provided a boost to UK companies who were major exporters, because it made their goods cheaper to overseas customers. On the other hand it increased the price of imported raw materials, pushing up domestic inflation, and the value of the pound became much less stable, making planning more difficult. A business buying large items of machinery from Germany, for example, may sign a contract for goods to be delivered and paid for up to a year later, perhaps. If, in the meantime, the pound strengthens in value against the Euro, the goods will be cheaper than expected.

Activity 5 **(15 minutes)**

Can you think of any other way a company may attempt to overcome the various economic problems that arise from world trade?

Social and cultural factors are another important PEST factor in the external environment for a marketing business. To some extent they interact with economic factors.

3 SOCIAL AND CULTURAL FACTORS

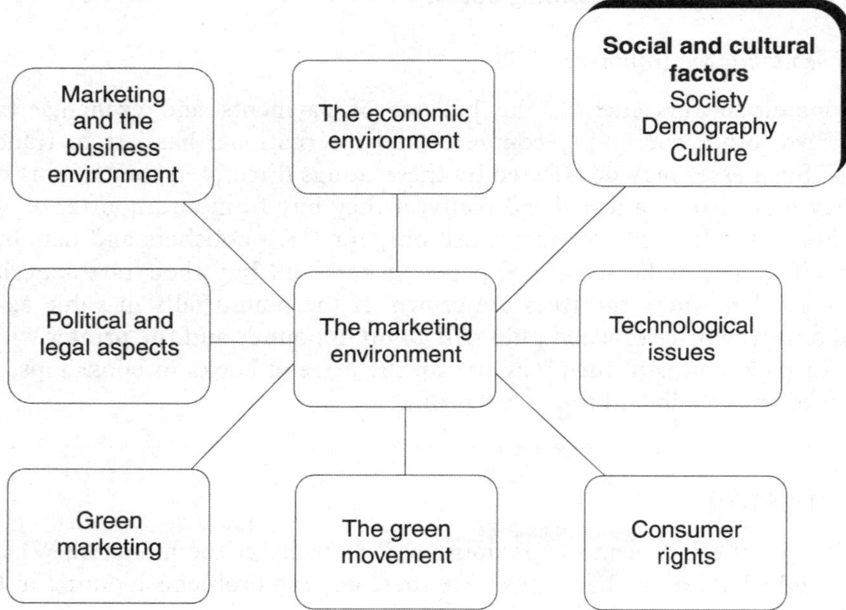

3.1 Society

Society provides the framework for human behaviour and conduct. Underpinning this is a set of attitudes and beliefs. We know that if we want to be accepted by others, we should behave in certain ways. For example, when a group of friends are drinking in a bar, it is normal for them to take it in turns to buy drinks for each other. If you accept drinks from other people but never buy any in return, you will not be popular! Businesses need to take account of these attitudes.

Activity 6 **(10 minutes)**

Think of five recent advertisements which play on social attitudes.

When a business is taking account of social influences, it should consider the following aspects.

(a) **Norms and values**, such as sharing. Families influence people strongly.

(b) **Lifestyles**, for example the young, free and single lifestyle or the respectable middle-aged lifestyle. These are often influenced by the media.

(c) The influence of **peer groups**. These are groups of people of your own age, status and so on, whom you tend to mix with. There is often pressure to conform, to be like your peers in your choice of clothes, restaurants and so on.

Activity 7 **(15 minutes)**

To what extent does marketing mould society, as opposed to society influencing marketing? You may wish to consider the impact of Sunday shopping, global brands such as Coca-Cola, and the targeting of computers at the young.

3.2 Demography

Definition

Demography is the study of population characteristics and population trends. It is about how many people there are, how old they are, the proportions of men to women and how the population is spread across the country.

Demographic factors affect what consumers are likely to want, and the quantities they will want. For example, if the population comprises mostly young adults, demand for baby care products may be high. When planning for the future, an organisation should consider the following factors.

(a) The rate of growth or decline of the national population.

(b) Population changes in particular regions.

(c) The age distribution of the population, both nationally and regionally. This will not only affect what people want. It will also affect what people can afford to buy, both individually and as a whole. If a country has a high proportion of retired people, who are not productive, the overall standard of living may be low.

(d) Where people live (cities, small towns or the countryside), whether people live alone or in families and so on. This will affect where goods should be sold.

Activity 8 **(20 minutes)**

Consider the following figures for the United Kingdom, which are in millions of people.

Age	*1971*	*1981*	*1991*	*1993*	*2001*
Under 16	14.2	12.5	11.7	12.0	12.4
16–39	17.5	19.7	20.4	20.3	19.7
40–64	16.7	15.7	16.6	16.8	18.3
65–79	6.1	6.9	6.9	6.2	6.8
80 +	1.3	1.6	2.1	2.3	2.6

What are the main trends? What are the main implications for organisations in (1) the health care sector and (2) the manufacturing sector, for example Coca Cola?

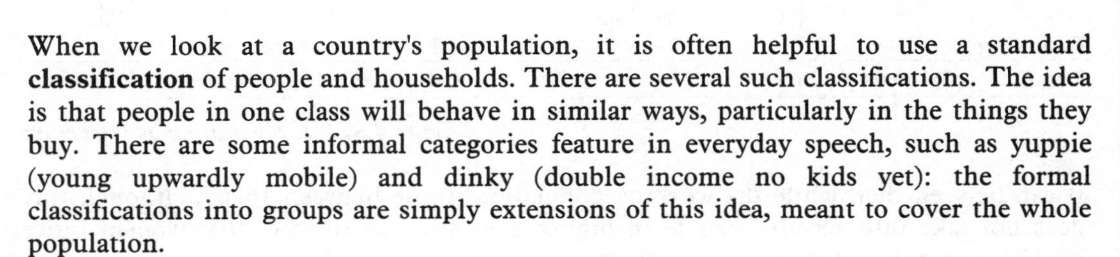

When we look at a country's population, it is often helpful to use a standard **classification** of people and households. There are several such classifications. The idea is that people in one class will behave in similar ways, particularly in the things they buy. There are some informal categories feature in everyday speech, such as yuppie (young upwardly mobile) and dinky (double income no kids yet): the formal classifications into groups are simply extensions of this idea, meant to cover the whole population.

An early example, which still has some uses, is the **socio-economic grouping** originally developed by the **UK Registrar General**. It is as follows.

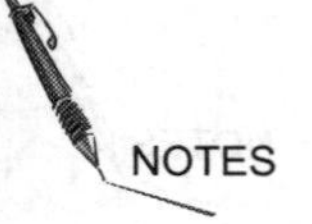

EXAMPLE: REGISTRAR GENERAL'S SOCIO-ECONOMIC GROUPINGS

I: Managerial and professional, such as lawyers and company directors

II: Intermediate managerial and technical, for example teachers and managers

III(i): Skilled non-manual

III(ii): Skilled manual workers, such as electricians

IV: Semi-skilled manual workers, such as machine operators

V: Unskilled occupations

A much more elaborate classification is Experian's MOSAIC scheme, which classifies UK consumers into 15 groups that are themselves further subdivided into 67 types. Another commonly used scheme is ACORN, which combines geographic, socio-economic and lifestyle groupings. **ACORN** stands for A Classification Of Residential Neighbourhoods.

There are other groupings that are based upon the status of the household and what stages people have reached in their lives. These are called **family life cycle** analyses, which again we will see in Chapter 6.

FOR DISCUSSION

What use could a housebuilder make of family life cycle analysis, and information on the number of people at each stage in the cycle, in planning the types of houses to build?

Age structure

The age structure of the population is of particular concern to planners and business organisations. In 1951, 10% of the population were over 65. This will rise to nearly 20% by 2021. It is perhaps interesting to note that the UK's population is ageing less quickly than, say, Japan. Here are some trends for the age structure.

Age	*2021 est %*	*2011 est %*	*Projected % change 1991–2011*	*1991 %*	*1981 %*	*% change 1981–1991*	*1961 %*	*% change 1961–1991*
Under 16	19.5	20.1	(1)	20.3	22.2	(8.5)	24.8	(18%)
16–39	30.5	30.0	(15)	35.2	34.9	0.8	31.4	12%
40–64	31.9	33.7	17	28.7	27.8	3.2	32.0	11%
65–79	13.6	11.7	(3.5)	12.0	12.2	(1.6)	9.8	22%
80+	4.5	4.4	21	3.7	2.8	32%	1.9	95%
Rounding		0.1		0.1	0.1		0.1	
Total	100.0	100.0		100.0	100.0		100.0	

Figure 4.8: UK population age structure

It can be seen that, while the working population (those between 16–65, although this does not take into account people in higher education, or the fact that women retire earlier than men) is fairly constant as a percentage, there is a shift in the relative proportion of elderly and young dependants. In 1961, 11.7% (9.8 + 1.9%) of the population were over 65. By 1991 this had risen to 15.7% (12% + 3.7%). The proportion of under 16s in the same period fell from 24.8% to 20.3% of the population. This has

been occurring since 1961 and has continued. This shift is important for the following reasons.

(a) The elderly dependants have different needs (for long term health provision, for example) to younger people whose needs are for education and so on. Planners must take this into account when allocating resources for social provision.

(b) The elderly, as a market segment, are likely to be increasingly important, not only because of their numbers, but because they are likely to be increasingly affluent.

(c) The decline in the number of young people will mean that organisations might have to change their recruitment policies or production methods. There will be fewer young people, and more competition for them. However, the fall in young people is more complex than a simple decline.

   (i) In 1971 there were 14.3 million under 16.

   (ii) In 1988 there were 11.5 million under 16.

   (iii) In 2001 it is projected that there will be 12.6 million under 16, before a slow fall and stabilisation.

The age structure, as with population size generally, depends on the **birth rate** and the **death rate**. Importantly, of course, the age structure depends not only on the current birth rate, but on that of previous years.

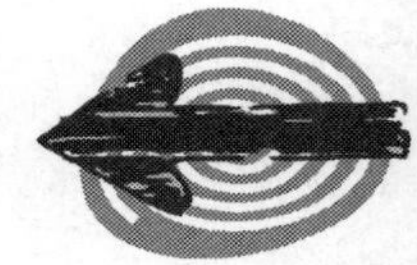

Demography has a big effect on culture, and cultures can influence demography. A mainly young society is likely to have a different culture from an elderly one, and culture influences people's decisions on whether or when to have children. The next section looks at several cultural issues.

3.3 Culture

> **Culture** is the sum total of the inherited ideas, beliefs, values and knowledge that make up the basis of social action.

Definition

A society's culture comprises three interdependent elements, as follows.

(a) The **ideological system** represents the ideas, beliefs, values and ways of reasoning that we accept. For example, most people accept that they have some responsibility not to endanger others through carelessness, and therefore accept (at least in theory) that they should drive carefully.

(b) The **technological system** comprises the skills, crafts and arts that allow us to make things. Thus one of the most important reasons why our culture today is very different from the culture of 500 years ago is that we have aeroplanes, computers, telephones and so on.

(c) The **organisational system** is the system which co-ordinates people's efforts. It includes the government, companies, families and social clubs.

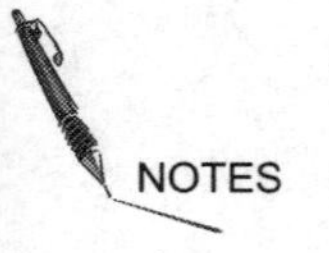

Activity 9 **(10 minutes)**

The role of the family and religion are two of the main indicators of what a culture is like. What do you think that the other main indicators are?

Businesses must take account of the culture of their society. It will determine what they can sell and how they should sell it. For example, an advertisement containing a shot of a semi-naked woman might be perfectly acceptable in some countries, but will be very offensive in others. Businesses must also pay attention to **subcultures**, the cultures of groups within a society.

Attitudes to pleasure

Many people have spare money to spend as they choose, and businesses want to attract that money to themselves. There are many different ways in which they can get people to spend on things they do not really need. One approach is to appeal to self-centredness, using slogans such as 'Go on, treat yourself'. Another approach is to emphasise the benefits to others, for example by emphasising that producers of the goods in poor countries are paid a good price for their output. Which approach is best will of course depend on the product, but it will also depend on the culture. Here are some pairs of opposed attitudes to pleasure.

Other-centredness	Self-fulfilment
Postponed gratification	Immediate gratification
Hard work	The easy life
Formal relationships	Informal open relationships
Religious orientation	Secular orientation

Activity 10 **(15 minutes)**

Assume that you are running a bookshop. Think of one way you could deal with each of the above attitudes to attract different customers.

Changes in culture

A business must not simply find out about the state of the culture it operates in, and leave it at that. **Culture can change**, and businesses need to notice these changes and adapt. For example, while belief in marriage has persisted, the belief that people should marry young has not: many women now have careers before they marry, and have children later than they used to.

EXAMPLE: BOOMERS BECOMING SIMPLIFIERS

'Instant gratification' and 'Boomers' have been almost synonymous for several decades. Don't have the cash? Whip out the plastic and think about the bill next month. That's been the mantra of most. However, there appears to be a culture change happening where conspicuous consumption and the over-accumulation of stuff has become almost an embarrassment for some Boomers.

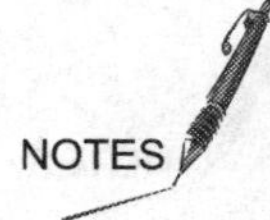

John Quelch, an associate dean at the Harvard Business School, calls this new type of consumer *the middle-aged simplifier*. Mr. Quelch says, 'This group consists of well-off people who are turning their backs on conspicuous consumption and the accumulation of stuff. They don't define their social status by the size of their McMansions or the number of Range Rovers in the garages. They value experiences over material possessions.'

While not associating this group with any particular generation, Quelch notes that the group includes 'empty-nester baby-boomers ... who are tired of heating unused spaces in cavernous mansions, now preferring smaller houses with architectural character and intimate spaces, more charm and less maintenance.'

Linda S. Thompson,
EVLiving.com, 9 November 2009

---

4 POLITICAL AND LEGAL ASPECTS

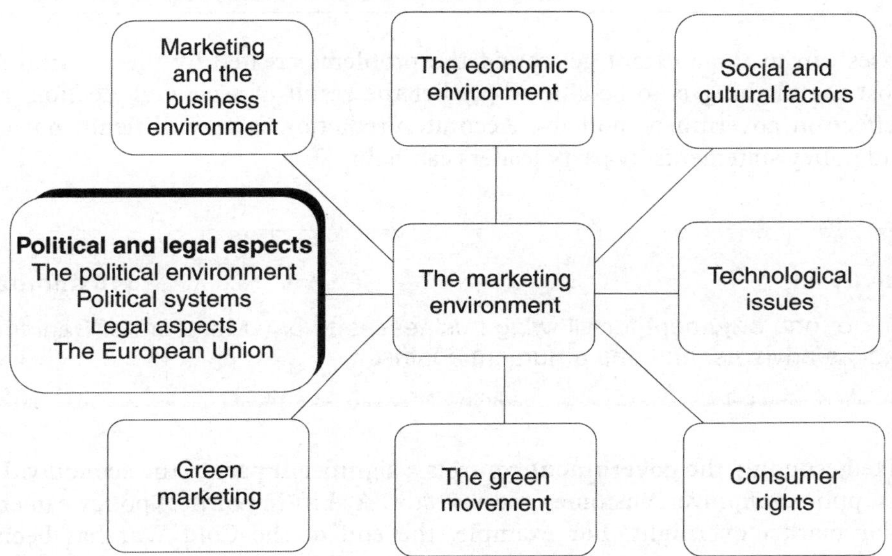

4.1 The political environment

Businesses, like everyone else, have to work within the **law**. Laws are made by Parliament for the good of society as a whole. What laws are made depends on which political party holds power. Therefore the political environment is important to businesses. However, this environment goes further than the election of governments. Although a government will come to power already committed to making certain changes, there are many other things which it might or might not do.

Businesses may, either individually or though trade associations, lobby for changes they would like. In the UK, **pressure groups** have an important role, and businesses can hire professional lobbyists who know how to persuade politicians to do things. Even beyond legislation, businesses must also be aware of general political attitudes. For example, some governments favour free enterprise, while others prefer central control, and even nationalisation of industries.

We will start by looking at how political systems can affect businesses. It is tempting to think that, because the UK's political system has changed only slowly over the years, with no revolutions since 1685, it can be ignored. In fact it has a big impact on business.

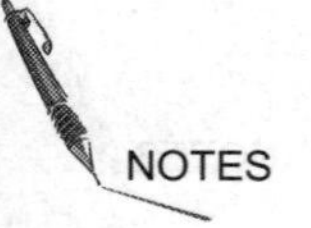

4.2 Political systems

The UK's political system has been remarkably stable, with no revolutionary changes for over 300 years. Over the same timespan, most European countries have experienced violent revolutions which have seriously disrupted their economies. UK businesses need not worry about revolutions. What they do need to worry about is the risk of dramatic changes in **government policy**, as one party replaces another in government at a general election. The UK system channels any urges for dramatic change into the voting system, which allows a change of heart by voters to change the whole direction of government.

FOR DISCUSSION

How might a UK car manufacturer be affected by a change of government (to the left or to the right)? You might consider the effect of changed policy towards, say, company cars, road-building, green issues, personal taxation and import restrictions.

Businesses can to some extent get round the problems created by the political system. The most useful thing is to be able to predict the result of a general election, and the likely effect on government policies. Accurate prediction is very difficult, but opinion polls and policy statements by party leaders can help.

> **Activity 11** **(10 minutes)**
>
> Think of one argument for allowing businesses to pay Members of Parliament to act as advisors, and one argument against it.

In a mixed economy the **government** controls a significant part of the economy. It is the largest supplier, employer, customer and investor. A shift in political policy can change a particular market overnight. For example, the end of the Cold War has been a big change for weapons makers.

Any business which operates abroad, or which has overseas suppliers or customers, needs to consider the **political environment** in the countries involved as well as in the UK.

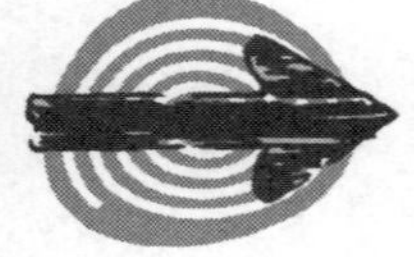

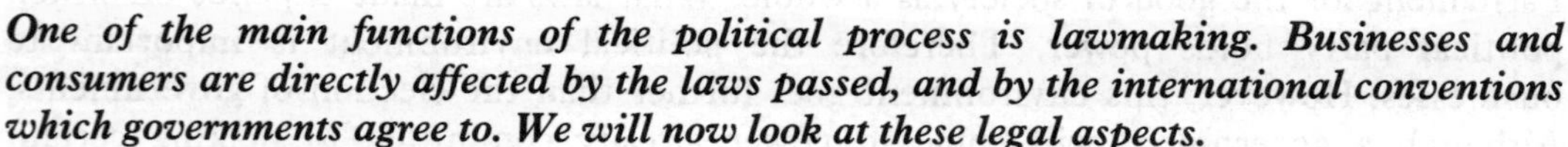

One of the main functions of the political process is lawmaking. Businesses and consumers are directly affected by the laws passed, and by the international conventions which governments agree to. We will now look at these legal aspects.

4.3 Legal aspects

Laws can affect businesses in the following different ways.

(a) **Dealings with customers** can be affected by laws on the sale of goods and services, on advertising and trade descriptions, on product safety and on shop opening hours.

(b) **How a business treats its employees** is affected by employment legislation and trade union law, largely designed to protect employees' rights. Thus there are strict rules on the dismissal of employees and on equal opportunities.

(c) **Dealings with shareholders** are affected by the Companies Acts, which lay down how information must be given in published accounts and what dividends may be paid.

(d) **The criminal law** can affect companies. Some offences can be committed by companies as separate legal persons distinct from their directors and employees.

Some laws apply to all businesses. Others apply only to particular types of business. An example is the Financial Services and Markets Act 2000, which affected sellers of insurance, pensions and other financial products.

Changes in laws are often predictable. The proposals may be part of a government's declared programme or part of an opposition party's manifesto. The process of enacting laws in the UK also gives businesses time to plan for proposed changes: there is likely to be a preliminary period of consultation, followed by the Parliamentary process. This process can itself take several months.

Businesses are affected by laws made outside the UK. For example, anyone doing business in the USA must take account of US law. Even a business which has no international dealings must take account of European Union law. We will now go on to look at the European Union.

EXAMPLE

The smoking ban, which took effect on 1 July 2007, has had major implications for a wide range of businesses. Bus shelter manufacturers have found an opportunity to develop new products *'smoking shelters'* which are modified to ensure that a certain percentage of the shelter is not enclosed. It has not been just bars and restaurants who have had to adjust to the new legislation but also venues as diverse as theme parks showing specific areas where smoking is permitted.

Bingo clubs are thought to be one of the main industries to suffer a downturn in trade directly in response to the ban. 50-60% of bingo players are smokers and it is anticipated that numbers visiting the clubs will fall. In addition, unlike pubs and clubs where smokers will be popping outside, bingo clubs make a large proportion of their revenue from people playing machines during breaks in the main games. Research conducted by the industry has shown that one in three players will go to clubs less often, one in ten will stop playing altogether and more than three in five will increase their online bingo spend. Gala, one of the largest bingo hall operators stated that if trends follow the same pattern as found in Scotland where smoking was banned prior to the UK they would need to close around 13 clubs.

In the first months, smoking cessation products such as gums and nicotine patches were seen to actively take advantage of increased promotional opportunities.

4.4 The European Union

Until 2004, the European Union (EU) comprised 15 countries: Austria, Belgium, Denmark, Finland, France, Germany, Greece, Ireland, Italy, Luxembourg, the Netherlands, Portugal, Spain, Sweden and the UK. On 1 May 2004 a further 10 countries joined: Cyprus, Czech Republic, Estonia, Hungary, Lithuania, Latvia, Malta, Poland, Slovakia, and Slovenia. In 2007 Romania and Bulgaria joined.

A key aim of the EU is the creation of a **single economic area** which is as good as a single country for the businesses and individuals in it. The idea is that businesses

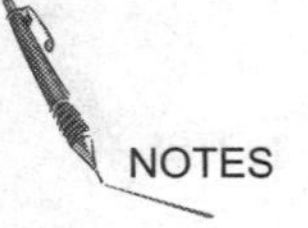

throughout the EU should be subject to the same laws, and that there should be no barriers to trade within the EU. The Euro is the currency of thirteen EU countries. Since it was first circulated in 2002 business between member countries has simplified.

EXAMPLE

If you have flown within the EU recently, you will have noticed the blue exit channel at your destination airport. This is for people travelling within the EU, and reflects the fact that there are no customs controls within the EU. This is of course far more important to a company sending lorryloads of goods abroad than to the average holiday traveller.

The EU has done many things to make the sale of goods in different countries easier, and to allow the free movement of capital and labour. Here are some examples.

(a) Setting common standards on **food labelling and hygiene**.

(b) Setting common standards for **information technology**.

(c) Making rules to ensure that when a **government** needs to buy something, all EU companies have an equal chance to supply and the home country's companies are not favoured.

(d) Liberalisation of **capital movements,** so that (for example) a UK investor can freely move money to another country and invest it in a business there.

(e) Removing of rules which limited access to **financial services**.

(f) Ensuring mutual recognition of **professional qualifications,** so that (for example) a French lawyer can practise in the UK without having to requalify as a UK solicitor or barrister.

(g) Giving all EU citizens the **right to work** anywhere in the EU.

Activity 12 **(15 minutes)**

A Japanese electronics company decides to set up a factory in the UK. Can you think of three political and three legal aspects that the company will need to be aware of which will impinge on the company and its products?

The last PEST factor is the technological one. We discuss it in the context of change since this is the area in which the greatest environmental developments are currently taking place.

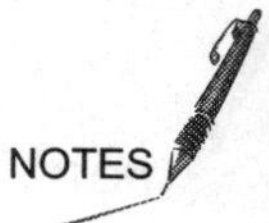

5 TECHNOLOGICAL ISSUES

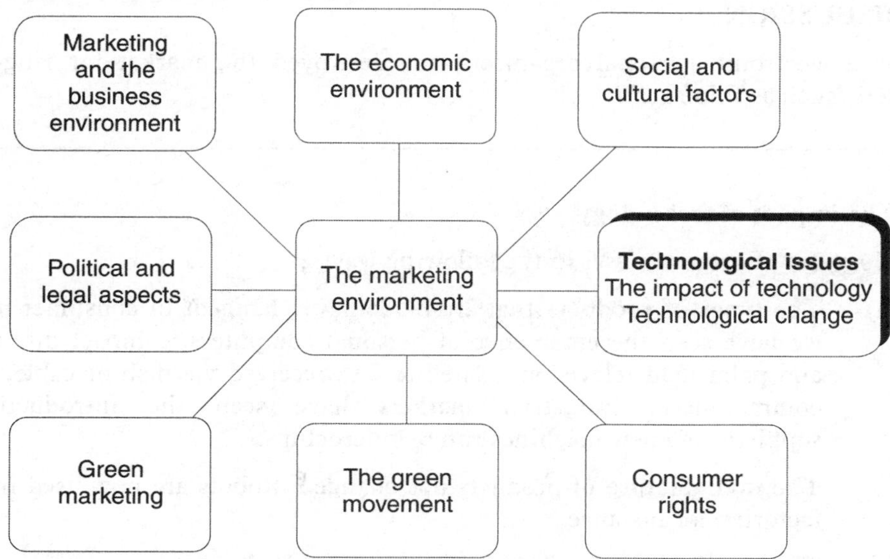

The Concise Oxford Dictionary defines technology as the application of scientific knowledge for practical purposes. It depends on knowledge which now often comes from scientific research and can be 'high tech', for example the use of micro chips. However, technology can also be 'low tech', for example child-proof tops on medicine bottles.

Of all of the environmental factors, technology is the most challenging for the marketing manager. Change is rapid, and a company which makes the right decisions early can get a big advantage over its competitors To stay ahead, companies need effective **research, planning** and **marketing** of new products. In some cases, if a new product is late, it may barely sell at all because better products have become available in the meantime. This has happened with personal computers: there would be little point in launching a new range of computers that did not use the most powerful processors are widely available.

EXAMPLE

The need to market the right technology, at the right time and to consider all the relevant factors, is illustrated by early domestic video systems. Initially, consumers could choose between the VHS system or the Betamax system. In the end VHS won, not because it was technically better nor because it was available sooner, but because the promoters of VHS ensured that lots of films were available on video in the VHS format.

A generation later, a similar contest took place between competing high defintion video systems.

Dixons, one of the UK's largest electrical chains were the first to de-list VCRs altogether by 2005. The company had first sold the product in 1978 but had found that since the early 1990s sales had fallen dramatically due to low price of DVR players and the rapid fall in price of DVD recorders.

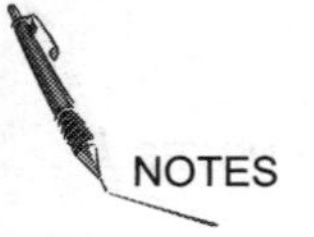

NOTES

FOR DISCUSSION

Why have electronic personal organisers not destroyed the market for ring-bound organisers (such as Filofaxes)?

5.1 The impact of technology

Technology can affect businesses in the following ways.

(a) The **types of products** that are made have changed. In consumer markets we have seen the emergence of personal computers, compact disc players and palm held televisions. Satellite TV, received via dish or cable, is now commonplace. Industrial markets have seen the introduction of sophisticated new machines run by microchips.

(b) The **manufacture** of products has changed. Robots are now used in many factories, for instance.

(c) The **quality** of products has improved with the use of automatic testing equipment that takes away human error.

(d) The way in which goods and services are **delivered** to the customer has changed, and one of the key influences on this has been the **Internet**. Automatic teller machines are now the main route by which people get cash from their banks. **Home shopping** is becoming easier and more widespread.

(e) The **availability** of goods has improved. The flow of goods can be monitored by the use of computerised point of sale equipment such as bar-code readers in shops. This information can be used to re-order goods automatically when stocks are low, and also to gather marketing information.

(f) Large scale **databases** to monitor customer behaviour are now possible. The Barclays Bank group of companies have access to a database of over 20 million potential customers and therefore can closely monitor the individual members of its market. **Direct mail** can be sent to the right people instead of to everybody.

(g) Technology has significantly changed **the way people work**. Computers are used not only to create documents and to store and process data, but also to **communicate** using electronic mail. Many people can now work at home and be linked to their employers electronically.

Activity 13 **(10 minutes)**

Growth in the use of mobile phones has been huge, and a very high proportion are used for private, rather than business, purposes. What impact has this technology had on people's lives? How might the technology be developed further?

Activity 14 **(15 minutes)**

Look at the direct mail that you or your family have received during the past few months. How do you think the senders obtained your names? How relevant are the products or services to you? Do you think that the senders have any idea of how old you are, of how much money you have or of your lifestyle?

5.2 Technological change

The effects of technological change can include the following.

(a) A fall in **costs**. The most dramatic example is **data processing costs**. The cost of working out how much a customer owes, or working out an employee's pay is now about 0.2% of what it was 40 years ago.

(b) Improved **quality**, especially in the area of **customer service**. If, for example, a customer telephones with an enquiry, that customer's details can be automatically displayed before the call is answered.

(c) **New products** and services. For example, telephone subscribers now get itemised bills.

(d) Easier **access** to products and services, for example home shopping by computer, use of the **Internet** to access information, shops and books.

Activity 15 **(10 minutes)**

Think of a company which you know something about. How has it changed over the past few years in response to new technology? How might it have to change over the next few years?

As technology has become more complex and the pace of technological change ever increases, so concern for the **rights of the consumer** has also become greater. The consumer has a right to be treated fairly in situations where power may seem to reside only in the big corporations marketing goods and services.

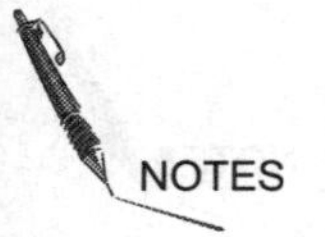

6 CONSUMER RIGHTS

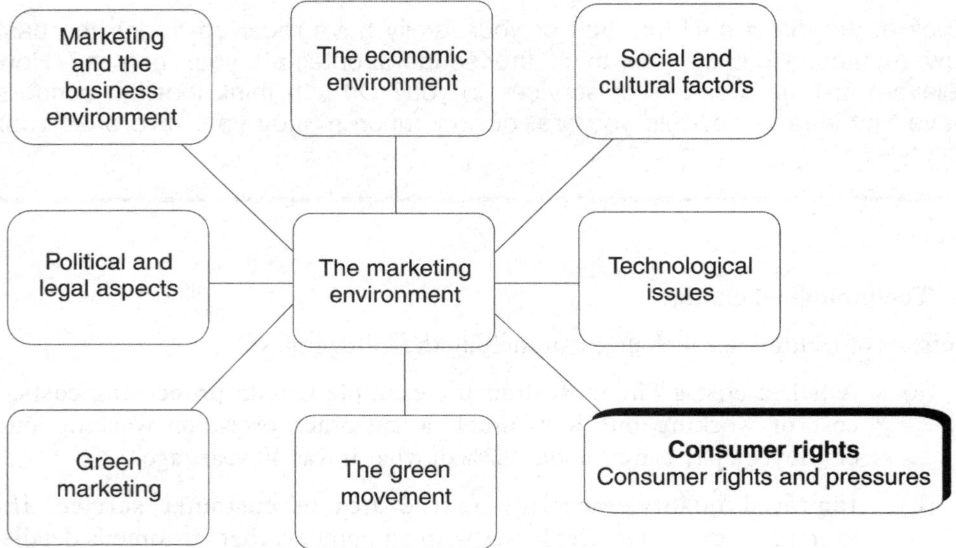

6.1 Consumer rights and pressures

The importance of customer care has been acknowledged as a result of the growth of **consumerism**. A number of consumer rights have been recognised, including the following.

(a) The right to be informed of the **true facts** of the buyer-seller relationship, for example:

  (i) The **true cost** of loans

  (ii) **Truth in advertising** (watchdog bodies vet any advertisement and consumers complain about advertisements to the Advertising Standards Authority).

(b) The right to be protected from unfair **exploitation or intrusion.** Consumers' trust in organisations must not be abused. For example, the sale of mailing lists to third parties can lead to consumers receiving vast quantities of 'junk' mail.

(c) The right to a particular **quality of life**. This right is focused increasingly on **environmental protection**, making suppliers aware of the implications of their actions on the eco-system, and the quality of water, air and so on.

Suppliers need to take careful note of these consumerist pressures to maintain a good **image and reputation** with customers and other important publics. This may militate against aggressive marketing tactics. The need to consider the best interests of customers should be paramount in a marketing strategy. The long-term view is necessary rather than attempting to maximise short-term profits.

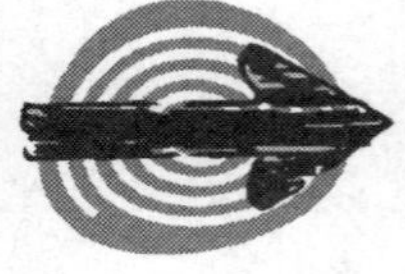

Technological developments are often seen as causing problems such as increased pollution and waste of natural resources. These factors affect everyone, not just the consumers of particular products. 'Green issues' are concerned with the whole planet, its populations and natural systems. We will now consider them.

7 THE GREEN MOVEMENT

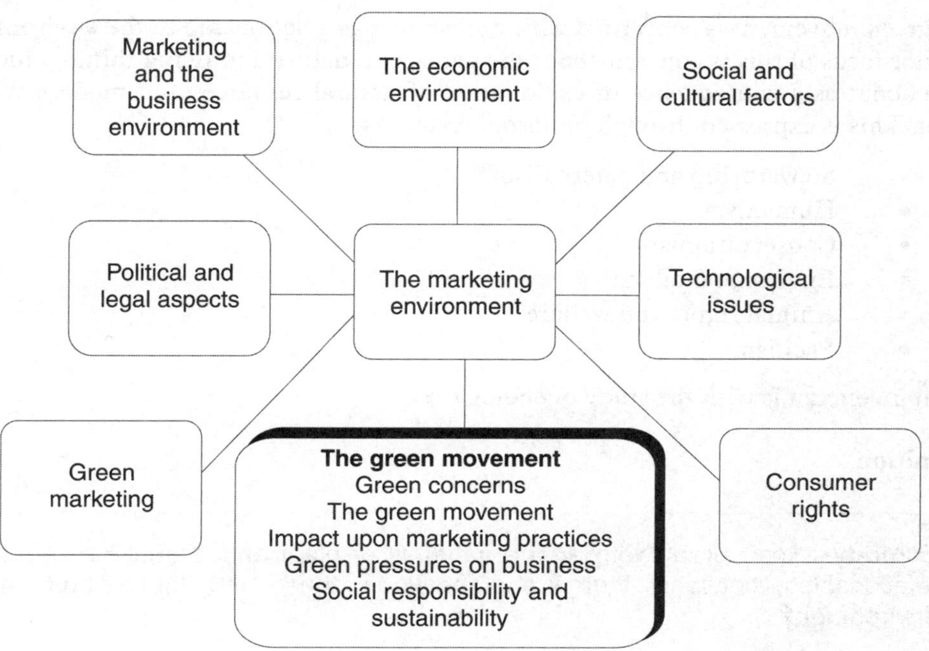

7.1 Green concerns

The modern **green movement**, although arising from concerns over pollution and overpopulation which are centuries old, was given major impetus by studies carried out in the 1970s into the effects of massive economic growth on the finite resources of the Earth. Initial predictions of impending disaster failed to produce a significant change in **public opinion** and policy making on green issues was largely stalled.

From the mid-eighties onwards, however, a series of **ecological disasters** (the emission at the Union Carbide plant at Bhopal, India, the Chernobyl nuclear reactor accident in the USSR, the Exxon-Valdez oil spill in Alaska, and the torching of the Kuwaiti oil fields at the end of the Iraqi invasion) reawakened public concern and sparked general public fears about environmental dangers. Other factors contributing to increased 'green consciousness' included scientific reports about the state of the North Sea, the forests of Central Europe and the droughts which afflicted several regions, all of which were linked to **environmental damage caused by modern industry**.

The end of the Cold War led to a search, on the part of the media and the public at large, for a substitute threat to the safety of the world. Scientific progress also enabled us to measure the hole in the ozone layer which had long been suspected. Pressure groups, agencies and prominent individuals began to play a part in bringing these issues to the public attention.

Fast air transport and new satellite **communication systems** give media such as television and newspapers fast access to, and rapid dissemination of information from, countries affected by environmentally-linked disasters, such as the Ethiopian famines. Satellite television transmission allowed the Live Aid concert to be seen all over the world. Events in countries in Eastern Europe, South America and Asia can be transmitted internationally, almost instantly, with the same technology. Consumers are aware of the importance of green issues. Products and services, and the ways in which they are marketed, are changing to reflect this growing consumer awareness.

Against this background the green movement has gained momentum and is having an increasing effect on the practice of marketing.

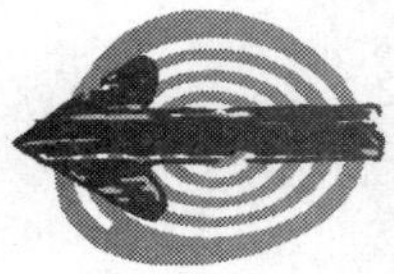

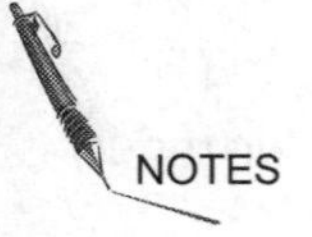

7.2 The green movement

The green movement is concerned with human beings' relationship to the **environment**. A major focus of this is concern about the damage to nature and living things which has come about as a consequence of exploitation of natural resources and modern ways of living. This is expressed through philosophical ideas.

- Stewardship and paternalism
- Humanism
- Conservationism
- Environmentalism
- Animal rights and welfare
- Pacifism

A major concern is with the study of **ecology**.

Definition

Ecology is concerned with all the varieties of plant and animal life and the relationships between them, and between these life forms and their environment.

Major themes of this way of thinking include the following.

(a) The environment is a 'web' of complex interconnected living (biological) and non-living (physical) systems.

(b) Everything, including pollution, goes somewhere into this 'web'.

(c) Nature has an inherent equilibrium or 'balance'.

(d) All exploitation of nature which upsets this balance will ultimately have a cost.

7.3 Impact upon marketing practices

Among the environmental issues which are likely to be seen as relevant to businesses are the following.

(a) **Resource depletion** may influence business operation by reducing the availability of raw materials through damage to soil, water, trees, plant-life, energy availability, mineral wealth, animal and marine species.

(b) **Genetic diversity** may not seem immediately important for business, but in fact the development of many important new varieties of plants and animals, and of medicines and the new bio-technology which enables commercially valuable materials of all kinds to be synthesised, depends crucially on the availability of wild species from which genetic resources can be drawn. In the development of high-yield and disease-resistant crop plants, for example, wild species are a critical resource.

(c) **Pollution concerns** are at the centre of most worries about the environment.

In order to take action to remedy these problems, the **polluter pays principle** was adopted by the OECD in the early 1970s.

7.4 Green pressures on business

Pressure for better environmental performance is coming from many quarters. Consumers are demanding a better environmental performance from companies. In recent surveys, it has been demonstrated that around three-quarters of the population are applying environmental criteria in many purchase considerations. A survey by *Which?* magazine found that 90% of the sample had considered green issues in relation to their consumption on at least one occasion within the past year. They also claimed to be prepared to pay a premium for green products.

Green pressure groups

Green pressure groups increased their influence dramatically during the late 20th century. Membership of the 13 largest green groups in the UK grew to over 5 million, with staff of over 1,500.

Groups have typically exerted pressure through three main types of activity.

(a) **Information based activities**: gathering and providing information, mounting political lobbies and publicity campaigns.

(b) **Direct action**: varying from peaceful protests and the activities of organisations such as Greenpeace through to the environmental terrorism of more extreme organisations.

(c) **Partnership and consultancy**: groups here aim to work with businesses to pool resources and to help them improve environmental performance.

7.5 Social responsibility and sustainability

Green marketing is founded on two main ideas: one is a response to and **responsibility** for the community; the other is **sustainability** – the idea that we must be aware of the need for resources to be marshalled and monitored so that the environment can continue to provide natural resources and to absorb and recycle the waste products of human consumption.

Social responsibility is based on two ideas.

(a) **The moral and ethical responsibilities of businesses**

Businesses must exist within and depend upon a society. While businesses control many of the resources available to society, the majority of the population actually contribute to the production of wealth, and justice demands that they share in its benefits. Society should not be asked to solve and pay for those problems which businesses cause, without help from those businesses. Businesses and business people are also socially prominent and must be seen to be taking a lead in addressing the problems of society.

(b) **The benefits to business of 'enlightened self-interest'**

In the long term, business concern over the possible damage which may result from some of its activities will safeguard the interests of the business itself. In the short term, **responsibility** is good for the image of the company – it is a very valuable addition to the **public relations** activities of a business. In addition, as pressure for legislation grows, 'self regulation' can avoid potentially disadvantageous legal restrictions.

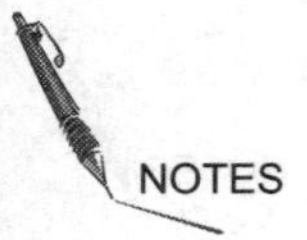

Definition

> **Sustainability** involves developing strategies so that the company only uses resources at a rate which allows them to be replenished in order to ensure that they will continue to be available, while at the same time emissions of waste are confined to levels which do not exceed the capacity of the environment to absorb them.

In relation to the development of the world's resources, policies based on sustainability seek the following.

- To pursue equity in the distribution of resources
- To maintain the integrity of the world's ecosystems
- To increase the capacity of human populations for self-reliance

---

EXAMPLE

Some business leaders have made a case for becoming ecologically and socially sustainable:

- 'Institutions that operate so as to capitalise all gain in the interests of the few, while socialising all loss to the detriment of the many, are ethically, socially and operationally unsound … This must change.' – Dee Hock, Founder, President and CEO Emeritus of Visa International, the credit card organisation.
- 'Far from being a soft issue grounded in emotion and ethics, sustainable development involves cold, rational business logic'. – Robert B. Shapiro, Chairman of Monsanto, the US multinational.
- 'The gap between rhetoric and reality is increasing. I would tell multinationals they have to watch out … they are much more vulnerable because they have to be accountable to the public everyday.' – Thilo Bode, Executive Director of Greenpeace.
- Explaining his company's forays into renewable energy and enhanced support for the communities where it does business: 'These efforts have nothing to do with charity, and everything to do with our long-term self interests … our shareholders want performance today, and tomorrow, and the day after.' – Sir John Browne, CEO of British Petroleum/Amoco.

Activity 16 **(20 minutes)**

Roy Brooks was an estate agent in Kensington, London who became famous in the 1950s and 60s for insanely honest property advertisements such as these.

> 'This DESIRABLE RESIDENCE has everything – dry rot, settlement, filthy decor, running cold water – sometimes where it was intended ...'
>
> 'So-called garden with possibilities – best solved by saturation bombing'
>
> 'Back bedroom suitable only for dwarf or placid child'
>
> 'A fussy purchaser would presumably have the gaping hole in the top bedroom ceiling – open to the sky – repaired'
>
> 'The gdn looks horrible but so would you if you'd been neglected for 20 yrs'

Gerald Ratner of Ratners Jewellers said in an after dinner speech that his company's earrings were cheaper than a prawn sandwich from Marks and Spencer and probably did not last as long.

Do you think it would be in the interests of manufacturers or customers to adopt this approach to marketing? Discuss this in class if possible, and design your own insanely honest advert for something that you have bought recently.

8 GREEN MARKETING

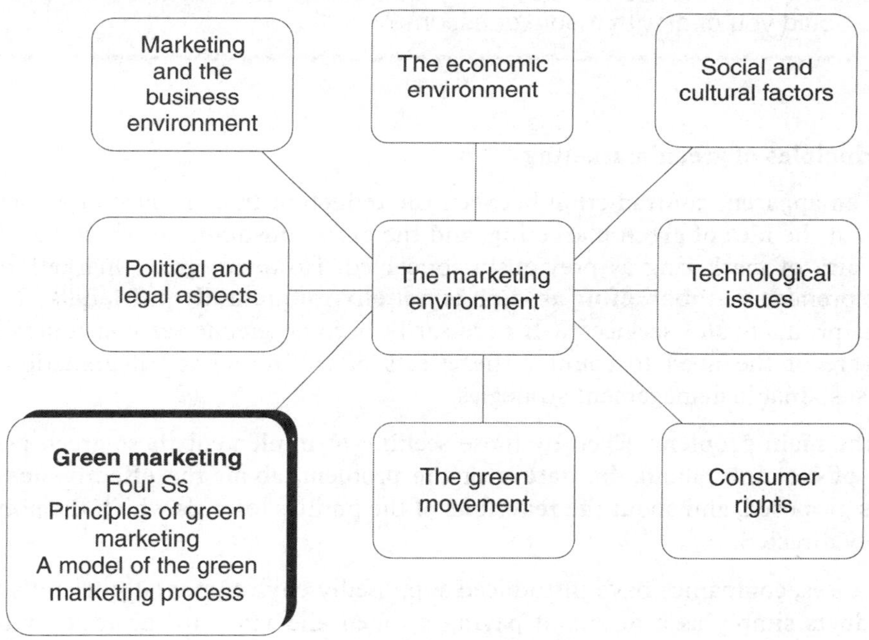

8.1 Four Ss

Getting marketing's four Ps (price, place, promotion and product) right leads to profit, according to orthodox ideas. Green marketing insists that the mix must be evaluated in terms of four Ss.

- Satisfaction of customer needs
- Safety of products and production for consumers, workers, society and the environment
- Social acceptability of a product and its method of production
- Sustainability of the products, their production and the other activities of the company

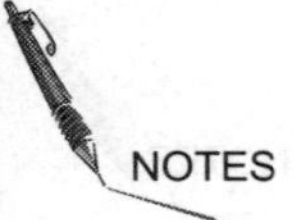
NOTES

A successful green marketer needs to:

(a) To understand the consumer's wants and needs

(b) To understand the environmental issues which are relevant to the company, customer, products and market environment

(c) To evaluate the degree to which green product attributes fit consumer needs

(d) To match price to consumer demand

(e) To develop strategies which identify and effectively meet consumer needs and competitor challenges in relation to green issues

(f) To promote the flow of environmentally-related information on consumers and product/service performance throughout the company

Activity 17 **(15 minutes)**

You are the product manager of Anti-Zit, a facial cleanser. You receive a phone call claiming that an entire consignment of Anti-Zit, now in the shops, has been contaminated by animal welfare activists who believe – wrongly – that the product is tested on animals. Due to controls that are known to be operating effectively it is highly unlikely in reality that more than a few bottles have been tampered with.

The media have the story already. What practical action should you take and how should you deal with media questions?

8.2 Principles of green marketing

There is an apparent contradiction between the reduction in consumption which lies at the heart of the idea of green marketing, and the extra consumption which has been the primary aim of marketing as previously conceived. However, green marketing begins from the premise that **marketing as such is not environmentally unfriendly**. There is a view that products and services will necessarily become greener as consumers become more aware of the need to counter the effects of environmental degradation and to develop sustainable management strategies.

One of the main problems faced by those seeking to implement these green policies is the lack of certainty about the **nature** of the problem, about the **effectiveness** of the remedies proposed, and about the **reactions** of the publics towards which the policies are ultimately directed.

In some cases, companies have introduced supposedly environmentally-friendly policies and products simply as a means of paying a token allegiance to the idea, or to try to garner extra sales. One possible consequence of this is moral fatigue: as with other issues in the past, the public may become disenchanted with the whole idea, or sceptical about claims to greenness which are made, in various ways, by almost every manufacturer or service provider.

8.3 A model of the green marketing process

The green marketing process requires the matching of those **internal variables** which the company can control with the strictures of the **operating environment** which the commercial decision-maker faces. Like conventional marketing, green marketing needs to deal with a blend of internal and external factors. These have been described as internal and external **'green Ps'** (that is, the green equivalent of the four Ps) to be used as a checklist to diagnose how well the company is succeeding in living up to targets for green performance.

Analysing the process

Inside the company, marketers need to attend to the following 'internal green Ps'.

(a) **Products.** A green audit needs to look at how safe products are in use, how safe they are when disposed, how long they last and what are the environmental consequences of materials used in manufacturing and packaging the product.

(b) **Promotion.** Using green messages in promotion. Establishing standards of accuracy and reliability.

(c) **Price.** Prices set for green products must reflect differences in demand; price sensitivity is also an important issue.

(d) **Place.** How green are the methods by which distribution takes place?

(e) **Providing information.** This needs to be related to internal and external issues bearing on environmental performance.

(f) **Processes.** Energy consumed, waste produced.

(g) **Policies.** Do they motivate the work force? Are there policies to monitor and react to environmental performance?

(h) **People.** Do they understand environmental issues and how the company performs in relation to these issues?

Outside the company, a different set of factors needs to be addressed. These might be referred to as 'external green Ps'.

(a) **Paying customers.** What are their needs in relation to green products and services? What information are they receiving about green products?

(b) **Providers.** How green are suppliers of services and materials to the company?

(c) **Politicians.** Public awareness and concern over green issues is beginning to have a strong influence on the legislation which appears, and this directly affects the conduct of business. A modern organisation must make this part of its concerns.

(d) **Pressure groups.** What are the main issues of concern? Which groups are involved and what new issues are likely to concern them?

(e) **Problems.** Which environmental issues have been a problem for the company, or part of the area in which it works, in the past?

(f) **Predictions.** What environmental problems loom in the future? Awareness of scientific research can be strategically vital.

(g) **Partners.** How green are my allies? How are business partners perceived? Will this pose problems?

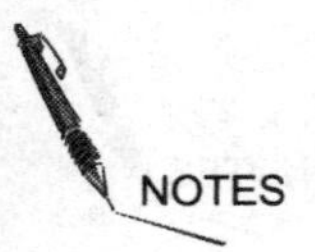

Chapter roundup

- A firm's business environment needs to be considered in terms of particular markets, internal organisational aspects and broad trends in society as a whole (PEST factors).
- Economic factors such as rate of growth, inflation, taxation rates and interest rates, at home and abroad, must be considered when devising marketing plans.
- Social and cultural factors such as demography, family relationships, religion and ideology will all affect consumers' responses to the product; the marketing effort must take account of these factors.
- To a large extent, the macro environment is determined by political and legal factors which the marketer can do little to influence. These factors may produce constraints on marketing activities; on the other hand, they may provide opportunities for new products and services necessary to enable citizens to stay within new laws (smokeless fuels, car seat belts and so on).
- Technology affects the types of products that are made, the way they are made, their quality, delivery and availability. Databases have been developed that illustrate customer behaviour in increasing levels of detail.
- Environmental issues have become more important over the last 10-20 years, with the emergence of the green movement and green economics. Environmental issues will have a direct and indirect impact on both marketing practices and on businesses in a more general sense.
- Environmental protection is now a key strategic issue and businesses setting up environmental management systems will probably use the guidance given by BS 7750 (as well as the quality standard ISO 9000).
- Green marketing practices must overcome a variety of barriers. A new 'green' orientation is required in obtaining marketing information, in marketing planning and in creating a green marketing process.

Quick quiz

1. Draw a diagram illustrating the market environment.
2. What is the purpose of a marketing audit?
3. List the major economic factors that the marketing manager must take into account.
4. In what ways may the economic factors of another country affect the marketing of a product made in the UK?
5. What demographic factor changes would increase the markets for comics?
6. How can the marketing manager of a charity use the public's desire for pleasure to raise funds?
7. What are the three levels of economic system?
8. List three ways in which EU law has affected the marketing environment.
9. How has technology affected the way people work?
10. How does technological change affect markets?

11 What environmental issues will impact upon marketing practices?

12 Define 'sustainability'.

13 What is BS 7750 and what does it involve?

14 What are the 'four Ss' of the green marketing mix?

Answers to Quick quiz

1 See section 1.3.

2 A marketing audit helps a firm to understand the internal environment.

3 Rate of growth, rate of inflation, level of unemployment, interest rates, taxation levels, personal saving, balance of payments, other countries, international barriers.

4 If the economy of the target country is doing well (eg low unemployment), the product is likely to do well as target customers can afford to spend money.

5 An increase in the birth rate, shifting the age distribution of the population towards younger people.

6 The marketing manager may appeal to the desire to help others and the feeling of satisfaction that this can bring.

7 Local environment
National environment
International (world) environment

8 Setting common standards (eg hygiene, labelling, IT).
All companies in all EU countries should have equal access to markets.
Free movement of labour and capital.

9 People are working with computers every day, using swifter communications such as e-mail, and may even work from home.

10 Costs may fall at the same time as quality is improved. New products may be made available, and customers have easier access to them.

11 Resource depletion, genetic diversity, pollution concerns.

12 Using resources only at a rate that allows them to be replenished, so they continue to be available, and controlling waste emissions.

13 It sets the standard for environmental management systems, hoping to prevent problems at source by encouraging companies to develop systems for managing their own environmental policy with regard to appropriate regulations.

14 Satisfaction of consumer needs
Social acceptability of products and production methods
Sustainability of products and methods
Safety of products and methods

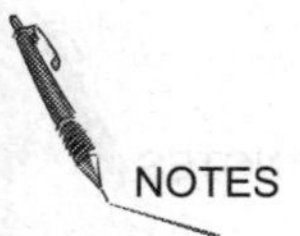

NOTES

Answers to Activities

1 **Micro**: suppliers; customers; intermediaries; competitors; other stakeholders

Macro: political & legal forces; social & cultural forces; technological forces; economic forces

2 (a) Tommy's Toys can expect more competition.

(b) Tommy's Toys might find it easier to compete as there may be a convergence of product standards.

3 (a) The airline industry: a number of airlines will compete to fly you from London to Glasgow.

(b) The railways: it is possible that two railway companies will compete to take you there.

(c) The car industry, if you have purchased a car.

(d) The bus industry: several bus firms will compete to drive you to Glasgow.

(e) The telecommunications industry. You may not need to travel at all, if the conference can be held via a video-conferencing system. BT and Mercury might compete to provide this service.

4 The rate of growth will determine the number of computers sold: if people have more money, and new businesses are being created, then sales should be good. The rate of inflation will affect costs, the price which can be charged and the profits made. The level of unemployment will affect demand: unemployed people are not likely to buy computers. Interest rates will determine the amount the company has to spend on financing its activities. If customers borrow money to buy computers, interest rates may also affect the willingness of customers to buy. The exchange rate will affect the cost of imported components and revenue from export sales. International barriers to trade and the state of other countries' economies will affect export sales.

5 A company may decide to open up a factory or offices overseas. Motor manufacturers have done this very successfully in order to gain advantages of low wage rates, taxation and get round import controls. There are also complex financial contracts that can be used to manage exchange rate risk but, like buying insurance, these require the payment of a kind of premium in advance.

6 Your answer will depend on what advertisements you have seen recently, but food and drink advertisements often centre on happy gatherings of families or friends and are often seasonally timed, to coincide with events such as Christmas. Many grocery advertisements feature children, exploiting the view that mothers should buy only the best for their offspring.

7 You will reach your own conclusions from your discussion.

8 In all groups except the 16–39 years olds, growth is predicted. The number of retired people will continue to rise with a marked growth in the 80 plus age group. The health care sector will be faced with an ageing population, but also with some growth in the child population. Child medicine and care of the elderly are likely to be the main areas for the sector to concentrate on.

The manufacturing sector will need to analyse forecast demographic patterns in order to assess likely demands for products suited to the various age groups. Coca-cola may be facing a declining market share as its key customer group is not expected to grow – product development may be called for to try and attract older customers.

9 The other main indicators of culture are language, education and material possessions.

10 A regular coffee evening with the occasional author as speaker and a club card allowing discounts would ensure that most attributes listed are met. Also ensure that there are books in stock on a wide range of subjects and an efficient ordering service for books not in stock.

11 An argument for allowing MPs to be paid advisors is that they will spend time on the work, in addition to their normal duties, and that time should be paid for. An argument against allowing payment is that MPs may spend too much time working for whoever pays them the most, and may ignore their duties to their constituents.

12 Examples of legal aspects which would impinge upon the company are health and safety laws, employment law and planning regulations. Examples of political aspects are grants for companies in certain areas of high unemployment, tax policy and relations between Japan and the UK (and EU) generally.

13 You will reach your own conclusions from your discussion, but most impacts relate to increased convenience.

14 Your name might have come from a list sold by another business you have had dealings with, from a membership list of an organisation you belong to, even from a telephone directory. The senders probably know something about you, if only the type of area you live in.

15 Your answer will depend on the company you have chosen. For example, a retailer might now use EFTPOS (Electronic Funds Transfer at Point of Sale); a firm is very likely to use the Internet for promotional purposes.

16 You might have made the point that Ratners' trading worsened following Mr Ratner's unguarded comments (though it was already in difficulties); that consumers want to believe that the purchase decisions that they make are good ones; but that it is undoubtedly in the interests of consumers that advertising should be honest; that to be 'honest' about a product might genuinely be to sing its praises if it is a really good one. There are many other points to make.

17 Hushing it all up and doing as little as possible is definitely not the answer in any crisis, as many organisations have found to their cost. Be completely open and give out as much information as possible to reassure the public that they are not at risk.

Briefly, the extent of the contamination, if any, should be ascertained. If it is not possible to demonstrate beyond doubt that the bulk of the consignment is uncontaminated (if tamper-proof bottles are not used, for instance) it should be entirely withdrawn from the shops and consumers should be asked to return bottles that have been sold already. The media and perhaps the public should be invited to inspect the company's testing facilities and, if security allows, the control procedures that are in place should be demonstrated. As long as the product and the company's practices are beyond reproach, the threat can be turned into an opportunity.

NOTES

Chapter 5 :

CUSTOMERS, BUYERS, CLIENTS AND CONSUMERS

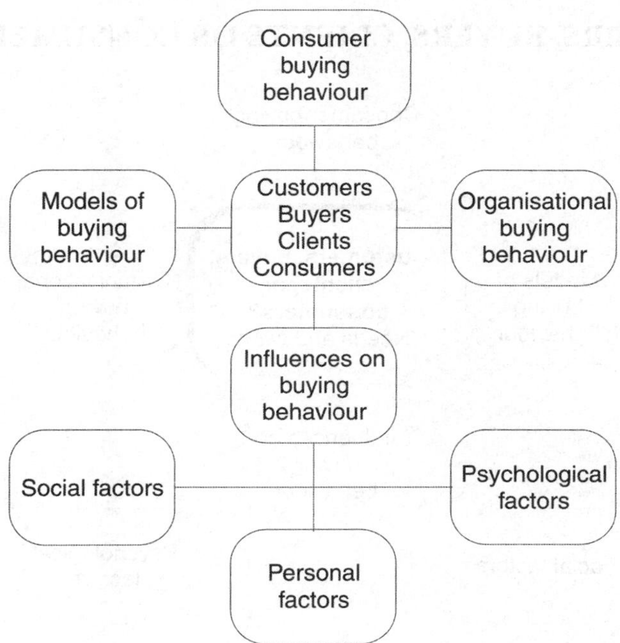

Introduction

The title of this chapter develops the idea that people have many roles in the process of purchasing products and services which are offered in the marketplace. We shall use the term 'customer' as a general label unless the specific term is more appropriate.

Customer orientation of the marketing function has achieved a level of such great importance in the recent past that almost every company has, or is aware of the necessity for, a **customer charter** of greater or lesser formality.

This should be seen as quite natural, as most modern definitions of marketing place the customer at the centre of the concerns of the business. It has also arisen from the commitment of organisations to **understanding customers**; their needs and wants and the way they satisfy them through purchasing behaviour.

This chapter examines the approaches to understanding customer behaviour which marketers find necessary and useful. These approaches take account of individual and social psychology and touch on the influences of economic factors. Clearly, this is a complex and sometimes profound area of study. The material below contains sufficient information for you to understand the approaches and to evaluate their contribution to marketing practice without getting bogged down in too much detail.

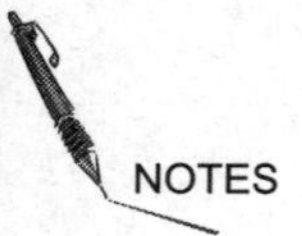

Your objectives

In this chapter you will learn about the following.

(a) The differences between customers, clients, buyers and consumers

(b) The importance of the main consumer behaviour models

(c) The main approaches to understanding customer behaviour

(d) The main issues in organisational buying

1 CUSTOMERS, BUYERS, CLIENTS OR CONSUMERS?

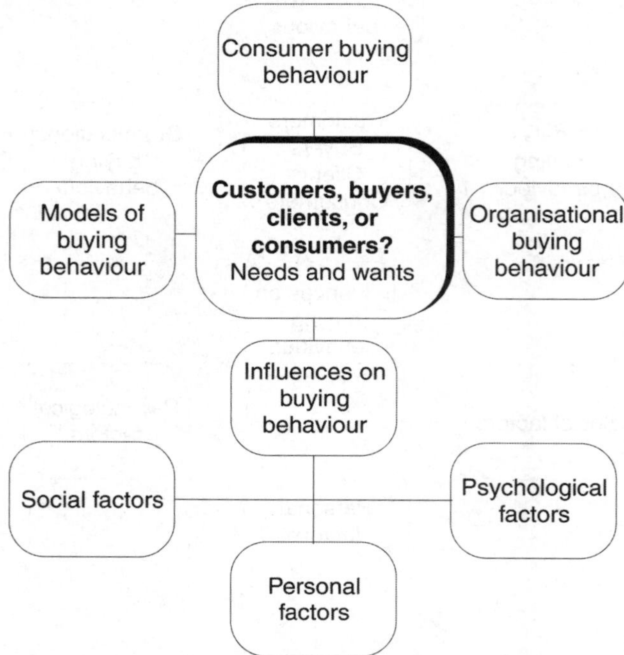

Whoever we are, we are all **consumers** of products and services throughout our lives. During our lifetime we are responsible for, directly or indirectly, significant decisions about **what** we buy, **when** we buy it, **where** we buy it, **how** we buy it and **why**. We shall spend, and have spent on us, hundreds of thousands of pounds, if not more.

The roles we occupy when purchasing a product or service may vary. What we are called when doing this is important. A crude distinction exists between the **customer,** who takes the decision to buy (and usually pays) and the **consumer**, who consumes the good. At a supermarket checkout, the customer for cat-food is the cat's owner: the consumer (we hope!) is the cat. However, in practice buying is a complex process in which people take many different roles.

Definitions

1. As a **customer**, we would engage in a purchase transaction with a supplier of goods. In a domestic context, these would be for our own or our family's consumption.
2. As a **client** we would be availing ourselves of a range of professional services such as accountants and solicitors.
3. As a **professional**, we would be exercising special skills in purchasing, often in large quantities and/or expending millions of pounds, as a part of our job on behalf of an organisation. For example, media buyers are professionals who purchase advertising space.
4. As a **consumer**, we are the end user of the product. A consumer may not be a customer and vice-versa. We do not necessarily take direct part in the purchase but, because we use up the product and gain some satisfaction or benefit from it, we may influence its purchase and/or its re-purchase. We are the end-user of the products.
5. When we are part of a group combining our influences we are known as a **Decision Making Unit** (DMU), for example children influencing the purchase of breakfast cereals; the adults in a family choosing a new carpet; or a group of colleagues of differing disciplines in an organisation. The latter DMU may have a very formal structure and the former have very little.

The above categories are not intended to be formal labels used as mutually exclusive descriptors but the differences indicated can be quite important to the marketer.

Activity 1 **(10 minutes)**

What other words can you think of which describe a particular relationship in a product or service transaction?

A poem by Rudyard Kipling refers neatly to the ideas given about the customer above:

I had six stalwart serving men
They taught me all I knew
Their names were What and Where and When
And Why and How and Who

So the questions:

What / Where / How / When } do we buy?

should be prefixed by:

Why do we buy { What / Where / How / When } we buy?

Coupled with who we are, answers to these questions could let the marketer know all that it is possible to know about us as customers, existing and potential. And this is so, because the marketer does not only want to know about the **behaviour** of customers, but also **why** they behave as they do and **what kind** of customers behave in ways that others do not.

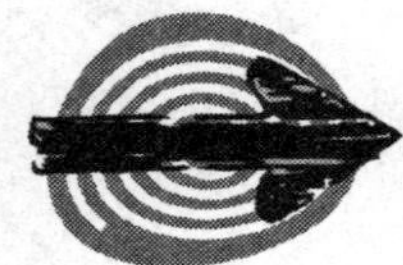

This chapter examines the factors which are influential in establishing the approaches of the marketer to ensure the provision of products and services which best meet the needs and wants of the market.

1.1 Needs and wants

It is important for us to distinguish between **needs** and **wants.**

Definition

Technically, a **need** is defined as a 'state of felt deprivation'. We recognise that there is an absence of something. As marketers we should only use it in the appropriate sense. Wants are those things which we perceive as having those characteristics which will fulfil a particular need, that is, which we imagine will satisfy us in some way that an alternative product may not.

For example, children may say that they **need** a drink. This may arise from them experiencing a physiological state of thirst – a need. If their mother or father tells them to get a glass of water (which would fulfil the physiological need), the child may refuse and say 'No! I don't **want** water, I **want** Pepsi. This demonstrates the essential difference which is critically important to marketers. The child cannot be said to need Pepsi-Cola in the true physiological sense. But it is certain that the child could want it very much.

The marketer's task is to recognise the basic need and, by crafting a marketing mix, shape that need towards a want for the organisation's product or service. We shall discuss further, in some detail, what constitutes a need later in the chapter.

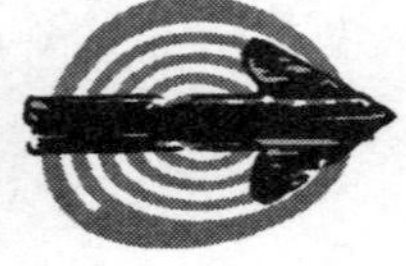

We will examine the complexity of these issues in the following sections.

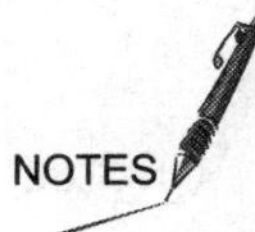

2 CONSUMER BUYING BEHAVIOUR

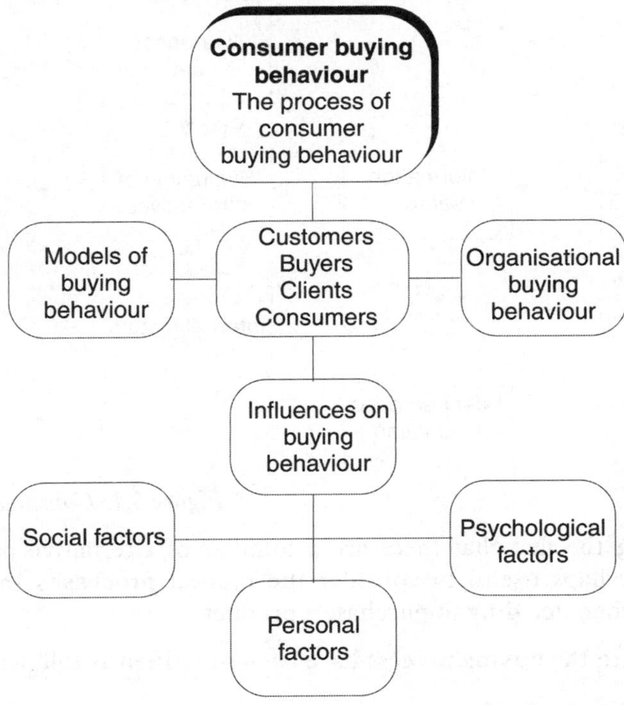

Definition

> **Consumer buying behaviour** can be defined as, 'the decision processes and acts of individuals involved in buying and using products or services.' (Dibb: *Marketing Concepts and Strategies*, 2001).

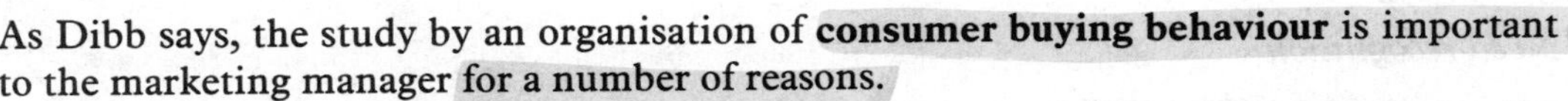

As Dibb says, the study by an organisation of **consumer buying behaviour** is important to the marketing manager for a number of reasons.

(a) The buyer's **reaction** to the organisation's marketing strategy has a major impact on the success of the organisation.

(b) If organisations are truly to implement the marketing concept, they must examine the main **influences** on what, where, when and how customers buy. Only in this way will they be able to devise a **marketing mix** that satisfies the needs of the customers.

(c) By gaining a better understanding of the factors influencing their customers and how their customers will respond, organisations will be better able to **predict the effectiveness** of their marketing activities.

2.1 The process of consumer buying behaviour

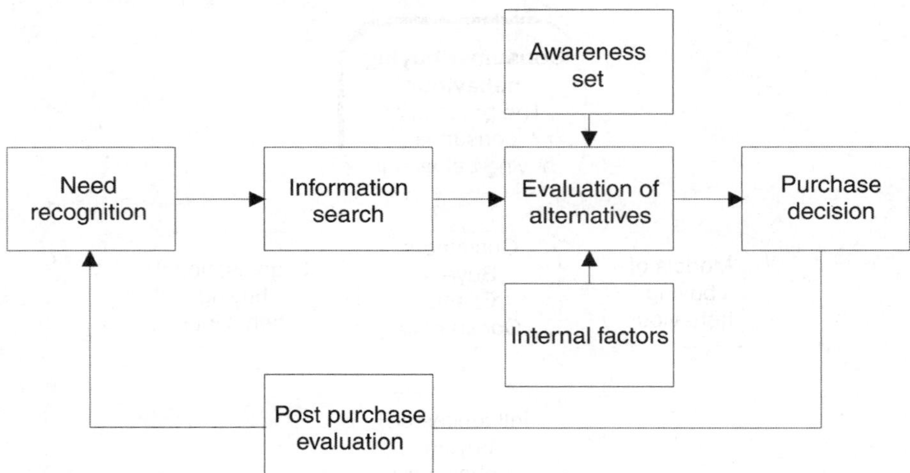

Figure 5.1: Consumer buying behaviour

Whilst recognising the fact that there are a number of alternative patterns of buying behaviour, it is perhaps useful to consider the **mental processes** through which the consumer moves when deciding to purchase a product.

The general stages in the buying process have been identified as follows.

- Need recognition
- Information search
- Evaluation of alternatives
- Purchase decision
- Post purchase evaluation

Each stage will be considered in turn and an example will be provided at the end of the section.

Need recognition

The process begins when the buyer recognises a need or problem. This can be triggered by internal stimuli, such as hunger or thirst, or external stimuli, such as social esteem. If the need rises to a threshold level it will become a **drive** and from previous experience the buyer will know how to satisfy this drive through the purchase of a particular type of product. Kotler states that the task for the marketer is to identify the circumstances and/or stimuli which **trigger** a particular need and to use this knowledge to develop marketing strategies which **stimulate consumer interest**.

Information search

Once aroused the customer will search for more information about the products that will satisfy the need. The information search stage can be divided into two levels. The first is **'heightened attention'**, where the customer simply becomes more receptive to information about the particular product category. The second stage is **'active information search'**. The extent of active search will depend on the strength of the drive, the amount of information initially available, the ease of obtaining additional information and the satisfaction obtained from the search.

The task for the marketer is to decide which are the major information sources that the customer will use and to analyse their relative importance. According to Kotler, consumer information sources fall into four groups.

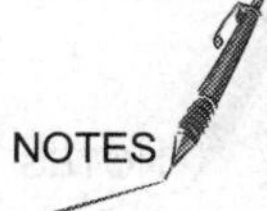

(a) **Personal sources:** family, friends, neighbours, work colleagues

(b) **Commercial sources:** direct mail, salespeople, packaging, displays

(c) **Public sources:** mass media, consumer rating organisations

(d) **Experiential sources:** handling, examining, using the product, seeing the product in use Use of the senses

A consumer will generally receive the most information exposure from commercial sources, but the most effective information exposure comes from personal sources. Each information source performs a somewhat different function. For instance, you may ask friends or work colleagues which camera they would recommend, or ask them to state their preference from a range of choice.

Through this information-gathering process the consumer will learn about **competing brands** and their relative pros and cons. This will enable the consumer to narrow down the range of alternatives to what has been called the '**choice set**'. The marketer's task is to get his or her brand into the customer's choice set.

Evaluation of alternatives

Trying to describe the process of evaluation of alternatives is not easy as there is no generally accepted single evaluation process. Most current models of evaluation take the view that the customer forms judgements largely on a conscious and rational basis.

Kotler states that, as consumers are trying to satisfy some need with the buying process, they will be looking for certain benefits and each product will be seen as a '**bundle of attributes**' with varying capabilities of delivering the benefits sought. The marketer should determine what importance the customer attaches to each attribute. In consumer marketing, the concept of **brand** is very important. Fundamentally, a brand is a promise that reassures the customer about the desirable attributes of the product, such as quality and privity. Marketers can extend this concept by promoting even more abstract ideas in association with the brand. These features that are claimed for the brand are called **brand values**. Thus, Rolls-Royce's brand values are said to be reliability, integrity and innovation.

In contrast with brand values, which are what the marketer wishes the customer to associate with the brand, customers themselves are likely to build up their own set of **brand beliefs** about the position of each brand with regard to each attribute. The sum of these brand beliefs will make up the **brand image**. The extent to which customers' brand beliefs echo the intended brand values determines the success of the marketing involved. Consumers will probably choose the brand that they think maximises benefits to them.

In order to ensure that the brand has the best chance of being chosen by the consumer, the marketer has a range of options for action including the following.

(a) **Modifying the brand.** Redesigning the product so that it offers more of the attributes that the buyer desires. Kotler calls this **'real repositioning'**.

(b) **Altering beliefs about the brand.** Kotler recommends that this course of action be pursued if the consumer underestimates the qualities of the brand. He calls this '**psychological repositioning**'.

(c) **Altering beliefs about competitors' brands.** This course of action would be appropriate if the consumer mistakenly believes that a competitor's brand has more quality than it actually has, and can be referred to as '**competitive repositioning**'.

(d) **Altering the importance weighting of attributes.** The marketer would try to persuade consumers to attach more importance to the product attribute in which the brand excels.

(e) **Calling attention to neglected attributes**, particularly if the brand excels in these attributes. ('Have you forgotten how good they taste?').

(f) **Shifting the buyer's ideals**. The marketer would try to persuade consumers to change their ideal levels for one or more attributes.

FOR DISCUSSION

People buy more on impulse than any other way.

Awareness set

Schiffman and Kanuk (1991) describe a model to show how 'set' works in consumers' brand choice.

(a) There will be some brands of which the individual will not be aware at all. This **unawareness set** will not impact on his decision.

(b) There will be a group of brands of which the customer is aware – his **awareness set** – and from which he will make his selection.

(c) Within the awareness set, there will be a group of brands which the consumer will call to mind and consider purchasing. This is called the **evoked set**.

There are further subsets, according to the individual's evaluation of the brands within the awareness set. By definition, the evoked set includes brands which have been positively evaluated, but there may also be:

(a) An **inert set** of brands, of which the individual is aware but about which he is completely indifferent. (Perhaps he has insufficient data to make a judgement or perhaps the evoked set of brands are already sufficient for his needs.)

(b) An **inept set** of brands of which the individual is aware, but about which he is negative – because of past bad experience, negative associations or poor reports.

EXAMPLE: CATEGORISING BRAND X

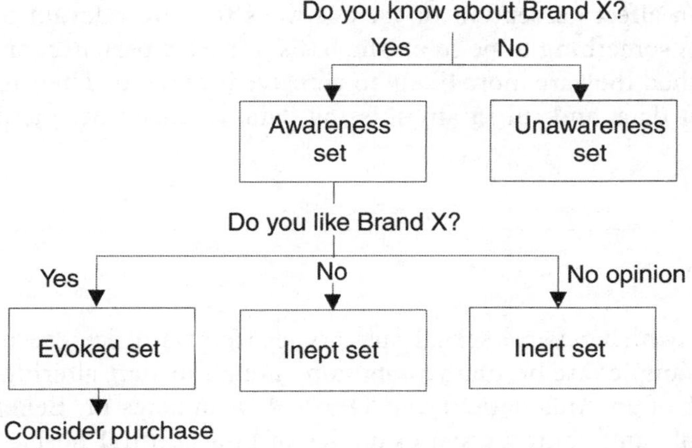

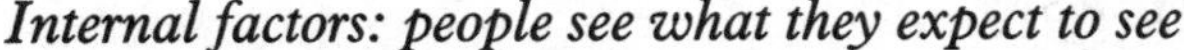

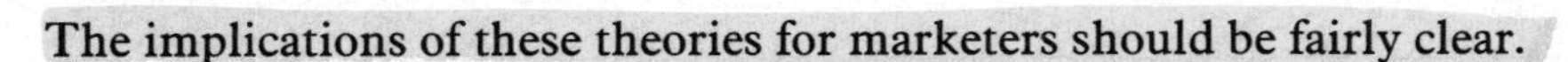

The implications of these theories for marketers should be fairly clear.

(a) Awareness sets represent consumer perceptions, so they can be a useful indicator of a brand's position.

(b) The presence of a brand in the **evoked** set of most consumers is very positive. Awareness campaigns would be required to remind the market of the brand's presence and key features, in order to keep it in the set.

(c) The presence of a brand in the **unawareness set** of most consumers would indicate the need for a marketing strategy to raise the brand's profile in the market place.

(d) The presence of a brand in the **inert set** of most consumers would indicate the need for a marketing strategy to persuade consumers to try the brand – by giving more information, stressing positive features, or offering samples or other promotional incentives to try the product.

(e) The presence of a brand in the **inept set** of most consumers would indicate the need to improve the product, or promotional message, to counteract its negative image.

FOR DISCUSSION

Advertising helps us keep abreast of what is good in the market place.

Internal factors: people see what they expect to see

Expectations are based on past experience, the knowledge derived from it (by learning), and the social and cultural influences associated with it.

Expectations create in each individual a readiness to respond in a learned/accustomed way to a given stimulus or group of stimuli. This readiness to respond is called the individual's **perceptual set**. If you are orientated towards art and music, you will respond more readily to artistic visual images and music, while you will tend to 'switch off' when mathematical formulae or scientific theories are put before you. Depending on

NOTES

your political convictions, you will be disposed to respond positively to some Party Political broadcasts and not to others.

Expectations can affect perception in various ways that are relevant to the marketer. If someone expects something to be so on the basis of past experience, or on the say-so of a trusted person then they are more likely to perceive it to be so. Their mind will filter out any inconsistent data, and fill in any missing data, to create the picture they expect to see.

EXAMPLE

Advertisements which reverse sexual stereotypes (female office executives ogling male collegues, for example) are becoming common enough to start altering expectations, but the appearances of an Aids patient and Death Row inmates on Benetton knitwear ads were questionable and controversial examples of how cultural norms can be flouted in spectacular fashion.

Part of the effect of expectation is that we categorise or classify people and objects according to experience. We learn categories or 'concepts,' such as male and female, animal, vegetable and mineral, good and bad, as we go through life and absorb cultural values. This then makes it simple for us to identify and label things and people in our perception.

This aspect has proved particularly interesting to marketers, because consumers evaluate fairly similar products and allocate them to distinct categories or 'sets', in order to simplify the purchase decision.

Purchase decision

Having evaluated the range of brand choices the consumer may have formed a purchase intention to buy the most preferred brand. However, some factors could intervene between the **purchase intention** and the **purchase decision**. The first factor is the attitude of others. If, for example, a friend or relative of the consumer expresses a strong negative opinion, this may influence the consumer to change his or her mind. Purchase intention is also influenced by unanticipated situational factors that may intervene between purchase intention and decision. Such factors could include a change in financial circumstances such as redundancy, or circumstances in which some other purchase becomes more urgent.

EXAMPLE: HOLIDAY RETAIL SALES LIKELY TO DEPEND ON PERCEIVED 'DEALS' AVAILABLE TO CONSUMERS

Consumers who find perceived deals are more likely to spend the same amount of money this holiday season as they did in 2008, according to the latest FYi online survey conducted this month by Michigan-based market research and strategy firm Intellitrends.

'Retailers that can help consumers feel like they are getting more for their money have a better chance of having a profitable shopping season,' said Marlene Stone, Intellitrends President and CEO. 'I think our survey shows that consumers are expecting to see significant discounts and sales this holiday season and they will take more time to make a purchase decision to ensure they are getting a perceived bargain.'

Businesswire.com, 19 November 2009

Post purchase evaluation

Having purchased the brand the consumer will experience some level of satisfaction or dissatisfaction, depending on the closeness between the consumer's **product expectations** and the product's **perceived performance.** These feelings will influence whether the consumer buys the brand again and also whether the consumer talks favourably or unfavourably about the brand to others.

Activity 2 **(20 minutes)**

Before reading on, think about a recent purchase of a fairly major item that you have made. Did you go through the stages listed above? Explain what the need was, how you searched for information and so on.

EXAMPLE

Imagine two different purchase scenarios, buying a car and buying a snack at a train station. The behaviour or possible thoughts of the consumer at each stage is likely to vary considerably.

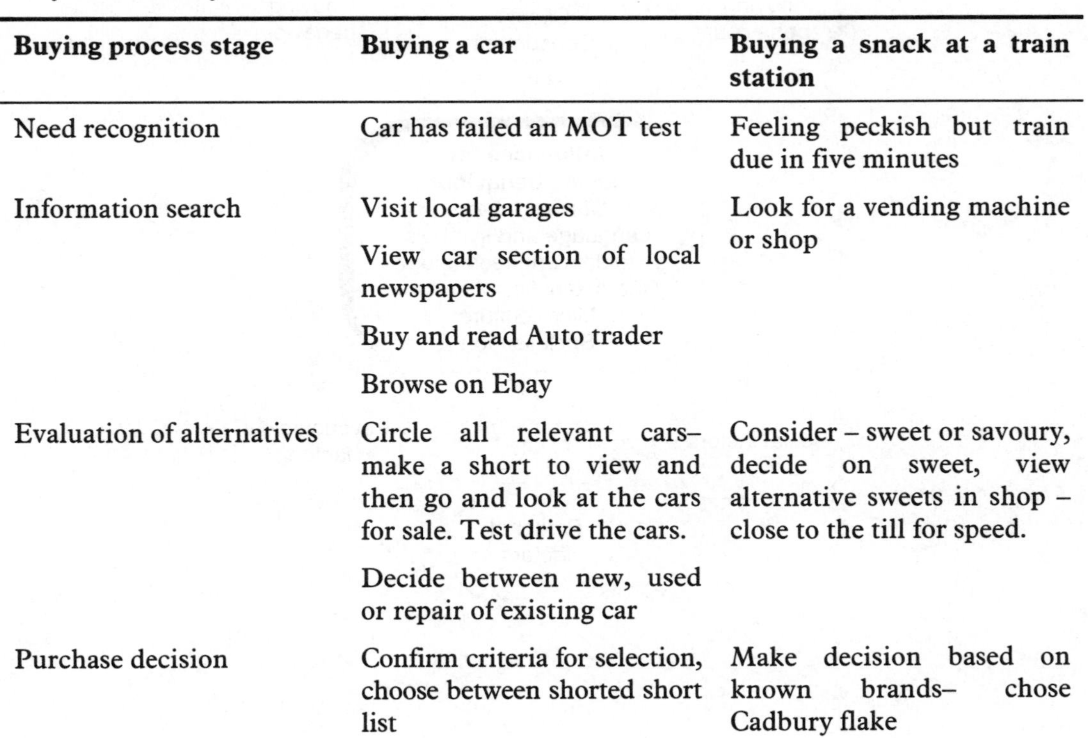

Buying process stage	Buying a car	Buying a snack at a train station
Need recognition	Car has failed an MOT test	Feeling peckish but train due in five minutes
Information search	Visit local garages View car section of local newspapers Buy and read Auto trader Browse on Ebay	Look for a vending machine or shop
Evaluation of alternatives	Circle all relevant cars– make a short to view and then go and look at the cars for sale. Test drive the cars. Decide between new, used or repair of existing car	Consider – sweet or savoury, decide on sweet, view alternative sweets in shop – close to the till for speed.
Purchase decision	Confirm criteria for selection, choose between shorted short list	Make decision based on known brands– chose Cadbury flake

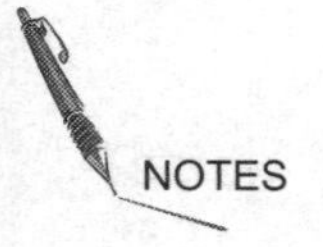

Buying process stage	Buying a car	Buying a snack at a train station
Post purchase evaluation	Thoughts about the car following the purchase, reliability, satisfaction with the drive, comments from friends.	regret as difficult to eat on the train due to the crumbly nature of the product– decide not to buy again for a train journey

It is highly probable that as you have been reading this you have thought of very different behaviours you may have shown at each stage. This is due to the range of influences we are subjected to as individuals and these will be covered in the next section.

It should also be apparent that both purchase scenarios are entirely different in their nature as the product could be one which requires lots of complex decision making because it is an important, expensive or risky purchase (known as a high involvement purchase). Alternatively, it may be less significant and routine and is referred to as a low involvement purchase eg chocolate bars. The type of purchase behaviour also differs depending on whether the purchase is familiar or unfamiliar, routine, an impulse or critical.

3 INFLUENCES ON BUYING BEHAVIOUR

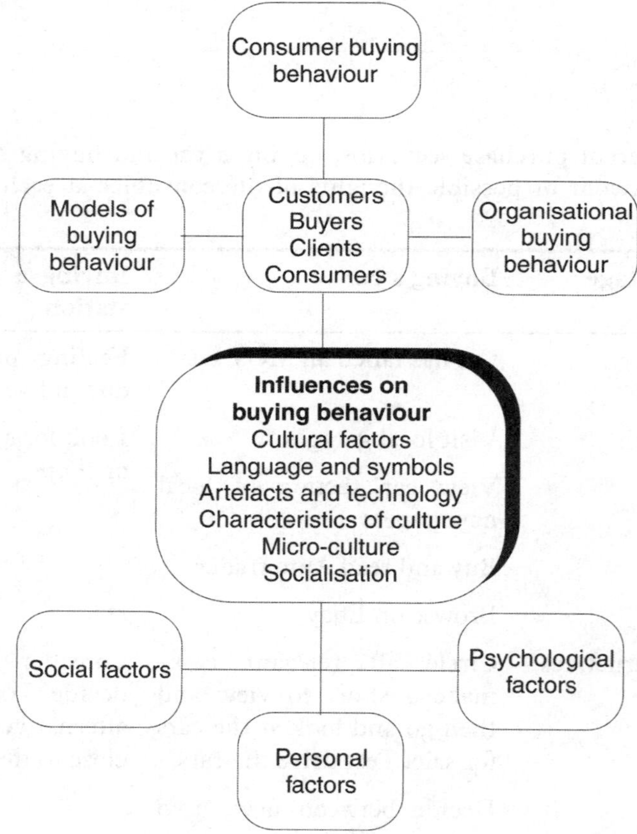

The 'core' process of consumer buying behaviour described above will be influenced by a number of outside variables. These variables have been classified by Wilson as follows, with the focus progressively narrowing.

- Cultural
- Social
- Personal
- Psychological

Each factor will be considered in more detail separately, but it is essential to remember that they are not mutually exclusive. Marketers must have a clear understanding of how the various factors interact and how they influence buyer behaviour, both separately and together.

3.1 Cultural factors

Definition

> **Culture** is a much broader concept than the sense in which it is most often used by people to refer to classical aesthetic or artistic pursuits. The term is used by sociologists and anthropologists to encompass the sum total of the learned beliefs, values, customs, artefacts and rituals of a society or group.

As suggested by our definition above, culture embraces the following aspects of social life.

(a) **Beliefs and values.** Beliefs are perceived states of knowing. We feel that we know about 'things', on the basis of objective and subjective information. Values are key beliefs which are:

  (i) Relatively enduring

  (ii) Relatively general – not tied to specific objects

  (iii) Fairly widely accepted as a guide to culturally appropriate behaviour

(b) **Customs**. Customs are modes of behaviour which represent culturally approved ways of responding to given situations. There are various types of social behavioural norms.

(c) **Rituals**. A ritual is a type of activity which takes on symbolic meaning, consisting of a fixed sequence of behaviour. Ritualised behaviour tends to be public, elaborate, formal and ceremonial – like religious services, marriage ceremonies, court procedures, even sporting events. Ritualistic behaviour, however, is any behaviour a person makes a ritual out of. You always do your makeup/shave/get up in the morning in the same way. Rituals commonly require **artefacts** (representing, for the marketer, products): think of the 'accessories' that attend a wedding, a football match, a Christmas dinner, a business conference.

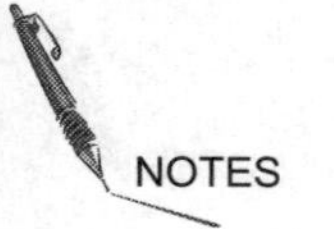

FOR DISCUSSION

Kissing and hugging on greeting are becoming increasingly common in the UK.

3.2 Language and symbols

Another very important element of culture, which makes the learning and sharing of culture possible, is **language**. Without a shared language and symbolism – verbal and non-verbal – there would be no shared meaning. The different languages of different cultures are an obvious means of distinguishing large groups of people. Language can present a problem to cross-cultural marketers as we shall see.

Symbols are an important aspect of language and culture. Each symbol may carry a number of different meanings and associations for different people, and some of these meanings are learned as part of a society's culture. The advertiser using slang words or pictorial images must take care that they are valid for the people he wants to reach and are up-to-date.

3.3 Artefacts and technology

Culture embraces all the physical 'tools' used by people for their physical and psychological well-being. In our modern society, the technology we use has a very great impact on the way we live our lives, and new technologies accelerate the rate of social change.

3.4 Characteristics of culture

Having examined the areas included in the definition of culture, we can draw together some of the underlying characteristics of culture itself. Culture comprises all the following.

(a) **Social**. Culture exists to satisfy the needs of people in a society.

(b) **Learned**. Cultural norms and values are taught or 'transferred' to each new member of society, formally or informally, by socialisation. This occurs in institutions (the family, school and church) and through on-going social interaction and mass media exposure in adulthood.

(c) **Shared**. A belief or practice must be common to a significant proportion of a society or group before it can be defined as a cultural characteristic.

(d) **Cumulative**. Culture is 'handed down' to each new generation, and while new situations teach new responses, there is a strong traditional/historical element to many aspects of culture.

(e) **Adaptive**. Culture must be adaptive, or evolutionary, in order to fulfil its need-satisfying function. Many factors may produce cultural change, whether slow or fast, in society: eg technological breakthrough, population shifts, exposure to other cultures, gradual changes in values. (Think about male-female roles in the West, or European influences on British lifestyles.)

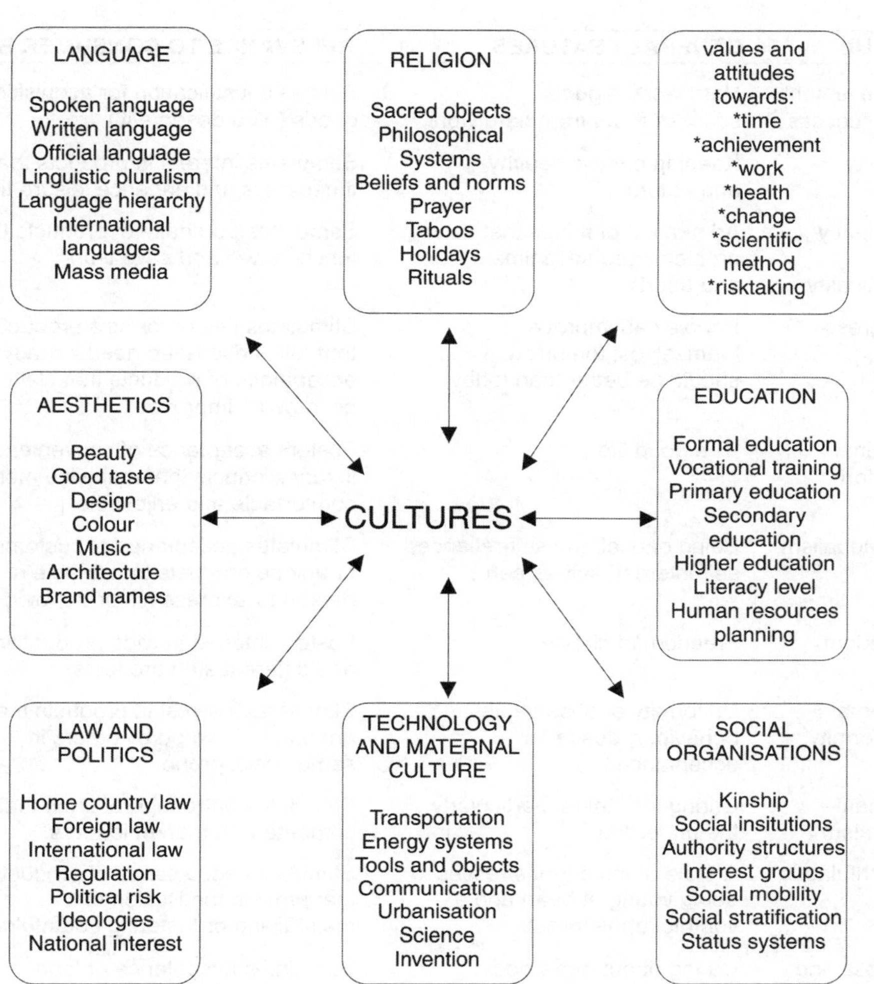

Figure 5.2: Characteristics of cultures

Activity 3 **(20 minutes)**

Schiffman and Kanuk give the following summary of American core values and their relevance to consumer behaviour. Consider how far they are applicable to your social culture. Which is the most important under each heading in each of the two right hand columns?

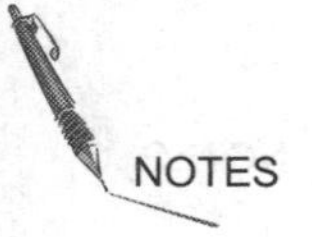

VALUE	GENERAL FEATURES	RELEVANCE TO CONSUMER BEHAVIOUR
Achievement and success	Hard work is good; success flows from hard work	Acts as a justification for acquisition of goods ('You deserve it')
Activity	Keeping busy is healthy and natural	Stimulates interest in products that are timesavers and enhance leisure time
Efficiency and practicality	Admiration of things that solve problems (eg save time and effort)	Stimulates purchase of products that function well and save time
Progress	People can improve themselves; tomorrow should be better than today	Stimulates desire for new products that fulfil unsatisfied needs; ready acceptance of products that claim to be 'new' or 'improved'
Material comfort	'The good life'	Fosters acceptance of convenience and luxury products that make life more comfortable and enjoyable
Individualism	Being oneself (eg self-reliance, self-interest, self-esteem)	Stimulates acceptance of customised or unique products that enable a person to 'express his or her own personality'.
Freedom	Freedom of choice	Fosters interest in wide product lines and differentiated products
External conformity	Uniformity of observable behaviour; desire for acceptance	Stimulates interest in products that are used or owned by others in the same social group
Humani–tarianism	Caring for others, particularly the underdog	Stimulates patronage of firms that compete with market leaders
Youthfulness	A state of mind that stresses being young at heart and a youthful appearance	Stimulates acceptance of products that provide the illusion of maintaining or fostering youthfulness
Fitness and health	Caring about one's body, including the desire to be physically fit and healthy	Stimulates acceptance of food products, activities, and equipment perceived to maintain or increase physical fitness

Figure 5.3: Values and consumer behaviour

FOR DISCUSSION

Drugs and alcohol abuse are clear evidence of an increasing pleasure principle in youth culture.

3.5 Micro-culture

Culture is a rather broad concept, embracing whole societies. It is possible to subdivide (and for marketers, further segment) a macroculture into micro-cultures (or **sub-cultures**) which also share certain norms of attitude and behaviour.

Definition

> A **micro-culture** is a distinct and identifiable cultural group within society as a whole: it will have certain beliefs, values, customs and rituals that set it apart while still sharing the dominant beliefs, values, customs and rituals of the whole society or 'mainstream' culture.

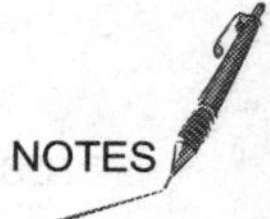

The main micro-cultures relevant to the UK are defined by in the following ways.

(a) **Class.**

(b) **Nationality**. Nationality refers to the birthplace of one's ancestors.

(c) **Ethnicity**. Ethnicity refers to broader divisions into for example Afro-Caribbean, white and Asian groups. There are identifiable differences in lifestyles and consumer spending patterns among these groups, but it is only relatively recently that attention has been given to reaching and serving ethnic minority market segments, as distinct from mass marketing.

(d) **Geography or region**. Even in such a small country as England, there are distinct regional differences.

(e) **Religion**. Adherents to religious groups tend to be strongly oriented to the norms, beliefs, values, traditions and rituals of their faith. Food customs are strict in religions such as Judaism, Hinduism and Islam.

(f) **Age.** Micro-cultures vary according to the period in which individuals were socialised, because of the great shifts in social values and customs in this century.

(g) **Gender**. We have already discussed gender roles in family buying behaviour, and their gradual erosion – despite which, marketers make frequent appeals to gender-linked stereotypes. The Career Woman and the New Man are perhaps the most important current micro-cultural markets segmented on this basis.

Marketers need to be aware of **micro-cultural variations**. Not all may be significant enough to be a basis for segmentation of the market for a particular product. Some may be particularly sensitive (eg marketing 'prohibited' foods to a religious group).

EXAMPLE

Domino's Pizza

'In the US, Domino's Pizza stresses its delivery system as a way to differentiate itself from other pizza companies, but abroad it is not so easy. In Britain, customers don't like the idea of the delivery man knocking on their doors – they think it's rude. In Japan, houses aren't numbered sequentially, so finding an address means searching among rows of houses numbered willy-nilly. In Kuwait, pizza is more likely to be delivered to a waiting limousine than to someone's front door. And in Iceland, where much of the population doesn't have telephone service, Domino's has teamed with a drive-in movie theatre chain to gain access to consumers. Customers craving a reindeer-sausage pizza – one of the most popular flavours – flash their turn signals, and a theatre employee brings them a cellular phone to order a pizza that is delivered to the car.'

Adapted by Cateora & Graham (International Marketing) from an article in *The Wall Street Journal*: 'The Most Successful Companies Have to Realise a Simple Truth: All Consumers Aren't Alike'

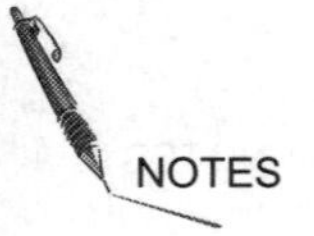

FOR DISCUSSION

What are the most important cultural values and/or infrastructure factors in your own country that impact on marketing practices and trends?

Marketers also need to avoid exaggerating the exclusivity of micro-cultures. Promotional strategies need not target a single micro-cultural membership, since each consumer is simultaneously a member of many micro-cultural segments.

Activity 4 **(30 minutes)**

(a) Find at least one example of marketing targeted at a segment of each of the above micro-cultures. You do not have to confine yourself to commercial enterprises or to TV advertising. The Metropolitan Police, for example, ran a recruitment drive using a poster that featured a white man chasing a black man - or so one concluded until one read the copy. Actually both men were policemen chasing an unseen villain.

(b) Visit shops or look through magazines that are not targeted at the micro-cultures into which you happen to fit. Make a note of the differences that you perceive.

3.6 Socialisation

Definition

Socialisation is 'the process by which the individual learns the social expectations, goals, beliefs, values and attitudes that enable him to exist in society'. In other words, socialisation is the process by which he acquires sufficient knowledge of a society and its ways to be able to function and participate in it.

The learning of gender-related, consumer and occupational roles is part of the socialisation process: what it means to 'be' or 'behave like' a girl or boy, what money is for, what 'buying' is, what 'work' is and what sorts of work different 'sorts' of people do.

The **family** is the earliest contact through which socialisation is achieved, although other socialising influences on children include formal **education**, **reference groups** (particularly peer groups, at a young age), and the **mass media**. Socialisation is an on-going process.

Consumer socialisation is the process by which children acquire the skills, knowledge and attitudes that enable them to function in society as consumers.

(a) Children observe the consumption behaviour of their parents or older siblings (while pre-adolescents), or their peers (once adolescents and teenagers), and model their own behaviour accordingly. This applies to specific brand attitudes/choices and pricing/budgeting skills, as well as to shopping behaviour: 'co-shopping' (parent and child shopping together) can encourage both sorts of learning.

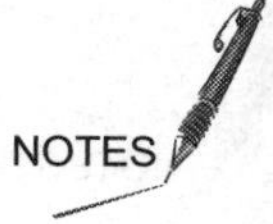

(b) Parents use consumption-related events to socialise children generally: promises of gifts or shopping expeditions are used as incentives to behave in a desired way; withholding of money for self-directed purchases is threatened as a deterrent to undesirable behaviour.

(c) Children are socialised into attitudes, values and motivations which are indirectly related to consumption: products or particular brands are means of satisfying socialised needs and wants. Socialisation creates consumer motivations.

We can therefore identify a number of agencies who are instrumental in the socialisation of individuals.

(a) The **family** is probably the most enduring and extensive source of influence, because it is here that the dependent child learns from his or her parents and siblings.

(b) **School** is an important source of values, particularly as they relate to other people.

(c) **Peer groups** exert influence which can control a person's social and emotional satisfactions, say by appointing a person unelected leader or by 'sending him to Coventry'.

(d) The **mass media** are extremely pervasive and have a profound effect on us all.

FOR DISCUSSION

Children rebel against their parents' examples of product and brand adoption more than they copy them.

Activity 5 **(20 minutes)**

List some of your favourite brands and examine them against a list which represents those which your parents would choose. What do you make of the similarities and/or differences?

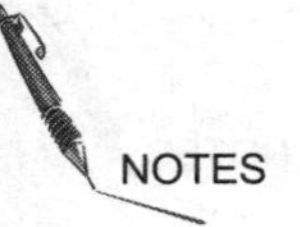

4 SOCIAL FACTORS

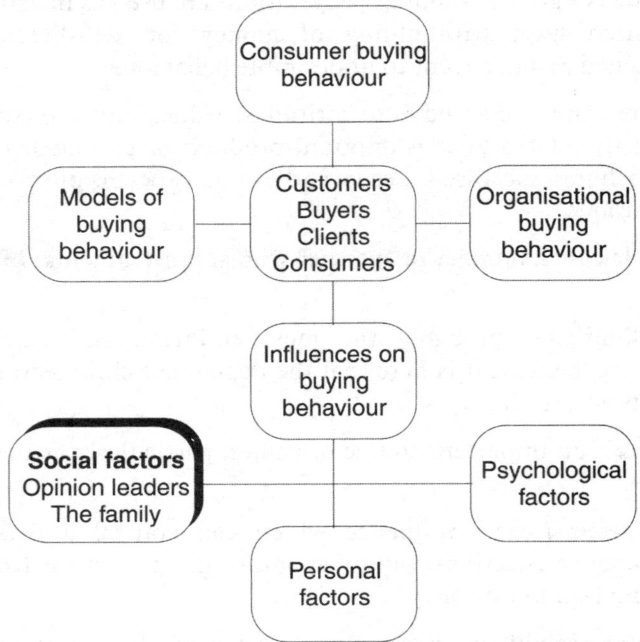

Within the context of culture, an individual is also influenced by a series of social factors, such as reference groups, family, social role and status, which can all have a direct effect on buying behaviour.

Reference groups have been defined as groups 'with which an individual identifies so much that he or she takes on many of the values, attitudes or behaviours of group members'. Four types have been identified.

(a) **Primary membership groups**, which are generally informal and to which individuals belong and within which they interact (family, friends, neighbours, work colleagues and so on).

(b) **Secondary membership groups**, which tend to be more formal than primary groups and within which less interaction takes place (trade unions, religious groups and professional societies are examples).

(c) **Aspirational groups**, to which an individual would like to belong.

(d) **Dissociative groups**, whose values and behaviour the individual rejects.

Activity 6 **(15 minutes)**

Higher National award holders constitute, presumably, one of your own aspirational groups. What other reference groups do you have? Divide them according to the above classifications.

4.1 Opinion leaders

With regard to reference groups, one of the marketer's tasks is to identify the groups with which individuals identify, and within these groups identify the opinion leaders.

Definition

> **Opinion leaders** are 'those individuals who reinforce the marketing messages sent and to whom other receivers look for information, advice and opinion.'

In addition, opinion leaders may communicate a marketing message to those members of the group who may have missed the original message. The marketer's task in identifying opinion leaders is made more difficult by the fact that opinion leadership is dynamic. At one time it was believed that opinion leadership was confined to a few prominent members of society, but increased understanding of the concept has shown that a person may be an **opinion leader** in certain circumstances but an **opinion follower** in others.

EXAMPLE: OPINION LEADERS ARE IMPORTANT MULTIPLIERS FOR INDUSTRY

From 2010 onwards opinion leaders will now be counted among the official list of admissible trade visitors (at the German International Sporting Goods Trade Fair) . . .

Opinion leaders who mediate between the consumer, trade and industry play an important role in the specialist trade in sports equipment – as well as athletes and trainers, they also include heads of ski schools and institutional buyers such as hospitals, the Red Cross and the police. As the name suggests, an opinion leader influences public opinion and helps guide consumers in their purchase decisions, thereby in the end also boosting the sales of retailers and producers. The significance of these opinion leaders is . . . that a large proportion of the exhibitors already count this group among their most important visitors, and even invite them to the trade fair.

fibre2fashion.com, 21 November 2009

4.2 The family

Another major social influence is the **family,** particularly with regard to the roles and relative influence exerted by different family members. Research has indicated three patterns of decision making within the family and identified the sorts of product categories with which each is typically associated, as follows.

(a) **Husband dominated**: life insurance, cars and television

(b) **Wife dominated**: washing machines, carpets, kitchenware and non living-room furniture

(c) **Equal**: living-room furniture, holidays, housing and entertainment.

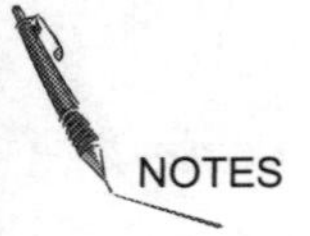

5 PERSONAL FACTORS

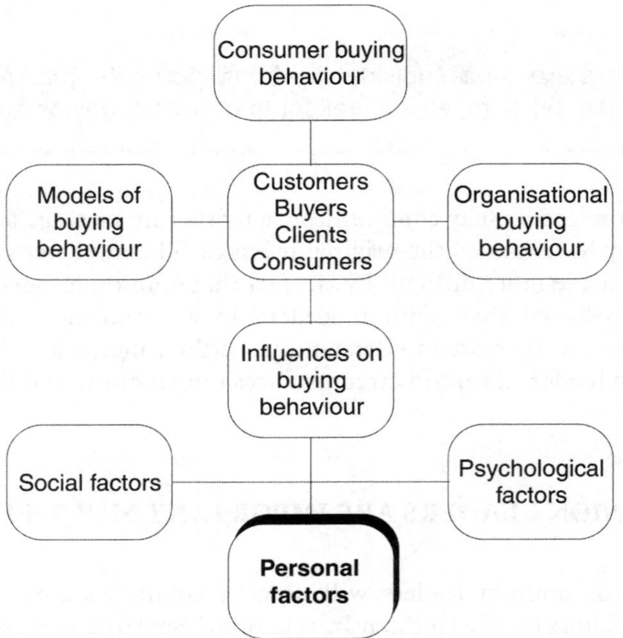

Influencing factors that can be classified as personal include such things as age and life cycle, occupation, economic circumstances and lifestyle.

Obviously, individuals will buy different types of product depending on age. This is particularly relevant to such products as clothes, furniture and recreation.

EXAMPLE

Chris Watt draws the following portrait of the **youth market** in the Australian marketing and advertising magazine *B & T Weekly* (5 July 2002).

- The youth market is extremely media-savvy and immediately dismissive of those who employ the standard tricks of the trade. Promoting a product as 'cool' in this market, is definitely not. They are cynical and untrusting of advertising and marketing promises.
- The fear of not belonging and the desire to be accepted are the key to understanding youth consumer behaviour. The flow-on effects of having a sense of belonging and control are the feelings of empowerment, confidence and independence – emotions highly sought by young people. Marketers must emphasise the elements within their product that evoke these emotions when communicating with this market.
- In the youth market more than any other, being seen to be 'on the cutting edge' has a major impact on the attention that a brand, product or service receives. Text messaging and the Internet are essential media of cutting edge communication, enabling the marketer to get closer to its market – and to fulfil their desires for instant interaction, gratification and belonging.

However, consumption may also be shaped by the stage of the **family life cycle** within which an individual falls. Two 25 year olds of equal income will have different spending patterns when one is married and the other is single.

A person's **occupation** will influence consumption and the task for marketers is to identify the occupational groups that have a strong interest in their products and services.

Buying patterns are also heavily influenced by an individual's **economic circumstances.** These are said to consist of the following.

(a) Spendable income; its level, stability and time pattern
(b) Savings and assets, including the percentage that is liquid
(c) Borrowing power and creditworthiness
(d) Attitude toward spending versus saving

However, people coming from the same subculture, social class and occupation may lead completely different lifestyles. A **lifestyle** is 'an individual's mode of living as identified by his or her activities, interests and opinions'. Marketers will search for relationships between their products and lifestyle groups. There are many different lifestyle classifications; an example is given in the table below.

Activity 7 **(30 minutes)**

(a) Read the table on the next page carefully. Where do you fit in? What about the members of your family and your friends and colleagues at work?

(b) See if you can think of one product or service that it would be easy to sell to a person in each of the lifestyle categories described.

(c) For each product or service identified in (b), think about how you would make the person in question aware of your company's brand.

Category	Comment
Upwardly mobile, ambitious	Seeking a better and more affluent lifestyle, principally through better paid and more interesting work, and a higher material standard of living. A customer with such a lifestyle will be prepared to try new products
Traditional and sociable	Compliance and conformity to group norms bring social approval and reassurance to the individual. Purchasing patterns will therefore be 'conformist'.
Security and status seeking	Stressing 'safety' and 'ego-defensive' needs. This lifestyle links status, income and security. It encourages the purchase of strong and well known products and brands, end emphasises those products and services which confer status and make life as secure and predicable as possible. These would include insurance, membership of the AA or RAC etc. Products that are well established and familiar inspire more confidence than new products, which will be resisted.
Hedonistic preferable	Places emphasis on 'enjoying life now' and the immediate satisfaction of wants and needs. Little thought is given to the immediate future

Figure 5.4: Lifestyle classifications

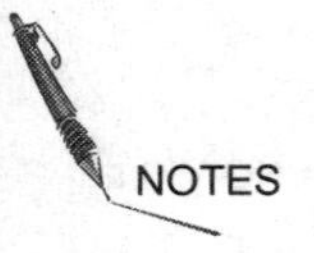

Activity 8 **(20 minutes)**

Assess a number of colleagues on the basis of the above schemes. Get the same ones to assess themselves. What do you make of any similarities or differences?

6 PSYCHOLOGICAL FACTORS

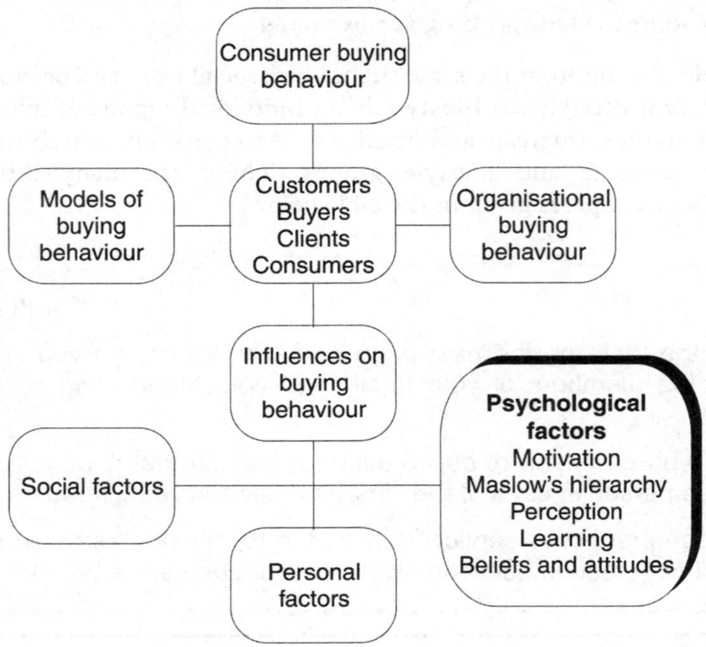

The process of buyer behaviour is also influenced by four major psychological factors: motivation, perception, learning, and beliefs and attitudes.

6.1 Motivation

Definition

Motivation has been defined as, 'an inner state that energises, activates, or moves, that directs or channels behaviour towards goals' (Assael).

Motivation arises from perceived needs. These needs can be of two main types – **biogenic** and **psychogenic**. Biogenic needs arise from physiological states of tension such as hunger, thirst and discomfort, whereas psychogenic needs arise from psychological states of tension such as the need for recognition, esteem or belonging.

A number of different theories of human motivation have been propounded which have differing implications for marketing and communications activity. These are given below. **Maslow's** is described at length as it is widely used and demonstrates how psychological models have much to offer the marketer.

Freud's theory of motivation assumes that the real psychological forces influencing people's behaviour are unconscious. Freud regards the process of growing up and accepting social rules as one which forces an individual to repress many of the natural

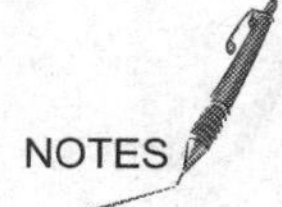

urges. These urges can never be eliminated or totally controlled, and can emerge in dreams, slips of the tongue or neurotic behaviour. From a marketing perspective, Freud's theory implies that people buy a product, not only for the rational reasons that they may state overtly, but also for a hidden set of underlying unconscious motives (such as the need for social esteem or belonging), that they may not articulate. The marketer, therefore, should be aware of the impact of all aspects of the product that could trigger consumer emotions that stimulate or inhibit purchase.

Herzberg developed a **'two factor theory'** of motivation that distinguishes between factors that cause dissatisfaction and factors that cause satisfaction. The task for the marketer is, therefore, to avoid 'dissatisfiers' such as, for example, poor after-sales service, as these things will not sell the product but may well 'unsell' it. In addition the marketer should identify the major satisfiers or motivators of purchase and make sure that they are supplied to the customer.

6.2 Maslow's hierarchy of needs

Maslow's theory of motivation seeks to explain why people are driven by particular **needs** at particular **times**. Maslow argues that human needs are arranged in a **hierarchy**, comprising, in their order of importance: **physiological** needs, **safety** needs, **social** needs, **esteem** needs and **self-actualisation** needs. As Maslow is seen as an important influence in understanding customer behaviour, we discuss it in some detail below.

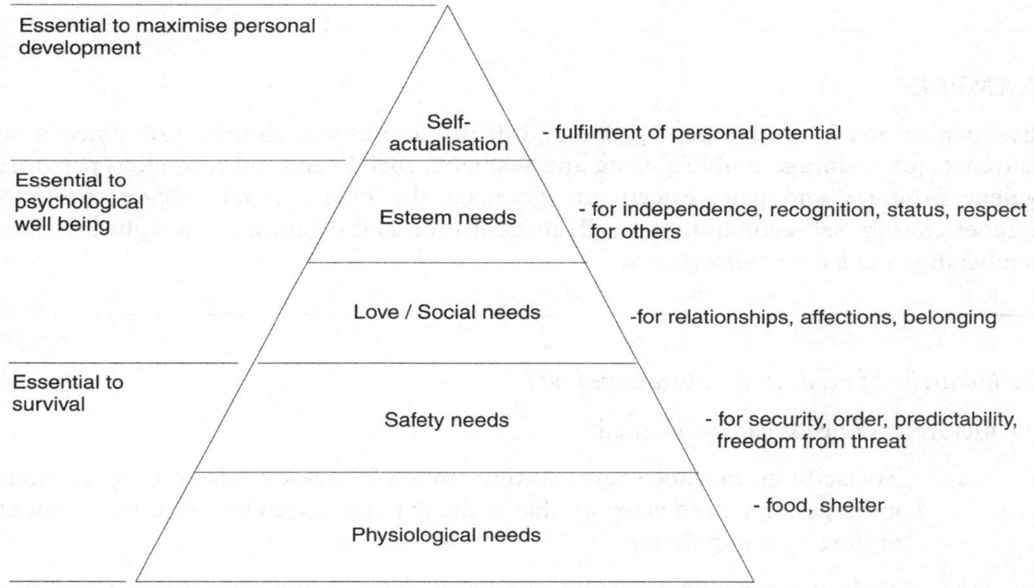

Figure 5.5: Maslow's hierarchy of needs

FOR DISCUSSION

'Love and security' are becoming stronger motivators of brand adoption than 'esteem'.

According to his theory, the lowest 'level' or need which is unsatisfied is **dominant**. Once it is satisfied, the next level 'up' becomes the dominant motivating impulse, until it in turn is satisfied – or until a lower-level need becomes dominant again, through renewed deprivation.

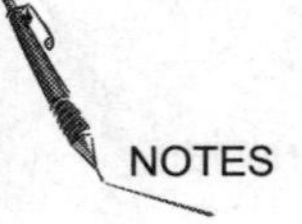

Since no need is ever completely satisfied, the levels overlap in practice, and more than one level of need may operate at the same time, but the **prime motivator** – the dominant impulse within the individual at a given time – is said to be the lowest level of need that is substantially unsatisfied.

Maslow's need categories are:

(a)	**Physiological** needs	–	food, water, air, shelter, sex
(b)	**Safety and security** needs	–	freedom from threat, good health, but also security, order, predictability, 'knowing where you are with people'
(c)	**Social** needs	–	for friendships, affection, sense of belonging
(d)	**Esteem or ego** needs	–	for self-respect and self-confidence, competence, achievement, independence, prestige and their reflection in the perception of others
(e)	**Self-actualisation** needs	–	for the fulfilment of personal potential: 'the desire to become more and more what one is, to become everything that one is capable of becoming'

EXAMPLE

Physiological needs can be met by food and drink, houses and clothes; safety needs by insurance, job training, double glazing and seatbelts; social needs by cosmetics, personal hygiene products and pets; esteem or ego needs by luxury items, bigger cars and designer clothes; self-actualisation needs by education and training services, health-club membership and career consultancy.

The hierarchy of needs as an operational tool

The hierarchy of needs can be adapted:

(a) To facilitate **market segmentation**, by enabling advertisers to focus their messages on a need category that is likely to be shared by a sizeable segment of the target population

(b) To facilitate **product/brand positioning**, by enabling advertisers to establish the product/brand in people's perception as the means to satisfy a particular need category.

Examples of segmentation and positioning by need category

Physiological needs: *Segment*
People concerned about health and fitness

Position
Benecol margarine positioned as almost a medicine

Safety needs:

Segment
Cautious people with responsibilities

Position
Creating the perception of Volvo as the safe car; insurance as safeguarding dependants

Social needs:

Segment
Young people

Position
Beer promoted as facilitating social interaction

Esteem needs:

Segment
High-income, high-status groups and lower income groups with aspirations

Position
Product as a sensible and refined choice – Marks & Spencer food promotions: 'This is not ordinary'

Self-actualisation needs:

Segment
People who are pleased with their status and achievements

Position
L'Oréal cosmetics because 'You're worth it'

6.3 Perception

Definition

> **Perception** is defined by Assael as 'the process by which people select, organise and interpret sensory stimuli into a meaningful and coherent picture.'

Physical stimuli are only one input to this process. There are also internal inputs from the individual himself, in the form of his own motives, expectations, personality, past experience and so on. This is why perception is so personal: each individual's viewpoint is unique, and will affect the way they act in a particular situation, or view an object or brand.

6.4 Learning

Learning describes changes in an individual's behaviour arising from experience. Theories about learning state that learning is the result of the interplay of five factors: drives, stimuli, cues, responses and reinforcement.

Definitions

A **drive** is a strong internal force impelling action, which will become a **motive** when it is directed to a particular drive-reducing stimulus object (the product). **Cues** are minor stimuli (such as seeing the product in action, favourable reactions to the product by family and friends) that determine when, where and how the person responds. Once the product is bought, if the experience is rewarding then the response to the product will be reinforced, making a repeat purchase the next time the situation arises more likely. Marketers must, therefore, build up demand for a product by associating it with strong drives, using motivating cues, and by providing positive reinforcement.

6.5 Beliefs and attitudes

Definition

A **belief** is 'a descriptive thought that a person holds about something'.

Beliefs are important to marketers as the beliefs that people have about products make up the brand images of those products.

Definition

An **attitude** comprises a person's enduring favourable or unfavourable cognitive evaluations, emotions, and action tendencies toward some object or idea.

Attitudes lead people to behave in a fairly consistent way towards similar objects. Attitudes can be regarded as **a short-cut in the thought processes** by ensuring that people do not have to interpret and react to every object in a fresh way. Attitudes settle into a consistent pattern and to change one attitude may entail major changes to other attitudes. Marketers, therefore, are advised to ensure that their product fits into people's existing attitudes rather than having to try to change attitudes.

EXAMPLE

Coca-Cola had to return to the original recipe when customers rebelled against the idea of a 'new' flavour.

7 MODELS OF BUYING BEHAVIOUR

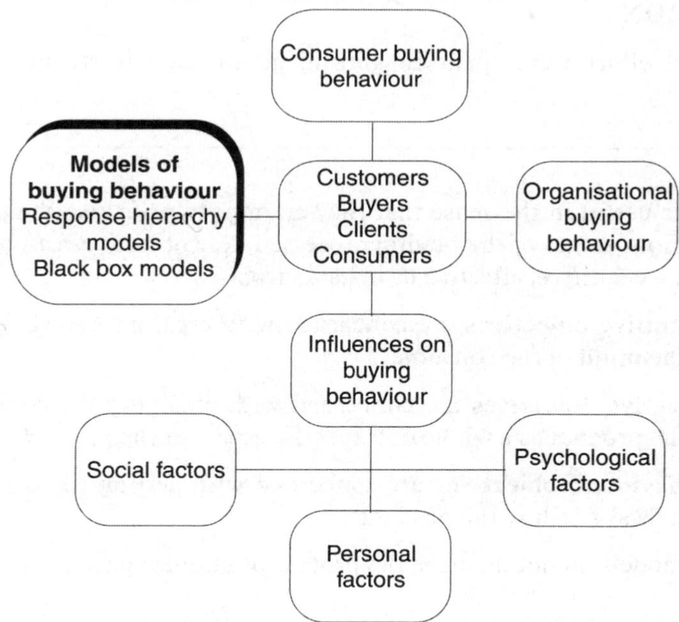

Given the complexity of the factors influencing consumer buying behaviour, can **models** be of any use in simplifying the process to make it more manageable for marketers, bearing in mind that their ultimate objective is to build repeat purchasing patterns on an ongoing basis?

One of the major ways in which models may help the marketer is to put some form of **framework** on the **thought processes** that the consumer goes through when buying. If marketers understand these thought processes then they are more likely to be able to develop communication activities that will effectively influence the consumer to buy a particular brand.

A number of different types of simple models have been put forward by way of explanation. These simple models can be classified into two major types – **response hierarchy models** and **black box models**.

7.1 Response hierarchy models

Response hierarchy models attempt to predict the sequence of stages that the consumer passes through on the way to a purchase. Here is an example.

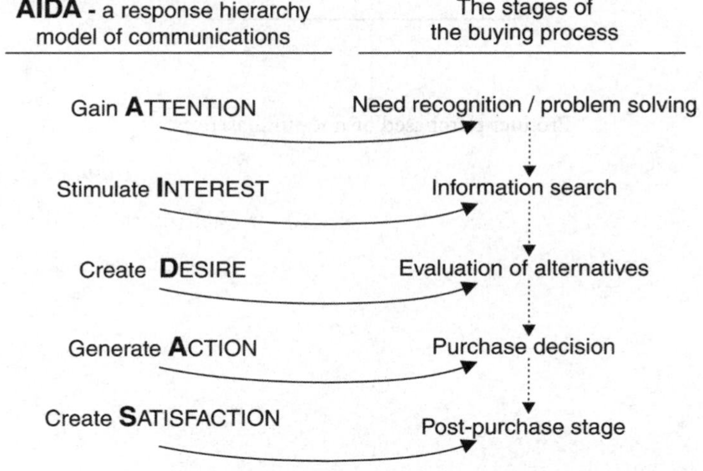

Figure 5.6: Response hierarchy model

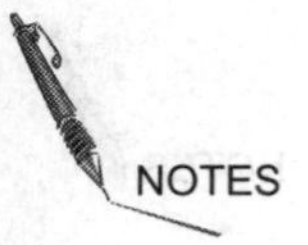

NOTES

FOR DISCUSSION

If less time and effort were spent in getting attention, advertising would be more effective.

These models are useful in the sense that they attempt to prioritise the **communication objectives** at various stages of the buying process. These objectives can be classified into three main areas – cognitive, affective or behavioural.

(a) **Cognitive objectives** are concerned with creating knowledge or awareness in the mind of the consumer.

(b) **Affective objectives** are concerned with changing the consumer's attitude to the product as a whole or a specific aspect of the product.

(c) **Behavioural objectives** are concerned with getting the consumer to act in some way (to buy the product).

However, such models do not describe the process of impulse purchase.

7.2 Black box models

These models are concerned with how people respond to stimuli, and as a result are often referred to as **stimulus-response models**. Such models do not attempt to explain the complexities of the customer's thought processes and the mind of the consumer is likened to a 'black box' which cannot be penetrated to find out what is inside. Therefore the intervening variables described in the previous section are ignored and the models focus on the **input** or stimulus (for example, advertising) and the **response** or output (purchase behaviour). The next diagram shows a simple black box model with an indication of examples of 'input' and 'output'.

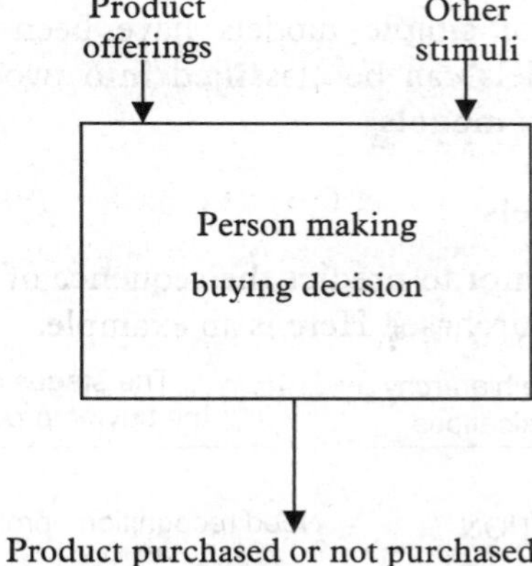

Figure 5.7: Black box model

8 ORGANISATIONAL BUYING BEHAVIOUR

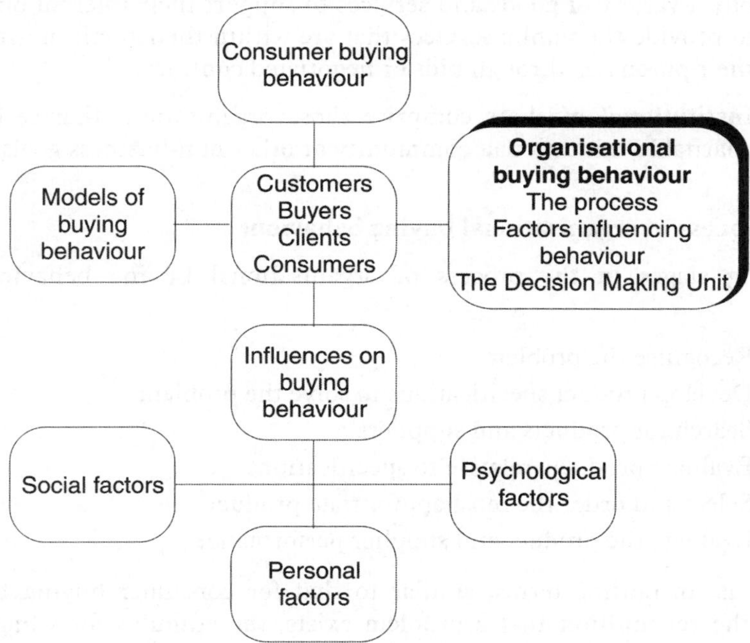

Definition

> **Organisational (or industrial) buying** may be defined as 'the decision-making process by which formal organisations establish the need for purchased products and services and identify, evaluate and choose among alternative brands and suppliers'.

A number of **differences between organisational and consumer markets** exist which mean that a modified approach needs to be taken when considering the process of buying behaviour.

Organisational markets normally comprise **fewer buyers**, with those buyers often being very concentrated (a few buyers are responsible for the majority of sales). Because of this smaller customer base and the importance and power of larger customers there is generally a **close relationship between buyer and seller** in organisational markets, with a great degree of **customisation and co-operation** on product specification and other requirements. Often organisational buyers are geographically concentrated.

The specific characteristics of organisational markets may vary according to the type of organisation that comprises the market.

(a) **Producer markets** comprise those organisations that purchase products for the purpose of making a profit by using them to produce other products or by using them in their own operations. This may include buyers of raw materials and of semi-finished and finished items used to produce other products.

(b) **Reseller markets** consist of **intermediaries** such as retailers and wholesalers who buy the finished goods in order to resell them to make a profit. Other than minor alterations, resellers do not change the physical characteristics of the products they handle.

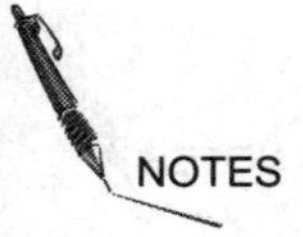

(c) **Government markets** comprise those national and local governments who buy a variety of goods and services to support their internal operations and to provide the public services that are within their remit, normally making their purchases through bids or negotiated contracts.

(d) **Institutional markets** comprise those organisations that seek to achieve charitable, educational, community or other non-business goals.

8.1 The process of organisational buying behaviour

The following stages in the process of organisational buying behaviour must be considered.

- Recognise the problem
- Develop product specifications to solve the problem
- Search for products and suppliers
- Evaluate products relative to specifications
- Select and order the most appropriate product
- Evaluate the product and supplier performance

This process is, in outline terms, similar to that for consumer buying behaviour. It begins with the **recognition** that a problem exists, the stimulus for which may come either from within or outside the company. The second stage of the process requires those people participating in the buying decision to **assess the problem** or need and determine what will be required to resolve or satisfy it. Here, the **DMU** comes into operation.

The third stage of the process is similar to that of **information search**; utilising trade shows, trade publications, supplier catalogues, and soliciting proposals from known suppliers. This should result in a list of alternative products which are then evaluated to ascertain whether they meet the product specifications. Suppliers may also be evaluated according to criteria such as price, service and ability to deliver.

The most appropriate product and supplier is then selected. In some cases an organisational buyer may select a number of suppliers in order to reduce the possibility of disruption caused by strikes, shortages or other failures of suppliers. The order will then be made, often with specific details regarding terms, credit arrangements, delivery dates and technical assistance or after sales service. The product and supplier will then be evaluated by comparing specifications regarding product quality and so on, and assessing the performance of the supplier in relation to the terms of the contract for the sale.

Activity 9 **(20 minutes)**

In the light of the above and earlier sections of this chapter see if you can draw up a list of similarities and differences between the purchase decision for an individual consumer and the purchase decision for an organisation.

You will also find some suggestions in the remaining sections of this chapter.

8.2 Factors influencing organisational buying behaviour

There are four main forces influencing the organisational buyer, shown below in order of progressively narrowing focus.

- Environmental
- Organisational
- Interpersonal
- Individual

Environmental forces include such factors as the level of primary demand, the economic outlook, the cost of money, the rate of technological change, political and regulatory developments and competitive developments. All these environmental forces must be monitored so as to determine how they will affect buyers.

Each **organisation** has its own objectives, policies, procedures, organisational structures and systems which may constrain the freedom of action of organisational buyers and this may in turn affect the decision-making process. For example, an organisation may insist on long-term contracts or may require special credit arrangements.

Interpersonal factors are important where the buying decision may involve a number of people. Within the buying group the use of power and the level of conflict could significantly influence organisational buying decisions.

Individual factors are the personal characteristics of the individuals in the buying group such as age, education, personality and position in the organisation. These will affect the decision-making process, and the seller must be aware of their potential influence.

8.3 The Decision Making Unit

One of the major differences between consumer and organisational buying behaviour is the fact that organisational purchase decisions are rarely made by a single individual. Normally purchasing decisions are made by a number of people from different functional areas, possibly with different statuses within the organisation. This obviously complicates the process of marketing and selling the product and it is important that the marketer is fully aware of the **composition of the buying group** and the relative importance to the purchase decision of the individuals within it.

A framework for considering these issues was provided with the concept of the **Decision Making Unit (DMU)** (Webster and Wind, 1972).

Definition

The **Decision Making Unit** is 'all those individuals and groups who participate in the purchasing decision process, who share some common goals and the risks arising from the decisions'.

There are six groups within the Decision Making Unit, as follows.

(a) **Users,** who may initiate the buying process and help define purchase specifications

(b) **Influencers,** who help define the specification and also provide an input into the process of evaluating the available alternatives

(c) **Deciders,** who have the responsibility for deciding on product requirements and suppliers

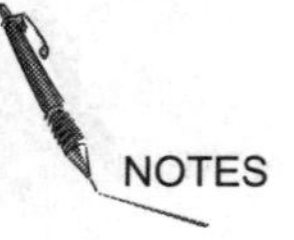

(d) **Approvers,** who authorise the proposals of deciders and buyers

(e) **Buyers,** who have the formal authority for the selection of suppliers and negotiating purchase terms

(f) **Gatekeepers,** who, by controlling the flow of information, may be able to stop sellers from reaching individuals within the buying centre

The size, structure and formality of the DMU will vary depending on the specific situation. However, the marketer has to consider five questions.

(a) Who are the **principal participants** in the buying process?

(b) In what areas do they exert the greatest **influence**?

(c) What is their **level** of influence?

(d) What **evaluative criteria** do each of the participants make use of and how professional is the buying process?

(e) To what extent, in large organisations, is buying **centralised**?

Activity 10 **(20 minutes)**

(a) Why might it be useful to target a promotional gift at a company director's secretary?

(b) In what circumstances might a negative post purchase evaluation by the users of a product have no impact on subsequent organisational buying decisions?

In the next chapter we look in more detail at one of the main processes of marketing, **segmentation**, which contributes to the effectiveness of the firm's approach to doing business. To do this well, the marketer has to have a keen appreciation of what makes the customer behave as they do. We should have some clear perceptions of this having just completed this chapter.

We are now well on the way to understanding the way that the marketing mix may be co-ordinated by the marketer to meet the needs of the customer and to achieve the company's goals.

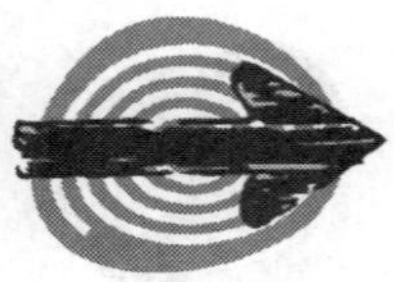

A detailed look at the components of the marketing mix begins in Chapter 7 as we examine the main factors through which a customer appreciates the company offering products and services.

Chapter roundup

- Marketers must have a clear understanding of the processes that customers go through when buying a product.
- This is true whether the product is bought by, or on behalf of, an individual consumer or by an organisation for production of other products or for re-sale purposes.
- The thought processes involved in buying, both individual or organisational, can be summarised in general terms as follows.
  - Recognition of problem
  - Information search
  - Evaluation of alternatives
  - Purchase decision
  - Post-purchase evaluation
- The extent to which a customer engages in any of, or all, these stages will depend on the value, scale and complexity of the product or service and the specific circumstances of the situation.
- Perception is selective, depending on external factors (the stimulus itself) and internal factors (the individual's experience, motives and interests).
- An awareness set is the group of products or services of which the customer is aware, hence members of this set are available for customer choice.
- A customer's self-image may lead to the choice of brands which support the customer's actual or desired self-perception: the way that customers think of themselves, or would like to see themselves.
- A brand image distinguishes a product from its competitors and is achieved by product positioning.
- A range of influencing factors can be identified which affect the buying process. They include, for example, biographic, behavioural, psychographic and economic variables. These must be recognised and understood by marketers in order that they are taken into account when constructing the offering as a combination of the components of the marketing mix.

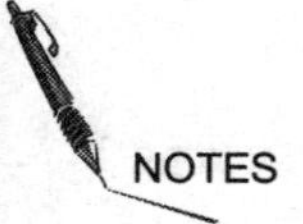

Quick quiz

1. Why is it important to study buying behaviour?
2. What are the five stages in the buying process?
3. In what ways can a marketer ensure that a brand has a good chance of being chosen by the customer?
4. Which four factors influence consumer buying behaviour?
5. What is an opinion leader?
6. Why should marketers not try to change attitudes?
7. What are the drawbacks of response hierarchy models?
8. What is a black box model?
9. List four types of organisational market.
10. What are the six stages in the process of organisational buying behaviour?
11. What four main forces influence the organisational buyer?
12. What are the six groups within the organisational DMU?
13. What are Maslow's need categories?
14. Give two main uses of the Maslow model for the marketer.

Answers to Quick quiz

1. It throws light on all the processes that combine to make and keep a customer.
2. Need, information, alternatives, purchase, post-purchase.
3. Modify brand beliefs, competitor beliefs, attribute weights, forgotten attributes, buyer's ideals.
4. Cultural, socio-economic, personal, psychological.
5. Those to whom others look for advice, opinions and approval.
6. Attitudes are enduring and difficult to change. It is more effective to develop product concepts which are in tune with target groups.
7. They do not account for all situations, eg impulse buying.
8. It demonstrates the principle of stimulus-response with an intervening variable.
9. Producer, re-seller, government and institutional.
10. Problem recognition, specify solution, product and supplier search, evaluate solutions, select and order, evaluate product and supplier performance.
11. Environmental, organisational, interpersonal, individual.
12. Users, influencers, deciders, approvers, buyers and gatekeepers.
13. Physiological, safety, love, esteem, self-actualisation.
14. Market segmentation and product positioning.

Answers to Activities

1 You could be a patron in a cinema, theatre or concert hall; a passenger on an airline, boat, bus or train; a patient at a chiropodist; a tenant in a flat. You can probably think of more. It is quite surprising that many of these special relationships are now described differently. Residents in care are often called clients instead of patients. Banks call us customers. The changes in name are brought about by a recognition of changes in relationships between supplier and customer (such as increased customer power).

2 The solution will depend upon your choice and your individual circumstances. If you have set down the five headings and given some thought to each, you may be surprised at what has happened. You certainly would not want to say 'I don't know why I bought this', especially if it were a large/special purchase.

3 The answer you give may depend on many things. Achievement and success are strongly held values in Western society. But, where there is high unemployment, for example, activity (having a job), independent of success by reference to traditional values, may be valued highly.

4 There is no direct solution for this for obvious reasons. Read the preceding text again carefully and satisfy yourself that you can really relate the concepts to the life that surrounds you.

5 Many of the brands that we buy are the same as those used in our parental home; many food brands are such. In the main, we still regard our parents (particularly mothers) as positive role references for food and household products. Saxa and Cerebos are two famous brands of table salt. In this product there is a tendency for us to buy the brand we had at home. Supermarkets own-branding is changing this somewhat.

Cosmetics are different. We almost go out of our way to be different in brand choice here. Targeting is very strong in this field.

6 Follow the classification given in the text and give some thought to your answers, especially with regard to the influences on your motivations.

7 Fashion, cosmetics, music, magazines and newspapers and cars could figure highly in the marketing strategies which are influenced by lifestyle factors.

8 Remember we are talking about self-perception which often includes an element of self-deception.

When you have puzzled about how your friends could possibly see themselves in the way that they do, tell them how you see yourself and ask them what they think about that!

9 There are similarities in that the problem recognition – post purchase behaviour model is generally appropriate to both. The main differences are likely to seen in the scale, cost and formality of purchasing behaviour. Out of these arise the critical consequences of purchase and supply. If the purchasing officers of a manufacturing organisation make a bad purchase the consequences can be catastrophic for the firm. It must be born in mind that the decision to purchase can depend on a number of people in a domestic group just as in a firm. The difference is that, in a firm the process is almost always a group decision and/or activity.

NOTES

10 (a) Because the secretary may be a gatekeeper
(b) There may be no alternative product known to the organisation.

There may be no part of the process which feeds back the failure.

Chapter 6 :
MARKET SEGMENTATION AND POSITIONING

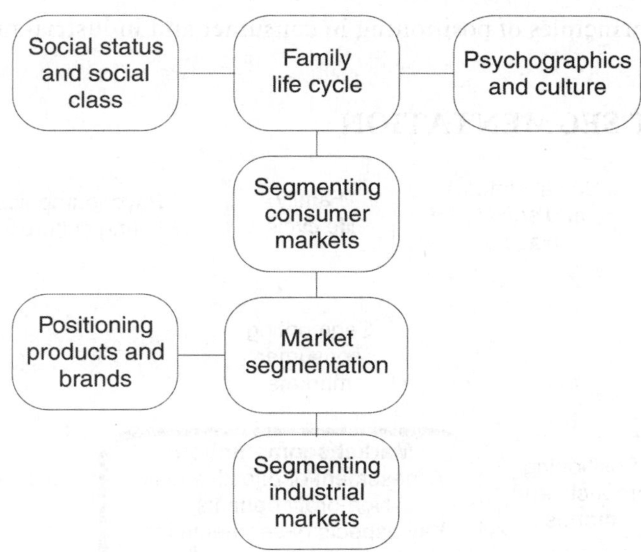

Introduction

Market segmentation enables firms to make the best use of the opportunities in the market for products and services. In this chapter we shall discuss the way the marketer approaches the issue of market segmentation, and provide the basis for your understanding of how you should go about it.

Continuing from our introduction to the **marketing mix** in Chapter 1, you will begin to see how the mix can be made to work more effectively in the light of market segmentation. Marketing mixes are segment-specific (which means that each segment may need its own marketing mix) and the process of segmentation impinges on all the components of the mix. The **product** design, **pricing** strategy, **promotional** mix and **choice of distribution channels** plus the other components of the services mix are all shaped to provide for the special needs of the target segment.

The main technique consists of dividing the broad view of the market into smaller groups by reference to one or more **characteristics** or **variables,** so that the supplier can concentrate specific resources on fulfilling each group's requirements. It should deliver a more attractive offering to the segment than would otherwise be the case.

To provide effective segmentation requires a great deal of **information** to be available, and so the process is very strongly connected to **market research**.

Market segmentation is almost always associated with **positioning**, and this topic is briefly discussed later in the chapter.

Your objectives

In this chapter you will learn about the following.

(a) Criteria used to segment markets

(b) The impact of segmentation variables on the marketing mix

(c) The importance of the segmentation process in marketing effectiveness

(d) Some of the sociological and psychological principles underlying the processes of segmentation

(e) The principles of positioning in consumer and industrial markets

1 MARKET SEGMENTATION

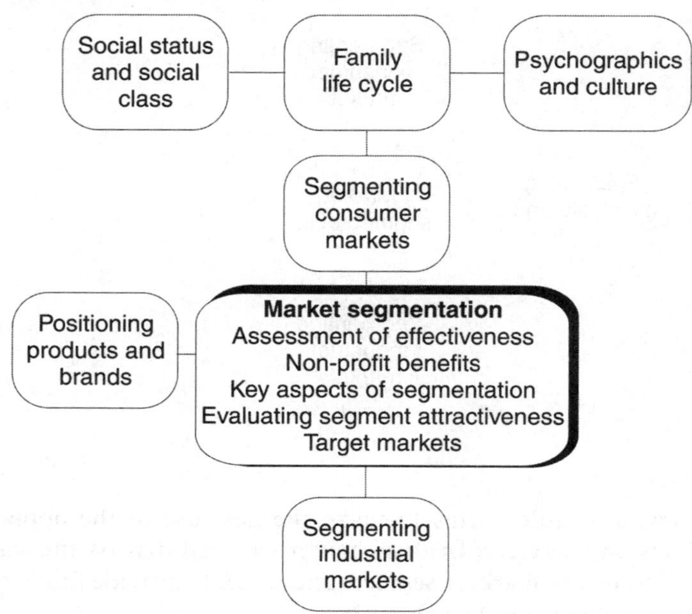

Definition

Market segmentation is 'the subdividing of a market into distinct and increasingly homogeneous subgroups of customers, where any subgroup can conceivably be selected as a target market to be met with a distinct marketing mix.'

(Kotler, 1994)

Customers differ according to age, sex, income, geographical area, buying attitudes, buying habits etc. Each of these differences can be used to segment a market.

Consumer and industrial buyers may be influenced by a wide range of factors and be in a variety of buying situations. A whole range of situational and background factors determine the outcome of a particular purchase opportunity.

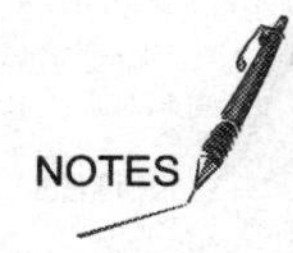

FOR DISCUSSION

Age is always a differentiating factor in considering market segments.

Marketing activity is more effective if groups can be identified and 'targeted' according to the marketing objectives of the company. This process is called **market segmentation** and it groups potential customers according to **identifiable characteristics** relevant to their **purchase behaviour**. Which segments are identified and selected depends on the **marketing objectives** pursued.

EXAMPLE: MILLENNIUM & COPTHORNE HOTELS TO OPEN FIRST STUDIO M BRANDED HOTEL IN SINGAPORE

http://www.millenniumhotels.com/

Millennium & Copthorne Hotels plc (M&C) today launched a new international hotel brand, Studio M, aimed at the new generation of savvy business and leisure travellers. Studio M is the latest addition to M&C's portfolio of brands and underscores the group's commitment to expanding its footprint in Asia.

The Studio M brand aims to offer both style and functionality to the well-travelled guest who relishes the urban contemporary lifestyle and demands access to fuss-free integrated technology and high connectivity.

The Studio M brand will be unveiled in Singapore soon when its first hotel opens in the second quarter of 2010.

A focus on elegantly restrained accommodation that offers a high degree of connectivity will set Studio M apart from current offerings. Savvy travellers will also enjoy using the hotel's unique open-air tropical deck, which offers private spaces in relaxed landscaped surroundings for both business meetings and leisurely conversations with friends. Guests will appreciate Studio M's locality within the vibrant Robertson Quay and Mohamed Sultan entertainment district, which offers abundant dining and leisure options.

'Studio M represents a new facet to the hospitality landscape in Singapore. The concept of smart business travel is evolving rapidly. There is increasing demand from this largely untapped market segment that craves a distinctive and unique experience from their hotel, even as they demand functional services like wireless connectivity. Studio M aims to fill this gap,' said Mr Kwek Leng Beng, Chairman of M&C.

hospitalitynet.org, 17 November 2009

The term one-to-one marketing addresses this very issue. Tesco currently holds one of the most sophisticated databases of consumers in the world. By collecting detailed patterns of buying behaviour through its Clubcard loyalty scheme, Tesco are able to specifically tailor marketing messages, promotional offers and work with manufacturers to ensure that stocked products appeal to their key consumer segments. Dunhumby the agency responsible for analysing Clubcard data, predicted that for most organisations only ten per cent of the stored information is actually being used to generate customer insight.

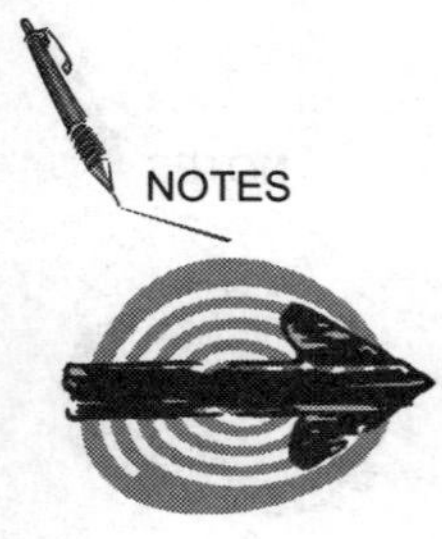

There are many possible characteristics of buyers which could be chosen as 'segmentation variables' and a variety of criteria which can be used to identify the most effective characteristics for use in market segmentation.

1.1 Assessment of effectiveness of market segmentation

Irrespective of the approach, there are a number of requirements for effective market segmentation.

(a) **Measurability** refers to the degree to which a characteristic can be quantified. The number of people who buy cars is known. How many people who do not buy cars of a given brand, could?

(b) **Accessibility** refers to the degree to which the company can focus effectively on the chosen segments using marketing methods. While we may be able to select what seems like the most appropriate target segment very clearly, we may not be able to identify the individuals or households involved, or communicate with them cost-effectively.

(c) **Substantiality** refers to the degree to which the segments are large enough to be worth considering for separate marketing cultivation.

Activity 1 **(20 minutes)**

Identify and evaluate, on the basis of the above factors, a segmentation design for a newly discovered supply of rare postage stamps.

1.2 Non-profit benefits of segmentation

(a) The identification of **new marketing opportunities** as a result of better understanding of consumer needs in each of the segments.

(b) **Specialists** can be appointed to develop each of the company's major segments.

(c) The marketing **budget** can be allocated more effectively, according to the needs and the likely return from each segment.

(d) **Precision marketing** approaches can be used. The company can make finer adjustments to the product and service offerings and to the promotional appeals used for each segment.

(e) Specialist knowledge and more focused effort may enable the company to **dominate** particular segments and gain **competitive advantage**.

(f) The **product assortment** can be more precisely defined to reflect differences between customer needs.

(g) Improved segmentation allows more **highly targeted marketing activity**.

(h) **Feedback and customer problems** are more effectively communicated. Producers develop an understanding of the needs of a target segment and expertise in helping to solve its problems.

1.3 Key aspects of segmentation

The important elements of market segmentation are as follows.

(a) While the total market consists of varied groups of consumers, each group consists of people (or organisations) with **common needs and preferences**, who may well react to 'market stimuli' in much the same way.

(b) Each market segment can become a **target market** for a firm, and would require a specific marketing mix.

A total market may occasionally be **homogeneous** but this is likely to occur only rarely. At one time, for example, the Coca Cola Company successfully sold one type of drink in one bottle size to a mass market (although it has since pursued market segments in the soft drinks market). Sometimes consumer differences may exist, but it may not be effective to analyse them into segments. A segmentation approach to marketing succeeds when there are identifiable **clusters of consumer wants** in the market.

Definition

> **Homogeneous** means consisting of parts which are all of the same kind. In marketing it is used to identify markets which are undifferentiated, neither by customer nor product. Heterogeneous means the opposite, where there is a high differentiation in demand or products.

Segmentation as a strategy is one of the most important marketing tools. **Consumer orientation** and **the marketing philosophy** rests on the recognition that within a particular market there will be any number of **sub-groups** with their particular needs and requirements.

Segmentation only makes sense if it is brings appropriate benefits.

(a) Segmentation should **increase benefits to consumers** by providing products, product features or attributes more closely matching their identified needs.

(b) Segmentation enables the firm to **identify those groups of customers who are most likely to buy**. This ensures that resources will not be wasted, and marketing and sales activity can be highly focused. The result should be lower costs, greater sales and higher profitability.

(c) Across an industry, segmentation will provide **greater customer choice** by generating a variety of products within a particular class from which consumers can choose.

The diagram below outlines the steps necessary in deciding whether to segment a market.

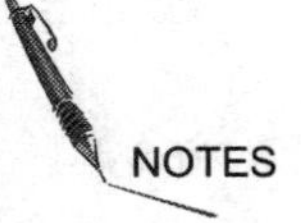

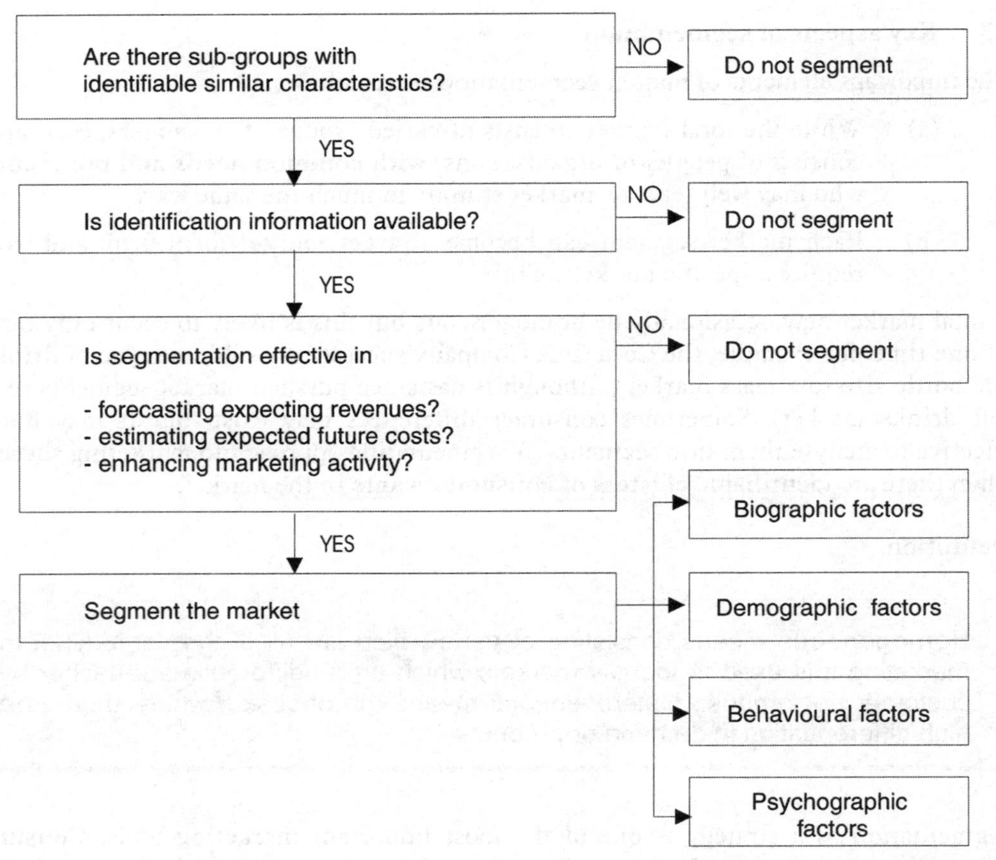

Figure 6.1: Market segmentation

FOR DISCUSSION

Segmentation is as much a benefit to the customer as it is to the marketer.

1.4 Evaluating segment attractiveness

A market segment will only be valid if it is worth designing and developing a unique marketing mix for that specific segment. The following questions are commonly asked to decide whether or not the segment can be used for developing marketing plans.

Criteria	Comment
Can the segment be measured?	It might be possible to conceive of a market segment, but it is not necessarily easy to measure it. For example, for a segment based on people with a conservative outlook to life, can conservatism of outlook be measured by market research?
Is the segment big enough?	There has to be a large enough potential market to be profitable.
Can the segment be reached?	There has to be a way of getting to the potential customers via the organisation's promotion and distribution channels.

Criteria	Comment
Do segments respond differently?	If two or more segments are identified by marketing planners but each segment responds in the same way to a marketing mix, the segments are effectively one and the same and there is no point in distinguishing them from each other.
Can the segment be reached profitably?	Do the identified customer needs, cost less to satisfy than the revenue they earn?
Is the segment suitably stable?	The stability of the segment is important, if the organisation is to commit huge production and marketing resources to serve it. The firm does not want the segment to 'disappear' next year. Of course, this may not matter in some industries.

A segment might be valid and potentially profitable, but is it potentially **attractive**?

(a) A segment which has **high barriers** to entry might cost more to enter but will be less **vulnerable to competitors.**

(b) For firms involved in **relationship marketing,** the segment should be one in which a **viable relationship** between the firm and the customer can be established.

Segments which are most attractive will be those whose needs can be met by building on the company's strengths and where forecasts for demand, sales profitability and growth are favourable.

Here is a comprehensive list of factors for evaluating market attractiveness.

Factors	Characteristics to examine
Market factors	• Size of the segment • Segment growth rate • Stage of industry evaluation • Predictability • Price elasticity and sensitivity • Bargaining power of customers • Seasonality of demand
Economic and technological factors	• Barriers to entry • Barriers to exit • Bargaining power of suppliers • Level of technology • Investment required • Margins available

Factors	Characteristics to examine
Competitive factors	• Competitive intensity • Quality of competition • Threat of substitution • Degree of differentiation
Environmental factors	• Exposure to economic fluctuations • Exposure to political and legal factors • Degree of regulation • Social acceptability

Figure 6.2: Factors for evaluating market attractiveness

It is important to assess company strengths when evaluating attractiveness and targeting a market. This can help determine the appropriate strategy, because once the attractiveness of each identified segment has been assessed it can be considered along with relative strengths to determine the potential advantages the organisation would have. In this way preferred segments can be targeted.

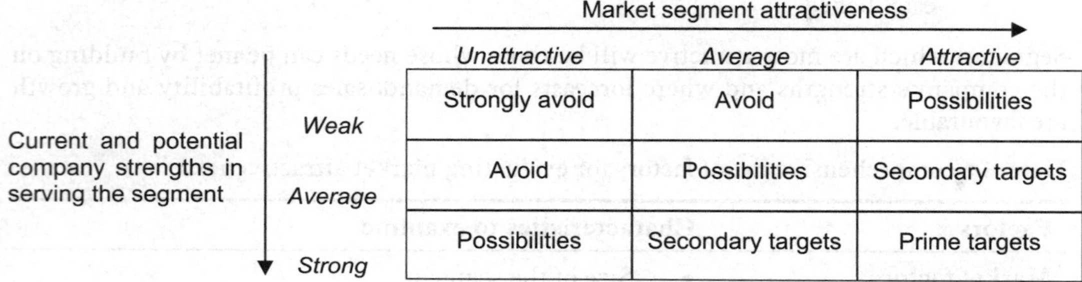
Market segment attractiveness

Current and potential company strengths in serving the segment	*Unattractive*	*Average*	*Attractive*
Weak	Strongly avoid	Avoid	Possibilities
Average	Avoid	Possibilities	Secondary targets
Strong	Possibilities	Secondary targets	Prime targets

Figure 6.3: Market segment attractiveness

1.5 Target markets

Having analysed the attractiveness of a segment, the firm will now choose one or more target markets.

Definition

A **target market** is a market or segment selected for special attention by an organisation (possibly served with a distinct marketing mix).

The marketing management of a company may choose one of the following policy options.

Policy	Comment
Undifferentiated marketing	This policy is to produce a single product and hope to get as many customers as possible to buy it; segmentation is ignored entirely. This is sometimes called mass marketing. It corresponds to the sales concept discussed earlier in this course book and is now unusual in advanced economies.
Concentrated marketing	The company attempts to produce the ideal product or small range of products for a single segment of the market (for example, *Rolls Royce* cars).
Differentiated marketing	The company attempts to introduce a wide range of product versions, each aimed at a different market segment (for example, the manufacture of different styles of the same article of clothing).

Figure 6.4: Target market policy options

EXAMPLE: A SHIFT TO ELECTRIC CARS WITH DRIVING MISSIONS?

For plug-in vehicle makers, 'a radical new form of market segmentation' holds the key to reaching beyond wealthy, green-minded early adopters, according to a report from McKinsey & Co. The common approach of trying to build a vehicle that can satisfy virtually all the driving needs for a large swath of consumers, if applied to the nascent market of plug-in hybrid and all-electric vehicles, may hinder its success, the consulting firm finds.

Instead, automakers should tailor plug-in vehicles for the primary 'driving missions' of specific consumer groups, McKinsey suggests. In other words, make a car that meets some of the needs of some customers. The researchers' conclusion, as explained in a McKinsey Quarterly article, rests on the argument that a carmaker can produce more economic vehicles—and develop more efficient advertising messages and go-to-market strategies—if it designs the battery pack (generally the most expensive portion of an electric car) according to a driver's particular needs. No more, no less.

'Driving missions' can be divided into two major groups: stop-and-go driving in town, and commuting. The latter, according to McKinsey, has higher energy storage requirements mainly because of 'the higher average driving speed, and thus air resistance, encountered on freeways.' (The firm says longer range is a less significant factor.) As a result, the researchers argue that cars designed to meet commuting needs will 'overserve' consumers using the cars for in-town driving at lower speeds and carry a higher price tag than what that group really needs to pay.

Josie Garthwaite, *businessweek.com*, November 19 2009

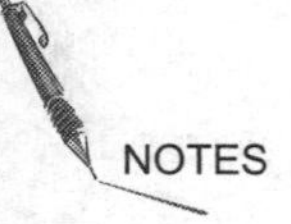
NOTES

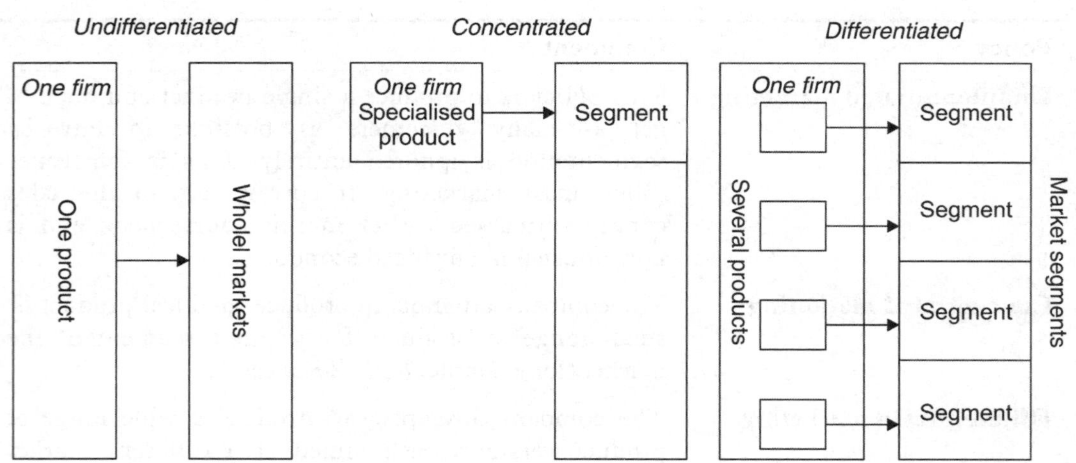

Figure 6.5: Target markets

The major **disadvantage of differentiated marketing** is the additional costs of marketing and production (more product design and development costs, the loss of economies of scale in production and storage, additional promotion costs and administrative costs and so on). When the costs of differentiation of the market exceed the benefits from further segmentation and target marketing, a firm is said to have over-differentiated.

The major **disadvantage of concentrated marketing** is the business risk of relying on a single segment of a single market. On the other hand, specialisation in a particular market segment can give a firm a profitable, although perhaps temporary, competitive edge over rival firms.

The choice between undifferentiated, differentiated or concentrated marketing as a marketing strategy will depend on the following factors.

(a) The extent to which the product and/or the market may be considered **homogeneous. Mass marketing** may be sufficient if the market is largely homogeneous (for example, for safety matches).

(b) The **company's resources** must not be over extended by differentiated marketing. Small firms may succeed better by concentrating on one segment only.

(c) The product must be sufficiently **advanced in its life cycle** to have attracted a substantial total market; otherwise segmentation and target marketing is unlikely to be profitable, because each segment would be too small in size.

Segmentation, as part of target marketing, looks certain to play an even more crucial role in the marketing strategies of consumer organisations in the years ahead. The move from traditional mass marketing to **micro marketing** is rapidly gaining ground as marketers explore more cost-effective ways to recruit new customers. This has been brought about by a number of trends.

(a) The **ability to create large numbers of product variants without the need for corresponding increases in resources** is causing markets to become overcrowded.

(b) The **growth in minority lifestyles** is creating opportunities for niche brands aimed at consumers with very distinct purchasing habits.

(c) The **fragmentation of the media** to service ever more specialist and local audiences is denying mass media the ability to assure market dominance for major brand advertisers.

(d) The **advance in information technology** is enabling information about individual customers to be organised in ways that enable highly selective and personal communications.

Such trends have promoted the developments in benefit, lifestyle and geodemographic segmentation techniques. Consumer market segmentation has developed so much in the last few years that the vision of multinational marketers accessing a PC to plan retail distribution and supporting promotional activity in cities as far apart as Naples, Nottingham and Nice is now a practical reality.

2 SEGMENTING CONSUMER MARKETS

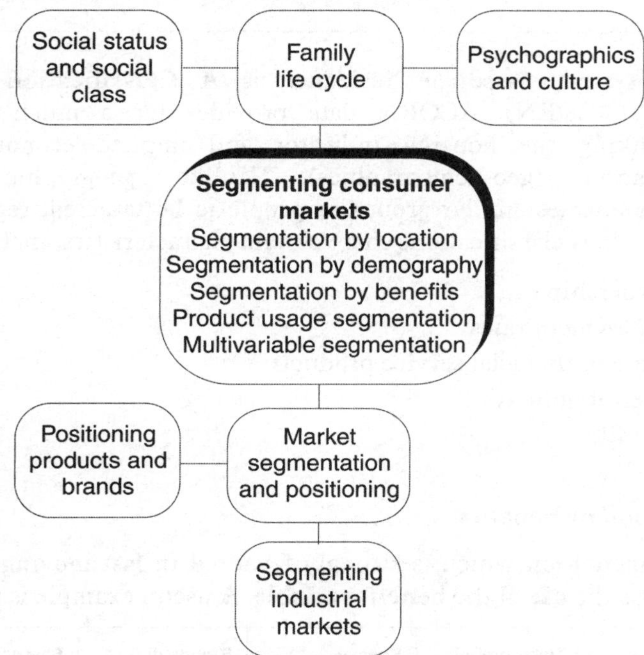

There are a number of ways which a consumer market can be segmented. Sometimes, more than one segmentation variable will be used (**multivariable segmentation**). Segmentation decisions have clear implications for other decision areas however, for instance, choice of advertising media.

2.1 Segmentation by location

This is based on **geographic location.** It may be important, for instance, for retailers who need to get to know about the different groups of customers within their catchment area. Segmentation by location can also be a feature of **international marketing strategy**, where marketing strategy is formulated around the different needs of various cultures, countries or regions. Needs and motives will be significantly influenced by a range of factors including climate, religion, culture and even geography. The opportunity to design an appropriate marketing mix and use sales staff familiar with a particular international market is vital for marketing success.

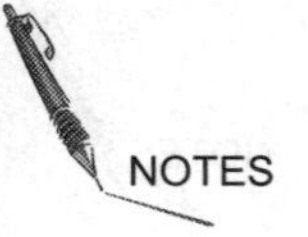

2.2 Segmentation by demography

The total size of the population defines the **total possible level of demand** for a product. With the formation of the Single European Market in 1992 the home market for UK companies became comparable in size to the US market.

The population is usually broken down into groups defined by demographic characteristics such as sex or 'age' (for example, the baby market, teenage market and senior citizens market). The total size of each segment will suggest possible levels of demand for corresponding products (rattles and prams, bicycles and motor cycles, retirement cottages and sea cruises). Another much used characteristic is the type of residence.

FOR DISCUSSION

The size of a house is a good indicator of the buying behaviour of its occupants.

A well known system based on residence is **A Classification of Residential Neighbourhoods** (ACORN). ACORN data provides for a much higher level of segmentation, linking the housing indicator and implied economic status with geographic location (geo-demographics). Unlike geographic segmentation, **geodemographics** enables similar groups of people to be targeted, regardless of where they live. These various classifications share certain characteristics, including:

- Car ownership
- Unemployment rates
- Purchase of financial service products
- Number of holidays
- Age profile

2.3 Segmentation by benefits

A method of segmentation which is strongly favoured in fast moving consumer goods (FMCG) markets is the use of the **benefit variable**. A useful example is shown below.

Segment name	Principal benefit sought	Demographic strengths	Special behavioural characteristics	Brands dis-proportionately favoured	Personality characteris-tics	Lifestyle characteris-tics
The sensory segment	Flavour, product appearance	Children	Users of spearmint flavoured toothpaste	Colgate, Stripe	High self-involvement	Hedonistic
The sociables	Brightness of teeth, fresh breath	Teens, young people	Smokers	Macleans, Ultra Brite, Thera-med	High sociability	Active
The worriers	Decay prevention	Large families	Heavy users	Crest	High hypo-chondriasis	Conservative
The independent segment	Price	Men	Heavy users	Brands on sale	High autonomy	Value-oriented

Figure 6.6: Benefit segmentation of the toothpaste market

NOTES

Activity 2 **(20 minutes)**

Check out the validity of the above table by asking a number of colleagues about their toothpaste purchases and see if you can agree the categorisations given. Do you find this a valid analysis? If they do not tally with your observations, how do you account for the variance?

2.4 Product usage segmentation

One of the oldest methods of identifying lucrative segments is by reference to **how much customers use**. In most markets the 80/20 rule applies. That is, 80% of a product or brand is bought by 20% of the customers. This is converted to a broader classification which uses the labels **Heavy User, Medium User, Light User**. Clearly the Heavy User Segment is a valuable and important target for marketers. On the other hand, there may be an attractive volume in the Light User Segment if the reason for light use can be clearly identified and the marketing mix can be manipulated in order to overcome the problem. Guinness have run many successful campaigns to make inroads into the non-user/light user segment.

FOR DISCUSSION

A person's hobby is a more reliable indicator of lifestyle than their occupation.

EXAMPLE

CACI is a company which provides market analysis, information systems and other data products to clients. It advertises itself as 'the winning combination of marketing and technology'.

As an illustration of the information available to the marketing manager through today's technology, here is an overview of some of their products.

Paycheck: This provides income data for all 1.6 million individual post codes across the UK. This enables companies to see how mean income distribution varies from area to area.

People UK: This is a mix of geodemographics, life stage and lifestyle data. It is person rather than household specific and is designed for those companies requiring highly targeted campaigns.

InSite: This is a geographic information system (GIS). It is designed to assist with local market planning, customers and product segmentation, direct marketing and service distribution.

Acorn: This stands for A Classification of Residential Neighbourhoods, and has been used to profile residential neighbourhoods by post code since 1976. ACORN classifies people in any trading area or on any customer database into 54 types.

Lifestyles UK: This database offers over 300 lifestyle selections on 44 million consumers in the UK. It helps with cross selling and customer retention strategies.

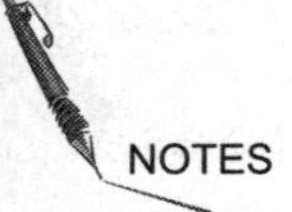

Monica: This can help a company to identify the age of people on its database by giving the likely age profile of their first names. It uses a combination of census data and real birth registrations.

ACORN has become a key tool now used by people looking to move home or find out more about their own neighbourhood. The website Upmystreet.co.uk uses this tool to provide free information about the type of neighbours found in an area. This website would prove highly useful to the small business such as a speciality cheese shop reliant on trade within a specific location.

2.5 Multivariable segmentation

One basis will not be appropriate in every market, and sometimes two or more bases might be valid at the same time. One segmentation variable might be 'superior' to another in a hierarchy of variables. There are thus **primary** and **secondary** segmentation variables.

EXAMPLE

An airport café undertakes a segmentation exercise of its customers. It identifies a number of possible segments.

- Business travellers
- Airport employees
- Groups
- Families
- Single tourists

Further analysis reveals that running through each of these categories is a more significant characteristic.

- Those in a hurry
- Those with time to spare

For marketing purposes, this later segmentation exercise is more useful as it may, for example, develop an 'express' menu.

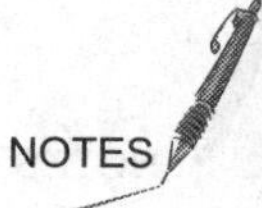

3 SOCIAL STATUS AND SOCIAL CLASS

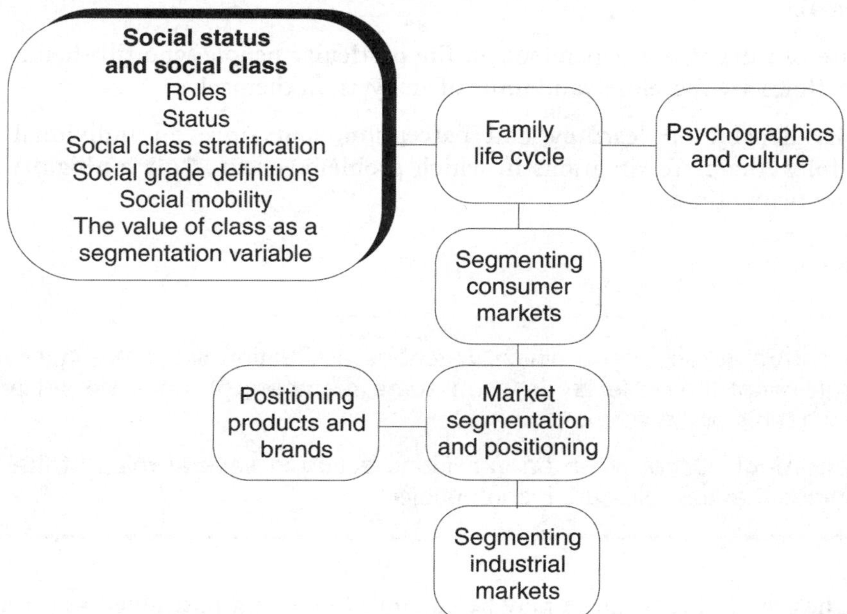

If we are to understand our customers we need to have some idea of how far individuals' thinking and behaviour, including their decision whether to become our customer, depend on their perception of and interaction with other people. In this section we will cover two particular ways in which we see ourselves, and behave, in relation to others; by adopting **roles** and **status**.

3.1 Roles

Definition

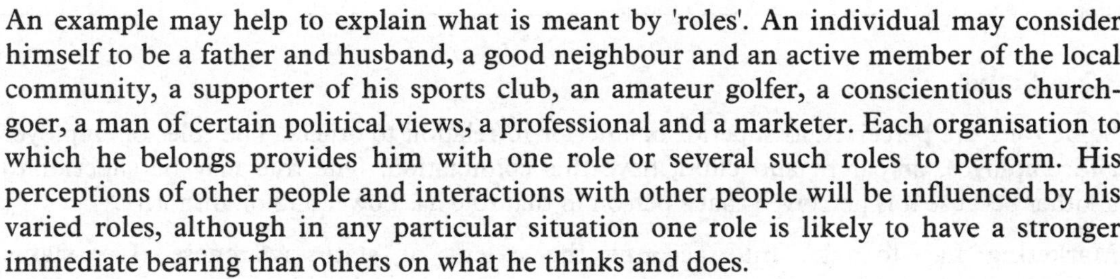

A **role** is the sum or 'system' of expectations which other people have of an individual in a particular situation or relationship. Role theory is concerned with the roles that individuals act out in their lives, and how the assumption of various roles affects their attitudes to other people.

An example may help to explain what is meant by 'roles'. An individual may consider himself to be a father and husband, a good neighbour and an active member of the local community, a supporter of his sports club, an amateur golfer, a conscientious church-goer, a man of certain political views, a professional and a marketer. Each organisation to which he belongs provides him with one role or several such roles to perform. His perceptions of other people and interactions with other people will be influenced by his varied roles, although in any particular situation one role is likely to have a stronger immediate bearing than others on what he thinks and does.

The other individuals who relate to him when he is in a particular role are called his **role set**. At work, he will have one role set made up of colleagues, superiors and subordinates, and any other contacts in the course of business: at home, he will have another role set consisting of family members, friends and neighbours.

Many products are purchased because they reflect or reinforce social roles. **Clothing** and **accessories** are bought as symbols of role, for example; people buy gifts for each other

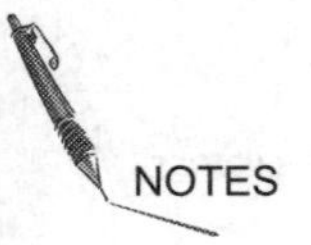

which reinforce the nature of their role relationship (intimate and familial or formal and professional).

The nature of roles is not dependent on the particular people who fill them: people fit into roles. Roles are therefore valid units of analysis, in themselves.

Since roles depend on learning and perception, and since an individual occupies multiple roles, there are situations in which problems occur. **Role ambiguity** and **role conflict** are two of these.

Definitions

Role ambiguity is a term which describes a situation when the individual is not sure what their role is, or when some members of their role set are not clear what his or her role is.

Role conflict occurs when an individual, acting in several roles at the same time, finds that the roles are incompatible.

Consider how a product's image may be enhanced by being positioned as (or associated with) the solution to such problems.

(a) A male manager will be in conflict between his role as manager in a recession (having to make staff cuts) and as a friend and drinking partner to 'the lads'. This man drinks a certain brand of beer with 'the lads' afterwards, as a symbol of the 'winning' role.

(b) A woman finds she cannot fulfil satisfactorily the (stereotyped) roles of worker and wife, because at the end of the day she cannot cook a 'proper' dinner, or get the laundry sweet-smelling enough. Fortunately, there are convenience products to help her. (There are lots of advertisements of this kind, and while they alienate most women, they appeal to a sense of role-related 'guilt' or inadequacy in some.)

FOR DISCUSSION

In young people, role conflict can be an important influence on their purchase decisions.

3.2 Status

Some roles are perceived as superior or inferior in relation to others. The roles of employer and employee, or parent and child, have this connotation. One role may be superior to another because it is perceived that a person in that role has power and/or authority.

Marketing has to take into account the extent of status-awareness. Low-status individuals in a status-conscious society may aspire to achieve higher status: products can be positioned accordingly. High status individuals may wish to be 'congratulated', or to emphasise the exclusivity and power of their position in society: **premium** quality (and price) products frequently appeal to this sense.

3.3 Social class: stratification of UK society

In practice, class strata or divisions are commonly derived from specific demographic factors

- Wealth/income – economic resources
- Educational attainment
- Occupational status

Social class, based on status, could be thought of as **a range of social positions in rank order**. Each class is then presumed to share a common level of status, relatively higher or lower than other classes in the 'hierarchy' of society. From a marketer's point of view, it is also possible to infer shared **values, attitudes and behaviour** within a social class. This makes social class an attractive proposition for market segmentation.

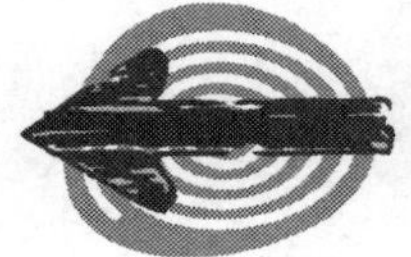

Various categorisations have been prepared, offering different ways of stratifying society, but we should note that 'class' is also a highly personal and subjective phenomenon, to the extent that people are 'class-conscious' or class-aware, and have a sense of belonging to a particular social group.

3.4 Social grade definitions

(a) Two-category schemes:

Producers of goods and services	***Managers and organisers***
Blue-collar Lower-class/working class	White collar Middle class

(b) Five or six category schemes

The most popular model for socio-economic segmentation is that produced by **JICNAR** (the Joint Industry Council on Newspaper Advertising Research). JICNAR's social grade definitions (A–E), correspond closely to what are called Social Classes I–V on the **Registrar General's Scale**.

Registrar General's Social Classes	**JICNAR Social Grades**	**Social Status**	**Characteristics of occupation**
I	A	Upper middle class	Higher managerial/professional eg lawyers, directors
II	B	Middle class	Intermediate managerial/administrative/ professional eg teachers, managers, computer operators, sales managers
III (i) non-manual	C1	Lower middle class	Supervisory, clerical, junior managerial/ administrative/professional eg foremen, shop assistants
(ii) manual	C2	Skilled working class	Skilled manual labour eg electricians, mechanics
IV	D	Working class	Semi-skilled manual labour eg machine operators
V			Unskilled manual labour eg cleaning, waiting tables, assembly
	E	Lowest level of subsistence	State pensioners, widows (no other earner), casual workers

Figure 6.7: Registrar General's Social Scale

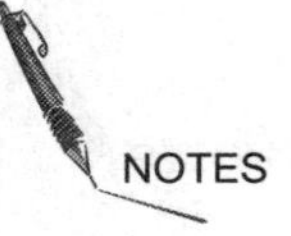

NOTES

(c) Some definitions also add a seventh stratum: **upper class,** consisting of the aristocracy (titled landowners) and the very wealthy (through ownership or investment). This stratum undoubtedly still exists in the UK, and this 1% of adult population is reckoned to own one quarter of the wealth of Britain!

The 2001 UK census used a new categorisation system, reflecting recent changes in the UK population. Chief among these is the increased role of women in the workplace.

New social class	Occupations	Example
1	Higher managerial and professional occupations	
1.1	Employers and managers in larger organisations	Bank managers, company directors
1.2	Higher professional	Doctors, lawyers
2	Lower managerial and professional occupations	Police officers
3	Intermediate occupations	Secretaries/PAs, clerical workers
4	Small employers and own-account workers	
5	Lower supervisory, craft and related occupations	Electricians
6	Semi-routine occupations	Drivers, hairdressers, bricklayers
7	Routine occupations	Car park attendants, cleaners

Figure 6.8: New social categorisation scheme

Activity 3 **(20 minutes)**

Why is social class of interest to the marketer? If you consider a number of your acquaintances, what differences in their life-styles and purchasing patterns can you account for by reference to their social class?

3.5 Social mobility

Definition

Social mobility is the tendency for individuals to move within the social hierarchy. Generally, such movement is associated with economic, educational or occupational success (upward mobility) or failure (downward mobilty).

Social mobility has several **implications for marketers**.

(a) People aspire to **upward mobility,** given a reasonable expectation of success, and will exhibit purchase and consumption patterns suitable to the class to which they aspire.

(b) The 'lower' classes will become a less significant proportion of the population (and therefore target market), as people move up out of them – assuming that the country's economy can support a widespread increase in per capita income.

3.6 The value of class as a segmentation variable

Consumer research has found some evidence that each of the social classes shares a number of **specific lifestyle factors** (attitudes, values, activities etc), and that these factors distinguish members of that class from members of all other classes. This theory has been used to determine the **appropriate marketing mix for each social stratum**, depending on researched buying preferences and habits. When banks, for example, have branded facilities for 'high net worths', they are targeting a class segment. 'Luxury' branded products and magazines catering for high-status readers are similarly positioned.

In particular, social class has been found to correlate with the following.

(a) **Tastes in clothing and fashion**
(b) **Home decoration**
(c) **Leisure activities**
(d) **Money management**

Such analyses must, however, be treated with caution in their use of 'social class' as a variable.

(a) Social class is not exactly or consistently **defined.**

(b) **Social mobility,** to the extent that a class group is defined, may make it difficult to use the concept in a meaningful way.

(c) Conventional gradings take into consideration the occupation of the head of the household, but with dual-income families, fluctuating family/household patterns, the mobility of labour and changes in employment circumstances (eg redundancy or insolvency), this may give a rather misleading picture.

FOR DISCUSSION

Class is a totally reliable indicator of purchasing behaviour.

4 FAMILY LIFE CYCLE

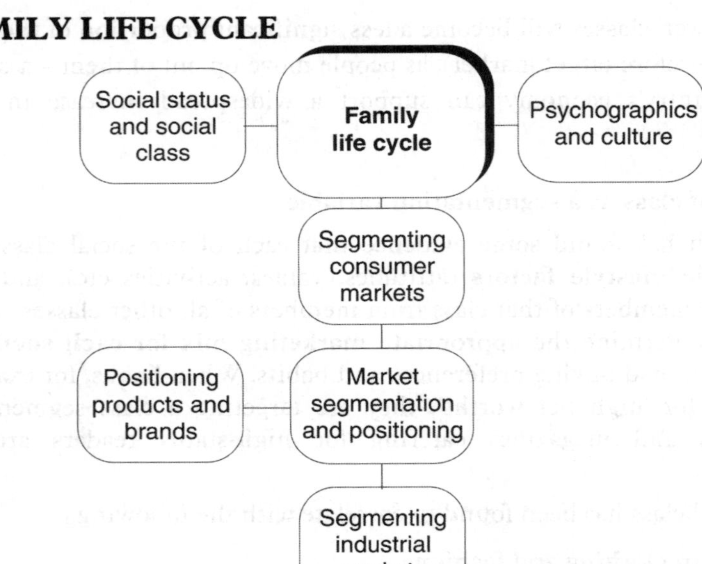

Family life cycle (FLC) is a method used by sociologists (and latterly consumer researchers) to classify family units in a way that is significant for social/consumer behaviour. It is frequently used as the basis of market segmentation, since it gives a composite picture of commonly-used demographic factors (marital status, family size, age, employment status) and their variation over time. You should be careful to distinguish in your mind between **life cycle analysis**, discussed here, and **life style analysis** (or psychographics), discussed in the next section, although both can be applied to the family in useful ways for marketing research and market segmentation.

Definition

> The concept of **family life cycle** is based on the idea that the structure, membership and lifestyle of a family change over time, with the age of the individual members. The family progresses through a number of common stages of development. Researchers note that the family's economic character — income, expenditure and consumption priorities — will also change.

Social variations and trends in the ages at which people marry (if they marry at all) and have children (if they have children) indicate that it would be misleading to relate life-cycle stage directly to age: specific age ranges are not normally determined, although ageing is inferred from the progressive stages.

There are various **models of the FLC** used by researchers, including different numbers of stages. One synthesis suggests nine stages, while a simpler synthesis suggests only five.

9-stage FLC		5-stage FLC	
I	Bachelorhood	I	Bachelorhood
II	Newly-married couples	II	Honeymooners
III	Full Nest I	III	Parenthood ('full nest')
IV	Full Nest II		
V	Full Nest III		
VI	Empty Nest I	IV	Post-parenthood ('empty nest')
VII	Empty Nest II		
VIII	Solitary survivor I	V	Dissolution
IX	Solitary survivor II		

Figure 6.9: Family Life Cycle

The profiles of the nine stages appear in Figure 6.10 below.

I	II	III	IV	V	VI	VII	VIII	IX
Bachelorhood	*Newly married*	*Full nest I*	*Full nest II*	*Full nest III*	*Empty nest I*	*Empty nest II*	*Solitary survivor*	*Solitary survivor(s) retired*
Young single people not living at home	Young, no children	Youngest child under six	Youngest child six or over	Older married couples, with dependent children	Older married couples, no children living with them, head of family still in labour force	Older married couples, no children living at home, head of family retired		
Few financial burdens Fashion/ Opinion leader Lead Recreation orientated Buy basic kitchen equipment, basic furniture cars, equipment for the mating game, holidays Experiment with patterns of personal financial management and control	Better off financially than they will be in the near future High levels of purchases of homes and consumer Durable goods Buy cars, fridges, cookers, life assurance, durable furniture, holidays Establish patterns of personal financial management and control	Home purchasing at peak Liquid assets/ savings low Dissatisfied with financial position and amount of money saved Reliant on credit cards, overdrafts etc Child dominated household Buy necessities washers, dryers, baby food and clothes, vitamins, toys books etc	Financial position better Some wives return to work Child dominated household Buy necessities ,foods, cleaning materials, clothes, bicycles, sports gear, music lessons, pianos , holidays etc	Financial position still better More wives work School and examination dominated household Some children get first jobs; others in further/ higher education Expenditure to support children's further/ higher education Buy new, more tasteful furniture, non-Necessary appliances, boats etc Holidays	Home ownership peak More satisfied with financial position and money saved Interest in travel, recreation, self education Make financial gifts and contributions Children gain qualifications; move to Stage 1 Buy luxuries home improvements eg fitted kitchens etc	Significant cut in income Keep home Buy medical appliances or medical care product which aid health, sleep and digestion Assist children Concern with level of savings and pension Some expenditure on	Income still adequate but likely to sell family home and purchase smaller accommodation Concern with level of savings and pension Some expenditure on hobbies and pastimes Worries about security and dependence	Significant in income Additional medical requirements Special needs for attention, affection, and security May seek sheltered accommodation Possible dependence on others for personal financial management and control

Figure 6.10: Profiles of Family Life Cycle stages

It is important to remember that the model of the family life cycle shown in the table displays the **classic route** from young single to older unmarried. In contemporary society, characterised by divorce and what may be the declining importance of marriage as an institution, this picture can vary.

There has therefore been some criticism of the traditional FLC model as a basis for market segmentation in recent years.

(a) It is modelled on the demographic patterns of industrialised western nations – and particularly America. This pattern may not be universally applicable.

(b) As noted above, while the FLC model was once typical of the overwhelming majority of American families, there are now important potential variations from that pattern.

(i) Childless couples	–	because of choice, career-oriented women and delayed marriage
(ii) Later marriages	–	because of greater career-orientation and non-marital relationships: likely to have fewer children
(iii) Later children	–	say in late 30s. Likely to have fewer children, but to stress 'quality of life'
(iv) Single parents	–	(especially mothers) because of divorce
(v) Fluctuating labour status	–	not just 'in labour' or 'retired', but redundancy, career change, dual-income etc
(vi) Extended parenting	–	young, single adults returning home while they establish careers/financial independence; divorced children returning to parents; elderly parents requiring care; newly-weds living with in-laws
(vii) Non-family households	–	unmarried (homosexual or heterosexual) couples
	–	divorced persons with no children
	–	single persons (mainly women, or older products of delay in first marriage)
	–	widowed persons (especially women, because of longer life-expectancy)

Therefore an alternative or modified FLC model is needed to take account of consumption variables.

(a) Spontaneous changes in brand preference when a household undergoes a change of status (divorce, redundancy, death of a spouse, change in membership of a non-family household)

(b) Different economic circumstances and extent of consumption planning in single-parent families; households where there is a redundancy; dual-income households

(c) Different buying and consumption roles to compensate/adjust in households where the woman works. Women can be segmented into at least four categories – each of which may represent a distinct market for goods and services:

- Stay-at-home homemaker
- Plan-to-work homemaker
- 'Just-a-job' working woman
- Career-orientated working woman

Activity 4 **(20 minutes)**

'The portrayal of non-traditional FLC stages in contemporary advertising of products and services is evidence that marketers are eager to expand their markets and make their products and services more relevant to varying family lifestyles.'

Identify examples of non-traditional FLC stages and circumstances in the advertising to which you are exposed.

5 PSYCHOGRAPHICS AND CULTURE

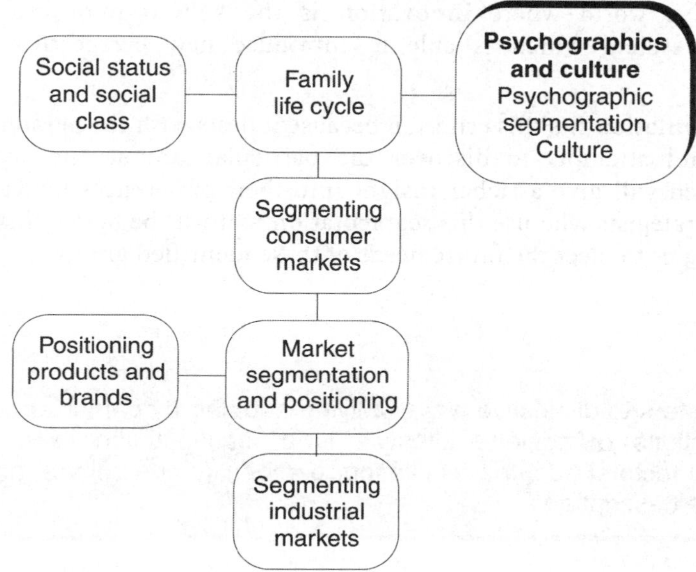

Definition

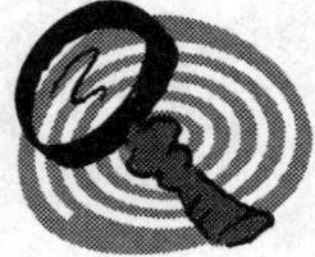

Psychographics is a form of consumer research which builds up a psychological profile of consumers in general, or users (or potential users) of a particular product. It is the main basis of psychological segmentation of a market, and appropriate product positioning.

Psychographics is also commonly referred to as:

(a) **Lifestyle analysis**

(b) **AIO analysis: Activities** (how consumers spend their time), **Interests** (or preferences) and **Opinions** (where they stand on product-related issues).

Psychographics is different from the following:

(a) **Demographics** consists of **quantitative data** about population characteristics like age, income, gender and location (as we have just seen). **Psychographics** tends to include **qualitative data** about motives, attitudes and values

(b) **Motivation research**. Psychographics includes qualitative factors, like motivation research, but the latter's findings are presented as quantified, statistical information in tabular format. They are also based on larger samples of the population reached through less intensive techniques like self-administered questionnaires and inventories.

5.1 Psychographic segmentation

Psychographics or lifestyle segmentation is a method which seeks to classify people according to their values, opinions, personality characteristics, interests and so on, and by its nature should be dynamic. The relevance of this concept is bound up in its ability to introduce various new dimensions to existing customer information, for example customers' disposition towards savings, investment and the use of credit, general attitude to money, leisure and other key influences.

In a competitive world where **innovation** is the key to improved organisational performance a system which is able to introduce new perspectives is worthy of investigation.

Lifestyle segmentation fits this criterion because it deals with the **person as opposed to the product** and attempts to discover the particular unique life style patterns of customers, which will give a richer insight into their preferences for various products and services. Strategists who use this segmentation tool will be better able to direct their marketing energies to meet the future needs of these identified groups.

Definition

Lifestyle refers to distinctive ways of living adopted by particular communities or sub-sections of society. Lifestyle is a manifestation of a number of behavioural factors, such as motivation, personality and culture, and depends on accurate description.

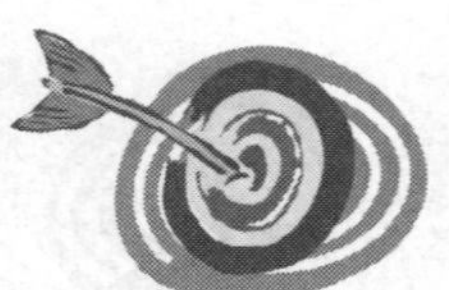

EXAMPLE: DUNNHUMBY: A LIFETIME OF LOYALTY?

Able to track the shopping habits of 16 million families through Tesco's Clubcard, loyalty scheme operator Dunnhumby is still one of the best examples of how data mining and analysis can be used to drive a retail business forward.

While some retailers crudely use data to try to increase sales, Tesco is able to deploy the insights generated within Dunnhumby to meet customer demands at every level.

Top-level lifestyle segmentation into one of six groups informs decisions on the grocer's strategy, such as the launch of new ranges at different price points. But the information is also used to decide the offers customers will receive down to an almost individual level, with 9 million variants of the quarterly Clubcard mailing distributed.

Dunnhumby director of strategy and futures Martin Hayward says: 'The focus has always been on satisfying customers. Tesco's mission is to earn the lifetime loyalty of its customers.'

Joanna Perry, retail-week.com, 20 November 2009

When the numbers of people following it are quantified, marketers can assign and target products and promotion upon this particular target lifestyle group. The implications of lifestyle for marketing, and the problems of definition involved, can perhaps best be illustrated by some examples.

One simple example generalises lifestyle in terms of four categories.

(a) **Upwardly mobile, ambitious**

People seek a better and more affluent lifestyle, principally through better paid and more interesting work, and a higher material standard of living. Persons with such a lifestyle will be prepared to try new products.

(b) **Traditional and sociable**

Compliance and conformity to group norms bring social approval and reassurance to the individual. Purchasing patterns will therefore be 'conformist'.

(c) **Security and status seeking**

'Safety' needs and 'ego-defensive' needs are stressed. This life-style links status, income and security. It encourages the purchase of strong and well known products and brands, and emphasises those products and services which confer status and make life as secure and predictable as possible. These would include insurance, membership of the AA or RAC etc. Products that are well established and familiar inspire more confidence than new products, which will be resisted.

(d) **Hedonistic preference**

The emphasis is on 'enjoying life now' and the immediate satisfaction of wants and needs. Little consideration is given to the future.

The **green movement** has become part of many life-style segments. Companies segment some clients according to whether they are 'pale' or 'dark' green in their attitude to the environment and therefore how significant environmentally friendly product attributes will be to the purchasing decision.

In a typical psychographic research study, an inventory is compiled, in which consumers are asked to react to a variety of statements – as individuals or as a family or household. They may be asked to react by degree of agreement (Do you strongly agree, agree, disagree or strongly disagree?) or by the importance they attach to a concept (is it very important, important, fairly important, unimportant?), or by the amount of time they spend on an activity or interest. Psychographic statements may be about general lifestyle or specific product categories, products or even brands: ideally the inventory would contain both.

Activity 5 **(20 minutes)**

Psychographic statements: Traveller's cheques

Individual/personal

Product specific	*General*
'Traveller's cheques are for people who are experienced travellers.'	'I think about my safety and security when planning a trip.'
'I almost always keep some traveller's cheques in my wallet.'	'I use a seat belt even when going to the local store for milk.'
'We wouldn't even go on an overnight trip without traveller's cheques.'	'When we go on holiday, our family is always shopping.'
'We really appreciate the peace of mind that traveller's cheques provide.'	'We use the hotel safe to store our valuables when away on a family trip.'

Family/household

What are the implications for a marketer of traveller's cheques of these statements?

Activity 6 **(15 minutes)**

Suppose you were considering the responses to the following questionnaire.

'Time spent' inventory

Please tick the box that best indicates how often you have engaged in the activity during the past 12 months.

	0 times	*1-4 times*	*5-9 times*	*10+ times*
Went to a library				
Went abroad on holiday				
Went to a museum				
Went to the cinema				
Watched television				

If 60% of your sample went to the cinema between one and four times in one year, but 100% watched TV 10+ times, where would you advertise your product?

5.2 Culture

Knowledge of the shared values, beliefs and artefacts of a society are clearly of value to marketers, who can **adapt** their products and appeals accordingly, and be fairly sure of a sizeable market. Marketers can also participate in the teaching process that creates culture, since mass media advertising is an important agent by which cultural meanings are attached to products, people and situations.

Culture is deeply embedded in everyday behaviour, but is susceptible to measurement to some extent.

(a) **Attitude measurement techniques**

(b) **Projective techniques**, depth interviews and focus group sessions

(c) **Content analysis** – examining the content of the verbal, written and pictorial communications of a society: what kind of people are shown in advertisements, what criteria are used in design (is the society verbal or non-verbal? does it favour simplicity or complexity?), what 'themes' and images recur etc;

(d) **Observation** of a sample of the population by trained anthropological researchers, in the field (eg in store), followed by inference of the underlying reasons for the observed behaviour;

(e) **Surveys** or 'value inventories', measuring personal values.

Cultural market segmentation tends to stress specific, widely-held cultural values with which the majority of consumers are expected to identify. Some products may have an appeal specific to a particular culture.

6 SEGMENTING INDUSTRIAL MARKETS

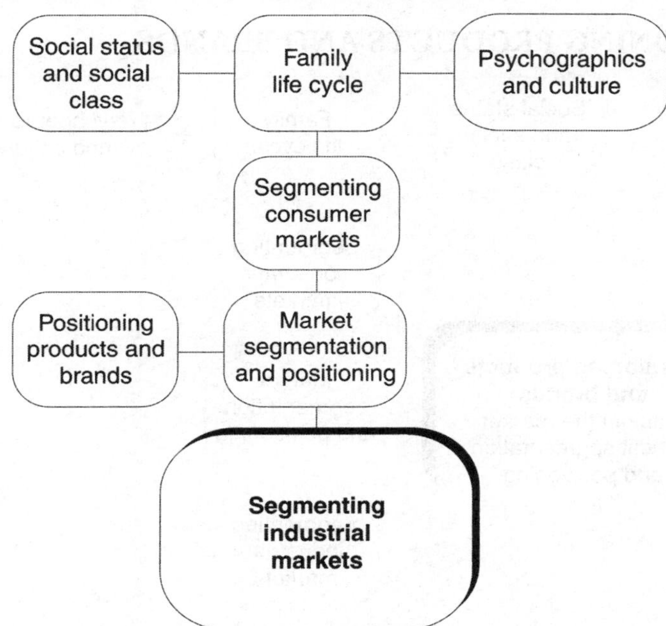

Although industrial markets are usually smaller and more easily identified than consumer markets, segmentation can still be worthwhile, allowing a modified marketing strategy to be targeted at specified groups within the total market.

A number of methods for **segmenting the industrial market** exist. Improved databases provide additional intelligence information allowing much tighter targeting of industrial customers.

(a) **By location**

Already covered under consumer segmentation, but many business sectors are concentrated in particular locations, for example steel in Sheffield, computer companies along the M4 corridor etc.

(b) **Customer size**

The size of a company either by turnover or employee numbers can give a broad indication of their needs for certain products, eg management training services.

(c) **Usage rates**

Customers can be segmented as heavy, medium or light users; this is most relevant in raw material and parts markets and the market for some industrial services, for example telecommunications and travel.

(d) **Industry classification (Standard Industry Classification (SIC))**

This classification indicates the nature of the business.

(e) **Product use**

Different products may be used in different forms or ways, for example an industrial organisation may buy a fleet of cars for use by its sales force, or to hire out to the public as the basis for its service. Different uses are likely to be associated with different needs.

7 POSITIONING PRODUCTS AND BRANDS

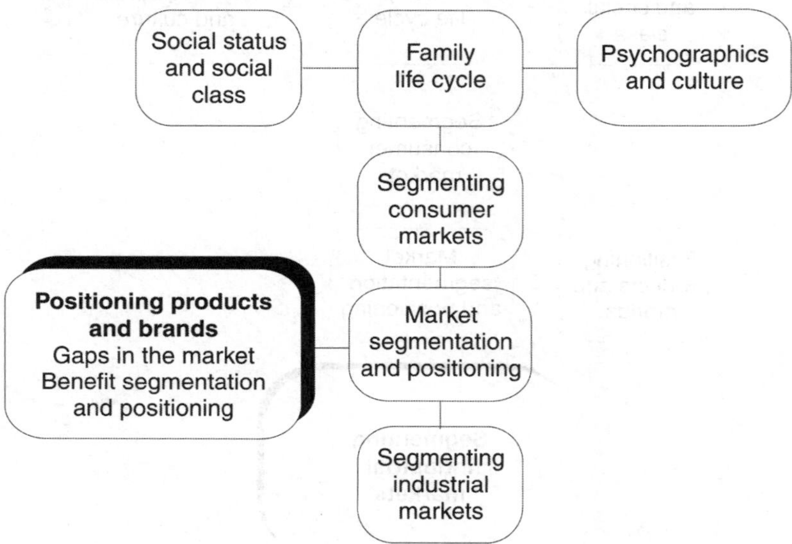

Definition

Positioning is the act of designing the company's offer and image so that it offers a distinct and valued place in the target customer's mind.

Brands can be **positioned** in relation to competitive brands on **product maps** in which relative positions are defined in terms of how buyers perceive key characteristics.

A basic **perceptual map** plots brands in perceived price and perceived quality terms.

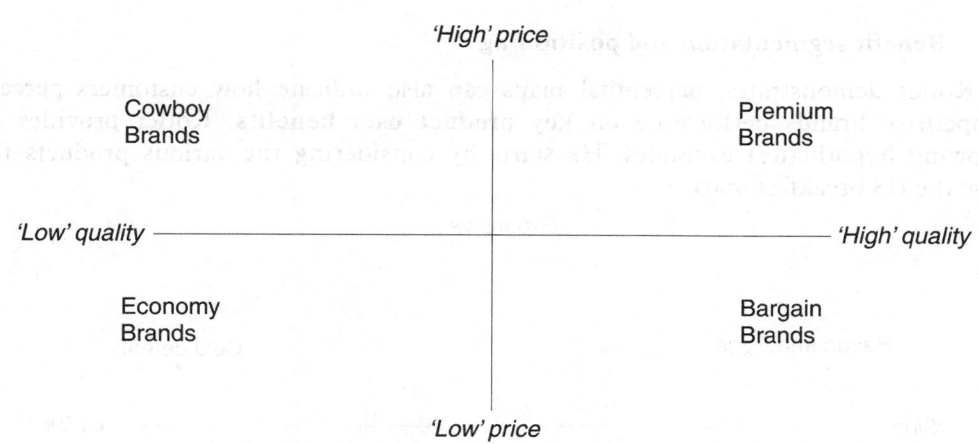

Figure 6.11: A perceptual map

Price and quality are clearly important elements in every marketing mix, but, in the customer's opinion, they cannot be considered independent variables. A 'high' price will almost always be associated with high quality and equally, low price with low quality. Thus, while everybody would like to buy a bargain brand, there is a problem to overcome. Will customers accept that a high quality product can be offered at a low price?

Public concern about such **promotional pricing** has resulted in the introduction of restrictions on the use of these techniques. Promotions have to be part of a genuine 'sale', and stores must provide evidence of this fact.

7.1 Gaps in the market

Market research into consumer perceptions can determine how customers locate competitive brands on a matrix.

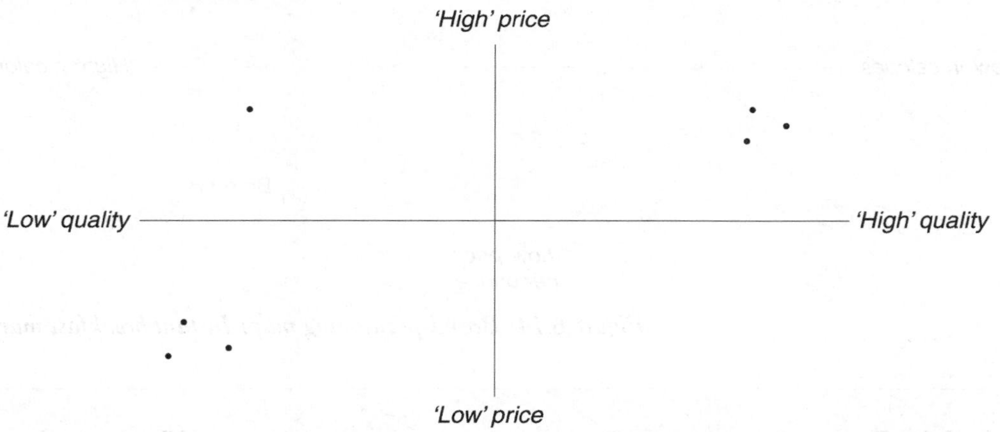

Figure 6.12: Restaurants in Anytown

The hypothetical model above shows a gap in the market for a moderately priced, reasonable quality eating place. This is evident between clusters in the high price/high quality and the low price/low quality segments.

It would be wise to think before acting on this assumption. Why does the gap exist? Is it that no entrepreneurial restaurateur has noticed the opportunity? Or is it that, while there is sufficient demand for gourmet eating and cheap cafes, there are insufficient customers to justify a restaurant in the middle range segment?

7.2 Benefit segmentation and positioning

As Kotler demonstrates, perceptual maps can also indicate how customers perceive competitive brands performing on **key product user benefits**. Kotler provides the following hypothetical examples. He starts by considering the various products that serve the US breakfast market.

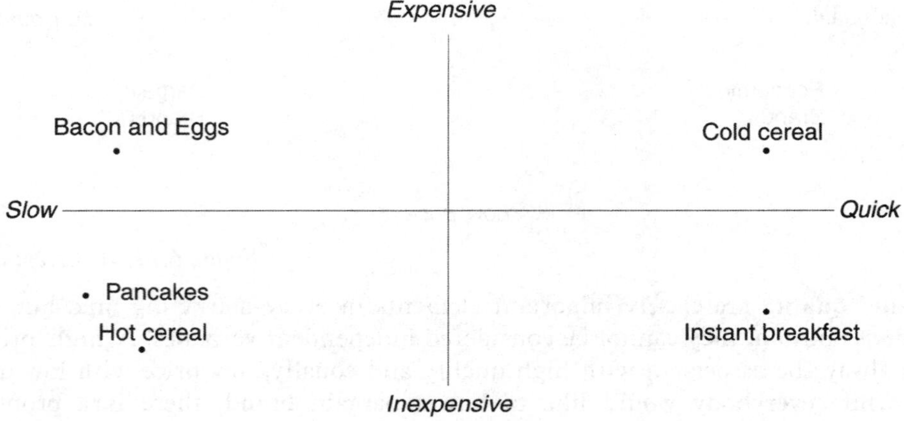

Figure 6.13: Product-positioning map: Breakfast market

A producer might be interested, for example, in entering the instant breakfast market. This is a sub-section of the breakfast market as a whole. It is necessary to plot the position of the various instant breakfast brands.

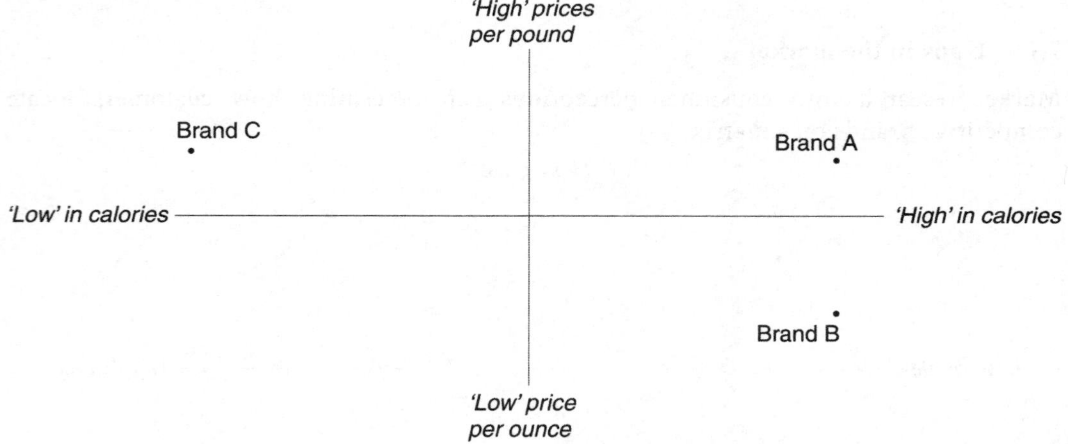

Figure 6.14: Brand-positioning map: Instant breakfast market

Activity 7 **(15 minutes)**

Figure 6.14 above indicates that there is an apparent gap. What type of brand would fill this gap? What is the major consideration after identifying the gap?

Segmentation can be used in the context of a marketing strategy in which positioning of products and re-positioning of a brand in the market plays a crucial part. Also very significant is customer buying behaviour. We addressed the critical area of analysing, understanding and responding to customer behaviour in Chapter 5.

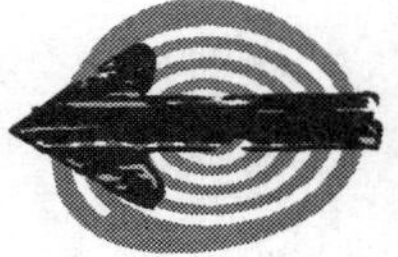

Definition

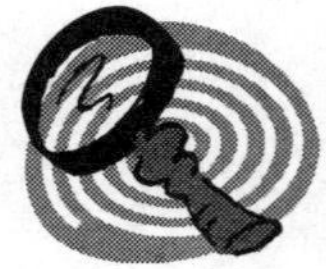

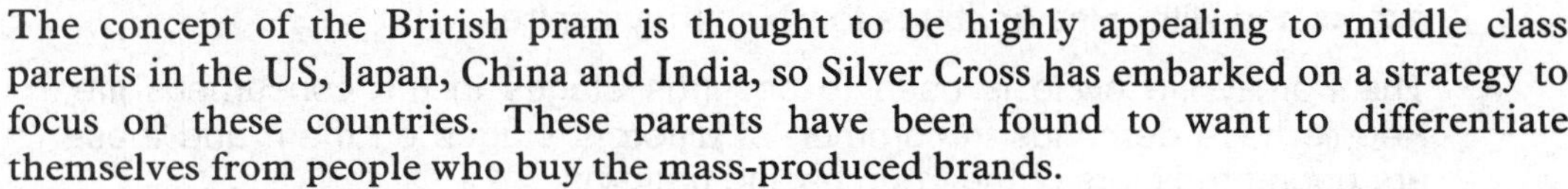

Re-positioning is the strategy of changing the customers' perception of a company or brand by reference to quality and/or price in order to take advantage of a market preference.

EXAMPLE

The pram manufacturer Silver Cross has been considered a heritage brand within the UK but from the mid 1990s began to be perceived as old-fashioned as other manufacturers introduced 'travel systems' which feature more compact and convenient pushchair, carrycot and car seat packages. Following several changes in ownership, the company is currently undergoing a re-branding exercise.

The concept of the British pram is thought to be highly appealing to middle class parents in the US, Japan, China and India, so Silver Cross has embarked on a strategy to focus on these countries. These parents have been found to want to differentiate themselves from people who buy the mass-produced brands.

The campaign has also actively sought high profile celebrity endorsement. Celebrities spotted pushing Silver Cross prams include Liz Hurley, Angelina Jolie and Maggie Gyllenhaal.

Finally, to supplement the Heritage range of traditional '*perambulators*', Silver Cross launched a new range of travel systems in 2007 to revitalise the brand and appeal to parents searching for a more modern Silver Cross. The product range launch was timed to coincide with an improved website to appeal to both consumers and retailer users.

Adapted from *The Sunday Times*, October 22 2006

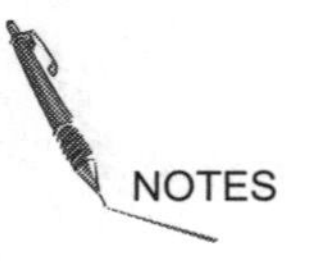

Chapter roundup

- Segmentation groups customers according to identifiable characteristics relevant to their purchasing behaviour.
- The tests for segmentation effectiveness are: measurable, accessible and substantial.
- Demographics is the discipline which describes the population. It enables the analysis of the population in terms of the characteristics which describe it such as age, gender, occupation, educational background etc.
- Geo-demographics combines demographic factors with geographical factors such as location of residence or business either locally (such as neighbourhoods by reference to post codes) globally (such as countries).
- Roles are the expectations which other people have for an individual in relation to his or her situation. They are important to marketers because people may buy products on account of the 'role signs' they display. A young man may buy a pipe because he believes that it makes him look more mature. Some people wear heavy-framed spectacles because they believe that others may consider them to be more serious or studious.
- Status, implying power and authority, is strongly associated with certain products such as motor cars. This association is useful to establish 'aspirational' products: those which people want because they are associated with roles or status to which they aspire.
- The Family life cycle is used to describe stages in the consumer's life. People have demands in common at different stages on them and these are good predictors of their purchasing patterns.
- Socio-economic groups define people by reference to their occupations. Occupation is a good indicator of earnings and educational background and so is good predictor of purchasing patterns. The Joint Industry Council on Newspaper Advertising Research (JICNAR) model is most often used in this regard.
- Biographics (facts about people such as age), behavioural factors (what people do, such as *when* they go shopping) and psychographics (the way people feel, their attitudes, interests and opinions) are three major variables of consumer segmentation.
- Psychographics are becoming more important, as is seen by models dealing with lifestyle.
- Cultural variables are becoming important because of the multi-racial and multi-cultural nature of our society and the trend to internationalisation and globalisation of firms and their markets.
- Segmentation is just as applicable to industrial markets as it is to consumer markets.
- Positioning is a way of indicating to customers how they should perceive a product in relation to other products on the market by reference to price, quality and status.

Quick quiz

1 What is market segmentation?

2 What are the main benefits of market segmentation to marketers?

3 Give an example of a geo-demographics model.

4 How are social roles shaped?

5 What is the impact of status-consciousness on marketing?

6 What demographic factors determine social class?

7 What are the relevant factors within socio-economic groups that aid segmentation?

8 What is social mobility? Give an example of how this has been in evidence in modern society.

9 How does social class translate into buying preferences?

10 What is meant by the Family Life Cycle?

11 What does 'psychographics' mean?

12 Why is psychographics important to marketers?

13 Give an example of the influence of an 'opinion' in determining group purchase behaviour.

14 What cultural factors may be used as segmentation variables?

15 Why are cross-cultural factors becoming more important to marketers?

16 What are the main components of the psychographic variables?

17 Describe some ways of segmenting industrial markets.

Answers to Quick quiz

1 The division of a market into a number of sub-sets by reference to one or more characteristics.

2 The ability to focus marketing activity and resources more effectively.

3 The ACORN model.

4 The expectations of others and the customs and informal rules of society.

5 It creates a market for aspirational products.

6 Family background, education, occupation.

7 Shared values, attitudes, behaviour.

8 The tendency for people to move from one classification to another by educational, occupational or marital changes. In the 1980's there was the phenomenon of the Young, Upwardly-mobile, Professional (YUPpies) who gave their stamp to a number of products.

9 By the process of social class transfer and aspirational products.

10 A model which characterises the stages most people go through in their life.

11 Describing individuals by reference to their feelings, attitudes, interests and opinions.

12 It provides an extra dimension of understanding customers' preferences for products and their likely responses to promotional messages.

13 The boycotting of South African products during the period of apartheid.

14 Language, beliefs and the norms of behaviour. There are also different implications of the demographic variables such as age and gender to consider.

15 Because of the multi-cultural development of societies and the internationalisation and globalisation of firms and their markets.

16 Beliefs, attitudes, interests and opinions.

17 By industry classification, size, turnover, number of employees, sector, business form, ownership, geographical location, etc.

Answers to Activities

1 The variables could be classified as trade and collector customers: in the former group, specialist 'Great Britain' dealers may be important. Collectors would be classified as 'serious'; geographically they could be world wide; they would need to be wealthy. They would probably be measurable by reference to previous purchases, accessible by mailing lists and/or the serious special interest magazines, substantiated by noting previous demand multiplied by the unit price of the stamps.

2 Such research is a generalisation which is usually derived from a large sample, perhaps over a long time scale. The chances are, if you asked enough people you would get some level of agreement. Any variance would possibly be because the above table has been based on a very large number which you would not be in a position to match. There is also another factor. There are a number of new brands which are not covered in the table. The tendency to buy 'own brands' has grown, and it is possibly independent of the variables used here.

3 There are many limitations to the usefulness to the marketer of social class per se. However, it is possible to make certain inferences from the shared values, attitudes, and interests of one class as distinct from another. Research has been able to relate certain consumer behaviour to class. But it is by no means absolutely certain when considering the individual. Your own research will probably confirm this. Social class must be used as a variable with caution.

Many students feel uncomfortable with this concept. It must be clear that marketers are not interested in class distinction as a value judgement. They are only interested in differentiating on the basis of how people behave in terms of purchasing.

4 The Nescafé Gold Blend coffee 'romances' are a good example. Financial services companies continue to focus their pension fund advertisements on early retirees.

5 Peace of mind and security are major features of these statements. These are strong elements in Barclaycard promotions. Also the role model of the experienced traveller could be usefully exploited

6 It rather depends on the product and the target segment. You may like to consider the difference between the impact of advertising in the two environments and the length of the advertisements. In the cinema they tend to be longer versions of the TV tapes. You may, of course, point out a flaw in the inventory. It does not make clear that 'watched TV' means 'watched commercials'. The respondents may ignore ads or watch the BBC channels for preference. Also, the response scales (0–10+) do not have the same significance for each activity. For example, to say that you watched TV 10+ times a year would not necessarily mean you could be classed as a regular TV watcher.

7 The analysis indicates a gap for a modestly priced slimmers' brand. You would have to establish that the anticipated demand for the product is sufficient for it to be a venture which would enable the company to meet is financial and other corporate goals.

In terms of positioning, you would probably want to consider the main points of the current competitive brand offerings. These are likely to be the brand identity, price and quality image of the brand leaders. Your launch programme has to compare your product in some way favourably with what is currently on offer. If you are up against, say, a Cadbury product as market leader with a long established and respected brand name, there is little point in just saying that you are the best! It could take some time before anybody would really believe you. You could say something positive about being new: high-technology; innovation; modern; imaginative. Pricing, provided your cost levels have been controlled, could be a significant differentiation but you would have to careful not to invade any positive quality message which you would wish to convey.

Targeting would follow from the positioning statement. If you go for the 'fresh-faced, new kid on the block' approach, you may wish to target the young market.

NOTES

Part C

The Extended Marketing Mix

Chapter 7 : PRODUCT

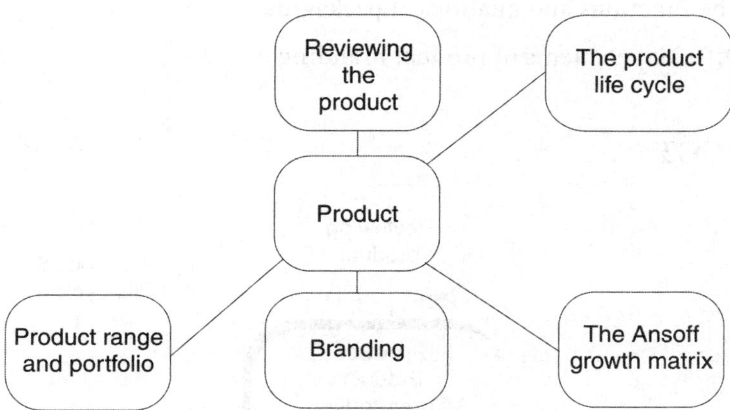

Introduction

This Chapter begins our analysis of the **components of the marketing mix**. It concludes in Chapter 13 where we talk about selling and direct marketing. We could consider the four Ps in any order (depending on the type of business), but we start with the **product**. This chapter begins by considering the **different types** of product that are made and gives an overview of possible ways of **sending products** out into markets.

In approaching the learning objectives, you should understand that it is more than the physical entity that we may take off the supermarket shelves. In marketing terms we see the product as **a package of attributes** which, together, constitute a uniquely relevant set of benefits to the customer. It is benefits which we must focus on. It is not the 'stainless steel' characteristic of a piece of equipment which the customer is interested in but the fact that it will not rust and therefore will not require replacing after a short period.

The **product life cycle** concept is useful for monitoring the progress of a product. We describe and criticise it in depth here.

Product portfolio planning looks at **product ranges** and how they can be managed. Important for allocating resources are product-market matrices such as the **BCG matrix**.

Innovation is vital: organisations must generate new products in order to survive in the long term. We look at where ideas come from, how new products are developed and tested, and how they gain a hold on the market.

Finally, brands are briefly introduced (there is more on branding in the chapter on promotion) and the use that is made of packaging is described.

The marketing mix of the 4Ps has been extended to 7Ps. We cover the 4Ps in Chapters 7 to 13. The extended marketing mix for services is covered in Chapter 15.

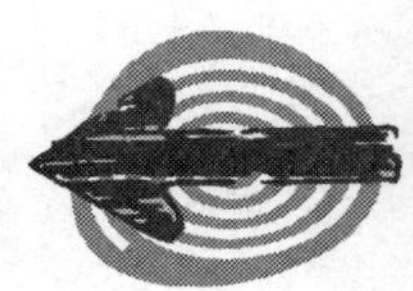

Your objectives

In this chapter you will learn about the following.

(a) What types of product there are and how they may be classified

(b) The validity of the product life cycle concept

(c) How a business manages its portfolio of products

(d) The importance of new products and how new products are developed

(e) The functions and qualities of packaging

(f) Different elements of product branding

1 PRODUCT

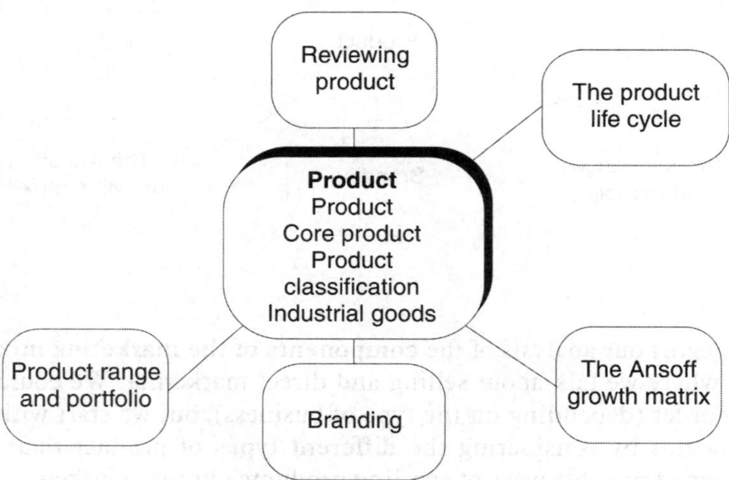

1.1 Product

It is mainly through the product that the customer or consumer experiences the output of all the activities of the firm. The customer is able to test the claims of the promotional promises and to respond accordingly. It is the time when the disposition to re-purchase, so much sought after by the supplier, begins to form. The cycle of goodwill has its pivot in the product.

The firm can only survive if it is consistently producing attractive and satisfying products that are based on the **requirements of the market** and provide **value**. They must keep up with the times in connection with the customer's needs and wants and the way they are fulfilled by reference to style, design, technology and materials. They must be aware of the **alternatives and substitutes** that constitute competitive offerings and respond to swings in **public opinion and behaviour** that may be nothing to do with the product itself but, often, more to do with political, economic and social issues.

Those unfamiliar with marketing probably think of a 'product' as a physical object. However, in marketing the term must be understood in a broader sense.

Definition

> A **product** is something that satisfies a set of wants that customers have. When you buy a set of wine glasses, for example, you are buying them because you want to drink wine and you prefer not to do so straight from the bottle. You may also want to impress your dinner guests with your taste, and choose to do so by possessing a particularly fine set of wine glasses.

A product may be said to satisfy needs by possessing the following attributes.

(a) **Tangible attributes**

- Availability and delivery
- Performance
- Price
- Design

(b) **Intangible attributes**

- Image
- Perceived value

These features are interlinked. A product has a tangible price, but for your money you obtain the **value** that you perceive the product to have. You may get satisfaction from paying a very high price for your wine glasses, because this says something about your status in life.

FOR DISCUSSION

People do not buy products, they buy what products do for them.

'When people buy drills, they want holes'. (Source unknown)

Philip Kotler says 'the product is a bundle of physical, service and symbolic particulars designed to deliver satisfactions'.

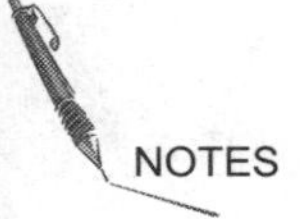

NOTES

1.2 Core product

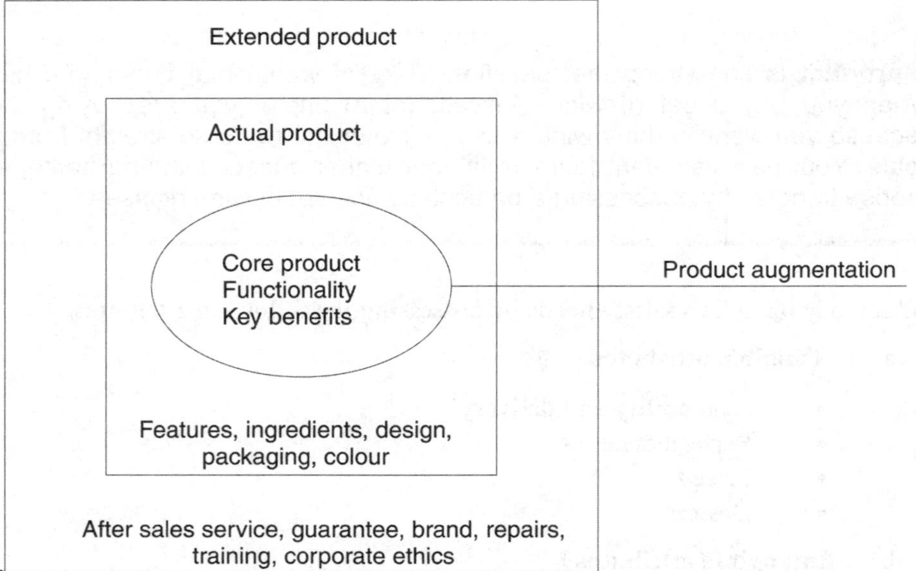

Figure 7.1: The total product

The concept of a 'total product' is built up from various layers. The core product is associated with what the product is designed to do. The actual product represents the improvements made to the basic core and these generally add different benefits provided by the product. The extended product are the additional elements which build trust and the reputation associated with the product.

Think about your brand of toothbrush as you follow this example. Colgate manufacture a wide range of different toothbrushes including children's character versions and adult manual and battery operated brushes. Toothbrushes generally are designed simply to clean teeth, the consumer need is to ensure that they maintain oral health and hygiene. To the consumer the benefits of this are obvious with very few individuals actually wanting to lose their teeth or gain a reputation for having bad breath! In consumer behavioural terms there is therefore a multitude of purchase risks associated with buying a relatively inexpensive everyday product. The reason Colgate produce a range of toothbrushes is that they are building a range of alternative 'total products' to meet the needs of different target consumers. The consumers who want to minimise their risk of bad breath would be most likely to choose the Colgate 360° because of the added features such as a tongue scrapper, raised, cupped and rounded bristles at different points in the brush head. Those consumers with sensitive teeth would opt for the Colgate sensitive version due to the product features associated with being gentle to the teeth and gums.

If you think about a basic complementary toothbrush you may have been given at a hotel or on an airplane, they generally are a plain, straight piece of plastic with hard and straight nylon bristles. This product will help you to clean your teeth but it is generally accepted that as they are designed for emergency uses to be used a couple of times and then disposed with. Essentially it is a 'core product'.

If you now think of a slightly upgraded version of a toothbrush, perhaps a retailer own brand basic version which is coloured, and has an angled neck and possibly rounded bristles. This toothbrush has distinct advantages because the colour makes it more aesthetically pleasing and additional features of the angled handle would mean that it is more comfortable to use and easier to reach back teeth. This product is 'augmented' by the additional features and represents the 'actual product'.

Next think of a premium brand of toothbrush such as those in the Colgate range. The brand is recognised as highly credible by consumers and is one of the key players in the market. The brand is synonymous with professionalism due to years of work by Colgate-Palmolive in ensuring the endorsement of the brand by dental practitioners, well designed and informative packaging, promotional activity, in-store presence and the use of guarantees, an educationally based website and customer information help-lines. The contribution of all these augmented elements represents the 'extended product' and benefits the consumers by providing confidence in the product they have purchased.

Definition

> **Augmentation:** the building up of benefits on the core product to increase the attractiveness and satisfaction factors for the consumer.

Each 'improvement' to the core product adds value. Such additions enable us to keep up to date with our competitors, or may enable us to differentiate the product in some way from competing products.

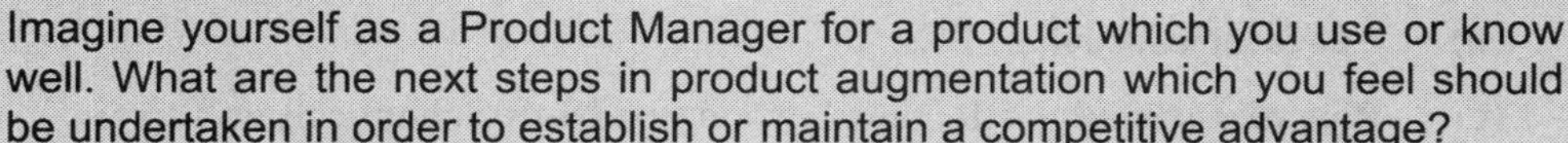

> **Activity 1** **(15 minutes)**
>
> Imagine yourself as a Product Manager for a product which you use or know well. What are the next steps in product augmentation which you feel should be undertaken in order to establish or maintain a competitive advantage?

Augmentation is part of a larger process which is called **product differentiation**. Making products different works for the marketer in two ways. On the one hand, it enables the **positioning and targeting** of products within market segments. On the other, it adds to the **competitive advantage** of the supplier. Taking a toothpaste example, the addition of an anti-plaque element makes the product more attractive to customers referred to in some models as 'the worrier' segment, which is willing to pay more for the extra security of dealing with the problems of plaque. The first manufacturer to add the anti-plaque element has, for a short time anyway, the advantage over competition. It is not long, of course, before every toothpaste contains the feature and the innovative producer will seek to extend the offering to include some other differentiator such as, in the example, a new kind of dispensing system. This may be attractive to a particular segment who is particular responsive to gadgets. Note that this does not change the efficacy of the toothpaste but it adds to the package of attributes in the offering to which we referred earlier.

1.3 Product classification: consumer goods

You have probably often heard the term **consumer goods**. It is used to distinguish goods that are sold directly to the person who will ultimately use them from goods that are sold to people who will use them to make other products. The latter are known as **industrial goods**.

Consumer goods may be classified as follows.

(a) **Convenience goods**. The weekly groceries are a typical example. There is a further distinction between staple goods like bread and potatoes, and impulse buys, like the unplanned bar of chocolate that you find at the supermarket checkout. For marketing purposes, brand awareness is extremely important in this sector. Advertising tries to make sure that when people put beans on their list they have in mind, for example, Heinz beans.

(b) **Shopping goods**. These are the more durable items that you buy, like furniture or washing machines. This sort of purchase is usually only made after a good deal of advance planning and shopping around.

(c) **Speciality goods**. These are items like jewellery or the more expensive items of clothing.

(d) **Unsought goods**. These are goods that you did not realise you needed! Typical examples would be the sort of items that are found in catalogues that arrive in the post.

1.4 Industrial goods

These may be classified as follows.

(a) **Installations,** for example, major items of plant and machinery such as a factory assembly line.

(b) **Accessories,** such as PCs.

(c) **Raw materials:** plastic, metal, wood, foodstuffs, chemicals and so on.

(d) **Components,** for example, the headlights in Ford cars or the Intel microchip in most PCs.

(e) **Supplies:** office stationery, cleaning materials and the like.

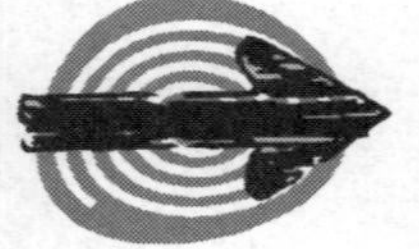

Products is a generic term and can, in many cases, include services for the practical purpose of marketing. However, there are some very specific aspects of service marketing which present particular marketing problems. Generally, from now on, we shall use the term products to cover both products and services unless there is a good reason for being specific. We look at services marketing specifically in Chapter 15.

2 REVIEWING THE PRODUCT

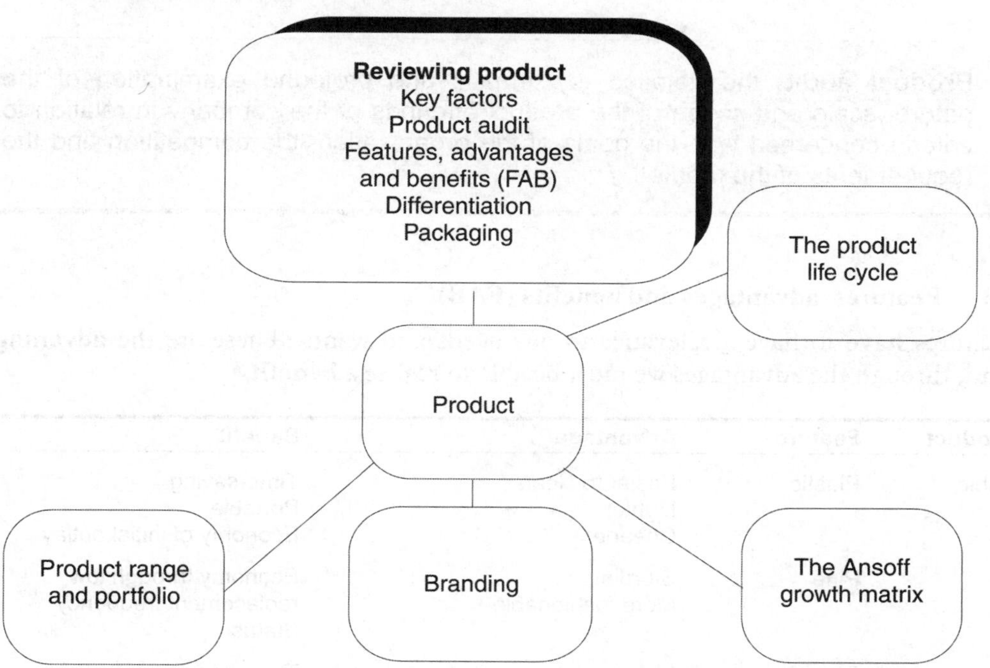

2.1 Key factors for consideration

The following constitute the main issues which concern the marketing manager's options in order to achieve the optimum offering to customers. We now consider the **product mix** within the marketing mix.

Product Mix

Range

Segmentation and positioning

Features, advantages and benefits (FAB)

Differentiation; – unfulfilled preferences

Branding

Packaging

Value

Product life cycle (PLC)

Portfolio analysis; (Boston Consulting Group Matrix)

Directional Policy Matrix (Ansoff)

Research and Development

New product development

Figure 7.2: The product mix key factors

2.2 The product audit

The marketer can use the above list of key factors to design the product audit.

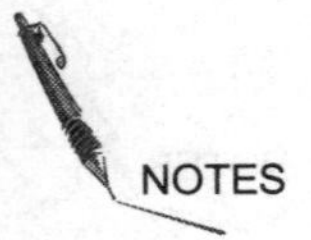

NOTES

Definition

Product audit: the detailed, systematic and profound examination of the nature, scale and scope of the product offerings of the company in relation to criteria concerned with the goals of the organisation, the competition and the requirements of the market.

2.3 Features, advantages and benefits (FAB)

Features **have** to have a relevance to our needs and wants. These are the **advantages**. And, through the advantages we must be able to realise a **benefit**.

Product	Feature	Advantage	Benefit
Table	Plastic	Easier to clean Lighter Cheaper	Time-saving Portable Economy of initial outlay
	Pine	Sturdier More fashionable	Economy through low replacement frequency Status
	Steel	More resistant to stains Will carry heavier weights	Time-saving Low replacement maintenance costs

Figure 7.3: Features, advantages and benefits (FAB) schedule

Clearly, this is a simplified examination of the product but it does illustrate the principle. In terms of the usefulness of the principle to the marketer, there is no real need to tell the market that plastic surfaces are easy to clean but it could be emphasised by the supplier that this advantage continues to deliver the time-saving benefit in an age when time is becoming a more and more precious commodity.

Notice that the advantage statements always contain a **comparative,** that is: fast; faster (comparative); fastest (superlative).

Easier

Lighter

Cheaper

Sturdier

More fashionable

More resistant

Heavier

Of course, this implies that it is being compared with something, another product. This is what enables the potential customer to construct a **value scheme** by which to judge the way that the benefits will help them.

Promotional messages should not dwell on the features of the product but should concentrate on the advantages so as to leave the potential customer in no doubt about what the benefits are.

Better for Your Health

Longer Lasting Flavour

More Miles per Gallon

Statements of advantage should be delivered to the customer clearly communicating what benefits the features deliver.

Activity 2 **(15 minutes)**

Choose a product with which you are familiar, or one that otherwise interests you and construct a FAB schedule for it.

Activity 3 **(20 minutes)**

Think of some products that have been superseded in your memory and construct an FAB chart for them and products which have ousted them.

2.4 Differentiation

Definition

Differentiation: the distinctiveness in the product or service being offered as perceived by the market by reference to any aspect of the marketing mix.

The attractiveness of difference is clear in many aspects of the market. Customers may like to have different products to those owned by their peers for a number of reasons: high fashion thrives on this. On the other hand uniformity appears to be the attraction in many teenage markets.

2.5 Packaging

Packaging has five functions.

(a) **Protection** of contents

(b) **Distribution**, helping to transfer products

(c) **Selling,** as the design and labelling serving promotional objectives

(d) **User convenience,** as an aid to use, storage and carrying, such as aerosol cans and handy packs

(e) To conform to **government regulations** especially on hygiene or content

Remember that goods are usually packaged in more than one form. Consumer goods might be packaged for sale to individual customers, but delivered to resellers in cartons or some similar bulk package.

FOR DISCUSSION

Packaging puts the price up unnecessarily.

Packaging must appeal not only to consumers, but also to **resellers.** A reseller wants a package design that will help to sell the product, but also one which minimises the likelihood of **breakage,** or which extends the product's **shelf life,** or makes more **economic use of shelf space.**

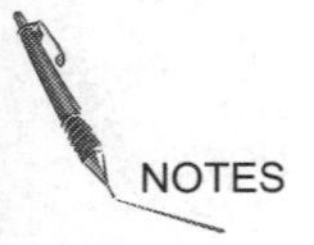

EXAMPLE: PACKAGING

In the mid-1960s, Heinz held a 95% share of the baby foods market in the UK, selling their food in tins. Gerber then entered the market and secured a wide distribution network, but needed a unique selling point for consumers. The USP they decided upon was glass jars instead of tins, in the belief that mothers would consider them to be more hygienic. This campaign was successful and Gerber gained a 10% share of the baby foods market (even though Heinz countered with their own range of foods in glass jars).

Many new products are actually developed because of new packaging capability for example squirty cream, pre-packed lunch kits and spray cooking oils. The core product had already existed but the development of the packaging enabled an entirely new use for the product.

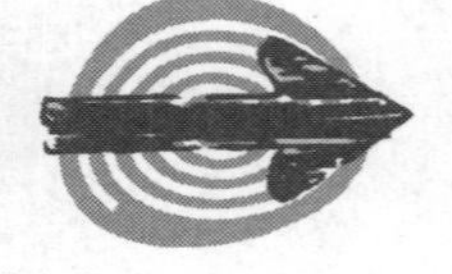

We shall now examine some very important frameworks where the product is a critical focus for marketing managers in creating their strategic plans.

3 THE PRODUCT LIFE CYCLE (PLC)

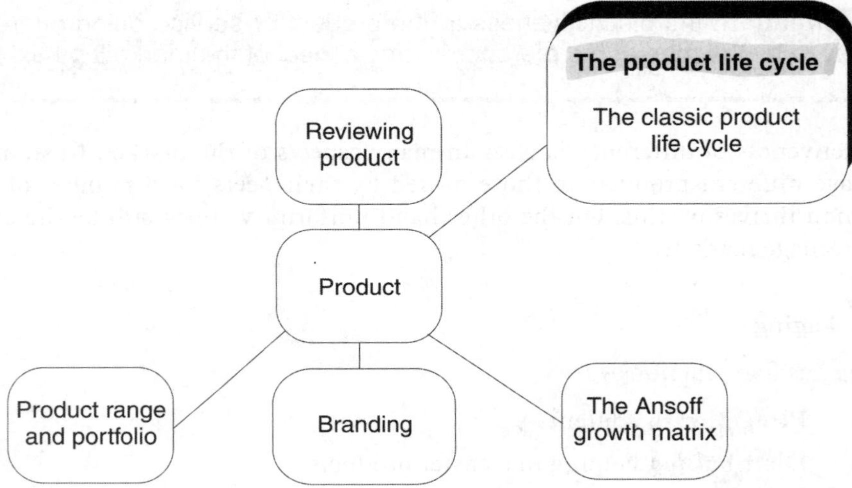

This concept is drawn from life-sciences. It asserts that products are born (or **introduced**), grow to reach **maturity** and then enter old age and **decline**.

3.1 The classic product life cycle

The **profitability** and **sales position** of a product can be expected to change over time. The product life cycle is an attempt to recognise distinct stages in a product's sales history. Here is the classic representation of the product life cycle.

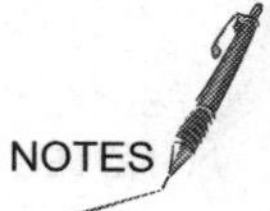

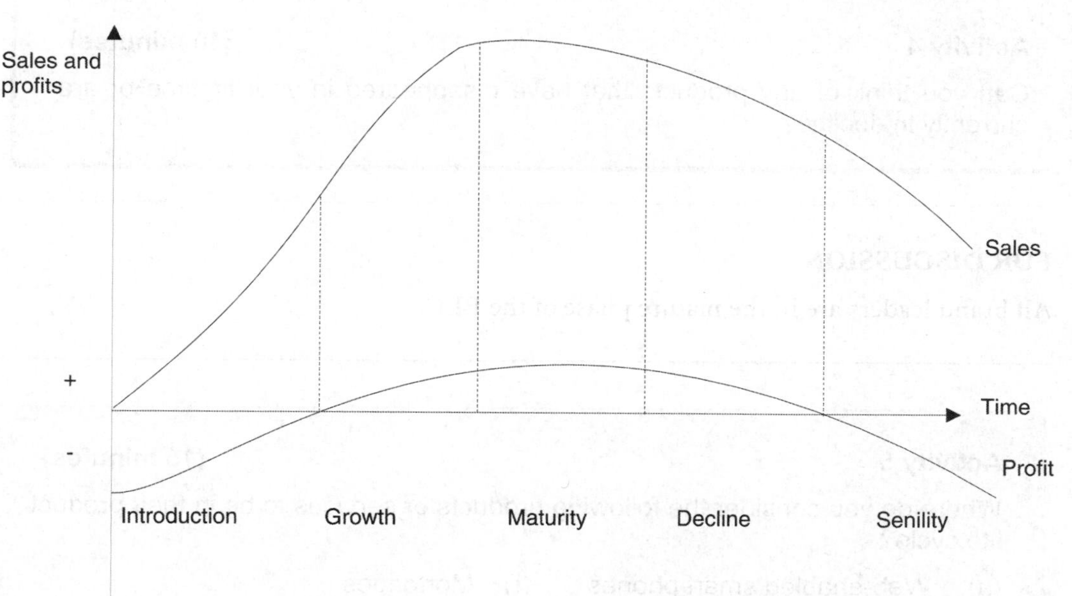

Figure 7.4: The product life cycle

Introduction

A new product takes time to find **acceptance** by would-be purchasers and there is a slow growth in sales. Only a few firms sell the product; **unit costs are high** because of low output; there may be early teething troubles with production technology and **prices may be high** to try to cover production costs and sales promotion expenditure. For example, pocket calculators, video cassette recorders and mobile telephones were all very expensive when launched. The product, for the time being, is a **loss maker**.

Growth

If the new product gains market acceptance, sales will eventually rise more sharply and the product will start to make profits. New customers buy the product and as **demand rises**, production increases and unit costs fall. Since demand is strong, prices tend to remain fairly static for a time. However, the prospect of cheap mass production and a strong market will **attract competitors** so that the number of producers is increasing. With the increase of competition, manufacturers must spend a lot of money on product improvement, sales promotion and distribution to obtain a strong position in the market.

Maturity

The rate of sales growth slows down and the product reaches a period of maturity which is probably the longest period of a successful product's life. **Most products on the market will be at the mature stage of their life.** Eventually sales will begin to decline so that there is **overcapacity** of production in the industry. Severe competition occurs, profits fall and some producers leave the market. The remaining producers seek means of **prolonging the product life** by **modifying** it and searching for **new market segments**.

Decline

Most products reach a stage of decline which may be slow or fast. Many producers are reluctant to leave the market, although some inevitably do because of falling profits. If a product remains on the market too long, it will become unprofitable and the decline stage in its life cycle then gives way to a 'senility' stage.

NOTES

Activity 4 **(10 minutes)**

Can you think of any products that have disappeared in your lifetime or are currently in decline?

FOR DISCUSSION

All brand leaders are in the mature phase of the PLC.

Activity 5 **(15 minutes)**

Where do you consider the following products or services to be in their product life cycle?

(a) Web-enabled smart phones
(b) Baked beans
(c) Home cinema television
(d) Cigarettes
(e) Carbon paper
(f) Mortgages
(g) Writing implements
(h) Car GPS systems
(i) Electric cars

Activity 6 **(15 minutes)**

There must be many products that have been around for as long as you can remember.

Think of some examples of products that go on and on from your own experience and try to identify what it is about them that makes them so enduring.

4 PRODUCT RANGE AND PORTFOLIO

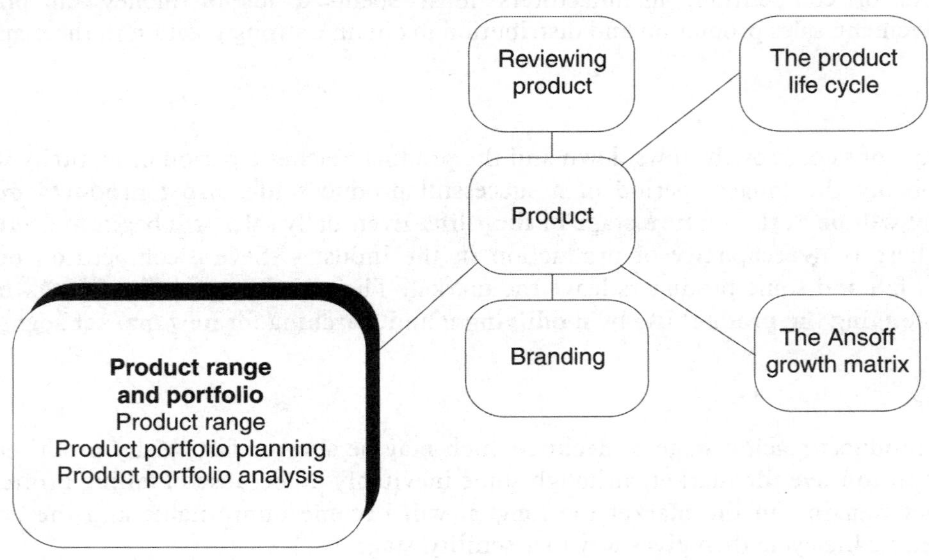

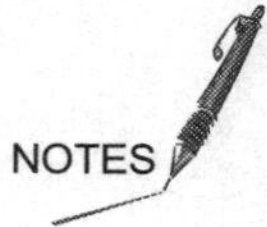

4.1 The product range

Definition

> **Range:** the number or scale of choice of the products or services offered by a supplier.

One of the first and obvious considerations is the number and types of products which an organisation produces. Generally, this is referred to as the product range (or portfolio). Each product range has two dimensions, width and depth. A wide range indicates a large number of different types of product. Depth means that different variations of a product are made, as in the example below.

Product A	Product B	Product C	Product D
Size 1	Size 1	Size 1	Size 1
Size 2	Size 2	Size 2	
Size 3	Size 3		
Size 4			

Figure 7.5: Product range: width and depth

Additionally, each product may have width.

Product A		
	Size 1	*Size 2*
Colour		
Yellow	X	X
Red	X	
Blue	X	
Green		X

Figure 7.6: Product: size and colour

As we are familiar with the concepts of segmentation and positioning, we shall not dwell on them here but it may be useful to consider how the range may be affected by reference to the following table.

	Product A	Product B	Product C	Product D
Market 1	X	X	X	X
Market 2	X	X		
Market 3	X		X	
Market 4	X			

Figure 7.7: Product range and market coverage

As may be seen from this table, Product A appears in all four markets and Market 1 takes all four products. Product D, although it only appears in Market 1 with (as we have seen) a shallow range, may have a turnover which makes it an important product for the firm.

The range is often used to **differentiate** the offering. It constitutes what customers refer to as **choice**. Range also operates to increase the likely catchment of customers.

The reduction in the range is sometimes referred to as **rationalisation**.

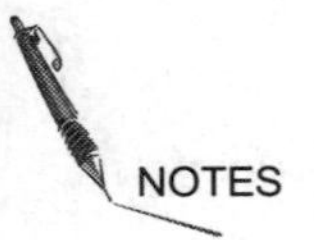

Definition

Rationalisation: the change in the scope of the company's offering (usually a reduction) brought about by a serious review of the demand for the product in the market and the product's contribution to the firm's objectives, both strategic and financial.

Rationalisation is brought about by evaluating the cost of stocking such a range and the **diseconomies of scale** in the production of small quantities of products at the ends of the distribution curve (otherwise thought of as 'specials').

In the context of the product audit, the range should be extensive enough to make the most of the **market segment opportunities** available, consistent with maintaining low **indirect costs** such as distribution and stockholding. The consideration of the **opportunity costs** of manufacturing and stocking low turnover items is important. In other words, what more profitable activity could be undertaken with the resources used up on such items?

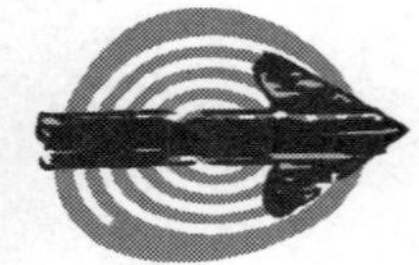

In the next part of the chapter we will deal with ideas concerning what it is that customers buy.

4.2 Product portfolio planning

Portfolio characteristic	Meaning
Width	Number of products
Depth	Average number of product variations
Consistency	Closeness of relationships in product range (eg end users, production, distribution)

Figure 7.8: The product mix

The product mix can be extended in a number of ways.

(a) By introducing **variations** in models or style

(b) By changing the **quality** of products offered at different price levels

(c) By developing **associated items,** eg a paint manufacturer introducing paint brushes

(d) By developing **new products** that have little technical or marketing relationship to the existing range

Managing the product portfolio involves more than the simple extension or reduction of the number of products. Maintaining balance between well established and new products, between cash generative and cash using products and between growing and declining products is very important.

4.3 Product portfolio analysis

The **product-market matrix** is a simple technique used to classify a product or even a business according to the features of the market and the features of the product. It is often used at the level of corporate strategy to determine the relative positions of businesses and select strategies for resource allocation between them. Thus, for example, a bank might apply such a technique to evaluate the relative position and profitability of

its corporate division and its personal division, its international division, its merchant banking division and so on. The most widely used approach is the **Boston Consulting Group (BCG) growth-share matrix.**

The BCG matrix

The BCG matrix, illustrated below, classifies products (or businesses) on the basis of their **market share** and the **rate of growth in the market** as a whole. Products are positioned in the matrix as circles with a diameter proportional to their sales revenue. The underlying assumption in the growth-share matrix is that a **larger market share** will enable the business to benefit from economies of scale, lower per-unit costs and thus **higher margins**.

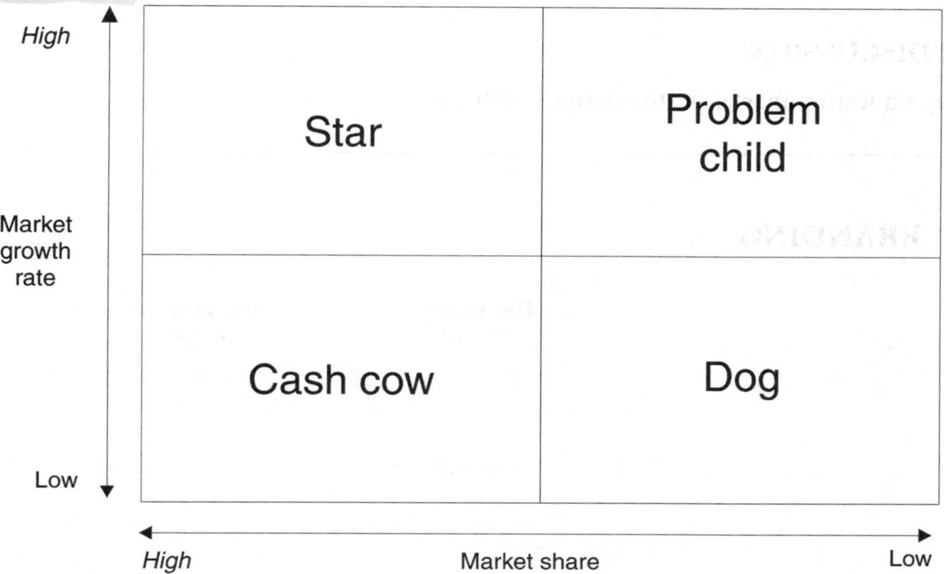

Figure 7.9: The BCG matrix

On the basis of this classification, each product or **strategic business unit** will then fall into one of four broad categories.

Definition

A **strategic business unit** (or SBU) is a section within a larger organisation which is responsible for planning, developing, producing and marketing its own products or services. A typical SBU is a division of the organisation where the managers have control over their own resources, and some discretion over their deployment.

(a) **The problem child** (or question mark): a small market share but in a high growth industry. The generic product is clearly popular, but customer support for the company brand is limited.

(b) **The star**: this is a product with a high market share in a high growth industry. By implication, the star has potential for generating significant earnings currently and in the future.

(c) **The cash cow**: a high market share but in a mature slow growth market. Typically, a well established product with a high degree of consumer loyalty. Product development costs are typically low and the marketing

campaign is well established. The cash cow will normally make a substantial contribution to overall profitability.

(d) **The dog**: a product characterised by low market share and low growth. Again, typically a well established product, but one which is apparently losing consumer support and may have cost disadvantages.

The framework provided by the matrix can offer guidance in terms of developing appropriate strategies for products and in maintaining a balanced product portfolio, ensuring that there are enough cash-generating products to match the cash-using products.

FOR DISCUSSION

Today's question marks are tomorrow's cash cows.

5 BRANDING

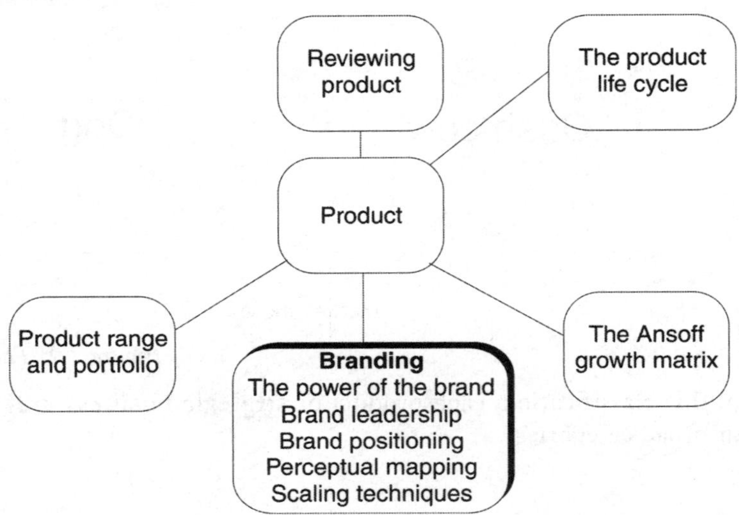

Definition

Brand: the device for distinguishing a product or service from all others. This may be a name, symbol or any other device which is unique to the company and is its legal entitlement. Branding is the practice and technique of creating, devising and communicating such a device.

A brand is shorthand for all the **FAB characteristics** which we associate with it. **Brand leadership** is the golden prize for the marketing manager and one which requires a massive effort of resources, imagination, persistence and above all consistency of value delivery.

Consider some of the major brands of today; Microsoft, Kellogg's, Cadbury's, Mars, Heinz; in the industrial sector ICI; in the retail sector, Marks & Spencer, Harrods, Sainsbury's. The very names speak volumes for the products and services which they

offer. A **brand name**, stands for things like quality, reliability, trust, status, and in the case of the food brands, wholesomeness, purity, nutrition.

> **Activity 7** **(20 minutes)**
>
> Write down the first 10 top brands from any product groups which come readily to mind. Against each, write the main characteristics which you feel, are appropriate. Give the list, without your choice of characteristics, to some friends and ask them to characterise each brand. Analyse the differences, if any, and account for the degree of similarity or otherwise.

5.1 The power of the brand

A brand name increases the value of the product in the eyes of the customers. They associate with the name, symbol, device or packaging, some other factor of value which is beyond the core product.

EXAMPLE

The marketing director of Heinz has said that the blue colour of the famous Heinz Beans tin was entirely inappropriate for a food product but they dare not change it. It was so deeply ingrained into the product image that customers would reject any distinct alternative and may well turn away from the product, not believing that the product in the can of the new colour would not be the same as the product in the established packaging. There were consumer tests run to see if customers would buy 'Kit-Kat', in a blue wrapper, very similar in shade to the Heinz blue. The customers to whom it was offered rejected it out of hand! The brand is a very powerful communicator when established.

FOR DISCUSSION

In some products, the packaging is more important than the content.

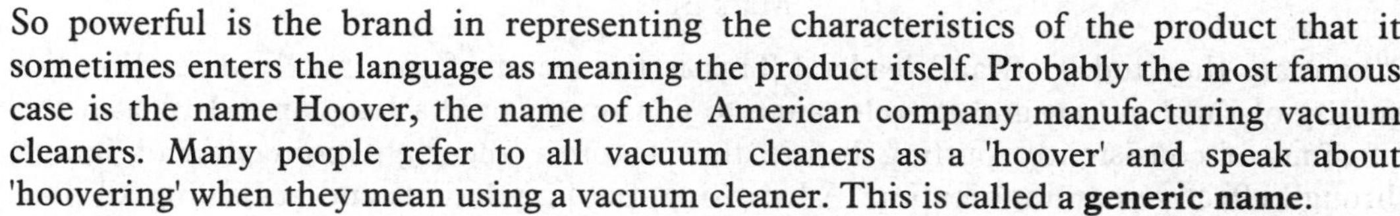

So powerful is the brand in representing the characteristics of the product that it sometimes enters the language as meaning the product itself. Probably the most famous case is the name Hoover, the name of the American company manufacturing vacuum cleaners. Many people refer to all vacuum cleaners as a 'hoover' and speak about 'hoovering' when they mean using a vacuum cleaner. This is called a **generic name.**

Definition

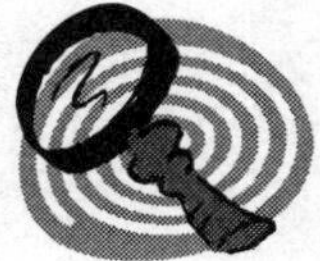

> **Generic name:** the name given to a product class such as analgesics (painkillers) rather than the product name (paracetamol) or the brand name (Anadin). In marketing, it has become the way of describing a brand name which has come to stand for the whole of the product class such as Hoover or Sellotape instead of vacuum cleaner or adhesive tape.

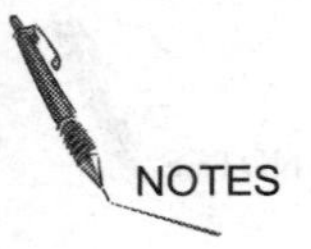

An important aspect of brand management is preventing the brand name from becoming generic. Once a brand name has become generic it loses legal protection, so competitors cannot be prevented from using it. More important, it loses its unique status in the minds of existing and potential customers. Brand loyalty is thus diminished.

5.2 Brand leadership

Definition

Brand leader: the brand which consistently holds the largest market share when measured by brand sales. You should note that there are some manufacturers who make a number of brands and therefore may be said to hold a larger share of the product market than the brand leader.

Activity 8 **(20 minutes)**

Make a list of brands which are commonly used in a generic way. Set beside them the brand names of the alternative products.

The world famous brands have not become so by accident. It takes great dedication on the part of the company who owns a brand to make it a household name.

Examine the following list of famous names which were the brand leaders of 1933.

Hovis Bread
Kellogg's Corn Flakes
Cadbury's Chocolate
Schweppes Mineral Waters
Brooke Bond Tea
Colgate Toothpaste
Kodak Film
Heinz Beans
Mars Bars

Where are they today? Brand leaders! This is the result of continually defending the **quality** of their output and its **relevance** to consumers over a long time. It is also the outcome of consistently putting before the customer the right **concept** and **image** through effective **communication**. Advertising, public relations and packaging all play their part in ensuring this continuity. Many customers could be said to buy some of these products instinctively. They are instinctively loyal to the brand name largely because it has never let them down in delivering the values that they cherish.

EXAMPLE

According to AcNielsen, the top 10 UK grocery brands in 2006 were:

	Brand	*Sales £000 to ...*	*30 Dec 2005*	*30 Dec 2006*
1	Coca Cola		897,248	942,391
2	Warburtons		437,034	514,341
3	Walkers		407,770	424,002
4	Hovis		347,363	403,126
5	Cadbury Dairy Milk		370,803	361,503
6	Nescafé		333,913	331,265
7	Andrex		310,585	326,646
8	Lucozade		254,267	296,216
9	Kingsmill		296,880	282,318
10	Robinsons		265,045	277,285

FOR DISCUSSION

Buying the right brand is more important than price.

Allied to this phenomenon are the concepts of **brand preference** and **brand loyalty**. In addition the behavioural concept of **brand switching** is clearly relevant.

Definitions

Brand preference: the degree to which customers express their inclination to select the brand of their choice by reference to their purchasing habits or by their asking for a given brand.

Brand loyalty: the extent to which consumers of a brand tend to re-purchase in the face of continuing availability of alternatives.

Brand switching: the disposition to change brands for marginal gains in price or perceived value.

Brand positioning: the strategy to ensure that the brand, in the eyes of the public, has a distinct position in the market with reference to quality, style, status, price or a combination of these.

These are important concepts in determining the **branding strategy**. It is necessary for a marketing manager to understand the reasons behind such preferences and loyalties in order to execute an appropriate policy, and the approach to keeping existing customers and to generating new ones.

5.3 Brand positioning

Brand positioning is one of the techniques which is critical in developing a **brand leader**. This is done through a series of activities in which the key elements of product perception are examined and subsequently tested in relation to key ideas which may be used in the **brand communication strategy**. Each brand should have a unique **niche,**

independent of the similarity of the substance of the products with which it competes. Discovering a niche in the market can be the first step in developing an effective brand.

5.4 Perceptual mapping

Figure 7.10: Perceptual mapping

In perceptual mapping, as illustrated, the product can be related to two dimensions of the way a customer views the existing market. Here we can see that there is a relatively low inhabitation of the medium quality/medium price area. This represents a potential niche for the 'no nonsense' type of product.

5.5 Scaling techniques

Further information can be derived from what are called **scaling techniques.**

Definition

> **Scaling techniques:** are derived from psychology and are used to determine the nature and intensity of an individual's attitudes towards objects or ideas: thus they are frequently called attitude scales. The most commonly used in market research into consumer behaviour are the Likert Scale, where respondents are asked to express their agreement or otherwise with a statement about the characteristics of a brand, and the Semantic Differential Scale, where the technique involves respondents indicating a notional value on a scale between two poles such as expensive/cheap. Examples are given in the diagram below.

> **Activity 9** **(20 minutes)**
>
> As a brand manager of Brand X shower gel, you are interested in determining the potential of creating a 'unisex' image for the product. How would you use perceptual maps and scaling techniques to examine this?

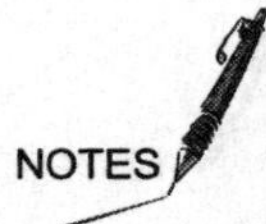

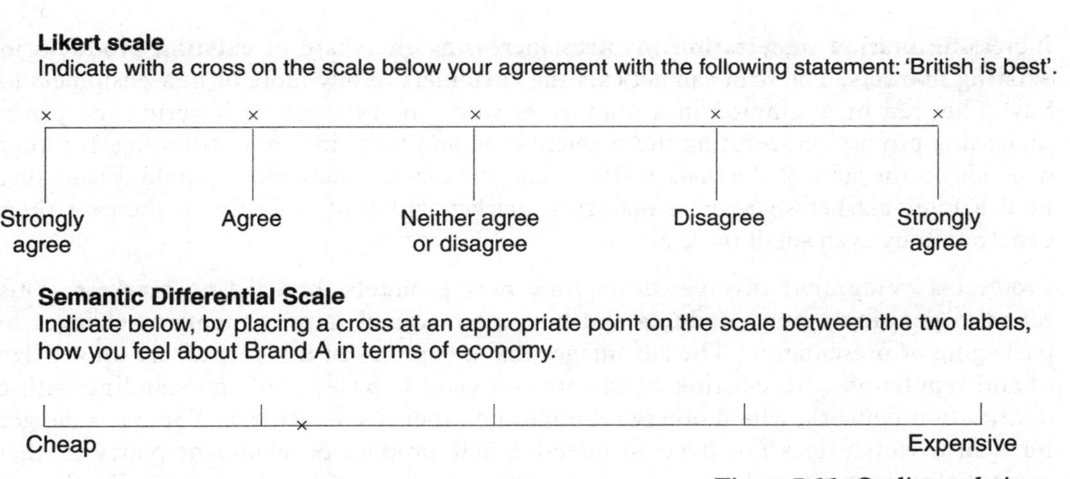

Figure 7.11: Scaling techniques

6 THE ANSOFF GROWTH MATRIX

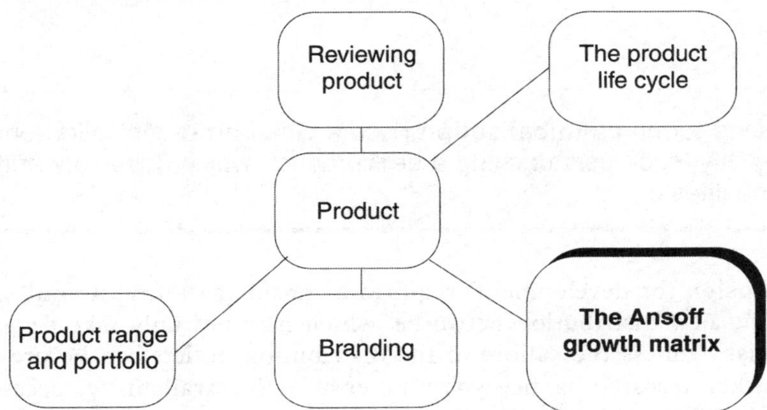

One of the most difficult things for an organisation to manage is **growth**. This is especially true of **small-to-medium size enterprises,** (SMEs), even those who have achieved success.

The **Ansoff matrix** is one of the most well-known and well used strategic frameworks for considering ways to achieve growth. In order to grow, companies may use various **combinations of product and market decisions.**

Ansoff demonstrates these options in a matrix as shown below.

Markets \ **Products**	Existing	New
Existing	Market penetration	Product development
New	Market development	Diversification

Figure 7.12: Ansoff matrix

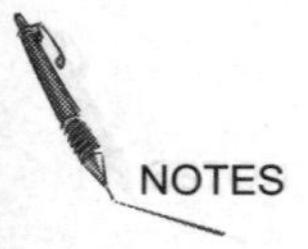

Increasing **market penetration** involves increasing the share of **existing products** in **existing markets.** The firm can get existing customers to buy more or new customers to buy. This can be attempted in a number of ways, for example by lowering the price; increasing promotion; refining the segmentation and targeting; re-positioning. It rather depends on the state of the market (PLC) and the market share already held. Firms that hold a high market share in a maturing market will find it costly to increase their penetration by even small increments.

Product development involves developing **new products** for **existing markets**. This refers to **genuinely new products** and not just marginal improvements or changes to packaging or presentation. The advantages that a firm has in this respect are knowledge of and reputation with existing customers and good knowledge of and standing with a distribution network, which otherwise might be expensive to achieve. There is a danger for a firm which does not have an effective new product development policy in that competitors may get in first. A further caution is to consider the **cannibalisation** of existing business. Customers may switch to the new product at the expense of sales in the existing one.

Definition

In marketing terms **cannibalisation** occurs when an organisation undertakes a new activity, such as launching a new product, which adversely affects their existing business.

Market expansion (or development) requires a considerable **investment** in setting up and developing new distribution networks, which may not only take time and money but also be risky unless the calibre of the distribution outlets can be pre-determined. Effective market research is necessary to ensure the availability, accessibility and suitability of an effective demand for the products in the new market.

Diversification involves the **highest risk** strategy for growth as it requires the development or acquisition of an entirely new product to enter an entirely new market. Extensive market research is necessary and a large commitment of time, resources and energy to the development of strong **customer and distribution relationships**.

In the Ansoff matrix, we can begin to see the coming together of many of the issues which have been discussed so far in this book. In particular in this chapter on products, you should have become familiar with key factors for evaluating the options offered by the matrix.

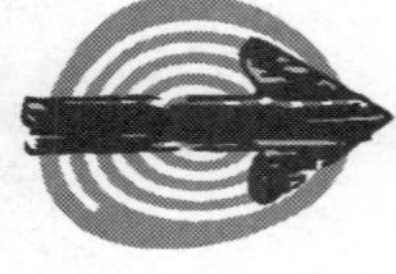

In the next chapter we turn our attention to another issue which has an important place of its own in the matrix, new product development.

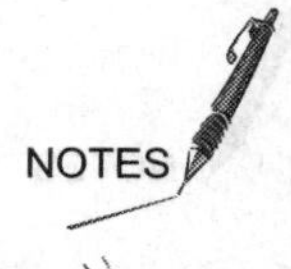

Chapter roundup

- A product can be either goods, or the performance of a service.
- A product is a package of attributes not confined to the physical entity.
- A product is a bundle of benefits designed to deliver satisfactions.
- Augmentation of the product is a way to differentiate it from competitors' products.
- Services are as much influenced by marketing considerations as products.
- The product audit is an important way for the management to keep in touch with the effectiveness of product policy.
- Features, advantages and benefits and the Unique Selling Proposition are important contributors to product differentiation.
- Branding is a major influence on the success of a firm.
- Scaling techniques are powerful ways of obtaining critical marketing information.
- PLC, BCG and Ansoff frameworks are very important in the strategic manipulation of product policy.
- The products is one of the major ways in which a company is judged by its markets.

Quick quiz

1 What do people want when they buy drills?

2 How are consumer goods classified?

3 What is augmentation?

4 What is a product audit?

5 What does FAB stand for?

6 How many functions is packaging said to have? Name them.

7 What is the PLC?

8 How many dimensions are there in a range?

9 What does rationalisation mean?

10 What are the categories given in the Boston Consulting Group Matrix?

11 By what, apart from a name, may a brand be represented?

12 Name two major scaling techniques.

13 What is the central observation on a Likert Scale?

14 What are the decision options in the Ansoff Matrix?

15 What is the highest risk option in the Ansoff Matrix?

NOTES

Answers to Quick quiz

1. Holes.
2. As convenience, shopping, speciality or unsought goods.
3. The building up of benefits on the core product.
4. A detailed and systematic examination of the product offering.
5. Features, advantages and benefits.
6. Five. Protection, distribution, convenience, selling and conformity with regulations.
7. Product life cycle.
8. Two main ones, width and depth, but these may represent further factors.
9. Generally speaking a reduction in the range for financial reasons.
10. Cash Cows, Stars, Question Marks (or Problem Children) and Dogs.
11. A symbol or any device.
12. The Likert Scale and Semantic Differential Scale.
13. Neither agree nor disagree.
14. Market penetration, product development, market development and diversification.
15. Diversification.

Answers to Activities

1. Use the model in the diagram to build up your idea of the product and add another benefit dimension which you feel will be attractive to the customer.
2. You should find sufficient guidance by re-reading the section on features, advantages and benefits.
3. Make sure that the advantages are given in statements which contain a comparative and that the benefits are not another way of stating an advantage; in other words they should not contain comparatives. Benefits are normally expressed in saving time, money or inconvenience or indicate factors which can be related to the Maslow Hierarchy of Needs such as esteem or security.
4. Two classic examples are manual typewriters and vinyl records. You will be able to think of more, such as audio and VHS cassettes.
5. Some of them are arguable but we suggest:

Introduction phase:	(i)
Growth phase:	(a), (c) & (h)
Mature phase:	(b), (f) & (g)
Decline phase:	(d) and (e).

6. See the list in the section on branding and ask yourself why they are so enduring: what do they offer that competing products do not offer or are not perceived to offer?

7 Although, as individuals, we may differ in our appreciation of various brands, there is likely to be some consistency in the positive/negative orientation of our collective opinion. The bases of any agreement are likely to be derived from:

(a) our use and experience of the product;

(b) who we know that uses it and what we think of them; and

(c) a belief born from the credibility of the brand about the products benefits.

Note that not all brands are seen as having a positive image.

8 You may have chosen Sellotape, Xerox, Biro, Levi's, Scotch tape. There are many more.

9 You may use something like masculine/feminine and young/old on a perceptual map concerning Brand X. Other factors could be examined by a statement such as 'The scent of Brand X is just as suitable for men as for women' placed on a Likert Scale. Place 'macho/feminine' on a Semantic Differential Scale.

NOTES

Chapter 8 :
NEW PRODUCT DEVELOPMENT

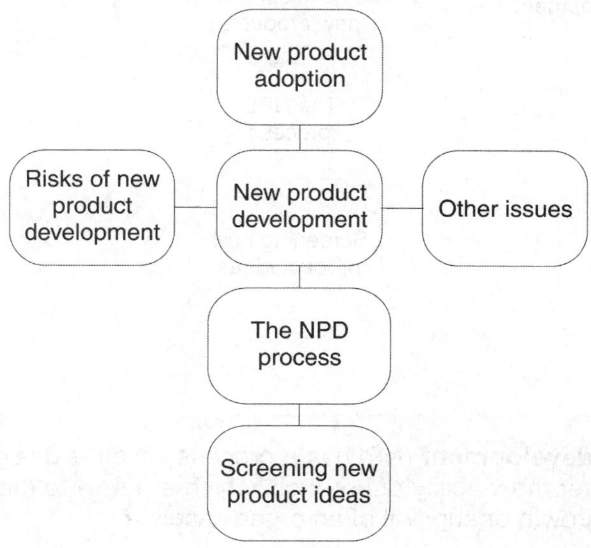

Introduction

All organisations need new products, even those which become great largely by a reliance on one product, or a very narrow product line.

We have said before that the majority of major brands are in mature markets, that is, markets with little or no growth. For the firm to continue to grow, **new products must be developed and exploited**. It is an option which, becomes more attractive as the cost of maintaining market share becomes greater and price pressures reduce profitability. For the smaller firm **new product development (NPD)** is a way of making a significant entry into an existing or new growth market.

Your objectives

In this chapter you will learn about the following.

(a) The implications of the changing environment and customer needs

(b) The bases of risk and new product failure rates

(c) Using the new product development process to examine a new product idea

(d) How the new product development process is handled within the organisation

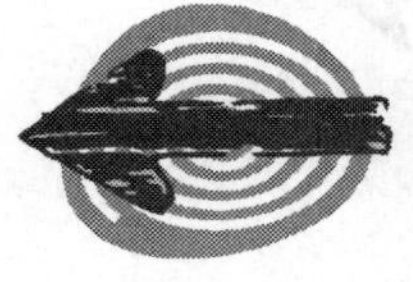

In Chapter 7 we reviewed the wide range of issues which make 'the product' such a critical influence on the future success of the firm. So it is entirely appropriate that we now devote a separate, short chapter to new products and how they are made important to the organisation.

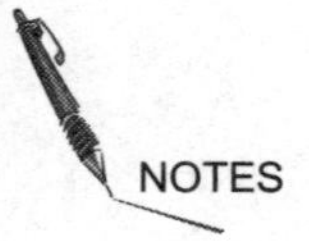

1 NEW PRODUCT DEVELOPMENT

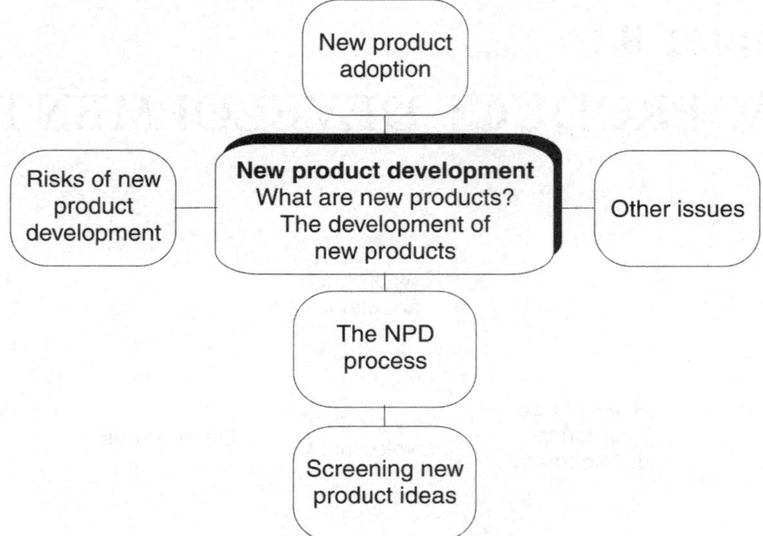

Definition

New product development (NPD) is a process which is designed to develop, test and consider the viability of products which are new to the market in order to ensure the growth or survival of an organisation.

The NPD process is well-known and it is seen by many as a costly exercise. For the successful firm it is realised as a necessary investment in the future of the firm and its **stakeholders.**

Definition

The word **stakeholder** is often used to denote all organisations, groups or individuals with whom the organisation has contact, or by whom the organisation's activities are otherwise influenced. They will include customers and consumers of its products and also the people that will influence the organisation, but who may not be customers or consumers themselves, such as suppliers. Pressure groups, politicians, charities, religious organisations and local authorities and other agencies can also be included in the definition.

Activity 1 **(10 minutes)**

Which large companies can you think of that have recently produced new products?

FOR DISCUSSION

Firms with only one product produce better value because they can concentrate all their resources on it.

1.1 What are new products?

New to the world

There are products which are **totally new** to everybody and tend to affect our purchasing behaviour considerably, for example laptop computers, mobile phones, DAB radio.

New to the company

Products which enable a company to enter a **new market** and possibly, because of their core competence, bring a new dimension to our quality of life: consider foodstuffs that have been imported to the UK for the first time.

New improvements

Products which are changed to a degree that affects our use of them: packaging improvements such as aerosols changed our usage patterns of many products.

There are other ways of looking at what constitutes a new product. A new product should:

- Open up an entirely new market
- Replace an existing product, almost entirely
- Broaden significantly an existing market

An old product is often considered new if it:

- Is introduced to a new market
- Is packaged in a significantly different way
- Uses a distinctly different marketing approach

Activity 2 **(15 minutes)**

Can you think of new products and new old products to fit into each of the above categories?

EXAMPLE

The Chartered Institute of Marketing warn that market places are becoming cluttered with minor product improvements that are easily and increasingly more quickly copied by competitors. The result is that consumers are bored with product developments and companies loose their competitive edge because they appear to be averse to innovation. The Apple iPod was described as the most innovative new product to emerge in recent years (some herald it to be the only true innovation since the Sony Walkman!). The rationale for its huge success has been due to the recognition that a problem existed for people who liked to listen to music on the go but didn't want to carry lots of CDs.

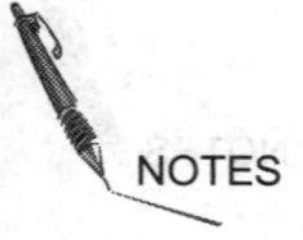
NOTES

The reason for this risk avoiding attitude is thought to stem from the fact that many marketers (and particularly brand managers) move roles after two years. NPD on a large scale can take an extraordinary amount of time and so there is not the opportunity for marketers to see projects through to completion and gain recognition for their contribution. Equally, only senior strategists would be in a position within the organisation to oversee such large scale projects and so concept development does not often have a clear home within the organisational structure.

Adapted from: *The Creative Dilemma: Successful Innovation in Fast-Changing Markets*, Chartered Institute of Marketing, Shape the Agenda paper

FOR DISCUSSION

Most so-called new products are just the old ones dressed up in a different way. Do you think the Hollywood film industry can be decribed as innovative?

1.2 The development of new products

The development of new and improved products emerges from two distinct organisational activities, **research and development** (R & D) and **NPD**.

Research and development

Definitions

Pure research is original research to obtain new scientific or technical knowledge or understanding. There is no obvious commercial or practical end in view.

Applied research is also original research work like (a) above, but it has a specific practical aim or application (eg research on improvements in the effectiveness of medicines).

Development is the use of existing scientific and technical knowledge to produce new (or substantially improved) products or systems, prior to starting commercial production operations.

EXAMPLE: NEW PRODUCT DEVELOPMENT THROUGH FOAM-FIBER TECHNOLOGY SYNERGY: MEDISPONGE(R) RBR WOUND CARE DRESSINGS

Filtrona Porous Technologies, manufacturer of custom fluid handling fiber and foam components for the medical device and healthcare industry, and a division of UK-based Filtrona plc, has recently developed a unique foam-fiber hybrid component for select medical and personal care markets, specifically wound care. Referred to as MediSponge® RBR, the patent-pending foam-fiber composite consists of a soft, highly absorbent foam with hydrophilic properties structurally enhanced by the addition of a fiber matrix . . .

Hydrophilic foam's presence as a wound dressing material has increased dramatically the last several years, featuring prominently in select advanced wound care settings. MediSponge RBR now expands the technology's application range within this market. To date, one delimiting characteristic of hydrophilic foam is its tensile and structural strength when wet, especially when exposed to moist or damp conditions for a substantial period of time . . .

Filtrona's new MediSponge RBR overcomes these limitations. MediSponge RBR incorporates to the foam media a fiber matrix that acts as a reinforcement or rebar-like structural enhancement. Versus the standard wet hydrophilic foam material, the average tensile strength, tear strength, and expansion properties may be improved by as much as 600 times, 40 times, and near 2 times respectively. These product technology enhancements among others make it an ideal material to consider for foam dressing applications for long-term advanced wound care.

reuters.com, 4 November 2009

New product development (NPD)

NPD has, potentially, the same commitment to research as R & D but here there is a **distinct commercial objective**. In all organisations that have some interest in NPD this can be seen in formal or informal activity. In the more formal structure there may be a **New Product Development Department** staffed by people who come from a mixture of technical and commercial backgrounds. They are given a clear brief for the development of concepts, processes and materials discovered or invented in the more remote R & D departments. This is an expensive commitment of very highly qualified staff and advanced capital equipment.

Less formal are the **NPD committees** comprising production, finance, marketing, human resource management and other personnel, which are the norm in some firms. Their job is to examine new product ideas and make decisions on how to proceed with the problem which is placed before them.

In the least formal, the process is left to the flash of inspiration or the lucky chance: when a new discovery comes out of the blue like the legend of the growth of penicillin on Fleming's sandwiches.

Sources of ideas

The driving forces behind NPD can either be **discovery** or **need.**

Some of the sources of new product ideas are given below. We can divide them into two main types: internal and external.

(a) **Internal to the organisation**

- Suggestion boxes
- Customer correspondence
- Sales records
- Customer complaints
- Salespersons' reports
- Competitive Activity reports
- NPD; departments
- R & D; departments

(b) **External to the organisation**

- Market research
- New product; agencies
- Inventors
- Patent agents
- Acquisition
- Licensing agreements
- Research institutions:
  - Academic
  - Trade
  - Industry
  - Charitable
  - Government
- Competitors

Some companies use the NPD process as a barometer of their virility in the industry. They are geared to new products as many people are to new gadgets. Other companies are **predators** or **parasites** on the research activities of the others. They are brilliant copyists of new technology and are able to work with great flexibility and speed. This is becoming a valid strategy called 'the close second, fastest follower' approach. It saves a great deal in resources in the development phase and exploits the promotional activity undertaken by rivals.

FOR DISCUSSION

How easy do you think it is for consumers to imagine improvements to a product? How easy is it for them to think of completely new products?

Activity 3 **(10 minutes)**

Suggestion boxes are not very well used in lots of firms. People just do not respond well to them.

Think of a better way of bringing in new product ideas from the workforce.

2 THE NPD PROCESS

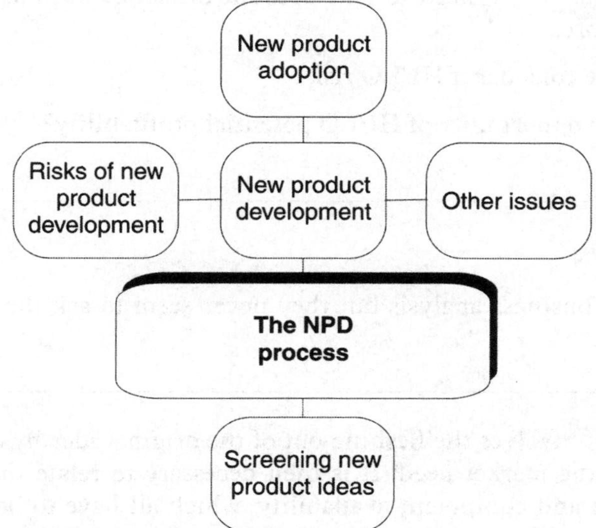

A sequence for this is as follows.

- Original concept
- Screening of ideas
- Business analysis
- Concept definition
- Product development
- Marketing mix issues
- Market testing
- Pilot launch
- Roll-out: full launch

We shall look briefly at some of these in more detail.

Original concept refers to the primary idea, the sources of which we have just discussed. As you might expect, a very large proportion of new ideas falls at the first hurdle. At the back of the marketing manager's mind is the thought that Kodak turned down the Xerox photocopying system while Rubik's Cube, an overnight craze which brought the manufacturer a fortune, was turned down several times by toy manufacturers at the Harrogate Toy Fair.

More straightforward concerns are: Has it been tried before? If so, what happened? Were there obstacles then which we are now able to overcome? If not, why not?

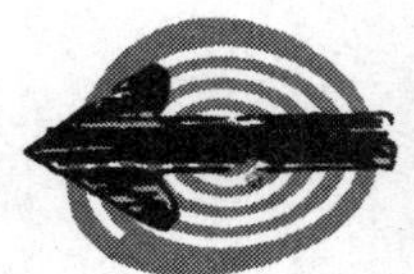

We will look in more detail at how to screen ideas later in this chapter.

Business analysis looks at the firm's resources and the market in order to evaluate the basis of risk assessment. Questions asked include the following.

(a) Is there a market of sufficient potential?

(b) What size is it?

(c) What is the PLC status?

(d) What is the growth rate?

(e) How inhabited is it?

(f) Who are the major players?

(g) What is the structure?

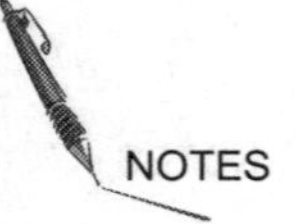

(h) Do we have a competitive advantage in the product? (Is there a clear USP potential?). We need to take account of factors such as costs, distribution, sales force?

(i) Can we consider it HI/LO risk?

(j) Is it an opportunity of HI/LO potential profitability?

FOR DISCUSSION

Firms may do the business analysis but they never seem to ask the customer how they feel about it!

Concept definition involves the fleshing out of the original idea by defining the criteria necessary to meet the market need. It is then necessary to relate these to the technical expertise and plant and equipment availability, which all have to be costed. The initial idea may have been changed somewhat in the commercialisation process and it is therefore necessary to keep in touch with the interests of the major players, including distributors as well as the final customer.

Product development here means the building of a concept into a production reality. This includes prototypes and dummy runs to ensure that the demands of the market can be met smoothly without causing inordinate pressure on other parts of the firm's systems.

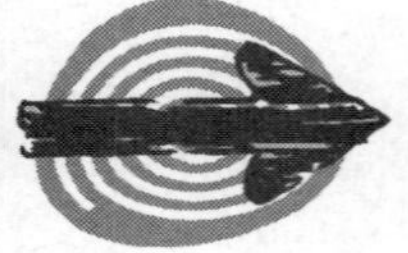

Before we go on to look in more detail at screening new product ideas, and the later stages of the NPD process, we will look at the general risks of NPD which the business analysis, concept definition and product development range of the NPD process are likely to throw up.

3 RISKS OF NEW PRODUCT DEVELOPMENT

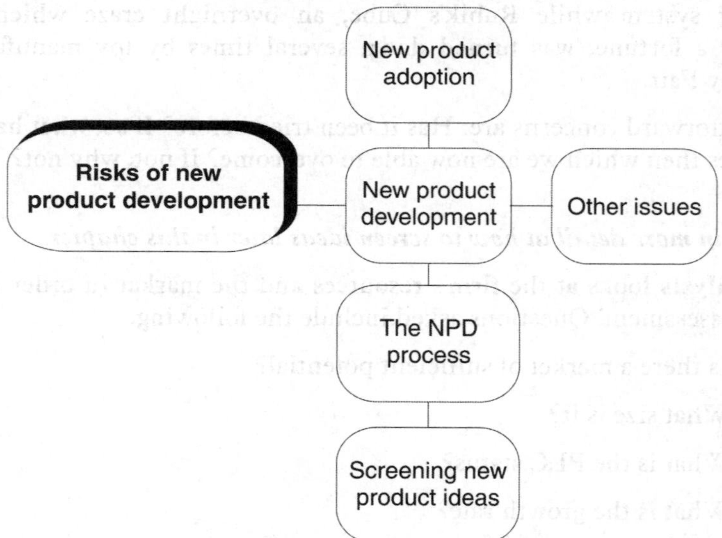

Although we have said that NPD is an essential recipe for a bright future, there are, increasingly, **risks** attached to it. These are mainly associated with new product **launch**

failure which is given by many estimates as around the 80% region. The other side of the coin, is the risk of **lost opportunity**.

The market is getting so difficult to manage for new products, that it is almost impossible to get long-term commitment from buyers. Competitors (especially the expert 'fastest followers') are coming into markets quickly, and product life cycles appear to be shortening as the pace of technology quickens. The main issues are given below.

(a) **Financial restrictions** may hold the product back.

(b) The **standing** of the firm in the market may be weak.

(c) Estimates of **potential** are often exaggerated.

(d) **Product championship** by a strong manager may override the recommendations not to proceed from other parties.

(e) A **skimming strategy** may be too ambitious.

(f) Competitive **defence** may be too strong.

(g) The **pace** of development may be too fast.

EXAMPLE

The footwear brand Crocs has been an international phenomenon since launching in July 2002 in the US. Originally designed as the perfect boat shoe they have now been adopted for a range of uses such as for the beach, gardening, to help with sore or problem feet, for those on their feet all day, pregnant women, the elderly etc. Manufactured in almost every conceivable colour, promotion is primarily related to comfort, as the rubber resin (Croslite) clogs mould to the feet when worn, and sanitation, as they are odour resistant.

The brand first became available in Europe in 2005 already supported by a wide celebrity following which despite the shoe frequently being described as ugly led to a fashion craze during the summer of 2006. This craze was not short lived with 2007 sales even higher and increasing numbers of retailers stocking the brand. Crocs became one of the most searched items to buy on the internet with specialist online retailers such as lookatmycrazyshoes.com experiencing eight-fold increases in site hits in 2007.

The growth in the shoes led to Crocs developing additional styles to expand their range of products such as off road versions, more feminine 'Mary Jane' styles, Wellingtons for children and flip- flops. The original 'Caymen' version of the shoe however remained the most widely stocked and the summer of 2007 saw widespread 'me too' competitor copies of this version. Crocs are in the midst of lengthy legal action taken against Holey Soles, a Canadian competitor version and ten other named companies for breach of intellectual property rights.

An even greater concern for the brand is the barrage of cheap unbranded plastic fakes that are sold via market stalls; discount retailers; beach shops and the internet. Although the fakes are sold at less than half the retail price, the danger for Crocs would be consumer opinion being based on the quality of these inferior products.

To protect the brand, crocs holds four separate legal patents and the Crocodile featured is a protected logo, meaning that consumers would be able to tell the true brand from the fakes.

Sources: Crocs.com, *The Times* 16 September 2006, *http://www.e-consultancy.com/news-blog/363141/fashion-searchers-snap-up-crocs.html*

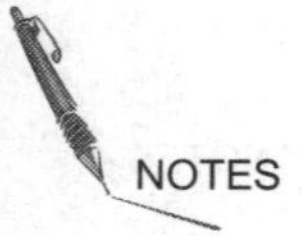

Definitions

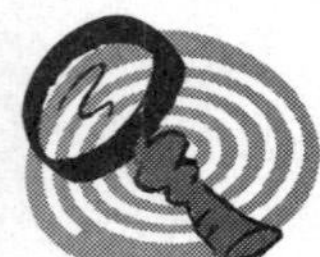

Product championship is a state of mind engendered in product managers and sales staff which places their products on pedestals. They defend them and will have nothing said against them. This is true even before the product has been launched. It is sometimes referred to as the 'new baby syndrome'.

Skimming strategy is an approach in which premium prices are used on the launch of a new product in an attempt to profit from the lead time over competition and on the basis that the early part of the market will always pay that bit extra at first for the new product. It is a natural expectation to re-coup the investment as early as possible.

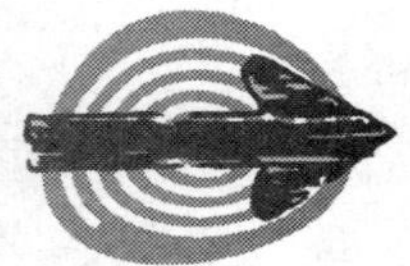

You may wonder, given the above, how or why new products ever get on to the market. The answer is that it is still the main way to ensure survival and growth and that firms have become much better at the part of the process called screening, analysis and testing. This we will now examine.

4 SCREENING NEW PRODUCT IDEAS

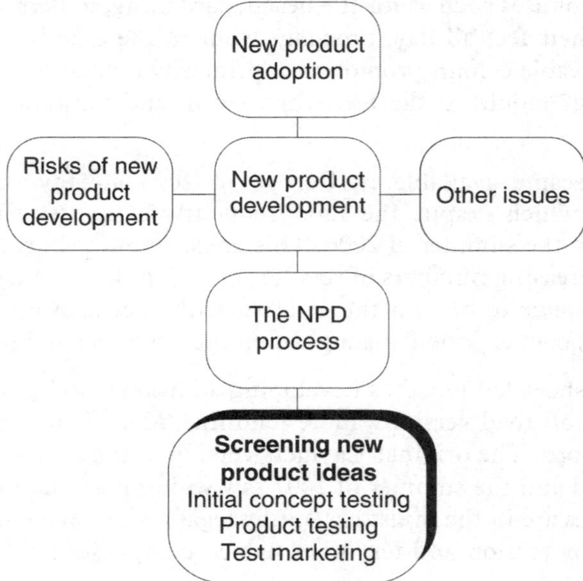

The **mortality rate of new products** is very high.

To reduce the risk of failure new product ideas should always be **screened**. There is some evidence that the product screening process is becoming more effective. On average, seven ideas will yield one successful product.

Initial assessment
Number of new ideas
Business analysis
Development
Test launch
Launch
Commercialisation
Time

Total costs
Costs
Initial screening of idea
Business analysis
Development
Testing
Launch
Cumulative costs curve
Timescale

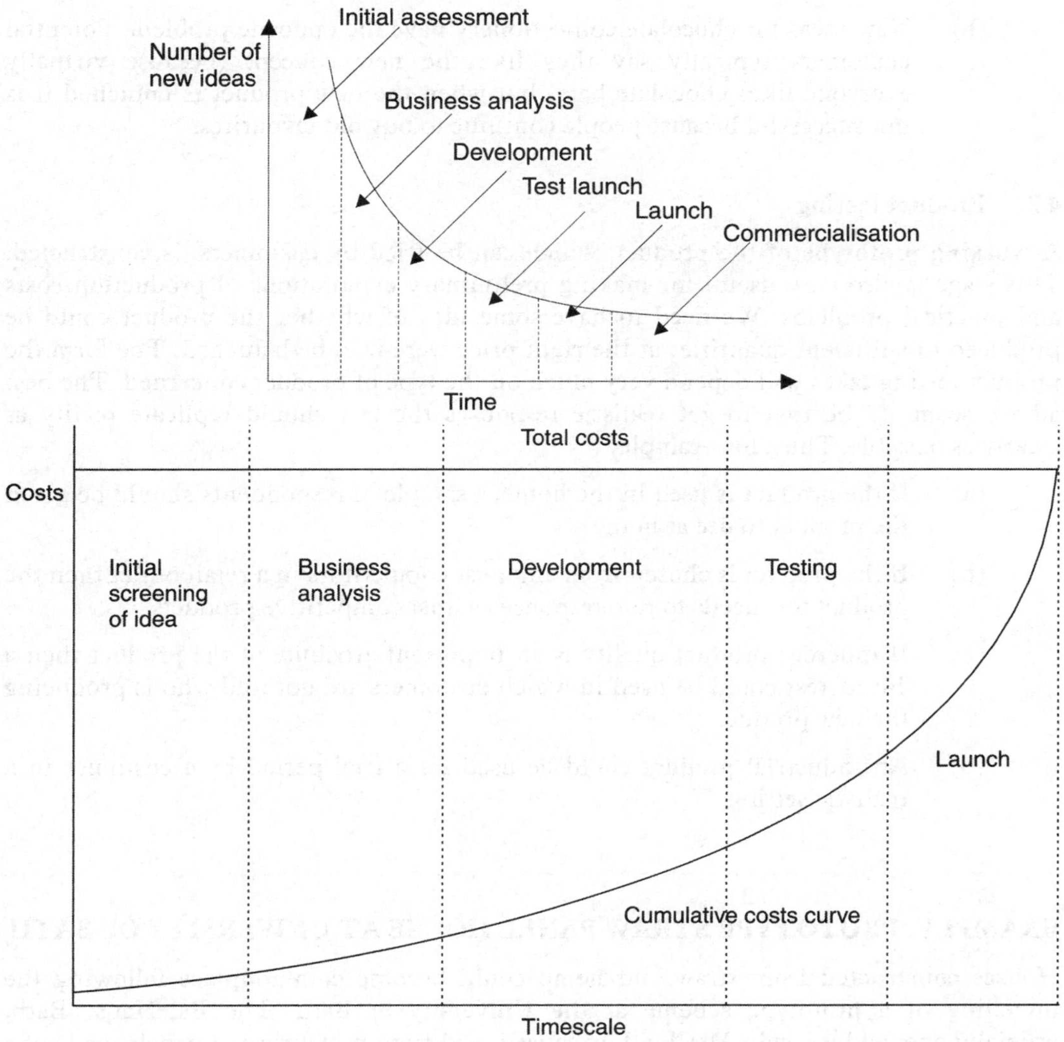

Figure 8.1: New product screening

Note the rapidly climbing costs towards the end of the process. Because of this many companies jump the **market testing phase.** The rationale for this is that what they lose by not doing it is often less than the costs of market testing. There is also the advantage of surprise and thus a longer lead time over competition.

New products should only be taken to advanced development if there is evidence of:

- Adequate demand
- Compatibility with existing marketing ability
- Compatibility with existing production ability

4.1 Initial concept testing

At a preliminary stage the concept for the new product should be tested on potential customers. It is common to use the company staff as guinea pigs for a new product idea. But it is difficult to get sensible reactions from customers. Consider the following examples.

(a) New designs for wallpaper. When innovative new designs are tested on potential customers it is often found that they are conditioned by traditional designs and are dismissive of new design ideas.

(b) New ideas for chocolate confectionery have the opposite problem. Potential customers typically say they like the new concept (because virtually everyone likes chocolate bars) but when the new product is launched it is not successful because people continue to buy old favourites.

4.2 Product testing

A **working prototype** of the product, which can be tried by customers, is constructed. This stage is also very useful for making preliminary explorations of production costs and practical problems. We need to have some idea of whether the product could be produced in sufficient quantities at the right price were it to be launched. The form the product testing takes will depend very much on the type of product concerned. The best advice seems to be that to get realistic responses the test should replicate reality as clearly as possible. Thus, for example:

(a) If the product is used in the home, a sample of respondents should be given the product to use at home

(b) If the product is chosen from amongst competitors in a retail outlet then the product test needs to rate response against competitive products

(c) If inherent product quality is an important attribute of the product then a 'blind' test could be used in which customers are not told who is producing the new product

(d) An industrial product could be used for a trial period by a customer in a realistic setting

---

EXAMPLE: PROTOTYPE STRAW PANEL HOUSE AT UNIVERSITY OF BATH

Houses constructed from straw and hemp could become commonplace following the unveiling of a prototype scheme at the University of Bath. The BaleHaus@Bath, officially opened by Kevin McCloud, is constructed from prefabricated panels made of a structural timber frame infilled with straw bales or hemp and rendered with a breathable lime-based system . . .

Previously the panels had only been used for cladding in larger framed buildings where there was no requirement for structural strength other than wind loading. For this building the panels are in a load bearing situation, where they have to support the building's weight and also provide racking strength to stabilise the building.

The prefabricated panels used in the BaleHaus have also undergone fire safety testing at the University of Bath which shows that they are safe even when exposed to temperatures over 1000°C. To reach the required standard the panel had to withstand the heat for more than 30 minutes. Over two hours later – four times as long as required – the panel had still not failed . . .

Stephen Kennett, *greenbuildingpress.co.uk*, 20 November 2009

4.3 Test marketing

The purpose of test marketing is to obtain information about how consumers react to the product in selected areas thought to be representative of the total market. This avoids

blind commitment to the costs of a full scale launch while permitting the collection of market data.

5 NEW PRODUCT ADOPTION

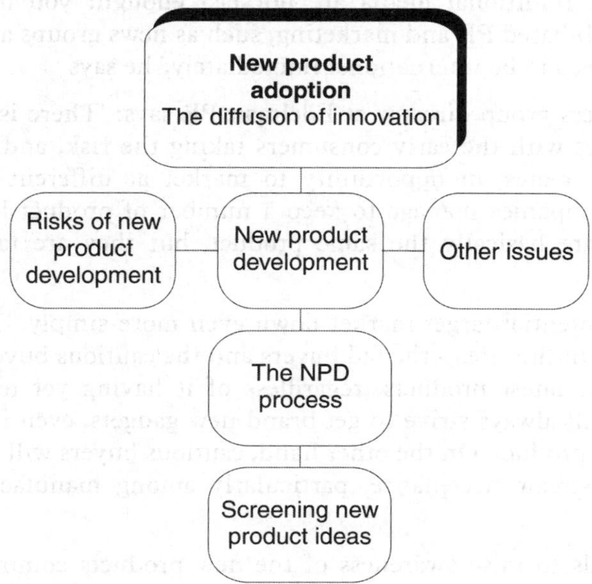

5.1 The diffusion of innovation

The diffusion of the new product refers to the spread of information about the product in the market place. Adoption is the process by which consumers incorporate the product into their buying patterns. The diffusion process is assumed to follow a similar shape to the PLC curve. Adoption is also thought usually to follow a 'normal' bell shaped curve. The classification of adopters is shown below.

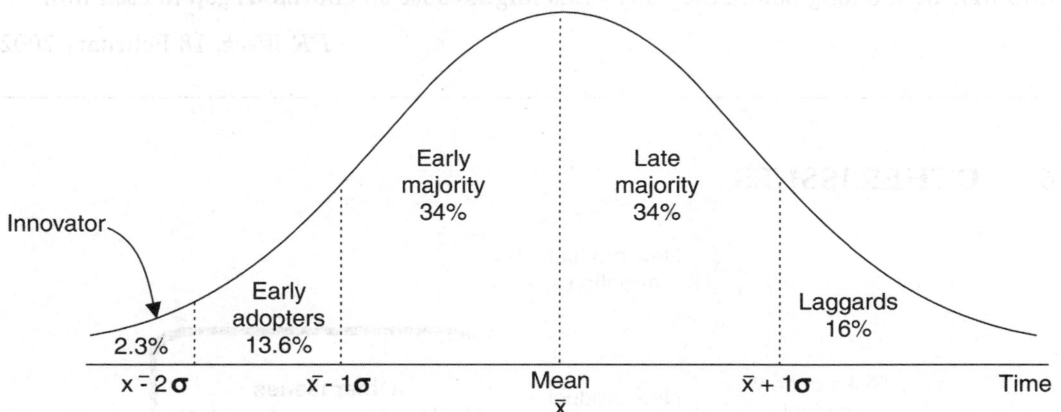

Figure 8.2: Adopters

Early adopters and innovators are thought to operate as opinion leaders and are therefore targeted by companies in order to influence the adoption of a product by their friends.

The main problem with this model is that the categories appear to add up to 100% of the target market. This does not reflect marketers' experience. Some potential consumers do not adopt/purchase at all. It has consequently been suggested that an additional category is needed: **nonadopters,** or **nonconsumers.**

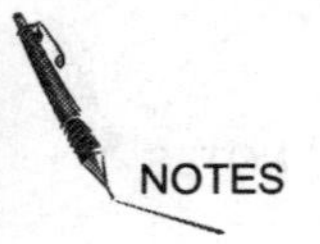

EXAMPLE

According to Chris Lewis, chief executive of Lewis PR, classic marketing theory does not really work for hi-tech products that have such short life-cycles that they are just fads. 'For fads, the traditional media are not fast enough; you need to use all the paraphernalia of web-based PR and marketing, such as news groups and web monitoring services. And you need to be international immediately,' he says.

Sue Rizzello, business group director at Edelman PR says: 'There is an adoption curve for new technologies with the early consumers taking the risk, and others being more conservative. This creates an opportunity to market at different levels to different audiences. Some companies manage to keep a number of product lines moving at the same time - they are basically the same product, but they are targeted at different audiences.'

Lewis breaks the potential target market down even more simply. 'There are generally two types of buyers in this area - the fad buyers and the cautious buyers. Fad buyers will usually snap up the latest products, regardless of it having yet to be proven in the marketplace, and will always strive to get brand new gadgets, even if this means that it replaces an existing product. On the other hand, cautious buyers will wait until there has been enough mainstream acceptance, particularly among manufacturers, before they make a purchase.'

When a client needs to raise awareness of the new products coming along while still generating income from existing product lines, this can mean two teams within an agency working in parallel. One team will be working on early adopters with the new product, while the other will stay on-message with the existing product for the mass market.

Rizzello says: 'There is a lot of energy that goes into creating marketing strategies that do not cannibalise the existing market. The timing of PR in this regard has to be very careful. A lot of energy also goes into managing upgrades so that people are not scared into waiting too long before they buy - this might cause an enormous gap in cash flow.'

PR Week, 18 February 2002

6 OTHER ISSUES

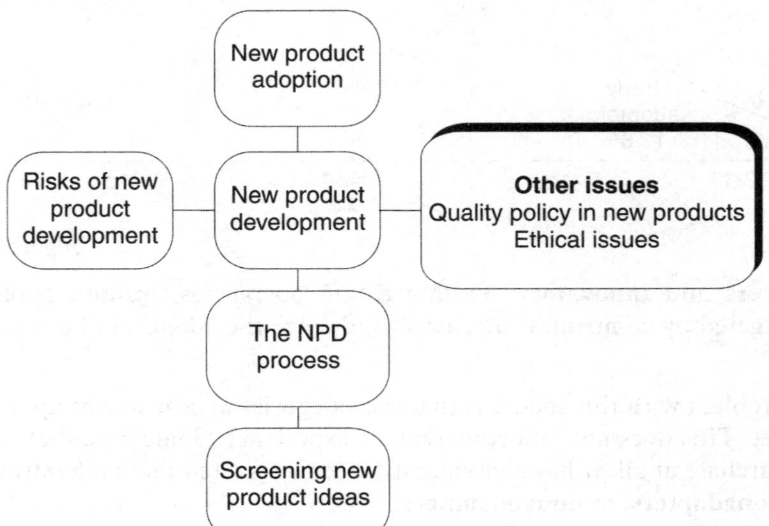

6.1 Quality policy in new products

This is an important policy consideration. Different market segments will require products of **different price and quality.** When a market is dominated by established brand names, one entry strategy is to tap potential demand for a (cheaper) lower quality item.

Customers often judge the quality of an article by its price. Quality policy may well involve fixing a price and then manufacturing a product to the best quality standard that can be achieved within these constraints, rather than making a product of a certain quality and then deciding what its price should be.

Quality should also be determined by the expected physical, technological and social life of the product for the following reasons.

(a) There is no value in making one part of a product good enough to have a physical life of five years, when the rest of the product will wear out and need to be replaced within two years.

(b) If technological advances are likely to make a product obsolescent within a certain number of years, it is wasteful and uneconomic to produce an article which will last for a longer time.

(c) If fashion determines the life of a product, the quality required need only be sufficient to cover the period of demand. The quality of fashion clothes, for example, is initially governed by their fashion life.

Quality policy must be carefully integrated with **sales promotion**. If a product is branded and advertised as having a certain quality, but customers then find that this is not true, the product will fail. The quality of a product (involving its design, production standards, quality control and after-sales service) must be established and maintained before a promotion campaign can use quality as a **selling feature**.

Notice that in terms of the marketing mix this is a clear example of consistency between product and promotion.

6.2 Ethical issues

As marketing people we should have some concept of the **responsibility** vested in us for delivering to the publics we serve.

This not to say that we are not to make a profit, nor to shirk the necessity for aggressive commercial action when required for the protection of our trading performance. We should, however, feel that what we are offering to the market is part of a **mutually beneficial exchange process.**

Nowhere are we more on trust in this regard than in the area of **new products**. It is our job to ensure that the products which we offer constitute a beneficial contribution to the consumer. They will make judgements in the form of re-purchase or promotion by word of mouth.

Clearly, this approach can be considered as less than an ethical issue. It can appear as feathering our own nests: **making sure that customers do come back** is one of the tenets of marketing.

Ethics is not a question of legality; it is a question of **fairness**. By keeping at the front of our minds that the new products which we work so hard to make successful should be part of the concept of **fair trading**, we shall be promoting a benefit for our customers and our companies. This is sometimes called **enlightened self-interest**.

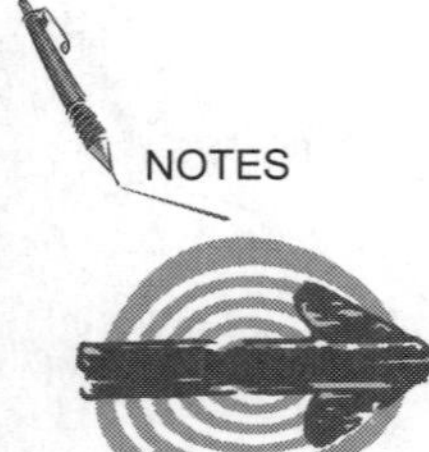

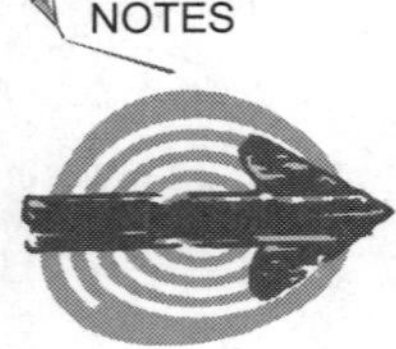

We have considered the development of new products as a part of the company's operation of the marketing mix. In the next chapter we consider the financial basis of marketing activity in the second level of the mix, pricing. It is the powerful combination of product and price which produces the concept of value, and that makes it all the more important to the marketing manager.

Chapter roundup

- New product development is a critically important issue.
- There are varying degrees of formality of the process in firms.
- The activities may be divided into R & D which comprises pure research and applied research and development.
- The NPD process covers issues from original concepts to the launch.
- The management of NPD is becoming more difficult: pressures on firms to launch new products are increasing, while at the same time risks are increasing.
- Effective development through all the stages of the NPD process may call for high levels of investment.
- Investment in the process is becoming less readily available as managements respond to the increasing risks.
- Successful managements are becoming more effective at the screening process.
- Ethical issues are important in new product policy.

Quick quiz

1. What is the main purpose of NPD?
2. Who are stakeholders?
3. What are products which are described as 'new to the world'?
4. What are the distinct organisational activities from which new products emerge?
5. Which department normally does pure research?
6. What does 'applied' mean in the research context?
7. What are two main driving forces behind NPD said to be?
8. What are two main types of source for NPD ideas?
9. Give four examples from each type of source of new product ideas.
10. How many parts are there to the NPD process model?
11. What failure rate % is given for new products?
12. What % of adopters are said to be in the 'early majority' group?
13. Which are the largest group, 'laggards' or 'innovators'?

Answers to Quick quiz

1 To ensure the growth or survival of an organisation.

2 Anybody who has a direct or indirect interest in the activities of the firm.

3 Products which are totally new to everybody and affect us significantly.

4 R & D and NPD.

5 R & D (although commercially motivated work will also be undertaken here).

6 Work which is done to solve a specific problem or achieve a specific objective such as produce a new product.

7 Discovery and need.

8 Internal and external.

9 Please refer to the lists in section 1.2.

10 In the model in the text there are nine parts, starting with original concept and culminating in roll-out: full launch.

11 80%.

12 34%.

13 Laggards are 16% and innovators are 2.3%.

Answers to Activities

1 The regular and rapid innovation from Apple is particularly noteworthy. This includes the various forms of the iPod and the iPhone. Another good example is the Toyota Prius hybrid drive car.

2 New product

Entirely new market	Fax machine
Replacing an existing product	Spin dryer
Broadening the market	PC innovations (almost daily!)

New old product

In a new market	Cider (Red Rock, for example)
New packaging	Spray Cooking Oil
New marketing	Hair gel

3 Part of the problem may be motivation and knowing that you can make a difference. If employees were informed of the importance of new products to the future of the company and therefore to their own future, this may be a start. In addition maybe a seat, in rotation, on the NPD committee would be an incentive. Also, a share option in the new product when launched.

Chapter 9 :

PLACE: THE IMPORTANCE OF DISTRIBUTION

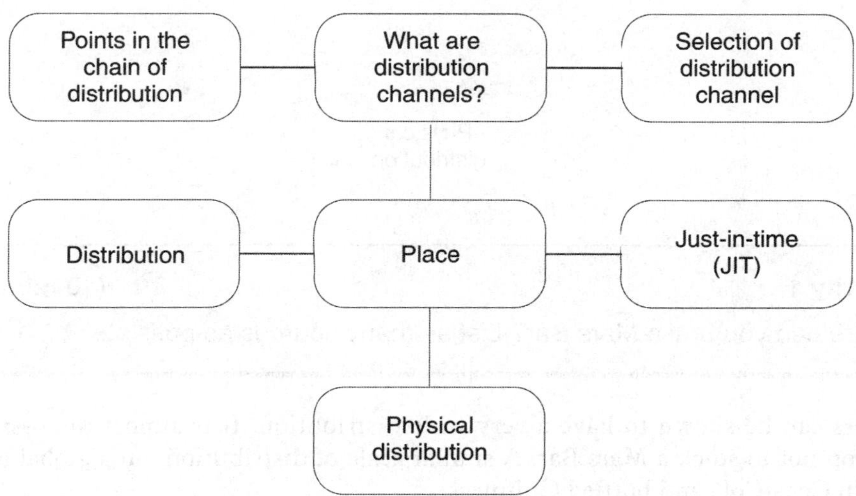

Introduction

No matter how sophisticated and well-thought out the other components of the marketing mix are, the company's fortunes will rise or fall on the effectiveness of its distribution policy. The customer's access to the product is a prime factor in the exchange process. Distribution may be a simple process or it may be highly complex and capital-intensive. **The purpose of distribution is to facilitate purchase.** Such a condition being achieved at a time and place that the combined effects of the marketing effort have worked to provide. Should the distribution strategy fail the whole investment so far may be wasted.

It is this critical aspect of the marketing mix which we are about to examine in the following pages.

Your objectives

In this chapter you will learn about the following.

(a) The importance of making goods easily available to the customer

(b) Identifying intermediaries and critically examining their role

(c) Analysing factors influencing the choice of channel intermediaries

(d) Critically examining the scope, key areas and goals of a physical distribution system

(e) Evaluating the importance of distribution and its role in the marketing mix

1 PLACE

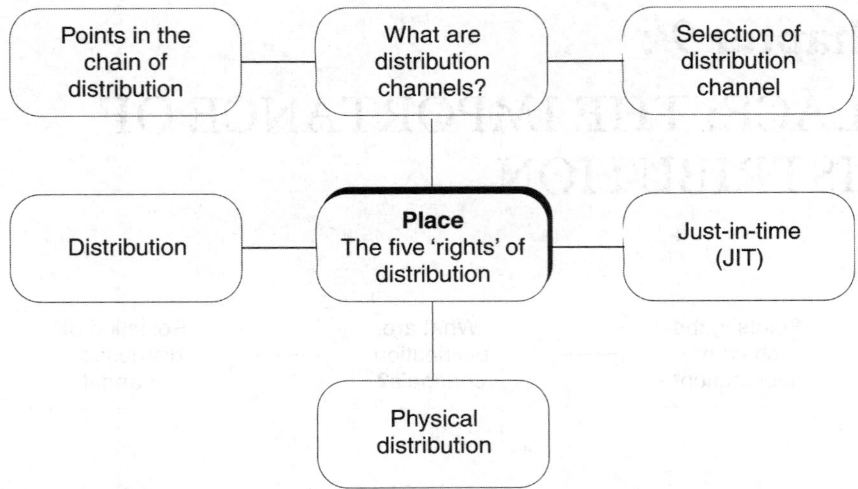

Activity 1 **(10 minutes)**

Where can you buy a Mars Bar? List as many sources as possible.

Mars Bars can be shown to have a very wide distribution. It is almost impossible for a sweet shop not to stock a Mars Bar. A similar scale of distribution, on a global level, can be seen in Coca-Cola and bottled Guinness.

This component of the marketing mix is essentially concerned with the **processes by which the product is made available to the consumer in a particular place**. Other more commonly used terms for 'place' include distribution, delivery systems and marketing; channels. The terms are often used interchangeably since all are related to making products available to the market. Although place is normally the last element in the list of marketing mix variables, its importance should not be underestimated, especially in provision of services. Marketing effort will be futile if the product is not actually in the right place at the right time so that a purchase can be made. Furthermore, effective and efficient distribution can be a crucial source of competitive advantage.

Distribution is often seen as the Cinderella of the marketing mix. In companies where distribution involves the physical transport of goods and stores, a lack of co-ordination by the marketing executive often results in inadequate control over the distribution function. However, the choice of a particular distribution policy, such as whether or not to use wholesalers, may result in the company delegating to intermediaries much of its marketing function, such as selling to the end user.

EXAMPLE: CLUB GLOVE STOPPING SALES TO E-TAILERS WITHOUT PHYSICAL STORES

Club Glove – maker of the most widely used golf travel bag on the PGA and Champions Tours – announces a new distribution policy aimed at minimizing excessive online discounting by limiting sales to only those e-tailers that also have a brick-and-mortar location.

Designed to support key green grass and big-box accounts like Edwin Watts, Dick's Sporting Goods, Golf Galaxy, Golfsmith, PGA Tour Superstores and Roger Dunn, among others, the new mandate helps Club Glove and its partners maintain price integrity and ensures consumers can more easily locate authorized dealers.

"We're not against online retail, but we are against the overcrowding and differences in both price and service that are so common in this sphere. Quite honestly, standard retail margins are not needed at the e-tail level," says company founder Jeff Herold. "An overwhelming number of hours and hard work are involved in running both sides of the manufacturing / retail equation. It just doesn't make sense for websites without a store front to claim the lion's share of the profits."

By limiting its online presence to established brick-and-mortar retailers with an e-commerce component, Club Glove is able to prevent its products from being discounted in a manner that undercuts some of its best partners.

Worldgolf.com, 18 November 2009

A profound influence on distribution in recent years has been the introduction of Just-in-Time (JIT) production and purchasing (this is linked to Total Quality Management.) We shall consider the impact of JIT in the final section of this chapter.

At this point, some definitions would be appropriate.

Definition

Distribution: a key marketing function: the process of getting products to consumers. Although some manufacturers can and do sell direct to consumers, practical considerations require most to use a distribution system composed of independent middlemen, usually wholesalers and retailers.

These intermediaries carry out critically important marketing activities, such as buying and selling, sorting and storing, transporting and financing products as they move from producer to consumer, all of which are necessary functions if products are to be found by consumers in the right place at the right time and at the right price.

Distribution can also refer to a measure of market penetration: the number of retail outlets which stock and sell a particular product as a percentage of all outlets that could possibly sell that product. *Pocket Marketing*

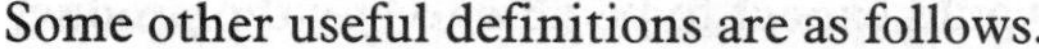

Some other useful definitions are as follows.

Definitions

Chain of distribution: the process which enables the flow of goods between the producer and the consumer.

Distribution channel: the means of getting the goods to the consumer.

Intermediary: any firm which buys from one post of the chain and sells to another in the process of transferring the goods from the producer to the consumer.

You can see from the definition of distribution that it does not only cover the physical distribution of products. It is concerned with all aspects of getting the product to the consumer, involving the choice of which outlets, channels and intermediaries to use. Some of those functions, particularly associated with physical distribution, may not be carried out or decided by the marketing department, but they are marketing led.

1.1 The five 'rights' of distribution.

There is a concept called the 'Five rights of distribution'.

The RIGHT product

In the RIGHT place

At the RIGHT time

In the RIGHT quantity

For the RIGHT price

These are what distribution does for the transaction. The **five rights** encapsulate the key roles of intermediaries. In the context of the statement, right has two meanings. Clearly it means correct or appropriate; it also refers to the right of the customer to expect such appropriateness.

Let us examine these ideas.

The **right product** means **the product which the customer asks for**, whether by brand or by type. The product which will fulfil the needs and wants of the customer as specified by them or as determined in the questioning of the salesperson. Remember the stage of the sale which was labelled **identifying the need**. There is also a legal concept of satisfactory quality which means rightness for purpose: the job for which it is required or described. If you ask for a particular brand in a shop, you have a normal expectation that, should the stockist not have that brand, there will be an alternative brand of a similar product, that is, a direct comparable alternative. To go back to Mars Bars, if the outlet was temporarily out of stock, you would not be surprised to be offered another similar bar, say Snickers.

FOR DISCUSSION

Shop assistants do not have sufficient product knowledge to know what is right for the customer.

The **right place** means **where the customer would expect to be able to buy the product** and **where the customer wants to buy the product.** A simple example would be that the seaside would be the appropriate place to sell buckets and spades, not, say, an inland clothes shop. A restaurant advertising outstanding cuisine would be expected to offer the best and not present the customer with a stained menu card offering only sausage, egg and chips.

The **right time** may be considered on a **seasonal basis**; the products which are seasonal such as produce in the greengrocer or fashion in the shops is subject to the customers normal expectations of timeliness. Christmas and Easter and back-to-school are other examples.

On a **twenty four hour basis** there are **expectations as to opening times**. You will be aware of the culture differences between the UK and mainland Europe in this regard. On the one hand, shop opening hours in the UK are far less restricted than in some

European countries, notably Germany. On the other hand, Sunday trading in the UK has until recently been subject to many more restrictions than in some European countries.

The **right quantity** is a clear expectation of customers. They **expect to be able to buy in convenient forms** and in **convenient amounts** for their rate of usage, storage and capacity to carry products. In fact the quantity aspect is one of the major ways that distribution adds value for the customer by breaking down the quantities which the manufacturer finds economical to produce into the quantities which the customer finds convenient to buy.

The **right price** is something we have discussed previously in an earlier chapter and specifically under the heading of the price expectation curve. Price is a function of the value concept. **Customers expect value** which is reflected by the relationship of price and performance. If we pay a high price we expect the product to give us something extra over a similar product for which we pay a lower price. The customer has a right to expect value. The customer also expects a range of prices. The **right price** is the price that **meets the customer's expectations and provides value.**

2 WHAT ARE DISTRIBUTION CHANNELS?

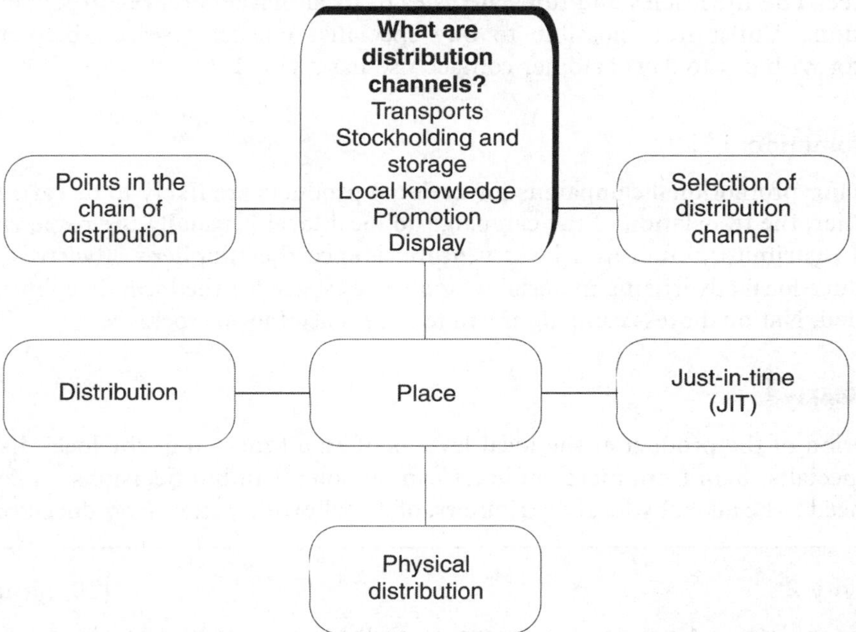

Independently owned and operated distributors may well have their own objectives, strategies and plans. In their decision making processes, these are likely to take precedence over those of the manufacturer or supplier with whom they are dealing. This can lead to **conflict**. Suppliers may solve the problem by buying their own distribution route or by distributing direct to their customers. Direct distribution is common for many industrial and/or customised systems suppliers and used to be common in some consumer markets, such as dairy products, insurance and newspapers; the rising cost of labour and where growth of out-of-town supermarket shopping has tended to reduce the incidence of such direct services. However, the growth of Internet retailing has led to a resurgence of direct distribution in some markets, including groceries.

In order for a product to be distributed a number of basic functions usually need to be fulfilled.

2.1 Transport

This function may be provided by the supplier or the distributor or may be sub-contracted to a specialist. For some products, such as perishable goods, transport planning is vital. The rent or buy decision on transport is important and has both financial and operational consequences.

2.2 Stockholding and storage

For production planning purposes an uninterrupted flow of production is often essential, so stocks of raw materials and components accumulate and need to be stored, incurring significant costs and risks.

For consumer goods, holding stock at the point of sale can be very costly especially in city centre retail locations. A good stock control system is essential, designed to avoid 'stockouts' while keeping stockholding costs low.

2.3 Local knowledge

As production has tended to become centralised in pursuit of economies of scale, the need to understand local markets has grown, particularly when international marketing takes place. The intricacies and idiosyncrasies of local markets represent key marketing information. Whilst it is possible to buy specialist market research help, the local distributor with day to day customer contact also has a vital role.

2.4 Promotion

While major promotional campaigns for national products are likely to be carried out by the supplier, the translation of the campaign to local level is usually the responsibility of the local distributor, often as a joint venture. Hence the supplier's advertising agency will produce local advertising material which leaves space for the local distributor's name to be added. National press campaigns can feature lists of local stockists.

2.5 Display

Presentation of the product at the local level is often a function of the local distributor. Again, specialist help from merchandisers can be bought in but decisions on layout and display need to be taken by local distributors, often following patterns produced centrally.

Activity 2 **(20 minutes)**

For many type of goods, producers invariably use retailers as middlemen in getting the product to the customer. Try to think of some of the disadvantages of doing this, from the producer's point of view.

3 POINTS IN THE CHAIN OF DISTRIBUTION

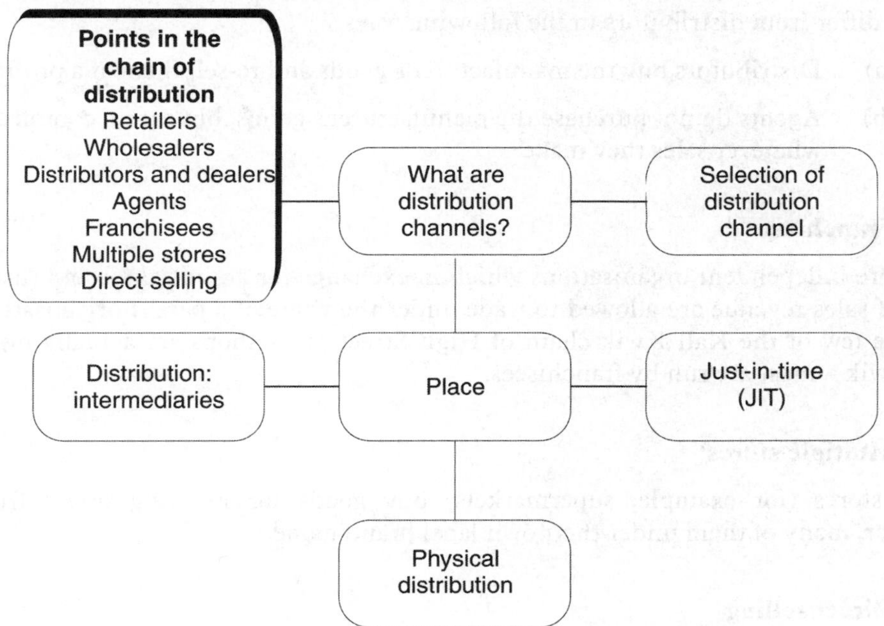

3.1 Retailers

These are traders operating outlets which sell directly to households. They may be classified by:

(a) Type of goods sold (for example, hardware, furniture)

(b) Type of service (self-service, counter service)

(c) Size

(d) Location (rural, city-centre, suburban shopping mall, out-of-town shopping centre)

Another classification is:

(a) **Independent retailers** (including the local corner shop, although independents are not always as small as this)

(b) **Multiple chains.** Some of these are associated with one class of product; others are variety chains, holding a wide range of different stocks; still others are voluntary groups of independents, usually grocers.

3.2 Wholesalers

These are intermediaries who stock a range of products from competing manufacturers to sell on to other organisations such as retailers. Many wholesalers specialise in particular products. Most deal in consumer goods, but some specialise in industrial goods (for example, steel stockholders and builders' merchants).

3.3 Distributors and dealers

These are organisations which contract to buy a manufacturer's goods and sell them to customers. Their function is similar to that of wholesalers, but they usually offer a narrower product range, sometimes (as in the case of most car dealers) the products of a single manufacturer. In addition to selling on the manufacturer's product, distributors often promote the products and provide after-sales service.

3.4 Agents

Agents differ from distributors in the following ways.

(a) Distributors buy the manufacturer's goods and re-sell them at a profit.

(b) Agents do not purchase the manufacturer's goods, but earn a commission on whatever sales they make.

3.5 Franchisees

These are independent organisations which in exchange for an initial fee and (usually) a share of sales revenue are allowed to trade under the name of a parent organisation. For example few of the Kall Kwik chain of High Street print shops are actually owned by Kall Kwik – most are run by franchisees.

3.6 Multiple stores

These stores (for example, supermarkets) buy goods for retailing direct from the producer, many of them under their own label brand name.

3.7 Direct selling

This can take place by various means:

(a) Mail order

(b) Telephone selling

(c) Door-to-door selling

(d) Personal selling in the sale of industrial goods

(e) A vertically-integrated organisation which includes both manufacturing and retail outlets

(f) Computer-shopping or TV shopping

The **Internet** has contributed to a process known as **disintermediation,** giving the consumer direct access to information that would otherwise require an intermediary, such as a sales person or retail outlet.

EXAMPLE

The potential of the Internet to serve as a channel for products and services is a real challenge for many brand-name bricks and mortar companies. Traditional bookshops find themselves challenged by companies such as Amazon and inceasingly groceryretailers such as Tesco who have sites with enourmous ranges of products. Stockbroking firms are seeing a tidal wave of on-line home investors using vehicles such as Charles Schwab's on-line dealing service. These comparatively young internet ventures have a culture of risk-taking that threatens to leave traditional companies behind. As a result, more and more companies are looking for Internet distribution experise. The DIY retailer B&Q found it necessary to launch an online store in order to retain a competitive edge but focusing more on large electrical products.

Activity 3 **(20 minutes)**

Choose a small town near you and identify the proportion of High Street shops that are branches of larger multiple retail chains.

4 SELECTION OF DISTRIBUTION CHANNEL

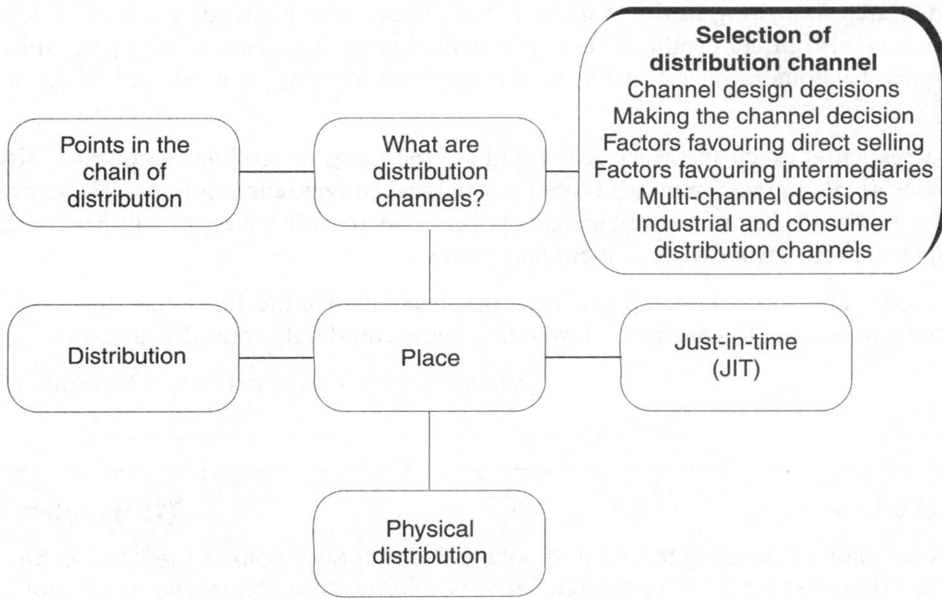

Choosing distribution channels is important for any organisation, because once a set of channels has been established, subsequent changes are likely to be costly and slow to implement. Distribution channels fall into one of two categories: **direct and indirect channels.**

Direct distribution means the product going directly from producer to consumer without the use of a specific intermediary. These methods are often described as **active** since they typically involve the **supplier making the first approach** to a potential customer. Direct distribution methods generally fall into two categories: those using media such as the press, leaflets and telephones to invite response and purchase by the consumer and those using a sales force to contact consumers face to face. This kind of distribution is, therefore, often referred to as 'direct to customer'.

Indirect distribution refers to systems of distribution, common among manufactured goods, which make **use of an intermediary;** a wholesaler, retailer or perhaps both. In contrast to direct distribution, these methods are often thought of as being **passive** in the sense that they **rely on consumers to make the first approach** by entering the relevant retail outlet. Dell computers have tried to avoid this problem by only selling directly to consumers.

EXAMPLE: DAIRY CREST TO RAMP UP FOOD HOME DELIVERY

Dairy company Dairy Crest is gunning to reach 250,000 customers by March for its home delivery, direct-to-customer Milk&More offer.

Dairy Crest already has 120,000 customers signed up to the scheme, which rolled out nationally this summer following a trial last year.

Shoppers at Milkandmore.co.uk are now offered a selection of staple foods delivered to their doorstep first thing in the morning. Dairy Crest, which already ran a milk delivery service, now also offers products such as bread, cheese, eggs, bacon, sausages, and fresh vegetables. Customers have until 9pm the previous evening to order online for a free next-day delivery.

Dairy Crest chief executive Mark Allen said . . . the range of products comprises 'distress purchases' that shoppers may need to go to the local convenience store for. He said: 'Our prices are akin to that of a convenience shop, so we are not trying to compete with the big supermarkets, rather with convenience stores.'

Allen said: 'The milk doorstep business has been in decline for some time and now represents less than 10% of the total, so our scheme could help stem this decline.'

Jennifer Creevy, retail-week.com, 6 November 2009

Activity 4 **(15 minutes)**

One factor influencing the choice between direct and indirect methods is the average order size for a product. State what you think the relationship might be between average order size and the occurrence (or non-occurrence) of direct distribution.

4.1 Channel design decisions

In setting up a channel of distribution, the supplier has to take into account:

- Customers
- Product characteristics
- Distribution characteristics
- The channel chosen by competitors
- The supplier's own characteristics

Customers

The number of potential customers, their buying habits and their geographical locations are key influences. The use of mail order for those with limited mobility (rural location, illness) is an example of the influence of customers on channel design. Marketing industrial components to the car industry needs to take account of the location of the car industry in the UK. Selling to supermarket chains in the UK is now very difficult as the concentration of grocery retailing into a few large chains has increased the power of the buyers: specialist centralised buyers can extract highly favourable terms from suppliers. Unless the supplier is successful in selling to the big chains, the product may only be available to small numbers of shoppers each week.

Product characteristics

Some product characteristics have an important effect on design of the channel of distribution.

(a) **Perishability**

Fresh fruit and newspapers must be distributed very quickly or they become worthless. Speed of delivery is therefore a key factor in the design of the distribution system for such products.

(b) **Customisation**

Customised products tend to be distributed direct. When a wide range of options is available sales may be made using demonstration units, with customised delivery to follow.

(c) **After-sales service/technical advice**

Extent and cost must be carefully considered, staff training given and quality control systems set up. Training programmes are often provided for distributors by suppliers. Exclusive area franchises giving guaranteed custom can be allocated to ensure distributor co-operation; the disadvantage of this is that a poor distributor may cost a supplier dearly in a particular area.

(d) **Franchising**

Franchising has become an increasingly popular means of growth both for suppliers like the Body Shop and for franchisees who carry the set-up costs and licence fees. The supplier gains more outlets more quickly and exerts more control than is usual with indirect distribution.

Distributor characteristics

The capability of the distributor to take on the distributive functions already discussed above is obviously an important influence on the supplier's choice.

Competitors' channel choice

For many consumer goods, a supplier's brand will sit alongside its competitors' products and there is little the supplier can do about it. For other products, distributors may stock one name brand only (for example, in car distribution) and in return be given an exclusive area. In this case new suppliers may face difficulties in breaking into a market if all the best distribution outlets have been taken up.

Supplier characteristics

A strong financial base gives the supplier the option of buying and operating their own distribution channel: Boots the Chemist is a prime example. The market position of the supplier is also important: distributors are keen to be associated with the market leader but the third, fourth or fifth brand in a market is likely to find more distribution problems.

Activity 5 **(15 minutes)**

What are three advantages to the manufacturer of factory shops where they sell their own products, often at reduced prices?

4.2 Making the channel decision

Producers have to decide the following.

(a) What types of distributor are to be used (wholesalers, retailers, agents)?

(b) How many of each type will be used? The answer to this depends on what degree of market exposure will be sought:

- Intensive - blanket coverage
- Exclusive - appointed outlets for exclusive areas
- Selective - few distributors, but restricted by location, size or status

(c) Who will carry out specific marketing tasks such as:

- Credit provision
- Delivery
- After sales service
- Training (sales and product)
- Display?

(d) How will performance of distributors be evaluated?

- In terms of cost?
- In terms of sales levels?
- According to the degree of control achieved?
- By the amount of conflict that arises?

To sum up, to develop an integrated system of distribution, the supplier must consider all the factors influencing distribution combined with a knowledge of the relative merits of the different types of channel available.

EXAMPLE

In 2002 Tesco lost a landmark four year legal battle with Levi Strauss for the right to sell Levi jeans in its UK stores. The argument posed by Levi was that being distributed in a supermarket environment undermined the brand image. The retailer was able to source the jeans from the US and sell them at half the recommended retail price. Following the ruling the retailer was still free to source the products for a time from Eastern Europe via the grey market.

FOR DISCUSSION

The retailer Poundland sells household brand names in its chain of 150 UK stores with everything stocked sold for just £1. Items sold tend to be discontinued stock or perishable food items. What are the advantages and disadvantages for branded manufacturers such as Cadbury making use of these distribution channels?

4.3 Factors favouring the use of direct selling

These are as follows.

(a) The need for an **expert sales force** to demonstrate products, explain product characteristics and provide after sales service. Publishers, for

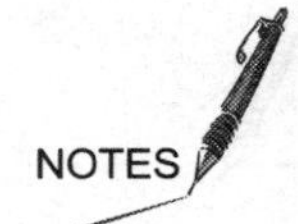

example, use sales reps to keep booksellers up to date with new titles, to arrange for the return of unsold books and so on.

(b) **Intermediaries** may be **unwilling** or **unable to sell the product**. For example, the ill fated Sinclair C5 eventually had to be sold by direct mail.

(c) **Existing channels** may be **linked to other producers**, reluctant to carry new product lines.

(d) The **intermediaries** willing to sell the product may be **too costly,** or they may not be maximising potential sales. This problem caused Nissan to terminate its contract with its sole UK distributor in 1991: Nissan believed that the distributor's pricing strategy was inappropriate.

(e) If **specialised transport requirements** are involved, intermediaries may not be able to deliver goods to the final customer.

(f) Where potential buyers are **geographically concentrated** the supplier's **own sales force can easily reach them** (typically an industrial market). One example is the financial services market centred on the City of London.

Activity 6 **(10 minutes)**

Why do you think that the Direct Line insurance company has been so successful?

4.4 Factors favouring intermediaries

These are as follows.

(a) **Insufficient resources** to finance a large sales force.

(b) A **policy decision** to invest in increased productive capacity rather than extra marketing effort.

(c) The supplier may have **insufficient in-house marketing expertise** in selling to retail stores.

(d) The **assortment of products** may be **insufficient** for a sales force to carry. A wholesaler can complement a limited range and make more efficient use of his sales force.

(e) **Intermediaries can market small lots as part of a range of goods.** The supplier would incur a heavy sales overhead if its own sales force took 'small' individual orders.

(f) Large numbers of **potential buyers spread over a wide geographical area** (typically consumer markets).

4.5 Multi-channel decisions

A producer serving both industrial and consumer markets may decide to use intermediaries for his consumer division and direct selling for his industrial division. For example, a detergent manufacturer might employ salesmen to sell to wholesalers and large retail groups in their consumer division. It would not be efficient for the sales force to approach small retailers directly, whereas industrial users will order very large quantities and may need advice about specialised detergents.

The distribution channels appropriate for industrial markets may not be suitable for consumer markets.

4.6 Industrial and consumer distribution channels

Industrial markets may be characterised as having fewer, larger customers purchasing more expensive products, some of which may be custom built. It is due to these characteristics that industrial distribution channels tend to be more direct and shorter than for consumer markets. It has to be remembered, however, that the most appropriate distribution channels will depend specifically on the objectives of the company regarding market exposure. There are specialist distributors in the industrial sector, which may be used as well as, or instead of, selling directly to the companies within this sector.

There are fewer direct distribution channels from the manufacturer to the consumer in the consumer market. Examples may be found in small 'cottage' industries or mail order companies. It is more usual for companies in consumer markets to use wholesalers and retailers to move their product to the final consumer.

(a) **Wholesalers** break down the bulk from manufacturers and pass products on to retailers. They take on some of the supplier's risks by funding stock. Recently in the UK there has been a reduction in importance of this type of intermediary.

(b) **Retailers** sell to the final consumers. They may give consumers added benefits by providing services such as credit, delivery and a wide variety of goods. In the UK, retailers have increased in power whilst wholesalers have declined. Retailing has also become more concentrated with increased dominance of large multiples.

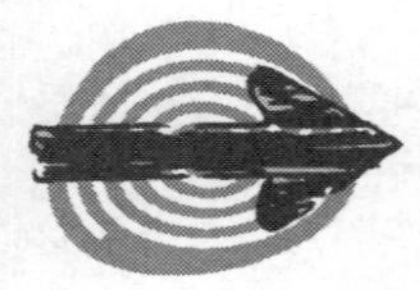

We have now considered some of the major factors which constitute the importance of 'place'. Although in practice distribution is normally managed by the operations management of a company it is still important to marketers. In all successful companies however, all operations are seen as being integrated in the firm's overall corporate marketing approaches.

5 DISTRIBUTION

5.1 Intermediaries

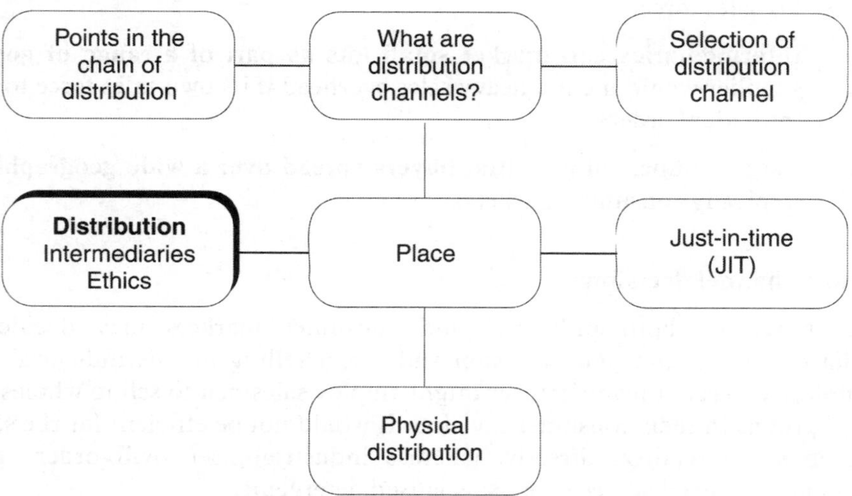

Figures 9.1 and 9.2 show distribution in a market with and without intermediaries.

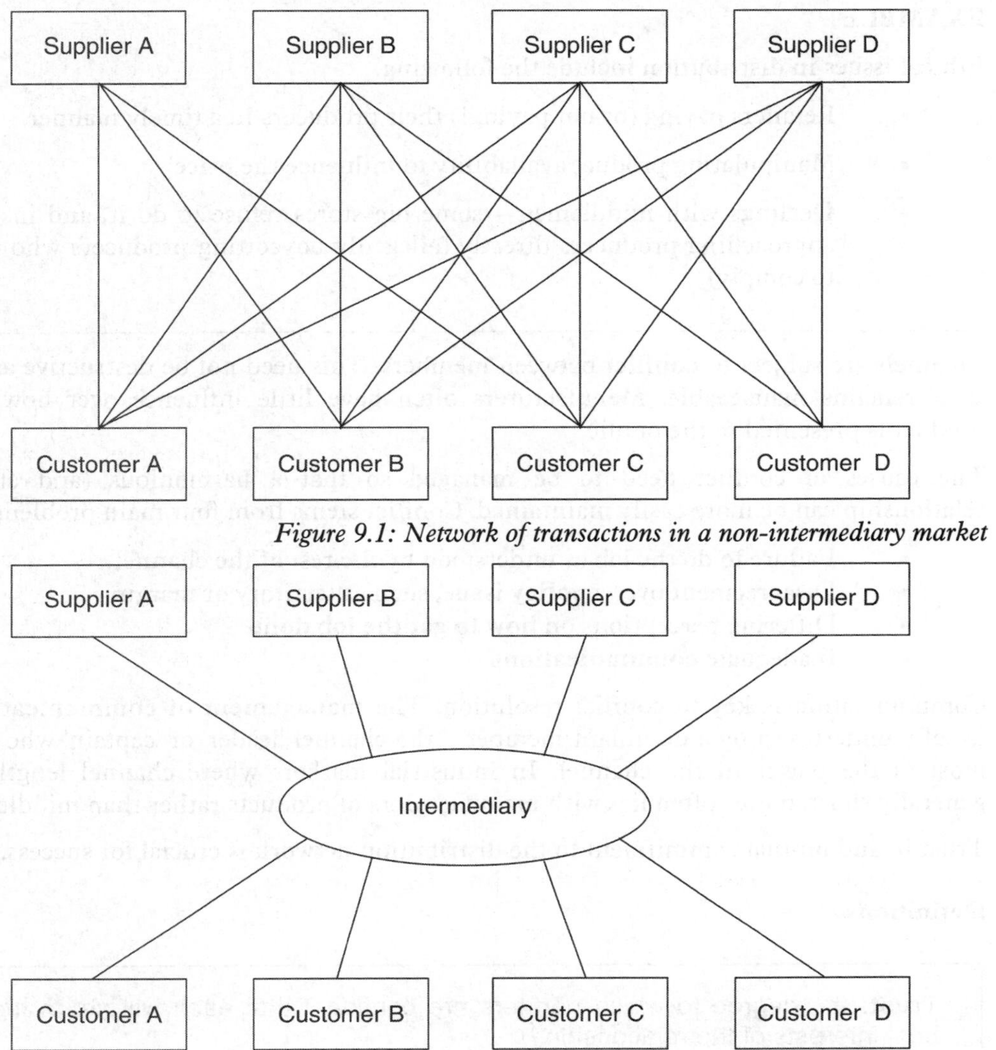

Figure 9.1: Network of transactions in a non-intermediary market

Figure 9.2: Network of transactions in an intermediary market

Figure 9.2 shows a simplified network which in itself demonstrates the logic of systems with intermediaries. Complexity is not the whole story. There are benefits from intermediaries which themselves add value to the offering.

Each stage of the distribution process adds value for the final consumer: the processes in manufacturing and conversion from raw materials to products; the packaging of small quantities and the convenience of shopping where the conditions are specially designed for our comfort and greater shopping pleasure; the ever increasing opportunities to shop at times of greater convenience. This is the added value which the system offers. It enables the manufacturers to concentrate their resources on the things they do best and operate with the economies of scale which enable the prices to be kept low.

5.2 Ethics in distribution

The market has to realise that distribution channel power is not equal. Different roles are played by retailers, wholesalers and agents. For example, in the UK, where in the grocery sector the concentration of retail power has gone furthest, the major supermarket chains are extremely powerful.

EXAMPLE

Ethical issues in distribution include the following.

- Retailers paying (or not paying!) their producers in a timely manner
- Manipulating product availability to influence the price
- Dealings with middlemen – some big stores refuse to do it, and insist on approaching producers directly (allegedly boycotting producers who refuse to comply)

Channels are subject to **conflict** between members. This need not be destructive as long as it remains manageable. Manufacturers often have little influence over how their product is presented to the public.

The causes of conflict need to be managed so that a harmonious (and ethical) relationship can be more easily maintained. Conflict stems from four main problems.

- Failure to do the job as understood by the rest of the channel
- Disagreement over a **policy issue**, such as territory or margin
- Differing perceptions on **how to get the job done**
- Inadequate **communications**

Communication is key to conflict resolution. The **management of communication** is usually undertaken by a dominant member – the channel 'leader' or 'captain' who holds most of the power in the channel. In industrial markets where channel lengths are generally short, power often lies with manufacturers of products rather than middlemen.

Trust in and mutual commitment to the distribution network is crucial for success.

Definitions

Trust: the degree to which partners are confident that each will act in the best interests of the relationship.

Commitment: the desire to maintain a valuable relationship.

The use of **trade promotions** and **trade advertising** by a company will be designed to keep the channel loyal. Techniques such as offering discounts to wholesalers, in return for extra promotion of the product, or extra shelf space, will help to increase sales as well (if the discount is passed on to the end consumer). Trade advertising in the form of brochures, leaflets and samples should focus on aspects such as margins, turnover, shelf space profitability and the level of manufacturer support.

6 PHYSICAL DISTRIBUTION

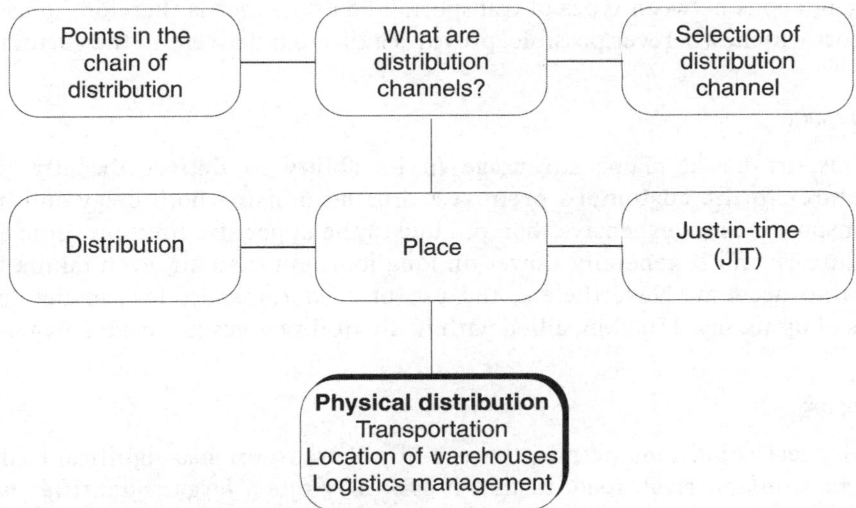

The cost of physically transporting goods has been estimated to be as high as 25% of the costs of an item. But logistics provide services to the customer in terms of availability, speed of delivery and convenience, which provide significant added value to the goods themselves. Logistics involves:

- Order processing
- Transportation
- Stock management
- Warehousing
- Customer services

In marketing, the distances involved mean that the time between placing an order and its delivery can be quite considerable, especially when compared to locally sourced supplies, and the cost significantly higher. A key concept in the management of logistics is that of customer service. Customer service involves defining adequate levels of performance for:

- Order cycle time (order to delivery)
- Accuracy of order processing
- Delivered quality of goods

It is thus concerned with getting the right goods (and all of them, with a mixed order), to the right person, at the right time, at a reasonable cost.

6.1 Transportation

Transport between markets is often the easier part of the problem, with good transport systems and infrastructure (roads, ports, airports, railheads and so on). Within a particular country however both the transport systems and the infrastructure may vary in quality considerably. Generally the more developed nations have reasonably efficient transport facilities internally but, as we look to the lesser developed countries, the quality of communications, availability of transport facilities, and the physical infrastructure may pose significant problems to the marketer looking at export markets.

Modes of transport

The marketer has to take into account the **cost** of transport. Temporary storage and handling form a significant part of the overall cost of transport so methods of transport which minimise them tend to be more competitive. The development of container

systems for road, rail, sea and air has reduced the amount of labour involved in transferring goods between types of transport. The preference is therefore to use a mode of transport which, wherever possible, provides a through delivery to the customer.

Road transport

Road transport has a major advantage in its ability to **deliver directly from the manufacturer to the customer's premises**, thus minimising both delay and handling. Road transport is more expensive than rail due to the upper size limit on vehicle loads in most countries, and is generally slower on long journeys than air, even taking handling transfer into account. Nevertheless, the use of road transport for smaller loads and distances of up to, say, 1500 km, allied with its **flexibility** gives it the advantage.

Rail transport

Where physical conditions permit, the use of rail transport has significant advantages over its main inland rival, road, in that it can carry much **larger quantities over long distances.** Over shorter distances the advantages of the load capacity are outweighed by the transfer costs on and off the rail network. Rail is not economical for short journeys. Bulky, low unit value items such as raw materials are more economically moved by rail where circumstances permit. Peugeot, for example, make use of the UK rail system to transport large quantities of their new cars to various sites. Gravel and sand are commodity products which also are transported using this method.

Water transport

Although little used in the UK for bulk transfer of items, water transport has **similar advantages to rail** and is widely used where geography allows. Where a suitable network of rivers and canals exists, inland waterways can bring the load nearer to the customer. Again the problem of transfer and handling may make this approach expensive. However, its **bulk carrying capacity** does provide significant cost advantages over long distances.

Air transport

Air transport is probably the **most expensive** of all four options for short journeys. The economics of air transport, together with handling costs, make air uncompetitive both in time and cost over short distances. The advantage of air transport lies in **speed** rather than cost, and this can be most effective over longer distances. Where high value, small unit size loads are being considered, air transport may be viable. Again this is a major consideration in exporting.

In particular, where **early speedy delivery** to a market can give **significant price advantages** (for example early flowers and vegetables can command a 10-fold price advantage over maincrop in many cases) air transport costs can be justified because of the high unit value of the goods. Similarly, where the customer is willing to pay a premium for speedy delivery, for example a spare part for a manufacturing plant, air transport can be justified. It is of course widely used for high value, low volume, perishable items such as pharmaceutical drugs.

The advantage of air transport, speed, can however be lost where delays at the airport in forwarding to the customer erode the time saving.

6.2 Location of warehouses

If a company is seeking to build or acquire a new warehouse, it must seek a general area and then a specific site in that area.

(a) Selecting the area will depend on the market potential. To minimise costs and improve delivery service (and thus increase sales), the warehouse should be sited in the middle of an area with high market potential. The size of the warehouse (that is, the amount invested) is also likely to influence the extent to which the market potential is exploited.

(b) The choice of site within an area will depend on:

   (i) The sites available

   (ii) Whether the customer will come to the supplier, or whether the supplier will deliver to the customer

   (iii) Local transport facilities (for instance, road, rail)

   (iv) Future development in the area

   (v) Whether a lease or a freehold is required

   (vi) Its geographical position within the market area

6.3 Logistics management

Logistics management includes **physical distribution** and **materials management**. It therefore encompasses the inflow of raw materials and goods together with the outflow of finished products. Logistics management has developed because of an increased awareness of:

(a) **Customer benefits** that can be incorporated into the overall product offering because of efficient logistics management.

(b) The **cost savings** that can be made when a logistics approach is undertaken.

(c) **Trends** in industrial purchasing that necessarily mean closer links between buyers and sellers, for example just-in-time purchasing and computerised purchasing.

Logistics managers organise inventories, warehouses, purchasing and packaging to product an efficient and effective overall system. There are benefits to consumers of products that are produced by companies with good logistic management. There is less likelihood of goods being out of stock, delivery should be efficient and overall service quality should be higher.

The logistics industry

Contracted-out distribution services require enormous trust, especially in the food business. Sensitive information must be exchanged between the retailer or manufacturer and the distribution company and responsibility for food safety and hygiene must be shared. However, contracting out offers great benefits in terms of flexibility and the elimination of the need for costly capital investment: hence the success of specialist distribution companies such as Hays and Norbert Dentressangle.

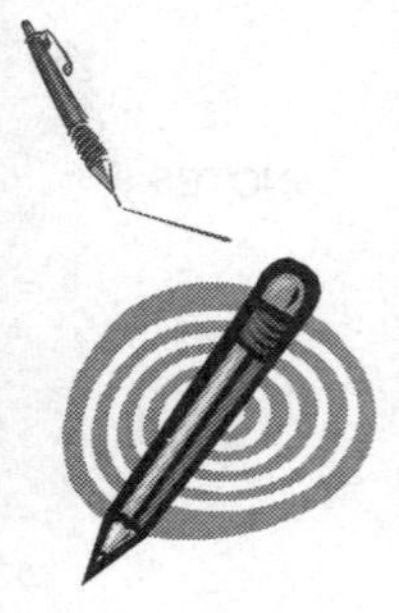

Activity 7 **(20 minutes)**

What factors have influenced the way goods and services are delivered by your own employer or an outlet you know well? Do you think that the choices made are all the right ones?

With the growth of the Single European Market, many firms are developing Europe-wide distribution systems and are ceasing to use merely national bases for distribution. The Channel Tunnel has made rail more cost effective for long journeys from the UK to Europe and beyond. Rail is not cost effective often for short distances, which is why lorries are preferred. Another factor affecting rail will be the increase in trade with Eastern Europe some of whose road networks, by Western standards, are poor.

7 JUST IN TIME (JIT)

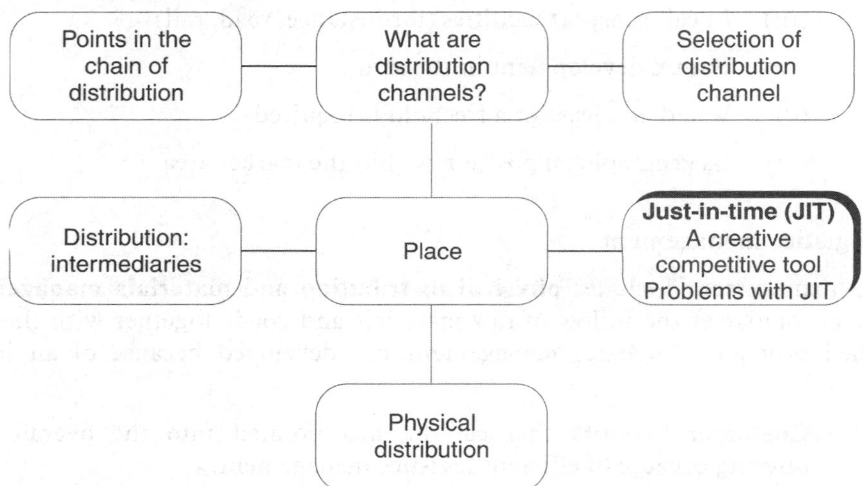

We have already said that **availability is a critical factor** in the formulation of the marketing mix. Increasingly, logistics management has been recognised for the advantages, in terms of customer benefits, which such an approach brings, along with saving in costs and improved company image. A more profound impact has been proposed, however, with the use of more creative and sophisticated systems bringing in not just new possibilities of improved delivery systems but also higher quality and increased profitability and efficiency.

7.1 A creative competitive tool

Just In Time (JIT) is a system of inventory control invented by the Japanese. The benefit is that it allows 'pull' in the market, in contrast to the traditional system of 'just in case'.

Definition

JIT: an inventory control system which delivers input to its production or distribution site only at the rate and time it is needed. Thus it reduces inventories whether it is used within the firm or as a mechanism regulating the flow of products between adjacent firms in the distribution system channel. It is a pull system which replaces buffer inventories with channel member co-operation.

JIT aims to: '**produce instantaneously**, with **perfect quality** and **minimum waste**.'

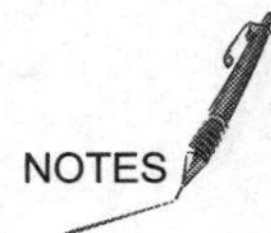

Issue	*Just in Case*	*Just in Time*
Official stocks	Maximum efficiency	Maximum efficiency
Stocks	Integral part of system - a necessary evil	Wasteful - to be eliminated
Lead times	Taken as given and built into production planning routines	Reduced to render small batches economical
Batch sizes	Taken as given and economic order quantity is calculated	Lot size of *one* is the target - because of flexible system
Production planning and control	Computer system models existing system and optimises within it. Information pull for hot orders	Centralised forecasts in conjunction with local pull control
Trigger to production	Algorithmically derived schedules. Hot lists. Maintenance of sub-unit efficiencies	Imminent needs of downstream unit via Kanban cards
Quality	Acceptable quality level. Emphasis on error detection	Zero defects. Error prevention
Performance focus	Sub-unit efficiency	System/organisation efficiency
Organisational design	Input-based. Functional	Output based. Product
Suppliers	Multiple; distant; independent	Single or dual sourcing. Supplier as extension

Figure 9.3: Traditional versus 'new' thinking

Synchronisation (or timing) is an essential component of such systems. A successful channel will require precise synchronisation between suppliers, through the production units to retailers and finally customers. This depends crucially on **information** being freely passed back and forth between channel members; suppliers need to be informed about raw material deliveries, and also the components delivered to manufacturers. For their part, manufacturers must be confident that their deliveries will arrive on time.

Customers need to be treated in a new way; loyalty is **no longer to be taken for granted.** Indeed, as consumers more and more realise the power they wield and become more sophisticated in the criteria they apply when evaluating and choosing products, manufacturers find that they must become responsive to these needs and also be able to adjust themselves rapidly in order to satisfy them. The keyword of the modern marketplace is **flexibility** and this is **coupled with profitability.**

This flexibility is now the key element in:

- The company meeting customer requirements
- The production process
- The company's organisation

JIT, it can be argued, even improves product quality. If suppliers are being provided with minimum resources and required to focus on using it to maximum effect, then it becomes even more important to get it 'right first time', since there is very little leeway in the resources available to do it again. **Right-first-time and just-in-time go together very well indeed!**

7.2 Problems with JIT

Problems with JIT have been identified, according to some commentators. These include the following.

(a) **Conflicts over customers.** Suppliers will often, of course, have commitments to other customers and this may well cause expensive and disruptive delays.

(b) **Conflicts with the workforce.** Excellent industrial relations are vital to the success of this system, as are flexible, sometimes multiskilled, workforces with a willingness to accept flexible work routines and hours, so that management can vary staffing arrangements. Single union deals, famously, are a sine qua non when Japanese companies establish UK operations and this is a major reason.

(c) **Disruption**. Because there is no slack in the system, disruption caused by weather, strikes, financial difficulty and so on cannot easily be dealt with: the whole downstream supply chain comes to a standstill.

JIT, then, is increasing as lean production becomes more important. Focusing as it does on consumer choice, company profit and strong company-supplier relations, this concept fits comfortably alongside other managerial developments such as Total Quality Management (TQM) and accelerating change in product markets.

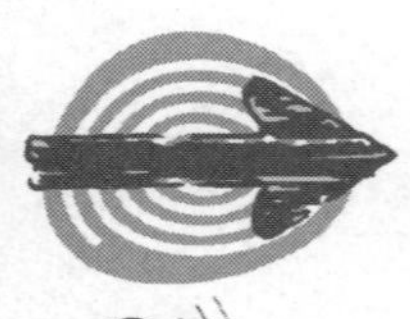

Our discussion of marketing mix variables continues in the next chapter, where we look at price.

Chapter roundup

- 'Place' is an integral part of the marketing mix and of equal importance to the other components.
- The chain of distribution describes the process which links the products to the customer.
- 'Place' is concerned with the channels and outlets, including physical distribution, stock handling, warehousing and transportation.
- There are five 'rights of distribution': product; place; time; quantity and price.
- There are many outlet types; of these the superstores are collectively increasing their power over manufacturers.
- Physical distribution involve logistics; management.
- Just-in-Time involves the creative use of availability as a competitive tool.
- Businesses can benefit by using distribution and the availability of their products as a source of competitive advantage.

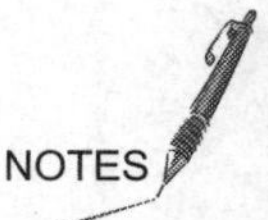

Quick quiz

1 Give an example of direct distribution in consumer markets.

2 What is another name in marketing for distribution?

3 What are the five rights of distribution.

4 What is the chain of distribution?

5 What are main types of intermediaries?

6 What is another word for the physical distribution element of the chain?

7 What are some of the factors favouring the use of intermediaries?

8 What would you say is the basis of the logic of using intermediaries?

9 What are the main elements of physical distribution?

10 What is the definition of Just-in-Time?

11 What are the main problems which have been identified with JIT?

Answers to Quick quiz

1 Fulfilment of Internet sales.

2 Place.

3 Product; place; time; quantity; price.

4 The process which enables the flow of goods to move from the producer to the consumer.

5 Wholesalers; distributors/agents; retailers.

6 Logistics.

7 Finance; alternative investments; know-how; small range; breaking bulk; complexity of network.

8 Doing away with complexity and adding value.

9 Stockhandling, warehousing and transportation.

10 An inventory control system which delivers input to production and/or procurement only at the rate and time that it is needed.

11 Conflict over customer; conflict with the workforce; problems over time scales.

Answers to Activities

1 Sweet shops; supermarkets; pubs; social clubs; sports clubs; railway stations; swimming pools; cafes; Post Offices; cake shops; etc.

2 Your answers might include some of the following points.

(a) The middleman of course has to take his 'cut', reducing the revenue available to the producer.

(b) The producer needs an infrastructure for looking after the retailers — keeping them informed, keeping them well stocked — which might not be necessary in, say, a mail order business.

(c) The producer loses some part of his control over the marketing of his product. The power of some retailers (for example, W H Smith in the world of book publishing) is so great that they are able to dictate marketing policy to their suppliers.

3 This depends on the town you have chosen, but you will probably find the proportion surprisingly high.

4 Other things being equal, if the order pattern is a small number of high-value orders, then direct distribution is more likely to occur. If there are numerous low-value orders, then the cost of fulfilling them promptly will be high and the use of intermediaries is likely.

5 They can sell surplus stock without reducing prices on the high street. They also save on the distribution costs of the products sold within the store and may gain customers who would not otherwise buy their products.

6 The access provided by the 0800 phone number and the very powerful promotional campaign are two important factors. Presumably what follows the enquiry call is efficient (process), the Telesales staff (people) are effective and the deal offered (product, price, value) is attractive.

7 There will be combination of factors to include: customer requirements; the firm's needs and objectives; cost relativities. Whether it is a good choice will depend partly on the cost/profit relationship but most importantly on customer satisfaction.

Chapter 10 : PRICING

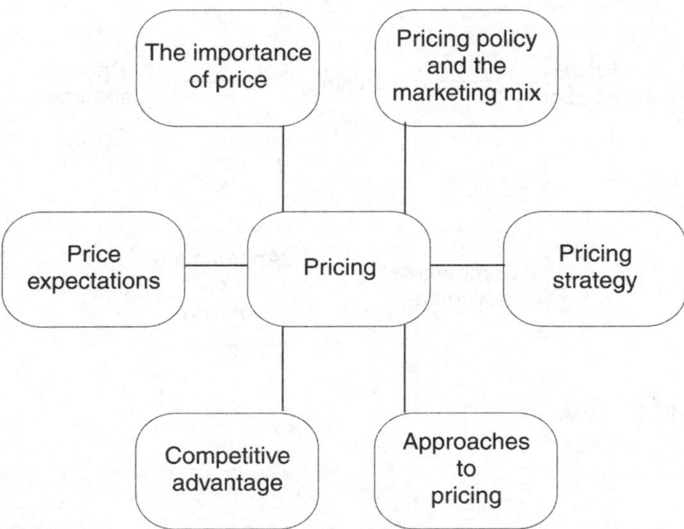

Introduction

From the marketing point of view there are two broad issues concerning price.

On the one hand, price is a unit of **revenue**.

On the other hand, price as an operational variable has a powerful **strategic role** to play. Marketing managers need to recognise that pricing (the **art and technique of deciding on price issues**) provides them with a tool which may be effectively combined with other components of the marketing mix to craft strategies of great variety.

In this chapter we will discuss in some detail the strategic implications of price in the marketing mix.

Your objectives

In this chapter you will learn about the following.

(a) The importance of price

(b) How prices are determined

(c) The relationship between types of costs and sales

(d) Different pricing strategies and their application

(e) Factors influencing pricing policies

(f) Ways in which organisations respond to price competition

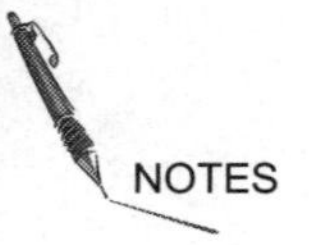

1 THE IMPORTANCE OF PRICE

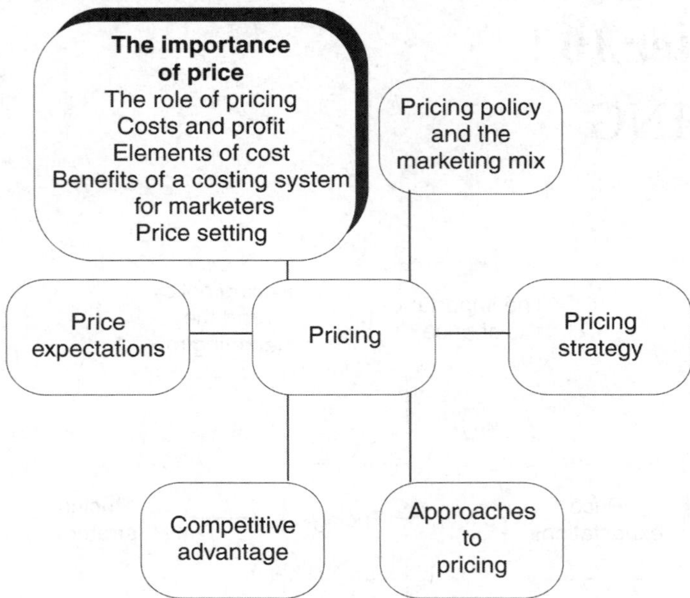

1.1 The role of pricing

Definition

Price can be defined as a measure of the value exchanged by the buyer for the value offered by the seller.

It might be expected, therefore, that the price would reflect the **costs to the seller** of producing the product and the **benefit to the buyer** of consuming it. Unlike the other marketing mix elements, pricing decisions affect profits through their impact on **revenues** rather than **costs**. It also has an important role as **a competitive tool** to differentiate a product and an organisation and thereby exploit market opportunities. Pricing must also be **consistent** with other elements of the marketing mix since it contributes to the overall **image** created for the product.

Activity 1 **(10 minutes)**

In what circumstances would you expect price to be the main factor influencing a consumer's choice?

Although pricing fulfils a number of roles, in overall terms price is set to produce the **level of sales** necessary to meet the **objectives** of the business strategy. Pricing must be systematic and at the same time take into account the internal needs and the external constraints of the organisation. Two broad categories of objectives may be specified for pricing decisions.

(a) **Maximising profits** is concerned with maximising the returns on assets or investments. This may be realised even with a comparatively small market share depending on the patterns of cost and demand.

(b) **Maintaining or increasing market share** involves increasing or maintaining the customer base which may require a different, more competitive approach to pricing.

Either approach may be used in specifying **pricing objectives**. They may appear in combination, based on a specified rate of return and a specified market share. It is important that stated objectives are consistent with overall corporate objectives and corporate strategies.

EXAMPLE

Over the last decade, a number of low-cost no-frills carriers have set up in business, for example EasyJet. To compete, British Airways set up its own low cost no-frills airline. However, to include these services under the British Airways name would have resulted in consumer confusion. Customers do not expect a no-frills service from BA, which has a strong, reliable, upmarket image. Therefore, the no-frills services were run under the 'Go' banner. Ironically, in May 2002 Go was bought out by its rival easyJet. BA's competitive strategy then led to EasyJet overtaking Ryanair, the Irish no-frills operator, to become Europe's biggest low-cost carrier! Periodically Easyjet andRyanair enter mini-price wars with tickets sold at specially low prices on selected routes.

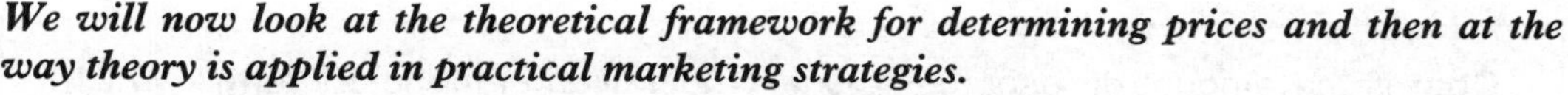
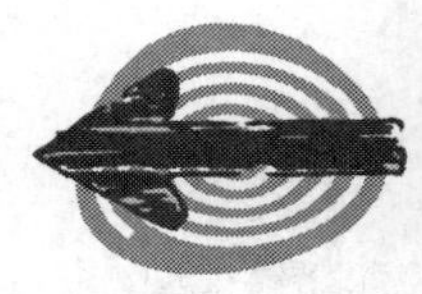

We will now look at the theoretical framework for determining prices and then at the way theory is applied in practical marketing strategies.

1.2 Costs and profit

As marketing people we do not have to be accountants! We do, however, need to understand some of the complexities of accounting methods insofar as they may affect our decisions, and because our actions influence the financial well-being of our organisations. Remember, part of one of the major definitions of marketing is '... to ... supply customer requirements ... **profitably**' (Chartered Institute of Marketing). It is also our responsibility to be aware of, and to contribute to the control of, costs.

Activity 2 **(10 minutes)**

The price of a product in the shops is made up of many elements. Consider the elements which constitute the price of a Mars bar on the shelf in a confectionery outlet.

Having completed Activity 2, you may be surprised to note just how many of the cost headings are marketing-related! Let us put those groupings into a simplified model.

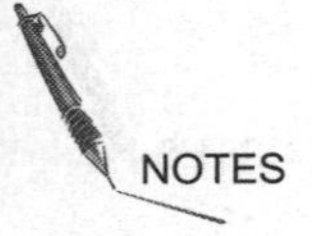

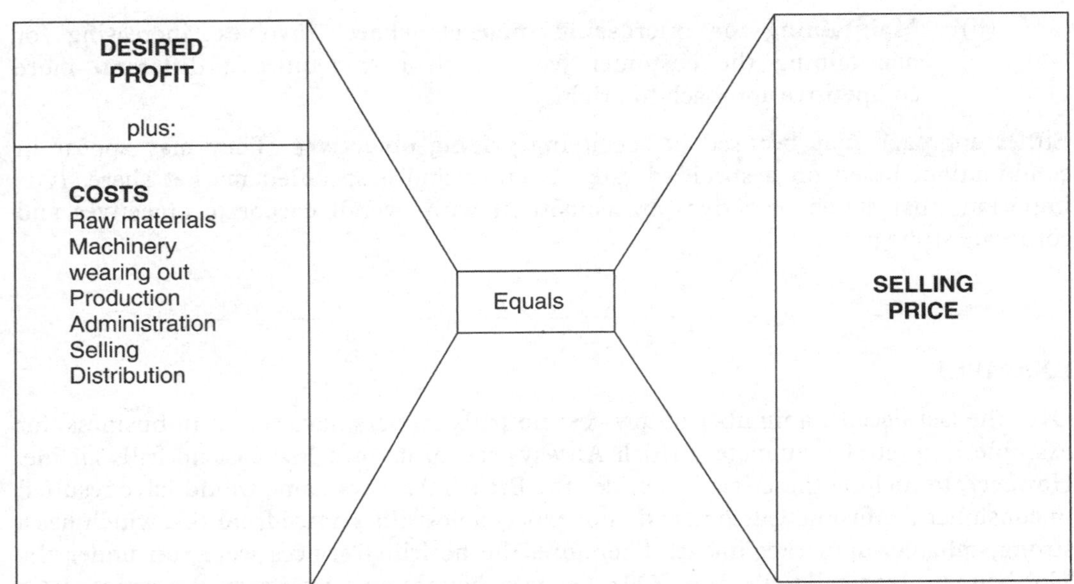

Figure 10.1: Cost-price model

Costs

Definition

> **Cost** is the amount of resources, usually quantified in monetary terms, which is allocated to preparing a product for offer to a market. In other words, everything we spend on making an offering before we add the element of profit.

Costs may be analysed into a number of categories and we shall discuss these categories in some detail later in the chapter.

What we must consider here is that cost is simply the price of **what we build in to the supplier's side of the offering.** It should be the case that all costs represent some aspect of the product or service which will be seen by the buyer as offering extra value. For example, binding a book in a hard binding costs more but it adds value; aesthetic to some people, functional to others. Consequently, the price is usually higher.

We can see then that **cost is a necessary component** in achieving a product or service of a level of attractiveness appropriate to a target market.

Profits

Profits are what enable a company to go on trading; developing new products; providing employment; paying dividends to investors, including pension funds, who can re-invest and maintain the flow of business which supports the activities of society. In general, we could say that profit is the outcome of delivering satisfactions to customers.

Definition

> **Profit** is the excess over costs in revenue. In other words, when we receive a sum of money from a sale whatever is left over when we have paid all our costs, is profit.

NOTES

Clearly, we can see much of what has gone before as having a bearing on our interests in marketing. The model in Figure 10.1 demonstrates the relevance of cost headings to the marketing function. The contribution that each heading makes to the offering through identifiable parts of the marketing mix is sufficient to confirm that the business of costs is very much our concern.

1.3 Elements of cost

Cost accounting involves the calculation of costs of products (or services).

Definition

A **product cost** is defined in the as 'the cost of a finished product built up from its cost elements' and therefore the total cost of a product/service consists of the following.

(a) The cost of materials consumed in making the product or providing the service.

(b) The cost of the wages and salaries (labour) of employees of the organisation, who are directly or indirectly involved in producing the product or providing the service.

(c) The cost of other expenses, apart from materials and labour costs. These include items such as rent and rates, electricity bills, gas bills, depreciation, interest charges, the cost of sub-contractors' services, office cleaning, telephone bills and so on.

Direct costs and indirect costs

Materials, labour costs and other expenses can be classified as **direct costs** or as **indirect costs.**

A direct cost is a cost that can be traced in full to the product, service, or department that is being costed.

Definition

Direct cost: expenditure that can be economically identified with a specific saleable cost unit.

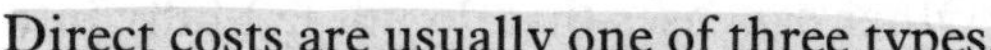

Direct costs are usually one of three types.

(a) Direct **material** costs are the costs of materials that are known to have been used in making and selling a product (or even providing a service).

(b) Direct **labour** costs are the specific costs of the workforce used to make a product or provide a service. Direct labour costs are established by measuring the time taken for a job, or the time taken in 'direct production work'.

(c) Other **direct expenses** are those expenses that have been incurred in full as a direct consequence of making a product, or providing a service, or running a department such as the quality control laboratory.

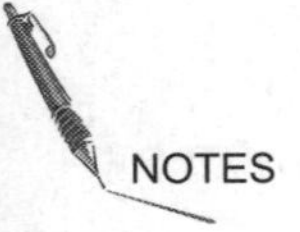
NOTES

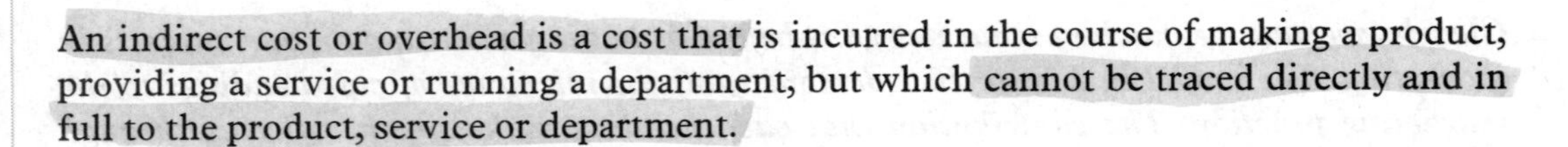

An indirect cost or overhead is a cost that is incurred in the course of making a product, providing a service or running a department, but which cannot be traced directly and in full to the product, service or department.

Definition

Indirect cost: Expenditure on labour, materials or services which cannot be economically identified with a specific saleable cost unit. Examples might include supervisor's wages, cleaning materials and buildings insurance.

You should now be able to specify whether an item of expenditure is a direct material cost, a direct labour cost, an overhead and so on. Try the following Activity to check that you can.

Activity 3 **(20 minutes)**

Classify the following as either direct material costs, direct labour costs, direct expenses or overhead (production, administration, selling or distribution).

(a) Rent, rates and insurance of a factory

(b) Time of skilled staff employed to set up production machinery for specific jobs

(c) Wages of packers, drivers and despatch clerks

(d) Advertising and sales promotion, market research

(e) Rent, rates and insurance of warehouses

(f) Materials specially purchased for a particular job

Functional costs

In a 'traditional' costing system for a manufacturing organisation, costs are classified as follows.

- Production or manufacturing costs
- Administration costs
- Marketing, or selling and distribution costs

Many expenses fall comfortably into one or other of these three broad classifications. Manufacturing costs are associated with the factory, selling and distribution costs with the sales, marketing, warehousing and transport departments and administration costs with general office departments (such as accounting and personnel). Classification in this way is known as classification by function. Other expenses that do not fall fully into one of these classifications might be categorised as 'general overheads' or even listed as a classification on their own (for example research and development costs).

Fixed costs and variable costs

A different way of analysing and classifying costs is into **fixed costs** and **variable costs**. Some items of expenditure are part-fixed and part-variable or 'semi-fixed' costs but, in cost accounting, semi-fixed or semi-variable costs are divided into their fixed and variable elements.

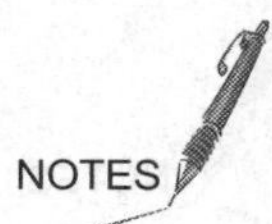

Definition

A **fixed cost** is the cost which is incurred for a period, and which, within certain output and turnover limits, tends to be unaffected by fluctuations in the levels of activity (output or turnover) whereas a variable cost is a cost which tends to vary with the level of activity.

The distinction between fixed and variable costs therefore lies in whether the amount of costs incurred will rise as the **volume of activity** increases, or whether the costs will remain the same, regardless of the volume of activity. Some examples are as follows.

(a) **Direct material costs** will rise as more units of a product are manufactured, and so they are **variable** costs that vary with the volume of production.

(b) **Sales commission** is often a fixed percentage of sales turnover, and so is a **variable cost** that varies with the level of sales (but not with the level of production).

(c) **Telephone call charges** are likely to increase if the volume of business expands, and so they are a **variable** overhead cost, varying with the volume of production and sales.

(d) The **rental** cost of business premises is a constant amount, at least within a stated time period, and so it is a **fixed cost** that does not vary with the level of activity conducted on the premises.

Controllable and uncontrollable costs

Costs which a business is able to control in the short term are generally direct costs or variable costs. Such costs may be avoided if output is lowered or particular activities not undertaken. **Controllable costs** are sometimes called **avoidable costs**. Note that a business faced with a sudden price increase of a raw material cannot control the increase, but it can reduce output and hence it can control its costs in total.

Costs which tend to be outside the short-run control of the business are **uncontrollable costs**. Many fixed costs are often uncontrollable or unavoidable in the short run. Although it is important to recognise that in the longer term all costs may be avoided since all decisions taken by managers can be avoided, in the context of **cost management** it is important to know which costs can be avoided in the short term, that is, the next financial period. Short-term avoidable costs are therefore controllable whereas long-term commitments are unavoidable. For example the costs of renting premises, business rates and security will have to be paid regardless of production and sales.

1.4 Benefits of a costing system for marketers

There are a number of benefits that a costing system can provide which include the following.

(a) The identification of profitable and unprofitable products, services, centres and so on

(b) The identification of waste and inefficiency

(c) Assistance in setting prices

(d) The provision of accurate stock valuations

(e) The analysis of changes in costs, volume and hence profit

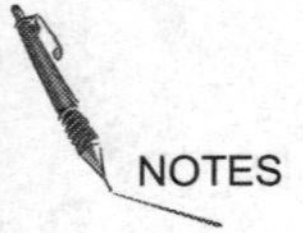

(f) Assistance in planning, control and decision making (budgets, pricing and so on)

(g) Evaluation of the effectiveness of decisions

The justification for a costing system must be that such **benefits** outweigh the cost of the system.

You may be wondering why, as a marketer, the costing aspects are relevant to you: after all, your main focus is the customer, and you might regard an inward looking concentration on costs and production processes as evidence of **product orientation**.

The essence of marketing, however, is that **customer needs are satisfied profitably**. In the long run, profit is achieved because sales revenue from goods and services exceeds the costs. Hence cost information is of vital importance to the marketer.

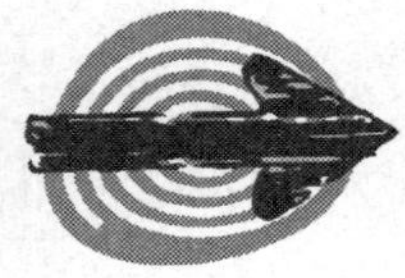

You should now share the view that the financial elements which we have discussed are important and useful to the marketer. You will have noticed also that the relationship between the product and service issues and price, costs and profit is a very strong one. This is a re-affirmation of the integrated nature of the marketing mix; a fact that we need to bear in mind constantly.

EXAMPLE

A survey from the Chartered Institute of Marketing suggests British marketers are lost when it comes to setting prices for their products.

According to the report, the most extensively used technique for pricing was 'face-to-face research'.

A report from consultants McKinsey observed that many firms set prices based solely on anecdotal evidence.

The introduction of the euro, in particular, has ensured that most European marketing managers faced a huge number of simultaneous price changes and very few 'anecdotal' guidelines to help structure their thinking.

There are three key constructs to consider when setting a price:

- The value of the offering to the customer (ie demand),
- The prices charged by competitors, and
- The organisation's costs of production.

But then comes a more subtle cost: that of changing prices in the first place. In many instances firms incur greater losses by increasing their prices than leaving them at the same level. Because the physical, labour and communication costs associated with a price change often exceed the marginal increase in revenues.

Hope is at hand, however.

- NCR launched Electronic Shelf Labels in the US, thus ensuring that supermarkets can cut the marketer out of the pricing task altogether. Prices are displayed in the supermarket on small LCD panels. As goods are scanned, computers at head office make a calculation based on the remaining supply of goods and the predicted demand and alter the price in each store.

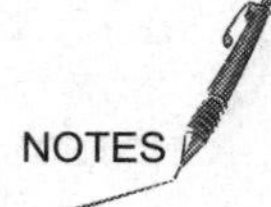

- Not to be outdone, Coca-Cola tested a prototype vending machine that increases the price of each can as the temperature gradually rises. Pure, perfect, elastic pricing will soon be ours and economists will rule the world! You have been warned.

Adapted from *Marketing*, 27 June 2002

1.5 Price setting in theory

Classical economic theory deals with a variety of possible market structures. The simplest is **perfect competition**. Under this structure, there are many buyers and many sellers all dealing in an identical product. Neither producer nor user has any market power and both must accept the price that is set by market forces of supply and demand. This is called the **equilibrium price** because it exactly balances supply and demand: there is no surplus production and no unsatisfied demand.

Conditions approaching perfect competition really only exist in commodity markets, though the principles may be applied in other circumstance to some extent. In markets where there is a degree of **monopoly**, suppliers are said to have **market power** because they are able to exert extensive influence over price. In modern economies, this power frequently arises from some aspect of **product differentiation.** Many small producers enjoy some market power by producing distinctly different products and they enjoy a degree of local monopoly.

A common market structure is **oligopoly**, under which there are very few suppliers. There tends to be very little price competition under oligopoly and prices tend to be very stable as a result. A simple explanation of this has two parts. First, a price cut by one supplier will be copied by all other suppliers in order to protect market share. Profit is thus reduced for all suppliers. Price cuts are therefore unlikely. Second, a price rise by one supplier will result in loss of market share since it will not be copied by the others. Price rises are therefore unlikely. These effects increase the likelihood of collusion between suppliers in order to co-ordinate price changes. This is illegal. Competition in such market conditions is likely to be restricted to non-price elements of the marketing mix. Thus the significance of product quality, promotion, personal selling and distribution and, in overall terms, branding, has grown.

In any market, **price elasticity** is important. Price elasticity measures the responsiveness of demand to changes in price. It is calculated as:

$$\frac{\text{\% change in sales demand}}{\text{\% change in sales price}}$$

Notice that, since a price cut usually enhances demand and *vice versa*, this calculation will always produce a negative answer, but the minus sign is usually ignored since it is only the magnitude that is important.

(a) When elasticity is greater than 1 (**elastic**), a change in price will lead to a change in total revenue so that

   (i) if the **price is lowered,** total **sales revenue will rise**, because of the large increase in demand

   (ii) if the **price is raised,** total **sales revenue will fall**, because of the large fall in demand.

(b) When elasticity is less than 1 (**inelastic**),

   (i) if the **price is lowered,** total **sales revenue will fall,** because the increase in sales volume will be too small to compensate for the price reductions

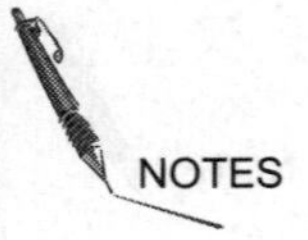

(ii) if the **price is raised**, total **sales revenue will go up** because the drop in sales quantities will be very small.

In some cases, however, other factors may influence price elasticity, so that previous responses to price changes no longer produce the same consumer responses. Products do not stay the same forever.

Activity 4 **(10 minutes)**

What are the limitations of price elasticity as a factor in determining prices?

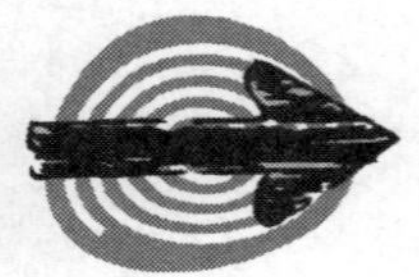

Having looked at price setting in theory, we will consider price setting in practice later in the chapter.

2 PRICING POLICY AND THE MARKETING MIX

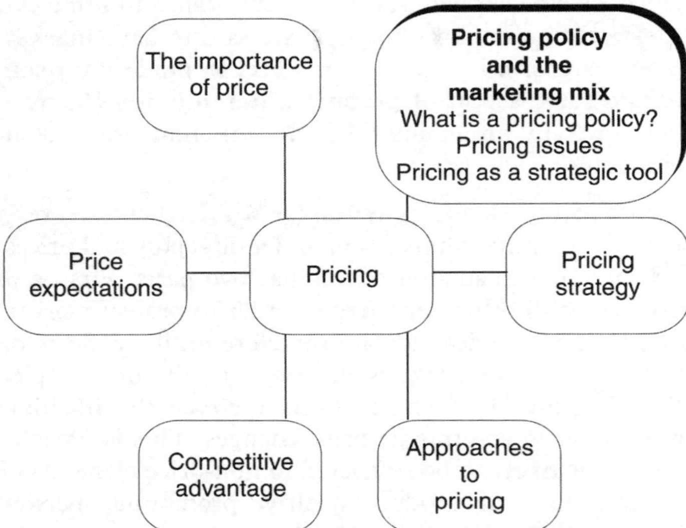

The critical nature of **price** in the consideration of the marketing operation is shown by the fact that it is normally stated as the second component of the marketing mix:

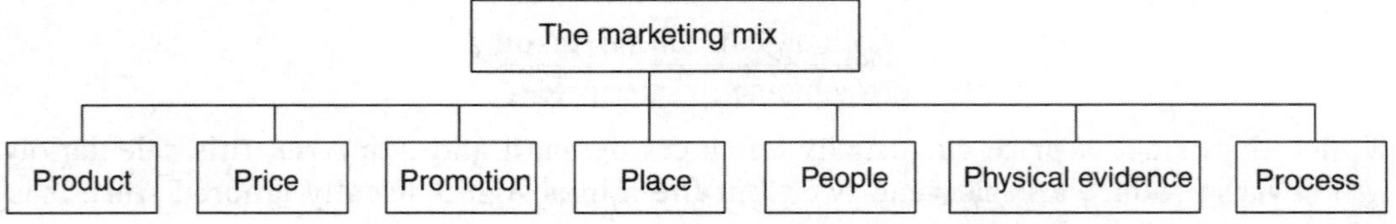

Figure 10.2: The 7Ps of the marketing mix

It is intimately connected to the issues we have discussed about the product in many crucial ways. It is these interconnections and their strategic implications that we examine in this chapter.

Definition

Price is the unit of revenue combining costs and profit at which a satisfactory exchange takes place in a transaction. When multiplied by volume it equals sales turnover.

Price, in common with all components of the marketing mix, never operates in isolation from the others but rather in more or less synergistic relationship with them.

2.1 What is a pricing policy?

Definition

Policy is a principle of how an organisation operates; how it does something consistently in a certain way as laid down by the management.

Mostly, such principles are set out formally in **written procedures** to which all employees are referred if in doubt as to how to take action: to this extent they may take the place of verbal instructions from managers, doing away with the need for them to be in lots of places at once. For example, very firm instructions may be laid down about opening new credit accounts or appointing a new supplier.

EXAMPLE

Very often such a 'policy' is extended from the internal sphere of operation to a public statement about how customers are treated such as the famous one used about its prices by the John Lewis partnership – 'Never Knowingly Undersold'. Or the known principle of sales policy operated for many years by Marks & Spencer with regard to the refund of the purchase price if a customer should be dissatisfied with a product. The availability of internet price comparison sites has meant, however, that companies like John Lewis have had to tighten the rules of their policies so as not to make a loss.

Pricing policy, therefore, is the outcome of **management decisions** about price which derive from internal operational considerations about costs and external, customer-focused considerations about **value**.

Activity 5 **(10 minutes)**

Can you think of any other policies about pricing which companies use?

2.2 Pricing issues

There are certain issues which must be addressed about price when an organisation approaches the problem of pricing a product for the market. They may be viewed through the following diagram.

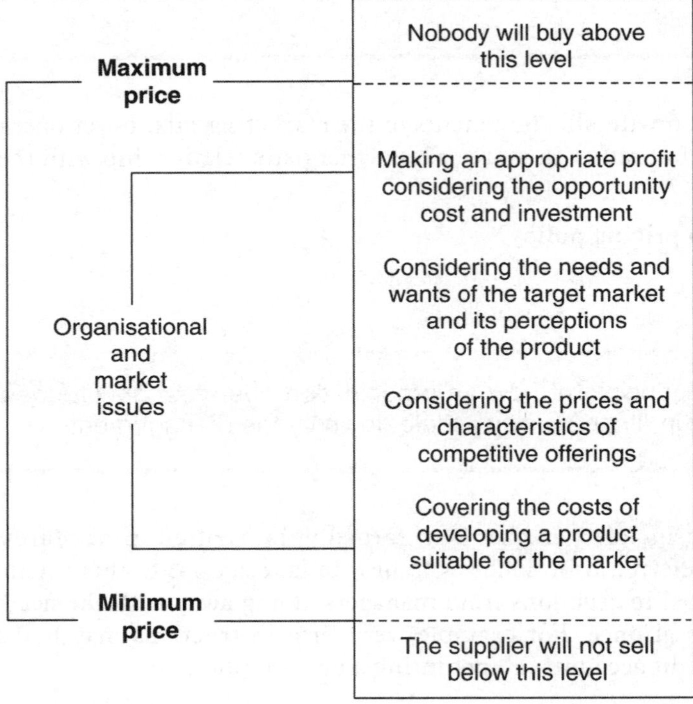

Figure 10.3: Pricing issues

Whatever is sold has a cost, even if it is an article which has been given to you. You can only sell it at the cost of not having it! This is called an **opportunity cost**. The value you receive from selling it may just be the money which is received for it – you value the money more than the product. On the other hand it may be the space which it takes up which you want and you are prepared to let it go cheaply. It may, of course, be a combination of the two factors and even include many more.

FOR DISCUSSION

A cynic is somebody who knows the price of everything and the value of nothing.

(Oscar Wilde)

What the above point is saying is that what a selling price represents is rarely as simple as an amount of money. A selling price is an amount of money which describes a **point in a process of exchange** in which two or more parties achieve **satisfaction.**

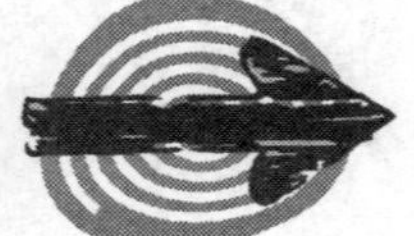

It is the mechanics of this complex exchange process which we will now examine.

2.3 Pricing as a strategic tool

As we have said previously, pricing is an important tool for the marketing manager to manipulate within the marketing mix in order to make the offering to the market attractive.

We shall examine the main ways in which this operates in a few moments but first of all, study this example.

EXAMPLE

How much are fish & chips?

A supermarket had on offer a frozen pack of two fish and two portions of chips for £1.69: as if this was not bargain enough, they also gave two packs for the price of one! This works out at 42.25p per serving.

Perhaps you visit the high street fish & chip shop and pay £4.25.

Perhaps you go to a local restaurant for a special occasion and choose from the menu *Dover Sole with French Fries, £18.95.*

There are restaurants which specialises in fish dishes and provide a very high level of service in elegant surroundings: ordering 'fish & chips', described in one way or another, can produce a bill for £35 and much more!

Very varied 'kettles of fish'! Purchase prices can vary according to a large number of factors which go far beyond the price of the basic raw materials. What we pay for is not the product in isolation but a package of attributes, which can include brand, occasion and outlet, all combining in a way which delivers a **set of satisfactions**. The particular specification of the required satisfactions may be unique; what one person will pay £1 for may be considered too expensive by another – or too cheap by a third.

FOR DISCUSSION

A transport café provides better value than a gourmet restaurant.

3 PRICE EXPECTATIONS

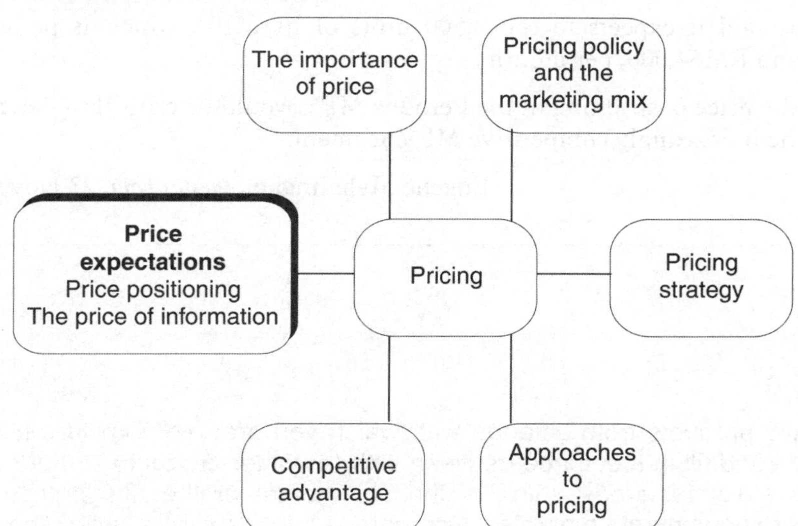

As consumers of many products, we become quite expert in the price of goods. We have a notional **range of prices** which enable us to categorise an offer as relatively expensive or inexpensive. If we use the terms 'dear' and 'cheap' we are usually applying a **value scale**

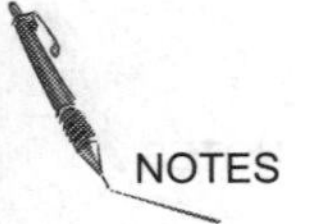

to indicate the benefit derived from the transaction. Age, occupation, educational background, where we live may all influence our buying patterns and this includes prices which we are prepared to pay.

3.1 Price positioning

We can refer to what is called a **price expectation model** to carry this idea further. First, let us look again at the concept of **price positioning.**

High price ———————————————————— Low price

In marketing we use this framework in the technique called **positioning,** where price is a prime variable.

Consider a market in which the product range in a market is represented at the two ends of the spectrum by Product A and Product Z.

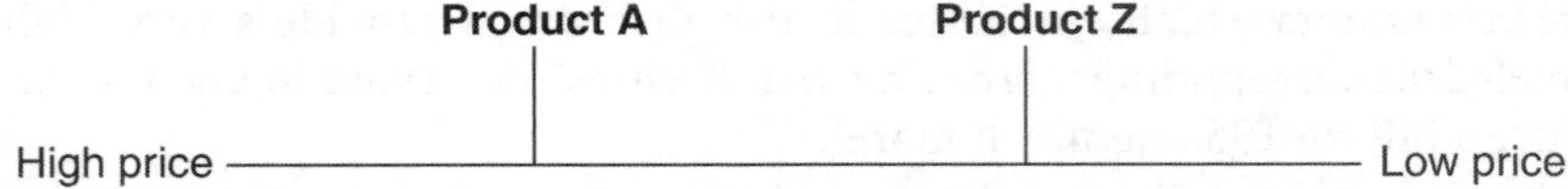

The **positioning** of a new product entering the market at a price anywhere in between tells the potential customers something about the intentions of the supplier in terms of the benefits from the product or service on offer in relation to Product A and Product Z. In the absence of any further information the customer forms a **perception** of the product.

EXAMPLE: MPVs ENGINE OF GROWTH IN MALAYSIAN CAR INDUSTRY

The local multi-purpose vehicle (MPV) segment is expected to see the biggest growth in sales in 2009, driven by the introduction of the Proton *Exora* in April and the launch of Perusahaan Otomobil Kedua Sdn Bhd's (Perodua) MPV today.

Frost & Sullivan was maintaining its earlier MPV growth forecast of 7.2% year-on-year to 57,000 units for 2009, said Albert Chow, the research firm's Asia-Pacific senior consultant for automotive & transportation practice . . .

Perodua has said it expects to sell 3,500 units of its MPV, which is priced between RM56,000 and RM64,000, per month . . .

Chow said the price positioning of the Perodua MPV would be critical in determining its success in the increasingly competitive MPV segment.

Eugene Mahalingam, *thestar.com*, 23 November 2009

Activity 6 **(20 minutes)**

Place two products from a range with which you are very familiar on a price spectrum and fill in the space between with the other products in that range. If you are stuck for ideas, think of the car market or the hi-fi equipment or computer equipment markets. Compare your spectrum with that of a colleague. Alternatively, ask somebody to construct a diagram similar to your own, given the same components.

Suppose you were looking for a second-hand car and were offered one described as 'tidy, in running order' which seemed to be about right at £500, when a friend said that you could have hers which is the same model and the same year for £50. Your first reaction would probably be 'What's wrong with it?'.

3.2 The price of information

It becomes clear that **information** is a key factor in the use of price in a tactical or strategic sense. And the following **price expectation curve** demonstrates this well.

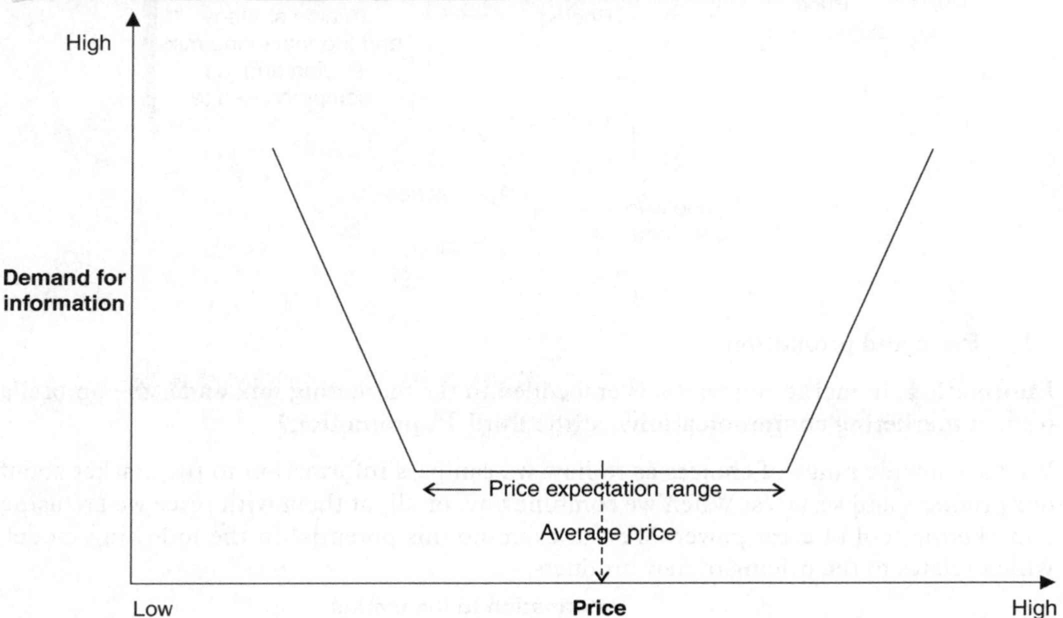

Figure 10.4: Price expectations curve

As price moves away from the average price and beyond the range of expectation which has been established by experience, then there is a rapidly growing demand for further information.

It follows that the more information which is given, relevant to the potential customers' needs, then the more likely that a higher price may be expected given that the information is supported by product performance. This concept leads us to examine the relationship between **information and price** in strategic terms.

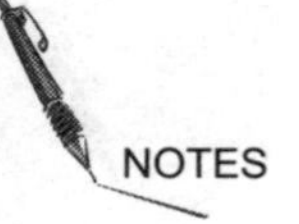

4 PRICING STRATEGY

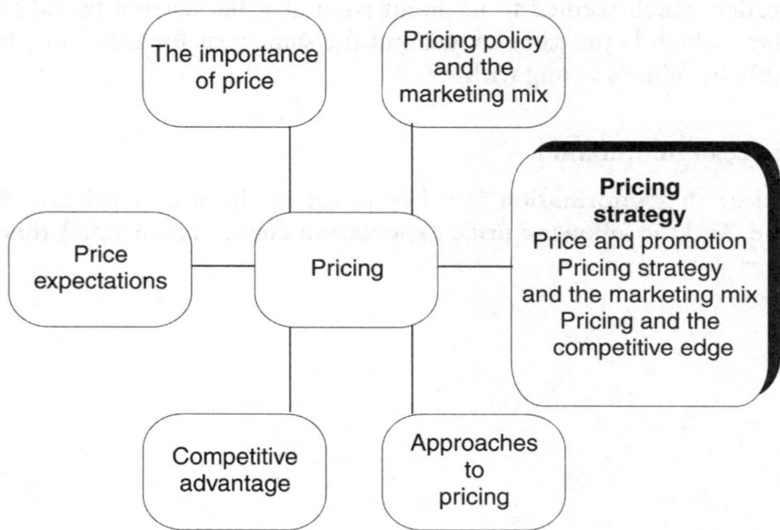

4.1 Price and promotion

Information, in marketing terms, is embedded in the marketing mix under the umbrella term of **marketing communications**, or the third 'P', **promotion**.

We have a wide range of choices as to how we can pass information to the market about our products and services. When we combine any, or all, of them with price we are using a marketing tool of great power. We can examine this potential in the following model, which relates to the pricing of new products.

		Information to the market	
		High	Low
Price	High	Rapid skimming	Slow skimming
	Low	Rapid penetration	Slow penetration

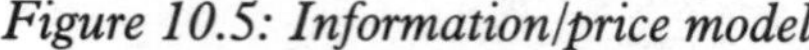
Figure 10.5: Information/price model

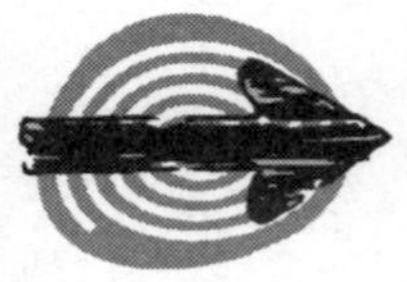

Skimming and penetration approaches are dealt with in more detail in Chapter 11.

As you can see, the high price/high promotion category produces a rapid **skimming strategy** which means that high profits may be achieved (given that the quality of the product is consistent with the high price) at a fast rate when the market is informed with high-powered promotional campaigns. Market penetration is enhanced by the combination of **low price** and **high levels of promotion.**

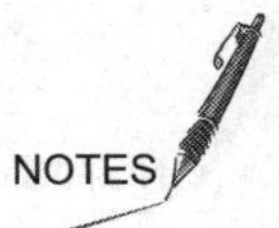

FOR DISCUSSION

It's always worthwhile waiting for the price to settle down before buying a new product.

4.2 Pricing strategy and the marketing mix

It cannot be repeated too often that the **components of the marketing mix never operate alone.** The Mix components, whether they be those of the product mix (the 4P's) or the services mix (the 7P's), always exist as a combination. Each component, however, may have a predominance in a given mix. Marketing mixes are segment-specific. The product may be specially designed for a given segment. Some segments may be very price sensitive and thus the price is the predominant component. The outlet may be the most critical factor.

Activity 7 **(20 minutes)**

Draw up your own matrix diagrams similar to that combining price and information in Figure 10.5 to show the combination of price with product, and with place (distribution).

Consider the following scenarios represented by different outlets.

Outlet A Low prices Top brands Well advertised Low quality staff Poor access No parking	**Outlet C** Low prices Top brands Well advertised Well-trained staff Good access Parking charge
Outlet B High prices Top brands Poorly advertised Well-trained staff Good access Free parking	**Outlet D** ? The output we do not yet know about because it is in a backstreet and does not advertise at all

You can see how each of the outlets A to C is operating price within the mix. The exception is D. This may have the lowest prices in the area but, because there is no effective communication, we just do not know about it.

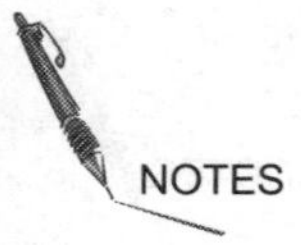

Definitions

Strategy is the way in which organisations meet their medium to long-term objectives by using their resources in certain ways.

Marketing strategy is the way in which organisations meet their marketing objectives by manipulating (fine-tuning) the interactions of the components of the marketing mix to achieve optimum customer response.

FOR DISCUSSION

In the long run, a 'bargain' seldom does either party any good.

4.3 Pricing and the competitive edge

As we have already discussed, pricing is a very powerful weapon in the marketer's armoury. One of the reasons that price is so significant is that, when considered alone, it is unarguable. That is, a product has either a lower or higher price than its competitor (unless of course they are the same!): it is not a matter of **opinion or preference** when only the price tag is under consideration.

One of the most dreaded possibilities in an industry or market is a **price war**. This is usually the outcome of a head-to-head conflict of the major players who are trying to achieve market supremacy. Prices are driven down, margins are reduced to the distributive chain and smaller players may go out of business. Quality may be reduced in order to cut costs to support the price reductions. Ranges are rationalised, reducing consumer choice. It is said to be a war which nobody wins, especially the consumer, because the outcome is often a **reduction of competition**. Look at many small town High Streets today. They have been stripped of the traditional sole trader providing for a local trade because of the intense competition of the national multiples.

EXAMPLE

The final book in the Harry Potter series led to arguments breaking out between Asda and the publisher Bloomsbury. Asda had criticised the publisher for over-pricing the book claiming that they were taking advantage of children with a RRP of £17.99. Asda had been advertising their price as £8.87. A public dispute erupted between the two parties with Asda claiming that the publisher had threatened to not supply books to them in time for the launch. A couple of days later Asda apologised publicly when it was revealed that the reason for the refusal of Bloomsbury to supply books was because the retailer owed them money.

Simultaneously, additional disputes were taking place within the world of book retailing because it was claimed that small independent retailers were planning to purchase copies of the much awaited novel from Tesco, Asda and Wilkinson because their advertised prices were cheaper than the wholesale price. The publisher was subsequently criticised for not protecting the value of the Harry Potter brand which has resulted in the

independent shops selling the book at a loss but still being required to hold typical midnight launch parties to retain their local reputations.

Activity 8 **(20 minutes)**

Look around the High Street in a convenient small town near to you with which you are familiar. Identify the outlets which have changed over the last few years. Note the type of outlets which have disappeared and the type which have taken their place and try to establish the reasons for the changes.

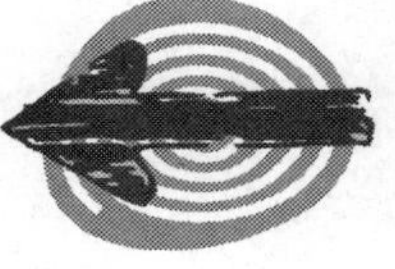

In the next section of this chapter we consider general approaches to pricing, or 'pricing in practice'.

5 APPROACHES TO PRICING

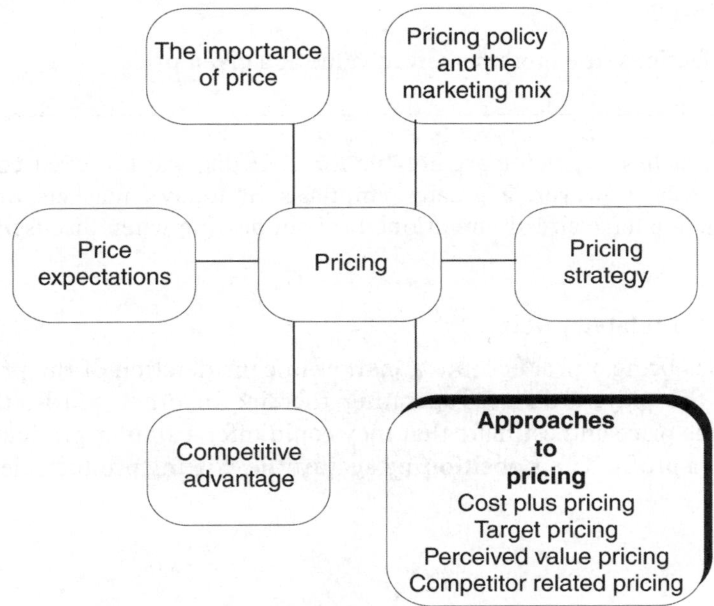

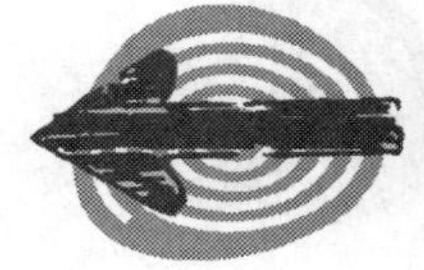

Organisations may follow a standard pricing formula, some of which are given below. Approaches to pricing are examined in more detail in the following chapter.

5.1 Cost plus pricing

Cost plus is the simplest method of pricing in which a standard or traditional **percentage is added** to the cost. This is often used when costs vary frequently. You may have experienced that produce is dearer on one day than it was the previous day because the wholesale price has changed. The trader adds the percentage that he knows will cover his costs and provide a profit margin.

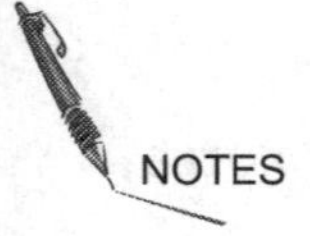

5.2 Target pricing

Target pricing is where an organisation pitches a price which will deliver a target profit or return on investment over a period. The use of **breakeven analysis** is very important here. We look at breakeven analysis in the next chapter.

5.3 Perceived value pricing

Perceived value pricing is the approach to pricing which is exemplified in the scenarios painted about the price of Fish & Chips earlier in the chapter. The components of the marketing mix, especially those specific to the services mix in the case of the Fish & Chips, are combined to build up a **perception of value** in the mind of the purchaser. A customer in a high class restaurant who orders something which is not on the menu may be charged extra for the privilege of being different and being allowed the self-indulgence. The head waiter makes up the price, which may be 300, 400 or 500% of the cost because he knows that the customer will value the special treatment and the additional service. This is one example of a **what the market will stand** approach to pricing.

FOR DISCUSSION

The more satisfactions, the more perceived value at a given price.

The above approaches to pricing are notable for their disregard of what **competitors** are charging. There is, however, a greater emphasis in today's markets on **competitor-related pricing**. We have already mentioned this in passing when discussing positioning earlier.

5.4 Competitor related pricing

Many companies bring a product into a market in consideration of the prices which are obtainable by the players already operating therein. In other words, they observe a product, note the price and estimate that they could offer a similar product and meet the price and make a profit. Their **positioning** against the existing products determines their approach.

Definitions

> **Price followers** are those entrants to a market who simply follow the existing players, very often pricing just below the market leader.
>
> **Price leaders** are those entrants who establish the going rate in a market thus providing a basis for others to follow.

Price leaders can be the market leaders too. They provide a **benchmark** in terms of the **economies of scale** on which they operate and also have entered the beneficial sector of the **learning (or experience) curve**.

Definitions

> **Economies of scale**, put simply, means that the larger the operation in terms of output, the smaller the costs for each unit of output.
>
> **Learning (or experience) curve**: the phenomenon, of which we all have experience, which demonstrates that, the more we do anything, the more efficient and effective we become at it. Practice not only makes perfect but also makes life easier. This idea has been applied to pricing by assuming that costs will fall as production of a new product builds up.

Price followers may have to forgo normal profit levels until they market leaders' level of competence.

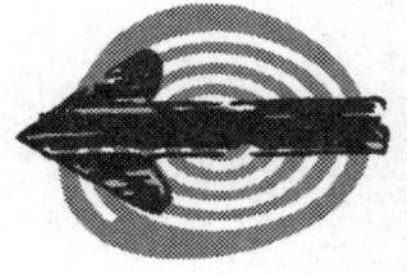

In tackling competition the work of Michael Porter is very important and we shall now discuss some of his ideas.

6 COMPETITIVE ADVANTAGE

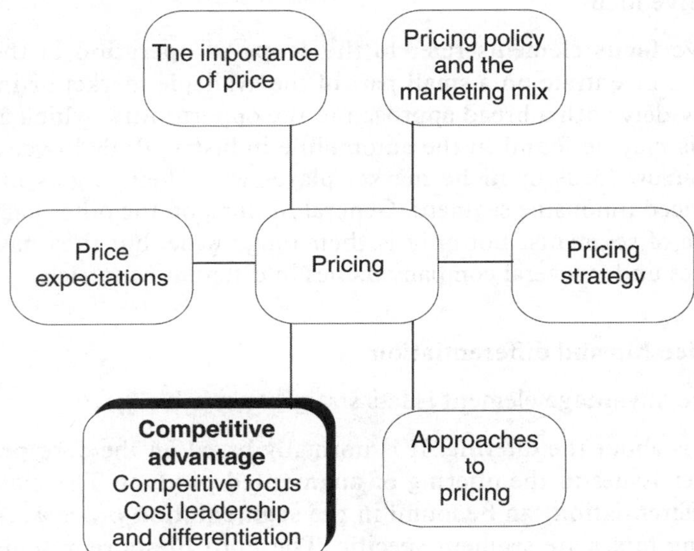

Michael Porter (*Competitive Advantage*, 1996) laid down the principle that firms should compete at one of two levels, either as **cost leaders** or as **differentiators.** Further they should do this in a **broad or narrow focus,** as the model below demonstrates.

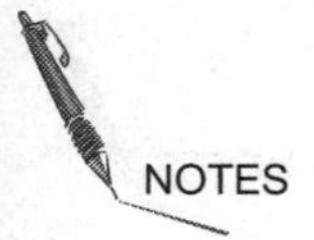

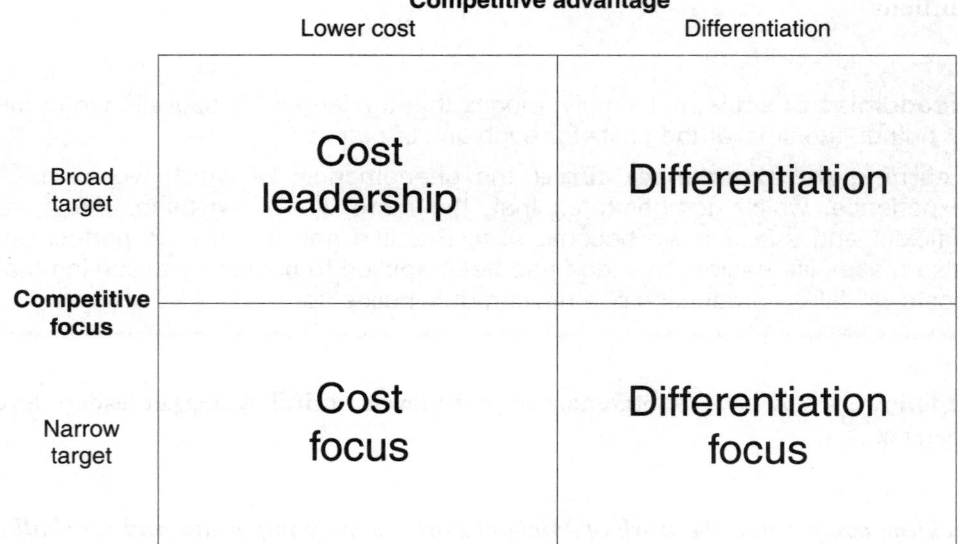

Figure 10.6: Competitive advantage

6.1 Competitive focus

The **competitive focus** elements refer to the **scope of operation** of the organisation. They can either concentrate on a small part of the available market or industry, or cast their net more widely with a broad approach to the opportunities which are appropriate. Examples of this may be found in the automobile industry. Rolls Royce are an extreme example of a narrow focus or niche market player with their targets in the very high quality, high-priced limousine segment. General Motors, on the other hand, provide cars for a wide range of segments: not only is their range wide, but they have a number of different marques under several company names in different countries.

6.2 Cost leadership and differentiation

The **competitive advantage** element is less straightforward.

Differentiation is about the offering. It is normally based on the **core product** but may rely on the wider issues in the offering or **augmented product**. The main factor which prompts the differentiation can be found in the **segmentation process**. As we have said before, marketing mixes are segment specific. The Ford Fiesta represents one model of car but small variations in the presentation of the 'package' render it more attractive to different sectors of the target group.

Cost leadership is an advantage which allows a number of strategic options best shown in the diagram below. 1, 2 and 3 are **cost leadership strategies**; column 4 represents **differentiation.**

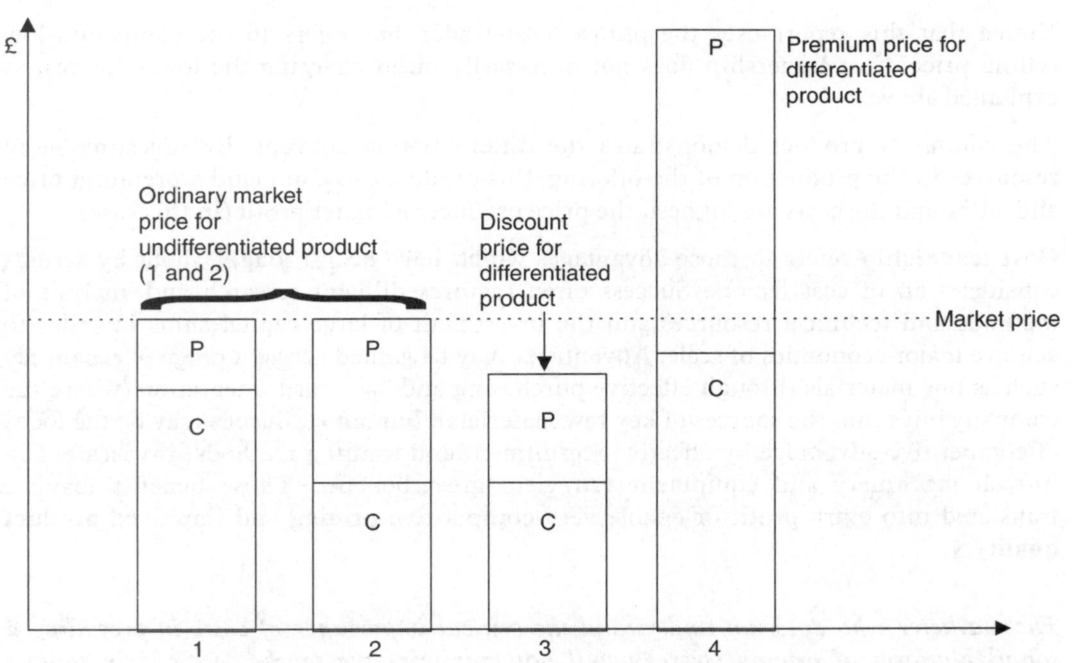

Figure 10.7: Cost leadership strategies

Column 1 shows the profit and cost profile of a product at average price in a market. Column 2 shows a product in the same market with a lower cost base and, at average price, is making more profit. The product in column 3 has the same cost base as the product in column 2 but is using this advantage to cut the price whilst maintaining the same profit margin as the product in column 1. A firm operating in column 1 would be at a severe competitive disadvantage.

EXAMPLE: SOLAR COMPANIES FOCUS ON NUTS AND BOLTS TO CUT COSTS

Even as solar companies cook up high tech ways to cut costs, the next push to make the renewable energy source more economical could come from workers who bolt panels onto rooftops and mount them across empty fields.

So far, panels – a system's most expensive piece – account for the biggest drop in the total cost, falling more than 50 percent from about $4.20 a watt in 2008.

Most U.S. and European makers are now selling panels near $2 per watt, while some low-cost Chinese players sell panels at about $1.85, said J.P. Morgan research analyst Christopher Blansett, while thin film maker First Solar Inc is the cost leader at about $1.50 or $1.55 per watt.

That decline has put a spotlight on installation, which now makes up a greater share of the total cost, and has prompted installers, developers and even panel makers to look for low-tech tricks, like quick fasteners and predrilled holes.

"There's no rocket science. It's literally doing things better and more efficiently," Blansett said.

Laura Isensee, *reuters.com*, 3 November 2009

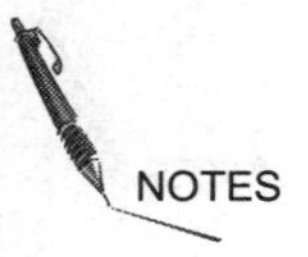

Notice that this report uses the phrase 'cost leader' but refers to the company's low selling price. Cost leadership does not necessarily mean charging the lowest prices, as explained above.

The column 4 product demonstrates the differentiation concept. By investing more resources in the production of the offering, this product can command a premium price and, although the costs are highest, the price produces a higher profit (in this case).

Cost leadership refers to those advantages which have been brought about by serious consideration of cost factors. Success often requires diligent research and analysis of methods and technical resources and the investment of large capital sums in order to achieve major economies of scale. Advantages may be gained across a range of **resources** such as raw materials through effective purchasing and backward integration (where the company buys into the sources of key raw materials); **human resources** may be the focus of competitive advantage by effective recruitment and training methods; **investment** in hi-tech machinery and equipment can yield great benefits. Those benefits may be translated into **extra profit** or enable very **competitive pricing** and improved **product quality**.

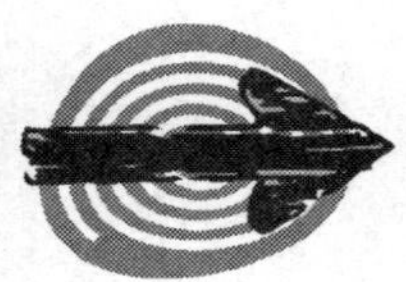

The marketer who does not understand the critical importance of costs in providing a sound platform of pricing strategy will not maximise the market options in today's competitive arena.

Chapter roundup

- Pricing, from the marketing point of view, is the operation of one of the components of the marketing mix and, in combination with the other components, produces a very powerful synergy in achieving marketing objectives.
- A cost is an amount of expenditure attributable to a specific product.
- Costs may be classified under many headings, allowing effective control.
- In marketing terms, price does not operate alone but always in interaction with the other parts of the marketing mix.
- Price is the unit of revenue combining costs and profit at which a satisfactory exchange takes place in a transaction.
- Price is also a signal of quality to the customer and a mechanism by which a product competes with alternatives in the market.
- Understanding the basis of costing is important to the marketing manager as it provides the basis of opportunity to make profit.
- Pricing, when used effectively in combination with the other components of the marketing mix, is a strategic tool used to construct an attractive offering for the target market.
- Cost leadership is the outcome of a number of competencies which enable organisations to compete at an advantage in the market.
- Differentiation depends on the crafting of a distinctive offering which responds with competitive advantage to the specialised wants of a market segment.

Quick quiz

1. What is pricing policy?
2. What is profit?
3. What is a cost?
4. State the elements of cost.
5. What is the offering?
6. What is price positioning?
7. What is the central observation on a price expectation curve?
8. With which components of the marketing mix may price be combined for strategic effect?
9. What are the main strategic effects of combining price with marketing communications?
10. What is marketing strategy?
11. What are the main pricing formulae used by organisations?
12. According to Porter, in his book *Competitive Advantage*, what are the principles on which firms should compete?

Answers to Quick quiz

1. The outcome of management decisions about price.
2. The excess of revenue over costs.
3. An objective measure of resources used.
4. Materials, labour and other expenses.
5. The package of attributes which can include brand, occasion, outlet and other factors which deliver satisfactions.
6. Pricing a product on a scale which represents the lowest and highest market prices.
7. Average price.
8. All of them!
9. Skimming and penetration are either rapid or slow depending on the levels of price and promotional activity.
10. The *how* of firms meeting their marketing objectives.
11. Cost plus; target pricing; competitor related pricing.
12. Cost leadership and differentiation with a broad or narrow focus.

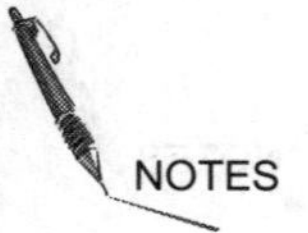

Answers to Activities

1 You might have identified a number of different factors here. Perhaps the most important general point to make is that price is particularly important if the other elements in the marketing mix are relatively similar across a range of competing products. For example, there is a very wide variety of toothpastes on the market, most of them not much differentiated from the others. The price of a particular toothpaste may be a crucial factor in its sales success.

2 Without being an expert it would be difficult to be exact but you may have come up with at least the following (and possibly more).

Raw materials	*Packaging*
Sugar	Wrapper
Flavourings	Counter pack
Cocoa, etc	Trade outer
Capital equipment	*Pallet*
Machinery costs	Shrink wrapping
Factory space	*Transportation*
Warehousing	To wholesaler
Discounts	*To retailer*
Wholesaler	*Selling*
Retailer	Media advertising
Administration and finance costs	Sales promotion material
Wages and salaries	Salespersons
Management information systems	Merchandisers
Banking charges and interest	Other marketing costs

3 (a) Production overhead
(b) Direct labour
(c) Distribution overhead
(d) Marketing overhead
(e) Distribution overhead
(f) Direct material

4 The main problem is that unless very detailed research has been carried out the price elasticity of a particular product or service is likely to be unknown.

5 There are many. Some are informal; unpublished. The ones you know about may include ESSO which has a price check system to ensure that its prices are always competitive and Safeway which offers a 10% discount to mothers with babies.

Look out for such embodiments of management decisions and you will find some interesting insights into how a company works.

6 The chances are that you will have chosen similar brands at the extremes of the spectrum but there is likely to be less consensus about those which cluster at the centre of the scale. The reasons for this are twofold. At the extremes of the spectrum the brands are very highly differentiated: towards the centre they may be less so. On the one hand some of the perception which you have constructed in your mind is a subjective (that is, particular to you) response to all the information which you know or believe about the product. On the other hand, the information which you and your colleague each have may differ and is not likely to be all that there is to know about each of the brands. What we don't know we often make up!

7 You may have shown price in combination with the quality of the product to produce high price/high quality offerings which would command a premium price and low price/ high quality which would constitute a bargain!

With regard to the combination of place and price you may have constructed a matrix which would be indicative of exclusive outlets (high price/few shops), or intensive distribution patterns (low price/many shops).

8 You may well find that the sole traders in the grocery, butchery, shoes, bakery, electrical and TV fields have reduced to be replaced by multiples and financial services. Most often, the reasons for the changes are put down to an inability to compete on price with a reduction of customer flow, revenue and profit which does not allow the trader to pay the increased costs, particularly rates. The overall outcome is a lower price for some things to the consumer but less choice and in many cases a lowering of the quality or loss of a special character of service.

NOTES

Chapter 11 :
PRICING FOR COSTS, SALES AND PROFIT

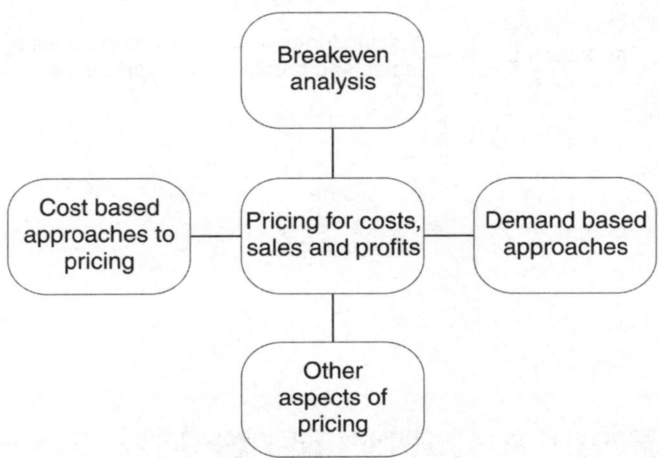

Introduction

In the previous chapter we referred to pricing as a strategic activity. We also defined terms such as costs and profit. We are now bringing costs and profit, together with **volume** (the amount of goods made or sold), under analysis in order to examine the effects they have on each other.

Pricing activity should consider three major factors:

- It must ensure that costs are covered
- It must take into account the effect of price on sales
- It should provide for a profit

This chapter concentrates on **breakeven analysis** as an analytical tool in pricing decisions and pricing techniques.

Your objectives

In this chapter you will learn about the following.

(a) Using the breakeven chart to aid pricing decisions

(b) A range of pricing techniques

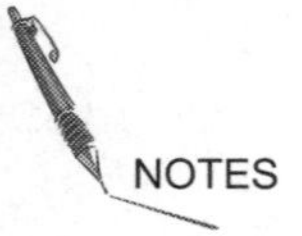

1 BREAKEVEN ANALYSIS

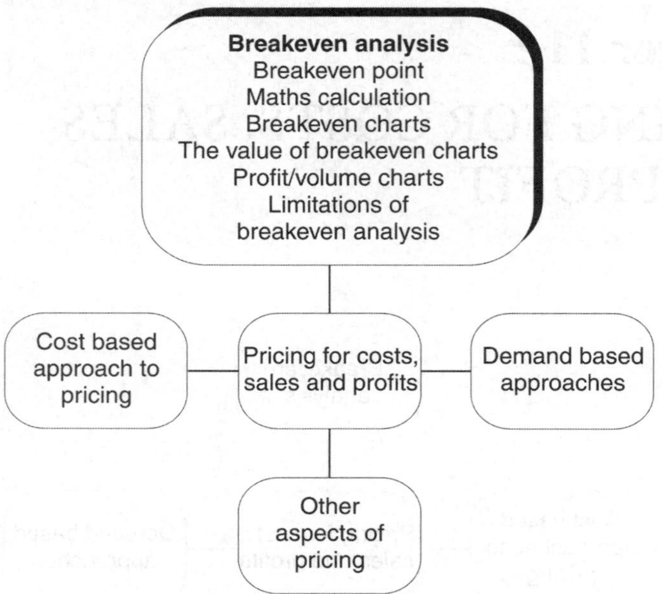

Definition

Breakeven analysis: is a technique for investigating the inter-relationship between costs, volume and hence profit. It is used to determine the effects on profit of changes in levels of production or sales volume at given costs and unit price. It is also known as cost-volume-profit (or CVP) analysis.

Marketers use breakeven analysis widely in price setting and especially for **new product pricing**. It is a technique which quickly provides useful impressions which can aid decision making.

1.1 Breakeven point

Breakeven analysis uses fixed and variable costs and revenue to work out the point, in a schedule of projected production or sales, at which **all costs will be covered**. This is called the breakeven point: sales beyond this will begin to yield profit.

Definition

The **breakeven point** is the volume level at which the revenue from sales exactly covers total fixed and variable costs at a specific price, that is, there is no profit or loss.

EXAMPLE: YOTA REACHES OPERATIONAL BREAKEVEN POINT

Russian WiMAX operator, Yota has announced that it has reached the operational breakeven point. This benchmark has been reached by Yota in less than 5 month after the start of the commercial operation of Mobile WiMAX network in Moscow and St Petersburg. In Ufa the network commercial operation has started in October.

In early October the subscriber base exceeded the point of 200,000 active users, while daily connection rate is 2,000.

Overall volume of data transferred through the Yota network in all three cities in September amounted to 1,848 TB.

"It took the company less than five months of network commercial operation to reach the operational breakeven point, - underlined Yota General Director Denis Sverdlov. - Our business experience may be used as a reference point for other Mobile WiMAX operators. It demonstrates that 4G broadband services business can be quite Next cities to be turned into commercial operation profitable".

Cellular-news.com, 8 November 2009

1.2 Maths calculation

The **breakeven point** can be calculated by using the following formula:

$$\text{Breakeven point} = \frac{\text{Fixed costs}}{\text{Price} - \text{variable costs}}$$

For example, if the fixed costs of making a product are £10,000 and the price is £10 per unit, with variable costs of £8 per unit there is £2 per unit available to go towards the fixed costs. So, it will require 5,000 units of sales to cover all costs.

$$\frac{£10,000}{£10-8} = 5,000 \text{ units}$$

FOR DISCUSSION

Explain the breakeven formula to a colleague, using different figures.

It is clearly very useful to be able to say how many items you will have to sell in order to start making a profit.

1.3 Breakeven charts

The breakeven point can also be determined **graphically** using a breakeven chart which shows approximate levels of profit or loss at different sales volume levels within a limited range. It shows on the horizontal axis the sales/output (in units or in value) and on the vertical axis values for sales revenue and costs. The following lines are then drawn.

(a) The **sales line**, which starts at the origin (zero sales volume = zero sales revenue) and ends at the point which signifies the expected sales.

(b) The **fixed costs line** which runs above and parallel to the horizontal axis, at a point on the vertical axis denoting the total fixed costs.

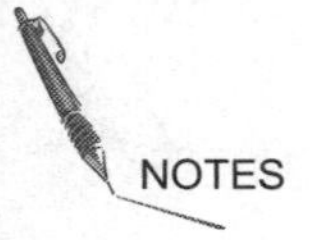

NOTES

(c) The **total costs line**, which starts at the point where the fixed costs line meets the vertical axis (at zero output), and ends at the point which represents, on the horizontal axis, the anticipated sales in units, and on the vertical axis the sum of the total variable cost of those units plus the total fixed costs.

The breakeven point is the intersection of the sales line and the total costs line. By projecting the lines horizontally and vertically from this point to the appropriate axes, it is possible to read off the breakeven point in sales units and sales value.

The number of units represented on the chart by the distance between the breakeven point and the expected (or budgeted) sales, in units, indicates the **margin of safety**.

WORKED EXAMPLE: A BREAKEVEN CHART

The budgeted annual output of a factory is 120,000 units. The fixed overheads amount to £40,000 and the variable costs are 50p per unit. The sales price is £1 per unit.

Construct a breakeven chart showing the current breakeven point and profit earned up to the present maximum capacity.

SOLUTION

We begin by calculating the profit at the budgeted annual output.

	£
Sales (120,000 units)	120,000
Variable costs	60,000
Contribution	60,000
Fixed costs	40,000
Profit	20,000

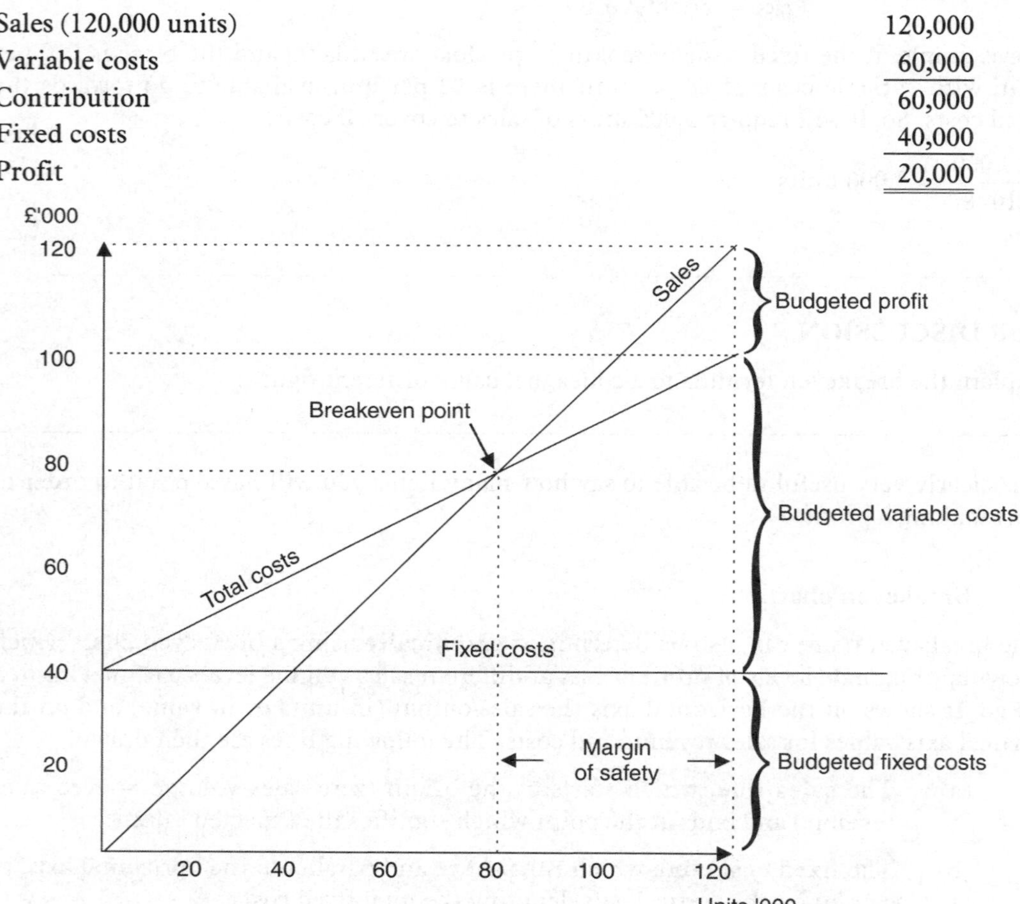

The chart is drawn as follows.

(a) The **vertical axis** represents money (costs and revenue) and the **horizontal axis** represents the level of activity (production and sales) in units.

(b) The **fixed costs** are represented by a straight line parallel to the horizontal axis (in our example, at £40,000).

(c) The **variable costs** are added to fixed costs, to give total costs. It is assumed that fixed costs are the same in total and variable costs are the same per unit at all levels of output.

The **line of costs** is therefore a straight line and only two points need to be plotted and joined up. Perhaps the two most convenient points to plot are total costs at zero output, and total costs at the budgeted output and sales.

(i) At zero output, costs are equal to the amount of fixed costs only, £40,000, since there are no variable costs.

(ii) At the budgeted output of 120,000 units, costs are £100,000.

	£
Fixed costs	40,000
Variable costs 120,000 × 50p	60,000
Total costs	100,000

(d) The **sales line** is also drawn by plotting two points and joining them up.

(i) At zero sales, revenue is nil.

(ii) At the budgeted output and sales of 120,000 units, revenue is £120,000.

The **breakeven point** is where total costs are matched exactly by total revenue. From the chart, this can be seen to occur at output and sales of 80,000 units, when revenue and costs are both £80,000. This breakeven point can be proved mathematically as:

$$\frac{\text{Required contribution} = \text{fixed costs}}{\text{Contribution per unit}} = \frac{£40{,}000}{50\text{p per unit}} = 80{,}000 \text{ units}$$

The **margin of safety** can be seen on the chart as the difference between the budgeted level of activity and the breakeven level.

We should include an important definition here.

Definition

> **Contribution:** sales value less variable cost of sales.

1.4 The value of breakeven charts

Breakeven charts may be helpful to management in **planning** the production and marketing of individual products, or the entire product range of their company. A chart gives a visual display of how much output needs to be sold to make a profit and what the likelihood would be of making a loss if actual sales fell short of the budgeted expectations.

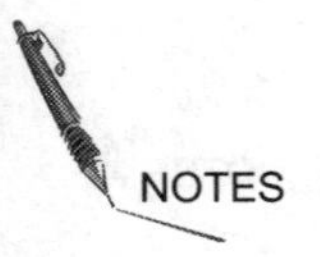

In practice, management is more likely to use breakeven analysis without bothering to draw charts.

Activity 1 **(30 minutes)**

Streamline Ltd budgets each year to sell 5,000 units of its product at a price of £4.80 per unit. Until this year, the variable cost of sale per unit had been £2 and fixed costs £9,800 per annum. With the introduction of new electronic equipment, however, variable costs have now been reduced to £1.40 per unit, although annual fixed costs have risen to £12,000.

Draw a breakeven chart to show the breakeven point and budgeted profit before and after the introduction of the new equipment.

1.5 Profit/volume charts

The P/V (profit-volume) chart is a variation of the breakeven chart which provides a simple illustration of the relationship of costs and profit to sales, and of the margin of safety. A P/V chart is constructed as follows (look at the chart on the next page as you read the explanation).

(a) 'P' is on the y axis and actually comprises not only 'profit' but contribution to profit (in monetary value), extending above and below the x axis with a zero point at the intersection of the two axes, and the negative section below the x axis representing fixed costs. This means that at zero production, the firm is incurring a loss equal to the fixed costs.

(b) 'V' is on the x axis and comprises either volume of sales or value of sales (revenue).

(c) The profit-volume line is a straight line drawn with its starting point (at zero production) at the intercept on the y axis representing the level of fixed costs, and with a gradient of contribution/unit (or the C/S ratio if sales value is used rather than units). The P/V line will cut the x axis at the breakeven point of sales volume. Any point on the P/V line above the x axis represents the profit to the firm (as measured on the vertical axis) for that particular level of sales.

WORKED EXAMPLE: P/V CHART

Cabbage Patch Ltd makes and sells a single product which has a variable cost of sale of £5. Fixed costs are £15,000 per annum. The company's management estimates that at a sales price of £8 per unit, sales per annum would be 7,000 units.

Construct a P/V chart.

SOLUTION

At sales of 7,000 units, total contribution will be 7,000 × £(8 – 5) = £21,000 and total profit will be £6,000.

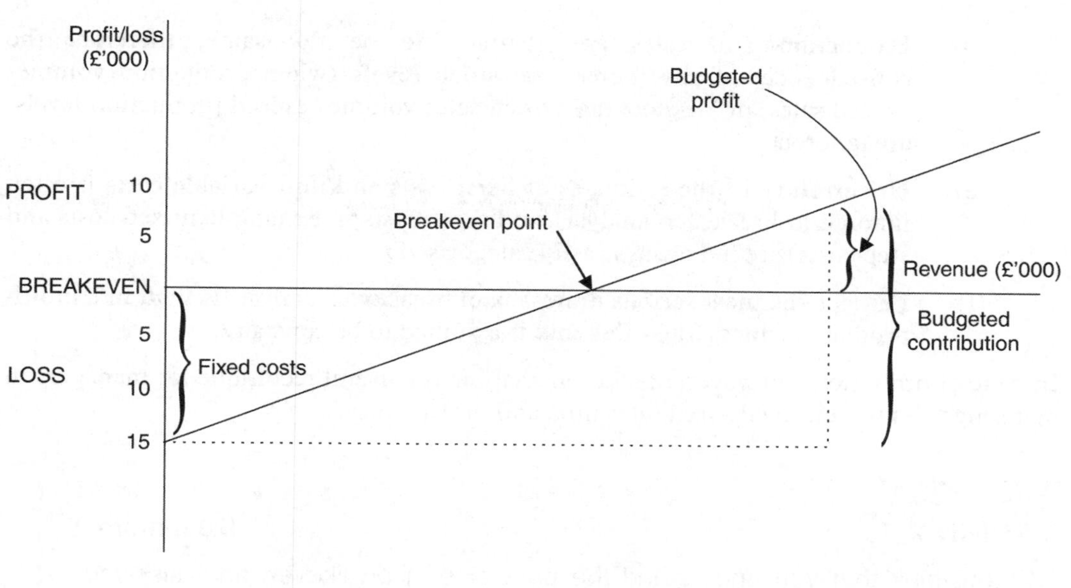

1.6 Limitations of breakeven analysis

Breakeven charts and breakeven arithmetic should be used carefully. The major **limitations of breakeven analysis** are as follows.

(a) A breakeven chart can only apply to one single product or a single mix (fixed proportions) of a group of products.

(b) It is assumed that fixed costs are the same in total and variable costs are the same per unit at all levels of output. This assumption is a great simplification.

   (i) Fixed costs will change if output falls or increases substantially (most fixed costs are **step costs**).

   (ii) The variable cost per unit will decrease where **economies of scale** are made at higher output volumes, and the variable cost per unit will also eventually rise where diseconomies of scale begin to appear at higher volumes of output (for example the extra cost of labour in overtime working).

Definition

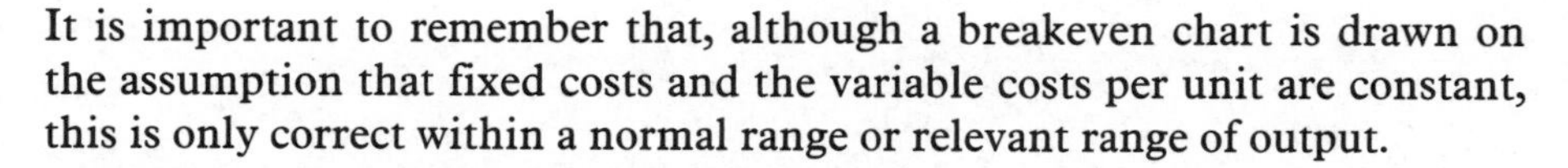

> **Economies of scale:** reductions in the average cost of producing a product in the long run as the output of the product increases.

It is important to remember that, although a breakeven chart is drawn on the assumption that fixed costs and the variable costs per unit are constant, this is only correct within a normal range or relevant range of output.

(c) It is assumed that **sales prices** will be constant at all levels of activity. This may not be true, especially at higher volumes of output, where the price may have to be reduced to win the extra sales.

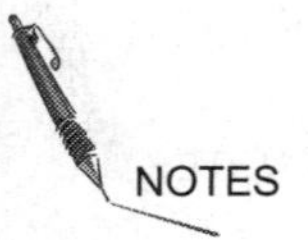
NOTES

(d) Production and sales are assumed to be the same, therefore the consequences of any increase in **stock levels** (when production volumes exceed sales) or 'de-stocking' (when sales volumes exceed production levels) are ignored.

(e) **Uncertainty** in the estimates of fixed costs and unit variable costs is often ignored in breakeven analysis, and some costs (for example mixed costs and step costs) are not always easily categorised.

(f) Perhaps the most serious drawback of breakeven analysis is that, in a multi-product business, the **sales mix** is assumed to be constant.

In spite of limitations, however, breakeven analysis is a useful technique for managers in planning sales prices, the desired sales mix, and profitability.

Activity 2 **(20 minutes)**

If you think that you understand the principles of breakeven analysis, you may be able to work out your own solutions to the following questions. Notice, by the way, that the questions deal with changes in selling prices, sales volumes, variable costs and fixed costs - hence the alternative term 'cost/volume/profit' analysis.

(a) If a company reduces its selling prices by 20%, but increases its sales volumes by 20% as a consequence of the price reduction, then profits will be unchanged.

True or false?

(b) If a company introduces automation into its work practices, so that

(i) unit variable costs fall; but
(ii) fixed costs increase substantially; so that
(iii) profitability at current sales volumes remains unchanged,

then the decision to automate would have been irrelevant to the future profitability of the company.

True or false?

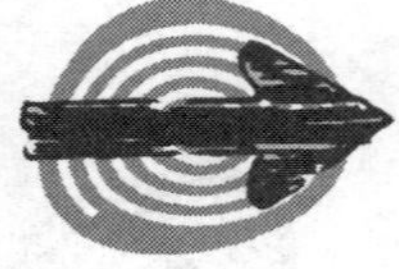

The price of a product or service is something which is frequently decided by the marketing manager and hence it is vital that you are aware of how to take pricing decisions. We have mentioned these issues before but now we can look at the accounting way of doing it.

2 COST BASED APPROACHES TO PRICING

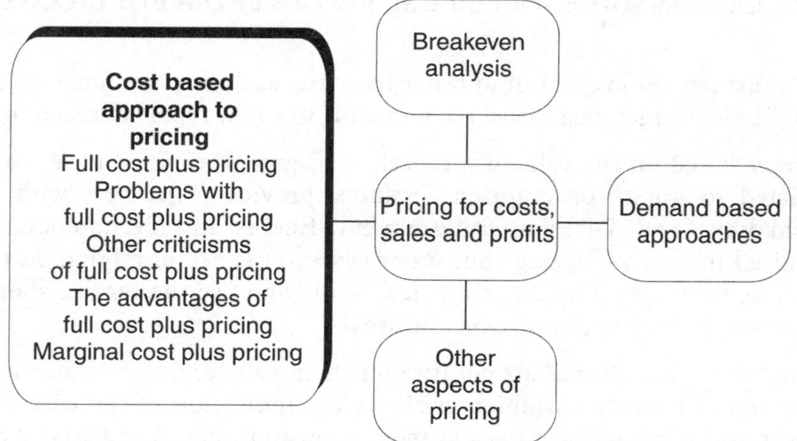

Pricing decisions must take account of a range of factors, including **demand and cost.**

Pricing decisions must have some regard for cost because the selling price of a product should exceed its average unit cost in order to make a **profit**. There are, of course, short-term situations where prices are kept deliberately low. **Loss leaders**, for example, are designed to attract custom for other products.

A major drawback of cost-based pricing models is the failure to take account of **demand factors.** The next section therefore considers demand-based approaches to pricing, including **competitors' pricing** and **price discrimination**.

Pricing decisions are, however, just one of the categories of marketing decision in the 'marketing mix' and pricing decisions should be taken within the framework of the overall marketing strategy.

2.1 Full cost plus pricing

A 'traditional' approach to pricing products is **full cost plus pricing**, whereby the sales price is determined by calculating the full cost of the product and then adding a **percentage mark-up** for profit. The term **target pricing** is sometimes used, which means setting a price so as to achieve a target profit or return on capital employed. Target pricing is therefore quite rigid, in the sense that a fixed, predetermined mark-up is added to cost so as to achieve the targeted profit or return.

In full cost plus pricing, the full cost may be a fully absorbed **production cost** only, or it may include some absorbed administration, selling and distribution **overheads**. The full cost might also include some **opportunity costs** as well, such as the opportunity cost of a production resource that is in short supply, for example skilled artists in the pottery sector.

A business might have an idea of the percentage profit margin it would like to earn and so might decide on an average **profit mark-up** as a general guideline for pricing decisions. This would be particularly useful for businesses that carry out a large amount of contract work or jobbing work, for which individual job or contract prices must be quoted regularly to prospective customers. However, the percentage profit mark-up can be varied to suit the circumstances.

The cost plus approach to pricing is commonly used in practice, but varying the size of the profit mark-up gives the pricing decisions much-needed **flexibility** so as to adapt to demand conditions.

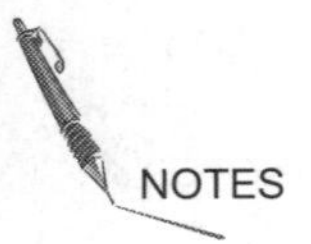

EXAMPLE: RESPONSIBLE WATER USE FLOWS FROM FULL-COST PRICING

Consumers must pay for every unit of water they use, and the price must reflect the cost of supplying it, the Conference Board recommends in a new report released today.

"Water charges based on the value of property – or any other fixed measure that is not directly related to water consumption – cannot provide consumers with clear price signals," said Len Coad, Director, Environment, Energy and Technology. "A cultural shift is required in how we manage our water system. Instead of relying on the tax base and allowing users to pay a below-cost price, those who use the service should pay the full cost of water, including capital expenditures."

Most Canadians pay less than $0.02 per litre for their water and wastewater service. Full-cost pricing would provide customers with a clear indication of the cost of providing water services and increase incentives to reduce consumption. As a basic step, universal water metering should be implemented immediately.

Cnw.ca, 27 November 2009

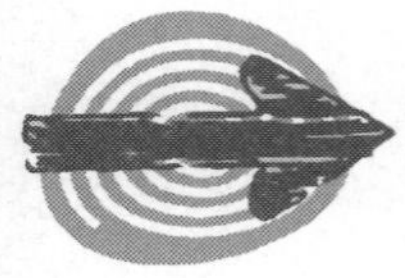

The basic principles and some of the practical problems with full cost plus pricing are illustrated in the following example. You might wish to attempt your own solution before reading ours.

WORKED EXAMPLE: FULL COST PLUS PRICING

Slidescale Ltd is about to quote a price for a contract which it is quite keen to win, provided that the price gives a reasonable profit on the work. If the company wins the contract, there is a good chance that a number of repeat orders will be made by the same customer within the next 18 months to two years.

The estimated costs of the contract would be as follows.

	£
Direct labour	2,500
Direct materials	6,000
Hire of equipment	500
Subcontractors' charges	1,200
Other direct expenses	300
Overheads	7,500
	18,000

The company sets its prices by adding a percentage mark-up for profit on to the full estimated cost of the contract, and the mark-up on its work for other customers tends to vary between 10% and 18%.

Determine the price which Slidescale should quote for this particular contract.

SOLUTION

There is really only one issue involved in this example, namely the **size of the profit mark-up**. The percentage profit margin is variable and presumably determined by management judgement, which in turn will be influenced by the following.

(a) The **wish to win the contract**, perhaps in the face of competition from rival companies.

(b) The likelihood of **repeat orders** and so further profits in the future.

(c) Whether the company has idle **capacity** or a full order book. When the company is busy, it can opt to quote higher prices, so that the profit margins on work that it obtains will be higher.

There is no 'correct' price, but the following points could be made.

(a) **The price should exceed full cost.** Companies must operate at a profit to survive and this means earning revenue that more than covers direct costs and a share of overheads.

(b) The company must make a judgement about **demand conditions** (competition, probability of repeat orders), the company's workload and order book, and even the nature of the work itself. For example, is it likely to be easy or difficult to do properly?

In this example, if we were to assume that Slidescale Ltd had some spare capacity and was quite keen to win the contract, a profit margin of around 10% might be recommended, giving a price of 110% × £18,000 = £19,800. But we should not ignore the other contract that may be being offered. If the size of the repeat order is much larger and we feel that it is important to obtain it, then we may be tempted to reduce our price still further.

Note that a margin of 10% on costs yields a profit of 9% of sales revenue.

2.2 Problems with full cost plus pricing

There are several serious problems with relying on a full cost approach to pricing, some of which have already been mentioned. These are as follows.

(a) The need to adjust prices to **market and demand conditions.**

(b) **Budgeting output volume,** which is a key factor in the fixed overhead absorption rate.

(c) Selecting a suitable **basis for overhead absorption,** especially where a business produces more than one product.

Perhaps the most important criticism of cost plus pricing is that it fails to recognise that since sales demand may be determined by the sales price, there will be a **profit-maximising combination of price and demand.** A cost plus-based approach to pricing will be most unlikely, except by coincidence of luck, to arrive at the profit-maximising price.

2.3 Other criticisms of full cost plus pricing

Further objections to full cost plus pricing can be listed as follows.

(a) We know how difficult it is to **budget** accurately, and a sudden slump in **demand** will result in difficulties in achieving the overall profit levels that were budgeted.

(b) When a company produces more than one product. The accountants will have to **allocate** the fixed costs of production to the different products. This is usually a fairly subjective allocation.

(c) It fails to allow for **competition.** A company may need to match the prices of rival firms when these take a price-cutting (or price-raising) initiative.

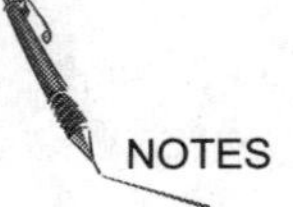

(d) A full cost plus price is a means of ensuring that, in the long run, a company succeeds in covering all its fixed costs and making a profit out of revenue earned. However, in the short term, it is **inflexible**.

2.4 The advantages of full cost plus pricing

The advantages of full cost plus pricing are as follows.

(a) Since the size of the profit margin can be varied at management's discretion, a price in excess of full cost should ensure that a company working at normal capacity will cover all its fixed costs and make a profit. Companies may benefit from cost plus pricing in the following circumstances.

   (i) If they carry out large contracts which must make a sufficient profit margin to cover a fair share of fixed costs.

   (ii) If the company must justify their prices to potential customers (for example for government contracts).

   (iii) If the company finds it difficult to estimate expected demand at different sales prices.

(b) It is a simple, quick and cheap method of pricing.

2.5 Marginal cost plus pricing

Instead of pricing products or services by adding a profit margin on to full cost, a business might add a profit margin on to **marginal cost** (either the marginal cost of production or else the marginal cost of sales). This is sometimes called **mark-up pricing,** which is another form of target pricing.

In practice, mark-up pricing is used in businesses where there is a readily-identifiable basic variable cost. Retail industries are the most obvious example, and it is quite common for the prices of goods in shops to be fixed by adding a mark-up (20% or 33.3%, say) to the purchase cost. For example, a department store might buy in items of pottery at £3 each, add a mark-up of one-third and resell the items at £4.

There are, of course, drawbacks to marginal cost plus pricing.

(a) Although the size of the mark-up can be varied in accordance with demand conditions, it is not a method of pricing which ensures that sufficient attention is paid to demand conditions, competitors' prices and profit maximisation.

(b) It ignores fixed overheads in the pricing decision, but the sales price must be sufficiently high to ensure that a profit is made after covering fixed costs.

3 DEMAND BASED APPROACHES

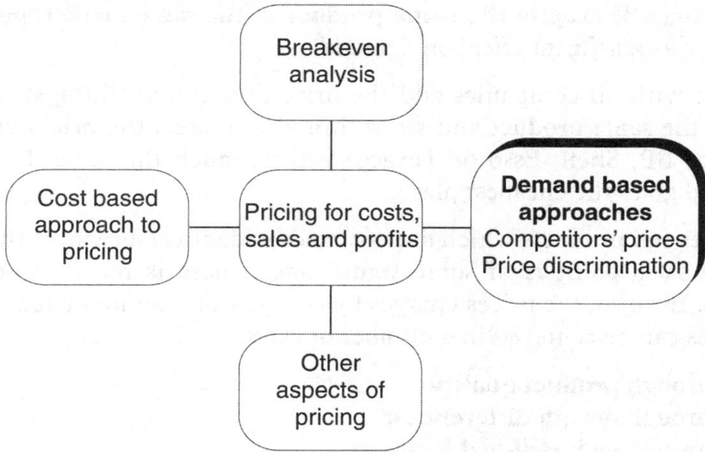

A difficulty with a demand-based approach to pricing is to find a balance between theory and practice.

(a) **Price theory** (or **demand theory**) is based on the idea that a connection can be made between price, quantity demanded and sold, and total revenue. Demand varies with price, and so if an estimate can be made of demand at different price levels, it should be possible to derive either a profit-maximising price or a revenue-maximising price.

(b) In practice, businesses might not make estimates of demand at different price levels, but they might still make pricing decisions on the basis of demand conditions and competition in the market.

Some larger organisations go to considerable effort to estimate the demand for their products or services at differing price levels by producing estimated **demand curves.**

For example, a large transport authority might be considering an increase in bus fares or underground fares. The effect on total revenues and profit of the increase in fares could be estimated from a knowledge of the demand for transport services at different price levels. If an increase in the price per ticket caused a large fall in demand, because demand was price elastic, total revenues and profits would fall whereas a fares increase when demand is price inelastic would boost total revenue, and since a transport authority's costs are largely fixed, this would probably boost total profits too.

Definition

Price elasticity of demand: a measure of the responsiveness of demand to changes in price: the percentage change in the quantity of a good demanded, divided by the percentage change in its price.

Activity 3 **(20 minutes)**

Moose Ltd sells a product which has a variable cost of £8 per unit. The sales demand at the current sales price of £14 is 3,000 units. It has been estimated by the marketing department that the sales volume would fall by 100 units for each addition of 25 pence to the sales price.

Establish whether the current price of £14 is the optimal price which maximises contribution.

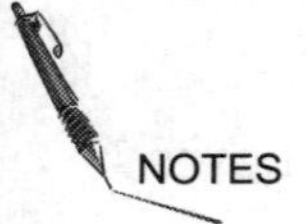

3.1 Competitors' prices

When competitors sell **exactly the same product** in the same market, price differences are likely to have a significant effect on demand.

This is the case with oil companies and the price of petrol at filling stations: different companies sell the same product and so, within a local area, the prices charged at each station (whether BP, Shell, Esso or Texaco) will be much the same. If they were not, customers would go to the cheapest place.

When companies sell products which are not exactly identical, or where the geographical location of the sales point is of some significance, there is more scope for charging different prices. Even so, the prices charges by competitors cannot be ignored altogether. Price differences can be achieved in a number of ways.

(a) Through **product quality**.
(b) Through **design differences.**
(c) Through **geographical location**.
(d) Through **brand loyalty**.

3.2 Price discrimination

Where a company can sell to two or more completely separate markets, it might be able to charge a different price in each market to maximise its profits because the demand function in each market might be different. Successful price discrimination depends on the ability of the company to prevent the **transfer** of goods by a third party from the cheap market to the more expensive one.

EXAMPLE: REEL TIME: THE INCREDIBLE SHRINKING WINDOW FOR MOVIE RELEASES

A decade ago, movie fans who wanted to forgo paying for pricey tickets and popcorn waited an average of five months before they could watch a film in their own living rooms. Today, the window between theatrical releases and distribution via DVD and other channels like cable television and the web has shrunk to four months or less – and in some cases has even disappeared, with films being made available through video-on-demand services the same day they debut …

The movie release window is a Hollywood construct where each distribution channel such as DVDs, cable television pay-per-view services and subscription channels like HBO, and Internet companies like Netflix get access to distribute films following their theatrical debut. Other forms of content have release windows as well: books, for example, have defined sales periods for hardcover versions before they are sold in paperback. In the movie industry, billions of dollars are at stake with regard to the timing of releases in various distribution channels. According to AC Nielsen, total U.S. and Canadian box office receipts totaled $9.78 billion in 2008. The same year, U.S. consumers spent $22.4 billion on DVD sales and rentals, according to a report by research firm Digital Entertainment Group.

"The decision of when to release a movie and to what channel is a strategic issue for the industry," says David Hsu, a management professor at Wharton. "At the end of the day, the studios are trying to maximize profits. The various distribution models revolve around maximizing the revenue from each type of consumer."

knowledge.wharton.upenn.edu, 24 November 2009

There are several ways in practice by which price discrimination can be exercised.

(a) **Negotiation with individual customers**. For example, customer A might buy a video cassette recorder for Firm X for £600 cash, whereas customer B might buy the same item and negotiate a discount for cash of, say, 10%.

(b) **On the basis of quantities purchased.** Bulk purchase discounts are a well-established form of price discrimination, offering favourable prices to large customers.

(c) **By product type**. Examples of price discrimination through product differentiation are to be found in meals in differently priced restaurants, supermarkets (as illustrated by Tesco's 'Finest' range, for example) or clothing (Donna Karan's 'DKNY' range).

(d) **By time.** Examples are services with peak time and off-peak tariffs, such as hotel accommodation in holiday resorts and charges for telephone calls.

(e) **By location.** Higher prices may be charged in some locations than in others so that a firm with several branches in various towns may set different prices in each branch. Branches in remote locations might set higher prices and in poorer areas they might set lower prices.

For price discrimination to be successful, certain **market conditions** must exist.

(a) The producer must enjoy a dominant position in the market, perhaps as a **monopolist** or as the provider of a product which commands a high degree of **customer loyalty**.

If this condition did not exist, customers faced with higher prices would switch to cheaper alternatives supplied by competitors.

(b) Where price discrimination is exercised on the basis of individual negotiation or by geographical area, there must be no opportunity for **rivals** to buy the product at the cheaper price and sell it at a competitive price to the higher priced market.

EXAMPLE

Examples of differential pricing

By market segment	By product version	By time

A cross-channel ferry company would market its services at different prices in England, Belgium and France. Services such as cinemas and hairdressers are often available at lower prices to old age pensioners and/or juveniles.	Software is written top-down and the full version is sold at a premium price. For less advanced users all the software company has to do is take features out: there is little extra cost.	Travel companies are successful price discriminators, charging more to rush hour commuters whose demand is inelastic at certain times of the day Other examples are off-peak travel bargains or telephone charges.

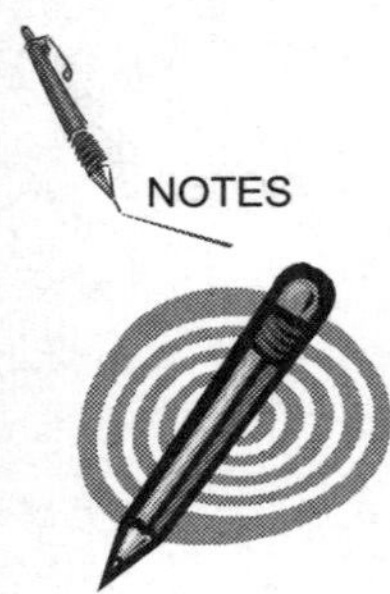

Activity 4 **(15 minutes)**

Can you think of three more examples of price discrimination and on which basis each is exercised?

The producer must also consider other factors.

(a) Can differential prices be **justified** to customers? For example, do the higher priced versions of the product offer added design features, extra materials, or a better quality of service?

(b) Is price discrimination **normal practice**?

(c) How much will the price **differential** be? If prices are going to be raised in one segment of the market, what will **customer reaction** be?

(d) Are the price differentials **cost based**, or are they determined purely according to **what the market will bear**?

FOR DISCUSSION

Good quality products are almost always offered at a high price. You get what you pay for.

Own label pricing: a form of price discrimination

Many supermarkets and multiple retail stores sell **own label products**, often at a lower price than established branded products. The supermarkets or multiple retailers do this by entering into arrangements with manufacturers.

For a manufacturer who is asked by a multiple retailer to quote a price for supplying goods in bulk under the retailer's own brand name, the pricing decision should be influenced by the following factors.

(a) Would the manufacturer become over-reliant on the multiple retailer as a customer? If the multiple retailer cancelled the contract, would the manufacturer's business survive?

(b) If the manufacturer would continue to produce his product under his own name as well as under the multiple retailer's name, would the products be similar or different in quality? If similar, what price difference should there be between the 'normal' output and the retailer's 'own brand'? In a market where demand is price elastic, a significant price difference could seriously affect sales of the higher priced 'normal' good.

4 OTHER ASPECTS OF PRICING

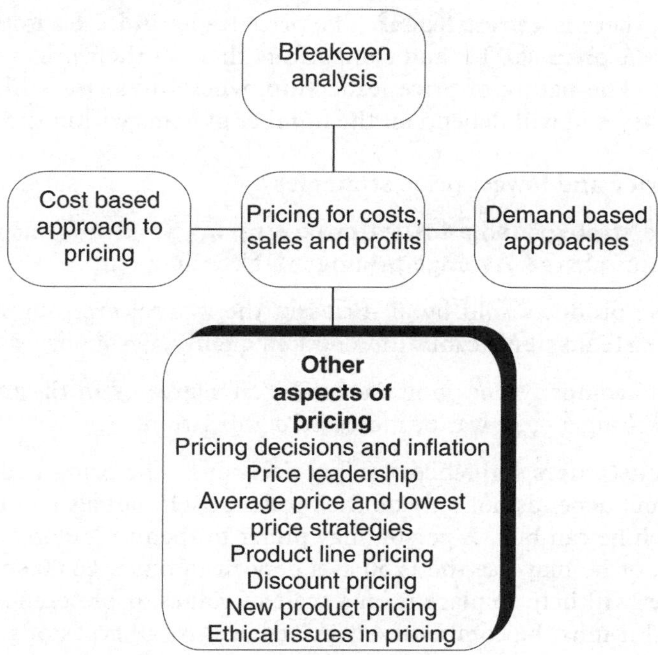

We have considered many different aspects of pricing but we now look at a different cost focus: inflation.

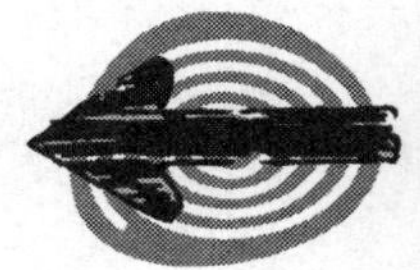

4.1 Pricing decisions and inflation

An organisation should recognise the effects of inflation on its pricing decisions. When its **costs are rising**, it must try to ensure that its prices are increased sufficiently and regularly enough to make an adequate profit.

There are several simple guidelines for **price reviews** during a period of inflation.

(a) **Fixed price long-term contracts should be avoided**. A long-term contract should include a price variation clause, which allows the supplier to raise the contract price to cover inflation.

(b) When one organisation sets its prices, it should decide **how long** it will be until the next price review.

(c) Prices should be **reviewed regularly**. The higher the inflation rate, the more frequent the price reviews should be.

(d) An organisation cannot assume that it can **pass on its cost increases** to its customers by raising prices.

(i) In a competitive market, competitors might opt to reduce their profit margins and place added emphasis on the **control of costs**.

(ii) Customers might **resist higher prices**, and so price increases would result in some fall in demand.

(e) When prices are reviewed, management must recognise that costs are likely to continue to rise, and so the new price levels ought to anticipate **future cost increases** up to the time of the next price review.

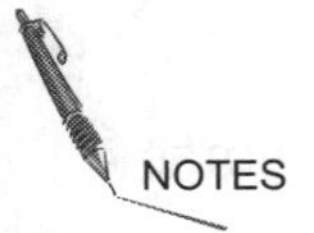

4.2 Price leadership

In some markets, there is a **price leader**. The price leader indicates to the other firms in the market what the price will be, and competitors then set their prices with reference to the leader's price. The nature of price leadership, where it exists, is likely to vary from industry to industry and will depend on the number of firms within the industry.

4.3 Average price and lowest price strategies

An **average price strategy** and a **lowest price strategy** are two forms of strategy based on what competitors charge. **Average pricing** might be adopted:

(a) If the products sold by all firms in the market are roughly the same, and there are no significant differences in quality, design or product content

(b) If the company does not wish to be an aggressor in the market, for fear of provoking a price war or increased competition.

The **attitude of customers** influences pricing decisions. The price a customer is willing to pay for a product depends not only on the product itself, but also on its relationship to other goods which he can buy. A person may prefer to spend £250 on a television, a hi-fi system, or a bed, or he may use the £250 as a deposit to buy a £6,000 car on credit. The price of a product will help to place it on a scale of values or preferences in the mind of the customer and it must be competitively priced against all types of goods and services to attract his custom.

A **lowest price strategy** might be associated with market aggression or low quality.

(a) When a major company in a competitive market pursues a lowest price strategy, it might provoke a response from rival companies, and start a price war. Relatively small firms, in contrast, might hope to build up a small share of the market without provoking a response from bigger competitors.

(b) Price is often a guide to quality, and low prices tend to indicate low quality.

4.4 Product line pricing

When a firm sells a range of related products, or a product line, its theoretical pricing policy should be to set prices for the products **which maximise the profitability of the line as a whole**. Problems which arise in product line pricing are as follows.

- Inter-related demand
- Inter-related cost
- The degree of competition

Inter-related demand occurs when two or more products in a line are either substitutes or complements. Tea and sugar (or sweeteners) are examples of complementary products: if the price of tea rises, the demand for sugar may well fall. Tea and coffee are examples of substitute products: if the price of tea rises, the demand for coffee may well rise. Before changing the price of one product, the firm's management should consider cross-elasticities of demand of different products in the range, in order to assess the effect of the price change on total demand for the product line.

Definition

> **Cross elasticity of demand:** a measure of the responsiveness of demand for one good to changes in the price of another: the percentage change in the quantity demanded for one good divided by the percentage change in the price of the other good.

4.5 Discount pricing

Definition

Discounts are reductions in list, advertised or quoted prices offered by sellers to buyers.

The reasons for discounts may vary from a small, one-off gesture because of a damaged package to a significant part of a firm's marketing strategy.

Discounts should be considered separately from low price strategies, which are a continuing feature of a firm's trading activity.

Discounts can be categorised as follows.

(a) **Quantity discounts** are those offered to encourage buying in larger amounts. Trade prices are often structured in this way.

(b) **Cumulative quantity discounts** extend over a period. They are designed to encourage continuing re-purchase of a product or brand or from an outlet.

(c) **Cash discounts** are offered when customers pay cash immediately in order to improve cash flow and/or to reduce administrative costs such as invoicing or the cost of running credit accounts.

(d) **Sale prices** are forms of temporary discounts used to clear lines from stock or stimulate sales of slow moving stock, damaged goods or products which have gone out of fashion or season.

(e) **Trade discounts** (retail and wholesale). Normally a traditional standard discount is given to a trade outlet in return for the activities which they contribute to the marketing effort.

FOR DISCUSSION

What are the likely effects on a regular line when special discounts are offered?

4.6 New product pricing

The pricing of new products requires that the principles discussed previously are considered very carefully.

The price has to cover costs and provide for profit at the same time as being seen as offering value to attract sufficient purchasers. Price is a signal, you will remember, of quality relative to competition. It has two time factors to contend with.

- Short-term, to get the product into the market
- Long-term, to ensure that it is a worthwhile venture for the company

Price skimming involves setting a high initial price for a new product (in order to take advantage of those buyers prepared to pay a high price for innovation) and then gradually reducing the price (to attract more price sensitive segments of the market).

This strategy is an example of price discrimination over time and is favoured in the following situations.

- Insufficient market capacity, and competitors cannot increase capacity
- Buyers are relatively insensitive to price increases
- High price perceived as high quality

Penetration pricing is pricing a new product low in order to maximise market penetration before competitors can enter the market.

The organisation sets a relatively low price for the product or service, to maximise sales by stimulating growth of the market and/or obtaining a larger share of it. This strategy was used by Japanese motor cycle manufacturers, for example, to enter the UK market. UK productive capacity was virtually eliminated, the imported Japanese machines could later be sold at a much higher price and still dominate the market.

Sales maximising objectives are favoured when the following apply.

- Unit costs will fall with increased output (in other words, there are economies of scale)
- The market is price sensitive and relatively low prices will attract more sales
- Low prices will discourage any new competitors

Effective **market research** will help in making the right tactical decisions in this regard.

FOR DISCUSSION

It is better to maximise profits in the short term than to risk sending the wrong quality signals to the market by launching at a low price.

4.7 Ethical issues in pricing

According to Dibb *et al* (2001), 'the emotional and subjective nature of price creates many situations in which misunderstandings between the seller and buyer cause ethical problems.'

As already mentioned, monopolistic market structures price competition may be avoided by **tacit agreement** leading to **concentration on non-price competition**. The markets for cigarettes and petrol are examples of this. Price-setting here is influenced by the need to avoid retaliatory responses by competitors resulting in a breakdown of the tacit agreement and so to price competition. Price changes based on real cost changes are led in many instances by a representative firm in the industry and followed by other firms. From time to time tacit agreements break down leading to a period of price competition. Whether agreements exist at all is hard to prove, as the competitors are exposed to the same market forces, so would expect to set similar prices. This is a problem for government agencies, such as the Office of Fair Trading, when attempting to establish if **unethical pricing agreements**, such as price fixing, exist.

Predatory pricing is another potential problem, when a company seeks to earn high profits at the (excessive) expense of its customers.

EXAMPLE

Dibb *et al* (2001) cite the example of Richard Branson who, when he launched Virgin Cola, advocated a relatively low price, arguing that consumers were paying a 'brand tax' premium whenever they bought leading cola brands.

Stelios Haji-Ioannou adopted a similar approach when the easyGroup launched easyCinema. The proposition addressed what Stelios referred to as 'rip off' cinema chains. He proposed an initial launch price of 20p for his 'no frills' cinema stating that consumers were paying over the odds to watch films and pay for ludicrously expensive popcorn and other additions. The venture failed however because he was unable to gain distribution rights to show movies from the major film companies due to his low price strategy.

Chapter roundup

- Breakeven, costs/sales and cost/volume/profit charts are valuable tools of analysis.
- There are limitations to these techniques.
- Pricing decisions should be taken with the marketing plan in mind.
- There are a number of important pricing techniques.
- Cost-based approaches to pricing tend to ignore demand factors.
- Price discrimination should be taken into account where appropriate.
- Pricing decisions should take account of competitors' prices.
- Inflation is an important influence on pricing decisions.
- All pricing strategies should attempt to optimise profit opportunity in the long term.

Quick quiz

1 What does C/V/P stand for?

2 What is the main weakness for marketers of a cost based approach to pricing?

3 What pricing method is based on relevant costs?

4 What is the significance of a monopoly situation for pricing decisions?

5 List some ways in which price discrimination can be exercised.

6 What problems can arise in product line pricing?

Answers to Quick quiz

1 Cost, volume, profit (analysis).

2 It ignores competition.

3 Machinery usage.

4 Following the market is not necessary; price elasticity can be judged.

5 By negotiation: quantities, product type, time, location.

6 Inter-related cost; inter-related demand; level of competition.

Answers to Activities

1

	Before		*After*
Fixed costs	9,800		12,000
Variable costs (5,000 units × £2)	10,000	(5,000 × £1.40)	7,000
Total costs	19,800		19,000
Revenue (5,000 units)	24,000		24,000

(a) Before the changeover, annual profit would be budgeted as £4,200 and the breakeven point (A) would be:

$$\frac{£9{,}800}{£(4.80 - 2.00)} = 3{,}500 \text{ units or } £16{,}800.$$

(b) After the changeover, annual profit should be £5,000 but the breakeven point (B) will be 3,529 units or £16,940.

2 (a) False.

The problem should be considered in terms of contribution, and it is helpful to use algebra.

Let: the current sales price = s
the variable unit cost = v
and the sales quantity = q

Total contribution = Contribution per unit (s – v) × Volume of sales (q)

$$= (s - v)q$$
$$= qs - qv$$

With the reduction in sales price to 0.8s and the increase in sales volume to 1.2q, total contribution would be

$$(0.8s - v)1.2q$$
$$= 0.96qs - 1.2qv.$$

Total contribution would be less, because sales revenue would fall (qs to 0.9qs) and total variable costs would rise (qv to 1.2qv).

If you do not follow the algebra, then put actual figures in for the factors in the question and work it through.

(b) False. Although total contribution and profits are unchanged at the current sales volume, the automation will have important consequences for any increase or fall in sales demand in the future, because the ratio of contribution to sales has increased. An increase in sales volume will now result in a faster rate of increase in profits (just as a fall in sales volume would reduce profitability at a faster rate).

3 Remember that the variable cost is £8 per unit

Sales price	*Unit contribution*	*Sales volume*	*Total contribution*
£	£	Units	£
13.00	5.00	3,400	17,000
13.25	5.25	3,300	17,325
13.50	5.50	3,200	17,600
13.75	5.75	3,100	17,825
14.00	6.00	3,000	18,000
14.25	6.25	2,900	18,125
14.50	6.50	2,800	18,200
14.75	6.75	2,700	18,225*
15.00	7.00	2,600	18,200

* Contribution would be maximised at a price of £14.75, and sales of 2,700 units.

The current price is not optimal.

4 Your answer will obviously depend upon your choice of product or service. You may have chosen air travel on the basis of both time and location. It is cheaper to fly to Glasgow from Heathrow than Birmingham despite the longer journey. Also on European flights you often have to stay over a Saturday night to obtain a cheaper fare. Clothes manufacturers often have a designer label, for which they charge high prices, and a cheaper range sold under a different name.

Chapter 12 : PROMOTION

Introduction

Promotion is concerned with communication between the seller and the buyer (an increasingly widely used, and probably more valid, name is **marketing communications**). Consequently it is the most visible aspect of marketing and, arguably, the most interesting. Promotion builds brands and we shall take a detailed look at branding in this chapter.

Promotion includes advertising, sales promotion activities, publicity or public relations, and the activities of the sales force. The fastest growing area, in the age of computers and telecommunications, is personal marketing. However, your first job if you choose marketing as a career may well be in the field of personal selling. All these topics are covered extensively below. This is a long chapter, but you will find it interesting.

Firms will use a combination of promotion methods and the optimal communications mix will depend on the nature of the product, the market and the customer. A manufacturer of industrial goods may rely more heavily on personal selling and sales literature, whereas a consumer goods manufacturer will use advertising and sales promotion.

Your objectives

In this chapter you will learn about the following.

(a) The communication process

(b) The purpose and objectives of advertising, the six stages of an advertising campaign, when advertising is likely to be successful and the advantages of using agencies

(c) The importance of branding

(d) Examples of sales promotion activities and the meaning of merchandising

(e) The ways in which publicity may be used for promotion

(f) Direct marketing and why it is growing in importance, and the techniques of direct mail and telemarketing

(g) The tasks and process of personal selling, how a sales force might be organised and the value of after-sales service

1 PROMOTION AND COMMUNICATING WITH CUSTOMERS

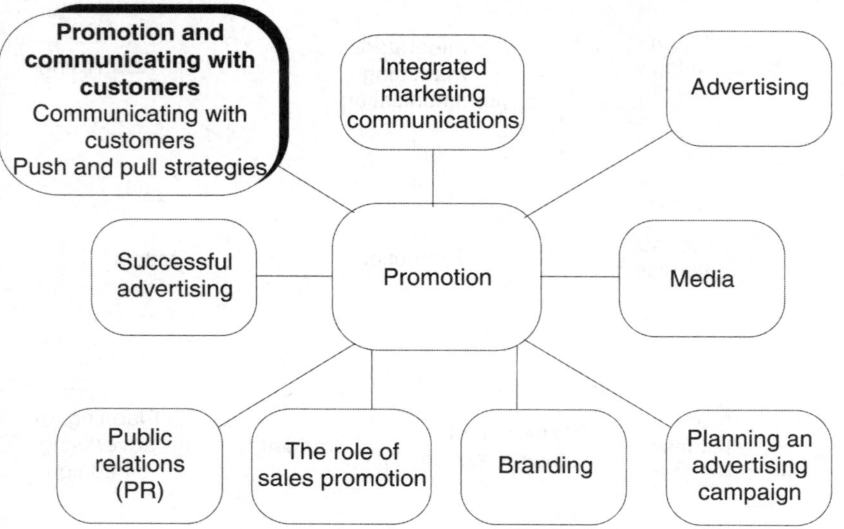

1.1 Communicating with customers

Definition

> **Marketing communications** is the process of both informing and educating users and dealers about the company, and of influencing attitudes and behaviour.

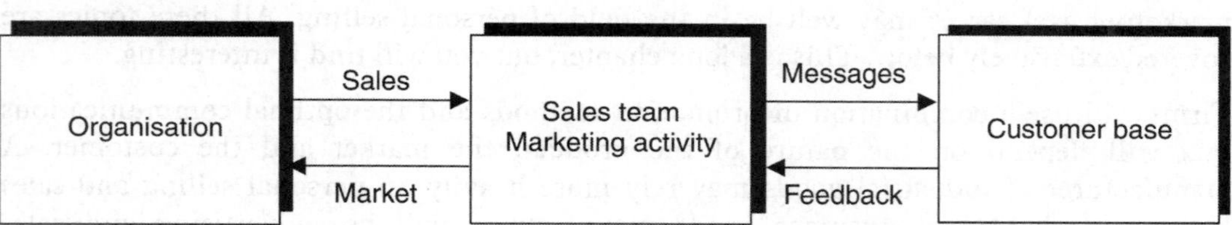

Figure 12.1: Marketing communication

Communication with customers involves many aspects of the marketing mix, but **promotion** is paramount.

Personal selling is not the only communication medium available to the organisation. In firms with a co-ordinated promotional strategy the activity of the sales team will be supported and supplemented by a combination of other communication tools. This combination is referred to as the **promotional mix**

EXAMPLE: SAINSBURY'S COPIES TESCO WITH BOGOF LATER DEAL

Sainsbury's has launched a trial to allow customers to claim the second item in BOGOF [buy one, get one free] deals at a later date, mirroring Tesco's BOGOF Later deal.

As part of the 'Buy Now- Free Next Time' initiative, customers will be given a coupon at the till point to claim the free item the next time they are in a Sainsbury's store ...

Sainsbury's trial follows the announcement from Tesco in October that it would offer staggered BOGOF deals but Sainsbury's has beat its rival to implementing the initiative, which is yet to go live in Tesco stores.

Sainsbury's customer director Gwyn Burr says: 'We know that 50% of shoppers take coupons and vouchers with them when they shop, and it's a really practical way for people to stretch their budgets, especially in the current economic climate. This new coupon promotion, together with the low prices and promotions we already have, means customers will get unbeatable value on the products that are most useful to them.'

Rosie Baker, *marketingweek.co.uk*, 17 November 2009

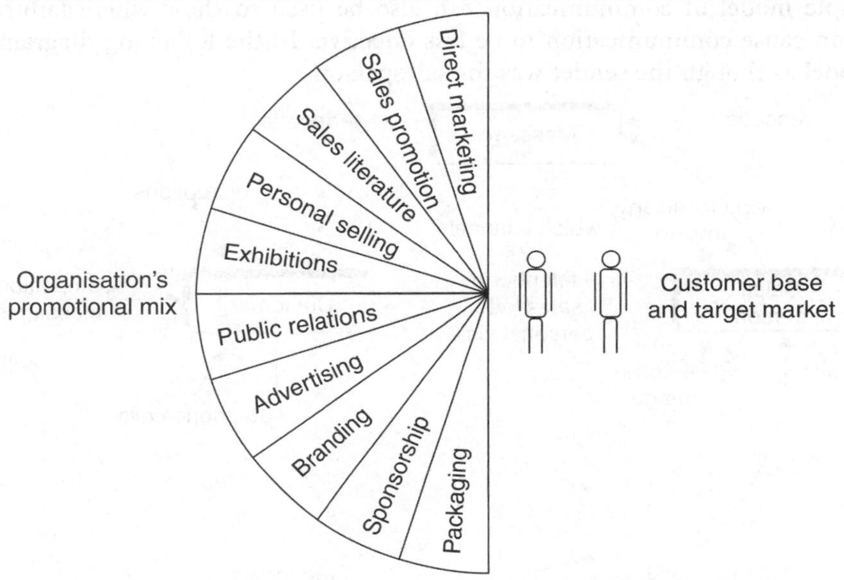

Figure 12.2: The promotional mix

These other communication tools are used to increase the **efficiency and effectiveness** of the sales effort. In combination, these represent the entire external communications activity of the organisation.

It is possible to use the same model of the **communication process** to describe one-to-one communication between friends, or a major multinational organisation communicating with its market place.

Effective communication requires several elements.

- A sender
- A receiver
- A message
- A communication channel or medium
- A feedback mechanism

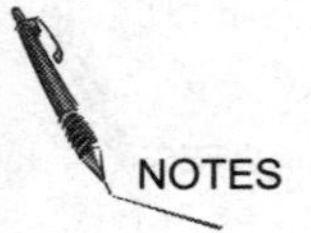
NOTES

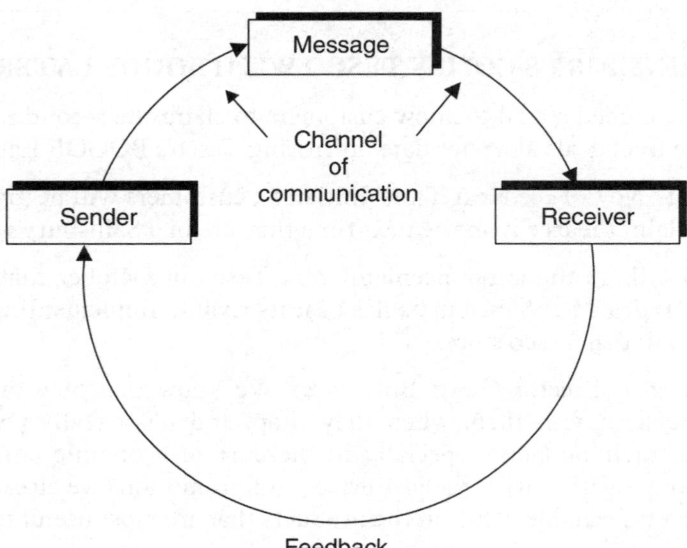

Figure 12.3: A simple model of communication

This simple model of communication can also be used to show where failures in the process can cause communication to be less effective. In the following diagram we look at the model as though the sender was the salesperson.

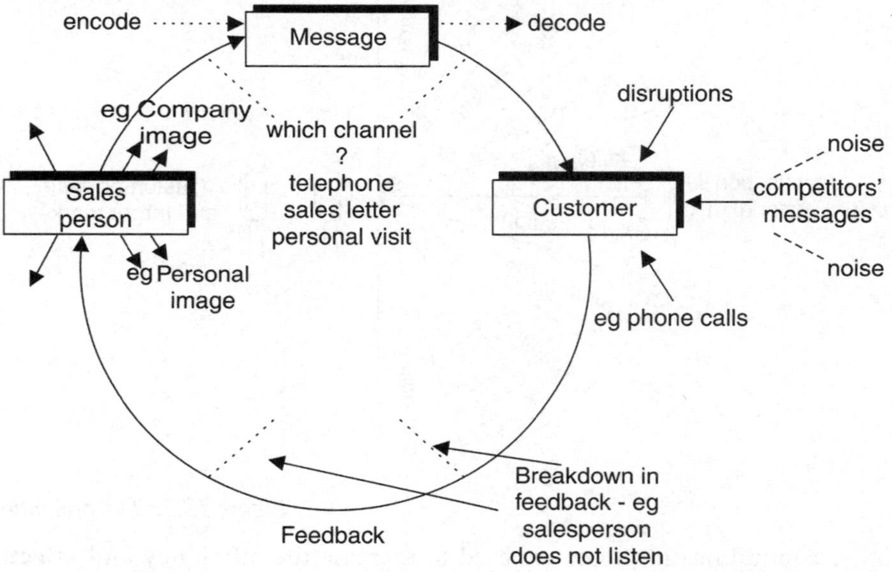

Figure 12.4: Model of communication showing the salesperson as the sender

The following table expands on the above diagram.

Element in process	How it can go wrong in personal selling
Sender	The salesperson transmits a personal and personified company **image**. The dress, the language used, and the car they drive creates that image. If it is **inconsistent** with the sales message or the customer's perceptions, communication can be adversely affected.
Message	The message has to be **encoded** and accurately **decoded** if it is to be effective. The words and pictures used can help or hinder this process.

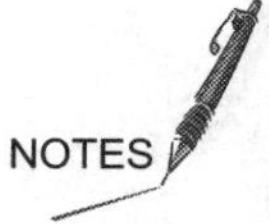

Element in process	How it can go wrong in personal selling
Channel	Choosing the **wrong channel** to transmit the sales message: an intrusive personal visit, instead of a phone call, or a phone call instead of a more effective personal visit.
Receiver	Much sales time and effort can be wasted talking to the wrong person. Ensuring the market has been **correctly targeted** and the **decision making unit** (DMU) identified, is essential to the selling process. Even when face to face with the decision maker, there will be distractions.
Feedback	The strength of personal selling lies in its ability to **modify the message** in response to customer **feedback**. If the feedback mechanism fails to work, selling loses its distinct advantage as a communication tool.

The salesperson has to be aware that as a communicator it is not just **what** is said which has an impact. **How** it is said, also speaks volumes. How something is said directly communicates the salesperson's attitude to customers and reflects the degree to which customer care is meant.

We shall be discussing personal selling in more detail later in the next chapter.

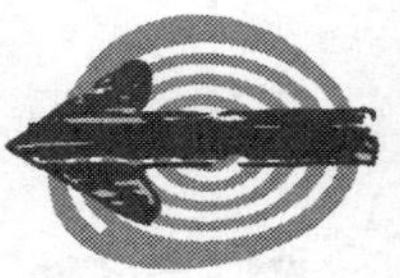

Activity 1 **(10 minutes)**

You have no doubt been browsing in a shop and found that you are constantly bothered by sales assistants wondering whether they can help you. You have also no doubt been ready to buy something in a shop and been infuriated that you cannot find anyone to help you.

How can this situation be analysed in terms of the communication process?

1.2 Push and pull strategies

The promotional mix is often described in terms of 'push' and 'pull' effects and towards whom the marketing strategy is emphasised. A balance is needed between the need to communicate with consumers, with distributors and with all other stakeholders.

Audience	Message focus
• Consumers, customers	Products and services
• Members of the marketing channel, such as dealers	Products and services
• All stakeholders, to raise the visibility of the organisation	The organisation

(a) A **pull effect** is when customers ask for the brand by name, inducing retailers or distributors to stock up with the company's goods.

(b) A **push effect** is targeted on getting the company's goods into the distribution network. This could be by giving a special discount on volume to ensure that wholesalers stock up with products that the company is promoting.

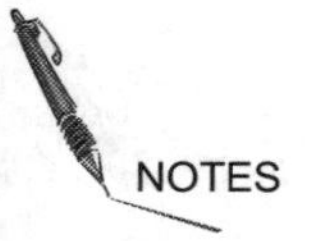

EXAMPLE

Continental, the German tyre group used a combination of 'push' and 'pull'.

- **Push** to the original equipment market, by supplying tyres to the big car manufacturers
- **Pull** via replacement tyres, with consumers tending to opt for the same brand

The tyre-fitting trade plays a large rôle in the route to the customer. Continental carries out a lot of push activity here, with incentive programmes, training and education to make sure that the fitters understand the brand segments (premium quality, economy, budget, own label). A greater challenge was to get consumers to think about tyres as more than those black things attached to their cars. TV and press advertising in Europe sought to change this perception.

Adapted from *Marketing Business*, January 2002

Perhaps the most obvious way in which the marketer can communicate with large numbers of potential customers is **advertising**. One of the aims of advertising is to create the 'pull' effect described above.

FOR DISCUSSION

Most customers do not have the opportunity to feed back their opinion to the supplier.

2 INTEGRATED MARKETING COMMUNICATIONS

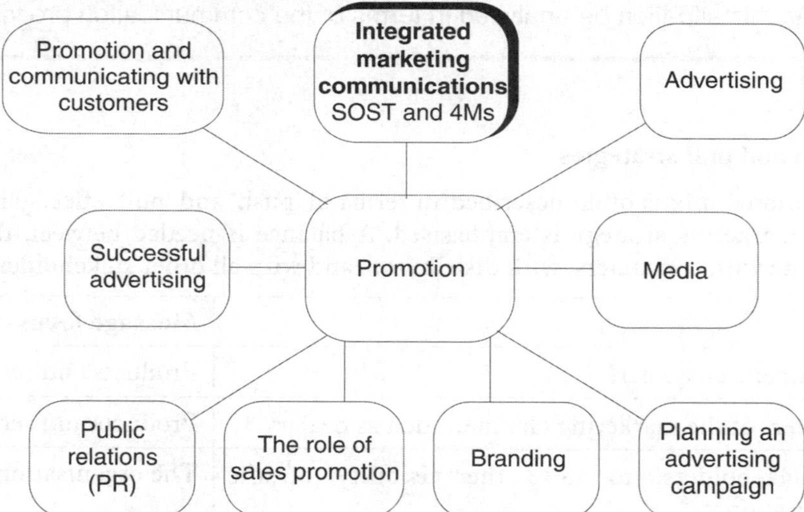

Promotion work is exciting because the aim is to **influence customers favourably** towards your organisation's products or services. It is not an exact science. It retains many of the characteristics of an art or a game. But in any game, there is great skill in co-ordinating all aspects. In the same way it is necessary to integrate all the promotional elements to achieve the maximum influence on the customer.

It is easy to understand, therefore, that there is a rapidly developing area of study known as **integrated marketing communications**. Integrated marketing communications

represents all the elements of an organisation's marketing mix that favourably influence an organisation's customers or clients. The concept promotes the use of a consistent message throughout the entire mix.

2.1 SOST and 4Ms

One technique that can be used for integrated marketing planning is known as **SOSTAC and 6Ms** (it is also described as **SOSTT**, or **SOST**, and **4Ms**, but the principle remains the same).

		Men: human resources
Situation		**M**oney: budget
Objectives		**M**achines: equipment
Strategy	+ 6Ms	**M**aterials: samples, brochures
Tactics		**M**inutes: time constraints
Action		**M**easurement: against initial objectives
Control		

- **Situation** What are the circumstances the company finds itself in?
- **Objectives** What are the key objectives to be met by the integrated marketing campaign?
- **Strategy** How is the objective going to be achieved?
- **Tactics** What are the operational details of the decided strategy?
- **Action** How should the strategy be implemented?
- **Control** Has the strategy met the objectives and if not what should be done?

3 ADVERTISING

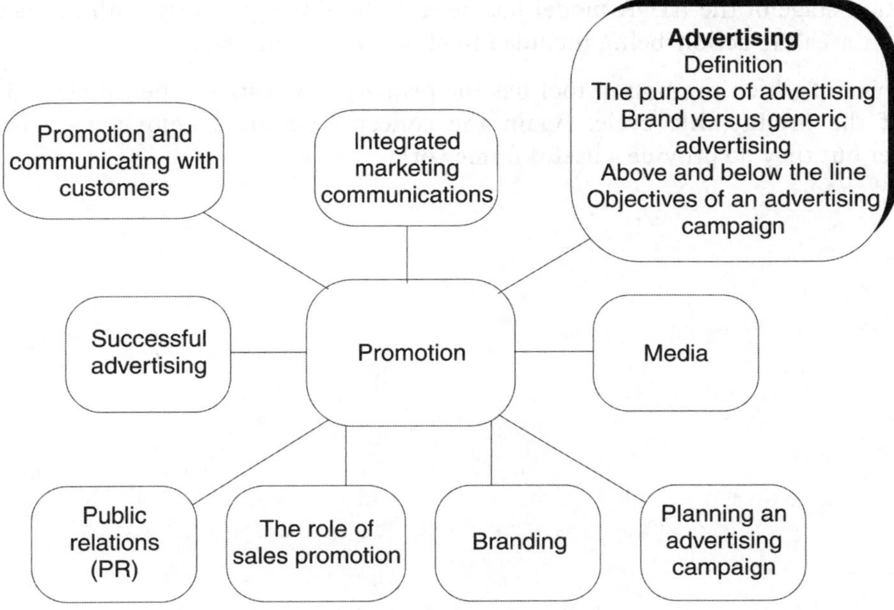

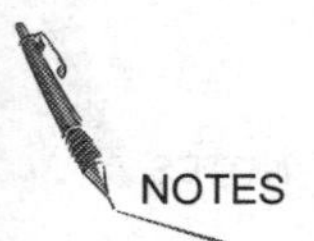

NOTES

Definition

Advertising is defined by the American Marketing Association as:

Any paid form of non-personal presentation and promotion of ideas, goods or services by an identifiable sponsor.

This definition clearly distinguishes advertising from personal selling and publicity (which is often not paid for and, even if it is, the sponsor does not openly present ideas or products).

Promotion, especially advertising, can be seen as attempting to move consumers along a **continuum** stretching from **complete unawareness** of the product to **regular usage** (brand loyalty). The **AIDA model** is a simple example of this approach known as the '**hierarchy of effects**' model.

Awareness → **Interest** → **Desire** → **Action**

These models assume that customers formulate a behavioural intention which then leads to actual purchasing behaviour.

A basic method of determining **which promotion tool is key to a particular situation** is to analyse what is happening using the AIDA model. The following diagram relates each stage of the promotion process to specific promotional tools. It will readily be recognised that such a diagram is useful only as a **broad guideline** and specific situations will require detailed solutions.

Desired response	Awareness	Interest	Desire	Action
Effective promotion tool	Advertising	Public relations	Sales promotion	Personal selling

Figure 12.5: AIDA model

The action stage of the AIDA model has been highlighted currently with an increasing regard for a 'call to action' being included in all marketing messages.

The choice of which promotion tool has the primary vote can also be influenced by the stage of the product life cycle. Again the concepts we are employing are broad in character but they do provide a useful framework.

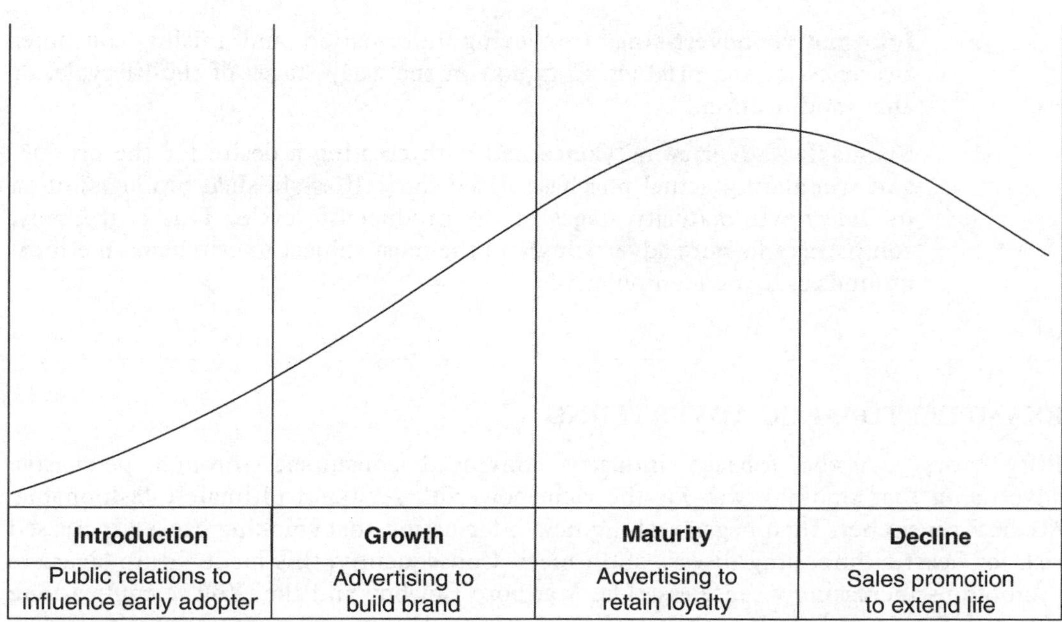

Figure 12.6: AIDA and the product life cycle

3.1 The purpose of advertising

Advertising is 'purposive communication' to a target market. It assists in selling by **drawing attention to the characteristics** of a product which will appeal to the buying motives of customers in the target segment of the market.

The following are examples of what advertising is mainly used for, couched in broad terms.

- To support sales increases
- To encourage trial
- To create awareness
- To inform about a feature or benefit
- To remind
- To reassure
- To create an image
- To modify attitudes
- To gain trade and sales staff support

Goals are general. It is necessary, for control purposes, to be specific and to express objectives in '**SMART**' terms, that is, Specific, Measurable, Achievable, Relevant and to a Timescale. Here are some examples.

(a) To support a sales increase on product X from 400,000 units to 500,000 units over the next 12 months.

(b) To raise awareness of service A amongst its target audience from its current level of 30% to 50% by the end of 200X.

(c) To reinforce retailer Z's image as a company which offers a good range of basic food products at value for money prices.

Advertising is targeted at specific audiences segmented by demographic, geographic, behavioural or lifestyle variables.

Advertising is often classed under one of three headings.

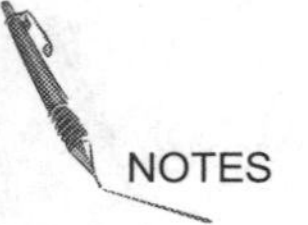

(a) **Informative advertising.** Conveying information and raising consumer awareness of the product. Common in the early stages of the lifecycle, or after modification.

(b) **Persuasive advertising.** Concerned with creating a desire for the product and stimulating actual purchase. Used for well established products, often in the growth/maturity stages of the product life cycle. This is the most competitive form of advertising and the most subject to criticism on ethical grounds as being manipulative.

EXAMPLE: TOBACCO ADVERTISING

Fifty years ago the tobacco industry convinced consumers through persuasive advertising that smoking was for the rich, powerful, sexy and ultimately fashionable. Medical researchers then began leaking new information that smoking caused increased risk for heart failure, lung disease and cancer. Consequently, this made future cigarette promotions increasingly senseless. The Marlboro Cowboy and the "You've come a long way, baby" chic and sleek sophisticate holding that Virginia Slim are now classified as "vintage" advertising. Although the methodology has changed, tobacco companies are still campaigning for customers and potential young recruits by dispensing logo merchandise and coupons.

Robin Rouse May, *Examiner.com*, 20 November 2009

(c) **Reminder advertising.** Reminding consumers about the product or organisation, reinforcing the knowledge held by potential consumers and reminding existing consumers of the benefits they are receiving from their purchase.

3.2 Brand versus generic advertising

It will only be worthwhile for an individual firm to advertise if it can **differentiate** its brands from competitors' in the eyes of the consumer. In the absence of **product differentiation** all advertising purchased by an individual firm would be **generic,** benefiting all producers equally at the firm's expense. This is a particular danger for commodity goods such as flour and sugar.

3.3 Above and below-the-line

The 'line' is one in an advertising agency's accounts above which are shown earnings on a commission basis and below which are shown earnings on a fee basis.

(a) **Above-the-line** advertising refers to adverts in media such as the press, radio, TV and cinema.

(b) **Below-the-line** advertising media include direct mail, exhibitions, package design, merchandising and so on. This term is sometimes regarded as synonymous with **sales promotion.**

3.4 Objectives of an advertising campaign

The more specific targets of a particular advertising campaign might be as follows.

(a) To communicate certain **information** about a product. This is perhaps the most important objective.

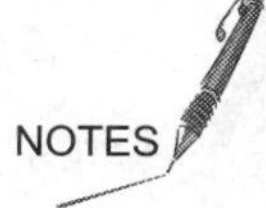

(b) To highlight specific features of a product which make it different from the competitors'. The concept of the **unique selling proposition** (USP) is that by emphasising a unique feature which appeals to a customer need, customers will be influenced to buy the product.

(c) To build up a **brand or company image** through corporate advertising.

(d) To reinforce **customer behaviour.**

(e) Influencing dealers and resellers to **stock** the items (on as much shelf-space as possible).

(f) In the case of government advertising, to achieve a **policy objective.**

Activity 2 **(20 minutes)**

Look through a magazine or watch commercial TV for a while and see if you can spot examples of each of these types of advertising.

4 SUCCESSFUL ADVERTISING

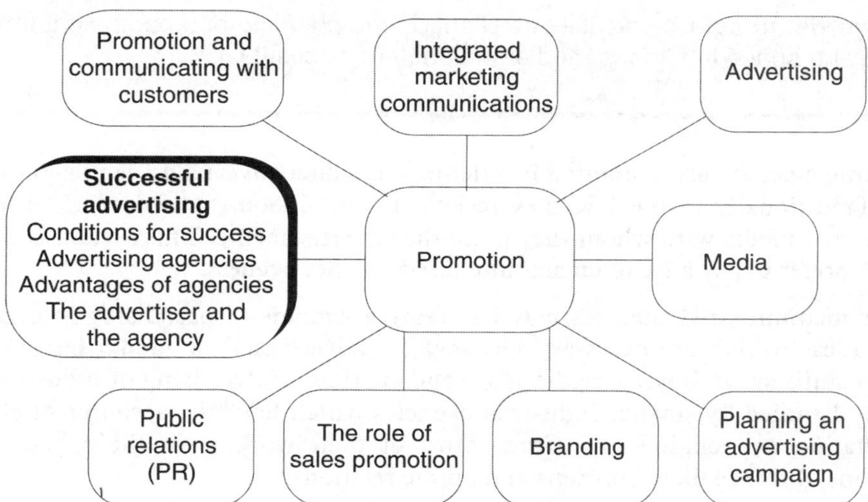

4.1 Conditions for success

The content of an advertisement is determined largely by the **objective** of the advertising and the **motivation** of the potential customer. An advertisement should present information which leads to a greater awareness of the product. It should be an attention-getter and may excite amusement or emotions such as fear, but inciting these feelings should not be allowed to be the only effect of the advertisement.

Advertising will be most successful if the following conditions apply.

(a) The product should have characteristics which lend themselves to advertising.

(i) It should be **distinctive and identifiable** (if it is not, a distinctive brand should be created).

(ii) It should stimulate **emotional buying** (emotive products such as medicine, insurance, cosmetics and products which can be made to

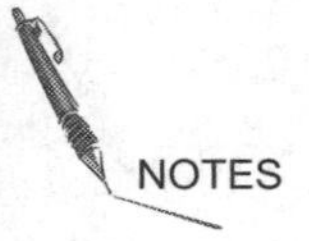

arouse social instincts, such as cars, alcohol, cigarettes and household appliances, can be advertised with great effectiveness).

(iii) If at the point of sale a customer can **refute** an advertising claim simply by inspecting the product, advertising will achieve no sales at all.

(b) There should be **consistency** throughout the sales operation. Advertising, the activities of salespeople and dealers, branding, packaging and pricing should all promote the same product image.

(c) There should be **co-operation** between advertising staff and all other activities in the company. Product design, production, distribution, selling and financial operations should all combine to achieve customer orientation and maximum selling efficiency.

4.2 Advertising agencies

Most large scale advertising involves not just an advertiser and the media owners, but also an advertising agency.

Definition

An **advertising agency** advises its client on the planning of a campaign and buys advertising space in various media on behalf of its client.

Advertising agencies are appointed by clients to conduct advertising campaigns on their behalf. Traditionally in the UK they receive a commission (of 10% or 15%) from the owners of the media with whom they place the advertisements. This system is changing as clients prefer to pay a fee or an amount based on effectiveness.

Large or medium sized agencies may be **creative agencies** (specialising in originating creative ideas, which are necessary for, say, TV advertising) or **media buyers** (whose specialist skills are in buying media space and air time). Advertising of industrial goods is usually handled by smaller industrial agencies which have the accounts of chemical, transportation and engineering firms. Most of their work is in the sphere of sales promotions, direct mail, exhibitions and public relations.

4.3 Advantages of agencies

The **advantages** of advertising agencies are as follows.

(a) From the media owner's point of view

(i) They reduce the number of organisations with whom they have to deal

(ii) Agencies are bound to conform to the **British Code of Advertising Practice** in order to obtain their commission

(b) From the advertiser's point of view

(i) An agency's **specialised services** are likely to be cheaper than an internal advertising department

(ii) An agency will have **broader contacts** with ancillary services such as printers and photographers

(iii) The advertiser receives **expert advice** (for example, from the agency's account executive)

(iv) Agency employees have a broad **experience** in the field of advertising

4.4 The advertiser and the agency

To take full advantage of the agency's services, the advertisement manager of the advertising company must:

(a) Have a working **knowledge** of advertising

(b) Be able to **negotiate** with the agency so that the proposed campaign will achieve the marketing aims of the organisation

(c) Transmit whatever **information** is necessary to the agency which may be of value in furthering the advertising campaign in the best interests of the organisation (for example, the annual report and accounts, copies of all the news releases and house journals, changes in products, packaging or distribution methods and news about R & D).

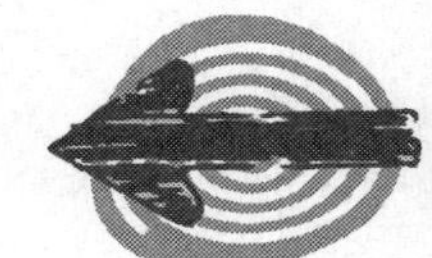

Before looking at other promotional activities we will be looking at the role of branding in the communications mix and product design.

Activity 3 **(15 minutes)**

The trade journal of the advertising industry is *Campaign*. This is targeted at people working in ad agencies but, although a lot of the gossip about individuals will go over your head, reading *Campaign* will give you a very strong flavour of the industry and some fascinating insights into what goes on behind the scenes. You will also become familiar with the industry's jargon and find articles that are directly relevant to your studies.

Your task, then, is to buy (and read) a copy of *Campaign* from time to time, or to study the website www.campaignlive.co.uk.

Once objectives are agreed between client and agency, the advertising campaign can be planned in detail. This will involve much collaboration between the two parties.

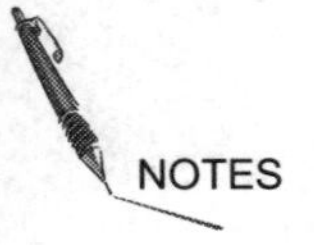

5 MEDIA

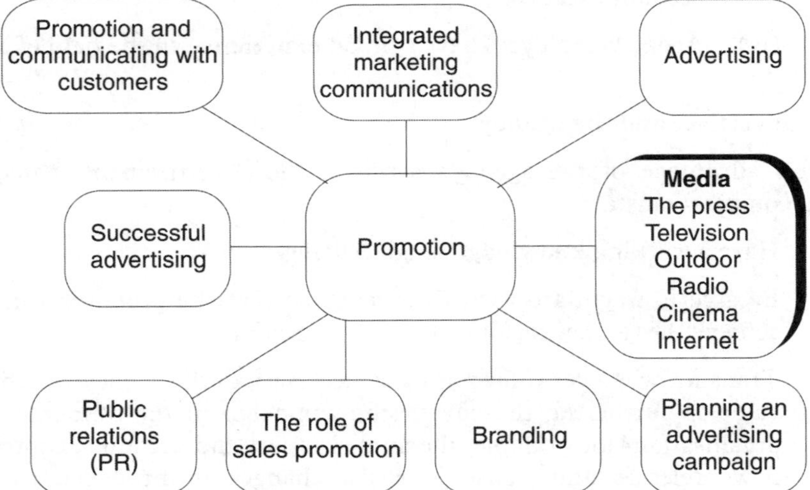

The UK is a media rich country. Specialist research agencies deal with sales and coverage.

(a) **The press**
(b) **Television**
(c) **Magazines**
(d) **Posters**
(e) **Radio**
(f) **Cinema**
(g) **Internet**

5.1 The press

The press is the largest media sector in the UK. Although some press spending will come under the heading 'classified advertising' (for example, recruitment, property, sales and wants), the bulk of the expenditure is on **display advertising**.

The press sector is divided into discrete segments, allowing for accurate targeting against specific audiences.

(a) *Newspapers*

Several further sub-divisions should be noted under this umbrella heading. Nationals divide into broadsheet and tabloid (or quality and mass market) and, as the name implies, offer national coverage. For a more tightly defined geographical coverage, morning or evening regionals are more appropriate and are perceived by their readers as speaking authoritatively from a local perspective.

(b) *Consumer magazines*

Readers of magazines tend to have more clearly defined characteristics than readers of newspapers, allowing for better segmentation and targeting.

(c) *Business-to-business magazines*

Whatever the trade sector, there is likely to be a number of specialist magazines catering for that sector.

(d) *Directories*

For small local service businesses entries in the relevant Yellow Pages and Thomson Local Directories are practically mandatory if they want to survive.

Press terminology

The media has its own specialist vocabulary. Although students are not expected to be media experts, comprehension of, and a degree of familiarity with, basic terms is useful.

Advantages and disadvantages of the press

The advantages and disadvantages of press media are summarised below.

	Advantages	Disadvantages	Comment
National newspapers	Reach large numbers of people Serious environment Short copy lead times Some colour availability	Short life Advertising clutter	
Regional newspapers	Reader loyalty Local features High coverage of geographical area	Lack of readership data Complex planning and buying	Good for test markets
Consumer magazines	Precise targeting of special interest groups Good colour reproduction	Long copy deadlines Lack of immediacy	Deliberate read
Business magazines	Read closely		
Directories	Source of reference on a local basis		A must for small local businesses

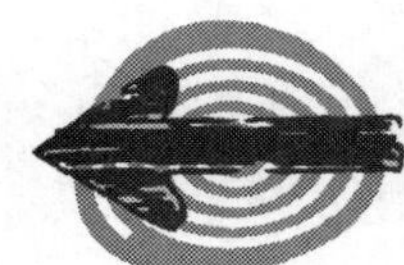

Although the press attracts the largest spend in media, television, with the addition of sound and movement to the message, is seen as the medium with the most impact.

5.2 Television

Television takes the next largest slice of the media cake after press. Television is a dynamic media sector, undergoing a period of rapid change.

Activity 4 **(15 minutes)**

This is another of those challenging 'watch TV' Activities.

This time, be on the look out for programme sponsorship.

Why do companies sponsor programmes?

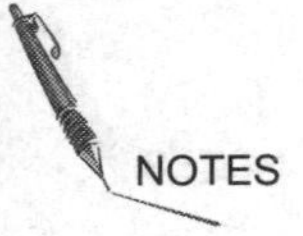

Television airtime is bought and sold either on a **spot-by-spot basis** or in packages of **airtime** with guaranteed audience delivery. With the latter, the scheduling of the advertisement is left to the television company, so some control over the airtime is lost.

Airtime is generally priced on the basis of **demand and supply**, with commercial breaks selling for what the TV market will bear. Peak spots, such as the centre break of Coronation Street, sell within a higher priced banding than do off-peak or early evening spots.

Television ratings (TVRs)

The unit of measurement by which television is bought and sold is the TVR or television rating. A TVR is a percentage measurement of how many within a specified audience (homes, adults, men) were watching at a specific point in time.

Television campaign media objectives will be couched in terms of **TVRs, coverage** and **opportunities to see.**

EXAMPLE: GOOGLE AND TIVO JOIN FORCES FOR ADVERTISING DEAL

It's not all bad news for TiVo today, as they've teamed with Google to create a sort of 'pay per click' advertising scheme for TV.

There's not much defense *(sic)* for the current television advertising model. It's behind the times at best, and advertisers really have no way to guarantee that their ads will be watched, let alone whether the ads will be effective. Thanks to an effort in tandem with TiVo, Google has a solution.

With second by second viewing data from TiVo, Google has created a television spin on their pay-per-click web based advertising. By using the data from TiVo, Google is able to determine exactly how many people watched each commercial, how many changed channels mid commercial, and how many fast forwarded right through it.

Using these statistics, customers buying ads through Google TV will pay for each ad based on the actual viewership. Under a more traditional advertising model, ads are bought based on the expected viewing data, with no regard for whether the advertisement is already watched.

Google hopes that this will help to create more appropriately targeted ads. By knowing exactly what gets watched and what doesn't, advertisers will have a better idea of what to see and viewers won't be barraged with ads for products irrelevant to them.

highdefdigest.com, 25 November 2009

Advantages and disadvantages of TV

The advantages and disadvantages of television as a medium are as follows.

Advantages	**Disadvantages**
Mass market coverage	Expensive production
Flexible by region	Expensive airtime Transient
Flexible by time of day	Some wastage Passive
Audio visual	Long lead times

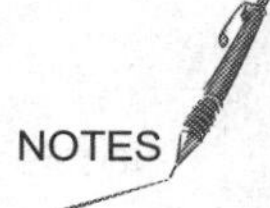

5.3 Outdoor

Outdoor as a medium covers posters (roadside and perimeter hoardings) and transport (rail/airport/underground/buses/taxis). Alongside cinema and radio, outdoor is often classified as a support medium.

Posters are bought and sold in terms of **sheet size**. This is an historical term which traditionally referred to the number of sheets of paper that were pasted to make up the poster.

Different poster sizes deliver different kinds of audience. Smaller sizes (4 sheets, 16 and 32 sheets and Adshels) are used in town centres to target shoppers and pedestrians. 48 sheets or the huge 96 sheets will target motorists and commuters on main roads in and out of cities.

Posters are a relatively **flexible** medium. They can be changed frequently and booked by the fortnight. In large cities, some electronic sites are also available.

The advantages and disadvantages of outdoor

Advantages	Disadvantages	Comment
High impact awareness	Long lead times	Good for building
Flexible by region	Limited prime sites	Good for teaser campaigns
High audience coverage in urban areas	Possible vandalism Some unsuitable environments	Reminder medium

5.4 Radio

The expansion of radio is likely to attract new advertising revenue to the medium. Previous criticisms that commercial radio has a downmarket profile have been overturned with the advent of new national commercial stations.

Advantages and disadvantages of commercial radio

Advantages	Disadvantages	Comment
Local targeting Immediacy	Lacks creativity Wallpaper syndrome	Good for local advertisers
Low cost High frequency		Support medium

5.5 Cinema

Cinema has experienced consistent growth in terms of popularity with the public. This has translated into a gain in advertising revenue for this medium.

The growth of Multiplex screen venues is one factor contributing to this success. The Cinema Advertising Association's research suggests another reason: that video, far from endangering cinema, has fuelled its growth.

Cinema advertising can be bought on a per cinema basis, or alternatively in packages (the London area, say, or Central Scotland).

Although one of the minority media, cinema can be important for targeting a young audience who are waiting to be entertained by big budget movies with high production values.

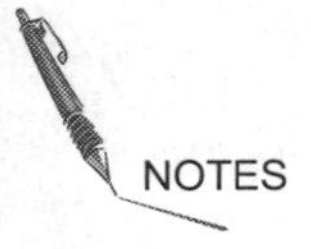

More recently, cinema advertising has become increasingly creative. An example is a first aid awareness campaigners using actors paid to sit in the audience, during the advertising slots prior to the film, they have been reported to get up from their seats and fake heart attacks and act as their helpless partners. The actors then apologise to the audience, show that they are ok and explain the purpose of their act. Such campaigns are particularly powerful because they are so shocking and create substantial additional discussion and 'word of mouth'. There has been criticism of these tactics however as some question whether it is ethical to shock in such a way.

Advantages and disadvantages of cinema

Advantages	Disadvantages	Comment
High attention span	Production expense	Another support medium
High impact	Low national coverage	
Regional flexibility		

5.6 Internet and online marketing

The **Internet** has evolved from being a toy for the computing elite to a genuinely useful tool for the marketing of services and products. In its most simple form the Internet can be regarded as being:

(a) **Electronic Mail** (e-mail) – the transferring of messages and files to other computers anywhere in the world, quickly and cheaply.

EXAMPLE

E-mail can double as advertising, by adding a 'signature' file message. Each time you send an email, the advertisement will follow.

From:	Promotions Inc
To:	elliot@hotmail.com
Sent:	26 May 2010 11:00
Subject:	Sale! Sale! Sale!

Dear Miss Elliot

Check out all the great homewares and gifts available on our website! You could qualify for our free prize draw.

Best wishes

Promotions Incorporated

Get the best deals online, whenever you want them!

This technique could be particularly useful when participating in a newsgroup discussion by a forum of 'surfers' who are interested in your field of business.

Viral marketing refers to the forwarding of email messages amongst consumers. It is a practice which has become increasingly popular and is often linked to sales promotional activities. The film industry makes much

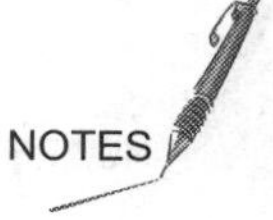

use of viral marketing with interested film buffs sharing information about new releases. The Samuel L. Jackson movie 'Snakes on a Plane' was said to use viral marketing to gain consumer interest whilst still being filmed. The infamous Blair Witch Project, filmed on a very limited budget by newcomers to the industry gained notoriety entirely as a result of an initial viral marketing campaign.

(b) **World Wide Web** – the 'shopping window to the world', the web pages and sites that you view and interact with on screen.

E-mail

E-mail is an incredibly flexible **communications** tool. It is easy to use, inexpensive and can send information quickly to another computer anywhere in the world. The advantage of e-mail is that you can send messages, documents or files directly from your computer and when they arrive at their destination they are in a form which may be edited on screen.

There are a number of direct **benefits for marketing** from e-mail technology. For example, customer e-mail addresses can be captured, stored and then used for e-mail-shots and **direct marketing activity**. Alternatively e-mail can be used to increase **speed and efficiency** in some promotion processes. Agencies can send visuals of brochures or adverts via e-mail, which makes proof reading and approval much quicker and cheaper than using couriers.

EXAMPLE

Business to business marketing is making the most use of email with 30% of decision-makers claiming to have been influenced by a sales-related email according to the research agency BMRB. This compares favourably to direct mail and the telephone, which scored 23% and 18% respectively in the same survey. Honda make use of this method to send offers to business prospects which tend to generate a respectable 6-8% response rate. Hay Group the global management consultancy has calculated that 31% of their clients open emailed newsletters with a third of those clicking though and reading the content. For B2B marketers a low outlay with a high response along with the ability to build relationships are major benefit to using email. Users also need to be aware however of the perils of unreliable and out of date address lists and the increasing use of anti-spam barriers. Equally important is the fact that in the UK B2B emails are not subject to the same legal restrictions as consumer focussed emails where only consumers who have opted to receive communications can be contacted.

Adapted from *Marketing*, 4 April 2007

Advertising and promotion on the world wide web

As in all media where you have people's attention, the potential for **advertising** on the world wide web is huge. This ranges from **banner advertising** on search engines to **co-operative advertising** on individual websites (for example, a distributor advertising on a manufacturer's website). Companies also promote themselves through the worldwide web. An Internet presence is usually the first step, and is generally a simple site to say what the company does (often referred to as a 'brochureware'). It may be an **online** version of the company brochure, or it may give more up-to-date information on the company's activities, products and services.

At this most basic level, there is limited added value the absolute minimum expected by individuals. Organisations have had to develop more creative means to persuade

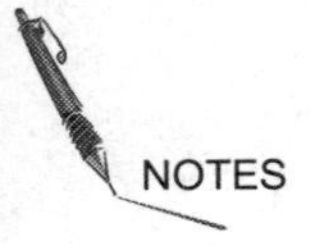

consumers to stay on their website and return. 'Stickiness' is a term used frequently by digital marketing agencies. It means creating a site which consumers will use for an extended period and return to. Increasing levels of interactivity provides added value and stickiness and is now possible in a range of alternative ways. Redbull were one of the first organisations to capitalise on this capability by putting reaction game style tests on their site. The advantage of this tactic was that it linked so well with the notion of the high energy drink. Many FMCG products are driving consumers to their websites by linking with on-pack competitions. For example, during 2007, Lurpak ran a competition to win a £500 Dualit kitchen accessory set every week. The competition used an on-pack entry code which could be used by consumers to enter the competition once they had registered on the website. Coca-Cola also ran a successful similarly designed competition where consumers could enter online with on-pack codes to win iPods and iTunes. The stickiness of the site was helped by the ability for individuals to watch a countdown to the hourly prize draws.

Pampers created added value through their website by focussing not on the products features and benefits but by investigating what parents would be most interested in at various stages of their babies development and providing an information service where they could develop a reputation for being experts in overall child development and advice. This information providing concept was also maintained through linked offline activities such as providing CDs of sounds of the womb to expectant mothers, direct mailings of child development booklets and vouchers for money-off coupons at the relevant life stage of the child.

EXAMPLE

For some the Internet is a necessary evil – others browse and surf the net with that obsessive drive that is peculiar to any new technology. But the Internet is not just any new technology. It is the most important communications development since the advent of the telephone, and like the telephone it has created its own culture and given birth to new businesses and new possibilities.

Early confusion about the Internet meant that many companies built their own websites after learning the rudiments of HTML. They had registered their company name and done everything by the book. The website went online and they all waited with bated breath. Nothing happened. No new business arrived and nothing changed, and they couldn't understand why.

E-commerce is a tidal wave; if you choose to participate you either 'sink or swim'. You must be daring enough in design to achieve something quite different from the ways things have been done in the past.

A website is a shopfront that must be located in the centre of town in the full gaze of everyone. A good one can make a small business as powerful and competitive as some of the largest players. It just needs flair and commitment to succeed. But to do so there are some measures that must be used. Marketing outside the web, in the press or even on the radio can alert the market to the website. The site itself should be properly identified by name, registered competently with the appropriate search engines and it must look good.

WEBSITE ESSENTIALS

- Integration with all company systems (ie back office)
- Speedy implementation
- Quick and easy updating by own staff to retain topicality
- Self producing audit records
- Promotion via the Internet
- Press and PR for website
- Attractive design but appropriate for the web
- Scope to interact with visitors
- Planned structure to include profitable business concept
- Control and maintenance by owner, without developer involvement

The appearance of a website is extremely important. Attractive and easy to fill interactive forms can lure a sales prospect into being a buyer. One has seconds in which to achieve this end. Too many graphics slow down the procedure. The experience of visiting and browsing through the shop and responding to the goods on offer must be clever, intriguing, quick and efficient. Millions of pounds worth of business is lost on the Internet every day as a result of so-called interactive websites that are difficult to operate and dull.

Adapted from *Management Accounting,* February 2000

FOR DISCUSSION

How far do you think the internet has developed since the article above was pubished in 2000?

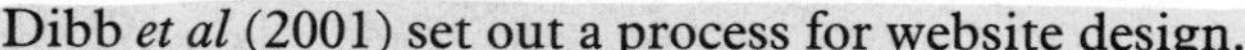

Dibb *et al* (2001) set out a process for website design.

1 **Planning the site's goals**
- Can our target customers access the Internet?

2 **Analysis of the required content**
- Relevant and interesting to target customers
- Stylish, eye catching but easy to follow

3 **Design and build the site**
- Branding/imagery consistent with product and other mix elements

4 **Implementation**
- Use of hypertext mark-up language (HTML)

5 **Maintenance and further development**
- Regular and accurate updates

Go on to the internet and find an example website layout.

Newspapers, which invested heavily in putting their content online, are at the forefront of experimenting with the new formats to attract advertising revenue to their sites.

The use of interactive banner adverts adds value to the advertisement by providing services such as:

- Entering a destination to show the cheapest fare
- Filling in an e-mail address to receive further information

So the Internet has become a medium for carrying advertising in its own right. However, companies need to be sure that the web provides the right environment and audience profile to meet marketing objectives.

The most common form of web advertising occurs when the advertiser uses a range of sites to drive visitors to a corporate site using one or more of the following:

- **Corporate Website Portal** eg Yahoo!
- **General news service** eg Sunday Times
- **Special interest site** eg lifestyle magazine
- **Internet promotional strategy**

Companies are still learning what works with web advertising, and what does not. There are two basic types of promotion associated with the Internet, **online** and **offline**.

Definitions

Online promotion uses communication via the Internet itself to raise awareness. This may take the form of links from other sites, targeted e-mail messages or banner advertisements.

Offline promotion uses traditional media such as TV or newspaper advertising to promote a website address (URL).

EXAMPLE

There are some tricks to offline promotion that can be used to help the customer in finding the information they need on a website. When advertising in traditional media such as a newspaper or magazine, it is beneficial to highlight a specific page that is related to the offline promotion and the interests of the audience. For example:

In an American magazine: www.jaguar.com/us

In a phone advert from a company that sells other products:
www.ericcsson.com/us/phones

For a specific digital camera: www.agfahome.com/ephoto

By doing this, the user will be sent directly to the relevant information without having to navigate through the corporate site.

A similar technique is to use a different sub-domain to the main domain, or register a completely different domain name which is in keeping with the campaign:

www.drivehonda.com rather than www.honda.com

www.fireandwater.com rather than Harpers and Collins Publishers

www.askntl.com to highlight that the site has the answers to questions such as: Who are NTL? What are their services?

Increasingly, promotion of the website in the offline media is not simply flagging the existence of the website as an afterthought via including the URL at the bottom of the advert, but highlighting the offers or services available at the website, such as special sales promotions or online customer service. Amazon commonly advertises in newspapers to achieve this.

Measuring the effectiveness of Internet advertising

This is based upon the behaviour of web users. When using the Internet, users will go through several stages:

1. **Be exposed** to a message (for example, through a banner advertisement)
2. Look for **more information** by clicking on the banner
3. **Go to the web page** of the advertiser

Based on this sequence, different types of advertisement effectiveness have been identified (listed by Pelsmacker *et al* (*Marketing Communications*, 2001). These can be measured for different online advertisements of the same advertiser, on a daily basis if required, to monitor web ad effectiveness.

- Total **ad impressions** (number of contacts made by the ad)
- '**Click throughs**' (contact by a user with advertisement)
- **Ad transfer** (successful arrival of a user at the advertiser's website)

Other online advertising methods

These include:

(a) Promotion in search engines and directories (such as Yahoo!). Your company may want to have its company website listed when a user types in a specific keyword, such as 'office equipment'. To achieve this, your website should be registered with each of the main search engines (Yahoo!, MSN, Infoseek, Netscape, Excite, for example). Research shows that most users will only bother looking at the first 10 listings thrown up by their search.

(b) Links from other sites. This involves making sure that your site is linked to as many related sites as possible.

(c) Using e-mail for advertising new products directly to customers.

The marketing mix and information technology

Even with the advent of information and communication technology (ICT), the marketing mix still provides a sound framework for generating marketing strategy. According to Dr Dave Chaffey (2002) 'the Internet provides many new opportunities for the marketer to vary the marketing mix'. Michael Porter has said: 'The key question is not whether to deploy Internet technology – companies have no choice if they want to stay competitive – but how to deploy it.'

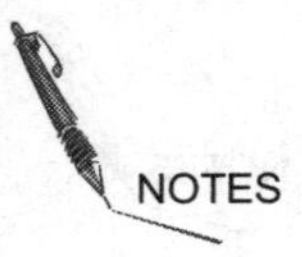

NOTES

EXAMPLE

If you are promoting packaged holidays, a strategy that is based solely on customers directly visiting your website would be ineffective. Instead holiday companies use affiliate arrangements and search engine marketing to drive visitors to their site. Furthermore, many consumers will go to neutral intermediaries such as LastMinute.com to find the best deal. For B2B, some large organisations such as General Electric post bids to tender on their own website.

As you know, the **Promotion** element of the marketing mix refers to how marketing communications are used to inform customers and other stakeholders about an organisation and its products. Some different approaches for looking at how the Internet can be used to vary the promotion element of the mix include:

(a) Reviewing new ways of applying each of the elements of the communications mix such as advertising, sales promotions, PR and direct marketing using **new media** such as the web and e-mail.

(b) Assessing how the Internet can be used at **different stages** of the buying process. For instance, the main role of the web is often in providing **further information**, rather than completing the sale.

(c) Using **promotional tools** to assist in different stages of customer relationship management, from acquisition to retention. In a web context this includes gaining initial visitors to the site, and then gaining **repeat visits.**

   (i) Reminders in traditional media campaigns of **why a site is worth visiting**, such as online offers and competitions

   (ii) Direct **e-mail reminders** of site proposition and offers

   (iii) **Frequently updated content**, including promotional offers or information that helps your customer.

The promotion element of a marketing plan also requires key decisions about **investment**.

(a) What is the balance between investment in site promotion, compared to site creation and maintenance? The e-marketing plan should **specify the budget** for each to ensure that there is a sensible balance.

(b) What is the investment in online promotion techniques, compared to offline promotion? Typically, offline promotion investment exceeds that for online promotion investment.

6 PLANNING AN ADVERTISING CAMPAIGN

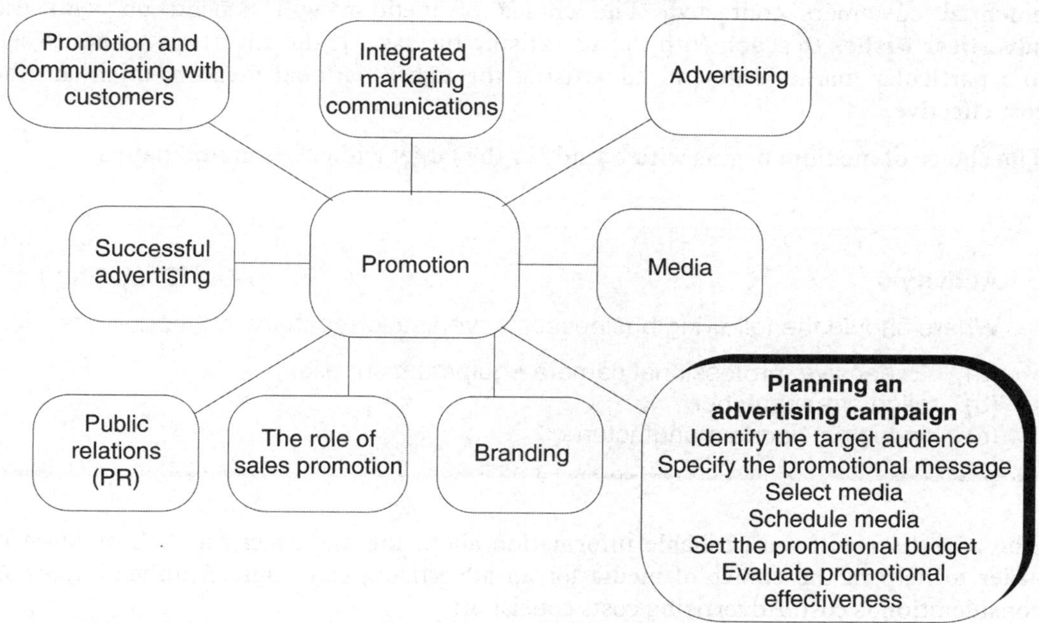

There are six distinct stages in an advertising campaign

6.1 Step 1: Identify the target audience

A list of dimensions which could be of use in identifying the target audience, depending on the type of product, is given below.

The target audience will be defined in terms of segmentation variables. The **psychographics** approach enables campaigns to be planned which emphasise how the brand has relevance for the lifestyle of the target audience.

These factors are particularly relevant when the aim of the campaign involves **persuasion** of the audience. Much advertising aims to accomplish very precise and limited changes in awareness of, or perceptions of, product attributes (**repositioning**).

For **industrial goods** the social and socio-psychological variables are still valid but are perhaps not as important as economic factors.

6.2 Step 2: Specify the promotional message

People are very specific about the advertisements to which they pay attention. Most of us have the opportunity to see hundreds of advertisements in many media each day, and cannot give our attention to each one.

The essence of specifying the promotional message lies in identifying the intended function of the campaign.

Each function can suggest an appropriate form for, and content of, the message. Messages are usually **tested** before use in qualitative group discussions with potential consumers.

6.3 Step 3: Select media

Media advertising means advertising through the media, which include national newspapers, regional newspapers, magazines and periodicals, trade and technical journals, directories, television, posters and transport advertising, cinema and radio. Each medium provides access to a certain type of audience.

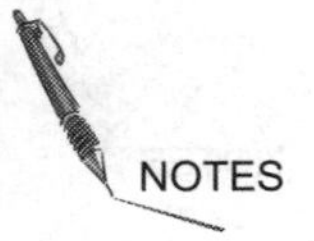

The medium used should be the one which will have the lowest **cost-per-head** of potential customers contacted. The choice of medium will depend on **who the advertiser wishes to reach** with the advertising message. If the advertiser wishes to sell to a particular market segment, advertising through a national medium might not be cost effective.

The choice of medium begins with a study of the target audience's **media habits**.

Activity 5 **(10 minutes)**

Where should the following businesses advertise to reach the right audience?

(a) Expensive, professional camera equipment supplier
(b) High street butcher
(c) Industrial goods manufacturer

The advertiser will want reliable information about the audiences for each medium in order to help in the choice of media for an advertising campaign. Another important consideration is cost. Advertising costs consist of:

- The cost of producing the advertisements
- The cost of exposure in the media

The costs of exposure are perhaps ten times the cost of production in consumer goods advertising.

The cost of a medium is measured by the **cost per thousand** criterion. If a full page advertisement in a national newspaper circulating to 2 million readers is £7,000, the cost per thousand is £3.50.

Activity 6 **(10 minutes)**

Cost per thousand is a very simple measure, which should be interpreted with caution. Why?

6.4 Step 4: Schedule media

An advertiser will not restrict his campaign to one advertisement in a single newspaper or one appearance of an advertisement on television. An advertisement must be **repeated** because many members of the target audience will miss it the first time it appears.

EXAMPLE: INFINITI CELEBRATES 20TH BIRTHDAY WITH YEAR-END CAMPAIGN

Luxury auto brand Infiniti is launching a new marketing campaign that celebrates the brand's 20th anniversary in the U.S., while offering leasing and financing offers.

The Web-centric "Limited Engagement Winter Event," running through Jan. 4, includes home page takeovers, in-market behavioral targeting on third-party automotive sites and, in a first for Infiniti, a sneak preview of TV creative on social media sites.

The new TV ads, via LA-based TBWAChiatDay, also further Infiniti's identification with Japanese art and design. The ads suggest, for instance, that Infiniti designers' use of sweeping arcs and lines on paper hails from Japanese shodo-style calligraphy.

The ads go on to show artful shots of fine wood, timepieces and vehicle elements all photographed to suggest jewelry (*sic*). Central to the campaign is an incentive of 0% financing up to 36 months, on everything under the Infiniti badge except for Infiniti G37 Convertible.

The media schedule includes spot TV in the top15 Infiniti brand markets starting No. 16 and network cable TV on Dec. 12. An additional Yahoo home page takeover unit will appear on November 17th, along with targeted digital home page takeovers on CNN, CNN Money and CNET News.

Karl Greenberg, *mediapost.com*, 6 November 2009

6.5 Step 5: Set the promotional budget

In an ideal world the budget for a campaign would be determined by a consideration of the four steps discussed so far. The budget needed is that which meets the **objectives** using the chosen media to convey the required message. In reality the constraint of **what the organisation can afford** is commonly paramount.

The promotional budget is often linked to sales using:

- A percentage of last period sales
- A percentage of expected (target) sales
- A percentage of past (or target) profit

6.6 Step 6: Evaluate promotional effectiveness

An advertising campaign can only be termed successful if it generates profit for the company. However, it is almost impossible to measure the effect on sales and profits by any direct means. The problem is that advertising never takes place in a vacuum and other events in the market place, such as competitors' actions, changing attitudes and relative price changes, swamp the advertising effect. It is therefore necessary to observe changes earlier on in the buying process, the assumption being that favourable changes in awareness and attitude will result in higher sales and profits.

This diagram indicates some measures of effectiveness.

Stage	*Relative*	*Ease of importance*	*Method of measurement*
Exposure	Low	High	Frequency and reach
Awareness			Consumer survey – recall
Attitude			Consumer survey – attitude test
Sales			Usually inferred from above
Profit	High	Low	Usually inferred from above

Figure 12.7: Measures of promotional effectiveness

Effective advertising often depends on giving a product a recognisable identity in the market place. **Branding** is the name given to this process of creating identity.

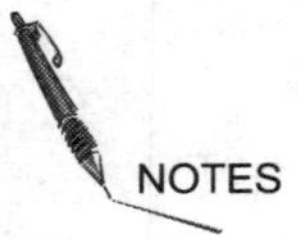

7 BRANDING

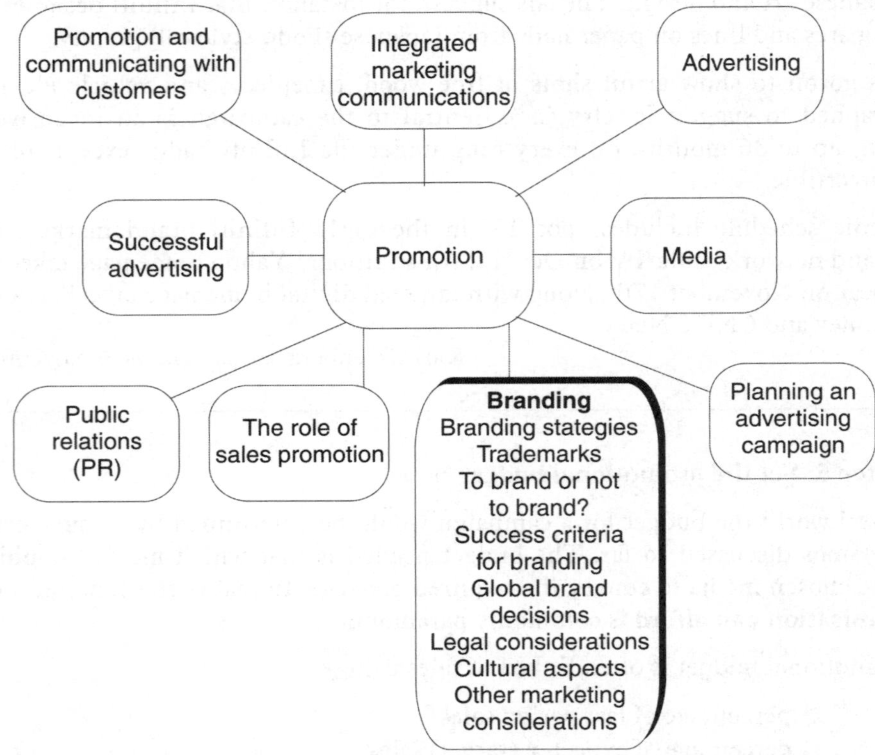

Expenditure on promotion gives rise to brands. We looked at brands briefly in Chapter 7 when we examined product strategies, but here we will look at branding in the context of promotional mix.

Definition

A **brand** is a name, term, sign, symbol or design intended to identify the product of a seller and to differentiate it from those of competitors.

Branding is a very general term covering brand names, designs, trademarks, symbols, jingles and the like. A **brand name** refers strictly to letters, words or groups of words which can be spoken. A **brand image** distinguishes a company's product from competing products in the eyes of the user.

A brand identity may begin with a name, such as 'Kleenex' or 'Ariel', but extends to a range of visual features which should assist in stimulating demand for the particular product. The additional features include typography, colour, package design and slogans.

Often brand names suggest desired product characteristics. For example, Fairy gives impressions of gentleness and hence mildness.

Activity 7 (20 minutes)

What characteristics do the following brand names suggest to you?

(a) (i) Brillo (scouring pads)
(ii) Pampers (baby nappies)
(iii) Cussons Imperial Leather (soap)
(iv) Kerrygold (butter)
(v) Hush Puppies (shoes)

(b) A publishing firm is considering producing a range of books. They are calling them the 'I Can't Believe I Made It To University' series. Can you foresee any problems with this brand?

The **reasons for branding** are as follows.

(a) It is a form of **product differentiation**, conveying a lot of information very quickly and concisely. This helps customers to identify the goods or services readily and thereby helps to create a customer loyalty to the brand. It is therefore a means of increasing or maintaining sales.

(b) **Advertising needs a brand name** to sell to customers. The more similar a product (whether an industrial good or consumer good) is to competing goods, the more branding is necessary to create a separate product identity.

(c) Branding leads to a **readier acceptance** of a manufacturer's goods by wholesalers and retailers.

(d) It facilitates **self-selection** of goods in self-service stores and also makes it easier for a manufacturer to obtain display space in shops and stores.

(e) It reduces the importance of **price differentials** between goods.

(f) **Brand loyalty** in customers gives a manufacturer more control over marketing strategy and of choice of channels of distribution.

(g) Other products can be introduced into brand range to '**piggy back**' on the articles already known to the customer (but ill-will as well as goodwill for one product in a branded range will be transferred to all other products in the range). Adding products to an existing brand range is known as **brand extension strategy**.

(h) It eases the task of **personal selling**.

(i) Branding makes **market segmentation** easier. Different brands of similar products may be developed to meet specific needs of different categories of users.

The relevance of branding does not apply equally to all products. The cost of intensive brand advertising to project a brand image nationally may be prohibitively high. Goods which are sold in large numbers, on the other hand, promote a brand name by their existence and circulation.

7.1 Branding strategies

Branding strategy	Description	Implication
Family branding	The power of the family name to help products	Image of family brand applicable across a range of goods
Brand extension	New flavours, sizes etc	High consumer loyalty to existing brand
Multi-branding	Different names for similar goods serving similar consumer tastes	Consumers make random purchases across brands

Brand extension denotes the introduction of new flavours, sizes and so on. New additions to the product range are beneficial for two main reasons.

(a) They require a lower level of **marketing investment.**

(b) The extension of the brand presents less **risk** to consumers who might be worried about trying something new. (Particularly important in consumer durables with relatively large investment such as a car, stereo system or the like.) Examples include the introduction of Persil washing up liquid and Mars ice cream.

Multi-branding: the introduction of a number of brands that all satisfy very similar product characteristics.

(a) This can be used where **little or no brand loyalty** is noted, the rationale being to run a large number of brands to pick up buyers who are constantly changing brands.

(b) The best example is washing detergents. The two major manufacturers, Lever Brothers and Procter & Gamble, have created a barrier to fresh competition as a new company would have to launch several brands at once in order to gain any noticeable market share.

Family branding: the power of the family name to assist all products is being used more and more by large companies, such as Heinz. In part this is a response to retailers' own-label goods. It is also an attempt to consolidate highly expensive television advertising behind just one message. Individual lines can be promoted more cheaply and effectively by other means such as direct marketing and sales promotions.

Cadbury re-branded a number of their individual products such as Caramel, Fruit & Nut all under their power brand name Cadbury Diary Milk. The move was designed to capitalise on the established success of their key brand and provide consistency of message.

7.2 Trademarks

A trademark is a **legal term** covering **words and symbols**. A legally protected mark can be a very valuable asset.

Activity 8 **(15 minutes)**

Think of some more examples on the same lines as Hoover and Xerox.

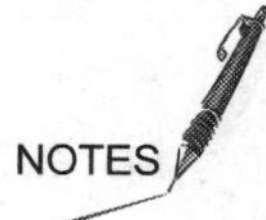

7.3 To brand or not to brand?

The **advantages** of branding include the following.

(a) Branding facilitates **memory recall**, thus contributing to self-selection and improving customer loyalty.

(b) In many cultures branding is **preferred**, particularly in the distribution channel.

(c) Branding is a way of obtaining **legal protection** for product features.

(d) It helps with **market segmentation**. (Take toothpaste for example: Crest is marketed to a health conscious segment, Ultrabrite is marketed for its cosmetic qualities.)

(e) It helps build a strong and positive **corporate image**, especially if the brand name used is the company name (for example, Kellogg's, Heinz). It is not so important if the company name is not used (for example, Procter & Gamble).

(f) Branding makes it easier to **link advertising** to other marketing communications programmes.

(g) **Display space** is more easily obtained and **point-of-sale** promotions are more practicable.

(h) If branding is successful, other **associated products** can be introduced.

(i) The need for expensive **personal selling** may be reduced.

(j) Brands can be considered a shorthand device with consumers knowing what to expect from the product because of the brand reputation. To put this into context imaging doing a weekly food shop in a foreign supermarket. The first few times this activity is likely to take ages.

Branding is not relevant to all products, only those:

(a) That can achieve **mass sales** – this is because of the high cost of branding and the subsequent advertising

(b) Whose **attributes** can be evaluated by consumers.

FOR DISCUSSION

Chocolate bars can be branded, but not concrete slabs; whisky can be branded, but not coal.

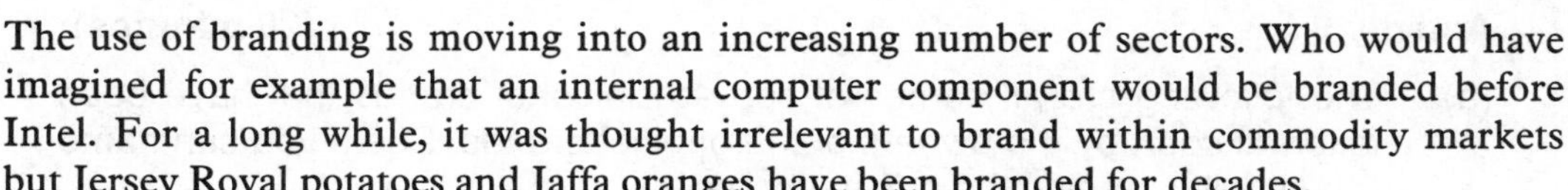

The use of branding is moving into an increasing number of sectors. Who would have imagined for example that an internal computer component would be branded before Intel. For a long while, it was thought irrelevant to brand within commodity markets but Jersey Royal potatoes and Jaffa oranges have been branded for decades.

7.4 Success criteria for branding

Branding should be a central and strategic part of both product and promotional planning.

NOTES

World-wide research suggests that the beneficial qualities of a brand name are that they should:

(a) Suggest **benefits,** for example, Ultrabrite toothpaste, Slimline tonic
(b) Suggest qualities such as **action or colour**, (for example, Shake 'n Vac)
(c) Be easy to pronounce, recognise and remember
(d) Be **acceptable** in all markets both linguistically and culturally
(e) Be **distinctive,** for example, Kodak
(f) Be **meaningful**. When Procter & Gamble wished to launch 'Crest Tartar Control' into South American countries, research found that there was no recognised Spanish translation for dental tartar.

7.5 Global brand decisions

For the international company marketing products which can be branded there are two further policy decisions to be made. These are:

(a) If and how to protect the company's brands (and associated trademarks)
(b) Whether there should be one global brand or many different national brands for a given product.

The major argument in favour of a **single global brand** is the **economies of scale** that it produces, both in production and promotion. But whether a global brand is the best policy or even possible depends on a number of factors.

7.6 Legal considerations

(a) Legal constraints may limit the possibilities for a global brand, for instance where the brand name has already been registered in a foreign country.
(b) Protection of the brand name will often be needed, but internationally is hard to achieve because:
   - In some countries registration is difficult
   - Brand imitation and piracy are rife in certain parts of the world.

There are many examples of **imitation** in international branding, with products such as cigarettes and denim jeans.

Worse still is the problem of **piracy** where a well known brand name is counterfeited. It is illegal in most parts of the world but in many countries there is little if any enforcement of the law.

Activity 9 **(20 minutes)**

(a) The following are all names of copy-cat alcohol brands that have been taken to court by the owners of the original brands. See if you can name (and spell correctly) the original brand.

Johnny Black
Raylas
Marabou
Zia Marina
M & B

(b) Why should the makers of the original sue the counterfeiters and what advantage is there for the counterfeiters in what they do?

7.7 Cultural aspects

Even if a firm has no legal difficulties with branding globally, there may be cultural problems, such as unpronounceable names, names with other meanings (undesirable or even obscene).

There are many examples of problems in global branding, for example Maxwell House is Maxwell Kaffee in Germany, Legal in France and Monky in Spain. But sometimes a minor spelling change is all that is needed, such as Wrigley Speermint in Germany.

7.8 Other marketing considerations

Many other influences affect the global branding decision, including the following.

(a) **Differences between the firm's major brand and its secondary brands.** The major brand is more likely to be branded globally than secondary brands.

(b) **The importance of brand to the product sale.** Where price, for example, is a more important factor, then it may not be worth the heavy expenditure needed to establish and maintain a global brand in each country; a series of national brands may be more effective.

(c) **The problem of how to brand a product arising from acquisition or joint venture.** Should the multinational company keep the name it has acquired?

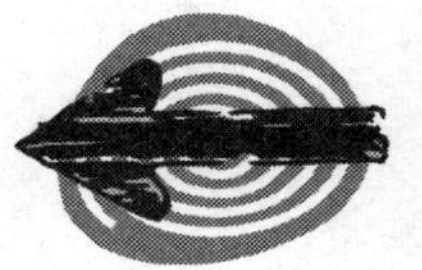

Whether the product is to be advertised or not, other forms of communication with potential customers will be necessary. This communication often takes the form of sales promotion.

8 THE ROLE OF SALES PROMOTION

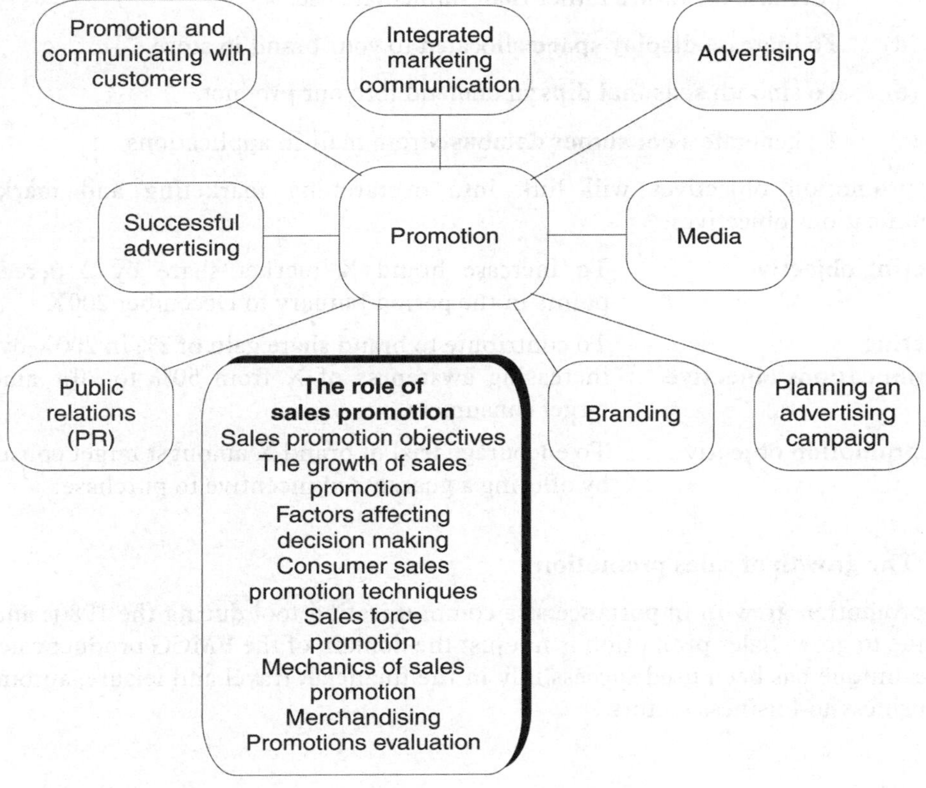

NOTES

Definition

Sales promotion: a range of tactical marketing techniques, designed within a strategic marketing framework, to add value to a product or service, in order to achieve a specific sales and marketing objective. Institute of Sales Promotion (ISP)

Sales promotion includes the notion of both **sales pull** and **sales push** techniques. Sales pull techniques encourage the consumer to buy, thus pulling sales through the chain of distribution via consumer demand. Sales push techniques either encourage the salesforce to sell products, or prompt the outlets to buy, ensuring the distribution pipeline is well loaded.

Be aware of the potential for confusion between the terms **promotion** (used as a synonym for communication techniques in general) and **sales promotion** (which is a specialist term reserved for the specific techniques described in this chapter).

8.1 Sales promotion objectives

The following are examples of consumer sales promotion objectives stated in broad terms.

(a) To increase **awareness and interest** amongst target audiences.

(b) To achieve a **switch in buying behaviour** from competitor brands to your company's brand.

(c) To encourage consumers to make a **forward purchase** of your brand, thus shutting out competitor purchase opportunities. A forward purchase is a purchase for future rather than immediate use.

(d) To increase **display space** allocated to your brand in store.

(e) To smooth **seasonal dips** in demand for your product.

(f) To generate a **consumer database** from mail-in applications.

Sales promotion objectives will link into overarching marketing and marketing communications objectives.

Marketing objective	To increase brand X market share by 2 percentage points in the period January to December 200X
Marketing communications objective	To contribute to brand share gain of 2% in 200X by increasing awareness of X from 50% to 70% amongst target consumers.
Sales promotion objective	To encourage trial of brand X amongst target consumers by offering a guaranteed incentive to purchase.

8.2 The growth of sales promotion

Sales promotion grew in importance as a communication tool during the 1980s and will continue to grow. Sales promotion is not just the domain of the FMCG product category. The technique has been used successfully in the financial, travel and leisure, automotive and business-to-business sectors.

8.3 Factors affecting decision making in sales promotion

The **market** in which the sales promotion is being run will affect the **choice of sales promotion technique**. Some sales promotion techniques lend themselves to specific types of market. For instance, **customer loyalty** programmes may be particularly appropriate in retail markets such as pubs, restaurants and petrol stations where there is a high propensity to **repeat purchase** from the same outlet.

The **nature** of the product or service being promoted will also affect the technique chosen. Consumers do not expect a 10% extra free offer on a bottle of Chanel No 5! However, this technique may work very effectively with instant coffee.

8.4 Consumer sales promotion techniques

Reduced price

Price promotions may take the form of a discount to the normal selling price of a product, or alternatively, offer the consumer more product at the normal price (20% extra free; three for the price of two).

EXAMPLE: DEBENHAMS CONFIRMS FOUR-DAY SPECTACULAR

Debenhams has confirmed that it will launch its pre-Christmas Spectacular on Wednesday, promising price cuts of £250m, more than the same Spectacular last year.

The department store – which factors in promotions as part of its annual budget – will slash prices by up to 25% for four days from Wednesday as revealed by Drapers.

Six weeks before Christmas, Debenhams will cut prices on tens of thousands of items across all categories in its 150 stores and online.

Debenhams is the first high street retailer to launch a blanket promotion in the run-up to Christmas and has fired the starter gun in the race to get customers shopping in the festive build up.

On the equivalent day last year, Debenhams kicked off a similar Spectacular which offered £200m of price-cuts and lasted for three days before being extended to cover the whole of the following weekend.

Marks & Spencer followed suit with a 20%-off promotion the following day, however, this year, M&S chairman Sir Stuart Rose vowed to remain full-price in the run up to Christmas.

Last year, retailers were forced in to a discounting war following a drop-off in consumer spend in the wake of the financial crisis.

Amy Shields, *drapersonline.com*, 16 November 2009

Cross-brand promotions may be regarded as a form of reduced price promotion as they offer the opportunity for the customer to sample the promoted product plus the complementary product at a discount (shampoo and styling mousse or teabags and biscuits are typical examples).

Coupons

Coupons are often used as a way of offering a current or future discount to the consumer. This is a highly versatile form of sales promotion and is more frequently being used at the point of sale such as on till receipts and are even available often on shelf edges.

Gift with purchase

'Gift with purchase' promotions are often referred to as **premium promotions**, as the consumer receives a bonus when he purchases. This promotion tends to be used with higher ticket goods and services, with the gift enhancing the quality of the original purchase. Cosmetic companies, such as Clinique, often use this form of promotion.

Orange have used this form of promotion when offering a free laptop if new customers sign up for two years to their broadband package. The promotion was first available though PC World and a few days later also in Curry's.

Competitions

This term covers any form of **prize promotion** and is popular with all types of organisations, from food and drink companies to travel agents, banks, and even charities.

Activity 10 **(20 minutes)**

Over the next few weeks, identify and note the different forms of sales promotion you encounter as you shop.

(a) Categorise the types of sales promotion into groups. Are certain types of promotion a characteristic of certain product categories?

(b) Are all the promotions appropriate to the products? Why?

(c) Try to distinguish the objectives of the different promotions. What are they and, in your opinion, are they being achieved?

Trade promotions

This category of promotion acts to encourage the distributor to stock or sell more of a product or service. In addition to the examples listed below, discounts and special terms may be used as part of the trade promotional armoury. In the Orange example above PC world were viewed by Currys as having an unfair advantage being able to offer the free laptop deal. Orange then provided the Curry's store brand a similar promotion.

Baker's dozen

This is a popular form of price promotion, where 13 items/cases/crates are offered for the price of 12.

Tailor-made promotion

Any of the standard consumer promotional techniques can be offered to a retailer as a tailor-made promotion exclusively for his store or group of stores. The offer of a tailor-made promotion can help a sales person in a negotiating position with a buying group.

Often, a tailor-made promotion will include promotional aspects for the retailer's sales staff to motivate them to push the promoted product at point of sale.

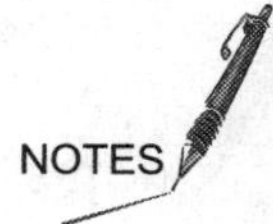

Mystery shoppers

Mystery shoppers are sometimes used as a trade motivator alongside a consumer promotion that has gained national distribution. All retail outlets are forewarned (as part of the promotion) that a mystery shopping team will be touring the country, checking that the consumer promotion is properly displayed and accurately described by sales assistants dealing with queries. Outlets satisfying the mystery shopper's judging criteria are rewarded. This is an important tactic as on average many retailers within the grocery industry only show promotions in 80% of the stores they are supposed to.

8.5 Sales force promotion

Incentives and competitions can be used as a means of motivating the salesforce to sell more. Trade and salesforce promotions may be designed in an attempt to maximise distribution.

EXAMPLE: BREWERY TELESALES PROMOTION

Here is an outline of a salesforce promotion that might be employed by a brewery.

Objectives	Gain trial of brewery house wines amongst selected targets Increase distribution and penetration of house wine Secure additional sales per call made
Individual sales targets	225 cases per telesales team 15 cases per telesales representative
Target market	Freehold and leasehold outlets
Mechanics	Buy one mixed case of New World house wines at the promotional discounted price of £32.50
Timing	10 week period commencing 18 March
Promotional support	One point of sales kit/case includes table top flyers, posters and an information leaflet on New World wine for bar staff training.
Sales incentive	Top 4 telesales staff and top team leader to stay overnight at West End five star hotel. Lunch, dinner, breakfast and theatre tickets included.

8.6 The mechanics of a sales promotion

All aspects of a sales promotion need to be considered very carefully before proceeding with the promotion itself. A poorly planned sales promotion is not just likely to backfire, it may self destruct causing irreparable harm to the company.

NOTES

EXAMPLE

The Hoover free flights episode is likely to remain the classic example of a badly designed sales promotion offer. Hoover offered free flights to anyone spending more than £100 on one of their products. As virtually all their products cost more than the minimum amount the offer was a fantastic success – in terms of sales. However press reports estimate that the promotion cost the company over £20 million in providing flights for all consumers who took up the offer. At first the offer was not honoured and the bad publicity forced Hoover into action. Several senior Hoover staff lost their jobs.

8.7 Merchandising

A manufacturer of consumer goods usually relies on **reseller organisations** to bring the goods to the point of sale with the consumer. This dependence on resellers for the sales volume of a product may be unsatisfactory to the manufacturer, who may try to take on some of the job of selling to the consumers. Manufacturer involvement in selling to consumers is achieved by advertising, packaging design or sales promotion offers. Another way of extending manufacturer involvement in selling is by means of **merchandising**.

Definition

> **Merchandising** techniques set out to achieve quick sales of goods, largely through the use of eye-catching presentation and display.

Merchandising is particularly relevant to retail goods marketing. It is concerned with putting the manufacturer's goods in the **right place** at the **right time**.

(a) Posters (for example, holiday posters in travel agents' offices);

(b) Showcards (for example, dispensers from which customers can take the product)

(c) Mobiles (display items suspended from the ceiling of, say, a supermarket)

(d) Dump bins : a product is dumped into a bin, suggesting a bargain offer

(e) Dummy packs

(f) Metal or plastic stands (to display the birthday cards of one manufacturer, say)

(g) Plastic shopping bags

(h) Crowners – the price tags or slogans slipped over the neck of a bottle.

8.8 Promotions evaluation

The results of a promotion should always be **measured against objectives.**

All sales promotions can be measured in terms of promotional **take-up**, for example, number of **vouchers redeemed**, or number of **competition entries** or **prize draw applications**. The absolute redemption figure should be expressed as a percentage of all possible redemptions in order to give a **benchmark** for future promotions.

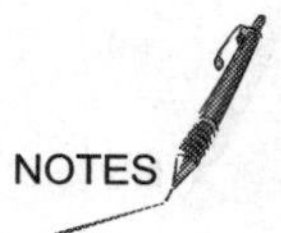

Electronic **household panel information**, which tracks shopping day by day, can give information about the overall level of promotional activity for a market or brand and show how this breaks down between different types of promotion.

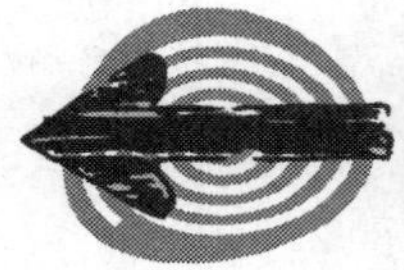

Media and sales promotion attract very large sums of advertisers' money. Public relations (PR) has a particular importance for companies with restricted budgets as well as the larger organisations. It is therefore a very useful area to understand.

9 PUBLIC RELATIONS (PR)

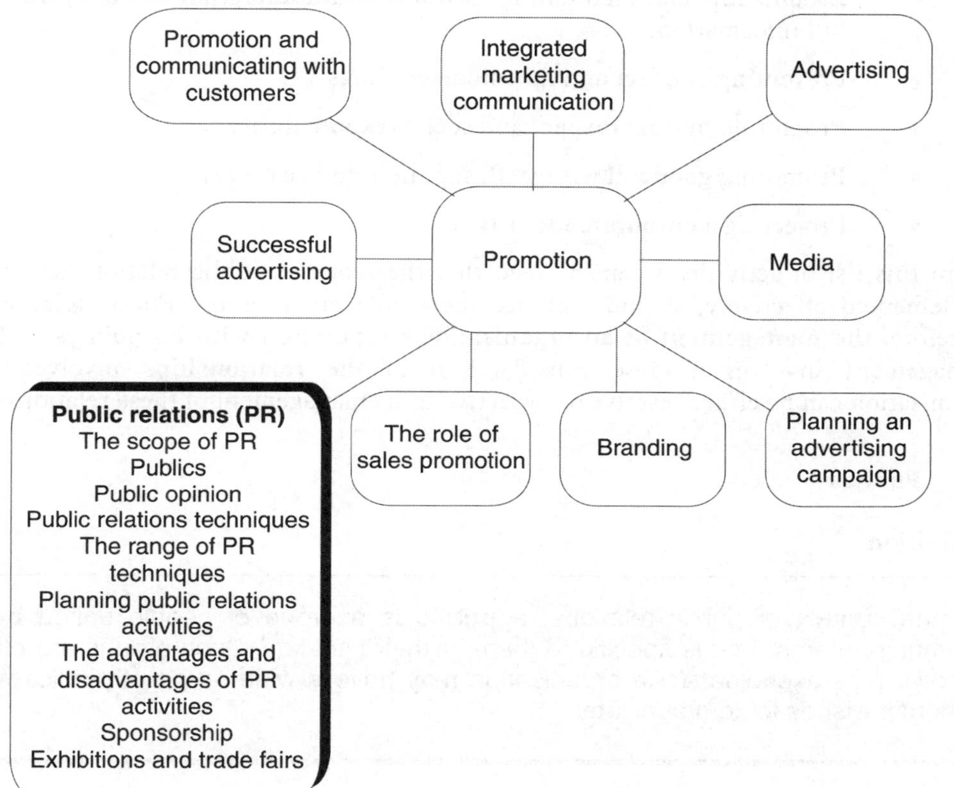

PR has been defined as 'the management of the corporate reputation'. Whilst this is a useful one-line summary it can be expanded.

Definition

> **Public relations** (PR): 'the planned and sustained effort to establish and maintain goodwill and mutual understanding between an organisation and its public.'
>
> Institute of Public Relations

9.1 The scope of PR

The scope of public relations activity is very broad. Below are a number of spheres in which PR activity would be appropriate.

- Government – national, local, international
- Business and industry – small, medium, large

NOTES

- Community and social affairs
- Educational institutions, universities, colleges
- Hospitals and health care
- Charities and good causes
- International affairs

Whilst the specific practice of the discipline of public relations will vary from sphere to sphere (and indeed, from organisation to organisation within each sphere) the following activities give a flavour of the work of a PR practitioner.

- Analysing **future trends** and predicting their consequences
- Establishing and maintaining two-way **communication** based on truth and full information
- Preventing **conflict** and misunderstandings
- Promoting mutual **respect** and social **responsibility**
- Promoting **goodwill** with staff, suppliers and customers
- Projecting a **corporate identity**

From this list of activities it can be seen that the scope of public relations activity, if implemented effectively, should embrace the whole organisation. Public relations is, therefore, **the management of an organisation's reputation with its publics** and this management involves a close consideration of the **relationships** involved. The organisation can be either reactive or proactive in its management of these relationships.

9.2 Publics

Definition

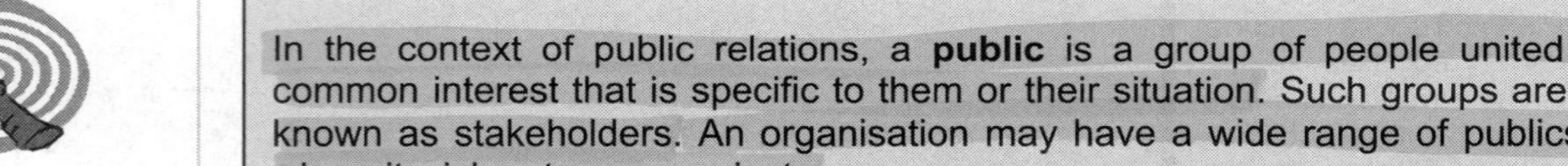

In the context of public relations, a **public** is a group of people united by a common interest that is specific to them or their situation. Such groups are often known as stakeholders. An organisation may have a wide range of publics with whom it wishes to communicate.

(a) Customers – existing, past and potential

(b) Members of the public in general

(c) The trade and distributors

(d) Financial public: shareholders, the City, banks, institutions and stockbrokers

(e) Pressure groups

(f) Opinion leaders

(g) The media as a special type of public as well as a channel of communication

(h) Overseas governments, EU bodies and international bodies

(i) Central and local government bodies, MPs and members of the House of Lords

(j) Research bodies and policy-forming units

(k) The local community

(l) Trade Unions

(m) Employees

By thorough research the PR practitioner can identify those groups which will be involved and concerned with the policies and actions of the organisation, and therefore whether those groups are likely to be particularly influential.

9.3 Public opinion

Once the relevant publics have been identified, the aim of public relations practitioners will be to influence the opinions of those publics.

Definition

> **Public opinion:** 'a consensus, which emerges over time, from all the expressed views that cluster around an issue in debate, so that this consensus exercises power.'

With regard to public opinion the role of public relations, and indeed of persuasive communication as a whole, is:

- To reinforce favourable opinions
- To transform latent attitudes into positive beliefs
- To modify and neutralise hostile or critical opinions

An important aspect of public opinion is the influence of **opinion leaders**.

(a) **Formal opinion leaders** are opinion leaders by virtue of their rank or position, such as Members of Parliament, newspaper editors, teachers or the clergy.

(b) **Informal opinion leaders** are opinion leaders by virtue of charisma, personality or background and exert a strong influence on their peers, friends or acquaintances.

In attempting to modify public opinion it seems sensible to concentrate on trying to influence opinion leaders who, in turn, are likely to spread understanding to ever widening circles of the general public.

EXAMPLE: TLG THOUGHT LEADERSHIP INDEX SAYS RADIO 'MOST INFLUENTIAL' MEDIUM

As UK businesses scramble to keep up with the demands of the Internet, new research suggests a far older form of communications remains much more influential.

A poll of 1,000 opinion leaders found radio had more influence than any other media on corporate reputation. Television came second and print third, while online languished in fourth place.

The Thought Leadership Index 2009 was compiled by corporate and public affairs consultancy TLG. Polling company Populus spoke to 1,000 chief executives and other business leaders, permanent secretaries across Whitehall and leaders in media and the public sector.

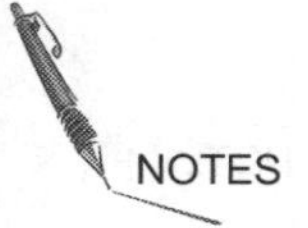

The research suggests radio owes its primacy to the BBC Radio 4 *Today* programme, which was seen as having far more impact on a company's reputation than any other – media title. BBC *News at Ten* and Channel 4 *News* were also considered highly influential.

Among print titles, the *Financial Times* (FT) was seen to have the most impact on a company's reputation, followed by *The Times* and *The Daily Telegraph*. Among online media, the BBC website was considered most influential, followed by the online operations of the FT and Bloomburg.

The index is now in its third year. TLG founder Malcolm Gooderham said: 'This year, for the first time, we have surveyed the influence of different media on brand reputation. Given the prevalence of new media companies being nominated as thought leaders, it may be surprising that the overwhelming winner in the media category is old media, and almost 100 years old at that.'

However, Gooderham suggested radio's reach and appeal was enhanced by innovations such as the iPlayer.

The opinion leaders were also asked to rank organisations according to their 'thought leadership' credentials. They ranked this year's top five thought leaders as Apple, Google, Microsoft, Amazon and GSK.

David Singleton, *prweek.com*, 24 November 2009

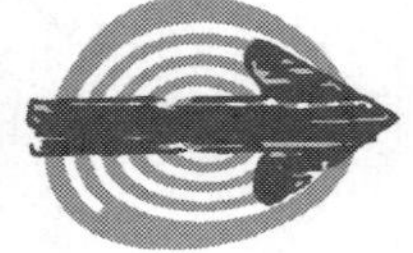

Having identified what a public is we will now go on to consider how it may be reached by PR practitioners.

9.4 Public relations techniques

Public relations programmes may be subdivided into **'contact'** and **'convince'** programmes. Two sequential steps frame the implementation of virtually any public relations programme.

(a) First, it is necessary to identify and contact the relevant target public.

(b) Then PR must convince that public of the merit of particular arguments, convince them to support specific ideas or causes, convince them to accept an organisation's proposals, or to behave in a particular manner.

The resulting communication process may be broken down into a number of stages.

- People are made aware of an idea or argument
- Their interest in it is aroused
- They are persuaded of its merits (and the potential benefits for themselves)
- They are shown how to respond and are encouraged to do so

You will note that these stages correspond with the **AIDA model.**

9.5 The range of PR techniques

PR employs a wide range of techniques, sometimes called a **media menu**. Inevitably some techniques will be more appropriate than others. It is possible, therefore, to classify the different types of techniques or media according to the type of project areas in which they appear to be most effective.

(a) **Consumer marketing support area techniques**

(i) Consumer and trade press releases

(ii) Product/service literature

(iii) Special events (in-store competitions, celebrity store openings, product launch events, celebrity endorsements)

(iv) Sport and, to a lesser extent, arts sponsorships

(b) **Business-to-business communication area techniques**

(i) Corporate identity design
(ii) Corporate literature
(iii) Trade and general press relations, both national and international
(iv) Corporate and product videos
(v) Trade exhibitions

(c) **Internal/employee communications area techniques**

(i) In-house magazines, employee newsletters
(ii) Speech writing for executives
(iii) Company notice boards
(iv) Briefing meetings

(d) **Corporate, external and public affairs area techniques**

(i) Corporate literature

(ii) Corporate social responsibility programmes and community involvement programmes

(iii) Local or central government lobbying

(iv) Industrial lobbying

(v) Local/national sponsorships

(e) **Financial public relations area techniques**

(i) Design of annual and interim reports

(ii) Facility visits for analysts, brokers, fund managers and other opinion formers

(iii) Organising shareholder meetings

While this is not a comprehensive list it does give an indication of the many types of PR techniques that can be used in various circumstances and how certain techniques will recur in various settings.

Activity 11 **(10 minutes)**

How could the fax machine, e-mail and/or video be used as an aid in employing the techniques listed below?

9.6 Planning public relations activities

There are seven stages in the planning and control process to ensure an effective and efficient PR programme.

- State the problem or aim
- Do the research
- Identify the public
- Choose the appropriate media
- Monitor the effects

- Look to the future
- Maintain financial checks

State the problem or aim

In generating the aims and objectives of PR activity we should use '**issue analysis**'. The issues will normally be external forces operating in the trading or community environment and by analysing them the organisation will hopefully have a clear idea as to how it will be able to accommodate or counter them. Some of the questions that the organisation will need to ask include the following.

- What is the issue?
- How might it affect the organisation?
- What is the organisation's stance on this?
- What are the existing external attitudes?
- Whom do we wish to influence?
- What new attributes do we wish to develop?

Once the answers to the questions are identified they can be translated into specific objectives.

FOR DISCUSSION

What could PR do for Cross Channel Ferries, with the Channel Tunnel being a direct competitor?

Do the research

Research, both formal and informal, is important in order to have as clear an understanding as possible of the issue or problem and its wider implications. As has been said, research should provide help:

- In **defining** public relations problems
- In **planning the programme**
- In the **implementation** of the programme
- In **evaluating** the programme

Identify the public

Having identified the issue and carried out research the organisation can then begin to identify who constitutes the public for the particular issue or problem, considering some of the factors described earlier in this chapter.

Choose the appropriate media

The PR practitioner can now consult the 'media menu' to ascertain the most appropriate techniques and media in order to reach the chosen public.

Monitor the effects

Without adequate mechanisms for monitoring and control it is impossible to know whether the objectives of the PR activity have been met. In particular observation should be made of the following.

(a) Any media coverage received, which may include an assessment of the number of column inches/minutes of broadcast coverage, the position of articles, the accuracy of the content and the use of key words or phrases.

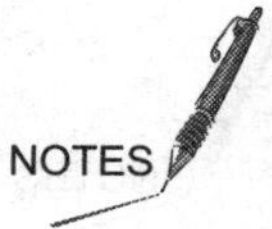

(b) Attendance at exhibitions together with the number of orders and enquiries received.

(c) Replies to response coupons included in advertorials.

(d) Telephone enquiries following the appearance of an article or broadcast programme.

(e) Response rates to a mailing.

Look to the future

As has been stated, the environment in which public relations activity takes place is dynamic and what is an important issue today may not be in the near future. In this case the PR practitioner must constantly be looking at the future trends in the environment and assessing current activities in the light of this.

Maintain financial checks

Constant vigilance in this area is needed if the public relations activity is to remain cost effective.

9.7 The advantages and disadvantages of PR activities

As we have seen, one of the main public relations techniques is **media relations** and we shall concentrate on this aspect of public relations as a means of weighing up the pros and cons of PR.

There are two main advantages inherent in effective media relations. First, there is no direct media cost, and second, the message is perceived to have a higher credibility than advertising. However, there is a downside in that the PR practitioner loses control over how the message is delivered.

However, the other side of the coin is that there is a great inherent risk in using media relations to generate editorial coverage, as opposed to advertising, because of the loss of control over how the message is presented.

Public relations agencies are generally hugely worthwhile in times of corporate crisis. The agency can manage the crisis management strategy to help regain (or retain) a positive corporate image.

EXAMPLE

2007 saw a bumper year for PR crises for a number of major UK companies. Bernard Matthews and the BBC came under extreme public criticism due to an outbreak of bird flu in the formers turkeys and the phone-in competition deception scandal for the latter. PR consultants were almost certainly involved in advising the companies in terms of their reaction to the adverse publicity they received.

Tesco provides a good example of a badly handled crisis also in 2007 when the retailers' petrol supply was contaminated resulting in drivers cars breaking down once they had filled up. The initial reaction of Tesco was to deny that there was a problem with their petrol leading to a large amount of negative press accusing the retailer of arrogance. When it was confirmed a few days later that there was a problem with Tesco petrol, the retailer was forced to issue full page newspaper ads and in-store posters apologising to customers.

In direct contrast, Mars handled a PR crises expertly. As a result of some leaked information it was reported that that company would be changing an ingredient in their Mars bar which meant that the confectionary would become unsuitable for vegetarians.

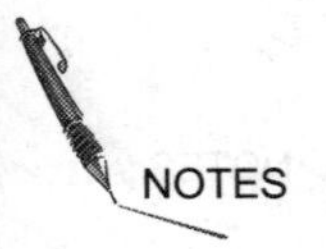

NOTES

The news angered vegetarian groups and led to mass press coverage. In response Mars apologised and also published the following statement on their website:

> 'At Mars UK we recently changed the source of some of the whey which is used in some of our chocolate products. We have received lots of feedback that this decision has made it difficult for some of you, especially those of you who are vegetarians, to continue to enjoy our products.
>
> We made a mistake. We apologise.
>
> The consumer is our boss. Therefore we listen to you and your feedback.
>
> As a company we value openness, honesty and diversity and we believe that anybody should be able to choose freely from our range of chocolate brands.
>
> But being sorry isn't enough. Therefore we commit to you today, that we at Mars UK will ensure that a selection of your favourite brands – Mars bars, Snickers bars, Galaxy and Maltesers, will be suitable for vegetarians in the near future. To this effect we are starting to change our manufacturing process today.
>
> We will keep you informed of our progress against this commitment through regular updates on this website. Please accept our apology and keep talking to us'

www.mars.co.uk

9.8 Sponsorship

In marketing terms, **sponsorship** is a form of marketing communication. It stands alongside media advertising, personal selling, public relations and other forms of sales promotion as a method by which companies can communicate with potential customers. There are many other influences on sales, and it is extremely difficult to isolate the effects of specific marketing activity on them. There are, however, several potential advantages of sponsorship.

(a) Distributor and customer **relations**

(b) The impact of sponsoring 'worthy' events can have a wide positive effect on the attitude of **potential customers** toward the company's services.

(c) Sponsorship has wider implications in public relations terms. It demonstrates good **corporate citizenship** and it may also have a positive impact on the company's employees.

EXAMPLE

Spiralling costs have meant that sponsors are increasingly prepared to consider involvement at the grassroots level rather than the higher cost 'glamour' events. This in turn encourages the development of sport over the long term, and appeals to today's socially responsible consumer who is looking for genuine involvement to overcome his cynicism about corporate motives. The Football Association in the UK, for instance, now has a limited number of sponsorship partners, who are expected to get involved at all levels of the game.

Sponsorship of television programmes has grown from nothing five years ago to being an hugely popular medium since Cadbury first sponsored Coronation Street. The practice has been popular in the US for decades.

9.9 Exhibitions and trade fairs

Britain has been fairly backward in its use of exhibitions and trade fairs and even the Birmingham NEC centre does not rival the foreign exhibition centres of Hanover or Geneva.

Exhibitions can be consumer focussed (eg the BBC's Good Food Show) or trade focused (eg the International Food Fair).

The advantage of exhibitions to the visitor

(a) The products can be **viewed** and **demonstrated**

(b) A wide range of **up to date products** can be seen in one place and **expert assistance** is available for answering queries

The advantages of exhibitions to the manufacturer

(a) They attract **many visitors** who are potential customers

(b) They are a valuable **public relations** exercise

(c) They are useful for **launching** a new product, or **testing** a market

(d) They **sell** the product

Disadvantages of exhibitions

(a) They are **costly** to prepare and operate

(b) They take **sales people away from normal selling duties** Exhibitions are more naturally suited to some products than to others. Where **demonstrations** are particularly valuable to the prospective customer (for agricultural equipment, for example) or at least **visual inspection** and **expert information** are required (for example, motor cars) exhibitions are a valuable means of sales promotion.

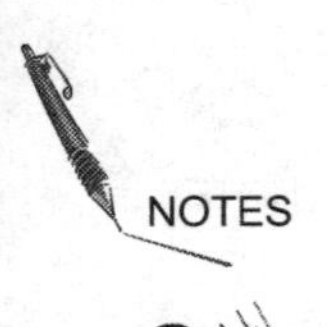

Chapter roundup

- Any effective communication relies on all the elements of the process working: the sender; the receiver; the message; the channel of communication; the feedback system.
- Promotion comprises advertising, sales promotion, publicity and the sales force's activities. Firms use varying combinations of these activities depending on the nature of their business.
- Promotional activity may have either a pull effect (whereby consumers ask distributors for the product) or a push effect (whereby distributors decide to stock it) or both.
- The AIDA model suggests that promotion moves consumers from Awareness to Interest to Desire to Action. Advertising may be informative, persuasive or reminding. It must be able to differentiate the advertised product rather than advertise the generic product class.
- Media includes TV, radio, cinema, outdoor and press, which is the largest media sector in the UK.
- This chapter also looked in some detail at the increasing significance of the Internet and online promotional methods.
- The six steps in an advertising campaign are: identifying the target audience; specifying the promotional message; selecting media; scheduling media; setting the promotional budget and evaluating promotional effectiveness. You should be able to discuss each of these steps, in particular the factors involved in selecting media, the factors affecting the promotional message and the difficulty of determining the optional amount of, and the effect of, advertising.
- Promotional expenditure creates brands. Branding is used to differentiate products and so build consumer and distributor loyalty. It is most relevant in marketing mass market items in competition with very similar generic products.
- *Sales promotion* activities have a more direct but possibly shorter term effect on sales than does advertising. There are many techniques, both push and pull, which you should be able to list and discuss.
- Promotion includes public relations exercises, including sponsorship, exhibitions and trade fairs. The purpose of this type of activity is not directly to increase sales but to increase and improve the profile of the firm and its products, particularly in its target market. PR in the form of media coverage of 'newsworthy' products/actions can be highly cost-effective. It can also be highly damaging in the wrong circumstances.

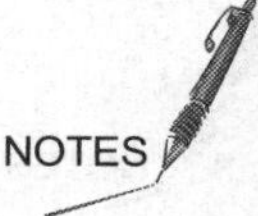

Quick quiz

1 What communication techniques might you expect to be used as part of the promotional mix?

2 In what way could poor encoding of a sales message impair sales performance?

3 What is a push effect, in promotional terms?

4 Distinguish between advertising and sales promotion.

5 What does AIDA stand for?

6 List three main types of advertising.

7 List the conditions for successful advertising.

8 What are the reasons for branding?

9 What legal matters are relevant to branding?

10 What are push and pull strategies?

11 Give examples of sales promotion activities aimed at

(i) the retailer;

(ii) the sales force.

12 What is merchandising?

13 What is the role of public relations?

14 What is a public?

15 What is the main disadvantage of PR?

16 Give reasons for engaging in sponsorship.

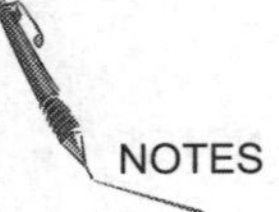

NOTES

Answers to Quick quiz

1 Direct marketing, sales promotion, sales literature, personal selling, exhibitions, public relations, advertising, branding, sponsorship, packaging.

2 Too much jargon may be used, or there may not be enough aids to visual interpretation to help customers decide what they want from a series of products (eg a clearly laid out product catalogue could help here).

3 A push effect is targeted at getting the company's goods into the distribution network.

4 Advertising is a general term for any paid form of non-personal presentation by an identifiable sponsor. Sales promotion is a specific range of tactical marketing techniques.

5 Awareness
Interest
Desire
Action

6 Informative
Persuasive
Reminding

7 See section 4.1.

8 See the beginning of section 7.

9 See section 7.6.

10 Pull: get the customer to buy

Push: encourage sales people or stockists

11 (i) Discounts or special terms
(ii) Incentives and competitions

12 Merchandising techniques set out to achieve quick sales of goods largely through the use of eye-catching presentation and display.

13 Management of the company's image in the view of its relevant public.

14 Any group of people who are united by a common interest.

15 Lack of control over how the message is presented after editing.

16 Improving customer relations, impressing potential customers, demonstrating corporate citizenship.

Answers to Activities

1 You could answer in considerable detail, but briefly, in the first case you may be sending out messages that you do not want to be bothered, but the sales assistant is either insensitive to them or deliberately misreads them. In the second case the organisation that you want to buy from fails to decode your message. Put from the other point of view you are taking in the shop's messages in the form of sales display and giving feedback in the form of your response to the goods. The channel is mainly body language.

4 The basic reason is clearly to do with the size and make up of the TV audience as determined by research. In many sponsorship deals, however, there is an expectation that there will be a matching of values between the programme and the image of the product. Cadbury's sponsors Coronation Street from the position of being 'the nation's favourite'.

5 (a) Photography magazines (small, specialist readership).
(b) Locally, for example in local newspapers.
(c) Trade magazine.

6 The advertisement might be reaching many people who will not be affected by it. Males might account for half the readership of a newspaper, so there is relatively little value in advertising female fashions to male readers.

Not all users of the medium will see the advertisement. Many TV viewers will leave the room during a commercial break; magazine and newspaper readers will not look at every advertisement.

7 As examples:

(a) (i) Shine, brilliance
(ii) Comfort, care
(iii) Luxury, tradition
(iv) Irish farms, happy cows, quality
(v) Comfort, soft leather

(b) The brand may alienate customers who had every confidence of making it to university. They may perceive the product as being aimed at 'dunces'. Or they may be amused, seeing the title as an example of post-modern irony.

8 The most successful examples of world-wide branding occur where the brand has become synonymous with the generic product: Cellophane, Sellotape, Aspirin, Kleenex, Filofax, Xerox. This can eventually, however, carry its own dangers. When the brand name has been adopted as the description of the generic product (such as Thermos for a vacuum flask) the manufacturer of the brand will no longer be able to protect it from misuse.

9 (a) Raylas is the probably the most difficult. This was an imitation of Bailey's Irish Cream. The others were pretending to be Johnnie Walker, Malibu, Tia Maria, and J & B whisky.

(b) The legal director of International Distillers and Vintners puts it like this.

'Brands are our most important assets. Through them we communicate the quality of our products to consumers. They represent a huge investment of time, effort, and money, that can be diluted, weakened, even destroyed by those who copy them.

Counterfeits or imitations can be sold cheaper. Their producers do not have to spend on advertising and marketing. Nor do they have to bother about the quality of the drink or the packaging.'

10 Individual answers will differ.

11 PR is a communication activity and fax, e-mail and video are major vehicles for communication. Fax/e-mail for invitations (and reminders) to exhibitions and conferences; press releases; lobbying activities. Videos have a part to play in virtually every category.

Chapter 13 : SELLING AND DIRECT MARKETING

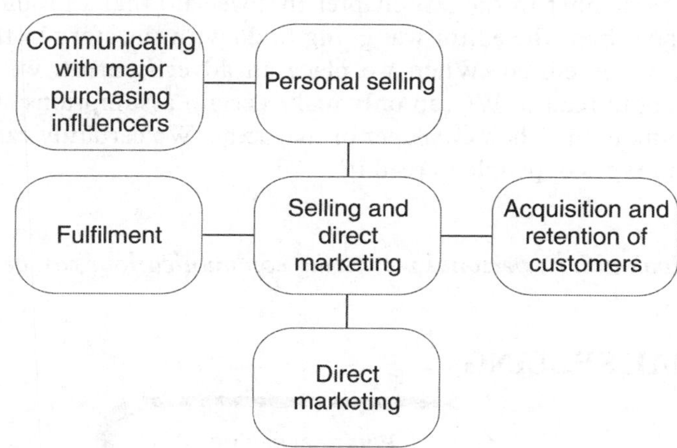

Introduction

In Chapter 12 we discussed the communications process and how it related to the marketing mix in general. The connections between promotion and products, and promotion and pricing, have been strongly emphasised. We came to understand the potential for increasing the effectiveness of promotional programmes by differentiating them on the basis of product class, PLC and markets and segments. We made the distinction between non-personal and personal promotional approaches. We continue our examination of marketing communications in this chapter by concentrating on the personal promotion techniques of selling and direct marketing.

Your objectives

In this chapter you will learn about the following.

(a) The role of the sales force

(b) The effective relationship between selling and the marketing mix

(c) The basis of managing the sales effort

(d) The effectiveness of the range of direct marketing options

(e) An effective direct marketing programme

Activity 1 **(15 minutes)**

Rank the components of the marketing communications mix in order of the amount of control that the advertiser has over the audience and the message.

Companies spend billions of pounds each year on promotion in the UK. It is clearly critical, therefore, for them to know what happens to it; to know what is effective and what is not. Therefore monitor the effects of a campaign. Another aspect of ensuring good value for the money spent is to exercise as much control as possible over the process. You will remember in the last chapter that we said that a problem with PR was that we did not know what the editor was going to do with the story in the press release, how it was going to be edited. When we place an advertisement, we cannot be sure exactly who is going to read it. We can only make certain assumptions about the type of people who are going to buy the newspaper or magazine. We certainly cannot say that we do not want certain types of people to read it!

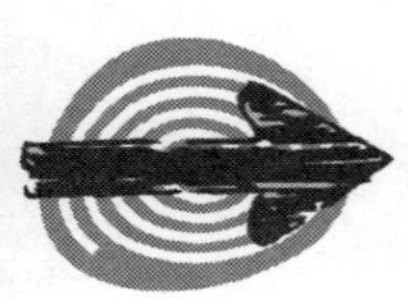

We now want to look at how personal marketing communications can be controlled.

1 PERSONAL SELLING

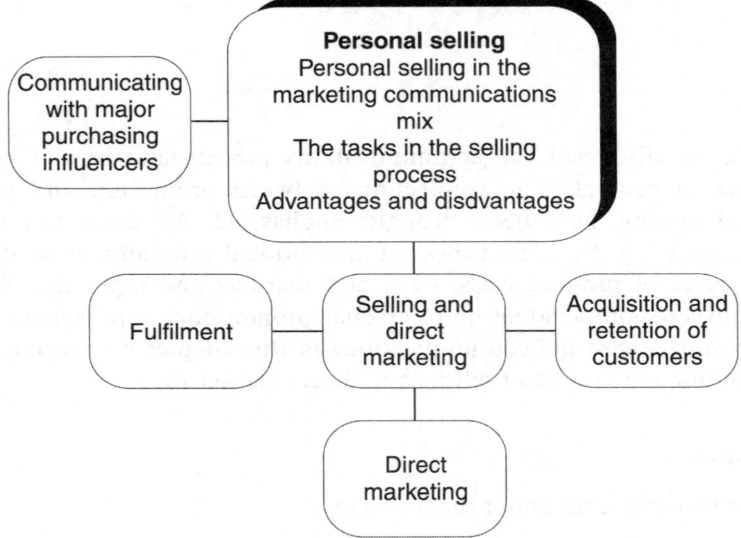

The techniques of personal selling and direct marketing are linked by the extent of the control they offer over the audience and the message.

(a) With **personal selling** we have the most control over who receives the message and a continuing interaction with the target audience which allows maximum flexibility of reaction in shaping the message.

(b) The techniques of **direct marketing** allow us to specify which households receive our message and, sometimes, which individual person. In some cases we can engage in a limited direct interaction which allows further control and monitoring.

FOR DISCUSSION

If only the salesmen would leave me alone, I would probably buy more.

1.1 Personal selling and its role in the marketing communications mix

Definition

> **Personal selling** is 'the presentation of products and associated persuasive communication to potential clients, employed by the supplying organisation. It is the most direct and longest established means of promotion within the promotional mix. (Baron *et al*, Macmillan Dictionary of Retailing 1991)

All organisations have employees with responsibility for contacting and dealing directly with customers and potential customers with a view to informing the public about the company's products. These employees provide a vital function to the organisation as they form a direct link to the buyers. When these employees have the specialist function of informing, convincing and persuading to buy, they are known collectively as the sales force.

Irrespective of the type of salesforce a company may use, the salesforce needs the support of other groups within the organisation if it is to operate efficiently and effectively. We can identify the following groups whose activities impact upon the effectiveness of the salesforce.

(a) **Top management** who can be increasingly involved in the selling process, particularly with big orders or key accounts.

(b) **Technical sales personnel** who supply technical information and service to the customer before, during or after the sale of the product.

(c) **Customer service representatives** who provide installation, maintenance and other services to the customer.

(d) **Office staff** including sales analysts, administrators and secretarial staff.

1.2 The tasks in the selling process

Personal selling is probably the area of the promotional mix that has the most stereotypes attached to it. The image of the 'travelling salesman' is an enduring one. However, this masks the reality that the term sales representative covers a broad range of positions, which vary tremendously in terms of tasks and responsibilities. These positions may be classified as follows.

(a) **Deliverer**, where the salesperson's job is predominantly to deliver the product.

(b) **Order taker**, where the salesperson passively takes orders from the customer.

(c) **Missionary**, where the salesperson is not expected or permitted to take an order but is expected to build goodwill or educate the customer in the use of the product. Medical representatives from pharmaceutical companies may fall into this category. Increasingly, their commercial effectiveness is monitored.

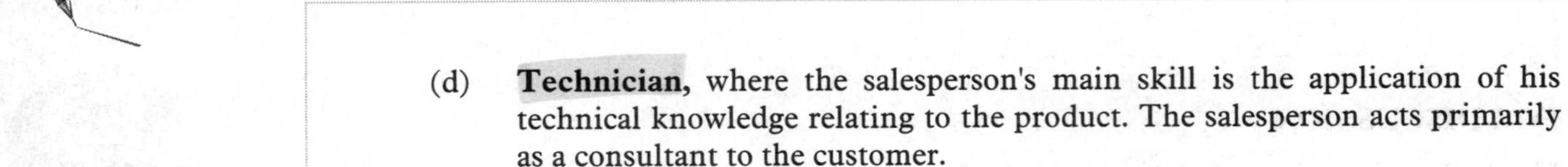

(d) **Technician,** where the salesperson's main skill is the application of his technical knowledge relating to the product. The salesperson acts primarily as a consultant to the customer.

(e) **Demand creator,** where the salesperson has to stimulate demand and creatively sell tangible or intangible products.

FOR DISCUSSION

An order taker is not a salesperson.

The degree of difficulty of the salesperson's tasks increases the nearer the person gets to being a demand creator. However, the art of selling in its narrowest sense is only one of a number of tasks that the salesperson may perform. They could perform as many as six different activities, as follows.

(a) **Prospecting:** gathering additional prospective customers in addition to sales leads generated by the company on his behalf.

(b) **Communicating:** communicating information to existing and potential customers about the company's products and services can take up a major proportion of the salesperson's time.

(c) **Selling**: approaching the customer, presenting, answering objections and closing the sale.

(d) **Servicing.** A salesperson may provide various services to the customer, such as consulting about their problems, rendering technical assistance, arranging finance and expediting delivery.

(e) **Information gathering.** The salesperson can be a very useful source of marketing intelligence due to the links with the end customer. Many salespeople are responsible for supplying regular reports on competitive activity within their particular sales area.

(f) **Allocating.** The salesperson may assist in evaluating customer profitability and creditworthiness, and may also have to control the allocation of products to customers in times of product shortages.

Whilst a salesperson may engage in all these tasks from time to time, the mix of tasks will vary according to the purchase decision process, company marketing strategy and the overall economic conditions of the time. For example, with regard to the influence that the buying decision process may have on the salesperson's mix of tasks, the skills needed for a straight rebuy situation (where the customer has bought the same product under the same conditions of sale in the past) will be totally different from those required to develop a new account.

1.3 The advantages and disadvantages of personal selling

Advantages

A number of **advantages** can accrue from using personal selling compared with other promotional tools.

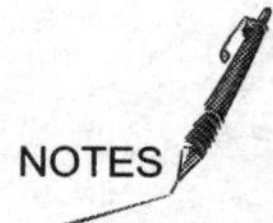

(a) Personal selling contributes to a **relatively high level of customer attention** since, in face to face situations, it is difficult for a potential buyer to avoid a salesperson's message.

(b) Personal selling enables the salesperson to **customise the message** to the customer's specific interests and needs.

(c) The two-way communication nature of personal selling allows **immediate feedback** from the customer so that the effectiveness of the message can be ascertained.

(d) Personal selling allows a **larger amount of technical and complex information** than could be communicated using other promotional methods.

(e) In personal selling there is a greater ability to **demonstrate** a product's functioning and performance characteristics.

(f) Frequent interaction with the customer gives great scope for the **development of long-term relations** between buyer and seller, making the process of purchase more of a team effort.

FOR DISCUSSION

If the marketing is good, you don't need salespeople.

Disadvantages

The primary disadvantage of personal selling is, of course, **the cost inherent in maintaining a sales force**. In addition, a salesperson can only interact with one buyer at a time. However, the message is generally communicated more effectively in the one-to-one sales interview, so the organisation must make a value judgement between the effectiveness of getting the message across against the relative inefficiency of personal selling in cost terms.

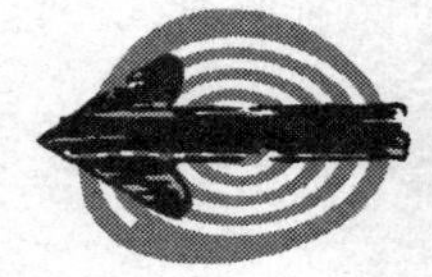

We have already discussed the Decision Making Unit (DMU). Part of the salesperson's job is to identify clearly the DMU so that the major purchasing influencers are involved in the communication process. The major purchasing influencers are the people who need to be informed, persuaded and convinced in the process of selling.

2 COMMUNICATING WITH MAJOR PURCHASING INFLUENCERS

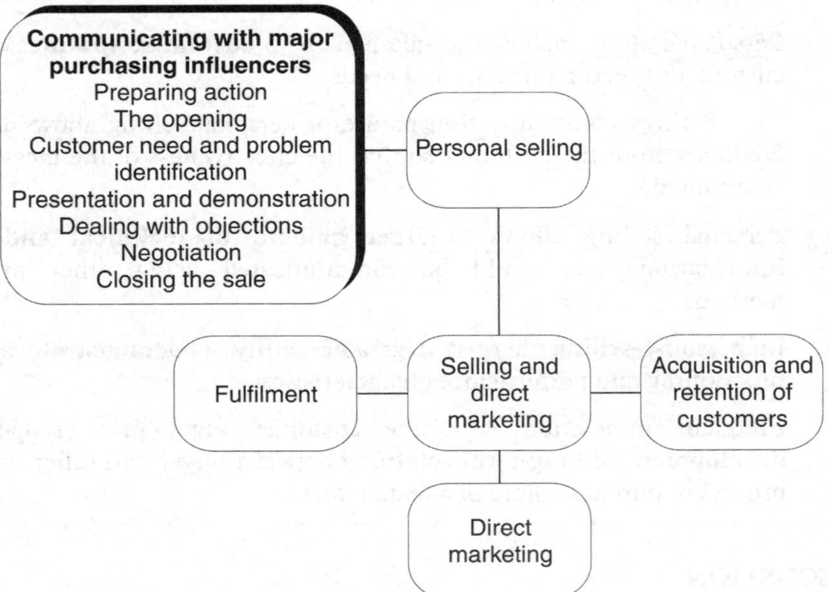

Personal selling may be divided into several distinct stages. Logically, these follow in sequence, but in reality the stages may be less distinct and the sequence disturbed.

2.1 Preparing action

For example, objections may occur during the presentation or during negotiations; similarly, if the salesperson perceives that the process of selling is going well an attempt to close the sale may be attempted at any stage. The salesperson's job begins before meeting the buyer – he or she has much to gain from careful preparation before the sales interview. This preparation could include **finding out as much about the buyer as possible,** both in terms of personal characteristics and the history of the trading relationship between the parties and also the specific requirements of the buyer and how the product being sold meets those requirements. In this way the salesperson can frame his or her sales presentations and prepare answers to objections in the most effective way.

At the other end, the selling process does not finish when the sale is made. Indeed, the sale itself may only be the start of a long-term relationship between buyer and seller which is cemented by the experience of an ongoing dialogue regarding product performance and after-sales service and support. However, for our purposes we will concentrate on the processes that occur when buyer and seller meet, considering each stage in turn.

2.2 The opening

As in any situation, first impressions are important so it is essential for the salesperson to open the sales meeting in a professional way. This takes two main forms. First, the salesperson is expected to be **businesslike in personal appearance and behaviour**. Second, the opening remarks set the tone of the whole interview.

2.3 Customer need and problem identification

The first objective that a seller has to accomplish is to **ascertain the circumstances of the customer.** Having ascertained this information the salesperson will be in a position

to highlight the product benefits that best meets the needs of the buyer. As most salespeople now sell a range of products this initial information-gathering regarding the specific requirements of the customer is of great importance if time is to be used in the most productive manner. The salesperson should, therefore, use 'open' rather than 'closed' questions to get the buyer to discuss his or her needs and problems. 'Open' questions are those which require more than just a one word or one phrase answer.

2.4 Presentation and demonstration

It is important at this stage to **emphasise the importance of benefits to the customer.** When buying products, customers are not motivated in the first instance by the physical features of a product but rather by the benefits that those features bring with them. Buyers are only interested in product features in as much as they provide the required benefits. It is important, therefore, for the salesperson to analyse his or her products and company, and by doing so identify all the relevant features and benefits. We can classify benefits into three categories: **standard benefits, company benefits** and **differential benefits.**

(a) **Standard benefits** are those which arise from the features of the company and its services.

(b) **Company benefits** arise from the links between the buyer and seller. Whenever a customer buys a product or service, he is simultaneously buying into a relationship with the seller on a number of levels, such as accounts departments regarding payments or service departments regarding installation or after-sales service. The buyer needs to have confidence in the selling company and will, therefore, be concerned about the company's reputation, quality of staff, and its willingness and ability to provide what it promises.

(c) **Differential benefits** relate to the offer of the seller relative to competing product offerings. Standard and company benefits may not be enough to persuade a buyer to commit to a sale, as in reality these benefits may not differ too much from competitors' offers.

However, not all benefits are equally attractive to the customer so the salesperson has to identify their relative appeal and then frame the offer around those appropriate benefits with the highest appeal. This is called **benefit analysis** and it is vital that it be carried out if the salesperson is to sell effectively.

FOR DISCUSSION

Benefits are not benefits if the customer does not see their relevance to his/her need.

Many selling situations involve risk for the buyer which may make him or her reluctant to buy even if the salesperson has put forward a very persuasive case. The buyer will want to reduce this risk and the salesperson has some weapons in the sales armoury to enable risk to be reduced. These include **reference selling, demonstrations, guarantees** and **trial orders.**

(a) **Reference selling** involves the **use of satisfied customers** in order to convince the buyer of the effectiveness of the product. It can be used very effectively to build the buyer's confidence in the product.

(b) **Demonstrations** also reduce the buyer's perceived risk because they **prove** the **benefits of the product** stated orally by the salesperson. It has been suggested that it is advisable to split the demonstration into two stages, the first involving a brief description of the features and benefits of the product and an explanation of how it works, and the second being the demonstration itself. The rationale for this is that it is often very difficult for the buyer to understand the principles of how the product works while at the same time watching it work.

(c) **Guarantees** of product reliability, after sales service and delivery can **build confidence** in the salesperson's claims and lessen the cost to the buyer should something go wrong.

(d) **Trial order** can also minimise perceived risk in the mind of the buyer as they allow sellers to **demonstrate their capability to satisfy requirements** at minimal risk. For the seller such tactics may be uneconomic in terms of finance and time in the short term, but the successful satisfaction of trial orders may secure a higher proportion of that customer's business in the long term.

(e) **Sale or return** allows the buyer to send the product back if it does not come up to expectations.

Activity 2 **(15 minutes)**

Name two examples of products or services where each of the five ways of reducing risk shown above may be used.

2.5 Dealing with objections

During the course of the sales interview there will be objections raised by the buyer, irrespective of the quality of the sales presentation. Objections should, however, be regarded by the salesperson in a positive and not a negative manner. Indeed, it can be argued that a successful presentation **should** create objections because it is arousing the interest of the buyer. By raising objections the potential buyer is asking for further information. Objections often highlight the issues that are important to the buyer, and as such should be regarded as opportunities.

We can classify objections into two main types – fundamental and standard. **Fundamental objections** occur when the **buyer fails to see the need** for the product or service on offer. **Standard objections** occur when the buyer recognises the need for the product but **wishes to delay making a positive decision.**

2.6 Negotiation

Definition

Negotiation: conferring with another with the view to compromising or agreeing on some issue.

In many selling situations both buyer and seller will have a degree of discretion regarding the terms of the sale, and therefore, negotiation will enter into the selling

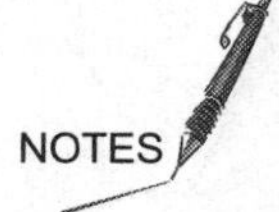

process as each party tries to get the best deal within the constraints under which they operate. The final deal that is struck will largely depend on two main factors: the **negotiating skills** of the participants and the **balance of power** between them.

2.7 Closing the sale

You could say that a sale is not closed until the cheque is in the bank, but for the purpose of this discussion we can afford to be less cynical! The sale is closed only when the buyer makes a firm commitment to place an order and the whole sales interview should be regarded as a process leading to a close.

Activity 3 **(15 minutes per role play)**

Set up a role playing exercise in which participants rotate the roles of buyer and seller. For guidance see the solutions and comments section.

2.8 Key Account Management

Key Account Management is an increasingly important role within organisations where major or more strategically important customers have been identified. Key account management is related to the concept of relationship marketing and it emphasises the need to develop positive relations with the most profitable 20% of customers. For example, a breakfast cereal manufacturer will probably find that the majority of their sales are to major retailers such as Tesco, Asda and Sainsburys. Because of the importance and power of these customers, it is likely they would need and warrant a great amount of sales time. For this reason, a key account manager would be assigned to each of these customers in order to better meet their needs, understand their requirements and behaviours such as order patterns and ensure a positive relationship is maintained. Smaller wholesaler groups or independent stores who place orders directly would not necessarily generate enough sales to justify such attention and may be dealt with by a sales office.

3 DIRECT MARKETING

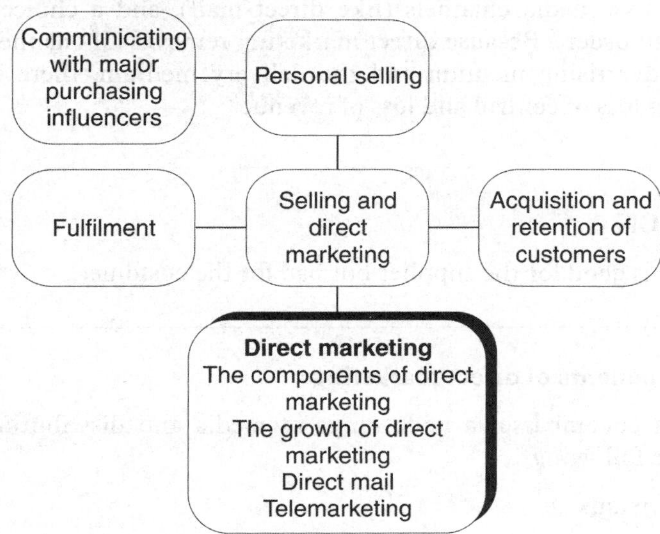

Drucker said that 'the sole purpose of a business is to create and keep a customer'. In brief, the aims of direct marketing are to **acquire** and **retain** customers. **Direct marketing** is also referred to as direct response marketing: we could say that response is its main purpose and techniques to achieve **response** are its key competence.

Definition

Direct marketing:

1 'The planned recording, analysis and tracking of customer behaviour to develop relational marketing strategies'.
Institute of Direct Marketing.

2 'An interactive system of marketing which uses one or more advertising media to effect a measurable response and/or transaction at any location'. Direct Marketing Association, U.S.

It is worth studying these definitions and noting some key words and phases.

(a) **Response:** direct marketing is about getting people to send in coupons, or make telephone calls in response to invitations and offers.

(b) **Interactive:** it is a two-way process, involving the supplier and the customer.

(c) **Relationship:** it is in many instances an on-going process of selling again and again to the same customer.

(d) **Recording and analysis**: response data is collected and analysed so that the most cost-effective procedures may be arrived at. Direct marketing has been called 'marketing with numbers'. It aims to take the waste out of marketing.

(e) **Strategy:** direct marketing should not be seen merely as a quick fix or a promotional device. It should be seen as a part of a comprehensive plan stemming from clearly formulated objectives.

Direct marketing creates and develops a direct relationship between the consumer and the company on an individual basis. It is a form of direct supply, embracing both a variety of alternative media channels (like direct mail), and a choice of distribution channels (like mail order). Because direct marketing removes all channel intermediaries apart from the advertising medium and the delivery medium, there are no resellers, therefore avoiding loss of control and loss of revenue.

FOR DISCUSSION

Direct marketing is good for the supplier but bad for the customer.

3.1 The components of direct marketing

Direct marketing encompasses a wide range of media and distribution opportunities which include the following.

- Television
- Radio
- Direct mail
- Direct response advertising

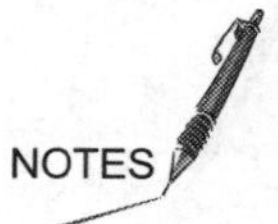

- Telemarketing
- Statement stuffers
- Inserts
- Take-ones
- Electronic media
- Door to door
- Mail order
- Computerised home shopping
- Home shopping networks

In developing a comprehensive direct marketing strategy, organisations will often utilise a range of different yet complementary techniques.

3.2 The growth of direct marketing

Over the recent past there has been a major increase in the amount spent on direct marketing activities. A number of factors have contributed to this growth and will undoubtedly play a significant part in the future.

The mainstay of UK society, the nuclear family, is no longer the dominant group within the population. If this trend continues it will lead to the emergence of new customer groups with a diverse range of needs, which will require a more individualistic marketing strategy.

Retailers within the UK have now become the custodians of that most important marketing tool, information. Not only has this further strengthened their hand in the manufacturer-retailer war, but it enables them to build up a much clearer customer profile and gives them the ability to utilise this in launching and targeting new goods and services more effectively.

The continued growth in acceptance and use of credit cards has provided financial institutions, multiple retailers and mail order companies with a plethora of personal information which, when merged with other data sources, transforms the art of marketing into a scientific skill. The ability to target tightly-defined customer groups has never been easier.

Activity 4 **(10 minutes)**

In the light of these comments, how effective do you think your bank is at targeting you and your personal financial needs?

There has been a significant rise in the real cost of **television advertising.** Whilst audiences have diminished, advertising rates have increased, pushing up the real cost of what is already a very expensive medium. The advent of satellite and cable television will further fragment the potential audience.

The development of **global markets** and the breaking down of **cultural boundaries** has opened up an entire new world of experience in terms of consumers who are more adventurous in their choice of goods and services.

Consumers are becoming more **educated** in terms of what they are purchasing and, as a consequence, are much more likely to try out alternatives. Own label brands have grown in significance, as consumers appreciate the parity in terms of value with major brands.

Most UK households now own a **telephone,** which has improved accessibility for the direct marketer.

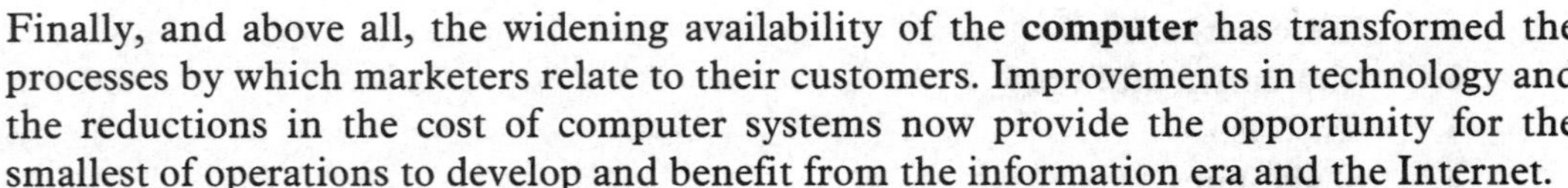

Finally, and above all, the widening availability of the **computer** has transformed the processes by which marketers relate to their customers. Improvements in technology and the reductions in the cost of computer systems now provide the opportunity for the smallest of operations to develop and benefit from the information era and the Internet.

EXAMPLE: MOBILE MARKETING

Consider the following lead-in from a special supplement in *The Guardian* in November 2009.

"We use them to take photos, receive emails, find the nearest restaurant, and navigate our way around an unfamiliar town. Oh, and to make calls as well. Mobile phones are becoming indispensable tools for modern living, and as their popularity grows, so too does their appeal for advertisers seeking a direct connection with consumers. In the UK, brands spent £28.6m on mobile campaigns in 2008, according to the Internet Advertising Bureau, the digital marketing trade body. That may be only a fraction of the £1.75bn spent on Internet advertising in the first half of 2009, but it is a growing number, driven mostly by 3G phones equipped with powerful Internet connections. The number of people using their mobiles to search online increased by 28% in 2008. In this special supplement we examine how the mobile advertising market is changing. We discover that SMS is still a powerful marketing tool, and look at how one company, Argos, is using it to drive sales. We ask what the future holds, and how new technology might make phones even more integral to our everyday lives. In the following pages an advertising professional looks at which campaigns work - and why - and offers up some tips. We also ask whether the year of the mobile has finally arrived, and talk to some who remain sceptical. On page 4 we examine the impact Apple's iPhone has had on the mobile industry and take a glimpse into a future that has already arrived in Japan. We also talk to a senior civil servant, who explains how the government is using mobile advertising to run high-profile campaigns aimed at the young, and evaluates their effectiveness."

James Robinson, *guardian.co.uk*, 9 November 2009

Activity 5 **(20 minutes)**

Conduct a small survey among your friends and family. How many of them have been targeted by companies selling over the telephone, by companies sending unsolicited catalogues and by motoring organisations during the past three months?

3.3 Direct mail

Direct mail has been the third largest and fastest growing advertising medium during the past 10 years. In this period, the number of mailings received by consumers has more than doubled.

Direct mail tends to be the medium of direct response advertising. It has become the synonym for it. The reason for this is that other major media, newspapers and magazines, are familiar to people in advertising in other contexts. Direct mail has a number of strengths as a direct response medium.

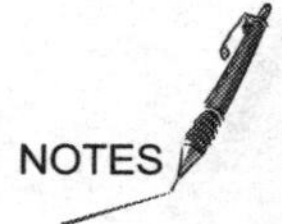

(a) The advertiser can **target** down **to the level of the individual.**

(b) The communication can be **personalised.** Known data about the individual can be used, whilst modern printing techniques mean that parts of a letter can be altered to accommodate this.

(c) **The medium is good for reinforcing interest** stimulated by other media such as TV. It can supply the response mechanism (a coupon) which is not yet available in that medium.

(d) The opportunity to use **different creative formats** is almost unlimited.

(e) **Testing potential is sophisticated**: a limited number of items can be sent out to a test panel and the results can be evaluated. As success is achieved, so the mailing campaign can be rolled out.

(f) What you do is **less visible to your competitors** than other forms of media.

There are, however, a number of weaknesses with this medium.

(a) It does **not offer sound or movement,** although it is possible for advertisers to send out audio or video tapes, and even working models or samples.

(b) There is obvious concern over the **negative association with junk mail** and the need for individuals to exercise their right to privacy,

(c) **Lead times may be considerable** when taking into consideration the creative organisation, finished artwork, printing, proofing, inserting material into envelopes where necessary and finally the mailing.

(d) The most important barrier to direct mail is that it can be **very expensive on a per capita basis**. A delivered insert can be 24 to 32 times more expensive than a full page colour advert in a magazine. It therefore follows that the mailshot must be very powerful and, above all, well targeted to overcome such a cost penalty (in many cases, though, this is possible).

The cornerstone upon which the direct mailing is based, however, is the mailing list. It is far and away the most important element in the list of variables, which also include the offer, timing and creative content.

FOR DISCUSSION

Most mail shots end up in the bin without being read.

Building the database

Definitions

A **database** is a collection of available information on past and current customers together with future prospects, structured to allow for the implementation of effective marketing strategies.

Database marketing is a customer-orientated approach to marketing, and its special power lies in the techniques its uses to harness the capabilities of computer and telecommunications technology.

A **prospect** is a person (or organisation) who is identified as having the potential to become a customer.

Building accurate and up-to-date profiles of existing customers enables the company:

- To extend help to a company's target audience
- To stimulate further demand
- To stay close to the customers
- To make its marketing effort more attractive

Recording and keeping an electronic database of customers and prospects and of all communications and commercial contacts helps to improve all future contacts.

Database applications

The database may be used to meet a variety of objectives with numerous advantages over traditional marketing methods. The range of database applications include:

- Focusing on prime prospects
- Evaluating new prospects
- Cross-selling related products
- Launching new products to potential prospects
- Identifying new distribution channels
- Building customer loyalty
- Converting occasional users to regular users
- Generating enquiries and follow-up sales
- Targeting niche markets

In order that the marketing specialists are able to make clear and informed marketing decisions, the marketing information must be:

- Comprehensive
- Accurate
- Simple to use

Buying lists from elsewhere

Over a period of time, the sources of data available to an organisation from its own database are finite and will ultimately diminish as customers cease to trade with the organisation. Therefore, it is necessary to go outside to other sources. These may include the following.

- The electoral register, possibly supplemented by geodemographic analysis
- Magazine subscription lists
- Membership lists of organisations such as the AA
- Questionnaire response lists
- Brokers offering list for purchase or rent
- Business directories such as Kompass

FOR DISCUSSION

Selling names and addresses is immoral.

Customer list evaluation

Some of the best lists to use will be those which are noted as 'mail responsive'. It is a proven fact that people who have responded by mail or telephone to anything in the past, will be more likely to do so again. Therefore, mail responsive lists are better then

compiled lists, which are made up from sources such as members of societies and business directories.

> **Activity 6** **(20 minutes)**
>
> You are the manager of a local sports centre which provides both indoor and outdoor sports facilities to your local community. Aware of the need to acquire more precise information on the customer base, you have been asked to identify the information needs to assist in a direct marketing strategy.
>
> Identify and justify the information you need in order that the sports centre will be able to undertake more cost-effective and targeted promotions in the future. You also need to consider how this information will be obtained.

3.4 Telemarketing

Definition

> **Telemarketing:** the planned and controlled use of the telephone for sales and marketing opportunities. Unlike all other forms of direct marketing it allows for immediate two-way communication.

Telemarketing is a quick, accurate and flexible tool for gathering, maintaining and helping to exploit relevant up-to-date information about customers and prospects. It can be utilised at all stages, from the point of building highly targeted mailing lists through to screening respondents to determine the best type to follow up, and thenceforward to supporting the salesforce in maximising customers' value throughout their lifetime.

Benefits of telemarketing

Telemarketing has the following advantages.

(a) It is **targeted**: the recipient of the call can be identified every time and the message appropriately tailored.

(b) It is **highly personal**: telemarketers can determine and respond immediately to the specific needs of individuals, building long-term personal and profitable relationships.

(c) It is **interactive**: since the dialogue is live, you can guide the conversation to achieve the desired results; the client's representative is in control.

(d) It is **immediate**: every outbound call achieves an immediate result, even if it is a wrong number or 'not interested'. Customers and prospects can be given 24 hour constant access to the company

(e) It is of a **high quality**: information can be gathered accurately, kept up-to-date and used to select and prioritise leads for follow up calls.

(f) It is very **flexible**: conversations can be tailored spontaneously as the representative responds to the contact's needs. There are no geographical constraints on calls which can be timed to suit the contact, providing the opportunity for maximum response levels.

(g) It is **accountable**: results and effectiveness can be checked continuously.

(h) It is **experimental**: campaign variables can be tested quickly and changes made whilst the campaign is in progress.

(i) It is very **cost effective**: when used professionally in the right application, all the above combine to create a highly effective marketing tool.

Problems with telemarketing

Despite the many attractions offered by telemarketing, there are a number of disadvantages. Firstly, it can be costly. There are few economies of scale associated with telemarketing, and techniques such as direct mail and media: advertising can work out cheaper. Labour overheads are potentially high, although this can be counterbalanced by operating the business from a central point.

A telemarketer can only contact around 30 to 40 customers in a day, whereas media advertising can reach a mass audience in a single strike. However, media advertising (giving an 0800 telephone contact number or the actual company number) married with telemarketing can be a very powerful combination.

If poorly handled, telemarketing may be interpreted by the customer, and more importantly the prospect, as intrusive. This may alienate the customer and lead to lost sales opportunities.

The telephone and mail preference service in the UK is a system by which households can choose not to be contacted via cold calling. This service is free and increasingly used by customers. BT even offers the ability to join the register of households for their customers as part of their website.

EXAMPLE: OFCOM LENGTHENS SILENT CALL TIME AFTER CBI MAKES CASE FOR OUTBOUND TELEMARKETING

Ofcom, the broadcasting and telecoms regulator, has agreed that firms using automatic diallers to make cold calls are to be given longer before they have to play a recorded message.

Automatic diallers can result in a silent call if more phones are answered than there are agents to handle them. To help remove the chance of a silent call, Ofcom has, until now, insisted that recorded messages have to be played within two seconds of the phone being picked up.

But this has now been amended so that the two seconds can begin after the person answering the phone starts speaking.

The move, which follows the Government's proposal last month to increase the fines on companies that flout silent call rules from £50,000 to a maximum of £2m, is in response to business concerns about the two-second rule's effects on outbound telemarketing.

In July the Confederation of British Industry issued a document arguing that the two-second rule would have a negative effect on business, as two seconds does not allow answering machine detection technology "sufficient time to operate".

Ofcom has amended the rule to "make it easier for diallers to detect when a call is being answered by a real person or an answering machine," Ofcom says in a statement on its website.

The change is bound to be controversial with consumer groups that have campaigned for silent calls to be banned entirely.

Two years ago Carphone Warehouse was fined £35,000 for silent calls while last September, Barclaycard received the current possible maximum fine of £50,000 for the same practice.

Noelle McElhatton, *marketingdirectmag.co.uk*, 04 November 2009

4 ACQUISITION AND RETENTION OF CUSTOMERS

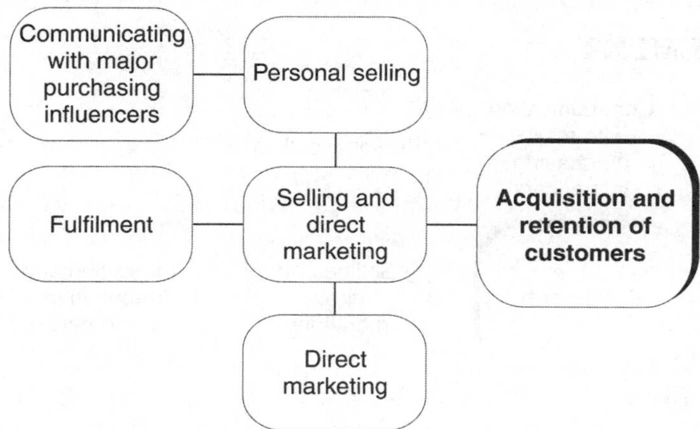

It was stated earlier that the sole aim of direct marketing is to acquire and retain customers. Many of the issues already discussed in this chapter have as their prime purpose acquisition and retention of customers. The process is summarised below.

(a) **Identify prospects.** The starting point in identifying and retaining customers is to build a database of existing customers. This will involve the profiling of customers into different categories, including:

- Socio-demographics
- Lifestyle
- Purchasing behaviour

Over a period of time however, there is a need to build upon the existing database. One method is to recruit new prospects on the basis of the characteristics which are similar to existing customers. This will be the case except where the organisation has exhausted a particular customer type and/or the organisation is launching a new product or service which is attractive to a different target audience. This may involve the buying in of an outside list to assist in the development of a new market.

(b) **Target media**. Virtually all media types may be utilised to acquire new prospects.

(c) **Selling the product**. The most important and costliest sale is the first sale.

(d) **Customer information and the database.** At this stage it is possible to build up a picture of the customer based upon existing and new key denominators.

(e) **Communication.** Regular contact with customers is a vital component of the direct marketing strategy.

(f) **Up-selling and cross selling.** Part of the direct marketing effort is to direct customers to more expensive products and/or longer-term commitments, as well as selling other products within the product range.

(g) **Increased customer value.** The success in any retention strategy is to realise that it is a two-way relationship. Perpetually attempting to sell more products is more likely than not going to irritate customers. Hence, a fine balance must be achieved between recognising individual customer needs at one level and the desire to sell more products at the other. Loyalty from the customer can be translated into customer value by demonstrating quality, trustworthiness, honesty and a deep interest in the customer's needs at every opportunity.

5 FULFILMENT

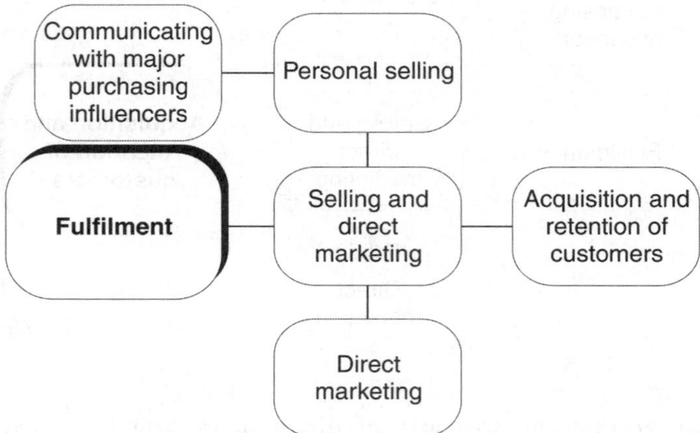

Perhaps the most important element, and the vital link in the direct marketing plan is the extent to which the promise to the customer is kept. Direct marketing by definition requires a response, and **fulfilment** is the act of servicing the customer's response. Cleary, fulfilment is an aspect of **place**, or distribution, but it has special importance for retail direct marketing since, in contrast to most retail selling, it involves direct doorstep delivery.

The act of fulfilment may take on a number of different activities including handling customer complaints, taking orders, offering advice and providing service and despatching goods. In all these cases, it is safe to assume that the customer requires a prompt, courteous and effective response.

Whether the fulfilment is carried out within the company or is handled by an external agency the area of fulfilment is a potential disaster area, where even the most professional organisations can come unstuck. Some problem areas are given below.

(a) **Inaccurate forecasting** by the organisation in the take-up of a particular offer.

(b) Fulfilment operations can lead to **extensive demands** upon the organisation **in terms of human resources and work space.** Organisations need to consider the trade-off between the costs of setting up the fulfilment service and the volume of business that will be generated by direct marketing activity.

(c) **Delays** in stock delivery and **pilferage** of stock can lead to **frustrated customers.**

(d) **Human error** when inputting data can result in the wrong items being despatched to the wrong address.

Such errors can lead to lost customers and ultimately lost profits. It is therefore crucial that any organisation embarking upon a direct marketing strategy is aware of the need for investment in its fulfilment policy, or it will not succeed.

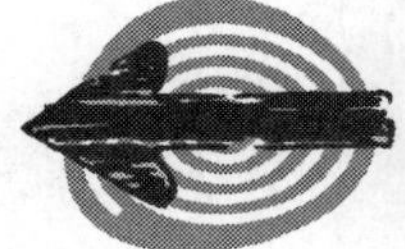

Direct marketing is an exciting synthesis of many of the concepts of the marketing communications mix and the new communications technology. Where the customer service component is assured through effective fulfilment, it will continue its spectacular growth.

Chapter roundup

- Personal selling is the direct presentation of products and associated persuasive communication to a potential buyer.
- The selling process comprises seven main stages: preparation; opening; problem identification; presentation; dealing with objections; negotiation; closing.
- The sales effort has to be managed effectively.
- Management is effected through organising; motivating; directing; training; and controlling the effort.
- Personal selling works because it can customise, simplify and condense large amounts of information effectively.
- It has the potential to create invaluable long-term customer relationships.
- The selling effort is a high level investment which requires effective management.
- Direct marketing is a personal, precise and powerful activity.
- The features can be summarised as customer focus; communication; cost effectiveness; convenience.
- Using new technology, it can harness many of the promotion concepts effectively.
- It is eminently more measurable because of new technology.
- It has the image of being intrusive on the customer.

Quick quiz

1. What are the major roles of the salesperson?
2. What are the main tasks of the selling effort?
3. What are the major phases of the selling process?
4. What are the main advantages of personal selling?
5. Why is personal selling seen by some as inefficient?
6. What are the major reasons for the growth of direct marketing?
7. How can a database assist in direct marketing?
8. What are the activities associated with creating fulfilment for the customer?
9. What are some of the disadvantages of direct marketing?
10. Name some well known direct marketing organisations.

Answers to Quick quiz

1. Deliverer; order taker; missionary; technician; demand creator.
2. Prospecting; communicating; selling; servicing; information gathering; allocating.
3. Preparing; opening; problem identification; presentation; dealing with objections; negotiating; closing; after sales service.
4. Customers' attention; customised messages; immediate feedback; handling large amount of complex information.
5. High cost; the salesperson can only interact with one buyer at a time
6. Changes in: family structures; retailing; credit cards; cost of TV advertising; global markets; branding; telephone usage; new low cost communications technology.
7. Focusing; evaluating; cross-selling; building customer loyalty; generating enquiries and follow-ups; targeting niche markets.
8. Promptness, courteousness and effectiveness: handling complaints; taking orders; giving advice; goods despatch; being available.
9. It is widely considered as intrusive.
10. Readers Digest; Betterware; Avon; Tupperware; K-tel.

Answers to Activities

1 In descending order:

personal selling

direct marketing

sales promotion

media advertising

public relations (PR)

(a) With PR we do not even control the message; it may be changed by the dictates of the editorial policy. It may not even be used, depending on the pressure of other stories on the day. Rarely, the power of competitive advertisers may influence the treatment.

(b) In media advertising, we cannot guarantee the ad being read. We have limited control over the audience; the positioning of the ad may be disadvantageous.

(c) With sales promotion we can make conditions to control who receives the benefit. We cannot be sure of the response. We do research and ask for information of the recipient which improves our market knowledge.

(d) With direct marketing we can be sure who receives the message by name. In some cases we can engage in a limited direct interaction which allows further control and monitoring.

(e) With personal selling we have the most control over who receives the message and a continuing interaction with the target audience which allows maximum flexibility of reaction in shaping the message.

2 Reference selling: double glazing, fitted kitchens. Demonstrations: hi-fi equipment, motor cars. Guarantees: video cameras, televisions. Trial order: luxury cars, mail order goods. Sale or return: drinks bought for parties, mail order goods.

3 Give some thought to the structure of this activity and you will enjoy it: do not and it is likely to collapse as a farce!

A group approach is most effective; five or six per group is about optimum size. Each member must develop a product. This is best achieved by writing up a FAB schedule. The seller has to know the product and its benefits very well. The seller should follow the selling process as given in the text; this will be the basis of the observers' assessments. In fact, a presentation outline should be prepared with this as the framework. The roles of buyer and seller are rotated amongst the members; the balance of the group act as observers: ideally the proceedings should be videoed. Avoid one member hogging the job of operating the camera. This role should be rotated too! Allocate a specific time for each pitch. A maximum of 10 to 15 minutes should be adequate, otherwise it can lose the tightness required for an effective cameo. The observers will comment on the effectiveness of the presentation. A sale is not a necessary outcome. Cussedness on the part of the buyer would be penalised! The buyer is expected to behave reasonably and with professionalism.

4 One way of measuring is to see how much of what your bank sends to you ends up in the bin! Arguably, the High Street banks are better at collecting information than using it intelligently; this is beginning to change as the banks become more marketing oriented.

5 The answer will obviously depend on your survey but it is doubtful that anyone will not have been contacted in at least two of these forms during the past three months.

6 Think in terms of the segmentation variables.

Biographic: age; sex; name and address (including postcodes); occupation; school/college; firm; shift worker?

Behavioural: sports played; attendance patterns; frequency; time; duration; other centres attended.

Psychographics: interests; opinions; attitudes (to, say, playing games with beginners/juniors/opposite sex).

Information could be obtained by questionnaire/interviews/competitions as well as some from secondary sources such as sports clubs and local authorities.

Part D

Market Segments and Contexts

Chapter 14 : TYPES OF MARKET

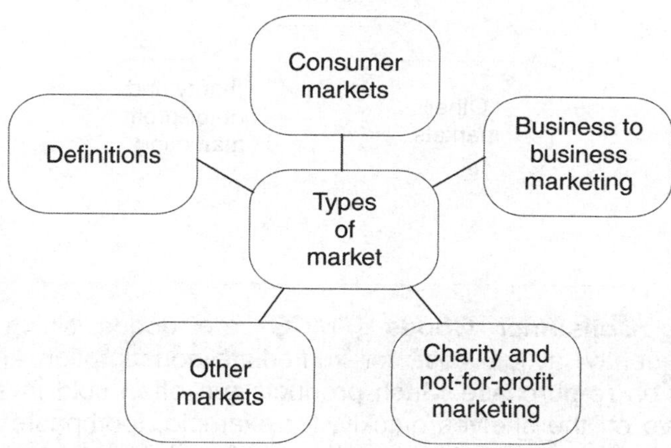

Introduction

The marketing concept and marketing mix will be applied in differing ways and to different segments, depending on what sort of market an organisation operates in. This leads us to consider other broad categories of market: FMCG, consumer durables and business to business, or industrial marketing.

This chapter also looks at non-profit making, government and re-seller markets.

Your objectives

In this chapter you will learn about the following.

(a) How the marketing mix can be applied in different types of market

(b) The differences in marketing products and services to organisations rather than consumers

1 DEFINITIONS

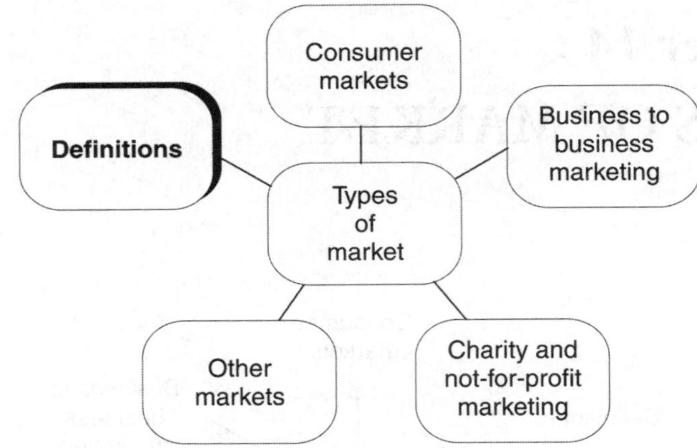

Definitions

Fast Moving Consumer Goods (FMCG) are goods which are bought relatively frequently, at low cost, for immediate consumption and often with high reliance on re-purchase. Such products are often sold in supermarkets and they move off the shelves quickly, for example, toothpaste and chewing gum. FMCGs require constant replenishment of in-store stocks.

Consumer durables or **shopping goods** are goods which are complex, purchased infrequently at relatively high cost and are expected to last a long time. Buying behaviour in this class often includes extensive searching, product comparison and reliance on new information.

Industrial consumables are products which are used up in the manufacture of goods but do not become an integral part of them. Examples are: protective packaging; cleaning materials; oil; drill bits. Such products have, relative to industrial durables, very low purchase importance, are poorly differentiated, are often unbranded and rely heavily on good distribution services. Like FMCGs they are often re-purchased without much formality.

Industrial durables are products which are normally high capital cost, complex and highly technical. There is a low frequency of purchase which requires high level approval and very often protracted negotiation.

Business-to-business (B2B) marketing refers to all business activities which are directed primarily at non-domestic markets. It therefore includes marketing products for industry, commerce, trade, distribution, professional outlets and individuals in such businesses.

2 CONSUMER MARKETS

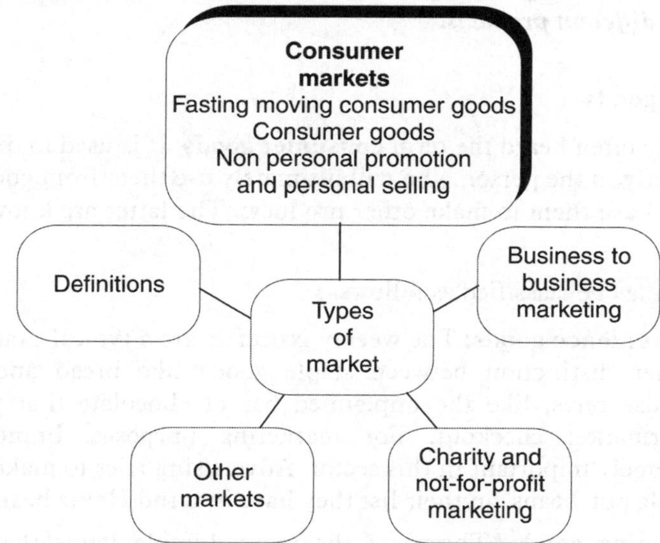

2.1 Fast-moving consumer goods

The FMCG market has the following features.

(a) The goods, whether they are tangible products or intangible services, are bought frequently. Examples are a daily newspaper and a bus ride.

(b) They are typically low priced and therefore are low risk purchases.

(c) Often they are the subject of an impulse purchase, such as a chocolate bar at a supermarket check out.

(d) Many of the goods in this category are basic items such as bread and tea.

(e) Purchasers will tend to make a minimal effort to satisfy the basic needs that FMCG meet, so they will readily accept alternative brands. If a packet of McVitie's Cheddars is not available, then rather than defer the purchase of cheese biscuits an alternative such as the retailer's own brand will be chosen.

The last point is particularly important to manufacturers: they must not only make a satisfactory product but must also make it **readily available** to the potential purchaser.

FOR DISCUSSION

Consider three FMCG products that you have brought in the last 24 hours. How closely did the goods that you bought match the characteristics listed above? To help you, fill in the chart below.

Product	*Frequent purchase?*	*Low price?*	*Bought on impulse?*	*Basic item?*	*Alternative if necessary?*
1………					
2………					
3………					

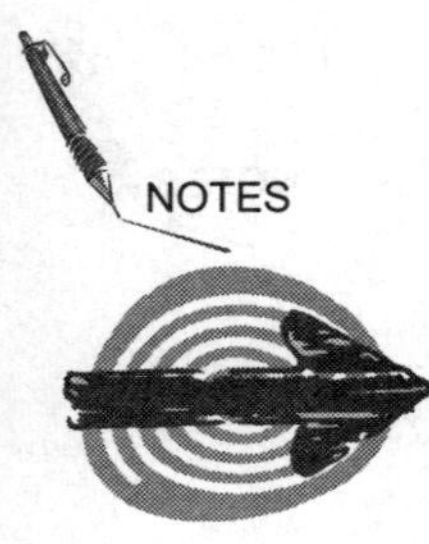

Examining the next market grouping, we will still be in the consumer sector but with the inclusion of quite different products.

2.2 Consumer goods

You have probably often heard the term **consumer goods**. It is used to distinguish goods that are sold directly to the person who will ultimately use them from goods that are sold to people who will use them to make other products. The latter are known as **industrial goods.**

Consumer goods may be classified as follows.

(a) **Convenience goods.** The weekly groceries are a typical example. There is a further distinction between staple goods like bread and potatoes, and impulse buys, like the unplanned bar of chocolate that you find at the supermarket checkout. For marketing purposes, brand awareness is extremely important in this sector. Advertising tries to make sure that when people put 'beans' on their list they have in mind Heinz beans.

(b) **Shopping goods.** These are the more durable items that you buy, like furniture or washing machines. This sort of purchase is usually only made after a good deal of advance planning and shopping around. Also known as consumer durables.

(c) **Speciality goods.** These are items like jewellery or the more expensive items of clothing.

(d) **Unsought goods.** These are goods that you did not realise you needed! Typical examples would be the sort of items that are found in catalogues that arrive in the post.

Activity 1 **(15 minutes)**

Think of three products that you have bought recently, one low-priced, one medium priced, and one expensive item. Identify the product attributes that made you buy each of these items and categorise them according to the classifications shown above.

Activity 2 **(15 minutes)**

Write down your experience of when you last purchased a speciality good. How did you gather information? What aspects did you consider to be important when making your decision?

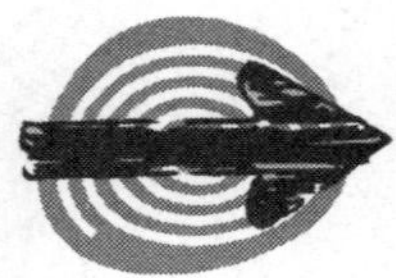

Business markets have their own particular needs. The main differences from consumer markets are the scale and consequent effort put into the purchasing decision.

2.3 Non-personal promotion and personal selling

There is a general relationship between non-personal promotion and personal selling across the classes of products which is demonstrated in the following model.

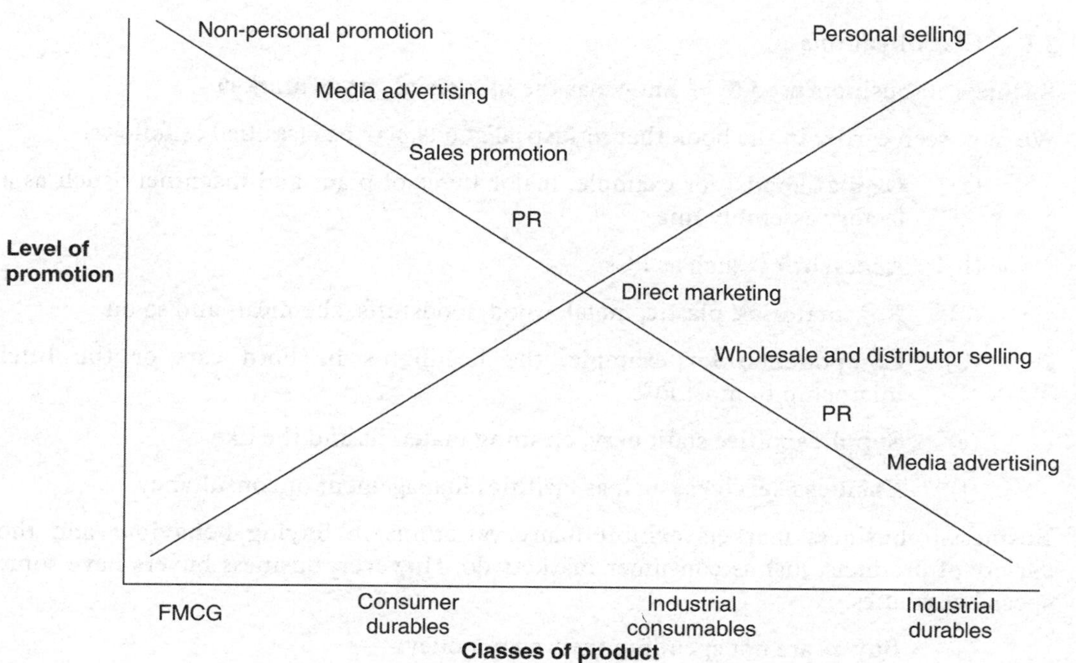

Figure 14.1: Relationship between non-personal promotion and personal selling

The model is useful for demonstrating the general principle that FMCGs do not rely heavily on personal selling as a form of promotion to the final customer. Of course, personal selling may be effective in selling FMCGs on a business-to-business basis: that is, from the manufacturer to the wholesaler and from the wholesaler to the retailer. On the other hand, personal selling is shown as very important in the promotional mix for industrial durables.

FOR DISCUSSION

Shopkeepers don't try to sell FMCGs, so the products have to sell themselves!

---

3 BUSINESS TO BUSINESS MARKETING

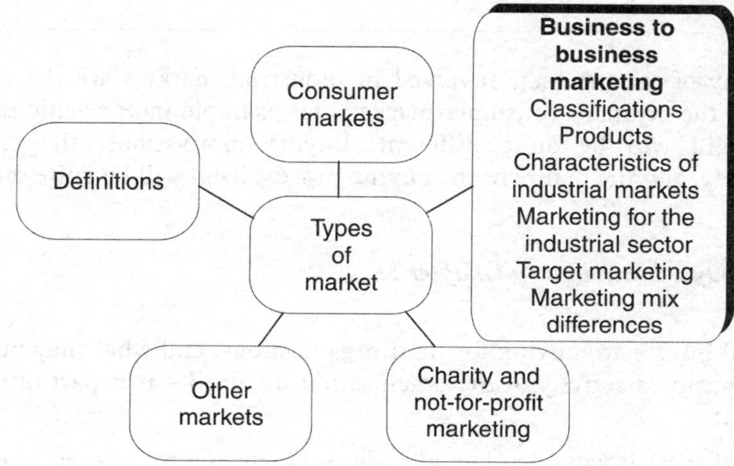

3.1 Classifications

Business-to-business used to be known as the **industrial goods market**.

We have seen earlier in the book that industrial goods may be classified as follows.

(a) **Capital goods,** for example, major items of plant and machinery such as a factory assembly line.

(b) **Accessories,** such as PCs.

(c) **Raw material:** plastic, metal, wood, foodstuffs, chemicals and so on.

(d) **Components,** for example, the headlights in Ford cars or the Intel microchip in most PCs.

(e) **Supplies:** office stationery, cleaning materials and the like.

(f) **Business services,** such as facilities management or consultancy.

Business-to-business markets exhibit many variations in **buying behaviour** and the variety of products, just as consumer markets do. However, business buyers have some special attributes.

(a) Buyers are not spending their own money.

(b) The buying decision making unit (DMU) may involve many people. (See Chapter 5.)

(c) Decision making may take a long time.

(d) The customer base is often small and easy to identify.

(e) Average order values and quantities are higher than in consumer markets.

(f) Personal contacts and relationships are often a key part of the buying decision.

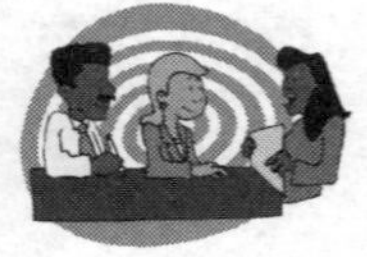

FOR DISCUSSION

A major mail order company is about to buy a computer system to handle all its sales, invoicing and customer accounts. The system is likely to cost about £5,000,000, and there are ten possible suppliers. How is the decision on which system to buy likely to be made? Who will need to be consulted? If you were one of the potential suppliers, what would you do to improve your chances of getting the order?

Although many of the products involved in industrial markets are the same as those bought within the ordinary consumer markets, for example motor vehicles, the reasons they are bought will be quite different. Buying motivations, the criteria which consumers apply, and the nature of the buying process itself will be quite different.

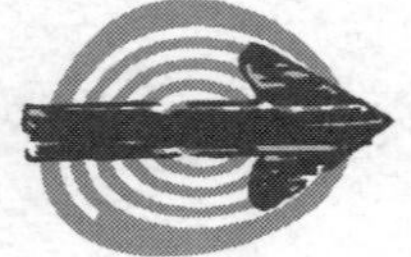

We looked at buyer behaviour in Chapter 5.

Organisational buyers are buying for their organisations, and what they buy is part and parcel of the business activity of the organisation involved – it is part of the process of earning a profit.

Industrial marketing involves widely varying products and services. It is not just about raw materials, or about the selling of specialised, heavy duty machinery or equipment.

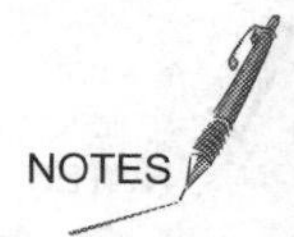

Industrial goods and services are bought by manufacturers, distributors and other private and publicly owned institutions such as schools and hospitals to be used as part of their own activities, rather than for resale.

3.2 Products

Industrial products are distinctive in several ways.

(a) **Conformity with standards**. Industrial products are often bound by **legal or quality standards**, and as a consequence, products within a particular group are often similar. Differentiation, which is such a key dimension of consumer goods, is more difficult here. At the same time, buyers lay down their own specifications to which manufacturers must adhere.

(b) **Technical sophistication**. Many products in this area require levels of complexity and sophistication which are unheard of in consumer products. Often the industry standard gradually influences the consumer equivalent as, for instance, in the case of power tools in the DIY market. After-sales and maintenance contracts have become essential in certain areas.

(c) **High unit values.** As a consequence of (a) and (b), many industrial goods, particularly capital equipment, are very often extremely costly items. Even in the case of supplies, although the unit value of components and materials may be comparatively low, the quantity required frequently means that individual orders and total sales to individual customers usually have a very high value.

(d) **Irregularity of purchase**. Machinery used to produce consumer goods is not bought regularly. Materials used to produce the goods certainly are, but components and materials are often bought on a contract basis, so that the opportunity to get new business may not arise very often.

3.3 Characteristics of industrial markets

Three kinds of economic activities have been defined.

(a) **Primary or extractive industries** cover activities like agriculture, fishing, mining and forestry.

(b) **Secondary or manufacturing industries** include manufacturing and construction.

(c) **The tertiary sector includes the service industries.** Services are becoming extremely important within our modern economy and services marketing is exerting a big influence on the way in which marketing is developing.

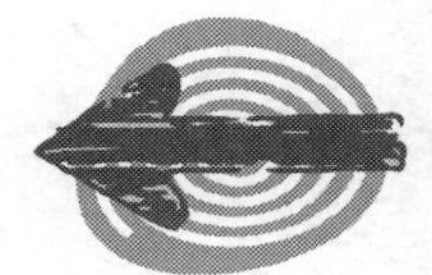

We look at services marketing in the next chapter.

3.4 Marketing for the industrial sector

A marketing orientation is just as valid within the industrial sector as it is in the consumer goods sector. Customers seek answers to their problems. Industrial products must be full of customer benefits.

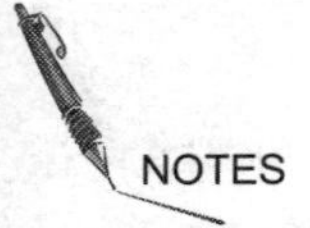

The marketing manager within the organisation

This implies a need for well co-ordinated activity, around a common, market-oriented, mission. Marketing management can:

- Act as catalysts within the firms
- Inform technical management about market trends
- Monitor competitive activity
- Inform corporate planning decisions
- Direct R & D

They are not simply concerned with customers, but in linking and co-ordinating various activities within the firm.

Special practices

Reciprocal trading is evident in some markets where buying and selling firms engage in reciprocal trading agreements. This closes markets off for newcomers and restricts trading.

Joint ventures often involve large industrial and commercial organisations which pool their resources in order to accomplish particular contracts. This may be necessary because of the scale of the project, or because of cultural, legal or technical advantages which the co-operation confers on both parties.

Consortiums are more permanent partnerships.

Project management involves special techniques to bring a single unique development to completion. Projects may involve research, design, manufacturing and logistic activities.

Turnkey operations may be similar to project management or may involve continuing responsibility to the customer for services and maintenance.

More and more **machinery is being leased rather than bought**. In the construction industry, leasing deals also involve lessors tying the machinery to exclusive purchasing of other items such as raw materials.

Licensing enables new products to be introduced to customers without the risks and high costs associated with the development and launch of a new product. It also significantly reduces the time to launch.

3.5 Target marketing

Business to business target markets tend to be easier to identify than consumer market segments, mainly because more **data is readily available** on businesses than on groups of people within the general public.

Much information about industrial markets is published in **government statistics**. Production statistics are available monthly and quarterly for manufacturing companies broken down into ten major **Standard Industrial Classifications (SICs)**, for example SIC3 is metal goods, engineering and textiles. Each major heading is broken down into smaller groups. Under each heading is given such detail as number of employees, number of establishments, value of shipments, exports and imports and annual growth rates.

Distribution statistics are available for retail outlets by type giving turnover and number of establishments, for instance.

> **Activity 3** **(20 minutes)**
>
> Find some examples of government publications which might provide a useful source of statistics.

Official statistics are also published by bodies such as the United Nations and local authorities.

3.6 Marketing mix differences

The industrial marketing mix differs from the marketing mix for consumer products. Often industrial products are not packaged for resale, prices tend to be negotiated with the buyer and distribution tends to be more direct. The promotional mix is also generally different in that consumer goods are often advertised heavily on TV and in mass media whereas industrial marketing companies tend to restrict advertising to trade magazines.

EXAMPLE

Business-to-business (B2B) magazines are used regularly for work purposes by more decision-makers than any other medium. 87% of decision-makers are regular users. B2B magazines dominate all other media in terms of usefulness to business decision-makers.

When asked, for eleven types of information, which medium was most useful, B2B magazines not only achieved the highest score in every case but also did so by wide margins.

The typical pattern was that, for a given type of information, the proportion of decision-makers who declared that B2B magazines were the most useful medium was usually around four to six times larger than for the medium in second place. The remaining eight media then tailed away with few people thinking them the most useful source.

The eleven types of information for which B2B publications were so pre-eminent were:

- Providing thorough coverage of your sector
- Helping you to stay in touch with what's going on in your sector
- Helping you to understand how your sector is changing
- Helping you to learn from the successes and mistakes of others
- Keeping you up to date with news of product launches
- Providing you with information about new products and services
- Helping you select new suppliers
- Looking for jobs, or helping you to keep up to date with the job market
- Helping you to spot new business opportunities
- Containing advertising which is useful to you
- Helping you to do your job better

Source: Periodical Publishers Association, 2002 survey

Much more reliance is placed on **personal selling.** Rarely will an industrial buyer purchase off the page, especially where capital goods are concerned. Whereas most FMCG are purchased on a self-service basis, industrial goods involve a great deal more

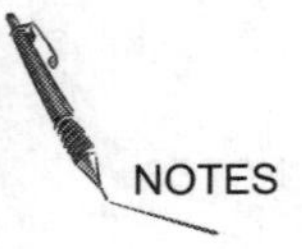

personal contact. Industrial marketers also use **exhibitions and demonstrations** to quite a high degree when promoting their products.

Product

Most business to business marketing mixes will include **elements of service** as well as product. **Pre-sales services** may involve technical advice, quotations, opportunities to see products in action and free trials. **After-sales service** will include just-in-time delivery, service and maintenance and guarantees. Products will also be **custom-built** to a much greater degree than for consumer marketing mixes. Frequently, products will have to be tested to laid down conditions. Packing will be for protection rather than for self-service. Some of these elements can comprise a powerful differential competitive advantage.

EXAMPLE

ICI offers laboratory testing of various metals so that industrial customers can be assured of the one most suitable for given corrosive conditions.

When buying machine tools, **efficiency features** can be the most powerful buying motive. Other product-unique features may be the ease of or safety of operation. If an operator can manage two machines rather than one, his potential output is doubled. **Training** of operators is another service often provided by manufacturers of industrial equipment.

Price

Price is not normally fixed to the same degree as in consumer markets. Particularly where products or services are customised, price is a function of **buyer specification**. Price is **negotiable** to a much greater extent and may depend upon the quantity, add-on services and features and sometimes the total business placed per year. Retrospective annual **discounts** act as loyalty incentives.

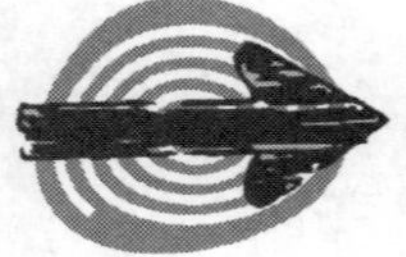

Trade discounts can apply in those cases where industrial and commercial goods are marketed through middlemen (see below on distribution). In some industrial markets, especially construction, prices are set under a tendering system.

Promotion

Within the promotional mix, **personal selling** is very important in business to business marketing. Some industrial products are quite complex and need explaining in a flexible way to non-technical people involved in the buying process.

Buying in business to business marketing is often a group activity and, equally, selling can be a team effort. Salespeople are expected to follow-up to ensure that the products are working properly and that the business buyer is perfectly satisfied. Where an industrial equipment manufacturer markets through an industrial dealer, the manufacturer's salesforce may be required to train the dealer salesforce in product knowledge.

NOTES

The **partnership approach** is present to a much greater degree in industrial selling, where the buyer needs information and services and the seller is seeking repeat business in the long term.

The types of **media** used for advertising differ greatly from those in consumer markets. Mass media are rarely used. Advertising is usually confined to **trade magazines**, which reach more precise targets. **Direct mail** is used to supplement personal selling.

EXAMPLE

The long neglected area of accurately targeted business-to-business direct marketing has been given a boost with the news that a system that classifies businesses according to their location has been launched.

B2B direct marketing has long been thought to have lagged behind consumer marketing, because of the lack of technology that classifies businesses geographically.

The Geodemographic Industrial Classification system claims to be the UK's first such product and has been developed by database marketing services consultancy Information Arts.

Simon Lawrence, joint managing director of Information Arts, said: 'B2B direct marketing is widely recognised for its poor levels of data accuracy and targeting and, to be fair, it is often because the availability of classification products is next to none, especially when compared with the business-to-consumer market.'

The system is based on the same principle as the consumer classification technology and was developed in response to the lack of accuracy and knowledge available when targeting businesses.

Brand Republic, 23 July 2002

Industrial exhibitions are popular as a means of personal contact with particular target markets, and factory visits are used as a means of engendering confidence in the manufacturer's abilities and standards. More industrial marketers are using PR, through agencies, as a means of gaining favourable publicity in the trade media and to build up their corporate images.

Place (distribution)

Business to business distributors are often employed, particularly for consumable and lower-value goods. **Business to business channels** are:

- Manufacturer → Business buyer
- Manufacturer → Agents → Business buyer
- Manufacturer → Business distributor → Business buyer
- Manufacturer → Agents → Business distributor → Business buyer

On-time delivery can be an extremely important requirement in industrial markets, especially where valuable contracts can be held up for want of a relatively small piece of equipment. In such circumstances the premium on delivery is so great that penalty clauses for lateness are invoked.

To summarise, here is a chart showing a baker's dozen of differences between business-to-business and consumer marketing.

	Area	Business-to-business marketing	Consumer marketing
1	Purchase motivation	Multiple buying influences Support company operations	Individual or family need
2	Nature of demand	Derived or joint demand	Primary demand
3	Emphasis of seller	Economic needs	Immediate satisfaction
4	Customer needs	Each customer has different needs	Groups with similar needs
5	Nature of buyer	Group decisions	Purchase by individual or family unit
6	Time effects	Long-term relationships	Short-term relationships
7	Product details	Technically sophisticated	Lower technical content
8	Promotion decisions	Emphasis on personal selling	Emphasis on mass media advertising
9	Price decisions	Price negotiated Terms are important	Price substantially fixed Discounts are important
10	Place decisions	Limited number of large buyers, short channels	Large number of small buyers Complex channels
11	Customer service	Critical to success	Less important
12	Legal factors	Contractual arrangements	Contracts only on major purchases
13	Environmental factors	Affect sales both directly and indirectly	Affect demand directly

Figure 14.2: Differences between business-to-business and consumer marketing

Powers, *Modern Business Marketing*, 1991

4 CHARITY AND NOT-FOR-PROFIT MARKETING

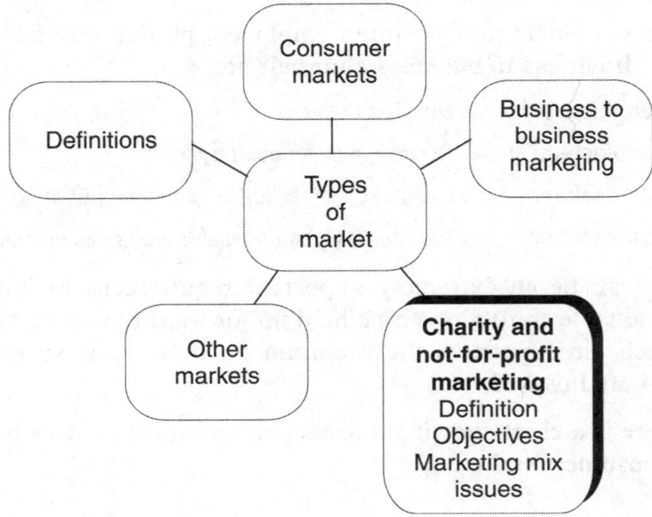

4.1 Definition

Although most people would 'know one if they saw it', there is a surprising problem in clearly defining what counts as a **not-for-profit (NFP) organisation**. Local authority services, for example, would not be marketing in order to arrive at a profit for shareholders, but nowadays they are being increasingly required to apply the same **disciplines and processes** as companies which are oriented towards straightforward profit goals.

We can define NFP enterprises by recognising that their first objective is to be **'non-loss' operations** in order to cover their costs, and that profits are only made **as a means to an end** (eg **providing a service**, or accomplishing some **socially or morally worthy objective**).

Definition

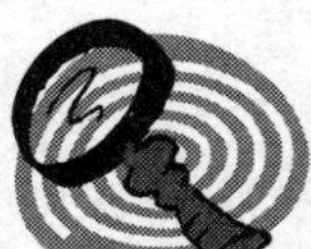

> A **not-for profit organisation** can be defined as: '...an organisation whose attainment of its prime goal is not assessed by economic measures. However, in pursuit of that goal it may undertake profit-making activities.'
>
> This may involve a number of different kinds of organisation with, for example, differing legal status — charities, statutory bodies offering public transport or the provision of services such as leisure, schools, health or public utilities such as water or road maintenance.

Dibb *et al* (*Marketing: Concepts and Strategies*, 2001) suggest that non-business marketing can conveniently be split into two sub-categories.

(a) **Non profit organisation marketing** eg hospitals and colleges

(b) **Social marketing** seeks to shape perceived beneficial social attitudes such as protecting the environment, saving scarce resources or contributing towards good causes

Marketing management is now recognised as equally valuable to profit orientated and NFP organisations. Schools, for example, often compete for funding and need to increase learner numbers if they are undersubscribed. Equally relevant to them is the need to retain a good reputation in order to attract the best staff. The tasks of marketing auditing, setting objectives, developing strategies and marketing mixes and controls for their implementation can all help in improving the performance of charities and NFP organisations. Whilst the basic principles are appropriate for this sector, differences in how they can be applied should not be forgotten.

4.2 Objectives

Objectives will not be based on profit achievement but rather on achieving a particular response from various target markets. The organisation will need to be open and honest in showing how it has managed its budget and **allocated funds** raised. **Efficiency and effectiveness** are particularly important in the use of donated funds.

> **Activity 4** **(15 minutes)**
>
> List possible objectives for NFP and charitable organisations.

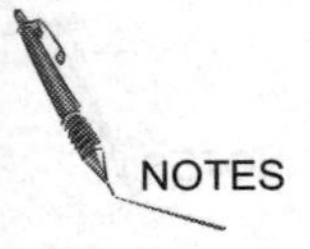

The concept of target marketing is different in the not-for-profit sector. There are no buyers but rather a number of different **audiences**. A **target public** is a group of individuals who have an interest or concern about the charity. Those benefiting from the organisation's activities are known as the **client public**. Relationships are also vital with **donors and volunteers** from the general public. In addition, there may also be a need to **lobby** local and national government and businesses for support.

EXAMPLE

The NSPCC frequently generates a lot of press attention for the use of shocking marketing communications (such as babies being shown with syringes) and possibly gains a majority share of publicity. With regards to their marketing, it has been said that the charity has become increasingly aggressive and it has been reported in the past that there have been complaints from people who donate regularly by direct debit that the charity sends increasingly shocking appeals in order to encourage them to donate more. Despite these claims the charity was found to exist on the most loved brands list compiled by Marketing magazines in a 2007 survey. Cancer Research UK is perceived even more favourably as a brand. It ranked as the most loved charity in position 19 in the list of overall brands. Much of the popularity for this charity is believed to come from the well received Race for Life events.

In an increasingly crowded not for profit sector, charities are needing to become increasingly inventive in order to compete for funds, the RSPCA for example have created mini reality TV ads designed to encourage viewers to call and raise money by voting for their favourite animal featured. The campaign features Simon Cowell and Fearne Cotton, popular hosts of reality TV shows.

Barnardos have worked for a few years with schools where younger children have been encouraged to grow beans and gain sponsorship per centimetre grown. This type of initiative is popular because it creates a sense of direct involvement with the charity and is highly targeted to an appropriate audience.

4.3 Marketing mix issues

Charities and NFP organisations often deal more with **services and ideas** than products. In this sense the **extended marketing mix** of people, process and physical evidence is important.

(a) **Appearance** needs to be business-like rather than appearing extravagant.

(b) **Process** is increasingly important, for example, the use of direct debit to pay for council tax reduces administration costs, leaving more budget for community services.

(c) **People** need to offer good service and be caring in their dealings with their clients.

(d) **Distribution channels** are often shorter with fewer intermediaries than in the profit making sector. Wholesalers and distributors available to a business organisation do not exist in most non-business contexts.

(e) **Promotion is usually dominated by personal selling.** Advertising is often limited to public service announcements due to limited budgets. Direct marketing is growing due to the ease of developing databases. Sponsorship, competitions and special events are also widely used.

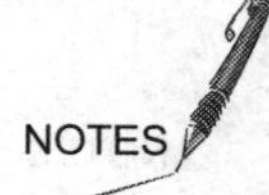

(f) **Pricing** is probably the most different element in this sector. Financial price is often not a relevant concept. Rather, opportunity cost, where an individual is persuaded of the value of donating time or funds, is more relevant.

Controlling activities is complicated by the difficulty of judging whether **non-quantitative objectives** have been met. For example assessing whether the charity has improved the situation of client publics is difficult to research. Statistics may be collated relating to:

- Product mix
- Financial resources
- Size of budgets
- Number of employees
- Number of volunteers
- Number of customers serviced
- Number and location of facilities

5 OTHER MARKETS

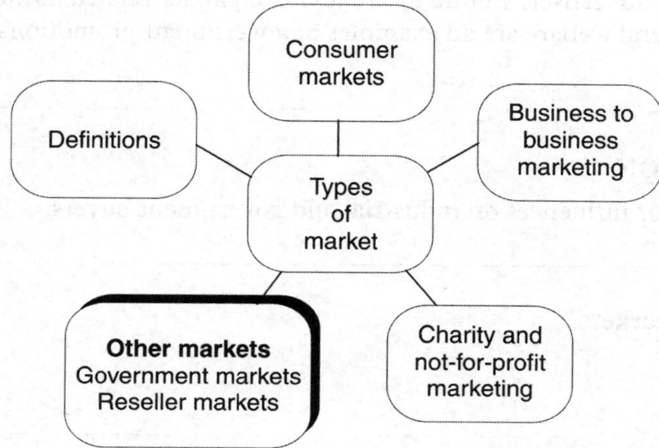

5.1 Government markets

The government offers a huge opportunity for many companies, many of whom rely on the government market for a large portion of their sales. Defence contractors are a key example, but governments also buy for schools, highways, hospitals, housing and information technology projects. A hospital purchaser of food, for example, has to search for a vendor whose food meets minimum quality standards, but whose prices are low.

Like consumer and industrial buyers, government buyers are affected by environmental and other factors, but a unique influence is that government activity is very carefully **scrutinised by outside observers.**

Government buyers are **accountable** to the public and perhaps as a result of this there is a lot of red tape to be cut through. The seller must identify **key decision makers** and understand the **buyer decision** process, much as for consumer or industrial marketing strategies.

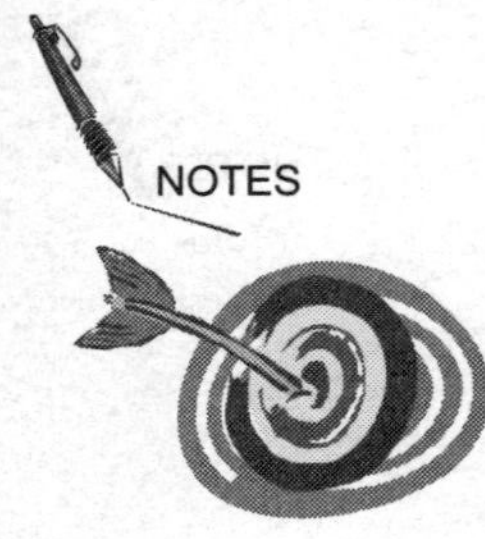

EXAMPLE

The government is often keen to attract new suppliers. Public purchasing accounts for around 11% of European GDP, and the information technology revolution is playing its part. The European Commission set a target of 25% of public procurement to be done via e-commerce by the end of 2003.

Total government spending is generally determined by **budget considerations** rather than commercial pressures or marketing decisions. They typically require suppliers to submit **bids**, and **price** is usually emphasised. With **product specifications** being carefully set out, differentiation is not a marketing factor.

Nevertheless, some companies, such as Eastman Kodak in the US, have set up separate departments to handle marketing to the government. This may lead to more proactive proposals of projects (rather than merely reactive responses to government requests).

Governments also are key marketers in their own right with the UK government being the single largest advertiser. Public awareness campaigns related to health, anti-drink, smoking and general welfare are all examples of government promotions.

FOR DISCUSSION

Compare the major influences on industrial and government buyers.

5.2 Reseller markets

Definition

The **reseller market** is all the individuals and organisations that resell or rent bought-in goods to others. They are essentially purchasing agents for their own customers. Most goods that are produced pass through some kind of reseller, such as a retailer or supermarket.

Reseller buyer behaviour is rather similar industrial buyer behaviour, but they have different influences. They buy products and brands that they think will appeal to customers. This affects what suppliers they choose, and the price they are prepared to pay. Buying is a **specialised function** in organisations such as supermarkets.

Resellers need to consider factors apart from just cost when choosing products for their outlets. These may include:

- Anticipated resale price and margin
- Appeal of the product to the customer
- Proposed marketing plan and advertising support
- Reputation of the selling company

The selling company therefore has to make sure that its product is an attractive proposition for the reseller. In the UK, the top supermarkets have a lot of power over their suppliers and have been criticised for using that power to negotiate deals that the supplier may have little option but to accept.

EXAMPLE

A recent example is the complaint by farmers in the UK over the low prices paid by the supermarkets for their meat (with no corresponding savings, it is alleged, being passed on the consumers).

Chapter roundup

- Three main types of market are fast moving consumer goods, consumer durables and industrial goods. Definitions are given at the beginning of the chapter.
- Business markets have their own particular needs, as the purchasing decision is often more complex and involves many people. Personal contact is often a key part of the buying decision.
- Industrial products are distinguished by technical sophistication, high unit values and irregularity of purchase.
- A marketing orientation is just as valid within the industrial sector as it is in the consumer goods sector, but the marketing mix differs.
- Consumer goods are often heavily advertised on TV, whereas industrial marketing may be limited to trade magazines or personal selling.
- Most business-to-business marketing often involves an element of adding value for the customer through service, such as after-sales maintenance agreements.
- Price in industrial markets is negotiable to a much greater extent.
- Not-for-profit marketing initiatives are aimed at achieving a particular response from target markets (donors, volunteers, for example) rather than achieving a profit objective. They often deal more with services than products.
- Government markets may be characterised by bureaucracy, but they are accountable to outside observers and so face many different pressures than those facing industrial or consumer markets. A low price is often the most important factor in the purchase decision.
- The reseller market is all the individuals and organisations (such as a supermarket) that resell or rent bought-in goods to others. Sellers to such organisations have to ensure that their product is an attractive purchase.

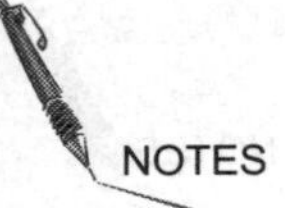

Quick quiz

1 What are the important features of fast moving consumer goods?

2 What are the distinctive characteristics of shopping goods?

3 How do business buyers differ from other consumers?

4 What level of personal selling is normally associated with FMCG?

5 How may industrial goods be classified?

6 Why are industrial products distinctive?

7 How does 'product' differ in industrial marketing when compared to consumer marketing?

8 Why is the extended marketing mix of people, process and physical evidence important in not for profit marketing?

9 What is the unique factor which characterises government markets?

10 Give an example of a reseller.

Answers to Quick quiz

1 Frequent purchase, low price, low risk, impulse buys, basic goods, minimal effort.

2 Shopping goods represent a bit more of a risk to consumers who become more willing to shop around as a result. They are infrequent, relatively expensive and long-lasting purchases.

Infrequent, expensive and long-lasting.

3 Buyers not spending own money; DMU may involve many people; lengthy process; customer base small, quantities and values high; importance of relationships and contacts.

4 Low to the domestic customer; medium to the trade customer.

5 Capital goods, accessories, raw materials, components, supplies and business services.

6 Conform with standards; sophisticated, high unit values, irregular purchases.

7 Product probably includes service as well as product (pre-sales and after sales)

8 Because such organisations often deal with services and ideas rather than tangible products. People, for example, need to offer a good service to their clients, be they hospital patients or the recipients of donations. Appearance has to be professional and business-like rather than extravagant (no corporate hospitality or lavish promotion, for example).

9 The fact that their purchasing decisions are scrutinised by outside observers, keen to see that Government resources are not squandered.

10 A retailer such as a supermarket.

Answers to Activities

1 and 2 The solutions will depend on your own experience. You may have gathered information from advertisements in various media, or from friends who had made similar purchases or from consumer reports such as *Which?* You may have been primarily concerned with, for instance, durability or fashion.

3 Examples of government publications include:

(a) The *Annual Abstract of Statistics* and its monthly equivalent, the *Monthly Digest of Statistics*. These contain a wide variety of data about manufacturing output, housing, population and so on.

(b) The *Digest of UK Energy Statistics* (published annually).

(c) *Housing and Construction Statistics* (published quarterly).

(d) *Financial Statistics* (monthly).

(e) *Economic Trends* (monthly).

(f) *Census of Population*. The Office for National Statistics publish continuous datasets including the *National Food Survey*, the *Household Survey* and the *Family Expenditure Survey*.

(g) *Census of Production* (annual). This has been described as 'one of the most important sources of desk research for industrial marketers'. It provides data about production by firms in each industry in the UK.

(h) *Employment Gazette* (monthly) giving details of employment in the UK.

(i) *British Business*, published weekly by the Department of Trade and Industry, giving data on industrial and commercial trends at home and overseas.

(j) *Business Monitor* (published by the Business Statistics Office), giving detailed information about various industries.

(k) *Social Trends* (annually).

4 Possible objectives include the following.

- Surplus maximisation
- Revenue maximisation
- Usage maximisation
- Usage targeting to make sure capacity is used properly
- Cost recovery
- Budget maximisation
- Satisfying staff and volunteers
- Satisfying the public

Answers to activities

1 and 2 Your solutions will depend on your own experience. You may have gathered information from advertisements in various media or from friends who have made similar purchases or from consumer reports such as *Which?* You may have been primarily concerned with fashion/looks or durability or fashion.

3 Examples of government publications include:

(a) The *Annual Abstract of Statistics* and its monthly equivalent, the *Monthly Digest of Statistics*. These contain a wide variety of data about manufacturing output, housing, population and so on.

(b) The *Digest of UK Energy Statistics* (published annually)

(c) *Housing and Construction Statistics* (published quarterly)

(d) *Financial Statistics* (monthly)

(e) *Economic Trends* (monthly)

(f) *Census of Population*. The Office for National Statistics publishes continuous datasets including the *National Food Survey*, the [illegible] Survey and the *Family Expenditure Survey*.

(g) *Census of Production* (annual). This has been described as one of the most important sources of desk research for industrial marketers. It provides data about production by firms in each industry in the UK.

(h) *Employment Gazette* (monthly) giving details of employment in the

(i) *British Business*, published weekly by the Department of Trade and Industry, giving data on industrial and commercial trends at home and overseas.

(j) *Business Monitor* (published by the Government Statistics Office), giving detailed information about various industries.

(k) *Social Trends* (annually)

4 Possible objectives include the following.

- Surplus maximisation
- Revenue maximisation
- Usage maximisation
- Usage targeting to make services available to as many as possible
- Cost recovery
- Budget maximisation
- Satisfying stakeholders
- Satisfying the public

Chapter 15 : SERVICES MARKETING

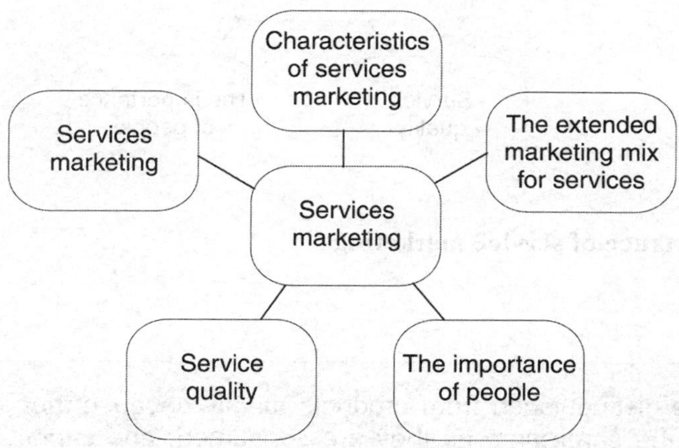

Introduction

'Product' is a generic term and can in many cases include 'services' for the practical purpose of marketing. The service sector has grown rapidly in recent years in the UK, both as an employer and in terms of its contribution to GDP.

There are certain basic characteristics of service industries which differentiate them from other business operations. These characteristics mean that the successful marketing and delivery of services requires attention to areas not really covered by the 4 Ps: who gives the service (people); how the service is given (process); the environment in which the service is given (physical evidence).

The nature of quality in services is complex. This chapter discusses what it is and how to measure it.

Your objectives

In this chapter you will learn about the following.

(a) The importance of having a separate marketing mix for services

(b) The features of services marketing

(c) The nature and characteristics of services, and what they imply for marketing strategy

(d) The importance of people in service industry

(e) The issue of service quality

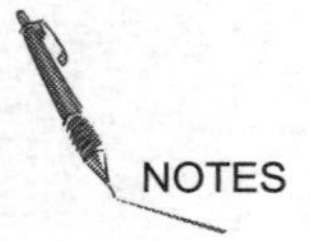

1 SERVICES MARKETING

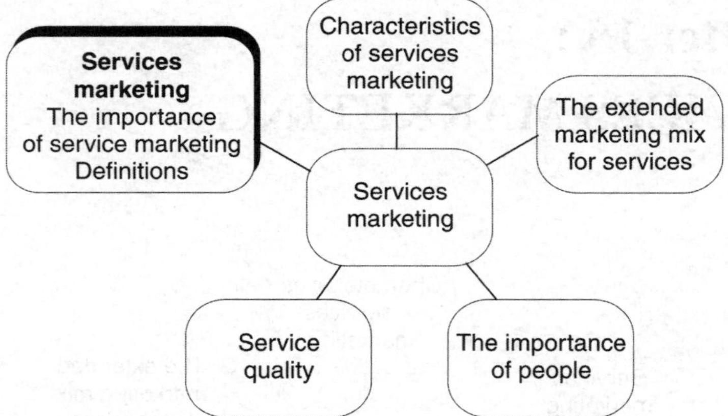

1.1 The importance of service marketing

Definition

Services are distinguished from products mainly because they are generally produced at the same time as they are consumed, and cannot be stored or taken away. An enhanced marketing mix needs to be deployed.

(a) **The growth of service sectors in advanced industrial societies.** More people now work in the service sector than in all other sectors of the economy and the major contributors to national output are the public and private service sectors. Invisible earnings from abroad are of increasing significance for Britain's balance of trade.

(b) **An increasingly market-oriented trend within service-providing organisations.** This has been particularly apparent within the public sector with the advent of internal markets, market testing and the chartermark.

It is often very difficult to distinguish between products and services because frequently there is a service element attached to many products such as a customer helpline in the bank of a food products. Retailers are actually by nature services but tend to be judged the quality of the products they sell.

EXAMPLE

The public sector in Britain includes service provision in the legal, medical, educational, military, employment, transportation, leisure and information fields. Increasingly, there is a focus on profits in many of these areas. The private sector embraces not-for-profit areas such as the arts, charities and religious and educational organisations and includes business and professional services in travel, finance, insurance, management, the law, building, commerce and entertainment.

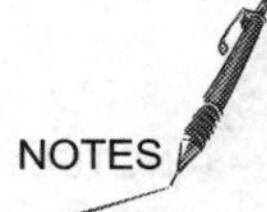

1.2 Services: some more definitions

(a) ' ... those separately identifiable but intangible activities that provide want-satisfaction, and that are not, of necessity, tied to, or inextricable from, the sale of a product or another service.' *Donald Cowell, The Marketing of Services*

(b) ' ... any activity of benefit that one party can offer to another that is essentially intangible and does not result in the ownership of anything. Its production may or may not be tied to a physical product.' *P Kotler, Social Marketing*

Marketing services faces a number of distinct problems, and as a consequence, the approach adopted must be varied, and particular marketing practices developed.

2 CHARACTERISTICS OF SERVICES MARKETING

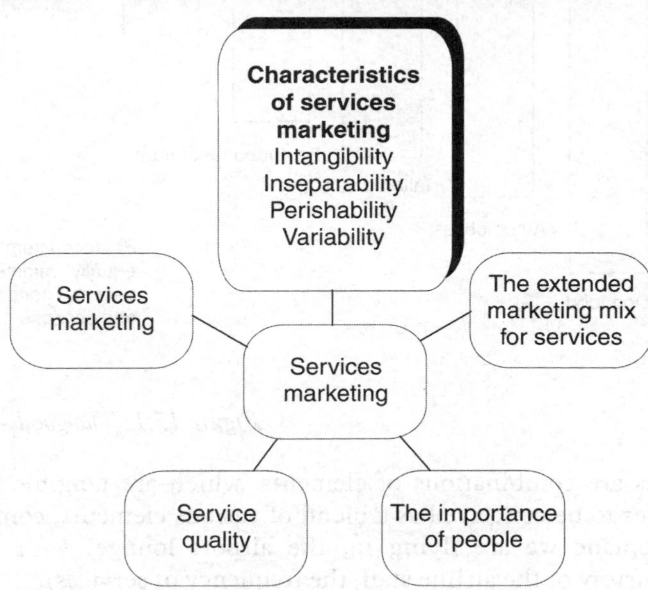

Characteristics of services which make them distinctive from the marketing of goods have been proposed. There are five major differences which we have encountered earlier in this book, but we will look at them in this chapter in detail.

- Intangibility
- Inseparability
- Perishability
- Variability

2.1 Intangibility

Intangibility refers to the **lack of physical substance** which is involved with service delivery. Unlike a product there is nothing to touch, feel or smell. Clearly, this creates difficulties and can inhibit the propensity to consume a service, since customers are not sure what they have.

It has been suggested that we view this insubstantiality as a **continuum,** as shown in the diagram below.

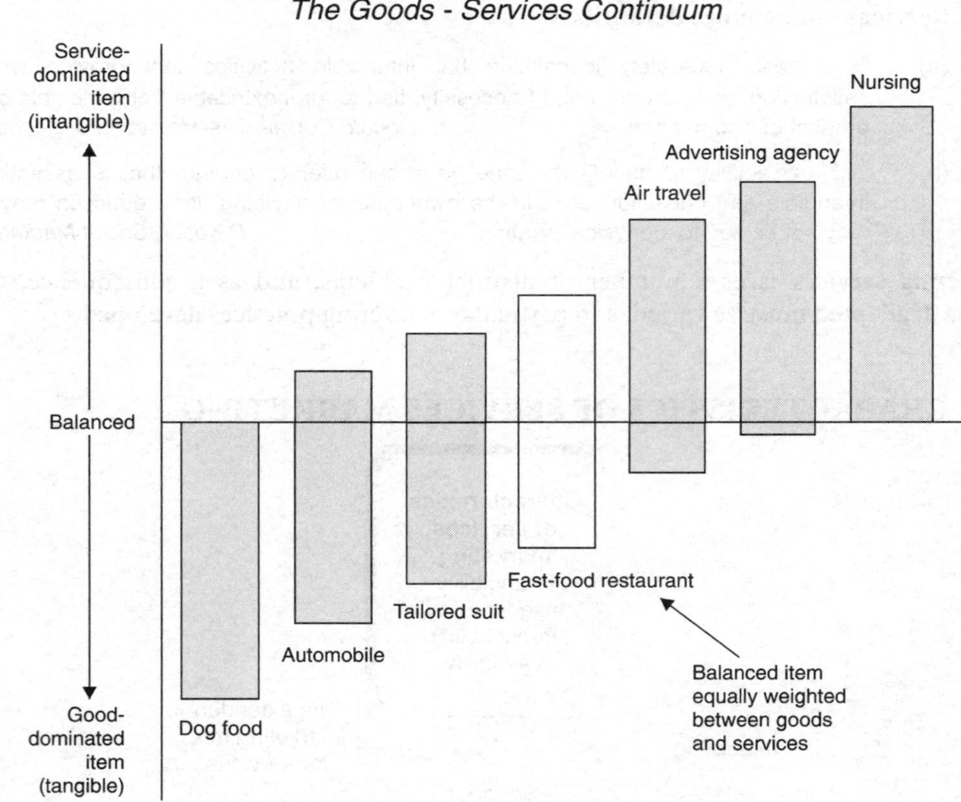

Figure 15.1: The goods-service continuum

Marketing entities are combinations of elements, which are tangible or intangible. A product then comes to be conceived as a blend of various elements, combining **material entities** (the aeroplane we are flying in, the airport lounge) with various sorts of **processes** (the courtesy of the airline staff, the frequency of services).

The intangibility may be countered in two ways.

- By the consumer seeking **opinions** from other consumers
- By the marketer offering the consumer something **tangible** to represent the purchase

Activity 1 **(15 minutes)**

A national charity wants to send out a mailshot to attract donations. Describe what you suggest receivers should find in the envelope. (Note: the charity faces the same problems as a typical service provider. The key is to overcome the lack of a physical product.)

Marketing implications

Dealing with the problems may involve strategies to **enhance tangibility**.

(a) **Increasing the level of tangibility**. When dealing with the customer, staff can use physical representations or illustrations to make the customer feel more confident as to what it is that the service is delivering.

(b) **Focusing the attention of the customer on the principal benefits of consumption.** This could take the form of communicating the benefits of purchasing the service so that the customer visualises its appropriateness. Promotion and sales material could provide images or records of previous customers' experience.

(c) **Differentiating the service and reputation-building.** This is achieved by enhancing perceptions of service and value through offering excellence in the delivery of the service and by promoting values of quality, service reliability and value for money.

EXAMPLE

The online retailer Amazon is a service provider with many intangible elements to its service. In order to provide reassurance and a more tangible dimension Amazon will focus on aspects such as the look and quality of the packaging and related paperwork they use when sending out goods to consumers. The retailer will also be able to use the physical look of their website and incorporate features such as order tracking so that the consumer gains more of an understanding of the service process.

With very few exceptions, credible online retailers will include a page on their website called something along the lines of 'About Us' where often there are photographs of actual shops, warehouses and other corporate premised to reassure consumers that although they are an online company, they are real, actually do have a physical representation and are not just a cyberspace image or are operating from a dodgy lounge.

Services do not result in the transfer of property. In the case of purchasing a product, there is permanent transfer of title and control over the use of an item. An item of service provision is often defined by the **length of time** it is available.

This may very well lessen the perceived customer value of a service, and consequently make for unfavourable comparisons with **tangible** alternatives. Attempts have been made to overcome this problem by providing **symbolic tangible items** which can be taken away and kept. Car brochures, theatre programmes and the plethora of corporate giftwares such as golf umbrellas, pens and keyrings are all examples of this.

Activity 2 **(10 minutes)**

What are the marketing implications of the lack of ownership of a service received?

2.2 Inseparability

A service often cannot be separated from the provider of the service. The **performance of a service often occurs at the same instant as its consumption.** Think of having dental treatment or going on a journey. Neither exists until actually consumed by the purchaser.

Activity 3 **(10 minutes)**

Consider a visit to the dentist to buy the product, dental treatment.

What is the importance of the three extra elements of the service mix to you as the customer?

Marketing implications

Provision of the service may not be separable from the provider. Consequently, increasing importance is attached to **values of quality and reliability** and a customer service ethic which can be transferred to the service provision. This emphasises the need for **customer orientation**, high quality **people** and high quality **training** for them.

Another implication relates to the role the consumer plays in creating a positive service experience. Imagine for example you visit a hair salon. It is very true to say that not all hairdressers are equally skilled and most people will at some point in their lives have a horror story to tell of an overzealous scissor wielding hairdresser. The issue in that instance for the salon is clearly one of improving training. There are occasions however when clients visit the salon with an unclear idea about the hairstyle they would like. Unless they are able to explain clearly what they would like, it is pretty much inevitable that they will be disappointed with the end result.

2.3 Perishability

Services cannot be stored. They are innately **perishable**. Performances at a theatre or the services of a chiropodist consist in their availability for periods of time, and if they are not occupied, the service they offer cannot be used later.

This presents specific marketing problems. Meeting customer needs in these operations depends on **staff being available** when they are needed. This must be balanced against the need to minimise unnecessary expenditure on staff wages. Anticipating and responding to **levels of demand** is, therefore, a key planning priority. There are two risks.

- Inadequate level of demand, accompanied by substantial fixed costs.
- Excess demand may result in lost custom through inadequate service.

Policies must seek to **match demand with supply** by price variations and promotions to stimulate off-peak demand.

EXAMPLE

The selling of last minute holidays is a way that tour operators manage to cope with the uneven patterns of supply and demand. Often holidays are sold with little or no contribution to hotel costs in order to fill aircraft seats.

2.4 Variability (or heterogeneity)

Many services face a problem of **maintaining consistency in the standard of output**. **Variability of quality in delivery** is inevitable, because of the number of factors which may influence it. This may create problems of operations management. For example, it may be difficult or impossible to attain:

(a) **Precise standardisation of the service offered**. The quality of the service may depend heavily on who delivers the service and when it takes place. Booking a holiday using standard procedures may well be quite different on a quiet winter afternoon than on a hectic spring weekend, and may well vary according to the person dealing with the client.

(b) **Influence or control over perceptions of what is good or bad customer service.** From the customer's perspective, it is very difficult to obtain an idea of the quality of service in advance of purchase.

Marketing implications

It is necessary to monitor **customer reactions** constantly and to maintain an attitude and organisational culture which emphasises three things.

- Consistency of **quality** control
- Consistency of **customer service**
- Effective staff **selection, training and motivation**

Other important matters

(a) Clear and objective **quality measures**

(b) **Standardising** as much as possible within the service

(c) The **Pareto principle** (80 per cent of difficulties arise from 20 per cent of events surrounding the provision of the service). Therefore, identify and respond most closely to these potential troublespots.

EXAMPLE

Despite the store being open until 10pm Monday to Saturday, ordering a new kitchen in Ikea varies considerably with regard to service levels if done after 8pm. After 8pm the call centre resposibile for delivery dates closes and so the service process is more complex for consumers.

3 THE EXTENDED MARKETING MIX FOR SERVICES

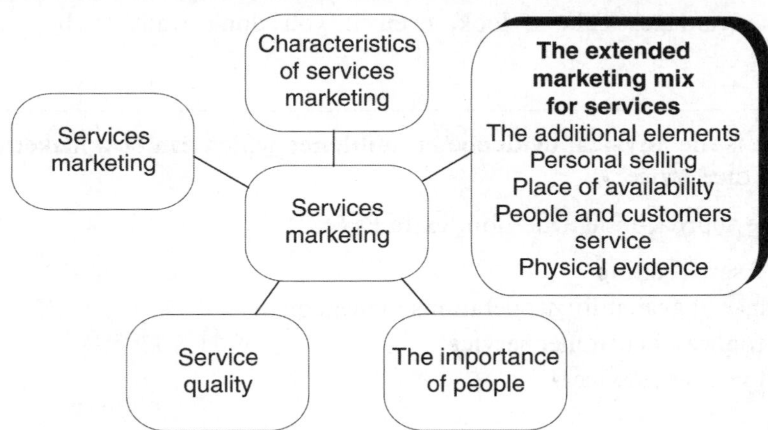

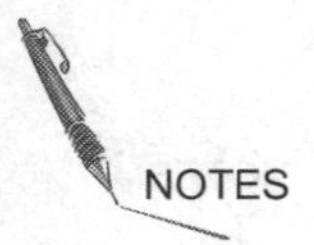

3.1 The additional elements

EXAMPLE

A service does not primarily involve a physical product. If you go on a train journey the ticket itself does not transport you to your destination, and you do not get to keep the train.

Most products have some element of service in them, too. If you buy a product over the telephone your purchase may be enhanced by friendly and helpful service from the telesales assistant. So where do **people** feature? And the telesales assistant may be able to offer that help because the ordering **process** is managed by a sophisticated customer and product database and a customer relationship management system.

The standard 4P approach to the marketing of products should therefore be extended for services to make 7Ps.

- People
- Process
- Physical evidence or ambience

in addition to product, price, place and promotion

Services are provided by **people** for people. If the people providing the service are wrong, the service is spoiled. In the case of a bus service, a cheap fare, a clean vehicle and a frequent service can be spoiled by a surly driver.

Services are usually provided in a number of sequential steps. This is **process.** The service can be spoiled or enhanced at any step in the sequence.

EXAMPLE

Efficient processes can become a marketing advantage in their own right. Dell's success is due as much to the remarkable efficiency of its ordering and customer information system as it is to the quality and manufacturing efficiency of its production system. The company's strapline is 'Easy as Dell', which refers to the process and sums up Dell's competitive advantage. Take a look, even if you don't want to buy a computer: www.dell.com.

Finally, there is the **physical evidence** or **ambience** which can be a maker or spoiler of experience of the service.

An alternative approach identifies four extra Ps.

- Personal selling
- Place of availability (operations management)
- People and customer service
- Physical evidence

3.2 Personal selling

Personal selling is very important in the marketing of services, because of the greater **perceived risk** involved and greater **uncertainty** about quality and reliability. The reputation of the supplier may be of greater importance, and the customer places greater

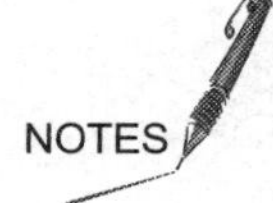

reliance on the honesty of the individual salesperson. When consumers seek reassurance, personal contact with a competent, effective representative may provide the necessary confidence. Conversely, inappropriate selling may generate increased anxiety. The electrical retail industry was disappointed when grocery retailers started selling TVs and other electrical items. They cited lack of sales advice as a problem associated with this distribution channel.

3.3 Place of availability

Place of availability is really covered by the distribution system, but there are special problems for services in **operations management**. The place and frequency of availability are key service variables but service resources must be used economically.

The level and quality of service are sensitive to the efficiency of the processes by which services are delivered. There are three key factors.

- **Capacity utilisation**: matching demand sequences to staff utilisation to avoid both the costs of overstaffing and the lost revenue of underprovision
- **Managing customer contact**, to avoid crowding and customer disruption, meet needs as they arise, and increase employee control over interactions
- **Establishing objectives within the not-for-profit sector**, for example, standards for teachers or medical staff

Interactions between customers are a key strategic issue. Customers often interact to gather information and form views about the service they are contemplating purchasing. Minimising exposure to negative feedback, and promoting the dissemination of positive messages about the service are important objectives.

3.4 People and customer service

For some services, the **physical presence of people** performing the service is a vital aspect of customer satisfaction. For example, staff in catering establishments are performing or producing a service, selling the service and liaising with the customer to promote the service, gather information and respond to customer needs. **Customer orientation** is needed in all sectors of organisational activity.

A customer orientation on the part of staff will be evidenced through:

- Appearance
- Attitude
- Commitment
- Behaviour
- Professionalism
- Skills
- Discretion

Customers will tend to use cues to establish a view about the organisation from the demeanour and behaviour of staff. The higher the level of customer contact involved in the delivery of a service, the more crucial is the **staff role** in adding value. In many cases, the **delivery of the service and the physical presence of the personnel** involved are completely inseparable.

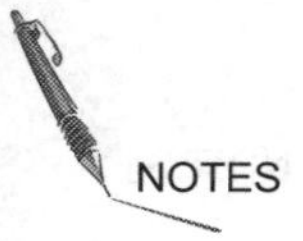

EXAMPLE: ORDER OF SERVICE

We British have been exercising our right to complain, according to the OFT. But how do you avoid bad customer service in the first place?

The British may not like complaining, but it seems we still do an awful lot of it. Nearly a third of UK consumers have made an official complaint in the past 12 months, involving an average sum of £930, according to research for the Office of Fair Trading (OFT).

The study, which involved more than 1,000 people around the country, found that of those who made a complaint 67% found the process stressful. Half of the stressed complainants said the outcome achieved was poor and, as a result, 48% would choose not to use the business again, while 74% would not recommend the company to others.

Customer satisfaction was greater when businesses had an easy-to-follow complaints procedure in place. In these circumstances 73% of complainants said they would do business with the offending firm again, and 57% claimed they would even recommend the firm to others.

guardian.co.uk/money/blog, 27 November 2009

Activity 4 **(10 minutes)**

All levels of staff must be involved in customer service. To achieve this end, it is vital for senior management to promote the importance of customer service. How do you think that this might be achieved?

3.5 Physical evidence

Physical evidence is an important remedy for the intangibility of the product. This may be associated with the service itself, (for example, credit cards which represent the service available to customers); built up by **identification with a specific individual** (a 'listening' bank manager); or incorporated into the **design and specification** of the service environment, involving the building, location or atmosphere.

Activity 5 **(10 minutes)**

What do you think that design can achieve in services marketing?

4 THE IMPORTANCE OF PEOPLE

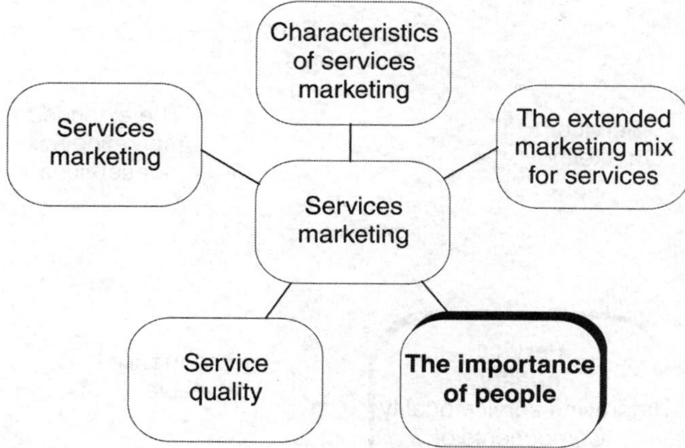

As a consequence of the importance of people, service marketing organisations have certain common areas of emphasis.

(a) Selection and training

(b) Internal marketing to promulgate the culture of service within the firm

(c) Ensuring conformance with standards

- Behaviour
- Dress and appearance
- Procedures
- Modes of dealing with the public

(d) Mechanising procedures where possible

(e) Constantly auditing personnel performance and behaviour

(f) Extending the promotion of the service and its qualities into the design of service environments and the engineering of interactions between staff and customers and among the customers themselves.

Activity 6 **(10 minutes)**

The role of people in services marketing is especially important. What human characteristics improve the quality of client service?

5 SERVICE QUALITY

Definition

Service quality is the totality of features and characteristics of that service which bears on its ability to meet customer needs.

Service quality is a significant basis which customers use for differentiating between competing services.

Quality can only be defined by customers. It occurs where a firm supplies products to a specification that satisfies their needs. Customer expectations serve as standards against which subsequent service experiences are compared.

5.1 Improving service quality

There are two ways firms can gain from improving their quality of service.

(a) **Higher sales revenues** and improved marketing effectiveness brought about by improved customer retention, positive word-of-mouth recommendations and the ability to increase prices.

(b) **Improved productivity and reduced costs** because there is less rework, higher employee morale and lower employee turnover.

Grönroos introduced the concept of 'perceived service quality' in 1982 and extended this in the development of his widely cited **model of service quality** in 1984.

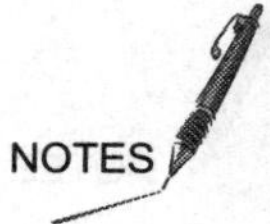

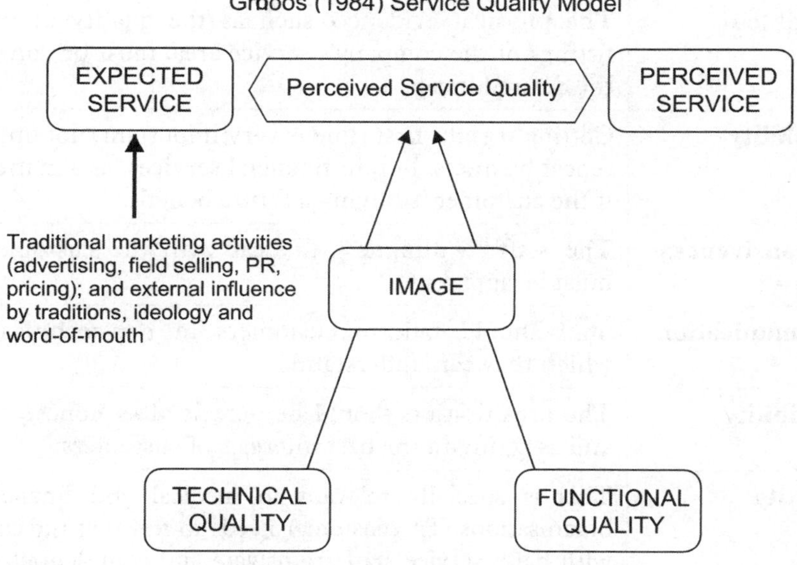

Figure 15.2: Grönroos (1984) Service Quality model

The model suggests that the quality of a given service is the outcome of an evaluation process where consumers **compare** what they **expected to receive** with what they **perceive** that they actually received. Consumer expectations are influenced by marketing mix activities, external traditions, ideology and word-of-mouth communications.

5.2 Components of service quality

In terms of perceived service quality, there are two principal components of quality, **technical** and **functional**, with a third, **image**, acting as a mediating influence.

(a) **Technical quality** is what the customer is left with, when the production process is finished. For example, in higher education this would be perceived as the level of attainment and understanding achieved at the end of the course. This can be much more easily measured by the consumer.

(b) **Functional quality,** on the other hand, is more difficult to measure objectively because it involves an evaluation of how the consumer receives the technical quality in the interactions between customer and service provider and other customers. Service quality is dependent both on what you receive and how you receive it.

Both expectations and perceptions are affected by the consumer's view of the company and by its **image**. If a consumer has a positive image of a university or lecturer but has a negative experience, for example a rather confused lecture, the consumer may still **perceive** the service to be satisfactory because he or she will find excuses for the negative experience.

NOTES

The major determinants of service quality can be seen to fit into a number of areas.

Tangibles	The physical evidence, such as the quality of fixtures and fittings of the company's service area, must be consistent with the desired image.
Reliability	Getting it right first time is very important, not only to ensure repeat business, but, in financial services, as a matter of ethics, if the customer is buying a future benefit.
Responsiveness	The staff's willingness to deal with the customer's queries must be apparent.
Communication	Staff should talk to customers in non-technical language which they can understand.
Credibility	The organisation should be perceived as honest, trustworthy and as acting in the best interests of customers.
Security	This is specially relevant to medical and financial services organisations. The customer needs to feel that the conversations with bank service staff are private and confidential. This factor should influence the design of the service area.
Competence	All the service staff need to appear competent in understanding the product range and interpreting the needs of the customers.
Courtesy	Customers (even rude ones) should perceive service staff as polite, respectful and friendly.
Understanding customers' needs	The use of computer-based customer databases can be very impressive in this context. The service personnel can then call up the customer's records and use these data in the service process, thus personalising the process. Service staff need to meet customer needs rather than try to sell products. This is a subtle but important difference.
Access	Minimising queues, having a fair queuing system and speedy service are all factors which can avoid customers' irritation building up. A pleasant relaxing environment is a useful design factor in this context.

Figure 15.3: Determinants of service quality

Once a firm knows how it is performing on each of the dimensions of service quality it can use a number of methods to try to improve.

(a) Development of a **customer orientated mission statement** and clear senior management support for quality improvement initiatives

(b) Regular **customer satisfaction research** including customer surveys and panels, mystery shoppers, analysis of complaints and similar industry studies for benchmarking purposes

(c) Setting and **monitoring standards** and communicating results

(d) Establishment of systems for customers **complaints and feedback**

(e) Encouragement of **employee participation**, ideas and initiative, often through the use of quality circles and project teams

(f) Rewarding **excellent service**

FOR DISCUSSION

What evidence do you see of firms implementing quality programmes and continually improving service quality?

Chapter roundup

- The extension of the service sector, and the application of market principles across many public sector and ex-public sector organisations, has made a large number of service providers much more marketing-conscious.
- Services marketing differs from the marketing of other goods in a number of crucial ways, and five specific characteristics of services marketing have been proposed:
  - Intangibility
  - Inseparability
  - Heterogeneity/variability
  - Perishability
  - Ownership
- An extended marketing mix has been suggested for services marketing. Here, we have taken an approach which analyses an additional 4Ps:
  - Personal selling
  - Place of availability
  - People and customer service
  - Physical evidence
- Service quality can be defined as the difference between what the customer expects and what he or she perceives him/herself to be receiving. Improved service quality leads to higher profits and is a key task for service marketers.

Quick quiz

1. What are the marketing characteristics of services?
2. What are the marketing implications of the intangibility of services?
3. What issues arise from the perishability of services being marketed?
4. How can the problems of lack of ownership be overcome in service marketing?
5. What are the additional 'Ps' in the service marketing mix?
6. In what areas should rigorous procedures be applied to take account of the importance of people in services marketing?
7. In what two ways can firms gain by improving their quality of service to customers?
8. What is 'quality' in marketing terms?

Answers to Quick quiz

1. Intangibility
   Inseparability
   Perishability
   Variability
2. The marketer needs strategies to increase tangibility, such as focusing the customer on the benefits of consumption and enhancing the service's reputation.
3. Services cannot be stored; staff must be available; demand must be anticipated; demand must match supply.
4. Symbolic tangible items may be given away instead (see also Activity 3).
5. People
   Process
   Physical evidence
   and:

   Personal selling
   Place of availability
   People/customer service
6. Selection and training; internal marketing; ensuring conformity with standards; mechanising procedures; monitoring performance.
7. Higher sales revenue
   Improved productivity and reduced costs
8. There are various definitions, but essentially it is defined by the consumer and is manifested when a consumer compares what he or she expected to receive with what they think they actually received.

Answers to Activities

1. You may well have received such a mailshot yourself. One sent by from the National Society for the Prevention of Cruelty to Children (NSPCC) contained five items in an envelope printed with a black and white photo of a sad and neglected little girl. The five items were as follows.

   (a) An A3 sheet folded to make a four A4 page letter printed in two colours and with more black and white photos of neglected children on paper with a recycled feel. The letter tells the story of Ellie, the child shown on the envelope, and in emotive language, asks for £15 and describes what good can be done with that money by the NSPCC.

   (b) An A5 size donation form printed on both sides. You can tick a box saying '£15' or fill in your own amount. You can give your credit card details. You can opt *not* to receive further mailings. On the other side, Ellie's story and NSPCC action is described again in a sort of brief 'photo-story'.

   (c) An envelope addressed to the Director of the NSPCC at a FREEPOST address (but suggesting that if you use a stamp it will save the NSPCC the postage).

   (d) A 'Thank You' card with a picture of Ellie smiling on the front, a further plea from the Director of the NSPCC, and a thank you message in a 'hand-written' typeface.

   (e) A car sticker saying 'Support the NSPCC'.

2 Possible marketing implications.

(a) Promote the advantages of non-ownership. This can be done by emphasising, in promotion, the benefits of paid-for maintenance, and periodic upgrading of the product. Radio Rentals have used this as a major selling proposition with great success.

(b) Make available a tangible symbol or representation of ownership (certificate, membership of professional association). This can come to embody the benefits enjoyed.

(c) Increasing the chances or opportunity of ownership (eg time-shares, shares in the organisation for regular customers).

3 *People:* it is very important what sort of person the dentist is. A good chairside manner is as critical to you as clinical training. If the dentist is caring, gentle, reassuring, the 'package' will be enhanced.

Physical evidence: start with the environment. It probably will be relaxing, decorated and furnished in good taste; perhaps a soporific and diverting aquarium; confidence inspiring by reference to the diplomas, the presence of white uniformed nurses; there will be impressive equipment, modern and with the appearance of high quality engineering.

Process: how we are received and dealt with. Kindly, efficiently, professionally, quickly but without haste. Are we expected in the appointments book; are we seen on time? Are we asked to make a further appointment and does the process takes us easily from the surgeon to the hygienist or the radiographer smoothly? As well as the professionalism and attentiveness of the staff, does the *system* work?

4 There must be continuous development of service-enhancing practice.

- Policies on selection
- Programmes of training
- Standard, consistent operational practices
- Standardised operational rules
- Effective motivational programmes
- Managerial appointments
- The attractiveness and appropriateness of the service offer
- Effective policies of staff reward and remuneration

5 Things design can do:

- Convey the nature of the service involved
- Transmit messages and information
- Imply aesthetic qualities, moral values, or other socio-cultural aspects of a corporate image
- Reinforce an existing image
- Reassure
- Engender an emotional reaction in the customer, through sensory and symbolic blends

6 The following are all dimensions of client service quality.

- *Problem solving creativity:* looking beyond the obvious and not being bound by accepted professional and technical approaches
- *Initiative:* anticipating problems and opportunities and not just reacting

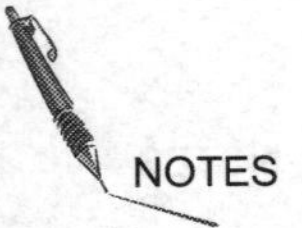

- *Efficiency:* keeping client costs down through effective work planning and control
- *Fast response:* responding to enquiries, questions, problems as quickly as possible
- *Timeliness:* starting and finishing service work to agreed deadlines
- *Open-mindedness:* professionals not being 'blinkered' by their technical approach
- *Sound judgement:* professionals such as accountants dealing with the wider aspects of their technical specialisations
- *Functional expertise:* need to bring together all the functional skills necessary from whatever sources to work on a client project
- *Industry expertise:* clients expect professionals to be thoroughly familiar with their industry and recent changes in it
- *Managerial effectiveness:* maintaining a focus upon the use of both the firm's and the client's resources
- *Orderly work approach:* clients expect salient issues to be identified early and do not want last minute surprises
- *Commitment:* clients evaluate the calibre of the staff and the individual attention given
- *Long-range focus:* clients prefer long-term relationships rather than 'projects' or 'jobs'
- *Continuity:* clients do not like firms who constantly change the staff that work with them — they will evaluate staff continuity as part of an ongoing relationship
- *Personality:* clients will also evaluate the friendliness, understanding and co-operation of the service provider

Chapter 16 : INTERNATIONAL MARKETS

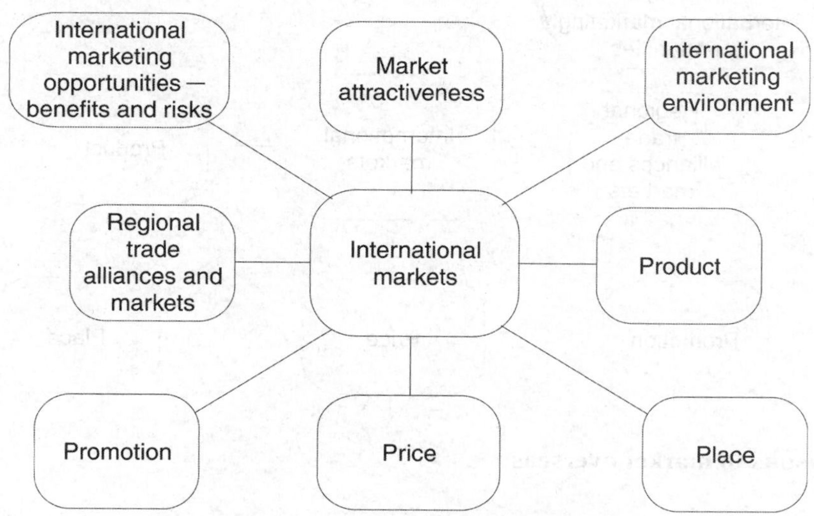

Introduction

Firms must deal with six major issues in international marketing.

- Whether to market abroad at all
- Which markets to enter
- The mode of entry
- Marketing programmes
- Marketing organisation
- Marketing mix

International marketing presents a new set of challenges for the marketer. First, the marketing **information needs** are great and cannot be satisfied as easily as at home. The marketing **environment** is different, with each country having its own characteristic laws and culture. Regional trade alliances between countries present difficulties and opportunities which must be addressed if the organisation's strategy is to be successful.

Key decisions relate to **adapting** the marketing mix and the **means** by which a firm will enter the overseas market.

Your objectives
In this chapter you will learn about the following.

(a) The background to and context of world trade

(b) Why companies and countries trade

(c) What is meant by international marketing

(d) Factors that influence the world trading environment, such as globalisation

(e) How the marketing mix can be adapted for international markets

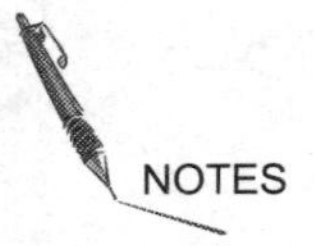

1 INTERNATIONAL MARKETING OPPORTUNITIES – BENEFITS AND RISKS

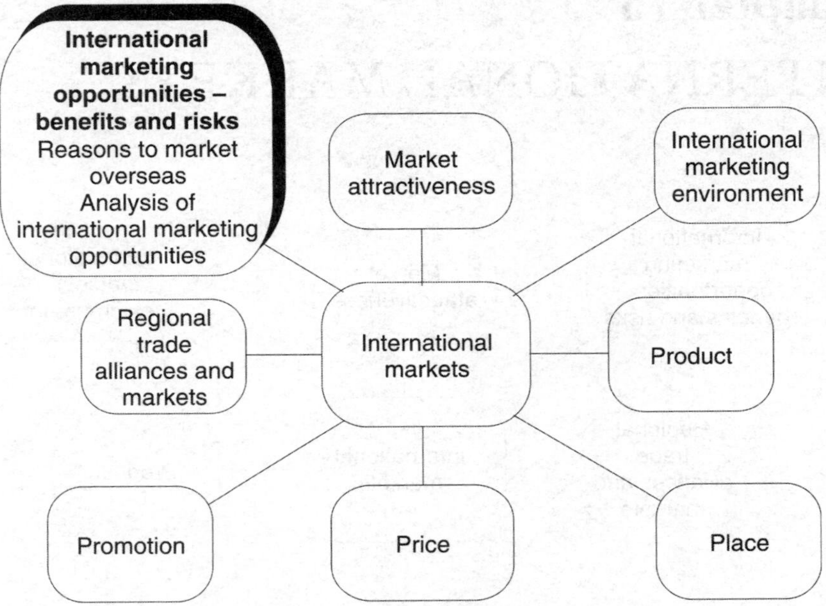

1.1 Reasons to market overseas

Definition

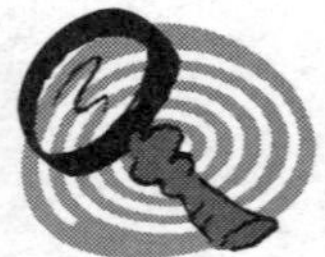

> **International marketing** (IM) refers to the marketing of goods and services in two or more countries.

Most businesses pursue profits. An overseas market or the global market offers larger profits. Companies will enter into international marketing for a number of different reasons.

(a) **Growth**. If the domestic market is static or growth is slow, or if competition is excessively fierce, a company may seek to explore new areas within which it can hope to compete or operate without competition.

(b) **Economies of scale**. Since volume of output and unit cost are related, increased volume may lead to lower-than-competitive costs. Expanding into international markets may provide the level of sales necessary to benefit from economies of scale.

(c) **International competition**. Markets of all kinds are becoming globalised. International trade becomes a necessity. In many industries, those who are unable to compete globally may find themselves reduced to subcontracting for the main players.

(d) **National necessity**. Imports must be paid for with foreign currency, and exports provide the means of acquiring this currency. Governments typically encourage exports.

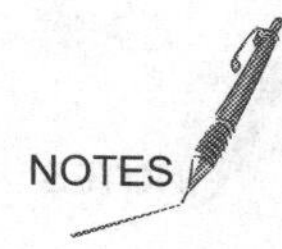

NOTES

EXAMPLE

Many firms could not survive at all without international trade. Volvo and SAAB, the Swedish car manufacturers, sell by far the majority of their output in overseas markets, as Sweden would be too small to support them. Some of the world's largest chemicals companies are Swiss, yet Switzerland is hardly a big enough market for them.

Other reasons to market overseas are these.

(a) The market for a product is **unquestionably a global one.**

(b) Overseas operations might be **cheaper than manufacturing at home**. However, differences in labour costs are not so great as is often imagined, especially when labour productivity is taken into account.

(c) **Competitors** are entering the overseas market.

(d) A company executive may recognise a **chance opportunity** while on a foreign trip. The firm may receive orders or requests for information from potential overseas customers.

(e) **Profit margins** may be higher abroad.

(f) **Seasonal fluctuations** may be levelled out (peak periods in some countries, for example those related to the weather, coincide with troughs in others).

(g) It offers an opportunity of disposing of **excess production** in times of low domestic demand.

(h) The firm's **prestige** may be enhanced by portraying a global image.

(i) **Stakeholder expectations** (eg a specified return on capital employed) may drive the decision.

Reasons for **avoiding involvement** in international marketing are these.

(a) Profits may be affected by **factors outside the firm's control** (eg due to fluctuation of exchange rates and foreign government actions).

(b) The necessary **adaptations** to the product will diminish the effects of economies of scale.

(c) **Anti-dumping duties** are more quickly imposed now than in the past, so overseas markets are less available as convenient places to sell excess stock at marginal cost.

Some **key factors** differentiating domestic and international marketing are outlined in the table below.

	Domestic	*International*
Social and cultural factors	Relatively homogeneous market 'Rules of the game' understood Similar purchasing habits	Fragmented, diverse markets Rules diverse, changeable and unclear Diverse purchasing habits
Economic factors	National price Uniform financial climate Stable business environment	Diverse national prices Variety of financial climates, ranging from very conservative to highly inflationary Multiple business environments, some unstable

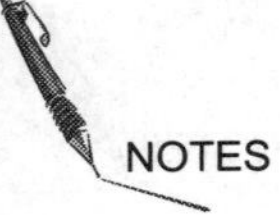

	Domestic	*International*
Competitive factors	Competitors' products, prices, costs and plans usually known	Many more competitors, but little information about their strategies
Political legal factors	Relative freedom from government interference Political factors relatively unimportant	Involvement in national economic plans Political factors often significant
Technological factors	Use of standard production and measurement systems	Training of foreign personnel to operate and maintain equipment

Figure 16.1: Factors differentiating domestic and international marketing

Before getting involved in international marketing, the company must consider both **strategic** and **tactical** issues.

(a) **Strategic issues**

(i) Does the decision to get involved in IM fit with the company's overall **mission and objectives**?

(ii) Does the organisation have the **resources** to exploit **effectively** the opportunities overseas?

(b) **Tactical issues**

(i) How can the company get to understand **customers' needs** and **preferences** in foreign markets?

(ii) Does the company know how to **conduct business** abroad, and deal effectively with **foreign nationals**?

(iii) Are there **foreign regulations** and associated **hidden costs**?

(iv) Does the company have the necessary **management skills**?

1.2 The analysis of international marketing opportunities

International markets could be analysed under headings described as the **12Cs.**

- Country
- Culture and consumer behaviour
- Concentration
- Communication
- Channels of distribution
- Capacity to pay
- Currency
- Control and co-ordination
- Commitment
- Choices
- Contractual obligations
- Caveats

Marketing into a foreign marketplace presents quite specific problems which should not be under-estimated even when the markets involved appear very similar.

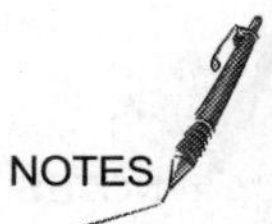

2 MARKET ATTRACTIVENESS

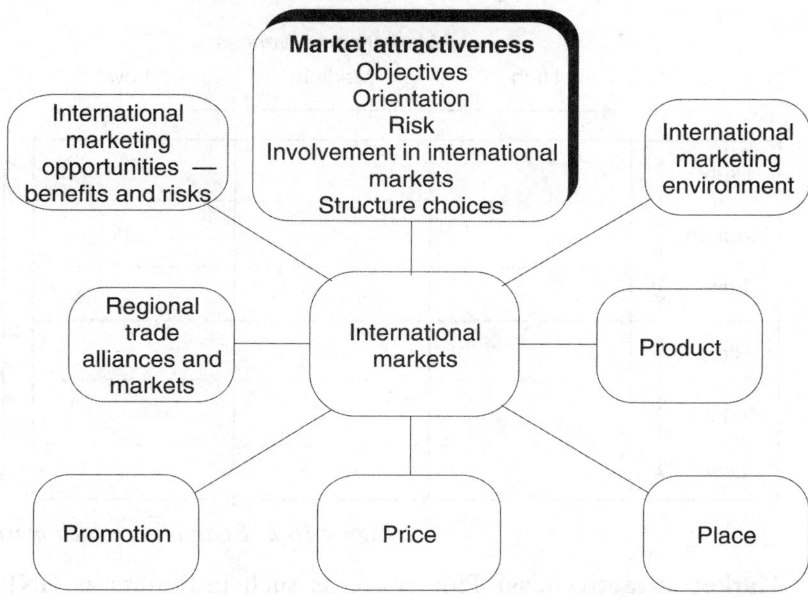

2.1 Objectives

The starting point for all successful strategic marketing planning must be the formulation of **objectives.** Defining objectives clarifies the **international orientation** of the firm. Failure to define objectives clearly may lead to a firm attempting to penetrate markets that involve activities which conflict with or detract from the firm's principal objectives. If there is a mismatch between **corporate objectives** and **foreign market opportunities** then either plans must be modified or objectives need to be reconsidered. Here are some examples.

(a) What proportion of total sales will be overseas?

(b) What are the longer term objectives?

(c) Will it enter one, a few, or many markets? In most cases it is better to start by selling in countries with which there is some familiarity and then expand into other countries gradually as experience is gained. Reasons to enter fewer countries at first include the following.

- Market entry and market control costs are high
- Product and market communications modification costs are high
- There is a large market and potential growth in the initial countries chosen
- Dominant competitors can establish high barriers to entry

(d) What types of country should it enter (in terms of environmental factors, economic development, language used, cultural similarities and so on)? Three major criteria should be as follows.

- Market attractiveness
- Competitive advantage
- Risk

The matrix below can be used to bring together these three major criteria and assist managers in their decisions.

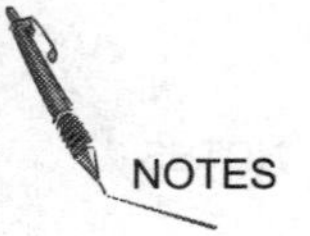

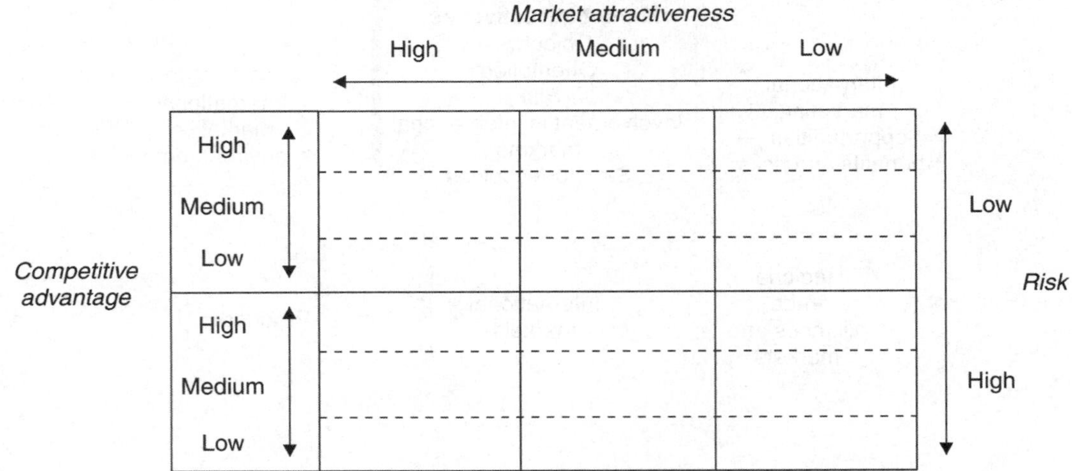

Figure 16.2: Evaluating which market to enter.

(a) **Market attractiveness**. This concerns such indicators as GNP/head and forecast demand, and market accessibility.

(b) **Competitive advantage**. This is principally dependent on prior experience in similar markets, language and cultural understanding.

(c) **Risk**. This involves an analysis of political stability, the possibility of government intervention and similar external influences.

The best markets to enter are those located at the top left of the diagram. The worst are those in the bottom right corner. Obtaining the information needed to reach this decision requires detailed and often costly **international marketing research** and analysis.

2.2 Orientation

A firm's basic international marketing orientation can be one of the following.

Ethnocentrism

Definition

> **Ethnocentrism** is a domestic country orientation in which IM is secondary to home marketing. Firms adopting this orientation will tend to adopt objectives which involve marketing the same products with the same marketing programmes in overseas countries as at home.

The approach simply ignores any inter-country differences which exist. Market opportunities may not be fully exploited with this orientation, or foreign customers may be alienated by the approach.

EXAMPLE

Pepsi experienced customer alienation when it attempted to mechanically import its global image into Russia. It lost ground to an obscure Swiss rival, Herschi, which used Russian sports stars and celebrities in its campaign.

Polycentrism (multidomestic)

Definition

> With **polycentrism**, objectives are formulated on the assumption that it is necessary to adapt almost totally the product and the marketing programme to each local environment. Thus the various country subsidiaries of a multinational corporation are free to formulate their own objectives and plans (bottom up planning).

Sometimes the outcome of this orientation is too much differentiation.

Geocentrism (or regiocentrism)

Definition

> **Geocentrism** is the synthesis of the two previous orientations. It is based on the assumption that there are both similarities and differences among countries, which can be incorporated into regional or world objectives and strategies. This approach favours neither the home approach nor total adaptation.

Geocentrism considers the issues of standardisation and adaptation on their merits so as to formulate objectives and strategies that exploit markets fully while minimising company costs.

Clearly geocentrism is preferable since it does not involve preconceived assumptions. It is usually firms with this orientation that use formal international strategic planning.

Companies which have successfully 'gone global' must plan to **maintain their competitive position.** Just as the company has to work to maintain a presence in the domestic market, the international market does not stand still.

EXAMPLE

Emerging markets such as India, China and Brazil are providing challenges for existing multinational corporations. These markets will be key arenas for competition in the future, with a new consumer base of hundreds of millions of people. Multinationals have tended to bring their existing products and marketing strategies to such markets without fully understanding the consumer market. When Revlon introduced its Western beauty

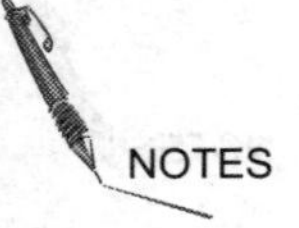

NOTES

products to China in 1976 and India in 1994, only the very top tier of the population could afford. it. Silver Cross are actually adopting this approach however with the launch of their prams in these markets specifically targeted at this consumer group. To compete more effectively with local producers, multinationals have to constantly re-think their strategies.

2.3 Risk

Definition

> In economic terms, **risk** is the potential volatility of returns on an investment, which is compensated for by a higher return. In other words, a rational investor will accept a higher risk in the hope of reaching a higher return.

In international marketing there are several categories of risk.

(a) **Political risk** relates to factors as diverse as wars, nationalisation and arguments between governments.

EXAMPLE

Heineken withdrew from Burma as a result of public hostility regarding the political situation.

(b) **Business risk.** This arises from the possibility that the business idea itself might be flawed. As with political risk, it is not unique to international marketing, but firms might be exposed to more sources of risk arising from failures to understand the market.

(c) **Currency risk.** This arises out of the volatility of foreign exchange rates. Given that there is a possibility for speculation and that capital flows are free, such risks are increasing.

(d) **Profit repatriation risk.** Government actions may make it hard to repatriate profits.

Assessing risk is not a straightforward exercise. A useful model is the **Business Environment Risk Index (BERI)**. A variety of environmental factors are scored between 0 and 4 (where 0 is unacceptable and 4 superior). These are then weighted, according to their significance. The total is added up and each country receives a score. A score of less than 40 would denote high risk.

2.4 Involvement in international markets

Firms develop through various stages of learning as commitment to IM grows. There are choices to be made along the way as to the extent to which a company commits itself to the international market. These stages are identified below.

(a) **Domestic marketing.** The firm is preoccupied with home marketing.

(b) **Pre-export stage.** A search is conducted and export opportunities are assessed.

(c) **Experimental involvement.** There is some limited involvement in exporting: unsolicited and easy-to-get orders are accepted.

(d) **Active involvement.** This indicates systematic analysis of export opportunities and expansion into foreign markets.

(e) **Committed involvement.** The firm allocates its resources according to opportunities in different countries.

Different levels of involvement in IM are shown below

Casual or accidental exporting		*Active exporting*		*Committed international marketing*
Occasional, unsolicited foreign orders are received. There is no real commitment to international marketing.	➔	The recognition that foreign markets exist. Attempts are made to cultivate sales across national boundaries. Little effort is made to consider foreign markets in the overall strategy. Minor adjustments may be made for foreign market product acceptance.	➔	Markets across national boundaries are a consideration in the marketing strategy. International marketing activities are an integral part of the overall marketing programme. Divisions or subsidiaries may be developed to serve the foreign target market better.

Figure 16.3: Levels of commitment to international marketing

2.5 Structure choices

There are five basic alternatives when entering a foreign market.

(a) **Simple exporting**, often based on the need to dispose of excess production for a domestic market, is the commonest form of export activity.

(b) The second main form is **licensing** based on patents, designs and trade marks.

(c) **Franchising** is the third main option. It is very similar to licensing, in terms of advantages and disadvantages, ie there is minimal risk, but also modest returns. **Joint ventures** are more likely to produce good returns, but they are much riskier.

(d) **Trading companies** may be established in the target countries.

(e) **Manufacturing abroad** may be undertaken. This will require major investment.

Exporting

Exporting can involve minimum effort, cost and risk and is relatively flexible. Exporting can be direct to buyers or more normally through **export organisations** of various kinds. An **export agent** acts as an intermediary between buyers and sellers, taking a commission from the transactions. Export merchants/export houses buy products from different companies and sell them to other countries.

In most cases these export organisations have long-established contacts in foreign countries and a purchasing headquarters. The exporter can thus deal in English, under

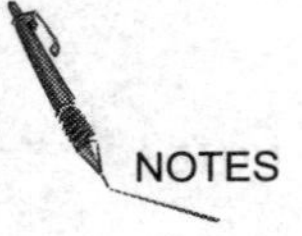

the English legal system, gets paid by a resident bank, is not involved in shipping and may not have to alter products in any way. It is simple and risk free, but naturally the rewards are not as potentially great as other options.

Activity 1 **(10 minutes)**

What would you suggest is the major danger in exporting?

Licensing

Licensing usually involves only a small capital outlay and this approach is favoured by small and medium sized companies. It is the least profitable method of entry, and has the least associated risks.

The licensee pays a **royalty** on every product item produced or sold in addition to a lump sum paid for the license. Licensing is used particularly when **local** manufacture, technical assistance and market knowledge offer advantages. It is an alternative to investing directly and is particularly advantageous if an overseas country should be politically unstable.

Licensing is also attractive for medium-sized companies wishing to launch a successful home market brand internationally. Fashion houses such as Yves St Laurent and Pierre Cardin have issued hundreds of licences and Löwenbrau has expanded sales worldwide without having to expend capital building its own breweries overseas.

Joint ventures

Joint ventures in Europe have become particularly prevalent since the advent of the EC. They involve **collaboration** with one or more foreign firms. They offer reduced economic and political risks and a ready made **distribution system**. Where there are barriers to trade, they may be the only way to gain entry to foreign markets.

Quite a number of vehicle manufacturers have initiated joint ventures or strategic alliances, including Chrysler with Mitsubishi and Alfa Romeo with both Nissan and Fiat.

EXAMPLE

British tobacco company Gallaher Group has formed a joint venture with American rival RJ Reynolds, which makes Camel cigarettes, worth an estimated $200m (£127m), to market American blend cigarette brands in Europe.

The joint venture deal is designed to help Gallaher grow in markets where it has little presence. The brands included in the deal include Benson & Hedges American Blend, Benson & Hedges Red and Reynolds, a new American blend in a unique 'slide-box' pack.

The deal initially covers four markets: France, Spain, Canary Islands and Italy. Certain markets, most notably Austria, are excluded from this agreement.

RJ Reynolds' financial contributions, which are expected to total in the region of $75m-$100m over the next five years, will balance Gallaher's contributions, which will include the value of the volume sales already being achieved by the Gallaher brands licensed to the joint venture.

The joint venture company, RJ Reynolds-Gallaher International SARL, will be headquartered in Switzerland. The joint venture company will receive manufacturing, sales, distribution and marketing support services from Gallaher.

Brand Republic, 16 July 2002

Following the smoking ban in some countries in Europe, industry experts predict however that the tobacco market is likely to shrink within Europe as a whole but grow significantly in the developing world. The tobacco industry is therefore likely to be reconsidering their overall global strategy.

Trading companies

This structure avoids involvement in manufacturing. A trading company simply buys in one country and sells in another country. It will sometimes also act as a consultant advising buyers and sellers on market conditions, quality/price issues etc. For example, long-established trading companies control much of the world's food market for commodities such as cereals or indeed any other items that are able to be stored in bulk and moved rapidly in response to shortages.

Direct ownership

Setting up a company in a foreign country may be appropriate if growth prospects and political stability make a long-term commitment attractive. **Manufacturing abroad** requires major investment and is only justified by very heavy demand. However, it may offer advantages such as those below.

- Lower labour costs
- Avoidance of import taxes
- Lower transport costs

These may be offset by the degree of **management effort** required and higher levels of risk. Multinationals will have **directly owned subsidiaries** in many countries. These can offer considerable operating and tax advantages. Some car manufacturers such as General Motors and Ford in the US import cars built by foreign subsidiaries.

3 INTERNATIONAL MARKETING ENVIRONMENT

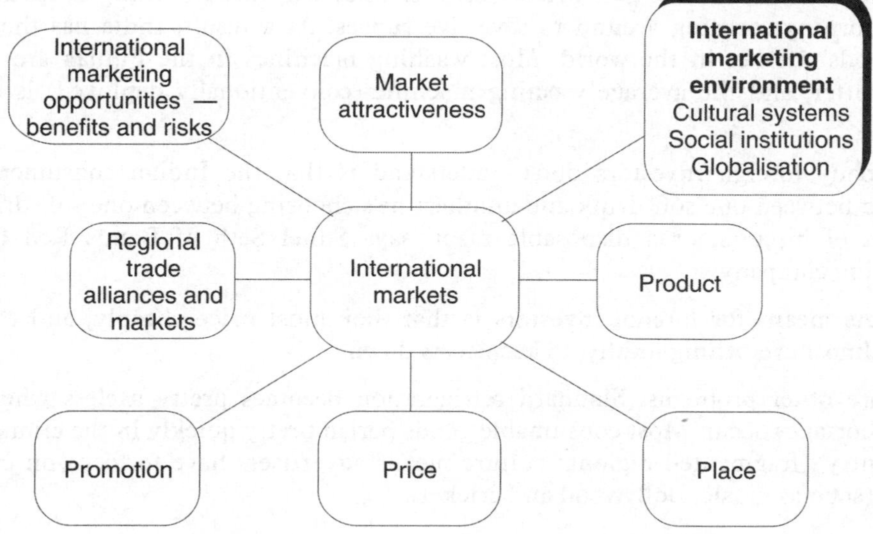

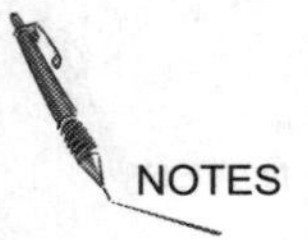

NOTES

3.1 Cultural systems

Even between neighbouring countries such as France and Spain, or Zimbabwe and South Africa, cultural differences can be very great. Marketing planning must consider the main aspects of cultural systems.

- Material culture
- Social institutions
- Belief systems
- Aesthetics
- Language

Material culture affects the following.

(a) The **level of demand**. For instance, a lack of electricity will restrict the demand for electronic items. An American firm set out to launch a best selling cake mix in the 1950s to Japan, only to find that Japanese kitchens were not equipped with ovens. In Spain, milk sold in supermarkets tends to be UHT rather than fresh whilst in the UK there is a widespread perception that fresh milk is best. The introduction of brands such as Cranvendale and the development of the 'Pure' (milk filtered to remove bacteria and retain freshness) has seen incredible growth and yet the concept would be meaningless in Spain.

(b) **Quality and types of products demanded**. Difference in disposable income influences the kinds of goods demanded. Note also the **symbolic** importance of particular goods which may be used primarily for **display,** for instance, the popularity of comparatively expensive western cigarettes and sunglasses in Communist China.

(c) **Functional characteristics**. Demand for snack food and the habit of 'grazing' has been stimulated in the UK by changes in the role of women, and in the activities which take place within the home.

(d) The **nature of products demanded**. 'Menu meals' are a product intended to help prepare quality food when time cannot be spared for shopping and cooking. This concept would be alien in countries where women traditionally stay at home to 'housekeep'.

EXAMPLE

Consumers in India are acutely price sensitive. They will think nothing of spending an entire morning scouting around to save five rupees. As a result, India has the largest 'used goods' market in the world. Most washing machines in the Punjab are used to churn butter, and the average washing machine (conventionally deployed) is over 19 years old.

'What many foreign investors don't understand is that the Indian consumer is not choosing between one soft drink and another; he's choosing between one soft drink and a packet of biscuits, or a disposable razor' says Suhel Seth of Equus Red Cell, an advertising company.

What this means for foreign investors is that they must price cheaply, and therefore source almost everything locally, to keep costs down.

There are other problems. Standard refrigeration becomes pretty useless when acute power shortages occur. Most consumable goods perish pretty quickly in the climate. And the country's fragmented regional culture means advertisers have to focus on common ground (such as music, Bollywood and cricket).

Is it worth the effort? Investors say that overcoming such obstacles has equipped them for success in any market in the world.

Adapted from the *Financial Times*, April 2002

3.2 Social institutions

Social institutions give a society its distinctive form, and develop around particular aspects of life experience, such as the care and education of children, or coping with conflict or suffering. The form of social institutions has profound implications for the ways in which goods are regarded, since they provide the foundations for value systems, and through them, attitudes and behaviour.

(a) **Social organisation**. Tightly knit family units, in which social roles are bound up with responsibility to the family, influence both the kinds of products demanded, and the ways in which purchase decisions are made.

(b) **Political structures.** The political system sets the agenda for consumption through policy and example.

(c) **Educational system**. Literacy is a key factor in promotional and advertising activity.

(d) **Family or household roles.** Roles played by family members in decision making are one area in which culture shapes consumption. Also, the way in which the household is actually used and regarded are very important for consumption. For instance, the modern household actually forms the focus for leisure activity far more than it did in the past.

Belief systems include religious, philosophical, and political ideologies. Generalised belief systems are all-pervasive, even in societies which consider themselves secularised. Our holidays and gift giving occasions are formed around the old religious calendar. The foods we eat reflect moral and aesthetic judgements as much as nutritional sense. Many religions proscribe particular forms of consumption, such as coffee, alcoholic drinks, 'provocative' clothes and certain music.

Aesthetics and what counts as beauty or ugliness is tied into quite specific values which a marketer must be aware of in a foreign culture.

Marketing literature is full of examples of linguistic faux pas, such as the Vauxhall Nova, which means 'doesn't go' in Spanish. Advertising slogans need to beware of the pitfalls of the local **language.** Successful slogans may not work in another language, or may be unintentionally funny or offensive.

Activity 2 **(15 minutes)**

Try to identify the marketing problems arising from national differences in:

(a) Language
(b) Consumption patterns
(c) Socio-economic factors
(d) Marketing practices and conditions.

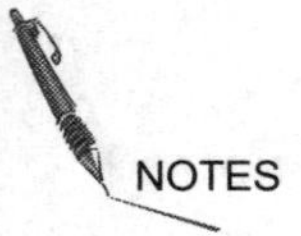

NOTES

EXAMPLE

National restrictions

'Sweden forbids all advertising aimed at children under 10; Greece bans TV toy advertising between 7am and 10pm; Britain is barring all ads aimed at children for 'unhealthy' foods; some countries require ads for sweets to carry a toothbrush symbol; others have rules intended to curb advertisers from encouraging children to exercise 'pester power'.

The same maze of national rules exists when it comes to promoting alcohol, tobacco, pharmaceuticals and financial services'.

There are proposals to set up a new body to deal with these issues, which are felt to be significant barriers to cross border trade within the EU.

On sponsorship, for example, the Netherlands was singled out as having particularly restrictive curbs on events sponsorship, while the UK and Denmark were seen to impose strict rules on broadcasting.

Price advertising and discounting is another area likely to get early attention. Measures are so disparate that cross-border campaigns using discounts are all but impossible ... In Germany, cash discounts are limited to 3% and the advertising of special offers is also restricted. Austria, Belgium and Italy also have strict regimes. In contrast, in Scandinavia, where the advertising law is more closely linked to consumer protection rather than unfair competition considerations, price advertising is encouraged – Swedish law, for example, promotes comparative price advertising between traders '

Source: *Financial Times*

3.3 Globalisation

Since 1945, the volume of world trade has increased. There have been two routes.

(a) **Import substitution**. A country aims to produce manufactured goods which it previously imported, by protecting local producers. This has had limited success.

(b) **Export-led growth**. The success of this particular strategy has depended on the existence of open markets elsewhere. Japan, South Korea and the other Asian 'tiger' economies (eg Taiwan) have chosen this route.

This has meant a proliferation of suppliers exporting to, or trading in, a wider variety of places. However, the existence of **global markets** should not be taken for granted in terms of all products and services, or indeed in all territories.

(a) Some services are still subject to managed trade (eg some countries prohibit firms from other countries from selling insurance). Trade in services has been liberalised under the auspices of the WTO.

(b) Immigration. There is unlikely ever to be a global market for labour, given the disparity in skills between different countries, and restrictions on immigration.

(c) The market for some goods is much more 'globalised' than for others.

    (i) Upmarket luxury goods may not be required or afforded by people in developing nations.

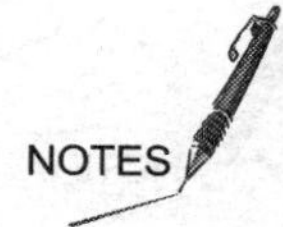

(ii) Some goods can be sold almost anywhere, but to limited degrees. Television sets are consumer durables in some countries, but still luxury or relatively expensive items in other ones.

(iii) Other goods are needed almost everywhere. In oil a truly global industry exists in both production (eg North Sea, Venezuela, Russia, Azerbaijan, Gulf states) and consumption (any country using cars and buses, not to mention those with chemical industries based on oil).

Some years ago, Harvard Business School professor Ted Levitt predicted the development of a '**global village**' in which consumers around the world would have the same needs and attitudes and use the same products. The whole debate about **globalisation** still goes on, with the attendant question of whether to **standardise or adapt** the marketing mix.

Definition

'Globalisation of markets' (Levitt, 1983) is an expression which relates first to demand: tastes, preferences and price-mindedness are becoming increasingly universal. Second, it relates to the supply side: products and services tend to become more standardised and competition within industries reaches a world-wide scale. Third, it relates to the way firms, mainly *multinational corporations* (ie those with operations in more than one country), try to design their marketing policies and control systems appropriately so as to remain winners in the global competition of global products for global consumers.

Some would say that **global marketing organisations** are rare. Industry structures change, foreign markets are culturally diverse, and the transformations brought about by developments in information technology mean that the world market is in a state of turbulence. The financial crisis in Asia caused significant political and economic unrest, for example. Continuing to follow the same marketing strategy can be risky. Global players must always seek new low cost production areas.

Activity 3 **(10 minutes)**

In what ways is an increasingly cross-cultural outlook becoming evident in UK consumers?

Here are some of the changes that have happened in the world market place:

(a) **Globalisation of business** – increased competition and global customers

(b) **Science and technology** developments (computing, telecommunications and information science)

(c) Mergers, acquisitions and **strategic alliances**

(d) Changing **customer values** and behaviour

(e) Increased **scrutiny** of business decisions by government and the public, with greater focus on ethical dimensions

(f) Increased **deregulation**, privatisation and co-operation between business and government

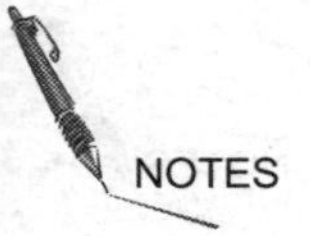

(g) Changes in **business practices** – downsizing, outsourcing and re-engineering

(h) Changes in the **social and business** relationships between companies and their employees, customers and other stakeholders

While more and more companies are competing in the world market place, most of them tend to focus on the developed markets of North America, Europe and Japan. A vast majority (86%) of the world's population resides in countries where GDP is less than $10,000 per head. Such countries offer tremendous marketing opportunities if the offering is presented correctly.

This leads on to the question of **market convergence** – how likely is it that consumers' tastes and preferences may converge? On the face of it, there is no reason why they should not, but in practice this is unlikely. Someone who lives in a very hot country is never going to want many sweaters, or be likely to go cycling in the midday sun just for the sake of getting some exercise.

FOR DISCUSSION

The average French high school student appears very similar to American students of the same age (clothing, eating and entertainment preferences). Take a student from Nigeria and compare him to one from Finland, however, and the story is likely to be different.

Other **global drivers** (factors encouraging the globalisation of world trade) include the following.

(a) **Financial factors** eg Third world debt. Often the lenders require the initiation of economic reforms as a condition of the loan.

(b) **Country/continent alliances,** such as that between the UK and USA, which fosters trade and other phenomena such as tourism.

(c) **Legal factors** such as patents and trade marks, which encourage the development of technology and design.

(d) **Stock markets** trading in international commodities. Commodities are not physically exchanged, only the rights to ownership. A buyer can, thanks to efficient systems of grading and modern communications, buy a commodity in its country of origin for delivery to a specific port. There is also a market in **futures**, enabling buyers to avoid the effect of price changes by buying for future delivery at a set price. This smoothes the process of international trade and lowers risk.

(e) The level of **protectionist** measures.

4 REGIONAL TRADE ALLIANCES AND MARKETS

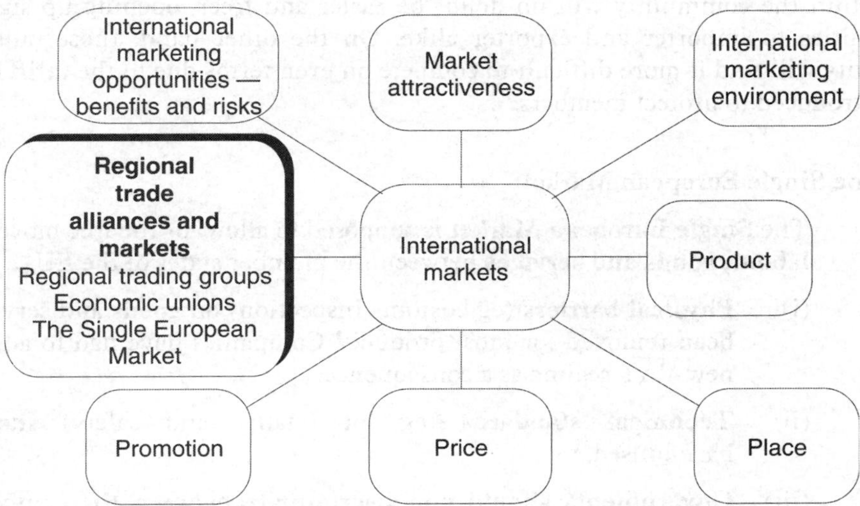

Trade between nations is of such significance that rules governing it have been established. Economic theory predicts mutual benefits for nations trading internationally but there are two opposing pressures.

- The desire to **expand the domestic economy** by selling to other nations
- The desire to **protect indigenous sources of employment** by restricting imports

4.1 Regional trading groups

Whilst the **World Trade Organisation** encourages free trade, the opposite force of **protectionism** has led to the creation of regional trading organisations, which seek to encourage trade between members but introduce hurdles to non-members. An example is the **EU**. These regional trading groups can take progressively more integrated forms.

- Free trade areas
- Customs unions
- Economic unions

Free trade areas have members who agree to lower barriers to trade amongst themselves. There is little other form of economic cooperation. Examples include **Mercosur** and the **Andean Community** in South America, and the **North American Free Trade Agreement**, comprising Canada, the USA and Mexico. In underdeveloped countries, attempts to form such associations have led to problems as members seek to protect their embryo economies, and fear the effects of free trade with member states.

Customs unions not only provide the advantages of free trade areas, but also agree a common policy on barriers to external countries. Currently the EU is the leading example of this type of union, and is seen as the prototype for other unions elsewhere.

4.2 Economic unions

The ultimate step is the submission of all decisions relating to trade, both internal and external, from member states to the union itself. **In effect the members become one for economic purposes.**

Since 31 December 1992 there has been a single European market. The EU has economic union as an aim.

NOTES

The effect of regional trade organisations, such as the EU is mixed. On the one hand, trade within the community will no doubt be easier and freer, opening up significant opportunities to importer and exporter alike. On the other hand, those outside the community will find it more difficult to compete on even terms due to the **tariff barriers** being introduced to protect members.

4.3 The Single European Market

(a) The **Single European Market** is supposed to allow for the free movement of **labour, goods and services** between the member states of the EU.

   (i) **Physical barriers** (eg customs inspection) on goods and service have been removed for most products. Companies have had to adjust to a new VAT regime as a consequence.

   (ii) **Technical standards** (eg for quality and safety) should be harmonised.

   (iii) **Governments should not discriminate** between EU companies in awarding public works contracts.

   (iv) **Telecommunications** should be subject to greater competition.

   (v) It should be possible to provide **financial services** in any country.

   (vi) Measures are being taken to rationalise **transport** services.

   (vii) There should be **free movement of capital** within the community.

   (viii) **Professional qualifications** awarded in one member state should be recognised in the others.

   (ix) The EU is taking a co-ordinated stand on matters related to **consumer protection**.

(b) At the same time, there are many areas where harmonisation is some way from being achieved.

   (i) **Company taxation**. Tax rates, which can affect the viability of investment plans, vary from country to country within the EU.

   (ii) **Indirect taxation (VAT)**. While there have been moves to harmonisation, there are still differences between rates imposed by member states.

   (iii) **Differences in prosperity**. There are considerable differences in prosperity between the wealthiest EU economy (Luxembourg), and the poorest (eg Latvia). The UK comes somewhere in the middle.

      (1) Grants are sometimes available to depressed regions, which might affect investment decisions.

      (2) Different marketing strategies are appropriate for different markets.

   (iv) **Differences in workforce skills**. Again, this can have a significant effect on investment decisions. The workforce in Germany is perhaps the most highly trained, but also the most highly paid, and so might be suitable for products of a high added value.

   (v) **Infrastructure**. Some countries are better provided with road and rail than others. Where accessibility to a market is an important issue, infrastructure can mean significant variations in distribution costs.

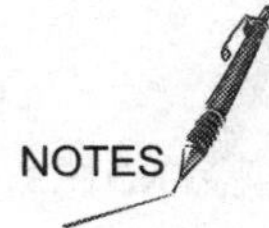

(vi) **Delays.** Single market regulation is still being introduced in some industries (insurance).

(vii) **Social differences.** The UK's welfare state is far less generous than Germany's.

Two other points about the EU are worthy of note.

(a) Bear in mind that the EU is much more than a single market and a free trade area. It has its own **Parliament**, elected from throughout the EU, **civil service** and **courts,** and it is one of the many political arrangements in which the countries of Western Europe are involved. It has a **political and constitutional** dimension largely absent from other free trading arrangements.

(b) The EU is in the process of expansion. Recent joiners have included Romania, Bulgaria and Slovakia, and candidates include Turkey (subject to various economic and political changes) Croatia and Macedonia. This expansion will have a significant impact on two areas.

(i) The EU's constitutional arrangements

(ii) The EU's budgetary arrangements. Already the agriculture budget is being cut. Funds also flow from the EU to economically depressed regions (eg parts of Greece). This may change.

Company planning for the Single European Market

The Department of Trade and Industry listed seven key questions of business strategy, which firms should face up to. These are especially pertinent to the **single currency**.

(a) How has the **market changed** for our business?

(b) Should we **shift** from being a UK firm with a UK market, to a European firm with a European market?

(c) If we became a European firm with a European market, would this alter the **scale of our operations**?

(d) In what ways will we become **vulnerable** in our existing markets to new or greater competition?

(e) Is our **management structure** suitable for exploiting new opportunities, and taking defensive measures against new threats?

(f) Should we be seeking **mergers or takeovers** to strengthen our market position, broaden our product range, or spread our financial risk?

(g) Who in the firm is going to be responsible for making the **key decisions** about how to exploit the single market opportunities?

Here are just a few possible implications for marketing and sales related operations.

(a) **Marketing**

- What new **customers** can be reached?
- Is the wider market **attractive**?
- What **market information** do we need, and how do we get it?
- Are our **products and services** suitable for the wider market?
- What will **competition** be like?

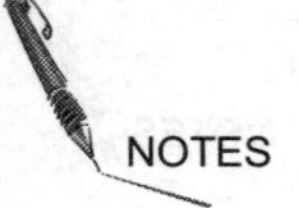

(b) **Sales**

- How can we **reach** the potential new customers?
- How can we **sell** into the new market?
- What sales **literature**, advertising and sales promotions will be needed?

(c) **Distribution**. What will be the distribution organisation for the new markets – eg, transport, warehousing, dealer agreements, delivery times etc?

(d) **Product development**

(i) What changes are needed to make our products and services more **attractive** to the new markets?

(ii) What **resources** will be needed to develop new products?

(iii) Is there scope for **collaborative ventures** in product development with other EU firms?

Cross border mergers

One of the results of the single European market has been a spate of **mergers**. Acquiring an overseas firm is an often-used mode of entry to European markets. Examples are as follows.

(a) Slowly but surely the European **defence industry** will be rationalised.

(b) Many UK water firms and rail firms are owned by French companies.

(c) Some firms, such as General Motors, already operate on a Europe-wide basis, with one model being sourced from one country. This offers the advantage of economies of scale.

(d) Some major UK retailers (eg Tesco) have sought to grow by acquiring retailers in other countries.

For a country like the UK, membership may bring mixed blessings.

(a) Over 50% of UK foreign trade is with other EU members, and the development of the EU will expand such trade and make it easier.

(b) Our largest market in terms of a single country is the USA, which takes some 13% of UK exports. The EU barriers to non-members such as the USA may result in retaliatory action.

EXAMPLE

A significant effect of EU progress has been the rush of multinationals setting up assembly or manufacturing plant within one or more member states, rather than importing into the EU. Thus France, Germany and the UK have seen considerable inward investment from US and Japanese firms, trying to avoid the barriers set in place from 1993. EU goods must be 80% sourced within the community to qualify as EU produced and thus avoid tariffs and quotas.

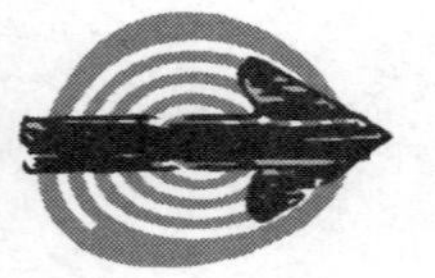

We will now look at the elements of the marketing mix in an international context.

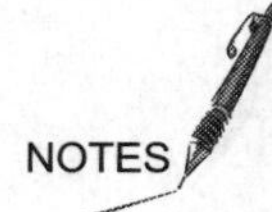

5 PRODUCT

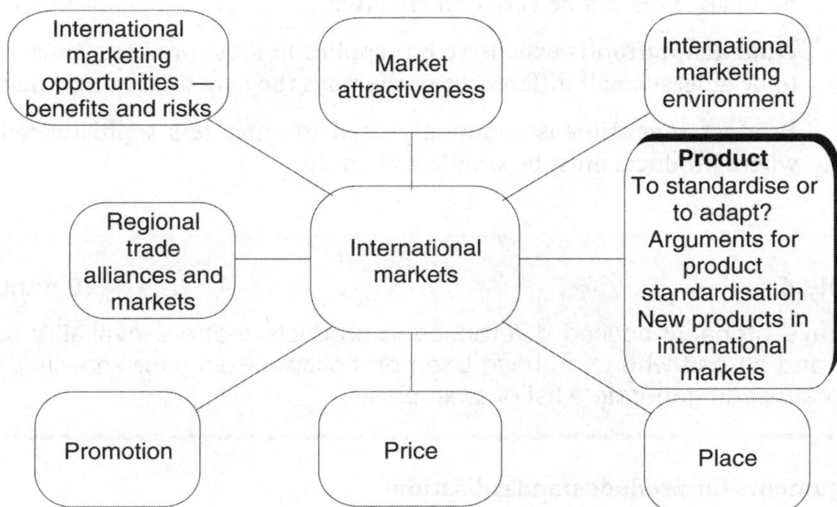

5.1 To standardise or to adapt?

Products successfully marketed within one country cannot necessarily be moved into an alien market without problems. Products have **symbolic** and **psychological** aspects as well as physical attributes. As a result, entry into a market with a different set of cultural, religious, economic, social and political assumptions may cause extreme reactions to a product concept or marketing mix.

The problem derives from an inherent tension between two important ideas in marketing. **Target marketing** and **segmentation** suggest that the way to maximise sales is to identify specific consumer needs and hence to **adapt** a product for a new foreign market. At the same time, it is impractical to create **separate products for every conceivable segment**, and it is more profitable to produce a **standardised** product for a larger market.

There are five suggested approaches to the problem of **adaptation** which are defined by decisions about the **product** and about **promotion**. They are summarised in the diagram below.

PROMOTION \ PRODUCT	Extension	Adaptation	New
Extension	Straight Extension	Product Adaptation	Product invention
Adaptation	Communication Adaptation	Dual Adaptation	

Figure 16.4: Approaches to the problem of adaptation

(a) **Straight extension** of product or promotion means that no significant change is made.

(b) **Product adaptation** is normally undertaken so that the product can either fulfil the same function under different conditions, as when an electrical device is adapted to conform to a different voltage, or to overcome cultural problems such as taste.

(c) **Communications adaptation** is a way of marketing an unchanged product to fulfil a different need as when garden implements are promoted as

agricultural equipment in less-developed countries where plot sizes tend to be small. This can be very cost effective.

(d) **Dual adaptation** is expensive but applies to most products since there tend to be at least small differences in the ways they are used in new markets.

(e) **Product invention** is commonly used to enter less sophisticated markets where products must be simple and cheap.

Activity 4 **(20 minutes)**

You have probably noticed differences in products that are available both at home and abroad when you have been on holiday. Pool your knowledge with classmates and generate a list of examples.

5.2 Arguments for product standardisation

(a) **Economies of scale**

(i) **Production**

- Plant confined to one country and used to maximum capacity rather than duplicated.
- Exporting rather than difficult licensing deals.

(ii) **Research and development.** Product modification is costly and time consuming.

(iii) **Marketing**. Promotion which can use the same images and theme in advertising is clearly more cost effective when only the soundtrack, or the printed slogan, has to be changed. Similarly, standardisation of distribution systems, salesforce training, aftersales provisions, and other aspects of the marketing mix can save a great deal of money.

EXAMPLE

Brewing is an industry with significant economies of scale. Apart from Heineken and Guinness, it is only recently that big brewers have become 'international'. There are a variety of aspects of this development.

(a) Beers are branded across markets. Stella Artois is available in the UK as a premium product, whereas in Belgium it is 'a decent modestly price lager'.

(b) Other firms are expanding by acquisition. Interbrew, the brewer of Stella Artois has purchased Labatt of Canada, to gain access to markets in North and South America.

(c) Big brewing companies see many European and American markets are stagnant: they are trying to revive them with imported or foreign brands.

(d) Firms co-operate in some markets but compete in others. (Guinness distributes Bass in the US, whilst competing with Bass in the UK.)

(e) The greatest potential seems to be east Asia, where beer consumption is rising by 10% pa and South America, where growth is 4% pa.

Ultimately, even if the beer market eventually becomes truly global, it will remain fragmented for a long time to come

(b) **Consumer mobility**. Finding a familiar brand name is important for the growing numbers of travellers moving across national boundaries.

EXAMPLE

Designing a new version of one product for each market is prohibitively expensive, but a company may want more than one product covering all markets. Nissan has been a pioneer in finding the right balance. It reduced the number of different chassis designs from 40 to 8, for cars destined for 75 markets.

(c) **Technological complexity.** The microelectronics market illustrates the inherent danger of diversity in technically complex products. Even the endorsement of powerful Japanese companies could not sustain the Betamax VCR system or non-standard PC systems. The international market selected VHS and IBM respectively.

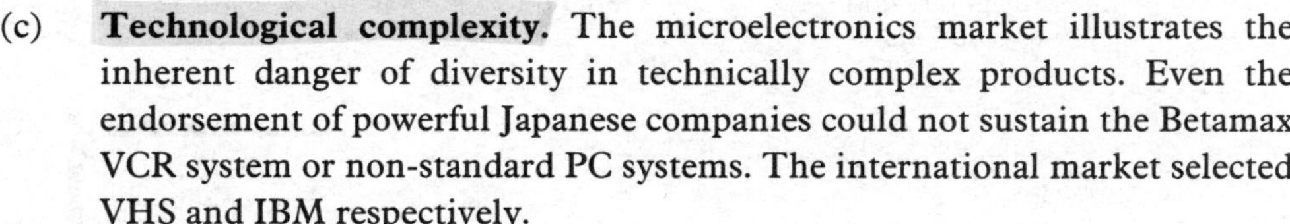

Activity 5 **(15 minutes)**

What are the arguments in favour of product adaptation?

5.3 New products in international markets

Product ideas, both internally and externally generated, must be screened in order to identify potentially marketable and profitable products. Product screening may be carried out at a centralised location, although this poses the threat of alienating management at remote subsidiary plants where many ideas may originate.

Criteria for product screening

Products are screened against the firm's capabilities and characteristics.

(a) **Producing the product.** This may involve existing resources or involve diversification.

(b) **Marketing the product**. If this can be accommodated within existing marketing resources, then so much the better. Formulating a new system could involve substantial outlay and disruption.

(c) **Researching the new market.** This might involve the deployment of existing resources, particularly if (as is likely) the firm is already established, and operating in a related area. If there is no related market involvement, there is greater uncertainty and hence risk.

(d) **Marketing internationally**. Orientation to a specific market will reduce the economies of scale involved in multinational marketing. Products are likely to be rejected if they cannot be produced for international markets.

(e) **Motivation to introduce and market the new product effectively.** What are the reasons for the new product being introduced and how well adjusted is the organisation to this process?

(f) **Organisational suitability to marketing the new product**. Are, for example, suitable support and maintenance systems available?

6 PLACE

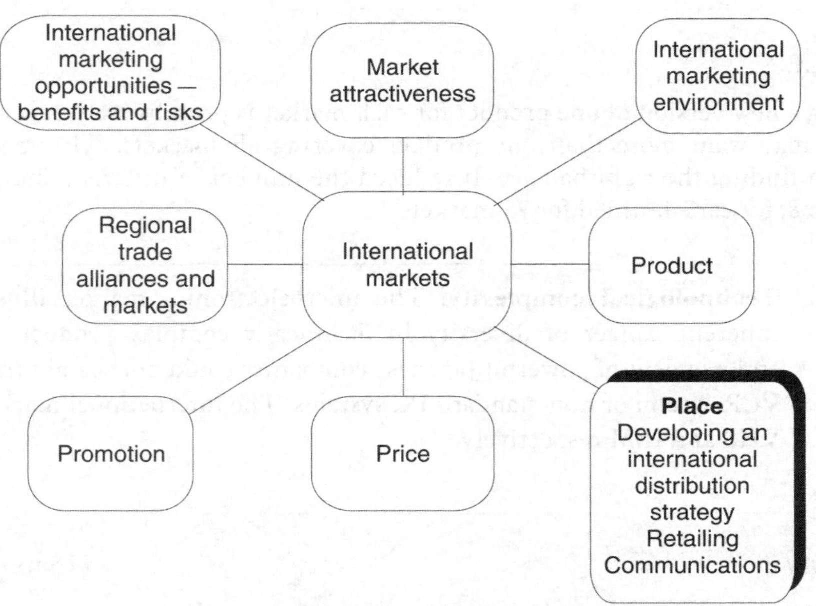

A range of factors affect the selection, establishment, and running of **international distribution systems**. A wide range of channels can be developed.

Using an **Export Management Company (EMC)** which handles all aspects of exporting can be an attractive option. It requires minimal investment and no company personnel are involved. The EMC already has an established network of sales offices, and extensive international marketing and distribution knowledge. From the company's point of view, however, there is a loss of control.

Another alternative is **export agents**. These provide more limited services than EMCs, are focused on one country and do not perform EMC marketing tasks but concentrate on the physical movement of products. The main problem here is that a company requires several agents to cover a range of markets.

Direct exporting can be attractive. In-house personnel are used, but they must be well trained and experienced. Also, the volume of sales must be sufficient to justify employing them.

Import middlemen, or distributors who are experts in their local market needs, can play a key part, being able to source goods from the world market to satisfy local needs. They operate to purchase goods in their own name, and act independently of the manufacturer. They are able to exploit a good access to wholesale and retail networks.

6.1 Developing an international distribution strategy

As in domestic marketing, there must be **consistency of purpose** in the way in which elements within the marketing mix operate. Some **key strategic areas** are involved.

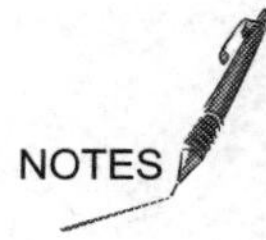

- **Distribution density** – exposure or coverage desired
- **Channel length**, alignment and leadership – number, structure and hierarchy relationships of the channel members
- **Distribution logistics** – physical flow of product

Distribution density

Distribution density depends on a knowledge of how customers select dealers and retail outlets, by segment. If less shopping effort is involved, as in the case of **convenience goods,** an extensive system would be appropriate. If more shopping effort is used, as in the case of premium priced goods, then a selective or exclusive system would be required.

Channel members

After strategy has been formulated, marketers must select **channel partners** capable of implementing the overall strategy. Since it can be difficult to change partners once contracted, this choice is very sensitive indeed.

Product and product line is also relevant. Perishable or short shelf-life products need shorter channels, and this bears on costs and hence profits. High tech products require either direct sales effort or skilled and knowledgeable channel partners.

Synergy arises when the components of a channel complement one another to the extent that they produce more than the sum of their individual parts. Such synergy may arise if, for example, the chosen partner has some key skill which allows quicker access to the market.

Logistics

Logistics systems are expensive and can be very damaging to corporate profitability if badly handled. There are several areas which are crucial to international logistics.

- Traffic and transportation management
- Inventory control
- Order processing
- Materials handling and warehousing
- Fixed facilities location management

Traffic and transportation management deals primarily with the main mode of transport involved in moving goods. Three main criteria are employed in this choice – lead times, transit time and costs.

Inventory control relates cost with service levels. Inventory reduces potential profit by using up working capital. The management aim here is to reduce inventories to an absolute minimum.

6.2 Retailing

There are certain key global trends in international distribution. Larger scale retailers are partly a consequence of economic development and growing affluence. Increasing car ownership, increasing fridge/freezer ownership and the changing role of women all encourage one-stop shopping.

International retailers like Marks and Spencer have developed for the same reasons. Companies saw limited growth opportunities at home, and moved to overseas markets. This allows manufacturers to build relationships with retailers active in a number of different markets. This **internationalisation process** is prompted by improved **data**

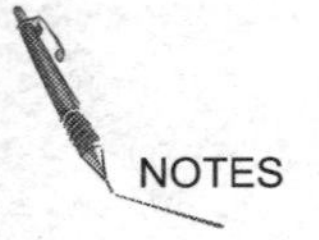

communications, new forms of **international financing**, more open **international markets** and **lower barriers to entry**. In the EU for instance, the Single European Market motivates retailers to expand overseas, as they see international retailers entering their domestic markets.

EXAMPLE

Over the last decade Tesco has become one of the leading global retailers. Although there may be some similarities, the retailer has had to adapt to local retail customs and has a diverse range of retail formats. In France for example, the UK 'booze cruise' market is catered for with few products other than alcohol being sold at their City Europe store near to the channel tunnel. In Prague, although food items are sold, the shop resembles a department store more than a supermarket. In holiday locations such as Minorca, small convenience stores in resorts appeal to UK tourists who like the familiarity of a home store. Tesco even operates fresh fish tanks in their Far East stores where consumers are used to purchasing living items from street markets rather than supermarkets.

The move to globalisation has been a long but successful process for the retailer. When launching a pilot store in the US, Tesco researched the market using a common US methodology by actually going to live with consumers in order to understand their buying habits. This activity would be virtually impossible within the UK where consumers are more guarded especially with regard to market research.

Direct marketing is growing rapidly all over the world, using IT systems to go direct to customers.

Information technology has had an enormous impact. Computerised retail systems allow better monitoring of consumer purchases, lower inventory costs and quicker stock turns alongside a better assessment of product profitability. They also make it possible to extend JIT ideas into the area of retailing. Internet selling is widely expected to revolutionise business.

6.3 Communications

Marketing communications face additional barriers internationally. The elements to be considered are as follows.

(a) **Push-oriented strategy**. In a domestic setting, this emphasises personal selling. This may be more expensive if employed abroad since minor equipment or supplies in large UK firms may be 'major equipment' overseas and require more involved personal selling effort. Also a long non-domestic channel, involving many non-domestic intermediaries, increase costs, reduces the effect of personal selling, and poses severe control problems.

(b) **Pull-oriented strategy** is characterised by a greater dependence upon advertising and is typically employed for FMCG marketing to very large market segments. It is generally more appropriate for long channels where relatively simple products are being sold. However, not all countries have the same access to advertising media and the quality of media varies greatly.

The use of key slogans used to great effect in one country can often be ridiculous when used in another country not only due to translation problems but maybe an innuendo or joke is lost within another culture. The famous Kentucky Fried Chicken slogan of 'Finger Licking Good' has been translated as 'Eat your fingers off' in Japan.

7 PRICE

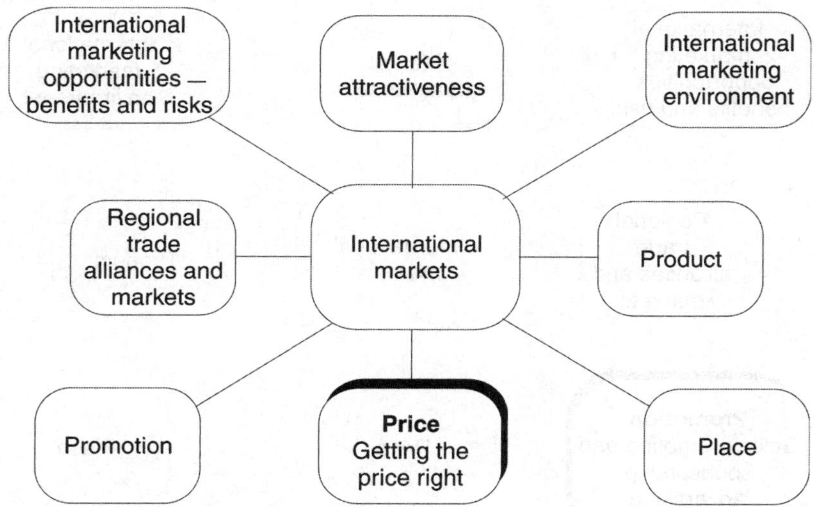

7.1 Getting the price right

Prices in foreign markets are likely to be determined by **local conditions,** with each market separate. The organisation's degree of control over pricing is likely to be higher if it has wholly owned subsidiaries in each of the markets, and lower if it conducts business through licensees, franchisees or distributors.

Activity 6 **(15 minutes)**

Market conditions are the most important influence on pricing. What other factors do you think influence pricing?

The **diversity of markets** within a region is important. If markets are unrelated, the seller can successfully charge different prices. Pressures for **price uniformity** often come from large groupings such as free trade areas or the EU and from increases in international business activity. Companies can control price in several ways.

- Direct distribution to customers
- Resale price maintenance
- Recommended prices
- Agreed margins between parent and subsidiary companies
- Centralised control over prices within several subsidiary companies

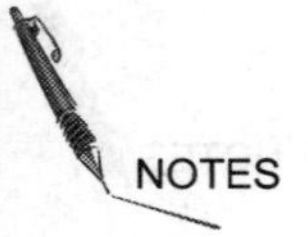

8 PROMOTION

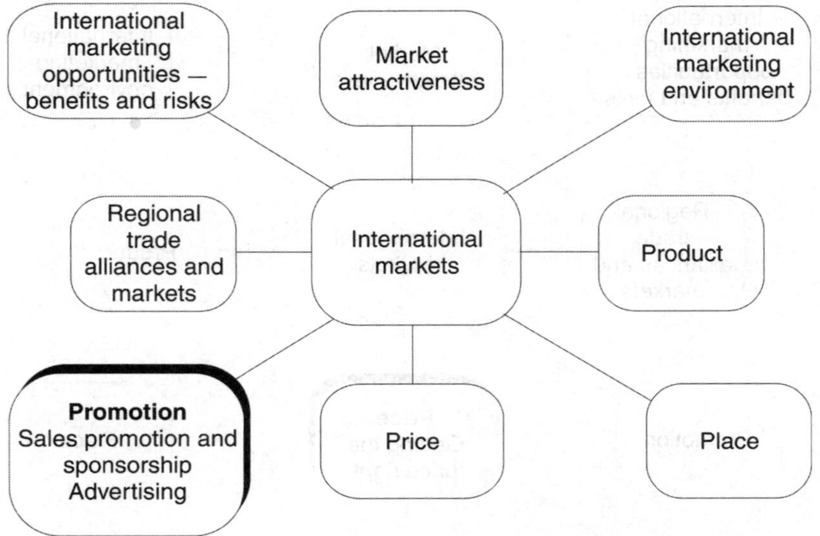

8.1 Sales promotion and sponsorship

Sales promotions may be affected by different retailing norms and government **regulations**. For example, coupons, much used in the UK and the USA, are prohibited in Germany and Greece. Reduction in price promotions are often restricted to a percentage of full price. As a consequence, standardising sales promotion tools is extremely difficult.

Sports promotions and sponsorships are widely used. The key methods involved are advertising during sports programming on TV, positioning of stadium or arena signs and sponsorship of individuals, teams or events. What type is used depends on the country involved, the circumstances and regulations which apply.

8.2 Advertising

Sources of **media problems**

(a) **Availability.** Media may be more important and effective in some countries than in others (for instance, cinema in India, radio in the USA), while there may be a lack of specific media in others.

(i) **Newspapers** may not be widely available because of low levels of literacy, or even specific policies on the part of the government.

(ii) **Magazines**, which are important for specialist products such as industrial machinery, may be very restricted.

(iii) **TV commercials** are restricted, or even banned in many countries, for instance advertising specifically directed at children is banned in some Scandinavian countries. It is also sometimes very difficult to gauge effectiveness because of missing or incomplete data.

(iv) **Billboards, direct mail** and other forms of promotion may be unfamiliar or ineffective (there is very limited usage of billboards in some formerly communist countries).

(b) **Financial aspects.** Costs may be very difficult to estimate in many countries, since negotiation and the influence of intermediaries is likely to be much greater. There may also be expectations of gift-giving in the negotiation process.

(c) **Coverage of media (or reach of advertising message).** This relates to the forms of media employed as well as the physical characteristics of the country. Inaccessible areas may rule out the use of direct mail, or posters; scarcity of telephones may rule out this form of advertising promotion. It may also be difficult to monitor advertising effectiveness.

Chapter roundup

- International marketing is an important area of marketing. There is a range of specific problems to be addressed.
- International marketing can be differentiated from domestic marketing and comprises strategic decisions. New markets may be sought for a variety of reasons.
- A firm's orientation towards international marketing will depend upon its objectives in the market, but can generally be characterised as ethnocentric, polycentric or geocentric.
- Market attractiveness is governed by factors such as wealth, demand and accessibility.
- The marketing environment is different in international marketing. Most aspects of cultural systems vary between countries, sometimes quite significantly.
- International marketing operations are affected by regional trade alliances and markets.
- Do these developments lead to globalisation - a single market for the world in which borders do not matter? Yes and no. A few products and industries are genuinely global. Many are not and national borders are still very relevant.
- Within the marketing mix, standardisation or customisation of the product must be considered.
- Distribution is a complex issue in international marketing, and a wide range of channels can be identified.
- Prices in foreign markets are likely to be determined by local conditions, with each market separate.
- Elements of the promotional mix must also be considered. Advertising media varies from country to country.

Quick quiz

1 What is international marketing?

2 Why might new markets be sought?

3 What are the 12Cs to be used when analysing international markets?

4 What is geocentrism?

5 What are the three major criteria to consider when deciding what country to enter?

6 What are the five basic choices of degree of involvement in a foreign market?

7 What is the significance of material culture in international marketing?

8 What is globalisation?

9 What is the basic aim of the single European market?

10 What are the arguments in favour of product standardisation?

11 What is product screening?

12 What affects a company's degree of control over the prices it may charge in foreign markets?

13 What media problems may arise in international marketing?

Answers to Quick quiz

1 International marketing is the marketing of goods and services in two or more countries.

2 Growth; economies of scale; international competition; national necessity

3 Country, culture, concentration, communication, channels of distribution, capacity to pay, currency, control, commitment, choices, contractual obligations, caveats

4 Geocentrism is an approach to international marketing which is based upon the assumption that there are both similarities and differences between markets that should be incorporated into marketing strategy.

5 Market attractiveness

Competitive advantage

Risk

6 Simple exporting

Licensing

Franchising/joint ventures

Trading companies

Manufacturing abroad

7 Material culture affects the level of demand, the types of product demanded, functional characteristics of preferred products and the nature of products demanded.

8 Globalisation refers to

(i) a convergence of tastes and preferences

(ii) standardised products and services

(iii) worldwide competition

(iv) the design of marketing policies

9 It is supposed to allow for the free movement of labour, goods and services between member states.

10 Economies of scale, consumer mobility and technological complexity

11 Product screening is the examination of product ideas in order to identify marketable and profitable products.

12 Control over prices is likely to be determined by local conditions, and whether the company has wholly owned subsidiaries in the foreign market or conducts the business via local agents.

13 Availability of media, financial aspects and media coverage.

Answers to Activities

1 The main problem for most companies is collecting the debts of their foreign customers. There is however a sophisticated system of export credit guarantee insurance that can be purchased, and certainly should be if exporting is to become a regular activity.

2 *Language*

A promotional theme may not be intelligible – or properly translatable – whether in words or symbols.

Consumption patterns

One country may not use a product as much as another (affecting product viability), or may use it in very different ways (affecting product positioning).

Socio-economic factors

Consumers in one country may have different disposable incomes and/or decision-making roles from those in another.

Marketing practices and conditions

Differences in retail, distribution and communication systems, promotional regulation/legislation, trade restrictions etc may affect the potential for research, promotion and distribution in other countries.

3 Consumers in the UK learn languages, drink wine as well as beer, cook with garlic and herbs, try other cuisines/music/arts. Newspapers exploit this trend, as do advertisements set in Italy and France: foreign or international 'style' is recognised as acceptable and desirable, rather than alien.

4 Answers will depend on individual experience.

5 Arguments in favour of product adaptation

(a) *Greater sales potential*, where this also means greater profitability, which it may not!

(b) *Varied conditions of product use* may force a company to modify its product.

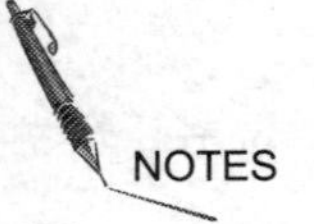

- Climatic variations, for instance cars produced for dry climates may suffer corrosion in wet ones
- Literacy or skill levels of users such as languages which can be used on a computer
- Cultural, social, or religious factors such as religious or cultural requirements for food products like halal slaughtering of New Zealand lamb for Middle Eastern Markets or dolphin-friendly tuna catching methods for Europe and the USA

(c) *Variation in market factors*. Consumer needs are in their nature idiosyncratic, and there are likely to be distinctive requirements for each group not met by a standard product.

(d) *Governmental or political influence*. Taxation, legislation or pressure of public opinion may force a company to produce a local product.

6 Other factors

(a) *Cost:* full cost of supplying goods to consumers. Relevant costs could include administrative costs, a proportion of group overheads, manufacturing costs, distribution and retailing costs.

(b) *Inflation*, particularly in the target market and in raw material suppliers.

(c) *Official regulations*. Governments may well intervene in pricing policies. This may involve *acceptable* measures such as import duties and tariffs, and generally *unacceptable* measures such as non-tariff barriers, import quotas and price freezes. Price controls may also be used.

(d) *Competition*. 'Price leaders' may well be undercut by competitors. The effectiveness of this policy will vary according to the significance of other marketing activities, and the capacity of competitors to match these.

Glossary

ACORN: a Categorisation of Residential Neighbourhoods.

Adoption process: similar to buyer behaviour ie the process of deciding to buy a product. Adopter categories can indicate the extent to which people are prepared to innovate and try out new products.

Advertising: the use of media to inform consumers about something and/or to persuade them to do something.

Advertising agency: acts on behalf of a client in planning a campaign and buys advertising space in various media.

AIDA: acronym denoting elements of a marketing communications strategy (to generate awareness, arouse interest, stir up desire and trigger action).

Ansoff Matrix: shows the four main growth strategies that are open to most organisations.

Applied research: original research work which has a specific practical aim or application (eg research on improvements in the effectiveness of medicines).

Attitude: a person's enduring favourable or unfavourable cognitive evaluations, emotional feelings and action tendencies toward some object or idea.

Augmentation: the building up of benefits on the core product to increase the attractiveness and satisfaction factors for the consumer.

Belief: a descriptive thought that a person holds about something.

Boston Consulting Group Matrix: used to analyse product mix performance, combining market share and market growth.

Bought-in goods: the reseller market is all the individuals and organisations that resell or rent bought-in goods to others. They are essentially purchasing agents for their own customers. Most goods that are produced pass through some kind of reseller, such as a retailer or supermarket.

Brand: the device for distinguishing a product or service from all others. This may be a name, symbol or any other device which is unique to the company and is its legal entitlement. Branding is the practice and technique of creating, devising and communicating such a device.

Brand leader: the brand which consistently holds the largest market share when measured by brand sales. You should note that there are some manufacturers who make a number of brands and therefore may hold a larger share of the product market than the brand leader.

Brand loyalty: the extent to which consumers of a brand tend to re-purchase in the face of continuing availability of alternatives.

Brand positioning: the strategy to ensure that the brand, in the eyes of the public, has a distinct position in the market with reference to quality, style, status, price or a combination of these.

Brand preference: the degree to which customers express their inclination to select the brand of their choice by reference to their purchasing habits or by their asking for a given brand.

Brand switching: the disposition to change brands for marginal gains in price or perceived value.

Breakeven analysis: a technique for investigating the inter-relationship between costs, volume and hence profit. It is used to determine the effects on profit of changes in levels of production or sales volume at given costs and unit price.

Breakeven point: the volume level at which the revenue from sales exactly covers total fixed and variable costs at a specific price, that is, there is no profit or loss.

Business-to-business marketing: refers to all business activities which are directed primarily at non-domestic markets. It replaces the concept of 'industrial marketing' or 'organisational selling'. It therefore includes marketing products for industry, commerce, trade, distribution, professional outlets and individuals in such businesses.

Cannibalisation: occurs when an organisation undertakes a new activity, such as launching a new product which adversely affects their existing business.

Circulation: the number of copies of a publication that are sold.

Commitment: the desire to maintain a valuable relationship.

Competitive advantage: factor which enables a firm to compete successfully with competitors on a sustained basis.

Competitor analysis: analysis of competitors' strengths and weaknesses, strategies, assumptions, market positioning, etc from all available sources of information in order to identify suitable strategies.

Consumer: the end user of a product service. May or may not be the customer.

Consumer buying behaviour: the decision processes and acts of individuals involved in buying and using products and services (Dibb).

Consumer durables: goods which are complex, purchased infrequently at relatively high cost and are expected to last a long time. Buying behaviour in this class often includes extensive searching, product comparison and reliance on new information.

Consumer goods: goods made for the household consumer, which can be used without any further commercial processing. Convenience goods are generally purchased in small units or low value (eg milk). Shopping goods have higher unit values and are bought less frequently (eg clothes, furniture). Speciality goods are those of high value which a customer will know by name and go out of his or her way to purchase. These distinctions are broad.

Consumer research: the study of the relationship between the personality of the consumer and the personality of the product. It looks at the consumer's motives, which may be unconscious but which still affect his or her choice of products. Techniques such as in-depth interviews and word association tests can be used to find out how consumers are really thinking.

Contact: ensuring that the customers know about a product or service. Distribution is ensuring that products or services are made accessible and available to consumers or buyers.

Contribution: sales value less variable cost of sales.

Corporate objectives: define specific goals for the organisation as a whole and may be expressed in terms of profitability, returns on investment, growth of asset base, earnings per share and so on.

Cost: the amount of resources, usually quantified in monetary terms, which is allocated to preparing a product for offer to a market. In other words, everything we spend on making an offering before we add the element of profit.

Cost per thousand: a measure of media cost, in terms of the price paid to reach an audience of one thousand readers. Cost per thousand rankings can be used to compare performance between press vehicles.

Coverage/reach/penetration: a measure of the percentage of the specified target who see an advertisement once during a campaign. By using a variety of newspapers and magazines within a campaign it is possible to build cover, since different consumers within the target audiences read different publications.

Cross elasticity of demand: a measure of the responsiveness of demand for one good to changes in the price of another: the percentage change in the quantity demanded for one good divided by the percentage change in the price of the other good. (*See* Price elasticity of demand)

Cues: minor stimuli (such as seeing the product in action, favourable reactions to the product by family and friends) that determine when, where and how the person responds.

Culture: a much broader concept than the sense in which it is most often used by people - to refer to classical aesthetic or artistic pursuits. The term is used by sociologists and anthropologists to encompass the sum total of the learned beliefs, values, customs, artefacts and rituals of a society or group.

Customer care: a fundamental approach to the standards of service quality. It covers every aspect of a company's operations, from the design of a product or service to how it is packaged, delivered and serviced.

Customer: the purchaser of a product/service. May or may not be the consumer.

Database: a collection of available information on past and current customers together with future prospects, structured to allow for the implementation of effective marketing strategies.

NOTES

Database marketing: customer-orientated approach to marketing. Its special power lies in the techniques its uses to harness the capabilities of computer and telecommunications technology.

Decision Making Unit (DMU): all those individuals and groups who participate in the purchasing decision process, who share some common goals and the risks arising from the decision.

Deming: system based on the improvement of products and services by reducing uncertainty and variability in the design and manufacturing processes through an unceasing cycle of product design, manufacture, test and sales, followed by market surveys to gain feedback, after which the cycle begins again with re-design.

Demography: the study of the population.

Development: the use of existing scientific and technical knowledge to produce new (or substantially improved) products or systems, prior to starting commercial production operations.

Differentiation: distinctiveness in the product or service being offered as perceived by the market by reference to any aspect of the marketing mix.

Direct cost: expenditure that can be identified with a specific saleable cost unit.

Direct marketing: a separately identified activity within the marketing spectrum. It combines direct mailing, off-the-page selling and a range of electronically supported systems such as telephone selling and Internet to become what is claimed to be the fastest growing area of marketing.

Direct marketing (1): the planned recording, analysis and tracking of customer behaviour to develop relational marketing strategies.

Direct marketing (2): an interactive system of marketing which uses one or more advertising media to effect a measurable response and/or transaction at any location.

Discounts: reductions in list, advertised or quoted prices offered by sellers to buyers.

Distribution (1): the process of getting products to consumers, usually via independent middlemen, such as wholesalers and retailers .

Distribution (2): a measure of market penetration: the number of retail outlets which stock and sell a particular product as a percentage of all outlets that could possibly sell that product.

Distribution chain: the process which enables the flow of goods between the producer and the consumer.

Distribution channel: the means of getting the goods to the consumer.

DMU: decision-making unit ie the people in a business who decide whether to buy a product.

Drive: is a strong internal force impelling action, which will become a **motive** when it is directed to a particular drive-reducing stimulus object (the product).

Durables: either industrial or consumer infrequently purchased high cost goods expected to last a long time.

Ecology: concerned with all the varieties of plant and animal life and the relationships between them, and between these life forms and their environment.

Economies of scale (1): the larger the operation in terms of output, the smaller the costs for each unit of output.

Economies of scale (2): reductions in the average cost of producing a product in the long run as the output of the product increases.

Ethnocentrism: a domestic country orientation in which IM is secondary to home marketing. Firms adopting this orientation will tend to adopt objectives which involve marketing the same products with the same marketing programmes in overseas countries as at home.

Family life cycle: the structure, membership and lifestyle of a family change over time, with the age of the individual members. The family progresses through a number of common stages of development. Researchers note that the family's economic character - income, expenditure and consumption priorities - will also change

Fast Moving Consumer Goods (FMCG): goods which are bought relatively frequently, at low cost, for immediate consumption and often with high reliance on re-purchase. Such products are often sold in supermarkets and they move off the shelves quickly, for example, toothpaste and chewing gum. FMCGs require constant replenishment of in-store stocks.

Five forces: external influences upon the actual and potential competition within any industry, which in aggregate determine the ability of firms within that industry to earn a profit.

Fixed cost: a cost which is incurred for a period, and which, within certain output and turnover limits, tends to be unaffected by fluctuations in the levels of activity (output or turnover).

Franchising: popular in retail and service industries, the franchisee supplies capital and the franchiser supplies expertise, a brand name and national promotion.

Frequency/opportunities to see (OTS): the number of times the target has a chance (or opportunity) to see the advert.

Generic name: the name given to a product class such as analgesics (painkillers) rather than the product name (paracetamol) or the brand name (Hedex). In marketing, it has become the way of describing a brand name which has come to stand for the whole of the product class, such as Hoover or Sellotape instead of vacuum cleaner or adhesive tape.

Geocentrism: the synthesis of the two previous orientations. It is based on the assumption that there are both similarities and differences among countries, which can be incorporated into regional or world objectives and strategies. This approach favours neither the home approach nor total adaptation.

'Globalisation of markets': (Levitt 1983) an expression which relates first to demand: tastes, preferences and price-mindedness are becoming increasingly universal. Second, it relates to the supply side: products and services tend to become more standardised and competition within industries reaches a world-wide scale. Third, it relates to the way firms, mainly *multinational corporations* (ie those with operations in more than one country), try to design their marketing policies and control systems appropriately so as to remain winners in the global competition of global products for global consumers.

Heterogeneous: a high differentiation in demand or products.

Hierarchy of effects: the steps in the process of persuading somebody to buy something. Models use the principle that the first effect is intended to be accomplished before the next.

Homogeneous: consisting of parts which are all of the same kind. In marketing it is used to identify markets which are undifferentiated, either by customer or product.

Indirect cost: expenditure on labour, materials or services which cannot be identified with a specific saleable cost unit. Examples might include supervisor's wages, cleaning materials and buildings insurance.

Industrial consumables: products which are used up in the manufacture of goods but do not become an integral part of them. Examples are: protective packaging; cleaning materials; oil; drill bits. Such products have, relative to industrial durables, very low purchase importance, are poorly differentiated, are often unbranded and rely heavily on good distribution service. Like FMCGs they are often re-purchased without much formality.

Industrial durables: products which are normally high capital cost, complex and highly technical. There is a low frequency of purchase which requires high level approval and very often protracted negotiation.

Industrial markets: business-to-business market (eg the sale of machine tools, consultancy advice etc).

Innovation: the process by which new products are brought to market.

Interest group: pressure group, or defensive group (eg trade union) promoting the interests of a group in society.

Intermediary: any firm which buys from one part of the chain and sells to another in the process of transferring goods from the producer to the consumer.

International marketing: the marketing of goods/services to two or more countries.

JIT: an inventory control system which delivers input to its production or distribution site only at the rate and time it is needed. Thus it reduces inventories whether it is used within the firm or as a mechanism regulating the flow of products between adjacent firms in the distribution system. It is a pull system which replaces buffer inventories with channel member co-operation.

Joint venture: an arrangement of two or more firms to develop and/or market a product or service. Each firm provides a share of the funding and has a say in management.

Learning (or experience) curve: the phenomenon that, the more we do anything, the more efficient and effective we become at it.

Lifestyle: distinctive ways of living adopted by particular communities or sub-sections of society. Life-style is a manifestation of a number of behavioural factors, such as motivation, personality and culture, and depends on accurate description.

Market: a group of consumers who share some particular characteristic which affects their needs or wants, and which makes them potential buyers of a product.

Market environment: all aspects of a market which affect the company's relationship with its customers and the patterns of competition.

Market positioning: the attempt by marketers to give the product a distinct identity or image so that it will be perceived to have distinctive features or benefits relative to competing products.

Marketing audit: part of the position audit which reviews the organisation's products, markets, customers and market environment: 'a comprehensive, systematic, independent and periodic examination of a company's or business unit's marketing environment, objectives, strategies and activities with a view to determining problem areas and opportunities and recommending a plan of action to improve the company's marketing performance' (Kotler).

Market segmentation: the sub-dividing of a market into distinct and increasingly homogeneous subgroups of customers, where any subgroup can conceivably be selected as a target to be met with a distinct marketing mix.

Marketing (1): the management process which identifies, anticipates and supplies customer requirements efficiently and profitably (Chartered Institute of Marketing).

Marketing (2): the sum of all those activities which, through exchange processes, bring about the satisfaction of customers' needs to the objective benefit of an enterprise in a mutually beneficial relationship (Middleton).

Marketing communications: the processes of both informing and educating users and dealers about the company and its objectives and of influencing attitudes.

Marketing management: the process of devising, implementing and monitoring the marketing plan.

Marketing mix: a phrase first used to describe the combination of Product, Price, Promotion and Distribution, the main variables which companies can manipulate in developing the offering to the market. Subsequently, these factors were incorporated in a model referred to as the 4Ps (Product, Price, Promotion & Place). In more recent times (1981), this was extended into the 7Ps by adding People, Physical Evidence and Process, to accommodate the factors important in the marketing of services.

Marketing planning: the process which identifies a marketing opportunity and the resources and actions needed in order to achieve a pre-determined objective.

Marketing orientation: a commitment to the needs of customers: 'marketing (focuses) on the idea of satisfying the needs of the customer by means of the product and the whole cluster of things associated with creating, delivering and finally consuming it' (Levitt).

Marketing research: includes investigating, describing and analysing markets (market research) and the analysis of the effects of the firm's competitors' marketing activities such as advertising.

Marketing strategy: the way in which organisations meet their marketing objectives by manipulating the interactions of the components of the marketing mix to achieve optimum customer response.

Matrix management: can be thought of as an integration of the product and market management approaches.

Merchandising: a method by which the manufacturer tries to ensure that a retailer sells as many of his products as quickly as possible. The manufacturer therefore gives advice to the retailer, either from the sales force or from full time merchandising specialists.

Micro-culture: a distinct and identifiable cultural group within society as a whole: it will have certain beliefs, values, customs and rituals that set it apart while still sharing the dominant beliefs, values, customs and rituals of the whole society or 'mainstream' culture.

Mission statement: a document in which an organisation gives one or all of: (a) its rationale for existing, (b) its long-term strategy, and/or (c) its values. Above all, the mission statement constitutes the organisation's view of its future.

Motivation: 'an inner state that energises, activates, or moves, that directs or channels behaviour towards goals' (Assael).

Negotiation: conferring with another with the view to compromising or agreeing on some issue.

New product development (NPD): a process which is designed to develop, test and consider the viability of products which are new to the market in order to ensure the growth or survival of an organisation.

Non-profit marketing: marketing activities undertaken by non-profit making organisations such as charities, government departments etc.

Offline promotion: uses traditional media such as TV or newspaper advertising to promote a website address (URL).

Online promotion: uses communication via the Internet itself to raise awareness. This may take the form of links from other sites, targeted e-mail messages or banner advertisements.

Opinion leaders: those individuals who reinforce the marketing messages sent and to whom other receivers look for information, advice and opinion.

Organisational (or industrial) buying: the decision-making process by which formal organisations establish the need for purchased products and services and identify, evaluate and choose among alternative brands and suppliers.

Penetration: *see* Coverage.

Perception: the process by which people select, organise and interpret sensory stimuli into a meaningful and coherent picture.

Personal selling: the presentation of products and associated persuasive communication to potential clients, employed by the supplying organisation. It is the most direct and longest established means of promotion within the promotional mix.

PEST factors: factors in an organisation's environment (political-legal, economic, social-cultural, technological).

Place: element of the marketing mix detailing how the product/service is supplied to the customer (distribution).

Policy: a principle of how an organisation operates. How it does something consistently in a certain way as laid down by the management.

Polycentrism: objectives are formulated on the assumption that it is necessary to adapt almost totally the product and the marketing programme to each local environment. Thus the various country subsidiaries of a multinational corporation are free to formulate their own objectives and plans (bottom up planning).

Positioning: the act of designing the company's offer and image so that it offers a distinct and valued place in the target customer's mind.

Pressure group: group of people who have got together to promote a particular cause (eg nuclear disarmament). Sometimes called a cause group. However, also used to mean any interest group.

Price: the unit of revenue combining costs and profit at which a satisfactory exchange takes place in a transaction. When multiplied by volume it equals sales turnover.

Price elasticity of demand: a measure of the responsiveness of demand to changes in price: the percentage change in the quantity of a good demanded, divided by the percentage change in its price. (*See* Cross elasticity of demand)

Price followers: those entrants to a market who simply follow the existing players, very often pricing just below the market leader.

Price leaders: those entrants who establish the going-rate in a market thus providing a basis for others to follow.

Product: element of the marketing mix: Anything that can be offered to a market that might satisfy a need or a want. It may be an object, a service, a place, an organisation, or an ideal.

NOTES

Product audit: the detailed, systematic and profound examination of the nature, scale and scope of the product offerings of the company in relation to criteria concerned with the goals of the organisation, the competition and the requirements of the market.

Product championship: a state of mind engendered in product managers and sales staff which places their products on pedestals.

Product class: broad category of product (eg cars).

Product cost: the cost of a finished product built up from its cost elements and therefore the total cost of a product/service.

Product differentiation: occurs when specific products or brands each have a specific combination of costs and benefits which a particular set of potential customers seek. This allows the product to be positioned in the market for specific customers.

Product life cycle: a model which suggests that sales of a product grow and mature and then decline as the product becomes obsolete and customer demands change. Applicable in some cases (eg horse-drawn transportation) but perhaps less so in others (eg corn flakes).

Production orientation: describes a company which makes what it thinks the customer will buy. It may make good products but will not take the trouble to find out whether there is a market for them.

Profit: the excess of revenue over costs.

Promotion: element of the marketing mix which includes all communications with the customer, thus including advertising, publicity, PR, sales promotion etc.

Prospect: a person (or organisation) who is identified as having the potential to become a customer.

Psychographics: a form of consumer research which builds up a psychological profile of consumers in general, or users of a particular product. It is the main basis of psychological segmentation of a market, and appropriate product positioning.

Public opinion: a consensus, which emerges over time, from all the expressed views that cluster around an issue in debate.

Public relations (PR): the planned and sustained effort to establish and maintain goodwill and mutual understanding between an organisation and its public.

Publics: in PR a group of people united by a common interest specific to them or their situation. Sometimes called stakeholders.

Pure research: a formal process which is mainly committed to research intended to discover new knowledge independent of the commercial value of such activity. (*See* also Research and development)

Quality: the totality of features and characteristics of a product or service which bears on its ability to meet stated or implied needs; fitness for use.

Range: the number or scale of choice of the products or services offered by a supplier.

Rationalisation: the change in the scope of the company's offering (usually a reduction) brought about by a serious review of the demand for the product in the market and the product's contribution to the firm's objectives, both strategic and financial.

Re-positioning: the strategy of changing the customers' perception of a company or brand by reference to quality and/or price in order to take advantage of a market preference.

Reach: *see* Coverage.

Readership: the number of an audience that have read one issue of a publication. The readership of any press vehicle is likely to be several times higher than its circulation.

Relationship marketing: focuses the firm's attention on customer retention with a view to building up a long-term relationship with a customer. A sale is not an end of a process but the beginning of a relationship. It is the successor to mass marketing, and is the process by which information about the customer is consistently applied by the company when developing and delivering products and services. Specially targeted promotions and product launches may be used to help build the relationship.

Research & development (R&D): in commercial organisations, this is generally concerned with applying technical or scientific knowledge to originate and develop new products. (*See* also Pure research)

Reseller market: all the individuals and organisations that resell or rent bought-in goods to others. They are essentially purchasing agents for their own customers. Most goods that are produced pass through some kind of reseller, such as a retailer or supermarket.

Risk: the potential volatility of returns on an investment, which is compensated for by a higher return. In other words, a rational investor will accept a higher risk in the hope of reaching a higher return.

Role: the sum or 'system' of expectations which other people have of an individual in a particular situation or relationship. Role theory is concerned with the roles that individuals act out in their lives, and how the assumption of various roles affects their attitudes to other people.

Sales promotion: a range of tactical marketing techniques, designed within a strategic marketing framework, to add value to a product or service, in order to achieve a specific sales and marketing objective.

Scaling techniques: derived from psychology and are used to determine the nature and intensity of an individual's attitudes towards objects or ideas: thus they are frequently called attitude scales. The most commonly used in market research into consumer behaviour are the Likert Scale, where respondents are asked to express their agreement or otherwise with a statement about the characteristics of a brand and the Semantic Differential Scale, where the technique involves respondents indicating a notional value on a scale representing the relationship between two poles of a characteristic such as expensive/cheap.

Segmentation (market segmentation): the subdividing of the market into distinct and increasingly homogeneous subgroups of customers, where any subgroup can be selected as a target market to be met with a distinct marketing mix.

Service quality: is the totality of features and characteristics of that service which bears on its ability to meet customer needs.

Services: distinguished from products because they are generally produced as they are consumed, and cannot be stored or taken away. For example, a bus is a product which is used to provide a service (transportation); the service is provided as you are consuming it (ie your trip from A to B). Also the standard of service differs each time it is produced (eg one bus driver may be a better or faster driver than another).

Skimming strategy: an approach in which premium prices are used on the launch of a new product in an attempt to profit from the lead time over competition and on the basis that the early part of the market will always pay that bit extra at first for the new product.

Social mobility: the tendency for individuals to move within the social hierarchy. Generally, such movement is associated with economic, educational or occupational success (upward mobility) or failure (downward mobility).

Social responsibility: is accepting responsibilities to the various publics of an organisation which go beyond contractual or legal requirements.

Socialisation: the process by which the individual learns the social expectations, goals, beliefs, values and attitudes that enable him or her to exist in society.

Societal marketing concept: is a management orientation that holds that the key task of the organisation is to determine the needs and wants of target markets and to adapt the organisation to delivering the desired satisfactions more effectively and efficiently than its competitors in a way that preserves or enhances the consumers' and society's well-being.

Stakeholders: a word used to denote all organisations, groups or individuals with whom the organisation has contact or by whom the organisation's activities are otherwise influenced. They will include customers, consumers and suppliers. They also will include pressure groups, politicians, charities, religious organisations and local authority and other agencies.

Strategic business unit (or SBU): is a section within a larger organisation which is responsible for planning, developing, producing and marketing its own products or services. A typical SBU is a division of the organisation where the managers have control over their own resources, and some discretion over their deployment.

Strategy: the way in which organisations meet their medium to long-term objectives by using their resources in certain ways.

Substitute: a good which can be substituted for another good, or an input which can be substituted for another input.

Substitute product: a good or service produced by another industry which satisfies the same customer needs.

Sustainability: developing strategies so that the business or entity only uses resources at a rate which allows them to be replenished in order to ensure that they will continue to be available.

Target market: market, or market segment to which an organisation offers goods/services; one or more segments selected for special attention by a business.

Technically: a **need** is defined as a 'state of felt deprivation'. We recognise that there is an absence of something. As marketers we should only use it in the appropriate sense. Wants are those things which we perceive as having those characteristics which will fulfil a particular need, that is, which we imagine will satisfy us in some way that an alternative product may not.

Technology: the knowledge which allows people to make and do things. Such knowledge often comes from scientific research and can be 'high tech', for example, the use of micro chips. However, technology can also be 'low tech', for example, childproof tops on medicine bottles.

Telemarketing: the planned and controlled use of the telephone for sales and marketing opportunities. Unlike all other forms of direct marketing it allows for immediate two-way communication.

Total Quality Management (TQM): Feigenbaum (1983) identifies Total Quality Management (TQM) directly with the customer. TQM is defined as the total composite product and service characteristics of marketing, engineering, manufacture and maintenance, through which the product and service in use will meet the expectations by the customer.

Trust: the degree to which partners are confident that each will act in the best interests of the relationship.

Unique selling proposition (or point) (USP): the aspect of a product, service, offering or transaction which distinguishes it from all others.

Variable cost: a cost which tends to vary with the level of activity.

World Trade Organisation (WTO): set up under the 1993 GATT agreement, the WTO is a body which adjudicates between countries to promote world trade.

NOTES

BPP
LEARNING MEDIA

Bibliography

Ansoff (1987) *Corporate Strategy* (2nd ed.). London: Penguin.

Assael, H. (1992) *Consumer Behaviour and Marketing Action* (4th ed.) Boston: PWS Kent.

Borden, N. (1964) 'The concept of the marketing mix' in G Schwartz (ed) *Science in Marketing.* New York: J Wiley and Sons pp 386 – 97.

Brassington, F., and Pettit, S. (2000) *Principles of Marketing* (2nd ed.) Harlow: FT/Prentice Hall.

Dibb, S., Simkin, L., Pride, W., Ferrell, O. (2001) *Marketing: Concepts and Strategies* (4th European edition) Boston: Houghton Mifflin.

Feigenbaum, A. (1986) *Total Quality Control.* New York: McGraw Hill.

Fill, C. (1999) *Integrated Marketing Communications.* London: Butterworth-Heinemann.

Grönroos, C. (1994) 'From Marketing Mix to Relationship Marketing'. *Management Decision,* Vol. 32, no. 2.

Gummesson, E. (1999) *Total Relationship Marketing: Rethinking Marketing Management from 4Ps to 30Ps*. Oxford: Butterworth-Heineman.

Jobber, D. (2007) *Principles and Practice of Marketing* (5th ed.) Maidenhead: McGraw Hill.

Johns, T. (1994) *Perfect Customer Care.* London: Arrow Books.

Kotler, P. (1994) *Marketing Management: Analysis, Planning, Implementation and Control.* (8th ed.) Englewood Cliffs: Prentice Hall.

Kotler, P. (2003) *Marketing Management: Analysis, Planning, Implementation and Control.* (11th International edition) Englewood Cliffs: Prentice Hall.

Levitt, T. (1960) 'Marketing Myopia'. *Harvard Business Review,* Vol 38 no. 4, July/August, pp 45-56.

Ohmae, K (1983) *The Mind of the Strategist: The Art of Japanese Business.* New York: McGraw Hill.

Palmer, A. (2001) *Principles of Service Marketing.* (3rd ed.) Maidenhead: McGraw Hill.

Pelsmaker, P., Gevens, M., van den Bergh, J. (2004) *Marketing Communications: A European Perspective*. Harlow: FT Prentice Hall.

Porter, M. (1980) *Competitive Strategy*. New York: Free Press.

Porter, M. (1985) *Competitive Advantage.* New York: Free Press.

Powers, T. (1991) *Modern Business Marketing.* St Paul; West Publishing Company.

Schiffman, L. and Kanuk, L. (1991) *Consumer Behaviour.* (4th ed.) Englewood Cliffs: Prentice Hall.

Schultz, D. (1991) *Integrated Marketing Communications: Putting it together and making it work.* New York: Contemporary Books.

Sheth, J., Mittal, B, Newman, B. (1999) *Customer Behaviour*. New York: Dryden.

Webster, F., and Wind, Y. (1972) *Organisational Buying Behaviour.* Englewood Cliffs: Prentice Hall.

Wilson, C., Gilligan, C., Pearson, D. (1992) *Strategic Marketing Managing: Planning, Implementation and Control.* London: Butterworth Heinemann.

Appendix: Edexcel Guidelines

Edexcel Guidelines for the BTEC Higher Nationals

This book is designed to be of value to anyone who is studying Marketing, whether as a subject in its own right or as a module forming part of any business-related degree or diploma.

However, it provides complete coverage of the topics listed in the Edexcel Guidelines for Mandatory Unit 4, Marketing Principles, of the BTEC Higher Nationals (revised 2010). We include the Edexcel Guidelines here for your reference, mapped to the topics covered in this book.

EDEXCEL GUIDELINES FOR UNIT 4: MARKETING PRINCIPLES

QCF Level 4

Aim

This unit aims to provide learners with understanding and skills relating to the fundamental concepts and principles that underpin the marketing process.

Unit

This is a broad based unit which provides the learners with the opportunity to learn to use the key principles of marketing.

First, the unit looks at the definitions of marketing and what is meant by a marketing orientation and the marketing process.

Next the learners consider the use of environmental analysis in marketing and undertake their own analyses at both macro and micro levels. They also investigate the importance of segmentation of the market and how this leads to the identification and full specification of target groups. Then they consider buyer behaviour and positioning.

The unit then looks at the main elements of both the original and the extended marketing mix. This includes an introduction to the concept of the product life cycle, new product development, pricing strategies, distribution options and the promotion mix.

Finally the unit allows learners to develop their own marketing mixes to meet the needs of different target groups. This is extended to include consideration of the differences when marketing services as opposed to goods. A range of other contexts is examined including the marketing to businesses instead of consumers and the development of internal markets.

On successful completion of this unit a learner will:

1 Understand the **concept and process of marketing**

2 Be able to use the concepts of **segmentation, targeting and positioning**

3 Understand the individual elements of the **extended marketing mix**

4 Be able to use the marketing mix in different contexts

Content		Covered in chapter(s)
1	**Concept and process of marketing**	
	Definitions: alternative definitions including those of the Chartered Institute of Marketing and the American Marketing Association, satisfying customers' needs and wants, value and satisfaction, exchange relationships, the changing emphasis of marketing.	1
	Marketing concept: evolution of marketing, business orientations, societal issues and emergent philosophies, customer and competitor orientation, efficiency and effectiveness, limitations of the marketing concept.	1, 2
	Marketing process overview: marketing audit, integrated marketing, environmental analysis, SWOT analysis, marketing objectives, constraints, options, plans to include target markets and marketing mix, scope of marketing.	1, 2
	Costs and benefits: links between marketing orientation and building competitive advantage; benefits of building customer satisfaction, desired quality, service and customer care, relationship marketing, customer retention, customer profitability, costs of too narrow a marketing focus.	3
2	**Segmentation, targeting and positioning**	
	Macro-environment: environmental scanning, political, legal, economic, socio-cultural, ecological and technological factors.	4
	Micro-environment: stakeholders (organisation's own employees, suppliers, customers, intermediaries, owners, financiers, local residents, pressure groups and competitors), direct and indirect competitors, Porter's competitive forces.	4, 5
	Buyer behaviour: dimensions of buyer behaviour, environmental influences, personal variables – demographic, sociological, psychological – motivation, perception and learning, social factors, psychological stimuli, attitudes, other lifestyle and life cycle variables, consumer and organisational buying.	5
	Segmentation: process of market selection, macro and micro segmentation, bases for segmenting markets ie geographical, demographic, psychographic and behavioural; multivariable segmentation and typologies, benefits of segmentation, evaluation of segments and targeting strategies, positioning, segmenting industrial markets, size, value, standards, industrial classification.	6
	Positioning: definition and meaning; influence over marketing mix factors.	
3	**Marketing mix**	
	Product: products and brands – features, advantages and benefits, the total product concept, product mix, product life cycle and its effect on other elements of the marketing mix, product strategy, new product development, adoption process.	7, 8
	Place: customer convenience and availability, definition of channels, types and functions of intermediaries, channel selection, integration and distribution systems, franchising, physical distribution management and logistics, ethical issues.	9

	Content	Covered in chapter(s)
	Price: perceived value, pricing context and process, pricing strategies, demand elasticity, competition, costs, psychological, discriminatory, ethical issues.	10, 11
	Promotion: awareness and image, effective communication, integrated communication process – (SOSTT + 4Ms), promotional mix elements, push and pull strategies, advertising above and below the line including packaging, public relations and sponsorship, sales promotion, direct marketing and personal selling, branding, interest and on-line marketing.	12, 13
	The shift from the 4Ps to the 7Ps: product-service continuum, concept of the extended marketing mix, the significance of the soft elements of marketing – people, physical evidence and process management.	7, 15
4	**Different marketing segments and contexts**	
	Consumer markets: fast-moving consumer goods, consumer durables, co-ordinated marketing mix to achieve objectives.	14
	Organisational markets: differences from consumer markets, adding value through service; industrial, non-profit making, government, re-seller.	14
	Services: nature and characteristics of service products – intangibility, ownership, inseparability, perishability, variability, heterogeneity – the 7Ps, strategies, service quality, elements of physical product marketing, tangible and intangible benefits.	15
	International markets: globalisation, cultural differences standardisation versus adaptation, the EU, benefits and risks, market attractiveness, international marketing mix strategies.	16

Learning Outcomes and assessment criteria

Outcomes	**Assessment criteria** **The learner can:**
LO.1 Investigate the **concept and process of marketing**	1.1 explain the various elements of the marketing process 1.2 evaluate the benefits and costs of a marketing orientation for a selected organisation
LO.2 Be able to use the concepts of **segmentation, targeting and positioning**	2 show macro and micro environmental factors which influence marketing decisions 2.2 propose segmentation criteria to be used for two products in different markets 2.3 choose a targeting strategy for a selected product/service 2.4 demonstrate how buyer behaviour affects marketing activities in two different buying situations 2.5 propose new positioning for a selected product/service
LO.3 Understand the individual elements of the **extended marketing mix**	3.1 explain how products are developed to sustain competitive advantage 3.2 explain how distribution is arranged to provide customer convenience 3.3 explain how prices are set to reflect an organisation's objectives and market conditions 3.4 illustrate how promotional activity is integrated to achieve its aims for the target market 3.5 analyse the additional elements of the extended marketing mix
LO.4 Be able to use the marketing mix in different **and contexts**	4.1 plan marketing mixes for two different segments in consumer markets 4.2 illustrate the differences in marketing products and services to organisations rather than consumers 4.3 show how and why international marketing differs from domestic marketing

Guidance

Links

This unit forms the basis of the HN Marketing Pathway linking with other marketing units: *Unit 17: Marketing Intelligence, Unit 18: Advertising and Promotion, Unit 19: Marketing Planning* and *Unit 20: Sales Planning and Operations.* There is also a link to the *Unit 1: Business Environment* in the area of stakeholders, effects of demand elasticity on pricing and external market factors. The unit also provides links to *Unit 30: Internet Marketing* and *Unit 41: Contemporary Issues in Marketing Management.*

Essential requirements

Appropriate textbooks

Employer engagement and vocational contexts

Centres should develop links with local businesses. Many businesses and chambers of commerce want to promote local business and are often willing to provide work placements, visit opportunities, information about businesses and the local business context and visiting speakers.

Index

Review Form – Business Essentials – Marketing Principles (7/10)

BPP Learning Media always appreciates feedback from the students who use our books. We would be very grateful if you would take the time to complete this feedback form, and return it to the address below.

Name: ______________________ **Address:** ______________________

____

____

How have you used this Course Book?
(Tick one box only)

☐ Home study (book only)

☐ On a course: college ______________

☐ Other ______________

Why did you decide to purchase this Course Book? *(Tick one box only)*

☐ Have used BPP Learning Media Texts/Course Books in the past

☐ Recommendation by friend/colleague

☐ Recommendation by a lecturer at college

☐ Saw advertising

☐ Other ______________

During the past six months do you recall seeing/receiving any of the following?
(Tick as many boxes as are relevant)

☐ Our advertisement

☐ Our brochure with a letter through the post

Your ratings, comments and suggestions would be appreciated on the following areas

	Very useful	*Useful*	*Not useful*
Introductory pages	☐	☐	☐
Topic coverage	☐	☐	☐
Summary diagrams	☐	☐	☐
Chapter roundups	☐	☐	☐
Quick quizzes	☐	☐	☐
Activities	☐	☐	☐
Discussion points	☐	☐	☐

	Excellent	*Good*	*Adequate*	*Poor*
Overall opinion of this Course Book	☐	☐	☐	☐

Do you intend to continue using BPP Learning Media Business Essentials Course Books? ☐ Yes ☐ No

Please note any further comments and suggestions/errors on the reverse of this page.

The BPP author of this edition can be e-mailed at: pippariley@bpp.com

Please return this form to: Pippa Riley, BPP Learning Media Ltd, FREEPOST, London, W12 8BR

Review Form (continued)

Please note any further comments and suggestions/errors below